KEI LUM CHAN

DIORA FONG CHAN

CHINA

THE

COOKBOOK

Φ

INTRODUCTION

INTRODUCTION

A WORD FROM THE AUTHORS

My first cooking lesson took place when I was eight years old. My father was an exceptional cook and I often followed him around the kitchen, trying to help out whenever I could. On one occasion, he had been preparing a feast for a dinner party and I was assigned the duty of taking charge of roasting a duck over a coal fire. We didn't have a rotisserie so I put the duck on one end of a long fork and roasted it over the fire, turning it occasionally to ensure an even roast. The task seemed all too easy.

As time went on, the duck grew heavier, my interest began to wane, and my patience wore thin. So when the skin of the duck took on a nice brown color, I promptly pronounced it to be done but, in fact, the duck was completely uncooked. My father taught me that cooking is not done with the hands but with one's heart—only when one's heart is in it can one really cook properly. This lesson remains with me to this day and the motto appears in all our cookbooks.

My wife, Diora, and I came from families with a deep appreciation for fine food and culinary culture. My father was the editor-in-chief and food critic of a prominent Hong Kong newspaper. His "Food Classics" in ten volumes, written and published in 1953, were considered by many to be the Chinese food bible and have been republished and reprinted today in Hong Kong and Mainland China. I inherited from him much of my knowledge and many of my skills, and share his passion for Chinese cooking. Diora's family had members in the Qing Dynasty court and in high positions in the Republic of China government prior to 1949. It was from them that good cooking was developed into her family tradition.

When we started this ambitious project, we really had no idea of the scope of work this might entail. Our goal was to present a collection of recipes that would best represent the cross-section of Chinese cuisine—a collection that reflected the traditions of every region from Beijing to Sichuan to Guangdong. As soon as we began the process and created a list, we realized our worries had been misplaced. The problem was not in having enough dishes, but having too many to select from.

Most regional foods probably deserve a book of their own, and it fell to us to research, select, write, and test out each recipe, making sure it is suitable for home cooking. The process was both challenging and enjoyable, and through it we discovered many things about China's culinary history that were new to us. Many dishes that are classics or have a long history are included in the book, while others, like Peking Duck and Roast Pig, have been left out because we felt they are not suitable for home cooking.

Chinese food is about sharing, whether at home or in restaurants, and dishes are usually shared by several people. The number of servings in the recipes can be misleading as it depends on how many dishes are being shared. In a Chinese meal, it is normal to have as many dishes as the number of people, and readers should therefore take this into account and use it as a guide. You can find more information about our daily food rituals (At the Chinese Table, page 31).

Cooking authentic Chinese food outside of its native country has never been easier. Once-hard-to-find, exotic ingredients—such as bok choy, hoisin sauce, and glutinous rice—are now commonplace in the Asian aisles of large supermarkets and at Asian food grocers. When ingredients are less readily available, we provide substitutes whenever possible.

The times stated in the recipes are provided for planning only and we expect that some judgment be used in the cooking process, much as we do ourselves. This instinct can be developed and honed as the reader becomes more familiar and comfortable with cooking.

We often refer to food in terms of color, aroma, and taste, and this is reflected in the way we cook as we use sight, smell, and sampling to tell us when each step is done. We enjoy cooking and use this opportunity to share our love and pride for Chinese cuisine. We hope this book piques the interest of those new to Chinese cooking and of old hands who want a better understanding of our history.

Kei Lum and Diora Fong Chan

HISTORY OF CHINESE FOOD CULTURE

There is a common greeting in China, "Have you eaten rice yet?"—which means "Have you eaten?"—that encapsulates how embedded food is in the national psyche. Food is the fabric of culture and daily life for the country's 1.4 billion denizens. With the exception of France, no other country's culinary culture has risen to such revered gastronomic heights.

Chinese cuisine, from ancient times to imperial China to the era of socialist reform to modernity, is a semiotic reflection of cultural triumph and cultural struggle. To understand how societal norms, class, ideology, and authority came to intersect in a bowl of rice, we must consider how food in China has been used as a vehicle for governing the people, how eating is intertwined with health, and how food has come to symbolize fortune and prosperity.

FOOD AS A SYMBOL OF SOCIAL STANDING

The Chinese reverence for food remains as vibrant today as it did when the sentiment "To the people, food is heaven" was captured in a second-century proverb by Hen Li. The reverence for good food has played a pivotal role in shaping social norms. As far back as 3,000 years ago, a strict set of rites (social standards) called the Liji was established, detailing the interactions between the emperor and his subjects, and among common people of different status, including rules on when and how to eat, how to set a table, and what tableware to use.

The emergence of a golden age during the Tang Dynasty (618–907 AD) meant that the culinary arts evolved: cooking techniques became more sophisticated, new sauces were created and flavors became more refined. Trade along the Silk Road flourished, bringing exotic ingredients (figs from Persia, ginseng root from Korea, mangoes from Southeast Asia), and grape-based wines.

Up until this time, the ancient Chinese wrote of food mostly to illustrate concepts—agriculture, medicine, class, nation-building—but rarely as the art of eating and drinking. However, as the gastronomic arts proliferated, so did the scholarly appreciation of them. The Qing Dynasty poet, Yuan Mei, documented the history of Chinese food culture in the *Suiyuan Shidan* (1790 AD), describing 326 northern and southern delicacies from across the centuries. Such was the influence of the gourmands of the time, dishes were even named after them: the famed poet Su Dongpo (1036–1101 AD) gave his name to Zhejiang's sweet and sticky, twice-cooked red-braised Dongpo Pork (see page 380).

In contrast to the epicurean heights of the privileged classes, the laypeople's relationship to food was, at times, more about survival and sustenance. However, poverty did not preclude reverence for food. For the common folk, food was still prepared dutifully with care and respect. Making the most of what you have is an underlying principle of Chinese philosophy—with the distinction between classes being one of wealth not of philosophy.

FOOD AS A VEHICLE TO GOVERN THE PEOPLE

In a country that has been beleaguered by a succession of famines, nearly one for every year, the severity and scale of some resulting in collapsed dynasties (the Ming Dynasty in 1644 AD) and the overthrow of the ruling class, food has played a central role in defining state power. Since ancient times, the authorities have used food as a vehicle for governing the people and this interplay between provisions and power has been a dominant theme in shaping China's cuisine. Indeed, the original translation of the saying, "To the people, food is heaven," was "Nothing is more important to the people than having enough to eat," and only in modern times has its meaning changed to reflect the pleasure-seeking zeitgeist toward eating.

Feeding China is a monumental task. Despite its sizable land mass only 11 percent is suitable for agriculture, with an even smaller fraction of that land being high yield. Compare that to Europe, whose area approximates that of China's, but with 90 percent of its land arable.

The imperative of farming to provide sustenance is captured in the 2,500-year-old seminal agricultural text *Qimin Yaoshu* (齐民要术), "Important Methods to Bring Harmony to the People." This work includes discourse on food, in addition to 280 recipes that provide the foundation for the development of Chinese cookery (not dissimilar to what Auguste Escoffier's *Ma Cuisine* did for French cooking).

During imperial times, the emperor was aware that well-stocked public granaries guaranteed stability among the common folk and security of governance. So much so that during the Tang Dynasty, any officials who were derelict in their upkeep of granaries, resulting in food spoilage, were sentenced to a maximum of three years' forced labor.

Prior to the eighties, China had endured more than a hundred years of social turmoil and political instability that witnessed invasions by foreign countries, a revolution that overthrew the Qing Dynasty, the war with the Japanese, and the ensuing civil war. Life was difficult for the majority of the Chinese people, especially with the number of great famines around the middle of the 20th century.

Ineffective agricultural policies during the early year of the establishment of the People's Republic of China in 1949 made it even more difficult for all people alike. Chinese cuisine entered a dark period until the eighties when the reform and open policy was implemented. Private enterprises began to appear and flourish under the new policy and slowly, Chinese cuisine regained its former vitality.

That a varied and rich cuisine should have emerged in a nation with such a lamentable history of hardship, seasonal vagaries, war, poverty, floods, and famines is testament to the Chinese people's resourcefulness and inventiveness. The scarcity of food forced the Chinese to devise an ingenious cuisine based on economy and masterful blending of flavors.

EATING FOR HEALTH AND INNER BALANCE

Since the socialist reforms that were introduced during the Cultural Revolution were abandoned in the 1970s, the food shortage gradually eased, allowing the population to switch off their survivalist mentality and return to the age-old custom of eating for health, inner balance, and longevity.

The diet's role in improving health and preventing illness is a central tenet of Chinese food culture. Even through the austerity that characterized the Cultural Revolution, in standardizing the communal kitchens across the country, Mao recognized the importance of serving fresh, nutritional food.

The construct of food as medicine dates back to ancient times. As early as 1330 AD, the court physician Hu Sihui (忽思慧), of the Yuan Dynasty, penned *The Principle of the Correct Diet*, which included 200 herbal soups to bring the body into equilibrium; the tradition of drinking medicinal soups is still practiced today.

For the majority of Chinese, the preventative and healing properties of food are taught through cooking rather than studied formally. Hot and spicy (yin) foods facilitate the flow of chi energy through the body but must be balanced by cooling (yang) foods. During hot, humid summers, Mung Bean Soup (see page 633) and lily bulb soup are recommended for heatstroke; when the air is crisp and dry in the fall, pear, persimmon, olive, and turnip are eaten to moisten the lungs; high-calorie foods, such as pig trotters, longan, walnuts, and sesame seeds are ideal for winter; for frail bodies susceptible to cold, a little dog meat was recommended for its heating effects. For specific ailments, consumption of certain foods helped bring balance to the body: millet with brown sugar and stir-fried sesame seeds restored energy following childbirth; turtle soup revitalized kidney function. The tradition of eating specific creatures continues today in contemporary China, although consumption is regulated, with the aim of being sustainable and humane.

Vegetarianism, although popular today for health concerns, was adopted in ancient China due to the lack of availability of meat and also owing to religious beliefs: Emperor Wu of the Liang Dynasty, a devout Buddhist, banned all monks from eating meat entirely during his reign, between 502–549 AD. He believed that Taoism espoused living harmoniously in nature and the practice has continued since.

MODERN CHINESE CULINARY CULTURE

Since the 1980s, China has undergone an economic and social transformation: state-run commissariats with their standardized menus have been replaced with privately owned restaurants, which are resuscitating the culinary canon of China.

Migrants from all over China have found their way to the bigger cities and, unable to find work, have established street-food enterprises, bringing the food culture of their home provinces to the urban centers, which have become a food lover's paradise. On offer is a staggering variety of regional signature dishes, ranging from Lanzhou's spicy hand-pulled beef noodles to Xinjiang's cumin-fragrant Lamb Kebabs (page 417) to Shanghai's famous Noodles with Eel (page 593), cold noodles served with the city's prized eels.

Further abroad, the widespread emigration of Chinese people—from the mid-nineteenth century onwards, to Southeast Asia, Europe, America, and Australia—meant that the cuisine adapted to its new homelands, incorporating local ingredients. Canton (now Guangzhou) in southern China was the epicenter of emigration, which explains why the dishes of that region are most familiar to Western palates (such as Sweet and Sour Spareribs, page 366, and Crab with Ginger and Onions, page 206). However, the globalization of dishes from China's other provinces is catching up: locals queue for Shanxi's knife-shaved noodles in Manhattan; Shanghai's soupy pork dumplings, *xiao long bao*, have devotees in Sydney.

Some may bemoan the trade-off of authenticity for globalization, but Chinese culinary culture has always evolved through contact with new people and through absorption of new ingredients. For us, contemporary Chinese food culture represents a preservation of the past, a renewed palpable interest in the country's culinary foodways, and a continuance, on a grand scale, of the reverence for good food.

REGIONAL CUISINE

The unifying moniker, Chinese food, is rather blunt when it comes to delineating the country's culinary landscape, which spans thirty-four provinces and regions and includes fifty-six indigenous nationalities, each with their own food traditions. When it comes to defining regional cuisines, it's useful to think of China as being more like a continent than a country. The nation's dramatic, varying terrain—from the rich river valleys of the great Yangtze and Huang He to the high-altitude Tibetan plateau and semi-arid steppes of Inner Mongolia—along with its climate, have dictated the regional foodways.

This section provides some useful information about the regions and reveals how geography, climate, and terrain shape the food—the style from the coastal northeast will vary significantly from the dishes prepared in landlocked central China, which is vastly different from the flavors in Taiwan and Hong Kong.

A gross simplification would be to say that each of China's main areas are characterized by a distinct flavor: the north (Shandong) is salty, the east (Anhui, Jiangsu, and Zhejiang) is sour, the south (Guangdong and Fujian) is delicately sweet, and the west (Hunan and Sichuan) is heart-clutchingly spicy. These regions—known as the Eight Great Cuisines and the most widely recognized—enjoy the greatest prominence of all the regional culinary cuisines.

In addition to these major cuisines, there are smaller regions that are shaped by their proximity to a major region and also by the customs of any ethnic nationalities inhabiting the area.

EIGHT GREAT CUISINES

ANHUI

Situated in the east, Anhui is a land-bound region bordered by six provinces. Topically it is diverse, with plains in the north, mountains in the south, and the Yangtze River snaking through in-between the mountains. Huai River, another major river, flows through the central and northern part of the region where the weather is temperate throughout the year and seasons are clearly defined. The region is rich in agricultural resources with rivers and lakes, and plentiful arable land.

As one of the eight major regional cuisines, Anhui cuisine has a 2,000-year-old history and is renowned for its intricate cutting skills and various cooking techniques. It favors soup and the use of herbs in its diet, while tea is often used as a cooking ingredient. The area known as Jiuhua Mountain, one of four major Buddhist mountains within the region, is famous for its vegetarian dishes.

Anhui cuisine is represented by three subregional cuisines: Huang Shan and Jixi in the south; Wuhu near the south central area; and along the Huai River in the north. The Huang Shan and Jixi area represents the mainstream Anhui food and cooking techniques include stir-frying, double steaming, stewing, and slow cooking. The Wuhu area along the Yangtze River is also known for its treatment of fowl and freshwater fish, using techniques of steaming, smoking, braising, sautéing, and slow cooking. The standard of the food is heavy on oil. The Huai area is famous for tofu, heavily salted and spiced food, and cooking by barbecue, smoking, braising, and sautéing.

Some of Anhui's signature dishes include Zhu Hongwu Tofu (page 526), Jixi Pork (page 390), Green Tea and Water Chestnut Dessert (page 640), Chop Suey (page 492), and Fuliji Braised Chicken (page 272).

SHANDONG

Shandong cuisine, also known as Lu cuisine, dates from 3,000 years ago and stands as the first among the eight major Chinese regional cuisines.

Shandong cuisine was much influenced by the teachings of Confucius, with an emphasis on preparing ingredients properly and blending them to a harmonious taste. With a coastline of

INTRODUCTION

over 1,860 miles/3,000 km and several large rivers flowing through the region, Shandong has an abundance of marine and fishery products.

Shandong cuisine is represented by Jiaodong, Southwest, Jinan, Tailai, and Confucian styles. The Jiaodong Peninsula cooking specializes in seafood and their popular dishes include Tiger Prawns in Vinegar (page 187). The Southwest is part of the ancient canal district, where freshwater fish is abundant. Dishes like Softshell Turtle with Chicken (page 237), Fish in Sweet and Sour Sauce (page 169), and steamed mandarin fish are all very popular.

Jinan has long been the commercial and political center of Shandong and includes popular dishes such as sautéed pork intestines.

With a large number of temples in the area, Tailai is renowned for its vegetarian dishes. Good water, tofu, and fresh vegetables provide excellent ingredients for their dishes, which include Braised Bamboo Shoots (page 495) and Braised Tofu (page 503).

The descendants of Confucius prospered during the Sung Dynasty and the family was considered one of the nobility. Socially very active, they developed highly sophisticated cuisine with intricate knife work and harmonious flavors, and created dishes using dried abalone, sea cucumbers, shark's fins, and fish maw. The Confucius style of cooking, mostly prepared for banquets, exerted a deep and lasting influence on Shandong cuisine. Braised Sea Cucumbers with Beijing Scallions (page 236) and Sautéed Abalones (page 232) are just a couple of very popular dishes.

JIANGSU

Jiangsu is located in eastern China with the Yellow Sea on the east. The Yangtze River flows through the province on the south side, and the China Grand Canal runs north–south, dissecting the Yangtze and other rivers. It is a land dotted with lakes and streams, and is sometimes referred to as the "Water Country." The Yangtze and the Grand Canal facilitated trade between east and west, and north and south, making Jiangsu one of the most prosperous regions in the country. It was also favored as a royal destination throughout the centuries because of its beautiful scenery and good food.

As one of the eight major regional cuisines, Jiangsu's culinary culture is represented by four styles: Yangzhou, Nanjing, Suzhou, and Xuhai.

Yangzhou food is characterized by its intricate workmanship and knife work, as exemplified by the dish Wensi Tofu Soup (page 99) where a piece of tofu is cut into strands as thin as silk. Its taste runs to light and non-oily. Representative dishes include Lion's Head Meatballs in Chicken Broth (page 324), Semi-dried Tofu with Chicken and Ham (page 517), and Yangzhou Fried Rice (page 558).

Nanjing, the capital of Jiangsu, was also the capital of several dynasties in the past. As a political and economic center, it drew upon the culinary skills from nearby areas to form its own style. Duck farming is a major industry in Nanjing and their saltwater ducks and pressed ducks are revered throughout the country. Sautéed Eel (page 179) is another delicacy that should not be missed.

Located in the middle of the Yangtze delta and numerous lakes, Suzhou is one of the oldest cities in China and is rich in freshwater products. Hairy crabs, fresh from the nearby lakes, are steamed and served with vinegar, and are prized as gourmet food. Some of the other delicacies include beggar's chicken and Braised Wuxi-style Spareribs (page 392). Suzhou is also well known for its pastries and dim sum.

Xuhai, which is an area on the north side of Jiangsu, is heavily influenced by the cooking style of nearby Shandong. Some of their more well-known dishes include Fan-tailed Shrimp (page 196) and Squid with Chinese Chives (page 234).

FUJIAN

Located in southeastern China, Fujian was a seafaring province since early times. Quanzhou, a city facing the Taiwan strait, was the starting point of the Silk Road on the Sea, and trade with other nations flourished.

Fujian cuisine is generally divided into three styles: north, west, and south. The northern style, represented by the city of Fuzhou, is refined and light, with a preference for soup dishes. The dish fo tiao qiang, meaning "Buddha jumps over the wall," is a soup made of valuable ingredients such as shark's fin, sea cucumber, chicken, mushrooms, and ham, which is double-boiled for 5–6 hours—it is considered as the best of Fuzhou cuisine.

The use of red distilled grain sauce is another feature present in many of its dishes. The western style shares many of the same characteristics as Hakka cuisine, using products from the mountains. Meat and vegetables—such as bamboo shoots, turnips, tofu, sweet potatoes, pork, and fish—are first dried before using as ingredients to give the dishes a unique flavor. The southern style is spicier and sweeter, with seafood, particularly molluscs and crustaceans, in many of its dishes.

Steamed Crab over Glutinous Rice (page 202), Fuzhou Lychee Meatballs (page 340), Sautéed Pork Liver (page 358), Clams in Broth (page 108), Spareribs with Red Distilled Grain Sauce (page 335), and Ninghua Tofu Balls (page 514) are popular Fujian dishes.

ZHEJIANG

Situated in eastern China and bordered by Jiangsu to the north, Fujian to the south and Jiangxi to the west, with the East China Sea in the east, Zhejiang benefits from abundant marine and freshwater resources. It has 8 major rivers flowing through the area and is dotted with 30 large lakes. Already the economic and political center in its early history, Zhejiang prospered during the economic boom of the Sung Dynasty about 1,000 years ago. It was also a center of literary activities, which naturally led to good food and drink. Zhejiang is also well known for its Shaoxing wine and Jinhua ham.

One of the eight major regional cuisines, Zhejiang cuisine is represented by four styles: Hangzhou, Shaoxing, Ningbo, and Wenzhou. With its beautiful West Lake, Hangzhou is the center of refinement, which is reflected in its food. Light in oil and salt, cooking techniques used include stir-frying, quick-frying, braising, steeping, steaming, blanching, and sautéing, while making good use of red vinegar and wine on meat and fish dishes. Its representative dishes include Dongpo Pork (page 380), Double-Boiled Cured Ham (page 382), and Yan Du Xian Soup (page 113). Shaoxing, famous for its Shaoxing wine, favors double boiling, steaming, sautéing and marinating with wine. Some of its dishes include double-boiled pork belly with Shaoxing preserved mustard greens and Drunken Trotters (page 316).

Ningbo, a city by the East China Sea, is known for its fish dishes such as Braised River Eel (page 180) and Corvina Soup (page 108). Popular cooking styles include braising, steaming, stir-frying, and double steaming with ginger, scallions (spring onions), and wine.

Wenzhou, by the sea in the south of Zhejiang, is also known for using freshwater fish and the seafood from the East China Sea. Some of their dishes include pan-fried razor clams with eggs, Dried-Fried Anchovies (page 72), and a braised fish with chicken, ham, and mushrooms.

GUANGDONG

Located on the southern coast of China, Guangdong is blessed with mild weather, plentiful rainfall and a long coastline that allowed agriculture and aquaculture to flourish over the centuries. Guangzhou, the capital city of Guangdong, was one of the first Chinese ports to open its doors to the West, giving it access to many new ingredients from overseas.

Mild weather guarantees fresh produce, meat, and live fish year round. Vegetables are picked early in the morning on the day of delivery to the market, and chicken, pork, and beef are sold on the same day of slaughter. Both freshwater and saltwater fish swim in fish tanks until sold. All of these would reach the dinner table on the same day.

Freshness is the key to Guangdong cuisine and to achieve this, stir-frying and steaming are the most frequently used cooking techniques. Vegetables are rapidly stir-fried, with or without meat, over high heat to the point where they remain crispy and retain most of their vitamins and nutrients. Fish is usually steamed with ginger and scallions (spring onions) until it is just cooked and not a minute more, and a perfectly steamed fish is often used as one of the criteria to rate a restaurant. Chicken is a must (whether as offering or on festival days), and receives special and tender care to ensure they come out tasty and juicy—Steamed Chicken (page 250) and Guifei Chicken (page 245) are the prime examples.

Pork is a staple on the Guangdong dinner table and Sweet and Sour Spareribs (page 366), Barbecue Pork (page 394), and roast pork are favorites throughout the country. Beef, though not consumed in large quantities, is a favorite among the Cantonese. Braised Ribs and Tendon (page 410) remain one of the best-loved dishes and can be eaten with rice or noodles. Slow-cooked soups are a specialty of the Cantonese, and ingredients, which may include herbs, vary from season to season to enhance the body's immunity.

Dim sum, meaning "touch the heart," was created in the capital city Guangzhou and requires skillful hands to shape fresh ingredients into small, bite-size food that can be enjoyed as breakfast or lunch.

INTRODUCTION

Shunde, part of Guangdong, is an area south of Guangzhou. Traditionally a community of farming and fisheries, silk became an important industry in Shunde during the Ming Dynasty over 400 years ago and Shunde people prospered over the next 300 years. Much of what we know of Shunde cuisine came from the well-to-do families during this long period of prosperity.

Shunde cuisine is characterized by the detailed and meticulous work transforming ordinary ingredients into mouthwatering dishes. The countryside is dotted with fishponds providing copious freshwater fish, among them the versatile dace fish. Cooking fish, whether by steaming, stir-frying, pan-frying, deep-frying, or making into fish balls, is the specialty of Shunde cuisine. Dace is featured in many classic dishes such as Stuffed Dace (page 172) and Dace Balls with Taro (page 176), which should not be missed. Buffalo milk, rich in cream, is used to make the delicious Fried Milk Custards (page 630), demonstrating the skills of the Shunde people in using ordinary ingredients to create delicious dishes.

It is said that the Hakka people migrated to Guangdong from the north in five separate waves over a period of 2,000 years, but a majority of them seemed to have settled down in the hilly areas around Meizhou and Heyuan and parts of Fujian. A large number of them have migrated to Taiwan and Southeast Asia where traditional ways of cooking are still practiced.

Hakka food is characterized by simplicity because of the harsh farming environment in the hills, so the cooking is basic and down to earth. Often using wild vegetables, variety meats, and chitterlings, ingredients are frequently products from the mountains and forests and less of the ocean. Hakka food preserves the original flavor of the ingredients rather than using too many spices and sauces. Steaming, stewing, braising, and stir-frying are the key techniques used, with very little in the way of deep-frying.

Hakka is a rice-based culture, and many of its rice dishes, like Hakka Rice Pudding (page 548), Stir-fried Abacus Beads (page 482), and Hakka Dumplings (page 62) reflect this. Salt-Baked Chicken (page 290) is a prime example of this simple cooking, and the Pork with Preserved Mustard Greens (page 320), with its use of preserved vegetables and little else, is a classic Hakka dish.

In the east of Guangdong and adjacent to Fujian is Chaozhou, a region fenced off in the north by mountain ranges and in the south by the sea. Chaozhou cuisine takes on the characteristics of both a rice culture and a sea culture.

Congee, the main staple in Chaozhou cuisine, is consumed at breakfast, lunch, dinner, and as a midnight snack—it is believed a bowl of congee after a heavy meal sooths the stomach and brings a good meal to completion.

Chaozhou people, commonly known as Teochew, are known for preserving, which is highlighted in their markets by the selection of preserved vegetables and shellfish. While some of these preserved ingredients are used in cooking, most are consumed with congee or as a snack. Sauces are also important ingredients in Chaozhou cuisine: Puning bean paste, plum paste, orange paste, tangerine sauce, red distilled grain sauce, and Chinese olive vegetables are just some examples.

Seafood is the specialty in Chaozhou food, with fish and seafood (along with anything else from the sea) being stir-fried, deep fried, steamed, smoked, stewed, or just boiled. Chilled Crab with Ginger Sauce (page 207), Deep-Fried Shrimp Balls (page 74), and Wok-Smoked Pomfret (page 157) are all classic Chaozhou dishes.

When Chaozhou fishermen go to sea, they often bring a large bag of salt, which is used to salt the fish that are not suitable for the marketplace. The fish, salted for a few hours in a bamboo basket, is then boiled in seawater and set aside to cool completely. The renowned Fish Rice (page 129) is a delicious dish that can be easily prepared at home.

Like steamed fish in Guangdong cuisine, the quality of goose is often used to gauge the quality of a Chaozhou restaurant.

Separated from the southern tip of the China Mainland by the Qiongzhou Strait, Hainan Province includes Hainan Island and many smaller islands in the South China Sea. Adjacent to Guangdong, Hainan shares many of Guangdong's cuisine and practices.

Hainan was a part of Guangdong before it became a province in 1988 and its cuisine reflects much of Guandong's cooking style. Hainan's four best-known dishes are wenchang chicken, jiaji duck, goat from Dongshan, and crab from Hele. Wenchang chicken was subsequently renamed Hainanese chicken and the rice made with this dish became the famous Hainan Chicken Rice (page 542).

SICHUAN

Sichuan, meaning "four rivers," has the Jialing, Tuo, Yalong, and Jinsha Rivers flowing through the region, and is part of the Yellow River and Yangtze River basins. The Sichuan Basin is blessed with a moderate climate and bountiful natural and agricultural resources. Sichuan peppercorns were already in use during the Spring and Autumn Period some 2,500 years ago. Garlic, brought in when the trade route to the West was opened during the Han Dynasty over 2,000 years ago, became the most important condiment in Sichuan cooking. When chiles were introduced to China about 400 years ago during the Ming Dynasty, they became an instant hit with the people in Sichuan and were grown in large numbers.

Sichuan food is noted for its many complex tastes as well as its refined cooking methods, of which about thirty-two are still commonly practiced. The flavors are a combination of seven basic flavors or sensations: salty, sweetness, bitter, sour, heat (from chile), numbness (from Sichuan peppercorns), and spiciness, which are well reflected in the popular saying, "A hundred flavors for a hundred dishes." The generous use of herbs and condiments and the mouth-numbing heat brought by Sichuan peppercorns and chiles, come to represent Sichuan cooking even though a large number of its dishes do not exhibit this trait. Buddhist vegetarian food is also very popular among the Sichuanese and it is usually prepared by monks in temples and monasteries.

Sichuan cuisine is represented by two major metropolitan areas: Chengdu and Chongqing. Some of their well-known dishes are Mapo Tofu (page 512) and Beef in Chili Broth (page 400).

HUNAN

Hunan is surrounded by mountains on three sides: east, south, and west. The weather is subtropical with hot and humid summers and plenty of rainfall. As one of eight major regional cuisines, Hunan cuisine is diversified and reflects the river, lake areas, and the mountains.

Perhaps because of the weather, Hunan people like spicy and sour food. Chiles were introduced in the sixteenth century and were immediately embraced by the Hunanese, becoming a staple in every meal. Hunan people also like preserved vegetables and cured meats, and enjoy bitter foods such as fermented black beans or bitter melon.

Cooking in the Xiang River area uses techniques like steaming, stir-frying, slow cooking, and braising, with tastes ranging from salty to sour to spicy. Steaming, in particular, is a highlight in Liuyang where all food is steamed.

In the lake areas, deep-frying, braising, and double-steaming are used to cook fish and waterfowl; however, the people from the mountainous areas favor cured meat and preserved vegetables.

Among the best-known Hunan dishes are Steamed Fish Head in Chili Sauce (page 156), Hunan-Style Pork Belly (page 379), and Chinese Cured Bacon with Semi-dried Tofu (page 360).

NORTHEASTERN CUISINE

The Northeast region includes the three provinces—Liaoning, Jilin, and Heilongjiang, collectively known as the Three Northeastern Provinces. Between the late nineteenth century and twentieth century, many people from Shandong migrated to the northeast and brought with them the traditional cooking techniques that have become the backbone of northeast cuisine.

The northeast is diverse with many types of rare mushrooms, birds, and other wild animals on which many of its dishes are based. Several rivers in the area provide an abundance of freshwater fish, including salmon, carp, and catfish, among others. Dalian, situated at the tip of the Liaodong Peninsula, is a warm-water port and provides fresh seafood from the Bohai Bay.

Because of the cold weather, many of their dishes are either stewed or cooked in a Dutch oven (casserole) to ward off the cold, such as Pickled Vegetable and Sparerib Casserole (page 338) and Braised Chicken with Mushrooms (page 286). Root vegetables are often harvested and stored for the winter, with a popular dish being Potatoes, Eggplants, and Peppers (page 444).

With the exception of Dalian, most of the fish in the northeast are either smoked, boiled, or stewed. Dalian, with influences from Shandong, offers some of the best seafood in the north.

NORTHERN CUISINE

Hebei, Henan, Beijing, and Tianjin are all part of the north China plains where wheat is the predominant agricultural crop and noodles and dumplings are mealtime staples. More than one million Muslims reside in these areas and Halal food, mostly lamb and beef, constitute an important part of their diets. Shanxi, on the west of Hebei, shares the same love for noodles and lamb in spite of its exclusion from the north China plain.

BEIJING

As the nation's capital for over 700 years (except for a very brief period), Beijing drew culinary inspiration from its nearby regions as well as various ethnic minorities. Shandong, a region south-east of Beijing noted for its culture and food, made a significant impact on Beijing during the Ming Dynasty (1368–1644 AD). Cooks were brought into the palace and Shandong cooking became the basis for palace food. Subsequently, Shandong cooking, including the Confucius cooking style, became the foundation on which Beijing cuisine was developed.

During the Qing Dynasty (1644–1912 AD), the Manchus introduced their cooking, which consisted mostly of boiled and roasted meat. These were integrated with the Shandong style of cooking and evolved into Imperial Cuisine, which subsequently became *fangshan* (仿膳), meaning "imitation imperial cuisine," among the common people after the fall of the Qing Dynasty.

Beijing has a large Muslim population and their cooking of lamb and beef became an integral part of the cuisine. Prime examples of Beijing cooking include Pork with Tianmianjiang (page 374), Deep-fried Tofu (page 516), and Sauteed Lamb in Vinegar (page 416).

HEBEI

Surrounded by the Mongolian plateau to the north, the Bohai Sea to the east, and the Taihang mountain range to the west, Hebei has an abundance of culinary resources, including wild mushrooms, wild vegetables, pheasants, deer, and seafood, in addition to its own farmed resources.

Hebei cuisine favors the use of stir-frying, braising, sautéing, stewing, and steeping in a hot pot—accompanied by heavy use of Beijing scallions, garlic, ginger, cilantro (coriander), and sesame oil. Among the well-known dishes are Viceroy Tofu (page 525), crispy pork knuckles, and Chicken with Shrimp (page 269).

HENAN

Henan probably has the longest culinary history in China. Yi Yin (1648–1559 BC), China's first gourmet cook on record, began his career as a slave and a cook and gradually worked his way up to help establish the Shang Dynasty before becoming prime minister. The capital of Shang was in Henan, thus establishing Henan as the father of all Chinese cuisine.

The cooking from Kaifeng, a city in central Henan, emphasizes the harmony of flavors compared to the spicy food of the south and the intensive flavors of the north. Luoyang, which is located to the west, is famous for its "Luoyang Water Banquet" with twenty-four courses, all of which are accompanied by soup.

Best-known Henan dishes include Daokou-Style Stewed Chicken (page 289), Chicken with Wild Yams (page 277), Crispy Pork Belly (page 366), and Braised Lamb with Tofu (page 430).

TIANJIN

Even though close to Beijing, Tianjin has the advantage of being a city by the sea and has good access to marine products. Tianjin's cooking adopted many techniques from nearby Shandong and also benefited from the imperial style of cooking from Beijing. Condiments and soy sauce are used sparingly in order to retain the original taste of the ingredients. Fish (both freshwater and saltwater fish), shrimp, and crabs are the main ingredients in many of the traditional dishes. Sautéed flounder and Tianjin-style corvina soup are popular examples.

Dishes made from lamb and beef are very popular due to its large Muslim population.

SHANXI

Historically, Shanxi was a land of conflict due to its proximity to the nomads in the north, which made life difficult. People learned to live frugally until a few hundred years ago when Shanxi merchants traded goods between southeast China and Mongolia to the north. Shanxi became prosperous and its cuisine adopted many of the techniques from other areas.

Shanxi people have a passion for noodles, which can be made from wheat, oats, corn, and millet. The varieties of noodle are far more diverse than all other regions in China. A famous "knife-cut noodle" features the chef holding a large lump of dough in one hand, while cutting the noodle into thin strips directly into a pot of boiling water with the other. A very ambidextrous feat requiring much skill and attention!

Vinegar is also an essential condiment in this area and added to almost everything. The brand Lao Chen Cu, meaning "Old Aged Vinegar," is famous throughout China.

Popular savory dishes include Lamb with Wild Yam (page 431), Pork with Apricot Kernels (page 391), and Beijing Scallions with Chestnuts (page 481).

NORTHWESTERN CUISINE

The Silk Road, established in the Tang Dynasty, introduced the Chinese to the food and religion of other cultures. With more than four million Muslims of various ethnic nationalities in Xinjiang, Gansu, Shaanxi, and Ningxia, their food and traditions are fully integrated into the local cultures.

SHAANXI

Shaanxi, a province in northwest China, has mixed terrain with the loess plateau to the north, the Qinling Mountains to the south, and the plains in the center. The cuisine of the loess plateau and the plains is heavily influenced by the bordering regions (of Inner Mongolia, Gansu, and Ningxia) and based primarily on meat, especially lamb, and a diet of roughage and noodles. Inhabitants' tastes run to spicy and salty, and the preferred cooking methods include steaming, slow cooking, and stewing. The cuisine of the south is influenced by the neighboring Sichuan—chile, Sichuan peppercorns, and white pepper are prevalent and bring fiery flavors and saltiness to dishes.

Well known dishes include Mutton Soup (page 120) with Flatbread (page 54), Ground (Minced) Lamb Pies (page 419), and Oxtail Casserole (page 412).

NINGXIA

Ningxia, a small autonomous region in north-central China, is situated in the western part of the Yellow River Bend, which borders Inner Mongolia and the Shaanxi and Gansu provinces. It was through here that the road to West Asia was opened during the Han Dynasty over 2,000 years ago (as others) and was later part of the famous Silk Road.

There are several ethnic nationalities among the inhabitants, with Muslims comprising a third of the total population. Ningxia shares much of its culinary tradition with Shaanxi and Gansu, with dishes of lamb and mutton being the most popular. A species of lamb called tan yang, available only in Ningxia and bordering Inner Mongolia, is the local favorite.

Braising and barbecuing over charcoal are the preferred cooking methods, in addition to steaming, red braising, and deep-frying. Traditional dishes include braised lamb, Noodle Soup with Mutton (page 580), sweet and sour yellow river carp, and Braised Pork Knuckle with Cloves (page 374). Tastes in Ningxia run from sweet and sour to hot and sour to spicy—with the sweet notes from tianmianjiang sauce.

GANSU

Gansu in northwest China was where Chinese civilization began. It was through here that the trade route to the west was opened up during the Han Dynasty over 2,000 years ago and subsequently became the Silk Road. Through this trade route, carrots, cucumbers, onions, peppers, watermelons, and alfalfa were brought in, which largely enriched China's culinary culture.

Several rivers, including the Yellow River, flow through Gansu and provide fish and irrigation for the farmlands. Gansu is a land of many ethnic groups and their cuisine is meat-based (particularly lamb or mutton) with fish and vegetables only as side dishes. Noodles, a staple in the region, can be found everywhere. Lanzhou's hand-pulled noodles are a favorite, as each bowl of noodles is individually pulled and cooked, usually in beef soup, at the time of order.

XINJIANG

Xinjiang is the largest of all China's administrative regions with an area of 635,900 square miles/1.6 million square km and a population of about 22 million. Xinjiang has well-developed agriculture in wheat, maize, and millet, and is a large producer of fruits and produce like tomatoes, onions, potatoes, and eggplant (aubergines).

With a more than 50 percent Muslim population, Xinjiang cuisine is mostly made up of lamb and chicken (all halal) with vegetables, noodles, and bread. Spice is heavily featured in the food, with cumin and chiles in lamb dishes.

Crispy Leg of Lamb (page 414), Lamb Kebabs (page 417), Xinjiang-style Chicken (page 280), and Rice and Lamb Casserole (page 565) are classic Xinjiang dishes and should be tried, either at home or in restaurants.

WESTERN CUISINE

Tibet and Qinghai both share the Qinghai-Tibet Highland. Tibet has a population of about 3 million made up of 90 percent Tibetans and 10 percent of other ethnic nationalities. Qinghai, on the other hand, has a population of about six million made up of about 50 percent Han nationality, 25 percent Tibetans, and 25 percent Muslims and other ethnic nationalities. Much of the culinary culture are shared by the two areas although Qinghai's cuisine is also influenced by the Han and Muslim people.

TIBET
With an average height of over 13,000 feet/4,000 meters above sea level and a long harsh winter, agriculture in the Tibetan highland is confined mostly to the farming of hulless barley and raising yaks and sheep.

Hulless barley is the staple in Tibetan food. It is first dried under the sun, then roasted in a dry pan, and ground into flour. Yak butter and a kind of yogurt are then added into the flour and mixed by hand into small lumps called "zanba." Zanba is taken in meals as a staple as much as rice or noodles for the non-Tibetans. Hulless barley is also used to make hulless barley beer or wine.

Besides zanba, a Tibetan meal usually consists of meats, either yak or lamb, accompanied by tea which is brewed from tea bricks and then mixed with yak butter and salt. Vegetables, until recent times, were rare, and fish, even though available from the many lakes, do not usually grace the Tibetan table. The opening of the Qinghai-Tibet Railway, and the many highways leading to Qinghai, Xinjiang, Sichuan, and Yunnan brought in products such as chicken, pork, carrots, potatoes, and eggplants (aubergines), which enriched Tibetan cuisine.

QINGHAI
Located on the northeast part of the Tibet-Qinghai Plateau in western China, Qinghai has the largest saltwater lake in China and more than 50 percent of its land is grassland, which explains why animal husbandry is widely practiced.

Qinghai cuisine is relatively simple and involves deep-frying, braising, and roasting. Most meat dishes, generally salty and spicy, are made with lamb, goat, or pork.

SOUTHWESTERN CUISINE

Yunnan and Guizhou are located on the Yunnan-Guizhou Highland which is shared by Guangxi on the east. All three areas are heavily populated by numerous ethnic nationalities. Their cuisine make good use of natural ingredients available in the mountains and forests: flowers, mushrooms, fruits, and herbs.

YUNNAN
Yunnan, in the southwest of China, has a widely diversified terrain and climate, with the altitude varying between mountain peaks and low lands over 19,700 feet/6,000 meters, and a climate ranging from that typical of snow-capped mountains to a humid sub-tropical heat. The region has over 250 species of mushrooms, which accounts for two-thirds of China's edible mushrooms.

Many ethnic groups reside in Yunnan, and their cooking is an important part of the local food. Flowers and fruits are often used as ingredients and add a new dimension to Yunnan cuisine. Mushrooms are essential to Yunnan cooking. Matsutake, ganba, porcini (cep), and chanterelle are just some of the prized mushrooms available fresh, and should definitely be tried. Some of the popular mushroom dishes include Fried Rice with Ganba (page 550), Sautéed Porcini Mushrooms (page 471), and Chanterelle with Tuberose (page 466).

Other dishes that should also be sampled are Yunnan Ham in Honeyed Sauce (page 332), Chicken with Papaya (page 278), and Dai Chicken with Coconut (page 282).

GUIZHOU
Located on the Yunnan-Guizhou Highland in southwest China, Guizhou is a mountainous region with a subtropical humid climate and inhabited by a number of ethnic groups.

Influenced by its diversity, the cuisine is characterized by the spiciness and sourness from the fermentation of ingredients. Ingredients such as chile, garlic, scallions (spring onions), mint, bay leaf, cumin, and Sichuan peppercorns are often mixed into a sauce and used as a dip. Fish in pickled soup is perhaps Guizhou's most famous dish but other popular dishes include rice in a bamboo tube and Chicken with Black Poplar Mushrooms (page 257). The famous Maotai wine is also a product of Guizhou.

GUANGXI

Adjacent to Guangdong Province, Guangxi is set on hilly terrain with the South China Sea to its south while bordering Vietnam to the west. Inhabited by many ethnic groups, the area boasts a diverse spectrum of culture. Guangxi cuisine is represented by the hilly area to the north around Guilin, where animals from the hills are considered delicacies, and their flavors tend to be heavy and slightly spicy. The coastal area also offers a bounty of fresh and dried seafood. Cooking by the various ethnic groups represents still another facet of Guangxi cuisine as ingredients like flowers, bamboo, and other natural products are used together with preserved vegetables and cured meats.

Guangxi is famed for its taro roots, water chestnuts, and Osmanthus flowers, which are often featured in various recipes. Dishes like Pork Belly with Taro (page 318), Stuffed Pumpkin Flowers (page 449), and Water Chestnut Soup with Osmanthus Sugar (page 626) are perfect Guangxi recipes to make at home.

CENTRAL CUISINE

Best known for the water resources, freshwater fish is a key part of Hubei and Jiangxi's cuisine.

HUBEI

Hubei, situated in central China with the Yangtze River flowing through from west to east, is dotted with freshwater lakes and has earned the title of "the province of a thousand lakes."

With abundant freshwater resources, the cooking of fish features in some of Hubei's signature dishes, the best known among them being Fish with Chinese Celery and Bamboo Shoots (page 152). Hubei people enjoy slow-cooked soups and Lotus Root and Sparerib Soup (page 114) is prepared in almost every home. Meat prepared with rice is popular and a classic dish is Meatballs with Glutinous Rice (page 330). A specialty vegetable known as purple brassica is ubiquitous in the Wuhan area, and Purple Brassica with Cured Pork (page 354) can be found in almost all restaurants.

JIANGXI

Situated northeast of Guangdong and east of Hunan, Jiangxi is surrounded by mountains on three sides with over 2,000 rivers flowing through the area. It is also the location of China's largest freshwater lake, the Boyang Hu, and fresh fish is the highlight of Jiangxi's cuisine, boasting more than 140 species of fish within these waters.

Jiangxi cuisine favors the use of red braising, steaming, double steaming, and stir-frying and its tastes run from spicy and salty to oil-rich, probably owing to the warm and humid climate and the culinary influences from the neighboring Hunan province. Some of Jiangxi's best-known dishes include Sautéed Fish Rolls (page 168), Braised Carp (page 159), Jiangxi-style Duck (page 293), and Pork with Sesame Seeds (page 370). Double-steamed soup is also a specialty of the area.

OTHER IMPORTANT CUISINES

BUDDHIST VEGETARIAN

Mahayana Buddhism, when introduced into China 2,000 years ago, was changed to Chinese Buddhism and remains a vibrant religion today alongside Taoism. Chinese Buddhism forbids killing and eschews the consumption of all meat and meat-derived products.

A unique aspect of Chinese Buddhist vegetarian dishes is the prohibitive use of certain ingredients. Garlic, onions, scallions (spring onions), garlic chives, and shallots produce a smell that is considered offensive and believed to be disruptive to those in meditation and learning, and are therefore banned from Buddhist vegetarian dishes. Harmony among the students in the group is important.

Temples throughout China offer vegetarian meals to visitors, and it is customary for believers, though not necessarily vegetarians, to partake, especially during certain festive days. On these occasions, you are likely to see dishes such as Vegetables with Red Bean Curd (page 476), Wheat Gluten with Chestnuts (page 481), Crispy Taro Roll (page 485), and Vegetarian Congee with Corn and Sweet Potato (page 490).

HONG KONG

Starting as a fishing village, Hong Kong developed a cuisine derived from various food styles as well as influences from Southeast and South Asia. Hong Kong's strength lies in its ability to assimilate ideas and techniques from others and make them its own. As a free port, Hong Kong has access to ingredients from all over the world, giving it the opportunity to create and preserve dishes that are uniquely Hong Kong.

Freshness is at the heart of Hong Kong cuisine. Vegetables are picked and sold on the same day, and meats are delivered to the market as soon as the animals are slaughtered. The best fish, whether freshwater or saltwater, are expected to be swimming in tanks to ensure freshness. It is customary for people to shop for food daily so that they may get the freshest vegetables and meat, and to cook them on the same day.

Some of Hong Kong's well-known dishes include Egg and Beef Rice Casserole (page 564), Baked Pork Chops over Rice (page 552), Soy Sauce Chicken (page 283), Jingdu Spareribs (page 336), and tasty Hong Kong-style Egg Tarts (page 648).

INNER MONGOLIA

When Genghis Khan led his army across the Mongolian highlands and through Central Asia, he brought with him horses and livestock. Everything else had to be transportable on pack animals, ready to move in an instant. A readily mobile army had no time to spare for cooking and food consisted mostly of dried meat and bread.

Traditionally, Mongolians were nomads, and they moved their base to where the grass was plentiful for their animals. Everything, including the yurt (Mongolian tent) in which they lived, had to be packed and ready to move the next day. They carried only the barest of utensils, which were to be used and packed away daily. Cooking often meant boiling or roasting a whole goat (or lamb), which would then be eaten with cheese and tea or wine.

Today's Mongolians are settled in cities and towns and no longer have to move for their livelihood, but their favorite foods remain very much the same despite influences from Sichuan and other regions. Visit a Mongolian family and you will be treated to endless cups of salty tea, served with roasted millet and cheeses. The food usually includes boiled mutton ribs and a salad of wild scallions (spring onions) or turnips. Goat liver sausage is a delicacy and, if available, should not be missed. Breakfast means a bowl of Millet Congee (page 575) accompanied by salad and cold cuts.

SHANGHAI

Shanghai started as a fishing village over 2,000 years ago and became the fiefdom of Lord Chunshen during the Spring and Autumn period (771–476 BC). It gained its current name during the Song Dynasty when it was named the Shanghai Town, meaning "the town upon the sea." The town prospered during the Ming Dynasty as an embroidery and trade center but it was not until the modern era when Shanghai became an international metropolis both in terms of finance and trade.

Shanghai cuisine consists of two styles: one which is developed locally and another which absorbs elements from nearby regions Anhui, Jiangsu, and Zhejiang. The local style is often characterized by its "oily, sweet, and intensive flavor." Typical dishes include Braised Red Meatballs (page 375), Fish in Distilled Grain Sauce (page 145), and Corvina with Scallions (page 174). The other style took from other regions the lighter, less oily way of cooking and includes dishes such as Kalimeris and Tofu Salad (page 50), "Vegetarian Crab with Tofu" (page 456), and Drunken Chicken (page 56).

TAIWAN

Located east of the China mainland, Taiwan was inhabited by Taiwanese aborigines until the mid-seventeeth century when the Han Chinese, mostly from Fujian across the strait and from Meizhou (which was considered as the home of the Hakkas), migrated from the mainland to escape the rule of the Manchus and became the largest ethnic group. Since 1949, people from other provinces, such as Jiangsu, Zhejiang, Hunan, and Sichuan, moved to Taiwan in large numbers, and some of their cooking styles have been integrated into Taiwanese cooking.

Taiwan cuisine is similar to much of Fujian and Hakka cooking. Sautéing, braising, steaming, and deep-frying are the major techniques with heavy use of soy sauce and sugar. Dishes such as Pork Belly in Soy Sauce (page 388), Squid with Chiles and Cilantro (Coriander, page 233) and braised Tofu with Preserved Mustard Greens (page 505) exemplify these cooking styles. Other dishes such as Vegetable Roll (page 522), Vermicelli with Tuna (page 599) and Taiwan-style Beef Noodles (page 576) are local Taiwanese creations.

AT THE CHINESE TABLE

Eating in China is rarely a solo occasion, whether taking a snack or something more substantial. Eating is as much about sustenance as it is about communing with others as an expression of love and respect. The careful preparation of a dish, perhaps a Winter Melon Soup (page 98), given as a tonic when one is run-down, or sweet fried sesame seed balls presented as a gift, is more of a sign of affection than an embrace or a kiss. Even something as simple as selecting the choicest morsel of food from a communal dish and placing it in another person's bowl is a mark of deference.

With the proliferation of street food vendors in China in the past three decades, the ritual of eating together is no longer confined to the home or restaurants. As beloved as a carefully prepared home-cooked meal or lavish banquet is to the Chinese people, a tasty quick snack, and the chance to socialize at all hours of the day and night, can be had on every street corner in China.

A hot meal traditionally starts the day: perhaps a bowl of rice porridge known as congee (pages 568–75) with fried dough sticks, popular all over the south; or hot fresh soy milk, a favorite morning staple of the Taiwanese; and then there is yum cha, the beloved tradition, in Guangzhou and Hong Kong, of eating dumplings and other small dishes while sipping tea. For a victual on the go, it may be da bing, a griddled wheat-flour pancake, topped with scallions (spring onions) and sesame seeds in Shanghai; Nanjing's jidan bing, a fried egg puff; or jian bing, an egg, lettuce, and hoisin crepe, arguably China's most obsessed-over breakfast street snack.

Lunch is no less varied. As with breakfast, it's often eaten in a hurry. It might be noodles, in a bowl topped with a piquant sauce and a little protein, such as spicy Sichuan Dan Dan Noodles (see page 590); the noodles may be stir-fried with a few greens and slithers of meat, such as Char Kway Teow (page 588); or they may be featured in a hearty bowl of soup (pages 86–123). Lunch may also be rice or steamed bread with a few basic accompaniments.

When it comes to dinnertime, a home-cooked family meal generally consists of a few simple, shared dishes. Chinese cuisine has a reputation for being elaborate and complicated, which may be true of banquet cookery, but everyday home cooking is satisfyingly straightforward and easy to attempt.

It's typical to have as many dishes as the number of people. Generally cold dishes are served first followed by hot dishes, progressing from light to heavy. A light broth or clear soup— perhaps taken as a tonic—may be served either at the beginning of a meal, as is the custom in Guangzhou, or at the end, which is the Sichuan way. Dessert is more often eaten on special occasions, where sweet soups—such as Red Bean Soup (page 644) and Black Sesame Soup (page 638)—or small pastries like Almond Cookies (page 653) are popular. In a formal banquet setting, the progression—from cold plates, wok dishes, braises, mains, rice, sweet soup, and fruit—is more strictly adhered to, but in smaller households, all of the dishes may be laid out on the table at the same time.

In this book, the number of servings is based on these traditional food customs of China. In other words, if a recipe indicates a serving for 4, this is to be shared at a table along with 3–4 other dishes as well as steamed rice. We appreciate the eating habits are slightly different in the West and recipes can be double for larger per serving portions but we encourage you to also try our customs, which allows for more variety and options at the table!

Modern-day cooks, with intrepid appetites and curiosity, and thanks to the wide availability of a vast array of Chinese ingredients, will be inclined to mix and match dishes from a variety of Chinese regions, similar to the way that foreign "Chinese" restaurants showcase the signature dishes from each province, and I encourage you to do the same when planning a meal using this book.

When deciding what to cook, whether creating a shared meal for two or ten, the ancient

INTRODUCTION

custom of balance and harmony still applies today. The meal should have a variety of contrasting flavors, textures, and colors, because much of the enjoyment of a Chinese meal is to be found experiencing a little of everything on offer.

Variety is truly the spice of life and we feel it's important to use the freshest of ingredients to create a well-rounded meal. For example, vegetables are often purchased from market stalls and fish and seafood are often live until the very moment the catch is purchased.

When cooking chicken, we always believe that starting with a whole chicken means you get fresher meat than when using cut up parts from the supermarket. We use thighs and breasts only when the dish calls for diced or filleted chickens. Also, when using whole chickens for recipes such as Drunken Chicken (page 56) or Hainan Chicken Rice (page 542), consider using corn-fed chickens, which will give the skin a beautiful yellow color.

I am aware that North Americans don't like bones, whether in fish or poultry, but that is the way of traditional Chinese cooking. We think chicken tastes better with bones and you will find this the case in many of the poultry and meat recipes. If you find it an issue, then we suggest for our readers to purchase filleted fish or boneless chicken and meat.

A balanced menu may consist of a cold bite, something stir-fried, a steamed plate, perhaps a braise; soft-textured foods should be offset by something crisp; there should be some dry dishes and some saucy ones; robustly flavored dishes (salty, spicy, fiery, pungent, oily, sour) should be countered with refreshing, delicate notes in another.

The meal should also be balanced in your ability and means to produce it; a menu in which every dish is a stir-fry that must be cooked at the very last minute, meant to be served piping hot, is not practical. In ancient times, when fuel was a precious commodity, it was traditional to cook an entire meal in the wok: raw rice and water lay in the base of the wok, then a stack of bamboo steamers was arranged on top, each tier containing steamed dishes or a soup. This ingenious method still applies to the modern cook who has limited room on the stove top.

On another practical note, when cooking for many, it's customary to increase the types of dishes with each additional person instead of scaling up the portions. However, it can be unrealistic for the beginner cook to attempt so many recipes, so use your judgment and simply increase the quantity of the servings. I would advise against upsizing stir-fries, though, as you risk overcrowding your wok, thus losing wok chi or hay (the prized seared taste that comes from a fiery, flaming-hot wok), and the ingredients will sauté instead of sizzle. If upscaling, cook the stir-fry in two batches. For special occasions, add another dish for the table. Use the servings in the recipes as a guide only because a complete meal will depend on how many dishes are being shared.

COOKING TECHNIQUES

A commendable dish relies, naturally, on the quality of its constituents. The aim of cooking is to showcase the pure flavor of the ingredients.

While stir-frying is the most common technique associated with Chinese cooking, it is but one of hundreds. The Chinese break down cooking styles to detail the finer complexities. We have outlined the most common methods, which may seem similar but the differences lie in the subtle details. Some techniques are used to create a desired texture, others to seal in moisture.

The preparation and organization of your ingredients will influence the execution of your cooking. In fact, the majority of a Chinese cook's time is spent preparing ingredients, rather than cooking them. There are more than 100 Chinese names for cutting techniques, with different ingredients requiring specific cuts. Ultimately, the aim is to cut ingredients so that they are the same size and shape for even cooking, and to slice meats for optimal tenderness.

BAKING (JU, 焗)
Baking is the method used to describe food that is cooked for a prolonged period of time using dry heat and often in an oven. See Walnut Cookies (page 654). Salt-baking (yan ju, 盐焗) is the term used when ingredients are encased in salt, with or without a sheet of paper in between, and baked in an oven or a dry wok until done. See Salt-Baked Chicken (page 290). Baking in low heat (xiao huo ju, 小火焗) is a technique, which uses hot air in an enclosed space like a pot or a wok with a lid. See Shrimp with Black Pepper and Basil (page 198).

BLANCHING (CUAN, 汆)
The ingredients are cooked in hot water or soup for a short period of time, then submerged in a bowl of cold water in order to retain the freshness and the original flavor. Ingredients, particularly vegetables, should be placed in boiling water so the cook can control the blanching time. Occasionally, meat or fish is placed in cold water and then boiled, but this only occurs when we want to arrive at an even temperature throughout the ingredients.

BOILING (BAO, 煲)
Ingredients are boiled in a large saucepan of water, reduced to lower heat, and simmered for 1–2 hours. See Lotus Root, Dried Octopus and Pork Soup (page 116).

BRAISING (HUI, 烩)
Braising often combines both dry- and moist-heat cooking: the ingredient is first seared at a high temperature, then transferred, with seasoning and some type of liquid, to a wok or saucepan and simmered for a short period of time. See Sautéed Mushrooms with Fish Puffs (page 138) or longer durations. Not surprisingly, the Chinese have several ways to braise food. Braising in a covered pot (men, 焖) means to stir-fry ingredients, usually meats, in a covered saucepan until slightly browned and then adding water so the dish braises over medium heat for a long period of time. See Pork Belly with Lotus Root (page 385). Braising in an uncovered pot (wen, 炆) is similar to braising in a covered pot but the food is thickened with a starch. See Catfish with Garlic, (page 173).

DEEP-FRYING (ZHA, 炸)
Deep-frying in oil is a popular Chinese cooking method as it cooks the ingredients within a short time. If a crispy crust is desired, deep-frying will be done twice. The ingredients will first be deep-fried until fully cooked and then removed from the oil briefly to lower the internal temperature of the ingredients and to let some of the moisture escape. The oil is then reheated to the desired temperature and the ingredients returned to the oil to deep-fry quickly to obtain a crispy crust without overcooking the ingredients. For very delicate ingredients such as shrimp (prawns), this may be done a total of three times. See Deep-Fried Shrimp (page 69). When deep frying and braising (ta, 塌), ingredients are first dipped in batter, then deep-fried or

pan-fried, and finally, braised or sautéed in a small amount of sauce. See Sautéed Deep-fried Tofu (page 516).

DOUBLE BOILING (DUN, 隔水炖)
Double boiling is to cook slowly through indirect heat without disturbing the food. The ingredients are combined and seasoned, with or without water, in a sealed container, which is then placed in a wok or steamer and steamed over high heat for 1–3 hours. More water may be added if needed. See Lion's Head Meatballs in Chicken Broth (page 324). When double boiling and inverting (kou, 扣), the ingredients are put into a sealed bowl until fully cooked and then inverted onto another platter to create a mound-like shape. Use a dish towel to hold the hot bowl, then cover the bowl with a plate and drain the sauce into another bowl. Invert the bowl to transfer the contents to the plate, then pour the sauce over the hot food. (Alternatively, just transfer the contents to a plate without inverting.) See Pork with Preserved Mustard Greens (page 320).

DREDGING (ZOU YOU, 走油)
Ingredients are lightly dredged in oil then heated over low or medium-low heat for about a minute to partially cook the ingredients in preparation for the next stage of cooking (which is usually stir-frying). Often used for meats and seafood such as shrimp (prawn), this method reduces the time for stir-frying and prevents ingredients from overcooking. See Shrimp and Longjing Tea (page 188). Another technique known as dredging in oil and sautéing (liu, 熘) has ingredients dredged in heated oil, then lightly sautéed with a thickened sauce. See Fish in Distilled Grain Sauce (page 145).

HONEYED SAUCE (MI ZHI, 蜜汁)
Sugar, either caramelized or in its natural state, is combined with ingredients and cooked over a long period so that the ingredients are coated with a sugared syrup. See Double-Boiled Cured Ham (page 382).

JELLIFYING (DONG, 冻)
Meat is first cooked over low heat until soft, and then chilled together with a meat broth until gelatinous. See Beef Jelly (page 58).

MARINATING (YAN PAO, 腌泡)
Ingredients are combined with seasonings to add flavor and to tenderize meat in preparation for the next step of cooking. See Sweet and Sour Spareribs (page 366). When marinating with wine (zui, 醉), precooked ingredients are soaked in wine for hours to acquire a strong wine flavor. See Drunken Chicken (page 56).

MIXING (BAN, 拌)
Raw or cooked ingredients are combined with seasonings and served immediately. See Lotus Root with Ginger (page 80).

PICKLING (YAN, 腌)
Raw fresh vegetables are mixed with salt and seasonings and left to ferment in a closed jar to pickle for several days. See Pickled Vegetables (page 49).

ROASTING (KAO, 烤)
Cooking by hot air in an oven. See Barbecue Pork (page 394).

RED BRAISING (HONG SHAO, 红烧)
Red braising is a special technique where ingredients are braised in a caramelized soy sauce and sugar mixture and take on a beautiful, deep red hue. See Hunan-Style Pork Belly (page 379). Dry braising (gan shao, 干烧) pre-processes the ingredient, usually by deep-frying, to reduce the natural juice so that it quickly absorbs more flavor in the subsequent step. The ingredient is braised in a sauce over medium heat, which is then reduced to a very thick sauce over high heat. See Fish in Chili Sauce (page 170). Soft braising (ruan shao, 软烧) also pre-processes the ingredient—but usually by blanching, scalding, or other means—and braises it in sauce over low heat until the sauce thickens. See Braised Tofu (page 503).

ROLL-CUTTING (GUN DAO, 滚刀)
Roll-cutting (or oblique cutting) is used for long vegetables, such as Asian eggplants (aubergines), carrots, and zucchini (courgettes). It makes attractive chunks and exposes more of the surface area of the vegetable for faster cooking. Hold the blade of the knife perpendicular to the board and cut straight down on the diagonal, then roll the vegetable a quarter-turn, and cut straight down again at the same diagonal angle. Continue rolling and cutting in this way all along the length of the vegetable. You can also cut large potatoes and tomatoes into oblique cuts. Just quarter them first to get easier pieces to work with. See Yan Du Xian Soup (page 113).

SCALDING (*ZHUO*, 灼)
Scalding is similar to blanching, but does not require submerging ingredients in cold water. Ingredients are thinly sliced and then dipped into boiling water to finish.

SHALLOW-FRYING (*JIAN CHAO*, 煎炒)
Shallow-frying uses less oil than deep-frying and lower heat than stir-frying, resulting in dishes that are often golden or crispy on the outside and tender on the inside. When shallow-frying, the ingredients should be fried on one side first and then flipped over and fried on the other side. Pan-frying (*jian*, 煎) means cooking and browning ingredients in a wok or pan with a small amount of oil. See Pot Stickers (page 70). When pan-baking (*luo*, 烙), ingredients are mixed with seasonings and starch and placed into a skillet (frying pan) until fully cooked into a pancake. See Noodlefish Pancake (page 168).

SLOW COOKING (*WEI*, 煨)
After bringing the ingredients (with water or sauce) to a boil, heat is reduced to low, and it cooks slowly to blend the flavor of the ingredients. See Braised Beef in a Casserole (page 409).

SMOKING (*XUN*, 熏)
Ingredients are precooked and then smoked in dry heat with smoke generated by heating tea, sugar, and rice. See Wok-Smoked Pomfret (page 157).

STEAMING (*ZHENG*, 蒸)
Once water is heated past boiling point (212°F/100°C), it changes its form into steam. Steaming is a very gentle cooking technique ideal for cooking seafood and other delicate items. More importantly, food cooks quickly without losing nutrients through leaching. Steaming is done by putting the ingredients into a heatproof plate or bowl, which is then placed on a rack inside a covered wok or steamer filled with boiling water. (Steaming is usually done over high heat to get the maximum steam to the ingredients.) I highly recommend steaming in a wok that can accommodate both small and large dishes; however, an electric steamer is also acceptable although steaming may be limited to smaller dishes. See Steamed Grouper (page 132).

STEEPING (*JIN ZI*, 浸渍)
Two popular steeping techniques are used in Chinese cooking, often to prepare fish. One is to steep in water (*jin*, 浸): bring a large saucepan of water to a boil, then turn off the heat, put ingredients into the water, and let the heat slowly cook to completion. This method is usually reserved for fish, but it can also be used for chicken as well. See West Lake-Style Fish (page 152). The other is to steep in oil (*shui jin*, 水浸): bring a large saucepan of oil to 350°F/180°C, then turn off the heat. Slowly lower the ingredients into the oil and steep until fully cooked.

STEWING (*DUN*, 不隔水炖)
Stewing is to cook slowly through direct heat. This is done by putting the ingredients together with seasoning, and broth or water, in a sealed container such as a Dutch oven (casserole) and placing the container directly over low or medium heat for several hours. See Lamb with Wild Yam (page 431).

STIR FRYING (*CHAO*, 炒)
One of the most popular frying techniques is stir-frying—ingredients are cooked in hot oil over high heat and stirred continuously until fully cooked. See Beef in Oyster Sauce (page 398). Stir-frying over very high heat (*bao*, 爆) is used to cook ingredients very quickly, usually without sauce. See Stir-Fried Pork Kidneys (page 363). Stir-frying with a small amount of oil (*bian*, 煸) means to rapidly stir-fry ingredients until most of the moisture is removed. Seasonings are added to complete the cooking. For some vegetables that have hard coverings, like beans, moisture is first removed either by roasting in a dry pan or deep-frying in oil, then stir-frying over high heat together with other ingredients. See Stir-Fried Green Beans (page 500).

EQUIPMENT

The great thing about Chinese cooking is that much of it can be prepared by hand: from making dumplings to preparing noodles and requires only a few essential items.

At a pinch you can prepare and cook Chinese food improvising with equipment you already have in your kitchen—you can stir-fry in a skillet (frying pan) instead of a wok, or use a cook's knife instead of a cleaver to cut ingredients, but I highly recommend investing in these traditional utensils to elevate your Chinese cooking. The items are affordable and their utility is not so specialized that you won't find them helpful in everyday cooking.

BAMBOO STRAINER
This strainer (sieve) is ideal for frying or straining but can be substituted with a regular strainer or even a slotted spoon.

CHOPSTICKS
It is not clear when and by whom chopsticks were invented, but the first pair of chopsticks was discovered in an ancient tomb in the city of Shangqiu (the then capital of Shang) and was made of bronze from the Shang Dynasty (1,766–1,122 BC). The first chopsticks were probably just a couple of sticks or branches used to pick up vegetables that were cooked in a cauldron, and did not survive the ages. For woks or skillets (frying pans) of hot oil, use wooden or metal (not plastic) chopsticks to stir food.

CLAY POTS
These vessels are perfect for slow-cooked stews, soups, and braised casseroles and can be used for serving as well. Before using a clay pot for the first time, be sure to fully submerge it in water and soak it for 24 hours.

CLEAVER
A cleaver is an indispensable item in the Chinese kitchen as every part of the knife can be used. In addition to cutting with the blade, the blunt top edge is excellent for pounding or tenderizing meats while the side of the blade can be used to crush garlic and ginger. A heavy cleaver should be used to chop bones (you may break the blade of a lighter one). Not all cleavers can be used to cut bones—look for a heavier knife, I prefer a quality stainless steel cleaver.

COOK'S THERMOMETER
The cook's thermometer is an essential tool to ensure that you are deep-frying at the right temperatures.

DISH TONGS
The dish tong is designed for removing hot, steamed small dishes from the steamer.

DUTCH OVEN (CASSEROLE)
A Dutch oven (casserole) is a large cast-iron or ceramic pot ideal for making soups, rice dishes, casseroles, and roasts. It can also be used as a substitute for a clay pot.

MEAT TENDERIZER
A meat tenderizer, also known as a meat mallet or meat pounder, is a durable, hand-held tool used to tenderize meat for cooking.

MORTAR AND PESTLE
A mortar and pestle can be used to crush spices such as peppercorns and to make pastes.

RICE COOKER
A rice cooker or rice steamer is a handy electric kitchen appliance designed to boil or steam rice. Rice cookers nowadays not only steam rice, but also make congee and stews. If you do not have a steamer, most rice dishes can also be prepared in a saucepan on a stove.

RICE PADDLE
A large flat spoon, often wood or plastic, used to stir and serve rice.

ROLLING PIN
Far more basic than their Western counterparts,

the Chinese rolling pin is nothing more than a 12-inch/30-cm dowel that can be used for rolling out dumplings.

SKEWERS
Wooden or metal sticks that can be used to hold pieces of meat together while grilling (griddling) or roasting.

SPICE BAG
Small, reusable cheesecloth (muslin) pouches are highly practical—they let larger, inedible herbs and spices impart their flavor during the cooking process without needing to be fished out by hand prior to serving.

SPIDER STRAINER
This type of strainer has a long handle attached with a wide shallow wire-mesh basket, used for removing hot food from liquid or for skimming foam off when making broths. A standard slotted spoon, though smaller, can be used as a substitute although it may require you to perform the task in batches.

STEAMER
The earliest pottery steamer (*zeng*, 甑) was unearthed during the excavation of the Hemudu Culture (5000–4500 BC). The earthenware had a flat base with many holes and was designed to sit on top of a cauldron (*li*, 鬲) that contained water. The steam from the heated water rose up through the holes to cook the food above, very much the same as steamers in modern kitchens.

The bamboo steamer has changed very little over the years. Cylindrical bamboo racks are stacked one upon the other so that multiple dishes can be prepared simultaneously. They are set in a wok filled with boiling water and commonly used to steam everything from rice dishes, and dumplings to fish and pork buns. Dishes can be cooked for different time periods, and more racks can be added along the way. Steaming is also a great way to preserve nutrients in food.

Bamboo steamers are available in a range of sizes and can be purchased online or in cookshops.

STEAMER RACK
Many recipes in this book—particularly those including fish and leafy greens—are steamed. When steaming, boiling water in the wok should never be high enough to touch the bottom of the plate. A metal steam rack is designed to sit in the wok and support a heatproof dish or bamboo steamer.

WOK
No other piece of equipment is as important to Chinese cooking as a wok. The wok with a round and concave bottom was a cauldron without l egs used in ancient times to cook meat and vegetables as offerings to heaven or for the entire community. When people started to build stoves in their homes, the wok was reduced in size to fit the stoves, and gradually evolved into the wok as we know it today. The heat concentrated in the bottom of the wok lets cooking be done rapidly to preserve the nutrients, the value of which was known to the Chinese long ago. When purchasing a wok, be sure to also get a wok lid, which comes in handy when steaming.

WOK RING
A wok ring rests on top of a burner to minimize movement of the wok while cooking. It's not essential but some people may find it useful.

WOK SPATULA
A metal wok spatula is used for stirring food in a wok, particularly fried rice, glutinous rice cakes, or anything that needs stirring in large quantities. A spatula (fish slice) can be used as well.

APPETIZERS & SALADS

APPETIZERS & SALADS

PREPARATION TIME: 15 MINUTES,
    PLUS 30 MINUTES SALTING TIME
COOKING TIME: 5 MINUTES
SERVES: 4

炝莴苣
CELTUCE
SALAD

- 2 STALKS CELTUCE
- ½ TEASPOON SALT
- 2 TABLESPOONS VEGETABLE OIL
- 1 TEASPOON SICHUAN PEPPERCORNS
- 1 TEASPOON GRATED GINGER
- 1 RED CHILE, SEEDED AND CUT INTO
  STRIPS
- 1 TABLESPOON LIGHT SOY SAUCE
- 1 TABLESPOON GRANULATED SUGAR
- 2 TABLESPOONS WHITE VINEGAR
- 1 TEASPOON SESAME OIL

This lettuce is grown for its mild and tasty stalk, which is often peeled, sliced, and stir-fried. It's available in Asian supermarkets, but celery makes an acceptable substitute.

* Trim off the leafy part and the base of the celtuce, leaving only the middle portion of the stems, and then peel off the outer layer to reveal the tender core of the stem. Discard the leaves. Cut the stems into 1½-inch/4-cm lengths, then cut into strips. Put the celtuce into a colander and sprinkle with the salt. Set aside for about 30 minutes, then pat dry with paper towels.
* Heat the vegetable oil in a wok or large skillet (frying pan) over low heat, add the Sichuan peppercorns, and stir-fry for 1–2 minutes until fragrant. Add the ginger and chile, then stir in the soy sauce, sugar, vinegar, and sesame oil to make a fragrant sauce. Turn off the heat. Mix the celtuce through the sauce while still hot. Serve either warm or cold.

REGION: GUANGDONG
PREPARATION TIME: 5 MINUTES
COOKING TIME: 5 MINUTES
SERVES: 2–4

凉拌苦瓜
BITTER MELON SALAD

- 1 BITTER MELON
- ½ TEASPOON SALT
- ½ TABLESPOON LIGHT SOY SAUCE
- ½ TABLESPOON BLACK OR BALSAMIC
  VINEGAR
- ½ TEASPOON SESAME OIL

* To prepare the bitter melon, use a paring knife or peeler to pare only the skin into spoon-size pieces. Discard the rinds and seeds.
* Bring a small saucepan of water to a boil over high heat, add the bitter melon, and blanch for about 30 seconds. Drain the melon, transfer to a bowl and mix with the salt while the melon is still warm. Set aside to cool.
* Mix in the soy sauce and vinegar, then drain the sauce from the bowl. Mix in the sesame oil and serve as a salad.

鸡丝凉皮
CHICKEN SALAD
WITH NOODLES

REGION: TIANJIN
PREPARATION TIME: 10 MINUTES,
  PLUS 20 MINUTES SOAKING TIME
COOKING TIME: 15 MINUTES
SERVES: 4

* Toast the sesame seeds in a small pan over medium heat and shake occasionally for 3–5 minutes, or until golden brown. Set aside.
* Place the chicken breasts in a collapsible pot or bamboo steamer over a pot of boiling water. Steam, covered, for 10 minutes, or until cooked through. Remove and set aside to cool, then shred the meat.
* Place the mung bean sheets in a large heatproof bowl, add boiling water to cover, and soak for 20 minutes until softened. Drain and refresh the sheets in cold water, then drain again. Trim away the firm part along the edges of the sheets and cut the sheets into strips. Put into a bowl and mix with the sesame oil.
* Combine the sesame paste with 2–3 tablespoons water in a small bowl to thin out. Add the soy sauce and sesame oil and mix well.
* Mix the chicken, noodles, and salad dressing in a large bowl, then season to taste. Transfer to a serving plate, sprinkle with salt and the toasted sesame seeds, and serve.

- 1 TEASPOON SESAME SEEDS
- 3 BONELESS, SKINLESS CHICKEN BREASTS
- 7 OZ/200 G DRIED MUNG BEAN SHEETS
- 1 TABLESPOON SESAME OIL
- SALT, TO TASTE

  FOR THE DRESSING:
- 1 TABLESPOON SESAME PASTE
- ½ TABLESPOON LIGHT SOY SAUCE
- 1 TABLESPOON SESAME OIL

青芥辣青瓜拌鸡丝
CHICKEN SALAD
WITH WASABI

REGION: HONG KONG
PREPARATION TIME: 5 MINUTES
COOKING TIME: 20 MINUTES
SERVES: 2

* Bring 4¼ cups (34 fl oz/1 liter) water and 1 teaspoon salt to a boil in a large saucepan over high heat. Add the chicken breast. Cover, turn off the heat, and steep the chicken for 15 minutes, or until cooked through.
* Remove the chicken and set aside to cool. Remove and discard the skin and shred the chicken.
* Toast the sesame seeds in a small pan over medium heat and shake occasionally for 3–5 minutes, or until golden brown. Set aside.
* Combine the wasabi, mayonnaise, and remaining ½ teaspoon salt in a bowl and mix well.
* Mix the chicken and cucumber in a salad bowl, add the wasabi sauce, and toss thoroughly. Sprinkle the toasted sesame seeds on top of the salad.

- 1½ TEASPOONS SALT
- 1 BONELESS, SKIN-ON CHICKEN BREAST
- 1 TEASPOON SESAME SEEDS
- 1 TEASPOON WASABI
- 3 TABLESPOONS MAYONNAISE
- 1 CUCUMBER, SEEDED AND CUT INTO 2-INCH/5-CM MATCHSTICKS

REGION: GUANGDONG
PREPARATION TIME: 10 MINUTES
COOKING TIME: 15 MINUTES
SERVES: 4

麻酱茄子
EGGPLANT SALAD
WITH SESAME SAUCE

- 1 TEASPOON SESAME SEEDS
- 2 EGGPLANTS (AUBERGINES), CUT INTO ½ × 2½-INCH/1 × 6-CM STRIPS
- 3 TABLESPOONS SESAME PASTE
- ½ TABLESPOON LIGHT SOY SAUCE
- 2 CLOVES GARLIC, CHOPPED
- 1 SCALLION (SPRING ONION), CHOPPED

* Toast the sesame seeds in a small pan over medium heat and shake occasionally for 3–5 minutes, or until golden brown. Set aside.
* Place the eggplants (aubergines) on a heatproof plate and put into a collapsible pot or bamboo steamer over a pot of boiling water. Steam, covered, for 15 minutes, or until tender. Drain the water in the plate and set aside to cool.
* Put the sesame paste and 2–3 tablespoons water into a small bowl and stir. Add the soy sauce and garlic.
* Drizzle the sauce over the cooled eggplants and top with the sesame seeds and scallion (spring onion).

REGION: HONG KONG
PREPARATION TIME: 15 MINUTES,
    PLUS 8 HOURS SOAKING TIME
COOKING TIME: 5–10 MINUTES
SERVES: 4

青瓜拌海蜇
JELLYFISH AND
CUCUMBER SALAD

- 1 TEASPOON SESAME SEEDS
- 7 OZ/200 G JELLYFISH, RINSED
- 1 TABLESPOON SALT
- ½ RED CHILE, SEEDED AND CHOPPED
- 1 CUCUMBER, SEEDED AND CUT INTO FINE STRIPS

FOR THE SAUCE:
- 3 TABLESPOONS RED VINEGAR
- 2 TABLESPOONS GRANULATED SUGAR
- 2 TEASPOONS LIGHT SOY SAUCE
- 2 TEASPOONS SESAME OIL
- SALT

* Toast the sesame seeds in a small pan over medium heat and shake occasionally for 3–5 minutes, or until golden brown. Set aside.
* To prepare the jellyfish, remove the gut and mouth on the underside of the umbrella, trim off the tentacles and arms, and scrape the skin to remove the mucous membrane. Rinse again thoroughly.
* Dissolve 1 teaspoon salt in 9 cups (76 fl oz/2.25 liters) water in a large bowl, and soak the jellyfish skin for 8 hours, changing the water twice and adding 1 teaspoon salt each time. Cut the jellyfish skin into ¼-inch/5-mm-wide strips.
* Fill a large bowl with ice-cold water and set aside.
* Bring a large saucepan of water to a boil over high heat, turn off the heat, and let the water cool down to between 160–175°F/70–80°C. Add the jellyfish strips and let stand for 1 minute until they curl. Use a slotted spoon to transfer the strips to the ice-cold water. When the strips regain their original thickness, drain and transfer to a bowl. Add the chile.
* To make the sauce, combine the vinegar, sugar, soy sauce, and sesame oil in a small bowl. Season with salt. Pour half of the sauce into the bowl with the jellyfish and set aside the remainder. Marinate the jellyfish for 5 minutes, then drain any excess liquid from the bowl. Stir the remaining sauce into the jellyfish mixture. Arrange the cucumber strips on a serving plate, then top with the jellyfish and toasted sesame seeds.

APPETIZERS & SALADS

泡菜

PICKLED
VEGETABLES

REGION: SICHUAN
PREPARATION TIME: 30 MINUTES,
 PLUS 2 HOURS COOLING TIME,
 PLUS 7 DAYS PICKLING TIME
SERVES: 4

* Sterilize a 12½-cup (100-fl oz/3-liter) pickling jar thoroughly by washing it in hot soapy water, and then drying it in a cool oven for at least 10 minutes.
* To make the pickling juice, bring 6¼ cups (50 fl oz/1.5 liters) water and the salt to a boil in a large pot. Set aside to cool completely, then pour into the sterilized jar.
* Put the Sichuan peppercorns and star anise into a spice bag and place in the jar. Add the ginger and chiles, then pour in the kaoliang wine.
* Bring a pot of water to a boil, add the beans, and blanch for 10 seconds. Drain and dry completely.
* Rinse and pat dry all the vegetables, then add them to the jar, making sure they are completely immersed. Seal the jar and leave to pickle for 7 days in a cool, dark place.

NOTES:
The pickling juice can be reused once all the vegetables have been consumed or removed. Reboil more salt in water and then set aside to cool. Just top up with the spice bag and salted water as required.
Always use a pair of clean chopsticks or tongs to remove vegetables from the jar and reseal the jar after opening.
If a white film begins to form on the surface of the juice, just add 1–2 tablespoons kaoliang wine and reseal the jar.

• ¾ CUP (4 OZ/120 G) STRING (GREEN) BEANS, STEMS TRIMMED
• ¼ CABBAGE, CUT INTO BITE-SIZE PIECES
• 8 OZ/225 G DAIKON RADISH, CUT INTO ½ × 2-INCH/1 × 5-CM BATONS
• 2 CARROTS, CUT INTO ½ × 2-INCH/ 1 × 5-CM BATONS
• 4 RED OR GREEN CAYENNE PEPPERS

FOR THE PICKLING JUICE:
• ⅓ CUP (3½ OZ/100 G) SALT
• 3–4 TEASPOONS SICHUAN PEPPERCORNS
• 2 STAR ANISE
• ¼ OZ/10 G GINGER (ABOUT ¾-INCH/ 2-CM-LENGTH PIECE), SLICED
• 2 RED CHILES
• 4 TABLESPOONS KAOLIANG WINE

糟毛豆

PICKLED
SOYBEANS

REGION: SHANGHAI
PREPARATION TIME: 10 MINUTES, PLUS
 4–5 HOURS MARINATING TIME
COOKING TIME: 35 MINUTES
SERVES: 6–8

* Bring 8½ cups (68 fl oz/2 liters) of water to a boil in a large pot. Add the Sichuan peppercorns, salt, and five-spice powder and simmer over medium heat for 5 minutes. Add the soybeans and simmer for 20 minutes. Turn off the heat and let the soybeans steep in the residual heat for another 10 minutes. Drain, then pat the soybeans dry with paper towels. Discard the Sichuan peppercorns.
* Combine the pickled wine sauce with ½ cup (4 fl oz/ 120 ml) cold water in a large bowl, add the soybeans, making sure they are immersed in the sauce. Marinate for 4–5 hours in the refrigerator, stirring the soybeans once or twice. Remove the soybeans from the bowl, season with salt to taste, and transfer them to a serving plate.

• 1 TABLESPOON SICHUAN PEPPERCORNS
• 1 TEASPOON SALT, PLUS EXTRA TO TASTE
• 1 TEASPOON FIVE-SPICE POWDER
• 2 CUPS (11 OZ/300 G) SOYBEANS, RINSED, DRAINED, AND SHELLED
• ½ CUP (4 FL OZ/120 ML) PICKLED WINE SAUCE

REGION: SHANGHAI
PREPARATION TIME: 15 MINUTES
COOKING TIME: 5 MINUTES
SERVES: 2
📷 PAGE 51

马兰头拌香干
KALIMERIS AND
TOFU SALAD

- ½ TEASPOON VEGETABLE OIL
- 12 CUPS (11 OZ/300 G) KALIMERIS INDICA OR ARUGULA (ROCKET), RINSED
- 2 PIECES SEMI-DRIED TOFU, RINSED
- ½ TEASPOON SALT, PLUS EXTRA TO TASTE
- 1 TABLESPOON SESAME OIL

This cold Shanghai salad dish is a popular appetizer in restaurants and homes. Grown on the riversides and roadsides of China, *Kalimeris Indica* (also known as Indian aster or Indian Kalimeris) has been nicknamed the "sidewalk chrysanthemum." This wild vegetable with blue-green leaves is highly nutritious and can be found frozen in Chinese supermarkets.

* Bring a saucepan of water to a boil over high heat. Add the vegetable oil and Kalimeris Indica and blanch for 1 minute. Drain and rinse under cold running water. Squeeze out any excess water.
* Bring fresh water to a boil in the same pan and add the semi-dried tofu. Simmer over medium heat for 1 minute, then drain.
* Use paper towels to absorb any excess water from both the tofu and Kalimeris Indica. Finely chop and put into a bowl, then add the salt and sesame oil and mix thoroughly. Adjust the seasoning to taste.
* Transfer to a serving plate or for a more formal presentation, fill a 3-inch/7.5-cm stainless-steel ring mold with the mixture, packing it tightly and pressing down firmly. Press out of the mold onto a plate to serve.

REGION: FUJIAN
PREPARATION TIME: 20 MINUTES, PLUS 2 DAYS PICKLING TIME
SERVES: 6-8

酱萝卜
PICKLED RADISHES
IN SOY SAUCE

- 2¼ LB/1 KG DAIKON RADISH, UNPEELED AND THINLY SLICED
- 1 TABLESPOON SALT
- ½ CUP (4 FL OZ/120 ML) LIGHT SOY SAUCE
- 3 TABLESPOONS DARK SOY SAUCE
- ½ CUP (3½ OZ/100 G) GRANULATED SUGAR
- 1 TABLESPOON SESAME OIL

* Combine the radish and salt in a large bowl and mix. Set aside for 15 minutes, then rinse under cold running water and drain.
* Combine the radish, soy sauces, and sugar in a large bowl and mix well. Cover and refrigerate for 2 days. Drain the sauce from the bowl and mix in the sesame oil. Transfer the radishes to a plate and serve.

KALIMERIS AND TOFU SALAD

REGION: SICHUAN
PREPARATION TIME: 10 MINUTES,
  PLUS 8 HOURS PICKLING TIME
COOKING TIME: 5 MINUTES
SERVES: 6-8

泡椒藕
PICKLED
LOTUS ROOTS

- 1 LB 2 OZ/500 G LOTUS ROOTS, PEELED
  AND ENDS TRIMMED
- ¼ OZ/10 G PICKLED RED CHILES
- ½ TEASPOON SALT
- 1 TABLESPOON GRANULATED SUGAR
- 1 TEASPOON GINGER JUICE
- 2 TABLESPOONS WHITE VINEGAR

* Use a chopstick to clean the channels and rinse under
  cold running water. Cut the lotus roots into ½-inch/
  2-mm-thick slices.
* Bring a large saucepan of water to a boil, add the lotus
  root slices, and blanch for 1 minute. Drain, then set aside
  to cool. Put the lotus root slices into a sterilized jar.
* Blend the chiles, salt, sugar, ginger juice, and vinegar
  in a bowl and stir until the sugar and salt have dissolved.
  Add this mixture to the lotus roots in the jar, seal, and
  pickle for 8 hours in the refrigerator, turning over the
  lotus roots once or twice during the pickling time.

REGION: HONG KONG
PREPARATION TIME: 10 MINUTES,
  PLUS 4 HOURS SOAKING TIME
COOKING TIME: 30-35 MINUTES
SERVES: 4

豆酥
SOYBEAN CRISPS

- ⅓ CUP (2 OZ/50 G) FRESH OR FROZEN
  SOYBEANS, RINSED
- ¼ TEASPOON SALT
- ¼ TEASPOON GRANULATED SUGAR
- ¼ TEASPOON LIGHT SOY SAUCE
- 1 TABLESPOON VEGETABLE OIL

* Soak the soybeans in 1 cup (8 fl oz/250 ml) water for
  4 hours.
* Put the soaked soybeans together with the soaking
  water into a blender or food processor, and blend until
  the soybeans are the texture of breadcrumbs. Strain
  through a strainer (sieve) lined with cheesecloth (muslin)
  to separate the granules from the milk.
* Preheat the oven to 275°F/140°C/Gas Mark 1.
* Transfer the soybean granules to a nonstick baking pan
  and bake in the oven for 25 minutes to dry out. Remove
  from the oven, then stir in the salt, sugar, and soy sauce.
  Gradually add the oil. Transfer the beans to a frying
  pan and pan-fry the dry soybeans over low heat for
  5-10 minutes until crispy. Remove from the heat, cool,
  and refrigerate until needed.

NOTE:
Soybean crisps are sometimes available in Taiwanese
food shops.

老醋花生
PEANUTS IN VINEGAR SAUCE

REGION: SHANXI
PREPARATION TIME: 10 MINUTES
COOKING TIME: 5 MINUTES
SERVES: 6

* Put the peanuts into a deep saucepan and add enough oil to cover them. Deep-fry the peanuts over low heat for 4–5 minutes until crunchy. Remove the peanuts with a slotted spoon and transfer to paper towels to drain. Put the fried peanuts into a bowl. Sprinkle with the kaoliang wine and stir to mix. Set aside to cool.
* Combine the vinegar, salt, sugar, soy sauce, and garlic in a bowl and stir well to dissolve the salt and sugar. Pour the sauce over the peanuts in the bowl.

- 1⅓ CUPS (7 OZ/200 G) PEANUTS
- VEGETABLE OIL, FOR DEEP-FRYING
- 1 TABLESPOON KAOLIANG WINE
- 4 TABLESPOONS BLACK OR BALSAMIC VINEGAR
- ½ TEASPOON SALT
- 2 TABLESPOONS GRANULATED SUGAR
- 1 TABLESPOON LIGHT SOY SAUCE
- 2 CLOVES GARLIC, CHOPPED

单饼
PANCAKES

REGION: BEIJING
PREPARATION TIME: 30 MINUTES,
  PLUS 35 MINUTES PROOFING TIME
COOKING TIME: 10 MINUTES
MAKES: 20

* To prepare a cold dough, put 1¾ cups (7 oz/200 g) all-purpose (plain) flour into a large bowl, add a scant ½ cup (3½ fl oz/100 ml) cold water, and stir with chopsticks until thoroughly mixed. Transfer the dough to a clean work surface and knead until smooth. Put the dough into the bowl, cover with a damp dish towel, and set aside in a warm place to proof for 20 minutes.
* To prepare a hot dough, put 2½ cups (11 oz/300 g) all-purpose (plain) flour into a large bowl, stir in 1 tablespoon oil, and then rapidly add 1 cup (8 fl oz/250 ml) boiling water. Stir with chopsticks until fully blended. Transfer the dough to a clean work surface and knead until smooth. (If it is too hot, wait until it is cool enough to handle—but do not allow the dough to become cold). Make 2–3 cuts on the surface of the dough to release some heat.
* Weigh out 14 oz/400 g of hot dough and 3½ oz/100 g of cold dough (save the rest to use another time). Sprinkle flour over the hot dough, place the cold dough on top, and knead the combination into a smooth dough. Put the dough into a bowl, cover with a damp dish towel, and set aside in a warm place to proof for 15 minutes.
* Divide the dough into two equal portions. Roll each piece into a long roll, then divide each roll into ¾-oz/20-g pieces. Using a rolling pin, roll each piece into a thin, round disk.
* Heat 1 teaspoon oil in a skillet (frying pan) over low heat. Add a disk and pan-fry for about 1 minute on each side until slightly brown. Transfer the pancake to a plate and repeat. The pancakes can be used as wrappers in other recipes such as Muxu Pork (page 351).

- 4¼ CUPS (18 OZ/500 G) ALL-PURPOSE (PLAIN) FLOUR, FOR DUSTING
- 1⅓ TABLESPOONS VEGETABLE OIL, PLUS EXTRA FOR FRYING

FLATBREAD

REGION: SICHUAN
PREPARATION TIME: 10 MINUTES,
  PLUS 2 HOURS PROOFING TIME
COOKING TIME: 15–20 MINUTES
SERVES: 6–8

- ½ TEASPOON SALT
- 2½ CUPS (10½ OZ/300 G) ALL-PURPOSE (PLAIN) FLOUR, PLUS EXTRA FOR DUSTING

* Combine the salt and scant 1 cup (7 fl oz/200 ml) warm water in a bowl and stir until the salt has dissolved.
* Put the flour in a large mixing bowl, gradually add the salt water, and knead into a smooth dough. Cover the bowl with a damp towel and set aside to proof for 2 hours.
* Dust a cutting board with flour, place the dough on the board and divide it into 4 equal pieces.
* Take a piece of dough and roll it into a long roll. Use a rolling pin to flatten the roll into a long, flat strip. Dust the surface of the flattened strip with a pinch of flour and roll it up. Stand the roll on one end and press down with a palm to make it into a round flatbread of about ½-inch/ 1 cm thick and 4 inches/10 cm in diameter. Repeat with the remaining dough pieces.
* Put the flatbreads in a dry skillet (frying pan) and heat over medium-low heat. Turn over the flatbreads every 3 minutes for about 15–20 minutes, or until cooked through.
* Flatbreads are dry and hard and can be stored in the refrigerator for up to 3 months.

棒棒鸡

BANG BANG

CHICKEN

REGION: SICHUAN
PREPARATION TIME: 5 MINUTES, PLUS
  10 MINUTES STEEPING TIME
COOKING TIME: 5 MINUTES
SERVES: 4

- 3 BONELESS, SKINLESS CHICKEN BREASTS
- ¼ OZ/10 G GINGER (ABOUT ¾-INCH/ 2-CM-LENGTH PIECE), SHREDDED

FOR THE SAUCE:
- 1 TEASPOON SESAME PASTE
- 2 TEASPOONS CHILI OIL
- 1 TEASPOON GRANULATED SUGAR
- 1 TEASPOON BLACK OR BALSAMIC VINEGAR
- 2 TABLESPOONS LIGHT SOY SAUCE
- ½ TEASPOON GROUND SICHUAN PEPPER
- 1 TEASPOON SESAME OIL

Bang bang chicken is a chilled, cooked chicken dish served with a spicy sauce that was traditionally served in the street markets of the Hanyang district. To prepare it, a mallet is used to pound the chicken breast before its shredded (hence the name).

* Put the chicken into a large saucepan with 8½ cups (68 fl oz/2 liters) water, bring to a boil, then turn off the heat. Cover and let the chicken steep in the hot water for 10 minutes. Remove the chicken and set aside to cool.
* Put the chicken on a cutting board and pound it with a rolling pin or a meat mallet for about 1 minute to loosen the fibers. Tear the chicken by hand into fine shreds, add it to a bowl, and mix in the ginger. Transfer to a serving plate.
* Mix the sauce ingredients in a separate bowl, then pour the sauce over the chicken, and serve.

银芽鸡丝
CHICKEN SALAD WITH
BEAN SPROUTS

REGION: SICHUAN
PREPARATION TIME: 15 MINUTES
COOKING TIME: 20 MINUTES
SERVES: 4

* Remove the seeds and roots from the bean sprouts, leaving only the stems. Bring a medium pot of water to a boil, add the sprouts and blanch them for 15 seconds. Drain and allow to cool.
* Combine the bean sprouts with the sesame oil and transfer to a serving plate.
* Bring a saucepan of water to a boil, add the cayenne pepper, and blanch for 15 seconds. Drain and allow to cool.
* Bring 6¼ cups (50 fl oz/1.5 liters) water to a boil in a pot over high heat. Add the chicken breasts and turn off the heat. Let the chicken steep in the hot water for 15 minutes, then remove, and drain. When cool enough to handle, tear the chicken into fine strips, mix with the cayenne pepper, and put on top of the bean sprouts.
* Combine the dressing ingredients in a small bowl, then adjust the seasoning to taste. Pour over the chicken and serve.

• 2½ CUPS (9 OZ/250 G) BEAN SPROUTS
• 1 TEASPOON SESAME OIL
• 1 RED OR GREEN CAYENNE PEPPER, SEEDED AND THINLY SLICED
• 2 BONELESS, SKINLESS CHICKEN BREASTS

FOR THE DRESSING:
• 2 CLOVES GARLIC, CHOPPED
• 1 TABLESPOON CHILI OIL
• 1 TEASPOON SESAME OIL
• ½ TABLESPOON LIGHT SOY SAUCE
• ½ TEASPOON GRANULATED SUGAR
• ½ TEASPOON ZHENJIANG OR BALSAMIC VINEGAR
• ¼ TEASPOON SALT

椒麻鸡翅
CHICKEN WINGETTES
WITH PEPPER SAUCE

REGION: SICHUAN
PREPARATION TIME: 10 MINUTES
COOKING TIME: 15 MINUTES
SERVES: 4

* Put the chicken wingettes into a saucepan and add enough water to cover them completely. Bring to a boil over high heat and blanch the chicken wings for 1 minute. Drain and rinse under cold running water.
* Put the chicken wings back into the pan. Add the ginger and enough water to cover completely. Bring to a boil, cover, and turn off the heat. Steep the wings for 12 minutes.
* Transfer the chicken wings to a large bowl of cold water and soak until cooled. Drain.
* Bring a saucepan of water to a boil over high heat, add the bean sprouts, and blanch for 15 seconds. Drain and rinse under cold running water. Scatter the bean sprouts onto a serving plate and place the chicken wings on top.
* Roast the Sichuan peppercorns in a small dry pan over a low heat for 2–3 minutes until fragrant. Transfer the peppers into a mortar, coarsely crush with a pestle, and transfer to a bowl. Add the salt, sugar, soy sauce, chicken broth (stock), scallion (spring onion), and sesame oil and mix into a sauce. Pour the sauce over the chicken wings. Serve immediately.

• 8 CHICKEN WINGETTES
• ¼ OZ/10 G GINGER (ABOUT ¾-INCH/ 2-CM-LENGTH PIECE), SLICED
• 3 CUPS (11 OZ/300 G) BEAN SPROUTS
• 1 TEASPOON SICHUAN PEPPERCORNS
• ½ TEASPOON SALT
• 1 TEASPOON GRANULATED SUGAR
• 1 TEASPOON LIGHT SOY SAUCE
• 2 TABLESPOONS CHICKEN BROTH (STOCK)
• 1 SCALLION (SPRING ONION), CHOPPED
• 1 TEASPOON SESAME OIL

REGION: SHANGHAI
PREPARATION TIME: 15 MINUTES, PLUS
  1 HOUR DRYING AND 26 HOURS
  MARINATING TIME
COOKING TIME: 35 MINUTES
SERVES: 4–6
📷 PAGE 57

醉鸡
DRUNKEN
CHICKEN

- 1 (4½-LB/2-KG) WHOLE CORN-FED CHICKEN
- 1 TABLESPOON SALT
- ½ CUP (4 FL OZ/120 ML) GOOD-QUALITY SHAOXING WINE
- 1 TABLESPOON GINGER JUICE
- ½ BROWN SUGAR BAR
- 1 GREEN APPLE, PLUS EXTRA SLICES TO GARNISH

This Shanghainese specialty may look simple in appearance, but it is deceptively bold, deep, and complex in taste. Drunken chicken is traditionally prepared by steaming or poaching the chicken, then marinating it in a wine broth for a full day. Because it's served cold or at room temperature, it makes a perfect summer dish.

* Trim off the fat from the chicken at the tail. Hang the chicken on a meat hook to dry for 1 hour. Pat the inside dry with paper towels.
* Put the chicken on a large heatproof plate. Rub all over with the salt, 1 tablespoon wine, and ginger juice and marinate in a cool place for at least 2 hours. Turn the chicken over once or twice. Do not refrigerate.
* Wrap the chicken in microwave-safe plastic wrap (clingfilm), leaving only the tail part uncovered. Place the chicken, breast facing upward, in a collapsible pot or bamboo steamer over a pot of boiling water. Steam, covered, for 23–25 minutes, or until cooked through.
* Turn off the heat but leave covered for another 5 minutes. Remove the chicken from the steaming plate, set aside to cool, then remove the wrap. Strain the juices from the plate and reserve for later. Cut the chicken into quarters and set aside.
* Pour the reserved steamed chicken juices into a pot and add an equal amount of water and the brown sugar bar. Bring the sauce to a boil over high heat and simmer for 3–4 minutes to dissolve the sugar completely.
* Transfer the sauce to a large bowl and let cool. Add an equal amount of Shaoxing wine.
* Core the apple, cut it into 8 pieces, and add to the sauce. Add the chicken, cover with plastic wrap, and marinate in the refrigerator for 24 hours.
* The next day, remove the plastic wrap, slice the chicken into smaller pieces, and arrange on a serving plate. Spoon some of the sauce over the chicken to keep it moist. Garnish with fresh apple, if desired.

REGION: HONG KONG
PREPARATION TIME: 10 MINUTES
COOKING TIME: 40 MINUTES
SERVES: 6–8

斋鸭肾

VEGETARIAN MOCK DUCK

- 14 OZ/400 G WHEAT GLUTEN, RINSED
- 2 CUPS (16 FL OZ/475 ML)
  VEGETABLE OIL
- 1 RED CHILE, CUT INTO THIN STRIPS
- 1 LICORICE ROOT
- 3 TABLESPOONS HOISIN SAUCE
- 1 TABLESPOON SHAOXING WINE
- 3 TABLESPOONS DARK SOY SAUCE
- 3 TABLESPOONS BROWN SUGAR

* Put the wheat gluten into a large saucepan and add enough water to cover it completely. Bring to a boil over high heat and blanch for 10 minutes. Drain and rinse under cold running water. Set aside to cool, then cut into ½-inch/ 1-cm cubes.
* Heat the oil in a wok or deep saucepan to 340°F/170°C, or until a cube of bread browns in 45 seconds. Add the gluten, in batches, and deep-fry for 3–4 minutes until light brown. Use a slotted spoon to carefully remove the gluten from the oil and drain on paper towels.
* Pour out most of the oil, leaving only 1 tablespoon in the wok. Reheat the oil over medium-low heat, add the chile, and stir-fry for 1 minute until fragrant. Add the licorice root and 1 cup (8 fl oz/250 ml) water, bring to a boil, reduce to low heat, and simmer for 10 minutes. Discard the licorice.
* Stir in the gluten, hoisin sauce, wine, soy sauce, and brown sugar. Increase to medium heat and stir-fry for 4–5 minutes until the sauce thickens and clings to the gluten.

REGION: NORTHEAST
PREPARATION TIME: 15 MINUTES,
  PLUS 12 HOURS CHILLING TIME
COOKING TIME: 2 HOURS 50 MINUTES
SERVES: 4

牛筋皮凍

BEEF
JELLY

- 11 OZ/300 G BEEF TENDONS,
  CUT INTO BITE-SIZE PIECES
- 11 OZ/300 G BEEF (ANY CUT),
  SLICED
- 1 TABLESPOON SICHUAN
  PEPPERCORNS
- 1 OZ/25 G GINGER (ABOUT 2-INCH/
  5-CM-LENGTH PIECE), SLICED
- 1 TEASPOON SALT, PLUS EXTRA
  TO TASTE
- ½ TEASPOON GRANULATED SUGAR

FOR THE DIPPING SAUCE:
- 2 TABLESPOONS BLACK OR BALSAMIC
  VINEGAR
- ⅛ OZ/5 G GINGER (ABOUT ½-INCH/
  1-CM-LENGTH PIECE), SHREDDED

* Put the beef tendons in a large saucepan and add enough water to cover them completely. Bring to a boil over high heat and blanch for 15 minutes. Skim any froth and scum off the surface. Use a slotted spoon to remove the tendons and rinse them under cold running water.
* Clean the pan, add more water, and bring to a boil over high heat. Blanch the sliced beef for about 30 seconds, remove, and drain. Set aside.
* Put the Sichuan peppercorns into a spice bag. Put the tendons in a large pot, add the ginger, spice bag, and 6¼ cups (50 fl oz/1.5 liters) water, and bring to a boil over high heat. Reduce to low heat and simmer, covered, for 2 hours.
* Add the sliced beef, salt, and sugar and bring to a boil. Simmer, uncovered, for another 30 minutes. Adjust the seasoning to taste. Discard the spice bag and ginger and pour the contents into a 9 × 13-inch/23 × 33-cm rectangular pan. Cover and refrigerate for 12 hours.
* To prepare the dipping sauce, combine the vinegar and ginger in a small bowl. To serve, cut the beef jelly into thin slices, transfer to a plate, and serve with the sauce.

APPETIZERS & SALADS

蒜泥白肉
PORK WITH
GARLIC SAUCE

REGION: SICHUAN
PREPARATION TIME: 10 MINUTES,
  PLUS 2 HOURS SALTING TIME
COOKING TIME: 1 HOUR
SERVES: 4–6

* Place the pork belly, skin facing down, on the cutting board. Trim the meat to an even thickness and scrape the skin clean, then rinse the pork under cold running water. Rub the salt into the pork and set aside for 2 hours.
* Combine the star anise, Sichuan peppercorns, cinnamon, and 1 cup (8 fl oz/250 ml) water in a large saucepan. Bring to a boil, reduce to low heat, and simmer for 10 minutes.
* Add the pork and enough cold water to cover completely and bring to a boil, uncovered, then reduce to medium-low heat, and simmer gently for 20 minutes.
* Cover, turn off the heat, and set aside for 20 minutes, or until cooked through. Remove the pork and let cool completely. Cut the pork into thin slices and arrange on a serving plate.
* To make the sauce, combine the ingredients and mix well. Pour over the sliced pork (or serve on the side as a dip) and top with cilantro (coriander).

• 1 (1 LB 5 OZ/600 G) SKIN-ON, BONELESS PORK BELLY
• 1 TABLESPOON SALT
• 2 STAR ANISE
• 1 TABLESPOON SICHUAN PEPPERCORNS
• 1 SMALL CINNAMON STICK
• ¼ BUNCH CILANTRO (CORIANDER), CHOPPED

FOR THE GARLIC SAUCE:
• 1 HEAD GARLIC, CLOVES SEPARATED, SKINS REMOVED, AND CHOPPED
• 1 TEASPOON GRANULATED SUGAR
• ¼ TEASPOON SALT
• 1 TABLESPOON CHILI OIL
• 1 TEASPOON SICHUAN CHILI OIL
• 2 TABLESPOONS SESAME OIL

菜肉馄饨
PORK AND VEGETABLE
WONTONS

REGION: SHANGHAI
PREPARATION TIME: 20 MINUTES, PLUS
  15 MINUTES MARINATING TIME
COOKING TIME: 20 MINUTES
SERVES: 4

* Combine the pork, soy sauce, salt, sugar, and 4 tablespoons water in a large bowl and marinate for 15 minutes.
* Bring a large saucepan of water to a boil over high heat, add the bok choy, and blanch for 2–3 minutes. Drain and rinse under cold running water. Chop the boy choy, squeeze out most of the water, and add to the pork. Stir in the cornstarch (cornflour) and sesame oil.
* Take a wonton wrapper and lay it flat on a cutting board. Put ½ tablespoon of the meat filling on one corner of the wrapper, fold the tip over the filling, and roll past the center. Fold the 2 ends horizontally with one end over the other. Dab a little water on the ends and press tightly to seal. Repeat with the remaining wrappers and filling.
* Bring a large saucepan of water to a boil, then add the wontons in batches. Return to a boil, add ½ cup (4 fl oz/ 120 ml) cold water, and return to a boil. Once the wontons float to the surface, use a slotted spoon to transfer them to a bowl. Serve.

• 11 OZ/300 G GROUND (MINCED) PORK
• ½ TABLESPOON LIGHT SOY SAUCE
• ½ TEASPOON SALT
• 1 TEASPOON GRANULATED SUGAR
• 1 LB 5 OZ/600 G GREEN BOK CHOY
• 1 TABLESPOON CORNSTARCH (CORNFLOUR)
• 1 TEASPOON SESAME OIL
• 1 LB/450 G SHANGHAI-STYLE WONTON WRAPPERS

REGION: GUANGDONG
PREPARATION TIME: 15 MINUTES
COOKING TIME: 15 MINUTES
SERVES: 4
📷 PAGE 61

錦卤馄饨
DEEP-FRIED
WONTONS

- 2 OZ/50 G GROUND (MINCED) PORK
- 2 OZ/50 G BARBECUE PORK (PAGE 394), CUT INTO THIN STRIPS
- 1 TEASPOON LIGHT SOY SAUCE
- ½ TEASPOON CORNSTARCH (CORNFLOUR)
- ½ TEASPOON GRANULATED SUGAR
- 1 TEASPOON SESAME OIL
- 8 WONTON WRAPPERS
- 3 CUPS (25 FL OZ/750 ML) VEGETABLE OIL
- SALT

FOR THE SWEET AND SOUR SAUCE:
- ⅓ CUP (2¾ OZ/75 G) BROWN SUGAR
- 5 TABLESPOONS RED VINEGAR
- 3 TOMATOES
- 5 OZ/150 G PRECOOKED CHITTERLINGS (PIG'S INTESTINES), CUT INTO THIN STRIPS

* To make the sauce, combine the sugar and vinegar in a small bowl, mix well, and set aside.
* Score the base of the tomatoes. Bring a small saucepan of water to a boil, add the tomatoes, and heat for 1–2 minutes. Immediately transfer to a bowl of ice water. When the tomatoes are cool enough to handle, peel away the skin. Cut into chunks and set aside.
* For the filling, combine both porks, soy sauce, cornstarch (cornflour), sugar, and sesame oil in a bowl.
* Fill a small bowl with cold water. Take a wonton wrapper and lay it flat on a cutting board. Put ½ tablespoon of the pork filling in the center of the wrapper. Lift the edges of the wrapper and twist to form a parcel. Dab a little water on the ends and press tightly to seal. Repeat with the remaining wrappers and filling.
* Heat the vegetable oil in a wok or deep saucepan to 350°F/180°C, or until a cube of bread browns in 30 seconds. Gently lower the wontons, in batches, and deep-fry for 1–2 minutes until golden. Use a slotted spoon to carefully remove the wontons from the hot oil and drain them on paper towels.
* Pour out most of the oil, leaving about 1 teaspoon in the wok. Add the chitterlings (pig's intestines) and tomatoes and stir-fry over medium heat for 2 minutes. Stir in the brown sugar and vinegar, and cook until the sugar has dissolved. Strain, if desired.
* Serve the wontons with the sweet and sour sauce.

NOTE:
The wontons can be frozen for up to a month. Spread out the uncooked wontons on a plate, freeze until firm, and then transfer them to a freezer bag. When ready to serve, place the frozen wontons into a saucepan of cold water and bring to a boil over medium-high heat. When the dumplings float to the surface, add ¼ cup (2 fl oz/60 ml) cold water and return to a boil.

DEEP-FRIED WONTONS

REGION: FUJIAN
PREPARATION TIME: 15 MINUTES,
    PLUS 20 MINUTES SOAKING TIME
COOKING TIME: 12 MINUTES
SERVES: 4

三角豆腐饺
TOFU
DUMPLINGS

- 3 DRIED BLACK MUSHROOMS
- 2 OZ/50 G GROUND (MINCED) PORK
- 1 SCALLION (SPRING ONION), CHOPPED
- 1 TEASPOON SALT
- ½ TEASPOON SESAME OIL
- ½ TEASPOON CORNSTARCH
  (CORNFLOUR)
- 1 LB 2 OZ/500 G FIRM TOFU, DRAINED
- 1 CUP (8 FL OZ/250 ML) CHICKEN
  BROTH (STOCK, PAGE 90)
- GROUND WHITE PEPPER, TO TASTE
- STEAMED RICE (PAGE 540), TO SERVE

* Put the mushrooms in a bowl, cover with cold water, and soak for at least 20 minutes, or until softened. Remove the mushrooms, squeeze dry, then discard the stems and chop.
* Combine the pork, chopped mushrooms, scallion (spring onion), ½ teaspoon salt, the sesame oil, and cornstarch (cornflour) in a large bowl. Use your hands to form 16 balls.
* Use a sharp knife to shave off a thin layer of the coarse outer skin of the tofu and cut it into 16 (4-inch/10-cm) square slices, each about ⅛ inch/3 mm thick. Cut a piece of cheesecloth (muslin) to the size of the tofu slices, put a piece of tofu on a square of cheesecloth and line up the edges. Put a pork ball in the center. Carefully lift one corner of the cheesecloth and fold over to the opposite corner to form a triangle with the pork ball inside.
* Press the 2 edges of the triangle tightly to seal the tofu dumpling. Remove the cheesecloth, trim the edges of the dumpling, and carefully transfer to a plate. Repeat with the remaining tofu and pork balls to make 16 dumplings in total.
* Place the dumplings on a heatproof plate and put into a collapsible pot or bamboo steamer over a pot of boiling water. Steam, covered, for 10 minutes until cooked through.
* Heat the chicken broth (stock) in a saucepan, season with the remaining ½ teaspoon salt, and pour over the dumplings. Sprinkle with white pepper and serve with rice.

客家茶粿
HAKKA
DUMPLINGS

REGION: HAKKA, GUANGDONG
PREPARATION TIME: 15 MINUTES,
   PLUS 10 MINUTES SOAKING TIME
COOKING TIME: 20 MINUTES
SERVES: 4

When immigrants migrated from the north to the mountainous regions near Jiangxi, Fujian, and Guangdong, most of them became Hakka farmers. Easy to make and carry, dumplings were a staple for farmers who worked in the fields. They also became a favorite dim sum to be served with tea.

* To prepare the filling, put the shredded radish into a colander. Squeeze out the excess liquid, then spread out on a skillet (frying pan). Cook over medium heat for 5 minutes, or until dried. Set aside.
* Soak the dried shrimp in a small bowl of cold water for 10 minutes. Drain, finely chop, and set aside.
* Combine the pork, soy sauce, cornstarch (cornflour), and white pepper in a large bowl. Set aside.
* Heat the oil vegetable in a large skillet over high heat, add the dried shrimp and ground pork, and fry for about 1 minute to brown. Reduce to medium heat and add the shredded radish, preserved turnip, salt, sugar, and sesame oil. Adjust the seasoning to taste. Remove from the heat and set aside.
* To make the dumpling wrappers, combine both flours in a large bowl. Make a well in the middle of the dry ingredients. In a measuring cup, combine ⅔ cup (5 fl oz/150 ml) just-boiled water, the salt, and oil and pour into the well. Using a dough scraper, gently push the flour toward the center and mix. Knead, adding about ½ cup (4 fl oz/120 ml) cold water slowly, little by little, to form a soft and pliable dough. Bring the dough together and use a rolling pin to roll into a long strip and cut into 8 equal pieces. Take 1 piece of dough and roll into a flat circle about ½ inch/2 mm thick. Take a spoonful of filling and place in the center of the dough wrapper. Close the dough over the filling to form a round ball. Repeat with the remaining wrappers and filling.
* Cut a sheet of aluminum foil into eight 3-inch/7.5-cm squares and brush with oil. Place a dumpling in the center of each square and put into a collapsible pot or bamboo steamer over a pot of boiling water. Steam, covered, for 12–15 minutes.
* Heat the 1 tablespoon oil in a skillet over medium-high heat until hot. Brush each dumpling with heated oil and serve immediately.

NOTE:
The dumplings can be frozen for up to a month. Spread out the uncooked dumplings on a plate, freeze until firm, and then transfer them to a freezer bag. When ready to use, defrost the dumplings on a baking sheet lined with wax paper and then prepare according to instructions.

- 9 OZ/250 G DAIKON RADISH, SHREDDED
- 5 TABLESPOONS DRIED SHRIMP
- 7 OZ/200 G GROUND (MINCED) PORK
- ½ TEASPOON LIGHT SOY SAUCE
- ½ TEASPOON CORNSTARCH (CORNFLOUR)
- ¼ TEASPOON GROUND WHITE PEPPER
- 1 TEASPOON VEGETABLE OIL
- 4 TABLESPOONS PRESERVED TURNIP, CHOPPED
- ½ TEASPOON SALT, PLUS EXTRA TO TASTE
- ½ TEASPOON GRANULATED SUGAR
- ½ TEASPOON SESAME OIL

FOR THE DUMPLING WRAPPERS:
- 1¼ CUPS (9 OZ/250 G) GLUTINOUS RICE FLOUR
- ¾ CUP (4½ OZ/130 G) RICE FLOUR
- ¼ TEASPOON SALT
- VEGETABLE OIL, FOR BRUSHING

REGION: SICHUAN
PREPARATION TIME: 15 MINUTES,
  PLUS 15 MINUTES MARINATING TIME
COOKING TIME: 30 MINUTES
MAKES: 48
📷 PAGE 65

红油炒手
SICHUAN-STYLE
WONTONS IN RED OIL

- 5 OZ/150 G GROUND (MINCED) PORK
- ½ TEASPOON LIGHT SOY SAUCE
- ¼ TEASPOON SALT
- ½ TEASPOON GRANULATED SUGAR
- ¼ NAPA CABBAGE (ABOUT 7 OZ/ 200 G), LEAVES SEPARATED
- ½ TABLESPOON CORNSTARCH (CORNFLOUR)
- ½ TEASPOON SESAME OIL
- 48 CANTONESE WONTON WRAPPERS
- 2 TABLESPOONS CRUSHED PEANUTS (OPTIONAL)
- 1 SCALLION (SPRING ONION)

FOR THE RED OIL:
- 1 TEASPOON WHITE SESAME SEEDS
- 1 TEASPOON CHOPPED GINGER
- 3 CLOVES GARLIC, CHOPPED
- ½ TEASPOON SALT
- 1 TEASPOON LIGHT SOY SAUCE
- 1 TEASPOON CHILI POWDER
- ½ TEASPOON SICHUAN PEPPERCORNS, CRUSHED
- 4 TABLESPOONS VEGETABLE OIL
- 1 TEASPOON SESAME OIL
- 1 TABLESPOON GRANULATED SUGAR

* Combine the pork, soy sauce, salt, sugar, and 2 tablespoons water in a bowl and mix well. Marinate for 15 minutes.
* Meanwhile, make the red oil. Toast the sesame seeds in a small pan over medium heat and shake occasionally for 3–5 minutes, or until golden brown. Set aside.
* Mix the ginger, garlic, salt, soy sauce, chili powder, and crushed peppercorns in a small heatproof bowl.
* Heat the oils in a small skillet (frying pan) over medium-high heat, then pour into the bowl. Stir in the sugar and toasted sesame seeds. Set aside.
* To make the filling, bring a large pot of water to a boil, add the cabbage leaves, and blanch for 5 minutes. Drain and rinse under cold running water. Chop the cabbage, squeeze out most of the water, and add to the pork. Mix well. Stir in the cornstarch (cornflour) and the sesame oil. Mix again.
* Take a wonton wrapper and lay it flat on a cutting board. Add about ½ tablespoon of the filling in the center of the wrapper. Fold into a triangle, then fold the two ends to the center. Seal the folds with a little water. Press the ends tightly and lay on a large plate. Repeat with the remaining wrappers and filling.
* Bring a large saucepan of water to a boil over high heat. Add the wontons, in batches, and cook for 3–4 minutes until they float to the surface of the water. Add ½ cup (4 fl oz/120 ml) cold water, increase the heat, and return to a boil. Cook the wontons until they float to the surface, then use a slotted spoon to transfer them to a bowl.
* Drizzle over the red oil, sprinkle over the crushed peanuts, if using, and scallion (spring onion), and serve immediately.

NOTE:
The wontons can be frozen for up to a month. Spread out the uncooked wontons on a plate, freeze until firm, and then transfer them to a freezer bag. When ready to serve, put the frozen wontons into a saucepan of cold water and bring to a boil over medium-high heat. When the wontons float to the surface, add ¼ cup (2 fl oz/60 ml) cold water and return to a boil.

SICHUAN-STYLE WONTONS IN RED OIL

REGIONS: BEIJING AND THE NORTHWEST
PREPARATION TIME: 15 MINUTES,
    PLUS 30 MINUTES STANDING TIME
COOKING TIME: 15 MINUTES
MAKES: 32 DUMPLINGS

羊肉水饺
LAMB
DUMPLINGS

FOR THE DOUGH:
- 5 CUPS (1 LB 2 OZ/500 G) SIFTED CAKE FLOUR

FOR THE FILLING:
- 11 OZ/300 G GROUND (MINCED) LAMB OR MUTTON
- 2 SCALLIONS (SPRING ONIONS), CHOPPED
- ½ TEASPOON GRATED GINGER
- 1 TEASPOON SALT
- 2 TABLESPOONS CORNSTARCH (CORNFLOUR)
- 1 TABLESPOON SESAME OIL
- 4 TABLESPOONS BLACK OR BALSAMIC VINEGAR, TO SERVE

* To make the dough, combine the flour with generous 2 cups (17 fl oz/500 ml) water in a large bowl and knead to form a smooth dough. Cover with a damp dish towel and let stand for 30 minutes.
* Meanwhile, make the filling. Combine the lamb, scallions (spring onions), ginger, salt, and 4 tablespoons water in a bowl and set aside for 10 minutes. Mix in the cornstarch (cornflour) and sesame oil.
* Divide the dough into 4 equal portions and use a rolling pin to roll each portion into a narrow strip. Divide each strip into 8 pieces. Roll each piece of dough into a thin round dumpling wrapper, about 2½ inches/6 cm in diameter and thinner at the edges.
* To fill the wrappers, put about 1 tablespoon of filling in the center of a piece of dumpling wrapper and moisten the round edge with water. Fold the wrapper over the filling, into a semicircle, and press to seal the top firmly. Using the thumb, forefinger, and middle finger, make small pleats on one side of the dumpling and press firmly to seal half of the dumpling. Repeat with the other side of the dumpling and seal well.
* Bring a large pot of water to a boil over medium-high heat. Add the dumplings, in batches, return to a boil, and cook for 5–6 minutes until the dumplings float to the surface. Add ¼ cup (2 fl oz/60 ml) cold water and return to a boil. Remove the dumplings with a slotted spoon and place in a bowl. Serve with the vinegar on the side.

NOTE:
The dumplings can be frozen for up to a month. Spread out the uncooked dumplings on a plate, freeze until firm, and transfer the dumplings to a freezer bag. When ready to serve, place the frozen dumplings into a saucepan of cold water and bring to a boil over medium-high heat. When the dumplings float to the surface, add ¼ cup (2 fl oz/60 ml) cold water and return to a boil.

猪肉蒸饺

PORK
DUMPLINGS

REGION: JIANGSU
PREPARATION TIME: 1 HOUR, PLUS
  30 MINUTES PROOFING TIME
COOKING TIME: 12 MINUTES
MAKES: 36

* To make the dough, put the flour into a large bowl and gradually add ⅔ cup (5 fl oz/150 ml) water. Stir with chopsticks until combined. (The dough may appear a little dry and flaky.) Bring the dough together in the bowl, then put it on a work surface and knead using a pushing and folding action for 3–4 minutes until the dough is silky and smooth. If the dough seems too sticky, add a little more flour. Put the dough back into the bowl and cover with a damp dish towel. Proof at room temperature for about 30 minutes.

* To make the filling, combine the pork, salt, soy sauce, and 3 tablespoons water and mix well, then marinate for 15 minutes. Add the chives, sesame oil, and white pepper to the pork and mix well. Stir in the cornstarch (cornflour).

* Dust a clean cutting board with flour and transfer the dough from the bowl onto the board. Knead the dough for about 1 minute and cut it into 3 equal portions. Take a piece of dough and roll it into a long rod shape about ¾ inch/2 cm in diameter. Divide the dough into 12 balls (about ¼ oz/10 g each). Repeat with the remaining pieces of dough.

* Take a dough ball and roll it by hand until smooth. Place it on the board, use your palm to flatten slightly, and then use a rolling pin to roll the dough into a round dumpling wrapper about 2¾ inches/7 cm in diameter. Repeat with the remaining dough balls.

* Put about 1 tablespoon filling in the center of a piece of dumpling wrapper, and moisten the round edge with water. Fold the wrapper over the filling, into a semicircle, and press to seal the top firmly. Using the thumb, forefinger, and middle finger, make small pleats on one side of the dumpling and press firmly to seal half of the dumpling. Repeat with the other side of the dumpling and seal well. Repeat with the remaining dumpling wrappers and filling.

* Line a collapsible pot or bamboo steamer with a small square of parchment (baking) paper, leaving some room on the sides for the steam to come through. Brush a little oil over the paper. Place the dumplings in the steamer and place over a pot of boiling water. Steam, covered, for 10–12 minutes until cooked through.

* For the dipping sauce, combine the vinegar and ginger. Serve the dumplings with the sauce.

FOR THE DOUGH:
* 2 CUPS (9 OZ/250 G) ALL-PURPOSE (PLAIN) FLOUR, PLUS EXTRA FOR DUSTING

FOR THE FILLING:
* 11 OZ/300 G GROUND (MINCED) PORK
* ½ TEASPOON SALT
* 1 TABLESPOON LIGHT SOY SAUCE
* 5 OZ/150 G CHIVES, CHOPPED
* 1 TABLESPOON SESAME OIL
* PINCH OF GROUND WHITE PEPPER
* 1 TABLESPOON CORNSTARCH (CORNFLOUR)
* VEGETABLE OIL, FOR BRUSHING

FOR THE DIPPING SAUCE:
* 4 TABLESPOONS BLACK OR BALSAMIC VINEGAR
* ¼ OZ/10 G GINGER (ABOUT ¼-INCH/ 2-CM-LENGTH PIECE), SHREDDED

NOTE:
The dumplings can be frozen for up to a month. Spread out the uncooked dumplings on a plate, freeze until firm, and then transfer them to a freezer bag. When ready to use, defrost the dumplings on a baking sheet lined with wax paper and then prepare according to instructions.

REGION: SHANDONG
PREPARATION TIME: 35 MINUTES,
  PLUS 30 MINUTES PROOFING TIME
COOKING TIME: 12 MINUTES
MAKES: 36

牛肉蒸饺
BEEF
DUMPLINGS

FOR THE DOUGH:
- 2 CUPS (9 OZ/250 G) ALL-PURPOSE
  (PLAIN) FLOUR, PLUS EXTRA FOR
  DUSTING

FOR THE FILLING:
- 11 OZ/300 G GROUND (MINCED) BEEF
- ½ TEASPOON SALT
- 1 TABLESPOON LIGHT SOY SAUCE
- 1 SMALL ONION, CHOPPED
- 1 TABLESPOON SESAME OIL
- PINCH OF GROUND WHITE PEPPER
- 1 TABLESPOON CORNSTARCH
  (CORNFLOUR)
- VEGETABLE OIL, FOR BRUSHING
- 2 TABLESPOONS BLACK OR BALSAMIC
  VINEGAR, TO SERVE

* To make the dough, put the flour into a large bowl and gradually add ⅔ cup (5 fl oz/150 ml) water. Stir with chopsticks until combined. (The dough may appear a little dry and flaky.) Bring the dough together, put it on a work surface, and knead using a pushing and folding action for 3–4 minutes until the dough is silky and smooth. If the dough seems too sticky, add a little more flour. Put the dough back into the bowl and cover with a damp dish towel. Proof at room temperature for 30 minutes.

* To make the filling, combine the beef, salt, soy sauce, and 3 tablespoons water in a bowl and mix well. Marinate for 15 minutes. Add the onions, sesame oil, and white pepper and mix well. Stir in the cornstarch (cornflour).

* Dust a clean cutting board with flour and transfer the dough from the bowl onto the board. Knead the dough for 1 minute and cut it into 3 equal portions. Take a piece of dough and roll it into a long rod shape about ¾ inch/2 cm in diameter. Divide the dough into 12 balls (about ¼ oz/10 g each). Repeat with the remaining pieces of dough.

* Take a dough ball and roll it by hand until smooth. Place it on the board, use your palm to flatten slightly, then use a rolling pin to roll the dough into a round dumpling wrapper about 2¾ inches/7 cm in diameter. Repeat with the remaining dough balls. To fill the wrappers, put about 1 tablespoon filling in the center of a dumpling wrapper and moisten the edge with water. Fold the wrapper over the filling, into a semicircle, and press to seal the top firmly. Using the thumb, forefinger, and middle finger, make small pleats on one side of the dumpling and press firmly to seal half of the dumpling. Repeat with the other side of the dumpling and seal well. Do the same with the remaining dumpling wrappers and filling.

* Line a collapsible pot or bamboo steamer with a small square of parchment (baking) paper, leaving some room on the sides for the steam to come through. Brush a little oil over the paper. Place the dumplings in the steamer and place over a pot of boiling water. Steam in batches, covered, for 10–12 minutes. Serve with the vinegar on the side.

NOTE:
The dumplings can be frozen for up to a month. Spread out the uncooked dumplings on a plate, freeze until firm. and then transfer them to a freezer bag. When ready to use, defrost the dumplings on a baking sheet lined with wax paper and then prepare according to instructions.

梁溪脆鳝
DEEP-FRIED
EEL

REGION: JIANGSU
PREPARATION TIME: 15 MINUTES
COOKING TIME: 10 MINUTES
SERVES: 6

- 1 (2-LB/900-G) FRESHWATER EEL
- ½ TEASPOON SALT
- 2 CUPS (16 FL OZ/475 ML) VEGETABLE OIL
- 2 OZ/50 G GINGER (ABOUT 3-INCH/ 7.5-CM-LENGTH PIECE), HALF CUT INTO THIN MATCHSTICKS AND HALF CHOPPED
- 2 SCALLIONS (SPRING ONIONS), STEMS CUT INTO THIN LENGTHS, GREENS CHOPPED
- 2 TABLESPOONS SHAOXING WINE
- 1½ TABLESPOONS LIGHT SOY SAUCE
- 4 TABLESPOONS GRANULATED SUGAR
- 1 TABLESPOON SESAME OIL

* Using a sharp knife, cut off and discard the eel's head. Cut the eel open down the entire length of the body and remove the spine. Rub the eel with the salt, rinse under cold running water, and pat dry with paper towels. Cut the eel into 3-inch/7.5-cm chunks and then vertically into ¼-inch/ 5-mm-wide strips.
* Heat the vegetable oil in a wok or deep saucepan to 340°F/170°C, or until a cube of bread browns in 45 seconds. Add the eel and deep-fry for 3 minutes until the skin is slightly crispy. Use a slotted spoon to carefully remove the eel from the oil. Reheat the oil, return the eel to the pan, and deep-fry for another 3–4 minutes until crispy. Remove the eel and drain on paper towels.
* Pour out most of the oil, leaving about 2 tablespoons in the wok. Add the chopped ginger and chopped scallion (spring onion) greens and stir-fry for 1–2 minutes until fragrant. Add the wine, soy sauce, and sugar and toss for 2–3 minutes until the sugar is dissolved and the sauce has thickened. Add the eel, mix well, and then add the sesame oil. Transfer to a plate and top with the remaining shredded ginger and scallions.

油爆虾
DEEP-FRIED
SHRIMP

REGION: SHANGHAI
PREPARATION TIME: 15 MINUTES
COOKING TIME: 15-25 MINUTES
SERVES: 4-6

- 14 OZ/400 G WHOLE FRESHWATER SHRIMP (PRAWNS), ABOUT 2-3 INCHES/5-7.5 CM LONG, INCLUDING HEAD
- 4¼ CUPS (34 FL OZ/1 LITER) VEGETABLE OIL
- 2 TABLESPOONS GRANULATED SUGAR
- 1 TABLESPOON GRATED GINGER
- 1 TABLESPOON SHAOXING WINE
- 1 TEASPOON LIGHT SOY SAUCE
- ½ TEASPOON SALT, PLUS EXTRA TO TASTE
- 1 TABLESPOON ZHENJIANG OR BALSAMIC VINEGAR
- 2 TABLESPOONS CHOPPED SCALLIONS (SPRING ONIONS)
- ½ TEASPOON SESAME OIL

* Prepare the shrimp (prawns). Using kitchen scissors, cut off the antennas and legs. Divide the shrimp into 4 portions.
* Heat the vegetable oil in a wok or deep saucepan to 340°F/170°C, or until a cube of bread browns in 45 seconds. Gently lower the shrimp, in batches, into the oil and deep-fry for 1–2 minutes until the bubbling of the oil begins to subside. Remove the shrimp and reheat the oil to 340°F/170°C, then deep-fry for another 1–2 minutes. Repeat the process (for a total of 3 times). Put the shrimp into a colander to drain off the excess oil. Repeat with the remaining shrimp.
* Pour out most of the oil, leaving 2 tablespoons oil in the wok. Heat the oil over medium heat, add the drained shrimp, sugar, and ginger, and stir-fry for 1 minute. Drizzle the wine along the inside of the wok, put in the soy sauce, salt, vinegar, and scallions (spring onions), and stir-fry for 1–2 minutes until quite dry. Finally, stir in the sesame oil and adjust the seasoning to taste.

REGION: SHANGHAI
PREPARATION TIME: 55 MINUTES, PLUS
  15 MINUTES MARINATING TIME
COOKING TIME: 20 MINUTES
MAKES: 24
[📷] PAGE 71

锅贴
POT
STICKERS

- 11 OZ/300 G GROUND (MINCED) PORK
- 1½ TEASPOONS LIGHT SOY SAUCE
- ½ TEASPOON SALT
- 1 TEASPOON GRANULATED SUGAR
- 1 SMALL NAPA CABBAGE (ABOUT
  1 LB 5 OZ/600 G), LEAVES SEPARATED
- 1 TABLESPOON CORNSTARCH
  (CORNFLOUR)
- 1 TEASPOON SESAME OIL
- 24 LARGE DUMPLING WRAPPERS
- 1 TABLESPOON VEGETABLE OIL
- CILANTRO (CORIANDER), TO GARNISH
  (OPTIONAL)

FOR THE DIPPING SAUCE:
- 2 TABLESPOONS ZHENJIANG OR
  BALSAMIC VINEGAR
- 1 TABLESPOON SHREDDED GINGER

Pot stickers, known as *jiaozi* in China, are a kind of meat- or vegetable-filled dumpling, commonly eaten across Asia. While the dumplings can be boiled, steamed, or fried, the popular method is to fry the dumplings in a little oil, add a bit of water, and then cover to steam and cook the filling. Once the water has evaporated, the dumplings are pan-fried on one side for a crispy outside texture.

* Combine the pork, soy sauce, salt, sugar, and 4 tablespoons water, and marinate for 15 minutes.
* Bring a large saucepan of water to a boil, add the cabbage, and blanch for 5 minutes. Drain and rinse under cold running water. Chop the cabbage and squeeze out most of the water. Mix thoroughly with the pork. Stir in the cornstarch (cornflour) and sesame oil and mix well.
* Fill a small dish with cold water and set aside. Lay a dumpling wrapper in your hand and place about 1 table-spoon of filling in the middle. Brush a little water on the edge of the wrapper, fold over into a semicircle, and seal the top by firmly squeezing the edges together. Start on one end of the semicircle and create pleats by pinching and pressing the edges tightly, about 10–14 pleats per dumpling. Repeat with the remaining wrappers and filling.
* To make the dipping sauce, combine the vinegar and the ginger in a small bowl and set aside.
* Heat the oil in a large skillet (frying pan) over medium heat, add the pot stickers and ½ cup (4 fl oz/120 ml) water, and cover the pan. Cook for 20 minutes until the water has been absorbed and the bottoms of the pot stickers are golden brown. Transfer to a serving plate, garnish with cilantro (coriander), if using, and serve with the dipping sauce.

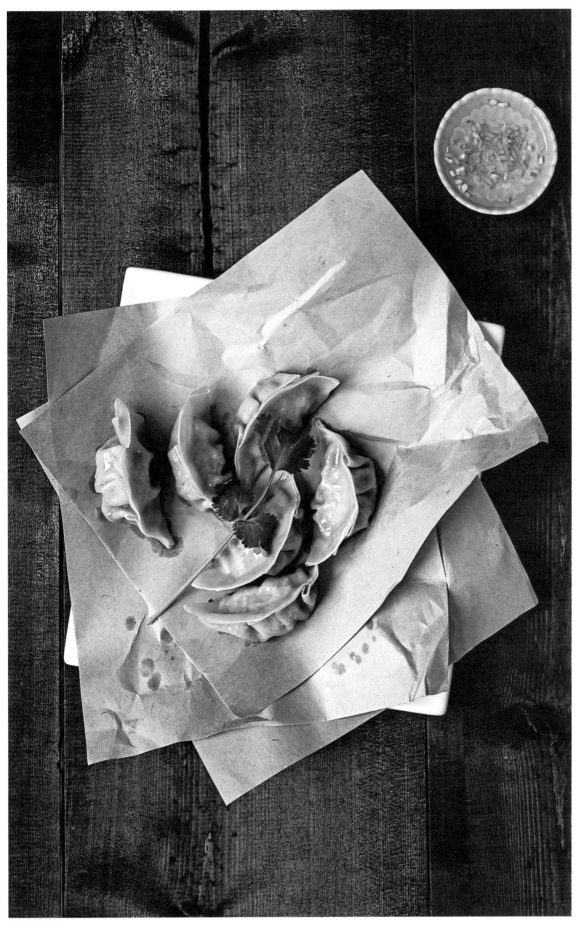

POT STICKERS

REGION: SHANGHAI
PREPARATION TIME: 5 MINUTES,
  PLUS 20 MINUTES SALTING TIME
COOKING TIME: 10 MINUTES
SERVES: 4

蜜汁凤尾鱼
DEEP-FRIED ANCHOVIES

- 1 LB 5 OZ/600 G GRENADIER OR ANY OTHER SMALL ANCHOVIES, HEADS AND STOMACHS REMOVED
- ½ TEASPOON SALT
- PINCH OF GROUND WHITE PEPPER
- 2 CUPS (16 FL OZ/475 ML) VEGETABLE OIL
- ¼ OZ/10 G GINGER (ABOUT ¾-INCH/ 2-CM-LENGTH PIECE), GRATED
- 2 CLOVES GARLIC, CHOPPED
- 3 TABLESPOONS GRANULATED SUGAR
- 1 TEASPOON FISH SAUCE
- 1 TABLESPOON SHAOXING WINE

* Rinse and drain the anchovies. Put the anchovies in a bowl, add the salt and white pepper, and set aside for 20 minutes. pat dry with paper towels.
* Heat the oil in a wok or deep saucepan to 350°F/180°C, or until a cube of bread browns in 30 seconds. Add the anchovies and deep-fry for 1–2 minutes until golden brown and crispy. Use a slotted spoon to carefully remove the anchovies from the oil and drain on paper towels.
* Pour out most of the oil, leaving about 1 tablespoon in the wok over medium heat. Add the ginger and garlic and stir-fry for 1 minute until fragrant. Stir in the sugar, fish sauce, and 2 tablespoons water and cook for 30 seconds until the sauce thickens. Add the anchovies and sprinkle in the wine. Stir gently until the sauce coats the fish. Serve immediately.

REGION: SHUNDE
PREPARATION TIME: 20 MINUTES
COOKING TIME: 10 MINUTES
SERVES: 4

顺德鱼腐
SHUNDE-STYLE FISH PUFFS

- 1 (14-OZ/400-G) DACE FISH, CLEANED, FILLETED, AND SKIN REMOVED
- ½ TEASPOON SALT
- 2 CLOVES GARLIC, CHOPPED
- ¼ TEASPOON GROUND WHITE PEPPER
- 4 TEASPOONS CORNSTARCH (CORNFLOUR)
- 4 EGGS, SEPARATED
- 1 CUP (8 FL OZ/250 ML) VEGETABLE OIL
- SWEET AND SOUR SAUCE (PAGE 169), TO SERVE

* Cut the fish fillets into slices, put them into a food processor, and process into a paste.
* Combine the fish, salt, garlic, and white pepper in a large bowl and stir with chopsticks in one direction until sticky. Add the cornstarch (cornflour) and egg yolks, then blend well. Beat the egg whites in a small bowl until foamy, then fold into the fish paste.
* Heat the oil in a wok or deep saucepan to 275°F/140°C, or until a cube of bread turns golden in 2 minutes. Add heaping teaspoons of the fish paste, in batches, using chopsticks to disperse the pieces rapidly to prevent sticking, and deep-fry for 3–4 minutes until light brown and puffed. Use a slotted spoon to carefully remove the fish puffs from the oil and drain on paper towels.
* Serve with the sweet and sour sauce.

NOTE:
Fish puffs can be refrigerated for 3–4 days and used in stir-fries, soups, or stews.

辣酒煮花螺
SNAILS IN
CHILI SAUCE

REGION: HONG KONG
PREPARATION TIME: 5 MINUTES,
   PLUS 20 MINUTES STANDING TIME
COOKING TIME: 5 MINUTES
SERVES: 4

* Combine the snails, salt, and enough water to cover completely. Let stand for 20 minutes, then drain and rinse.
* Bring a large saucepan of water to a boil over high heat. Add the snails and blanch for 15 seconds. Drain and set aside.
* Heat the oil in a wok or large skillet (frying pan). Add the shallots, ginger, garlic, chiles, and peppercorns and stir-fry over medium heat for 1 minute until fragrant. Add the chili bean paste, sugar, fish sauce, and wine and bring to a boil. Add the snails, increase to high heat, and stir-fry for another 2 minutes.
* Transfer to a large serving platter and garnish with the chopped scallions (spring onions).

• 1 LB 5 OZ/600 G FRESH MARINE SNAILS IN SHELLS
• 2 TABLESPOONS SALT
• 2 TABLESPOONS VEGETABLE OIL
• 2 SHALLOTS, CHOPPED
• 1 TABLESPOON GRATED GINGER
• 3 CLOVES GARLIC, FINELY CHOPPED
• 2 MILD RED CHILES, CHOPPED
• 1 TEASPOON WHITE PEPPERCORNS, CRUSHED
• 1 TABLESPOON CHILI BEAN PASTE
• 2 TEASPOONS GRANULATED SUGAR
• 1 TEASPOON FISH SAUCE
• ½ CUP (4 FL OZ/120 ML) SHAOXING WINE
• 1 TABLESPOON CHOPPED SCALLIONS (SPRING ONIONS)

虎皮虾包
SHRIMP EGG ROLLS
IN TOFU SHEETS

REGION: SICHUAN
PREPARATION TIME: 20 MINUTES
COOKING TIME: 5 MINUTES
SERVES: 4

* Rinse the shrimp (prawns) under cold running water and pat dry with paper towels.
* Bring a saucepan of water to a boil, add the peas, and blanch for 1 minute. Drain and rinse under cold running water. Set aside.
* Combine the shrimp, peas, pork fatback, ham, water chestnuts, salt, wine, white pepper, and half the egg white in a bowl. Divide the filling into 8 portions.
* Place the tofu sheet on a cutting board and slice it into eight 4-inch/10-cm squares. Take a tofu square, brush with the remaining egg white, and put a portion of the shrimp filling in the center. Roll halfway, tuck in the edges, and roll to the end. Repeat with the remaining sheets and filling.
* Heat the vegetable oil in a wok or deep saucepan to 325°F/160°C, or until a cube of bread browns in 1 minute. Add the egg rolls and shallow-fry for 2–3 minutes until golden brown. Use a slotted spoon to carefully transfer the egg rolls onto paper towels. Transfer to a serving plate and drizzle the sesame oil over the egg rolls. Serve immediately.

• 9 OZ/250 G UNCOOKED SHRIMP (PRAWN), SHELLED AND DEVEINED
• ⅓ CUP (2 OZ/50 G) PEAS
• 2 OZ/50 G PORK FATBACK, FINELY CHOPPED
• 1 OZ/25 G HAM, FINELY CHOPPED
• 5 WATER CHESTNUTS, PEELED AND CHOPPED
• ¼ TEASPOON SALT
• 1 TEASPOON SHAOXING WINE
• PINCH OF GROUND WHITE PEPPER
• 1 EGG WHITE, BEATEN
• 1 SHEET TOFU SKIN
• 1 CUP (8 FL OZ/250 ML) VEGETABLE OIL
• 1 TEASPOON SESAME OIL

REGION: CHAOZHOU
PREPARATION TIME: 40 MINUTES,
  PLUS 2 HOURS CHILLING TIME
COOKING TIME: 10 MINUTES
MAKES: 18
📷 PAGE 75

炸虾枣
DEEP-FRIED
SHRIMP BALLS

- 1 LB 5 OZ/600 G UNCOOKED SHRIMP (PRAWNS), SHELLED AND DEVEINED
- 1 TEASPOON COARSE SALT
- 1 EGG WHITE
- ¼ TEASPOON FERMENTED SHRIMP PASTE
- ¼ TEASPOON SALT
- ½ TEASPOON GRANULATED SUGAR
- ¼ TEASPOON GROUND WHITE PEPPER
- 1 TEASPOON CORNSTARCH (CORNFLOUR)
- 1½ OZ/40 G PORK FATBACK, FINELY CHOPPED
- 4 FRESH OR CANNED WATER CHESTNUTS, FINELY CHOPPED
- 3 CUPS (25 FL OZ/750 ML) VEGETABLE OIL
- CHAOZHOU TANGERINE SAUCE OR SWEET AND SOUR SAUCE (PAGE 169), TO SERVE

* Put the shrimp (prawns) into a colander, add the coarse salt, and use your hands to mix together. Rinse under cold running water, then drain. Put the shrimp on a clean dish towel, roll up to cover, and refrigerate for 1 hour.
* Remove the shrimp from the refrigerator and place on a cutting board. Using the back of a meat cleaver or a heavy knife, flatten the shrimp. Chop the shrimp repeatedly with the blunt edge of the knife until a paste is formed. (Alternatively, use a food processor.)
* Combine the paste and egg white in a large bowl. Stir with chopsticks in one direction until the paste is sticky and gluey in consistency. Add the fermented shrimp paste, salt, sugar, white pepper, and cornstarch (cornflour) and mix thoroughly. Using your hands, take handfuls of the paste and slap it against the bowl repeatedly until the texture becomes elastic and gluey. Add the pork fatback and water chestnuts.
* Wet one hand with water, pick up a handful of shrimp, squeeze it through the opening between the thumb and forefinger to form a ping-pong-size ball. Using the other hand, dip a spoon in water and scoop the shrimp ball onto a plate. Repeat with the remaining shrimp mixture. Refrigerate the shrimp balls for at least 1 hour.
* Heat the oil in a wok or deep saucepan to 340°F/170°C, or until a cube of bread browns in 45 seconds. Add the shrimp balls, in batches, and deep-fry for 4–5 minutes until golden brown and crispy. Use a slotted spoon to carefully remove the shrimp balls from the oil and drain on paper towels. Serve with Chaozhou tangerine or sweet and sour sauce.

DEEP-FRIED SHRIMP BALLS

REGION: TAIWAN
PREPARATION TIME: 20 MINUTES,
  PLUS 10 MINUTES MARINATING TIME
COOKING TIME: 5 MINUTES
MAKES: 16

蚵仔卷
OYSTER
ROLLS

- 11 OZ/300 G OYSTERS, SHUCKED
  AND DRAINED
- 1½ TEASPOONS CORNSTARCH
  (CORNFLOUR)
- 5 OZ/150 G GROUND (MINCED) PORK
- 1 TEASPOON SALT
- ½ TEASPOON GRANULATED SUGAR
- ¼ TEASPOON GROUND WHITE PEPPER
- 2 CUPS (16 FL OZ/475 ML) VEGETABLE
  OIL
- 6 CHINESE CHIVES, CUT INTO
  ½-INCH/1-CM LENGTHS
- ½ TEASPOON SESAME OIL
- 2 TABLESPOONS SWEET POTATO
  OR TAPIOCA STARCH
- 1 SHEET TOFU SKIN
- 1 EGG, BEATEN

* Using your hands, rub the oysters with 1 teaspoon
  cornstarch (cornflour) and pick out any fragments of shell.
  Bring a saucepan of water to a boil over high heat and
  blanch the oysters for 15 seconds. Drain and set aside in
  a bowl. (If using large oysters, cut them in half.)
* Combine the pork with salt, sugar, white pepper, and
  ½ teaspoon cornstarch in a bowl and marinate for
  10 minutes.
* To make the filling, heat 1 tablespoon oil in a wok or large
  skillet (frying pan) and stir-fry the pork mixture over
  medium-high heat for 2 minutes, or until cooked through.
  Stir in the chives and the sesame oil. Transfer the pork-and-
  chive mixture to the bowl with the oysters. Add the sweet
  potato starch and 2 tablespoons water and mix well. Divide
  the filling into 16 equal portions.
* Trim the tofu skin into a large 16-inch/40-cm square, then
  cut into 16 small equal-size squares. Take 1 tofu square,
  brush with the beaten egg, and put a portion of the shrimp
  filling in the middle. Roll halfway, tuck in the edges, and
  continue to roll to the end. Repeat with the remaining
  squares and filling.
* Heat the remaining vegetable oil in a wok or deep
  saucepan to 340°F/170°C, or until a cube of bread browns
  in 45 seconds. Add the oyster rolls, in batches, and deep-
  fry for about 1 minute until golden brown and crispy. Use a
  slotted spoon to carefully remove the rolls from the oil and
  drain on paper towels. Serve immediately.

炸鸡酥络
DEEP-FRIED CHICKEN PATTIES

REGION: BEIJING
PREPARATION TIME: 20 MINUTES
COOKING TIME: 20 MINUTES
SERVES: 4

* Bring 2 cups (16 fl oz/475 ml) water to a boil in a large saucepan. Add the ginger, scallion (spring onion), salt, and Sichuan peppercorns and boil for 5 minutes. Add the chicken, cover, and turn off the heat. Steep the chicken for 10 minutes, or until cooked through. Remove the chicken and set aside to cool.
* Remove and discard the chicken skin and tear the flesh into fine shreds. Divide the shredded chicken into 20 portions.
* Heat the oil in a wok or deep saucepan to 340°F/170°C, or until a cube of bread browns in 45 seconds. Put a portion of shredded chicken in the palm of one hand, flatten it as much as possible, and carefully slide it into the hot oil. Deep-fry the chicken for 2–3 minutes until golden brown. Use a slotted spoon to carefully remove the chicken mesh from the oil and drain on paper towels. Repeat with the remaining chicken portions.
* Sprinkle with ground Sichuan pepper while hot. Season with salt to taste and set aside to cool before serving.

- ⅛ OZ/5 G GINGER (ABOUT ½-INCH/ 1-CM-LENGTH PIECE), CRUSHED
- 1 SCALLION (SPRING ONION), SLICED INTO 2-INCH/5-CM LENGTHS
- 2 TABLESPOONS SALT
- ½ TEASPOON SICHUAN PEPPERCORNS
- 3 BONELESS, SKIN-ON CHICKEN BREASTS
- 2 CUPS (16 FL OZ/475 ML) VEGETABLE OIL
- ¼ TEASPOON GROUND SICHUAN PEPPER

蜜烧鸡肝
BARBECUE CHICKEN LIVERS

REGION: GUANGDONG
PREPARATION TIME: 10 MINUTES,
    PLUS 30 MINUTES MARINATING
COOKING TIME: 20 MINUTES
SERVES: 4

* Trim the fat from the surface of the chicken livers, tear out any blood vessels, and rinse thoroughly under cold running water. pat dry with paper towels. Combine the livers and the barbecue sauce ingredients, mix well, and marinate for 30 minutes.
* Meanwhile, soak 4 bamboo skewers in a bowl of water for at least 10 minutes (this prevents them from burning in the broiler/grill). Drain.
* Combine the glaze ingredients in a bowl and stir in 1 tablespoon hot water. Set aside.
* Preheat the oven to 375°F/190°C/Gas Mark 5.
* Thread 4 chicken livers onto each skewer. Grease a baking pan with a little oil and arrange the liver skewers in the pan. Roast on the middle shelf of the oven for 10 minutes until just cooked through. Remove from the oven and brush all of the livers with a coating of the glaze.
* Set the oven to broil (grill) and broil the livers on the top shelf for 3 minutes. Use tongs to flip the skewers over, brush with another coating of the glaze, and broil for another 2 minutes. Remove from the oven. Use a fork to carefully push the livers onto a serving plate. Serve hot.

- 16 CHICKEN LIVERS
- VEGETABLE OIL, FOR GREASING
- 4 SKEWERS

FOR THE BARBECUE SAUCE:
- 6 TABLESPOONS SUGAR
- 1 TEASPOON FIVE-SPICE POWDER
- 2 TABLESPOONS HOISIN SAUCE
- ½ TEASPOON SHAJIANG POWDER
- ½ TEASPOON LIGHT SOY SAUCE
- 2 TABLESPOONS SHAOXING WINE
- 2 TABLESPOONS CHOPPED GARLIC
- 2 TABLESPOONS CHOPPED SHALLOTS
- 1 TABLESPOON GINGER JUICE

FOR THE GLAZE:
- 2 TABLESPOONS MALTOSE
- 2 TABLESPOONS GRANULATED SUGAR
- 1 TABLESPOON MIRIN

REGION: SHANGHAI
PREPARATION TIME: 10 MINUTES,
  PLUS 10 MINUTES SOAKING TIME
COOKING TIME: 20 MINUTES
SERVES: 6-8

羊肚菌毛豆烤麸
MOREL MUSHROOMS
AND KAOFU

- 7 OZ/200 G KAOFU (BRAN DOUGH)
- 1 TABLESPOON GINGER JUICE
- 12 DRIED MOREL MUSHROOMS
- 1¼ CUP (11 OZ/300 G) PODDED
  SOYBEANS, RINSED
- 1 CUP (8 FL OZ/250 ML)
  VEGETABLE OIL
- ¾ OZ/20 G GINGER (ABOUT
  1-INCH/2.5-CM-LENGTH PIECE),
  SHREDDED
- ½ RED BELL PEPPER, SEEDED AND CUT
  INTO ½-INCH/1-CM DICE
- 1 TABLESPOON SHAOXING WINE
- 1 TABLESPOON OYSTER SAUCE
- ¼ TEASPOON SALT
- 1 TEASPOON GRANULATED SUGAR
- ½ TEASPOON SESAME OIL

* Tear the kaofu (bran dough) into teaspoon-size pieces.
  Place in a small saucepan, add the ginger juice and enough
  water to cover completely. Bring to a boil over high heat
  and blanch the kaofu for 1 minute. Drain and rinse under
  cold running water until cooled. Squeeze the kaofu dry and
  remove excess water with paper towels. Set aside.
* Put the mushrooms in a bowl, cover with ½ cup (4 fl oz/
  120 ml) cold water, and soak for at least 10 minutes, or until
  softened. Remove the mushrooms, squeeze dry, and discard
  the stems. Strain the mushroom soaking water into a bowl
  and reserve for later use.
* Bring a large saucepan of water to a boil, add the soybeans,
  and blanch for about 5 minutes. Drain and rinse under cold
  running water, then peel and set aside.
* Heat the oil in a wok or deep saucepan to 340°F/170°C, or
  until a cube of bread browns in 45 seconds. Add the kaofu
  and deep-fry for 2–3 minutes until lightly golden brown.
  Use a slotted spoon to carefully remove the kaofu from the
  oil, pressing down on them to squeeze out excess oil, then
  transfer to a plate lined with paper towels.
* Pour out most of the oil, leaving about 1 tablespoon in the
  wok. Add the shredded ginger and stir-fry over medium heat
  for 1 minute until fragrant. Add the bell pepper, mushrooms,
  wine, oyster sauce, salt, sugar, and the reserved mushroom
  soaking water and bring to a boil over high heat. Put in
  the kaofu and simmer over medium heat for 5–10 minutes
  until the sauce thickens. Finally, stir in the soybeans and
  sesame oil.

鱼汤萝卜糕
TURNIP
PUDDING

REGION: SHUNDE
PREPARATION TIME: 20 MINUTES
COOKING TIME: 1 HOUR 30 MINUTES
SERVES: 4-6

Daikon radishes are also known as Chinese turnips and hence the misnomer of the recipe title. We've provided instructions for the traditional method of using fresh fish soup, but feel free to use 4 tablespoons of concentrated fish stock to save on time and commence the recipe from step 2.

* To make the fish soup, heat the oil in a large saucepan over medium heat, add the ginger slices, and stir-fry for 2–3 minutes until fragrant. Add the fish and brown on one side for 2 minutes, then turn over and brown for another 2 minutes. Add the wine, white peppercorns, and 3 cups (25 fl oz/750 ml) boiling water. Bring to a boil over high heat and simmer, uncovered, for 30 minutes until only 4 tablespoons liquid remains. Remove from the heat, strain the soup into a bowl, and set aside.
* To make the turnip pudding, soak the dried shrimp in a bowl of cold water for 5 minutes until softened. Drain, chop, and set aside.
* Combine the daikon radishes, salt, sugar, and white pepper in a large saucepan and cook over low heat for 10 minutes until the daikon is translucent. Add the fish soup and stir.
* Remove from the heat. Once the radish has cooled, gradually add the flours and stir constantly until a paste is formed.
* Heat 1 tablespoon oil in a wok or large skillet (frying pan) over high heat, add the ground (minced) pork and dried shrimp, and stir-fry for 1 minute. Put in the cured pork and duck liver sausage and stir-fry for another 30 seconds, then remove from the heat. Add the stir-fried ingredients to the saucepan with the radish paste and mix well. Transfer the mixture to an 8-inch/20-cm steaming pan and place in a collapsible pot or bamboo steamer over a pot of boiling water. Steam, covered, for 1 hour. (Add more water to the pot if needed.)
* Uncover, then sprinkle with the toasted sesame seeds and cilantro (coriander) and press down so they stick to the pudding. Cover and turn off the heat. Let stand for 30 seconds, then remove the turnip pudding and set aside to cool completely.
* Once cooled, cut into ½-inch/1-cm-thick squares (only cut as much as will be served. The remainder can be refrigerated). Heat the remaining 2 tablespoons oil in a small skillet over medium heat and fry the squares for 3 minutes until slightly brown, then flip and cook for another 3 minutes, or until slightly brown. Serve with chili sauce on the side.

- 1½ TABLESPOONS DRIED SHRIMP
- 2¼ LB/1 KG DAIKON RADISH, SHREDDED
- 1 TEASPOON SALT
- 1 TEASPOON GRANULATED SUGAR
- ½ TEASPOON GROUND WHITE PEPPER
- 1½ CUPS (7 OZ/200 G) RICE FLOUR
- 4 TABLESPOONS GLUTEN-FREE RICE FLOUR
- 3 TABLESPOONS VEGETABLE OIL
- 3½ OZ/100 G GROUND (MINCED) PORK
- 2 OZ/50 G CURED PORK, CHOPPED
- ½ DUCK LIVER SAUSAGE, CHOPPED
- 1 TEASPOON TOASTED SESAME SEEDS
- 2 STALKS CILANTRO (CORIANDER), CHOPPED
- 1 TABLESPOON CHILI SAUCE, TO SERVE

FOR THE FISH SOUP:
- 1 TABLESPOON VEGETABLE OIL
- ½ OZ/20 G GINGER (ABOUT 1-INCH/2.5-CM-LENGTH PIECE), SLICED
- 1 (5 OZ/150 G) FRESHWATER FISH, CLEANED AND RINSED
- 1 TABLESPOON RICE WINE
- 30 WHITE PEPPERCORNS

REGION: HENAN
PREPARATION TIME: 40 MINUTES
COOKING TIME: 10 MINUTES
SERVES: 4
📷 PAGE 81

抓皮春卷
EGG
ROLLS

- 2 CUPS (16 FL OZ/475 ML) VEGETABLE OIL, PLUS 1 TABLESPOON FOR FRYING
- 2 OZ/50 G PORK TENDERLOIN, SLICED INTO ⅛-INCH/3-MM STRIPS
- ½ TEASPOON SALT, PLUS EXTRA TO TASTE
- 2 TEASPOONS LIGHT SOY SAUCE
- 2 TEASPOONS RICE WINE
- 3½ OZ/100 G CHIVES, CUT INTO ¾-INCH/2-CM LENGTHS
- 8 EGG ROLL WRAPPERS
- 1 TEASPOON CORNSTARCH (CORNFLOUR)

* Heat 1 tablespoon oil in a large skillet (frying pan) over medium-high heat, add the pork, and stir-fry for 4–5 minutes until cooked through.
* Combine the salt, soy sauce, and wine and add it to the mixture. Stir-fry for another 1 minute. Adjust the seasoning to taste, then transfer to a plate and set aside to cool.
* Add the chives to the pork and mix. Divide the filling into 8 equal portions.
* Place an egg roll wrapper on a cutting board, place a portion of filling at one end, and roll the wrapper into a 4-inch/10-cm-long egg roll, folding in the edges as you roll. Repeat with the remaining egg roll wrappers and filling. Combine the cornstarch (cornflour) with 1 tablespoon water in a small bowl. Dab the edges of the egg roll with the cornstarch water and seal.
* Heat the 2 cups (16 fl oz/475 ml) oil in a wok or deep saucepan to 350°F/180°C, or until a cube of bread browns in 30 seconds. Carefully lower the egg rolls into the hot oil, in batches, and deep-fry for 2 minutes, turning, until golden and crispy. Use a slotted spoon to carefully transfer the egg rolls to a plate lined with paper towels. Serve immediately.

REGION: SHANDONG
PREPARATION TIME: 10 MINUTES
COOKING TIME: 5–10 MINUTES
SERVES: 4

姜拌藕
LOTUS ROOT WITH GINGER

- 1 LB 2 OZ/500 G LOTUS ROOTS, PEELED AND ENDS TRIMMED
- 2 TEASPOONS LIGHT SOY SAUCE
- 1 TABLESPOON BLACK OR BALSAMIC VINEGAR
- 2 TEASPOONS SESAME OIL
- ¼ OZ/10 G GINGER (ABOUT ¾-INCH/2-CM-LENGTH PIECE), GRATED
- ¼ TEASPOON SALT

* Use a chopstick to clean the channels and rinse under cold running water. Cut the lotus roots into ⅛-inch/3-mm-thick slices.
* Combine the soy sauce, vinegar, and sesame oil in a bowl.
* Bring a saucepan of water to a boil, add the lotus root slices, and blanch for 1 minute. Drain, then transfer to a heatproof bowl. Mix with the ginger and salt, then cover with aluminum foil. Place the bowl in a collapsible pot or bamboo steamer over a pot of boiling water. Steam, covered, for 5 minutes, or until tender.
* Remove the foil, transfer the lotus roots to a plate, and drizzle the sauce on top.

EGG ROLLS

REGION: CHAOZHOU
PREPARATION TIME: 15 MINUTES,
  PLUS 30 MINUTES SOAKING TIME
COOKING TIME: 30 MINUTES
SERVES: 4

卷煎
GLUTINOUS
RICE ROLLS

- ¾ CUP (5¾ OZ/160 G) GLUTINOUS RICE
- 6 DRIED BLACK MUSHROOMS
- 1 TABLESPOON DRIED SHRIMP
- 2 TABLESPOONS VEGETABLE OIL
- 3½ OZ/100 G GROUND (MINCED) PORK
- 1½ TABLESPOONS PRESERVED TURNIPS,
  COARSELY CHOPPED
- 1 TABLESPOON LIGHT SOY SAUCE
- 1 TEASPOON GRANULATED SUGAR
- 1 (20-INCH/50-CM) SHEET TOFU SKIN,
  CUT INTO 4 EQUAL SQUARES

* Soak the glutinous rice in a heatproof bowl of hot water for 30 minutes.
* Meanwhile, put the dried mushrooms in a bowl, cover with cold water, and soak for at least 20 minutes, or until softened. Remove the mushrooms, squeeze dry, and discard the stems. Roughly chop and set aside.
* Drain and rinse the rice under cold running water. Return the rice to the bowl, add enough hot water to cover, and place the bowl in a collapsible pot or bamboo steamer over a pot of boiling water. Steam, covered, for 25 minutes, or until the rice is fully cooked. Set aside to cool.
* Meanwhile, soak the dried shrimp in a small bowl of water for about 10 minutes. Drain and coarsely chop.
* Heat 1 tablespoon oil in a wok or large skillet (frying pan) over high heat. Add the pork and stir-fry for 1 minute until slightly browned. Put in the mushrooms, shrimp, preserved turnip, soy sauce, and sugar and toss thoroughly for 30 seconds. Remove from the heat and combine with the rice.
* To make the rolls, place a tofu square on a clean work surface. Put a quarter of the rice mixture along one edge of a sheet, and roll, folding both ends towards the center. Repeat with the other 3 sheets and remaining filling. Place the rolls, seam-side down, in a collapsible or bamboo steamer over a pot of water. Bring to a boil and steam, covered, for 3 minutes.
* Heat the remaining 1 tablespoon oil in a wok over medium-low heat, add the steamed rolls, and fry for 2–3 minutes, or until crispy. Cut into 2-inch/5-cm lengths, transfer to a serving plate, and serve.

黄金丸子
GOLDEN MEATBALLS

REGION: HONG KONG
PREPARATION TIME: 20 MINUTES
COOKING TIME: 10 MINUTES
SERVES: 4

* Put the shrimp paste into a bowl and use chopsticks to stir in a single direction for 1 minute, or until gummy. Set aside.
* Combine the pork, salt, sugar, soy sauce, and 6 tablespoons water in a separate bowl and set aside.
* Place the salted fish on a heatproof plate, then put the plate in a collapsible pot or bamboo steamer over a pot of boiling water. Steam, covered, for 3 minutes. Carefully remove the plate from the pot and set aside to cool. When cool enough to handle, remove the bones and use a fork to mash the fish into a pulp.
* Add the shrimp, mashed fish, and cornstarch (cornflour) to the pork mixture and stir until fully combined. Using wet hands, form the mixture into 1-inch/2.5-cm meatballs.
* Heat the oil in a wok or deep saucepan to 340°F/170°C, or until a cube of bread browns in 45 seconds. Add the meatballs, in batches, and deep-fry for 2–3 minutes until golden brown and cooked through. Use a slotted spoon to carefully remove the meatballs from the oil and drain on paper towels.

- 11 OZ/300 G UNCOOKED SHRIMP (PRAWNS), SHELLED, DEVEINED, AND FINELY CHOPPED INTO A PASTE
- 11 OZ/300 G GROUND (MINCED) PORK
- 1 TEASPOON SALT
- ½ TABLESPOON GRANULATED SUGAR
- 1 TABLESPOON LIGHT SOY SAUCE
- ¼ OZ/5 G CHINESE SALTED FISH
- 1½ TABLESPOONS CORNSTARCH (CORNFLOUR)
- 2 CUPS (16 FL OZ/475 ML) VEGETABLE OIL

棗核肉
STUFFED JUJUBE DATES

REGION: ANHUI
PREPARATION TIME: 15 MINUTES,
  PLUS 10 MINUTES SOAKING TIME
COOKING TIME: 5 MINUTES
SERVES: 4

* Combine the pork and half the egg white in a bowl, season generously with salt, and mix well. Set aside. (Reserve the remaining egg white for another use.)
* Meanwhile, soak the jujube dates in a bowl of water for 10 minutes until soft. Drain, then cut open the dates to remove the seeds. Lightly dust the inside and outside with cornstarch (cornflour) and stuff them with the pork filling.
* Using your hands, gently squeeze close the opening of the dates. Dust the dates with cornstarch.
* Heat the oil in a wok or deep saucepan to 300°F/150°C, or until a cube of bread browns in 1½ minutes. Add the stuffed dates, in batches, and deep-fry for 1 minute until golden brown. Use a slotted spoon to carefully remove the dates from the oil and drain on paper towels
* Combine the sugar, vinegar, soy sauce, and ⅔ cup (5 fl oz/150 ml) water in a small saucepan and bring to a boil over high heat. Mix 1 teaspoon cornstarch with 1 tablespoon water in a small bowl and stir this mixture into the pan. Bring to a boil, stirring, for about 30 seconds to thicken the sauce. Transfer to a serving plate and serve.

- 5 OZ/150 G GROUND (MINCED) PORK
- 1 EGG WHITE, BEATEN
- 2 CUPS (9 OZ/250 G) JUJUBE DATES
- 2 TABLESPOONS CORNSTARCH (CORNFLOUR)
- 2 TABLESPOONS GRANULATED SUGAR
- 1½ TABLESPOONS ZHENJIANG OR BALSAMIC VINEGAR
- 1 TABLESPOON LIGHT SOY SAUCE
- 2 CUPS (16 FL OZ/475 ML) VEGETABLE OIL
- SALT

REGION: SICHUAN
PREPARATION TIME: 5 MINUTES
COOKING TIME: 35 MINUTES
SERVES: 6-8

红油猪耳
PIG'S EARS IN CHILI SAUCE

- 2 PIG'S EARS, SCRAPED CLEAN, RINSED, AND DRAINED
- ⅛ OZ/5 G GINGER (ABOUT ½-INCH/ 1-CM-LENGTH PIECE), SLICED
- 2 TABLESPOONS VEGETABLE OIL
- 1 TEASPOON SICHUAN PEPPERCORNS
- 1 STAR ANISE
- 2 CLOVES GARLIC, CHOPPED
- 1 TEASPOON SALT
- 1 TABLESPOON LIGHT SOY SAUCE
- 2 TABLESPOONS RED CHILI OIL
- ½ TEASPOON BLACK OR BALSAMIC VINEGAR
- 1 TABLESPOON SESAME OIL

* Combine the pig's ears, ginger, and enough water to cover it in a medium saucepan. Bring to a boil over high heat, then reduce to low heat, cover, and simmer for about 30 minutes. Remove the pig's ears from the saucepan and put them in a colander to drain.
* Heat the oil in a wok or large skillet (frying pan). Add the Sichuan peppercorns and star anise and stir-fry over low heat for about 2 minutes until fragrant. Use a slotted spoon to remove the spices and discard. Add the garlic, salt, soy sauce, chili oil, vinegar, and sesame oil and stir over low heat for another 1–2 minutes. Slice the pig's ears thinly and arrange on a plate. Drizzle the sauce over the ears and serve.

REGION: HUNAN
PREPARATION TIME: 15 MINUTES,
    PLUS 20 MINUTES STEEPING TIME
COOKING TIME: 25 MINUTES
SERVES: 4

芥末薄片肉
PORK WITH
MUSTARD SAUCE

- 1 (14-OZ/400-G) PORK TENDERLOIN, WITH ABOUT 20–30% FAT
- 3½ OZ/100 G STRING (GREEN) BEANS, TRIMMED AND CUT INTO 1½-INCH/ 4-CM LENGTHS
- ¼ TEASPOON SALT
- 1 TABLESPOON SESAME OIL
- 1 TEASPOON MUSTARD POWDER
- 4 CLOVES GARLIC, GRATED
- ⅛ OZ/5 G GINGER (ABOUT ½-INCH/ 1-CM-LENGTH PIECE), GRATED
- 2 TABLESPOONS LIGHT SOY SAUCE
- 2 TEASPOONS BLACK OR BALSAMIC VINEGAR

* Put the pork into a large pan with enough water to cover it completely. Bring to a boil, then reduce to low heat and cook for 20 minutes until the meat is cooked through. Remove the pan from the heat, cover, and steep the pork in the hot water for 20 minutes.
* Remove the pork using a slotted spoon and transfer it to a cutting board. Cut it into 2½ × 1¼-inch/6 × 3-cm slices with a thickness of ½ inch/2 mm.
* Bring a saucepan of water to a boil, add the string (green) beans, and blanch for 1 minute. Drain and rinse under cold running water. Transfer the beans to a bowl and mix with the salt and ½ tablespoon sesame oil. Put the dressed beans on a plate, then cover them with the pork slices.
* Add 1 tablespoon water to the mustard powder in a bowl and stir to make a mustard. Mix in the garlic, ginger, soy sauce, vinegar, and the remaining ½ tablespoon sesame oil. Drizzle the mustard sauce over the pork and beans.

APPETIZERS & SALADS

夫妻肺片
BEEF OFFAL IN CHILI SAUCE

REGION: SICHUAN
PREPARATION TIME: 5 MINUTES
COOKING TIME: 1 HOUR
SERVES: 4

* Put the tripe and heart in a large saucepan and add enough water to cover them. Bring to a boil over high heat and blanch for 5 minutes. Drain, rinse under cold running water, and return to the pan. Pour in 8½ cups (68 fl oz/2 liters) water and add the beef shin, star anise, five-spice powder, and wine. Bring to a boil, reduce to medium-low heat, and simmer for 40 minutes until tender.
* Remove the beef shin, tripe, and heart from the pan and set aside to cool. Cut them into slices and set aside.
* Put the peanuts in a small dry skillet (frying pan) and toast over low heat for 4–5 minutes until golden. Remove and crush lightly, then set aside. Using the same skillet, toast the sesame seeds for 4–5 minutes until golden and remove. Toast the Sichuan peppercorns for 2–3 minutes until fragrant, transfer to a mortar, and grind to a coarse powder with a pestle.
* To make the sauce, combine the ingredients and 1 tablespoon lukewarm water and mix well. Pour the sauce over the meat and serve.

- 3½ OZ/100 G BEEF TRIPE
- 3½ OZ /100 G BEEF HEART
- 3½ OZ /100 G BEEF SHIN
- 2 STAR ANISE
- 1 TABLESPOON FIVE-SPICE POWDER
- 1 TABLESPOON SHAOXING WINE

  FOR THE SAUCE:
- ¼ CUP (1 OZ/30 G) SHELLED RAW PEANUTS
- 1 TEASPOON WHITE SESAME SEEDS
- 1 TEASPOON SICHUAN PEPPERCORNS
- 1 TEASPOON GRANULATED SUGAR
- 1 TEASPOON LIGHT SOY SAUCE
- 1 TEASPOON CHILI OIL
- ½ TEASPOON SESAME OIL
- ½ TEASPOON SALT

木耳烤麸
KAOFU WITH BLACK FUNGUS

REGION: SHANGHAI
PREPARATION TIME: 20 MINUTES
COOKING TIME: 10 MINUTES
SERVES: 4

* Cut a third of the ginger into slices and shred the rest.
* Bring a saucepan of water to a boil and add the kaofu (bran dough) and ginger slices. Reduce to low heat and simmer for 1 minute, then use a slotted spoon to remove the kaofu and set aside to cool. Discard the ginger slices. When the kaofu is cool enough to handle, use your hands to squeeze out the water. Place on paper towels to drain.
* Bring a saucepan of water to a boil, add the fungus, and blanch for 2 minutes. Drain and set aside.
* Heat the vegetable oil in a wok or deep saucepan to 340°F/170°C, or until a cube of bread browns in 45 seconds. Add the kaofu and deep-fry for 4–5 minutes until golden brown. Use a slotted spoon to remove the kaofu and drain on paper towels.
* Pour most of the oil out, leave about 1 tablespoon in the wok. Heat over high heat, add the shredded ginger, and stir-fry for 30 seconds, until fragrant. Stir in the kaofu, bell peppers, and fungus. Sprinkle in the wine. Add the oyster sauce, salt, and sugar and toss well. Add the sesame oil, stir, and adjust the seasoning to taste. Serve cold or warm.

- ½ OZ/20 G GINGER (ABOUT 1-INCH/2.5-CM-LENGTH PIECE)
- 7 OZ/200 G KAOFU (BRAN DOUGH), TORN INTO BITE-SIZE CHUNKS
- ¾ OZ/20 G DRIED BLACK FUNGUS, SOAKED IN WATER AND DRAINED
- 1 CUP (8 FL OZ/250 ML) VEGETABLE OIL
- ½ RED BELL PEPPER, SEEDED AND CUT INTO SMALL CHUNKS
- ½ GREEN BELL PEPPER, SEEDED AND CUT INTO SMALL CHUNKS
- 1 TABLESPOON SHAOXING WINE
- 1 TABLESPOON OYSTER SAUCE
- ½ TEASPOON SALT, PLUS EXTRA TO TASTE
- 1 TEASPOON GRANULATED SUGAR
- ½ TEASPOON SESAME OIL

SOUPS

牛肉高汤
BEEF BROTH

- 1 LB 5 OZ/600 G BEEF SHORT PLATES
- 4½ LB/2 KG BEEF BONES
- 2 CARROTS, SLICED
- 2 ONIONS, QUARTERED
- ¼ OZ/10 G GINGER (ABOUT ¾-INCH/
  2-CM-LENGTH PIECE), SLICED
- ½ CINNAMON STICK
- 4 CLOVES
- 3 STAR ANISE
- 1 TABLESPOON WHITE PEPPERCORNS,
  CRUSHED
- SALT, TO TASTE

* Preheat the oven to 400°F/200°C/Gas Mark 6. Arrange the bones in a roasting pan and roast for 1 hour.
* Put the beef plates into a large saucepan and add enough water to cover it completely. Bring to a boil over high heat and blanch the beef for 10 minutes. Drain and rinse under cold running water.
* Put the bones, beef plates, and the remaining ingredients (except salt) in a large saucepan and add 16 cups (135 fl oz/ 4 liters) water. Cover, bring to a boil over high heat, and cook for 30 minutes. Skim the froth and scum off the surface, reduce to low heat, cover, and simmer for 2 hours. Add salt to season.
* To store, strain the cooled broth (stock) into a large container, cover, and refrigerate for up to a week (it can also be frozen for 3 months). Skim off the layer of fat formed on the surface before using.

鸡汤
CHICKEN BROTH

- 1 (3¼-LB/1.5-KG) CHICKEN,
  QUARTERED
- 11 OZ/300 G LEAN PORK, CUT INTO
  SMALL CHUNKS
- 2 OZ/50 G CHINESE CURED BACON,
  CUT INTO SMALL CHUNKS
- ¼ OZ/10 G GINGER (ABOUT ¾-INCH/
  2-CM-LENGTH PIECE), SLICED

* Combine all the ingredients and 16 cups (135 fl oz/4 liters) water in a large saucepan, bring to a boil, and cook over high heat for 20 minutes. Skim the froth and scum off the surface, reduce to low heat, cover, and simmer for 4 hours. Set aside to cool.
* To store, strain the cooled broth (stock) into a large container, cover, and refrigerate for up to a week (it can also be frozen for 3 months). Skim off the layer of fat formed on the surface before using.

猪骨高汤
PORK BROTH

REGIONS: ALL
PREPARATION TIME: 10 MINUTES
COOKING TIME: 3 HOURS 30 MINUTES
MAKES: 8½ CUPS (68 FL OZ/2 LITERS)

* Put the bones, spareribs, chicken in a large saucepan and add enough water to cover them completely. Bring to a boil over high heat and blanch the bones for 10 minutes. Drain and rinse thoroughly under cold running water.
* Place all the ingredients in a large saucepan with 12 cups (101 fl oz/3 liters) water and bring to a boil over high heat. Skim the froth and scum off the surface and boil for 15 minutes. Reduce to low heat and simmer for 3 hours, or until reduced to about 8½ cups (68 fl oz/2 liters) broth (stock). Set aside to cool.
* To store, strain the cooled broth (stock) into a large container, cover, and refrigerate for up to a week (it can also be frozen for 3 months). Skim off the layer of fat formed on the surface before using.

- 4½ LB/2 KG PORK BONES
- 11 OZ/300 G PORK SPARERIBS
- 1 LB 5 OZ/600 G CHICKEN (BREAST OR THIGH), BONE-IN
- 2 OZ/50 G GINGER (ABOUT 3-INCH/7.5-CM-LENGTH PIECE), SLICED
- 2 SCALLIONS (SPRING ONIONS), HALVED
- ½ CUP (4 FL OZ/120 ML) RICE WINE
- 1 TEASPOON WHITE VINEGAR

鱼高汤
FISH BROTH

REGIONS: ALL
PREPARATION TIME: 10 MINUTES
COOKING TIME: 40 MINUTES
MAKES: 3 CUPS (25 FL OZ/750 ML)

* Heat the oil in a large saucepan over high heat, add the ginger, and fry for 1–2 minutes until fragrant. Add the fish and brown over medium heat. Sprinkle in the wine, add 4¼ cups (34 fl oz/1 liter) boiling water, and bring to a boil. Reduce to medium heat and simmer for 30 minutes. Set aside to cool.
* To store, strain the cooled broth (stock) into a large container, cover, and refrigerate. Use within 2–3 days.

- 1 TEASPOON VEGETABLE OIL
- ⅛ OZ/5 G GINGER (ABOUT ½-INCH/ 1-CM-LENGTH PIECE), SLICED
- 1 LB 2 OZ/500 G ANY WHITE FISH, CLEANED
- 1 TABLESPOON RICE WINE

REGIONS: ALL
PREPARATION TIME: 15 MINUTES
COOKING TIME: 45 MINUTES
MAKES: 4¼ CUPS (34 FL OZ/1 LITER)

虾高汤
SHRIMP BROTH

- 11 OZ/300 G SHRIMP (PRAWN) HEADS AND SHELLS
- 2 TABLESPOONS VEGETABLE OIL
- 8 CLOVES GARLIC, CHOPPED
- 5 SHALLOTS, CHOPPED
- 6 DRIED CHILES, CHOPPED
- 3 TABLESPOONS DRIED SHRIMP, SOAKED IN A BOWL OF WATER UNTIL SOFTENED AND CHOPPED
- 1 TEASPOON SHRIMP PASTE
- 3 CUPS (25 FL OZ/750 ML) CHICKEN BROTH (STOCK, PAGE 90)

* Rinse the shrimp (prawn) heads and shells in cold running water and drain. Heat a skillet (frying pan) over low heat, add the heads and shells, and roast for 10 minutes.
* Heat the oil in a large skillet over low heat, add the garlic, shallots, and dried chiles, and stir-fry for 1–2 minutes until fragrant. Add the dried shrimp, shrimp paste, and the shrimp heads and shells, and stir-fry for 1–2 minutes until fragrant. Pour in the chicken broth (stock) and 1 cup (8 fl oz/250 ml) water and bring to a boil over high heat. Boil for 30 minutes. Strain, then set aside to cool.
* To store, pour the broth into a large container, cover, and refrigerate. Use within 3–4 days.

REGIONS: ALL
PREPARATION TIME: 10 MINUTES,
    PLUS 20 MINUTES SOAKING TIME
COOKING TIME: 1 HOUR 30 MINUTES
MAKES: 4¼ CUPS (34 FL OZ/1 LITER)

素汤
VEGETABLE
BROTH

- 2 OZ/50 G DRIED BLACK MUSHROOMS
- 2 OZ/50 G DRIED STRAW MUSHROOMS
- 2 CARROTS, CUT INTO CHUNKS
- 6¼ CUPS (1 LB 2 OZ/500 G) SOYBEAN SPROUTS

Unlike standard vegetable broths (stocks), this unique broth (stock) is made in accordance with the Buddhist vegetarian principle and suited for many of the vegetarian recipes in the book.

* Put the black mushrooms in a bowl, add ½ cup (4 fl oz/ 120 ml) cold water, and soak for at least 20 minutes, or until softened. Remove the mushrooms, squeeze dry, and discard the stems. Set aside, reserving the soaking water.
* Put the straw mushrooms in a bowl, add 1 cup (8 fl oz/ 250 ml) water, and soak for 20 minutes. Remove and rinse the mushrooms, reserving the soaking water.
* Put all the ingredients into a large saucepan, add 4¼ cups (34 fl oz/1 liter) water and the mushroom soaking water, and bring to a boil over high heat for 15 minutes. Reduce to low heat, cover, and simmer for 1 hour 15 minutes. Set aside to cool.
* To store, strain the stock into a large container, cover, and refrigerate for up to a week. (It can also be frozen for 3 months.)

蛋花汤
EGG FLOWER SOUP

REGION: GUANGDONG
PREPARATION TIME: 5 MINUTES
COOKING TIME: 5 MINUTES
SERVES: 4

* Bring the chicken broth (stock) to a boil in a saucepan. Slowly drizzle in the beaten eggs and use chopsticks to stir in one direction, making strands of egg. Season with salt and stir in the scallions (spring onions), then serve in a tureen or individual bowls.

- 4¼ CUPS (34 FL OZ/1 LITER) CHICKEN BROTH (STOCK, PAGE 90)
- 2 EGGS, BEATEN
- SALT, TO TASTE
- 2 SCALLIONS (SPRING ONIONS), CHOPPED

护国菜羹
PATRIOTIC SOUP

REGION: CHAOZHOU
PREPARATION TIME: 10 MINUTES
COOKING TIME: 10 MINUTES
SERVES: 4-6

Monks from a Chaozhou monastery served this soup to the last emperor of the Sung Dynasty, who was pursued by the Mongols towards the end of the thirteenth century. The recipe has evolved over time and now includes chicken broth (stock) but vegetable broth can also be used.

* Bring a saucepan of water to a boil over high heat, add the sweet potato leaves, and blanch for 1–2 minutes. Drain and rinse under cold running water.
* Heat the vegetable oil in a wok or large skillet (frying pan) over medium heat, add the sweet potato leaves, and stir-fry for 2 minutes. Transfer the leaves to a blender or food processor together with the chicken broth (stock) and puree. Pour into a large saucepan, then add the mushroom halves. Bring to a boil over high heat and boil for 5 minutes. Add the salt and sesame oil.
* Mix the water chestnut flour with 3 tablespoons water in a small bowl and stir this mixture into the soup. Bring to a boil, stirring, for 30 seconds to thicken the soup. Adjust the seasoning to taste, then transfer to a tureen or serving bowl and serve.

- 2¼ LB/1 KG SWEET POTATO LEAVES, TENDER LEAVES ONLY
- 1 TABLESPOON VEGETABLE OIL
- 3 CUPS (25 FL OZ/750 ML) CHICKEN BROTH (STOCK, PAGE 90)
- 10 STRAW MUSHROOMS, SLICED IN HALF
- 1 TEASPOON SALT, PLUS EXTRA TO TASTE
- 1 TEASPOON SESAME OIL
- 1 TABLESPOON WATER CHESTNUT FLOUR OR CORNSTARCH (CORNFLOUR)

BITTER MELON SOUP WITH PINEAPPLE SAUCE

REGION: TAIWAN
PREPARATION TIME: 10 MINUTES
COOKING TIME: 1 HOUR
SERVES: 2

- 2 BONELESS, SKINLESS CHICKEN BREASTS, CUT INTO LARGE CHUNKS
- ½ CUP (1 OZ/25 G) DRIED ANCHOVIES
- 4 TABLESPOONS PRESERVED PINEAPPLE PASTE
- 1 SMALL BITTER MELON, PREFERABLY WHITE, SEEDED, HALVED LENGTHWISE, AND CUT INTO ¾ × 1½-INCH/2 × 4-CM STRIPS
- 1 TEASPOON RICE WINE
- ½ TEASPOON SALT, PLUS EXTRA TO TASTE

* Put the chicken in a medium saucepan and add enough water to cover it completely. Bring to a boil over high heat and blanch for 1 minute. Drain the chicken and set aside.
* Put the dried anchovies into a large saucepan, add 5 cups (40 fl oz/1.2 liters) water, and bring to a boil. Cook over medium-low heat for 15 minutes until the liquid has reduced by half.
* Add the chicken and the preserved pineapple paste, cover, and simmer over low heat for another 30 minutes, or until the chicken is cooked through. Stir in the bitter melon, increase to medium heat, and cook for another 5 minutes. Season with the wine and adjust the salt to taste. Serve in individual bowls.

鸡茸雪蛤

HASMA AND CHICKEN SOUP

REGION: HONG KONG
PREPARATION TIME: 20 MINUTES,
    PLUS 8 HOURS SOAKING TIME
COOKING TIME: 20 MINUTES
SERVES: 4–6

- ¼ OZ/10 G HASMA
- 1 TABLESPOON GINGER JUICE
- 1 BONELESS, SKINLESS CHICKEN BREAST, FINELY CHOPPED INTO A PASTE
- 1 EGG WHITE
- 2½ CUPS (20 FL OZ/600 ML) CHICKEN BROTH (STOCK, PAGE 90)
- ½ TEASPOON SALT, PLUS EXTRA TO TASTE
- 1 TEASPOON GROUND WHITE PEPPER
- 2 TABLESPOONS WATER CHESTNUT FLOUR OR CORNSTARCH (CORNFLOUR)
- 1 TEASPOON SESAME OIL
- 1 TABLESPOON CHOPPED HAM
- 1 BUNCH CILANTRO (CORIANDER), LEAVES ONLY

* Soak the hasma in 2 cups (16 fl oz/475 ml) water for about 8 hours, or until the hasma looks like a ball of cotton. With a pair of kitchen tweezers, carefully pick out and discard any grit.
* Bring a saucepan of water to a boil, add the hasma and ginger juice, and blanch for 5 minutes. Drain and set aside.
* Put the chicken breast in a large bowl, then use chopsticks to stir in the egg white.
* Bring 1 cup (8 fl oz/250 ml) chicken broth (stock) to a boil in a small saucepan. Pour the hot broth into the bowl of chicken paste and stir in a single direction until fully combined. Set aside.
* Pour the remaining 1½ cups (12 fl oz/350 ml) chicken broth into the saucepan, bring to a boil, and add the hasma. Reduce to low heat and simmer for 3 minutes.
* Combine the water chestnut flour with 4 tablespoons water in a small bowl. Stir the mixture into the soup. Reduce to low heat, gradually add the reserved chicken paste broth, and then stir gently. Season with salt and white pepper.
* Add the sesame oil, then ladle the soup into a tureen. Garnish with the chopped ham and cilantro (coriander) and serve.

上汤蕹菜钵
WATER SPINACH
SOUP

REGION: CHAOZHOU
PREPARATION TIME: 5 MINUTES
COOKING TIME: 10 MINUTES
SERVES: 4

* Heat the oil in a large saucepan over medium heat, add the garlic cloves, and cook for 2–3 minutes until lightly browned.
* Add the chicken broth (stock) and salt and bring to a boil. Add the water spinach and boil, uncovered, for 5 minutes. Transfer to a tureen or ladle into individual bowls to serve.

- 1 TABLESPOON VEGETABLE OIL
- 3 CLOVES GARLIC, HALVED
- 3 CUPS (25 FL OZ/750 ML) CHICKEN BROTH (STOCK, PAGE 90)
- 1 TEASPOON SALT
- 1 LB 5 OZ/600 G WATER SPINACH, CUT INTO ¾-INCH/2-CM SECTIONS

西洋菜陈肾猪肉汤
PORK AND WATERCRESS
SOUP

REGION: GUANGDONG
PREPARATION TIME: 15 MINUTES,
   PLUS 1 HOUR SOAKING TIME
COOKING TIME: 2 HOURS 30 MINUTES
SERVES: 4–6

* Put the dried duck kidneys in a bowl of cold water and soak for about 1 hour.
* Put the pork in a large saucepan and enough water to cover it completely. Bring to a boil over high heat and blanch for 5 minutes. Skim the froth and scum off the surface, if needed. Drain and rinse under cold running water. Set aside.
* Combine the pork, duck kidneys, ginger, and 12½ cups (100 fl oz/3 liters) water in a stockpot, cover, and bring to a boil over high heat. Boil for 15 minutes, then reduce to medium-low heat, and continue to cook for another 1½ hours.
* Add the watercress and jujube dates, bring to a boil, and cook for another 30 minutes. Season with the salt.
* Remove the pork from the soup and transfer to a cutting board. When cool enough to handle, slice into smaller pieces. Put the pork in a tureen, add the soup, and serve with soy sauce on the side.

- 2 DRIED DUCK KIDNEYS
- 1 (1 LB 5-OZ/600-G) PORK SHOULDER, SKIN-ON, RINSED
- ⅛ OZ/5 G GINGER (ABOUT ½-INCH/ 1-CM-LENGTH PIECE), SLICED
- 1¾ LB/800 G WATERCRESS
- 2 JUJUBE DATES, PITTED
- 1 TEASPOON SALT
- LIGHT SOY SAUCE, TO SERVE

REGION: SICHUAN
PREPARATION TIME: 20 MINUTES,
  PLUS 20 MINUTES SOAKING TIME
COOKING TIME: 15 MINUTES
SERVES: 6
📷 PAGE 97

酸辣汤
HOT AND SOUR
SOUP

- 4 DRIED BLACK MUSHROOMS
- ¼ CUP (⅛ OZ/5 G) DRIED BLACK FUNGUS
- 3½ OZ/100 G LEAN PORK, CUT INTO STRIPS
- 2 TEASPOONS SALT
- ½ TEASPOON CORNSTARCH (CORNFLOUR)
- 7 OZ/200 G FIRM TOFU, DRAINED
- ½ TEASPOON GRANULATED SUGAR
- ⅔ CUP (3½ OZ/100 G) SLICED BAMBOO SHOOTS, DRAINED
- 2 TABLESPOONS WATER CHESTNUT FLOUR OR CORNSTARCH (CORNFLOUR)
- 1 EGG, BEATEN
- 5 TABLESPOONS RED VINEGAR
- ½ TABLESPOON GROUND WHITE PEPPER
- 1 TEASPOON SESAME OIL
- 2 CUPS (11 OZ/300 G) COOKED EGG OR RICE NOODLES (OPTIONAL)
- CILANTRO (CORIANDER), TO GARNISH (OPTIONAL)

* Put the mushrooms and black fungus into two separate bowls, cover with cold water, and soak for at least 20 minutes, or until softened. Drain both. Remove the mushrooms, squeeze dry, and discard the stems. Thinly slice, then set aside. Tear the black fungus into small pieces.
* Combine the pork, ¼ teaspoon salt, and the cornstarch (cornflour) in a bowl and set aside.
* In a separate bowl, combine the tofu, ¼ teaspoon salt, and enough cold water to cover and soak for 15 minutes. Drain, cut into thin strips, and set aside.
* Bring 4¼ cups (34 fl oz/1 liter) water to a boil in a large saucepan and add 1 teaspoon salt and the sugar. Put in the mushrooms, black fungus, and bamboo shoots. Drop the pieces of pork, using chopsticks to gently disperse them to prevent sticking. Do not stir.
* Mix the water chestnut flour with 4 tablespoons water in a small bowl, stir until dissolved, and pour slowly into the soup, stirring continuously. Add the tofu and reduce to medium-low heat.
* Hold a strainer (sieve) over the soup and slowly pour the beaten eggs into the strainer. At the same time, move the strainer in a circular motion over the soup so that the beaten egg is strained into the soup in a continuous line. Let sit for 1 minute, do not stir.
* Stir in the vinegar and white pepper, then add the sesame oil. Divide the noodles, if using, among the bowls. Ladle over the hot soup and garnish with cilantro (coriander), if using. Serve.

HOT AND SOUR SOUP

REGION: GUANGDONG
PREPARATION TIME: 10 MINUTES,
    PLUS 20 MINUTES SOAKING TIME
COOKING TIME: 1 HOUR 5 MINUTES
SERVES: 4

冬瓜汤
WINTER MELON
SOUP

- 2 DRIED BLACK MUSHROOMS
- 2 DRIED SCALLOPS
- 4¼ CUPS (34 FL OZ/1 LITER) CHICKEN BROTH (STOCK, PAGE 90)
- 2 OZ/50 G LEAN PORK, CUT INTO ½-INCH/1-CM DICE
- 7 OZ/200 G WINTER MELON, PEELED AND CUT INTO ½-INCH/1-CM DICE
- ¼ OZ/10 G GINGER (ABOUT ¾-INCH/ 2-CM-LENGTH PIECE), CRUSHED
- 1 TEASPOON SALT, PLUS EXTRA TO TASTE

* Put the mushrooms into a bowl, cover with cold water, and soak for at least 20 minutes, or until softened. Cut the mushrooms into ½-inch/1-cm pieces.
* Meanwhile, combine the dried scallops and ½ cup (4 fl oz/120 ml) cold water in a small bowl and soak for 15 minutes. Strain, then remove the small hard muscle. Reserve the soaking water.
* Bring the chicken broth (stock) to a boil in a large saucepan. Add the scallops, soaking water, mushrooms, pork, winter melon, ginger, and 2 cups (16 fl oz/475 ml) water and return to a boil. Reduce to low heat and cook for 1 hour. Add the salt, adjust the seasoning to taste, then transfer to a tureen to serve.

REGION: BUDDHIST VEGETARIAN
PREPARATION TIME: 5 MINUTES,
    PLUS 4 HOURS SOAKING TIME
COOKING TIME: 2 HOURS
SERVES: 4

冬瓜海带汤
WINTER MELON
AND KELP SOUP

- 1 CUP (8 OZ/225 G) DRIED MUNG BEANS
- ¼ OZ/10 G DRIED KELP
- 1 TEASPOON VEGETABLE OIL
- ⅛ OZ/5 G GINGER (ABOUT ½-INCH/ 1-CM-LENGTH PIECE), SLICED
- 3 CUPS (25 FL OZ/750 ML) VEGETABLE BROTH (STOCK, PAGE 92)
- 7 OZ/200 G WINTER MELON, PEELED AND CUT INTO 1½ × 1¼ × ½-INCH/ 4 × 3 × 1-CM PIECES
- ¼ TEASPOON SALT, PLUS EXTRA TO TASTE

* Cover the mung beans with cold water and soak for 4 hours. Drain thoroughly.
* Meanwhile, cover the dried kelp with cold water and soak for 30 minutes. Clean the kelp, then drain and cut it into 1-inch/2.5-cm sections.
* Heat the oil in a saucepan over medium heat, add the ginger, and stir-fry for about 30 seconds until fragrant. Add the vegetable broth (stock), mung beans, kelp, and winter melon and bring to a boil. Reduce to medium-low heat and simmer for 2 hours. Add the salt, adjust the seasoning to taste, and transfer to a tureen to serve.

西湖莼菜汤
WATER SHIELD
SOUP

REGION: ZHEJIANG
PREPARATION TIME: 10 MINUTES, PLUS
  10 MINUTES MARINATING TIME
COOKING TIME: 10 MINUTES
SERVES: 4

* Bring a large saucepan of water to a boil, add the water shield, and blanch for 30 seconds. Drain, then transfer to a tureen.
* Combine the chicken and ½ teaspoon salt in a heatproof bowl and marinate for 10 minutes. Add the ham. Place in a collapsible pot or bamboo steamer over a pot of boiling water. Steam, covered, for 5 minutes, or until fully cooked. Remove and set aside to cool.
* Remove the skin from the chicken breast and cut both the chicken and ham into fine strips.
* Heat the chicken broth (stock) in a saucepan, add the remaining ½ teaspoon salt, then pour the broth into the tureen. Garnish with the chicken and ham.

- 9 OZ/250 G WATER SHIELD
- 1 BONELESS, SKIN-ON CHICKEN BREAST
- 1 TEASPOON SALT
- 1 OZ/25 G JINHUA OR SMITHFIELD HAM
- 2 CUPS (16 FL OZ/475 ML) CHICKEN BROTH (STOCK, PAGE 90)

文思豆腐羹
WENSI TOFU
SOUP

REGION: JIANGSU
PREPARATION TIME: 25 MINUTES,
  PLUS 20 MINUTES SOAKING TIME
COOKING TIME: 2 HOURS 10 MINUTES
SERVES: 4

* Put the dried mushrooms into a bowl, cover with cold water, and soak for at least 20 minutes, or until softened. Remove the mushrooms, squeeze dry, and discard the stems.
* Place the tofu on a cutting board, then halve it. Cut each half lengthwise into 3 equal pieces for a total of 6 pieces.
* Put 1–2 tablespoons water on a piece of tofu and thinly slice. Gently lean the side of the knife against one end of the row so that the tofu slices lie on their sides. Sprinkle more water on the tofu slices and cut them into very thin, hair-like strands. Put the tofu strands into a large bowl of cold water and use chopsticks to gently disperse them. Repeat with the remaining tofu pieces.
* Fill a stockpot with 8½ cups (68 fl oz/2 liters) water, add the black mushrooms, soybean sprouts, and ginger, and bring to a boil. Reduce to low heat and simmer for 2 hours, or until reduced by half. Strain the soup into a large pot, then discard the mushrooms and sprouts.
* If using fresh straw mushrooms, trim the bottom of each. For fresh or canned, rinse and cut the mushrooms into quarters. Add the mushrooms to the pot and bring to a boil over high heat. Season with the salt and transfer to a tureen. Gently lift the tofu strands using chopsticks and drop them into the soup. Disperse the strands gently. Drizzle a little sesame oil over the soup and serve.

- 2 DRIED BLACK MUSHROOMS
- 9 OZ/250 G SILKEN TOFU
- 6¼ CUPS (1 LB 2 OZ/500 G) SOYBEAN SPROUTS, RINSED
- ⅛ OZ/5 G GINGER (ABOUT ½-INCH/ 1-CM-LENGTH PIECE), SLICED
- ⅓ CUP (ABOUT 2 OZ/50 G) STRAW MUSHROOMS
- ¼ TEASPOON SALT
- SESAME OIL

REGION: JIANGSU
PREPARATION TIME: 10 MINUTES,
   PLUS 20 MINUTES SOAKING TIME
COOKING TIME: 10 MINUTES
SERVES: 4

爆氽

BRAISED FISH
WITH SOUP

- 2 DRIED BLACK MUSHROOMS
- 9 OZ/250 G GRASS CARP (OR ANY
  FIRM FISH) FILLETS, CUT INTO
  ½-INCH/1-CM PIECES
- 1 TABLESPOON LIGHT SOY SAUCE
- 1½ TABLESPOONS SHAOXING WINE
- 4 TABLESPOONS VEGETABLE OIL
- 1 CUP (8 FL OZ/250 ML) CHICKEN
  BROTH (STOCK, PAGE 90)
- ⅓ CUP (2 OZ/50 G) SLICED BAMBOO
  SHOOTS, DRAINED
- ⅛ OZ/5 G GINGER (ABOUT ½-INCH/
  1-CM-LENGTH PIECE), SLICED
- 1 SCALLION (SPRING ONION), CUT
  INTO 1½-INCH/4-CM LENGTHS
- SALT, TO TASTE
- STEAMED RICE (PAGE 540), TO SERVE
  (OPTIONAL)

This popular and tasty dish from Jiangsu is perfect when
you're looking for a light, yet warming dish. It can be served
on its own as a nourishing and satisfying soup or with rice
as part of a family-style meal.

* Put the mushrooms into a bowl, cover with cold water,
  and soak for at least 20 minutes, or until softened.
* Meanwhile, combine the fish, soy sauce, and 1 tablespoon
  wine in a bowl and marinate for 5 minutes. Pat-dry with
  paper towels.
* Heat the oil in a wok or large skillet (frying pan) over
  medium-high heat, add the marinated fish, and fry for
  1–2 minutes until golden brown on both sides. Transfer
  to a plate lined with paper towels.
* Remove the mushrooms, squeeze dry, and discard the
  stems. Slice the mushrooms, then set aside.
* Put the chicken broth (stock) in a saucepan and bring to
  a boil. Add the fish, bamboo shoots, ginger, scallion (spring
  onion), mushrooms, and the remaining ½ tablespoon wine.
  Reduce to low heat and simmer, covered, for 5 minutes.
  Season with salt and serve with rice.

REGION: BUDDHIST VEGETARIAN
PREPARATION TIME: 5 MINUTES,
   PLUS 30 MINUTES SOAKING TIME
COOKING TIME: 25 MINUTES
SERVES: 2

烩银耳

SNOW FUNGUS
SOUP

- 2 DRIED SNOW FUNGUS (ABOUT 1¼
  OZ/30 G)
- 2 CUPS (16 FL OZ/475 ML) VEGETABLE
  BROTH (STOCK, PAGE 92)
- 1 TEASPOON SHAOXING WINE
- ½ TEASPOON SALT, PLUS EXTRA
  TO TASTE

* Cover the snow fungus in hot water and soak for about
  30 minutes. Rinse the snow fungus and trim off the firm
  part at the base. Tear the fungus into smaller pieces.
* Combine the vegetable broth (stock) and snow fungus in a
  saucepan and bring to a boil. Reduce the heat and simmer,
  partially covered with a lid, for 20 minutes. Add the wine
  and salt. Adjust the seasoning to taste, then transfer to
  individual serving bowls.

雪花鱼丝羹

FISH AND EGG
WHITE SOUP

REGION: ZHEJIANG
PREPARATION TIME: 25 MINUTES,
    PLUS 20 MINUTES SOAKING TIME
COOKING TIME: 10 MINUTES
SERVES: 4

* Put the mushrooms into a bowl, cover with cold water, and soak for at least 20 minutes, or until softened. Remove the mushrooms, squeeze dry, and discard the stems. Thinly slice and set aside.
* Sprinkle ½ teaspoon salt on the fish fillets and finely chop into a fish paste. (Alternatively, process in a food processor.) Add 4 tablespoons cornstarch (cornflour) to a shallow bowl, add the fish, and generously coat.
* Divide the fish paste into 3 portions. Take a portion and use a floured rolling pin to roll the paste into a thin disk. Repeat with the remaining portions.
* Bring a saucepan of water to a boil over high heat, add the fish disks, and blanch for 1 minute. Drain, then rinse under cold running water until cool. Cut into strips.
* Beat the egg whites in a small bowl until fluffy.
* Heat the chicken broth (stock) in a large saucepan, add the fish, bamboo shoots, mushrooms, and remaining ½ teaspoon salt, and bring to a boil.
* Mix 1 tablespoon cornstarch with 1 tablespoon water in a small bowl and stir this mixture into the soup. Add the beaten egg whites and bring to a boil, stirring, for 30 seconds to thicken the soup.
* Sprinkle in a pinch of white pepper, adjust the seasoning to taste, and transfer to a tureen. Garnish with the ham and chopped scallion (spring onion).

- 2 DRIED BLACK MUSHROOMS
- 1 TEASPOON SALT, PLUS EXTRA TO TASTE
- 1 (1 LB 5-OZ/600-G) CORVINA (YELLOW CROAKER), CLEANED, FILLETED, AND SKIN REMOVED
- 5 TABLESPOONS CORNSTARCH (CORNFLOUR)
- ALL-PURPOSE (PLAIN) FLOUR, FOR DUSTING
- 2 EGG WHITES
- ½ CUP (2¼ OZ/65 G) SLICED BAMBOO SHOOTS, DRAINED
- 2 CUPS (16 FL OZ/475 ML) CHICKEN BROTH (STOCK, PAGE 90)
- GROUND WHITE PEPPER
- ½ OZ/15 G JINHUA OR SMITHFIELD HAM, CUT INTO THIN STRIPS, TO GARNISH
- 1 TEASPOON CHOPPED SCALLION (SPRING ONION), TO GARNISH

REGION: HONG KONG
PREPARATION TIME: 10 MINUTES, PLUS
   10 MINUTES STANDING TIME
COOKING TIME: 20 MINUTES
SERVES: 4

粟米鱼肚羹
FISH MAW AND
CORN SOUP

- ⅛ OZ/5 G GINGER (ABOUT ½-INCH/
  1-CM-LENGTH PIECE), SLICED
- 2 SCALLIONS (SPRING ONIONS),
  HALVED
- 3½ OZ/100 G DRIED FISH MAW, RINSED
- 5 OZ/150 G GROUND (MINCED) PORK
- 1 TEASPOON SALT, PLUS EXTRA
  TO TASTE
- ½ TEASPOON CORNSTARCH
  (CORNFLOUR)
- ¼ TEASPOON GROUND WHITE PEPPER
- 1⅔ CUPS (14 FL OZ/400 ML) CHICKEN
  BROTH (STOCK, PAGE 90)
- 1 (14-OZ/400-G) CAN CREAMED CORN
- 1 TEASPOON WATER CHESTNUT FLOUR
  OR CORNSTARCH (CORNFLOUR)
- 2 EGGS, BEATEN
- ½ TEASPOON SESAME OIL

* Combine the ginger, scallions (spring onions), and 4¼ cups
  (34 fl oz/1 liter) water in a large saucepan, bring to a boil
  over high heat, and cook for 5 minutes. Add the fish maw,
  return to a boil, then cover and turn off the heat.
  Set aside for 10 minutes.
* Drain the fish maw in a colander and rinse under cold
  running water. Squeeze out the excess water and cut
  into bite-size pieces. Discard the ginger and scallions.
* Combine the pork, ½ teaspoon salt, the cornstarch
  (cornflour), and white pepper in a large bowl.
* Pour the chicken broth (stock) into a separate saucepan
  and bring to a boil. Add the pork, corn, and ½ cup (4 fl oz/
  120 ml) water, then use chopsticks to break up the pork.
  Return to a boil, add the fish maw and the remaining ½
  teaspoon salt, and cook for about 3 minutes.
* Mix the water chestnut flour with 1 tablespoon water in
  a small bowl and stir this mixture into the soup. Bring to
  a boil, stirring, for 30 seconds to thicken the soup. Slowly
  drizzle in the beaten eggs and use chopsticks to stir in one
  direction, making strands of egg. Add the sesame oil and
  season with salt to taste. Transfer to a tureen and serve.

REGION: HONG KONG
PREPARATION TIME: 10 MINUTES
COOKING TIME: 40 MINUTES
SERVES: 4

鲩鱼豆腐汤
GRASS CARP AND
TOFU SOUP

- 2 TABLESPOONS VEGETABLE OIL
- 1 (1-LB/450-G) GRASS CARP TAIL OR
  ANY FRESHWATER FISH, CLEANED AND
  PATTED DRY
- ⅛ OZ/5 G GINGER (ABOUT ½-INCH/
  1-CM-LENGTH PIECE), SLICED
- 1 TEASPOON WHITE PEPPERCORNS,
  CRUSHED
- 1 TABLESPOON SHAOXING WINE
- 14 OZ/400 G FIRM TOFU, DRAINED AND
  CUT INTO 1-INCH/2.5-CM CUBES
- 1 TEASPOON SALT, PLUS EXTRA
  TO TASTE
- LIGHT SOY SAUCE, TO SERVE

* Heat the oil in a skillet (frying pan) over medium heat,
  add the fish, and fry for 3–4 minutes on each side
  until browned.
* Add the ginger and peppercorns, sprinkle in the wine, and
  cook for 30 seconds. Increase to high heat, pour in 3 cups
  (25 fl oz/750 ml) boiling water, and bring to a boil. Add the
  tofu, reduce to medium heat, and simmer for 30 minutes.
  Add the salt, then adjust the seasoning if necessary.
* Ladle the fish and tofu onto a serving plate, then pour
  the broth into a tureen. Serve with light soy sauce
  on the side.

酸汤鱼

CATFISH IN
PICKLED SOUP

REGION: GUIZHOU
PREPARATION TIME: 10 MINUTES
COOKING TIME: 40 MINUTES
SERVES: 4

Traditionally, this soup was prepared in a large stockpot and simmered for hours before the fish was added. This version of the recipe can be prepared in a fraction of the time by preparing the soup stock with the fish.

* Combine the fish and 1 teaspoon salt in a bowl and transfer to a colander to drain. Set aside.
* Meanwhile, score the base of the tomatoes. Bring a small saucepan of water to a boil, add the tomatoes, and heat for 1–2 minutes. Immediately transfer to a bowl of ice water. When the tomatoes are cool enough to handle, peel away the skin. Put the tomatoes in a food processor or blender and puree.
* Bring 3 cups (25 fl oz/750 ml) water to a boil in a large saucepan. Add the soybean sprouts and simmer for 5 minutes. Use a slotted spoon to transfer the bean sprouts to a tureen and set aside.
* Put the pickled vegetables into the saucepan with the liquid from the soybean sprouts and stir in the pureed tomatoes, garlic, ginger juice, chili powder, sugar, and remaining 1 teaspoon salt. Return to a boil, reduce to low heat, and simmer for 20 minutes.
* To make the dipping sauce, combine all the ingredients in a small bowl and set aside.
* Add the fish and lemon juice to the broth (stock) and cook over medium heat for about 15 minutes until the fish is cooked through. Stir in the sesame oil, season with extra salt to taste, and transfer the soup to the tureen. Serve with the dipping sauce on the side.

- 1 (2-LB/900-G) CATFISH, CLEANED AND CUT INTO 1-INCH/2.5-CM CHUNKS
- 2 TEASPOONS SALT, PLUS EXTRA TO TASTE
- 2 TOMATOES
- 2½ CUPS (7 OZ/200 G) SOYBEAN SPROUTS, RINSED
- ½ CUP (5 OZ/150 G) PICKLED VEGETABLES, CUT INTO ¾-INCH/2-CM PIECES
- 4 CLOVES GARLIC, SLICED
- 1 TABLESPOON GINGER JUICE
- ½ TEASPOON CHILI POWDER
- 1 TEASPOON GRANULATED SUGAR
- 2 TABLESPOONS LEMON JUICE
- 1 TEASPOON SESAME OIL

FOR THE DIPPING SAUCE:
- 1 SCALLION (SPRING ONION), CHOPPED
- 1 TABLESPOON LIGHT SOY SAUCE
- 1 TEASPOON CRUSHED RED PEPPER FLAKES
- 1 TEASPOON SESAME OIL

REGION: GUANGDONG
PREPARATION TIME: 25 MINUTES, PLUS
  15 MINUTES MARINATING TIME
COOKING TIME: 5 MINUTES
SERVES: 4
[📷] PAGE 105

鲜虾馄饨
SHRIMP WONTON
SOUP

- 5 OZ/150 G GROUND (MINCED) PORK
- ½ TEASPOON LIGHT SOY SAUCE
- ½ TEASPOON SALT
- ½ TEASPOON GRANULATED SUGAR
- 5 OZ/150 G UNCOOKED SHRIMP
  (PRAWNS), PEELED AND CHOPPED
- ½ TABLESPOON CORNSTARCH
  (CORNFLOUR)
- 1 TEASPOON SESAME OIL
- 12 CANTONESE WONTON WRAPPERS
- 1 OZ/25 G YELLOW CHIVES, CUT
  INTO ¾-INCH/2-CM LENGTHS
- 2 CUPS (16 FL OZ/475 ML) CHICKEN
  BROTH (STOCK, PAGE 90)

In the Western world, there's no dish more synonymous with Chinese cuisine. The wontons are cooked separately to prevent the loose starch from the wonton sheets from thickening the chicken broth (stock).

* To make the wonton filling, combine the pork, soy sauce, salt, sugar, and 1½ tablespoons water in a bowl and marinate for 15 minutes. Mix in the shrimp (prawns), then stir in the cornstarch (cornflour) and sesame oil.
* Fill a small bowl with cold water. Put 1 tablespoon of the filling on one corner of a wrapper, fold the tip over the filling and roll past the center of the wrapper. Fold the 2 ends horizontally with one end over the other. Use a little water to seal the 2 ends, then press tightly together. Place on a tray or large plate lined with wax paper. Repeat with the remaining wrappers and filling.
* Bring a large saucepan of water to a boil over high heat. Carefully drop in the wontons, in batches, simmer over medium heat, and cook for 4–5 minutes, or until they float. Place the wontons into individual serving bowls and top with the yellow chives.
* Bring the chicken broth (stock) to a boil in a saucepan, then ladle it over the wontons. Serve.

SHRIMP WONTON SOUP

发菜海蚌汤

CLAMS AND BLACK MOSS SOUP

- 2¼ LB/1 KG MANILA CLAMS
- 1 TABLESPOON SHAOXING WINE
- 3 CUPS (25 FL OZ/750 ML) CHICKEN BROTH (STOCK, PAGE 90)
- ½ OZ/15 G DRIED BLACK MOSS
- ½ TEASPOON SALT

* Using a clam knife (or a short, dull knife), hold the clam firmly in your hand and insert the knife between the top and bottom shell. Carefully work the knife around to cut through the hinge muscle and pry open the shell. Detach the clam, then slice in half. Repeat with the remaining clams, then rinse under cold running water.
* Heat a saucepan of water to about 150°F/70°C, turn off the heat, add the clam slices, and soak for 1 minute. Drain.
* Combine the clams, wine, and 2 tablespoons chicken broth (stock) in a bowl and mix well. Marinate for 5 minutes, then drain.
* Meanwhile, soak the black moss in a small bowl of water for 10 minutes until softened. Remove, rinse, and squeeze out the excess water. Place in a heatproof bowl with 4 tablespoons chicken broth and put into a collapsible pot or bamboo steamer over a pot of boiling water. Steam, covered, for 5 minutes, then drain.
* Place the black moss on one side of a tureen and the clams on the other side.
* Bring the remaining chicken broth to a boil in a saucepan, add the salt, and pour over the moss and clams.

宋嫂鱼羹
SONGSAO-STYLE
FISH SOUP

REGION: ZHEJIANG
PREPARATION TIME: 25 MINUTES,
   PLUS 20 MINUTES SOAKING TIME
COOKING TIME: 40 MINUTES
SERVES: 4

This dish dates back 900 years to the Song Dynasty.
A woman named Song was selling her fish soup by West
Lake, where the emperor happened to be. He sampled and
praised the soup and shortly after, she opened a restaurant
that soon became one of the most famous culinary
destinations in Hangzhou.

* Combine the fish bones, sliced ginger, and 3 cups
  (25 fl oz/750 ml) water in a large saucepan. Bring to a boil,
  then reduce to medium heat, and cook for 30 minutes.
  Strain the broth (stock) through a fine-mesh strainer
  (sieve) into a bowl.
* Put the mushrooms into a bowl, cover with cold water, and
  soak for at least 20 minutes, or until softened. Remove the
  mushrooms, squeeze dry, and discard the stems. Thinly slice
  and set aside.
* Meanwhile, combine the fish fillets, ½ teaspoon salt, and
  the ginger juice and marinate for 10 minutes. Drain the
  fish and place on a heatproof plate, skin side facing down.
  Place in a collapsible pot or bamboo steamer over a pot
  of boiling water. Steam, covered, for 6–7 minutes, or until
  cooked through. Pour out any water that has collected
  on the plate, then carefully remove the skin and any fine
  pinbones from the fish. Shred the fish and set aside.
* Beat the egg whites in a bowl until fluffy. Set aside.
* Heat the oil in a saucepan over medium-high heat, add the
  shredded ginger, mushrooms, and bamboo shoots, and stir-
  fry for about 2 minute, or until fragrant. Drizzle in the wine.
* Pour in the reserved fish broth, white pepper, and the
  remaining 1 teaspoon salt and bring to a boil. Gently stir
  in the fish and turn off the heat.
* Hold a strainer (sieve) over the soup and slowly pour the
  beaten eggs into the strainer. At the same time, move the
  strainer in a circular motion over the broth so that the
  beaten egg strains into the broth in a continuous line.
  Let sit for 1 minute, do not stir. Put the soup back over
  low heat and stir in the vinegar.
* Mix the water chestnut flour with 2 tablespoons water in
  a small bowl and stir this mixture into the soup. Bring to
  a boil, stirring, for 30 seconds to thicken the soup. Season
  with salt to taste.
* Ladle the soup into a tureen and garnish with the ham and
  scallions (spring onions). Stir the soup just before serving.

- 1 (14-OZ/400-G) MANDARIN FISH
  OR ANY FIRM WHITE FISH, CLEANED,
  FILLETED, AND BONES RESERVED
- ¼ OZ/10 G GINGER (ABOUT ¾-INCH/
  2-CM-LENGTH PIECE), ½ SLICED AND
  ½ SHREDDED
- 5 DRIED BLACK MUSHROOMS
- 1½ TEASPOONS SALT, PLUS EXTRA
  TO TASTE
- 1 TABLESPOON GINGER JUICE
- 2 EGG WHITES
- 1 TABLESPOON VEGETABLE OIL
- 10 SLICED BAMBOO SHOOTS,
  SHREDDED
- 1 TABLESPOON SHAOXING WINE
- ¼ TEASPOON GROUND WHITE PEPPER
- 1 TABLESPOON RED VINEGAR
- 1 TABLESPOON WATER CHESTNUT
  FLOUR OR CORNSTARCH
  (CORNFLOUR)
- 2 TABLESPOONS SHREDDED JINHUA
  OR SMITHFIELD HAM, TO GARNISH
- 2 SCALLIONS (SPRING ONIONS),
  SHREDDED, TO GARNISH

REGION: ZHEJIANG
PREPARATION TIME: 10 MINUTES
COOKING TIME: 30 MINUTES
SERVES: 4

雪菜大汤黄鱼
CORVINA
SOUP

- 1–2 CORVINA (YELLOW CROAKER) FISH (ABOUT 1 LB 5 OZ/600 G), CLEANED AND RINSED
- ⅓ CUP (2 OZ/50 G) SLICED BAMBOO SHOOT, DRAINED
- 4 TABLESPOONS VEGETABLE OIL
- ¼ OZ/10 G GINGER (ABOUT ¾-INCH/2-CM-LENGTH PIECE), SLICED
- 1 TABLESPOON SHAOXING WINE
- 3 SCALLIONS (SPRING ONIONS), 2 KNOTTED AND 1 SHREDDED
- 3½ OZ/100 G PICKLED POTHERB MUSTARD STEMS, CUT INTO ½-INCH/1-CM LENGTHS
- ½ TEASPOON SALT, PLUS EXTRA TO TASTE

* Use a sharp knife to make 3 slashes on each side of the fish.
* Bring a small saucepan of water to a boil, add the bamboo shoots, and blanch for 2 minutes. Drain and rinse under cold running water. Slice and set aside.
* Heat 3 tablespoons oil in a wok or large skillet (frying pan) over medium heat, add the ginger, and stir-fry for 1–2 minutes until fragrant. Add the fish, increase to high heat, and cook for 2–3 minutes on each side until browned.
* Sprinkle in the wine, then add 3 cups (25 fl oz/750 ml) boiling water and the knotted scallions. Reduce to medium heat, cover, and simmer for about 10 minutes. Discard the scallion (spring onion) knots. Stir in the bamboo shoots, pickled potherb mustard, salt, and remaining 1 tablespoon oil. Return to a boil over high heat and cook for 4–5 minutes until the soup becomes milky and the fish is cooked through. Season with extra salt to taste.
* Transfer to a tureen and sprinkle with the shredded scallion.

REGION: FUJIAN
PREPARATION TIME: 15 MINUTES
COOKING TIME: 5 MINUTES
SERVES: 4

鸡汤氽海蚌
CLAMS IN BROTH

- 12 MANILA CLAMS
- 2 TABLESPOONS SHAOXING WINE
- 3¾ CUPS (31 FL OZ/925 ML) CHICKEN BROTH (STOCK, PAGE 90)
- 1½ TABLESPOONS LIGHT SOY SAUCE
- ¼ TEASPOON SALT

* Using a clam knife (or a short, dull knife), hold the clam firmly in your hand and insert the knife between the top and bottom shell. Carefully work the knife around to cut through the hinge muscle and pry open the shell. Detach the clam, then slice into 2 smaller pieces. Repeat with the remaining clams, then rinse under cold running water.
* Bring a small saucepan of water to a temperature of 150°F/70°C, turn off the heat, add the clam slices, and soak for about 1 minute. Drain.
* Place the clams in a bowl, then stir in the wine and set aside for 5 minutes. Drain, then return the clams to the bowl, add ¾ cup (6 fl oz/175 ml) chicken broth (stock), and soak the clams for another 5 minutes. Drain. Divide the clams evenly between 4 bowls.
* Bring the remaining 3 cups (25 fl oz/750 ml) chicken broth to a boil in a large saucepan, then add the soy sauce and salt. Pour the broth over the clams in the bowls and serve.

拆鱼豆腐羹
FISH AND TOFU
SOUP

REGION: SHUNDE
PREPARATION TIME: 15 MINUTES,
  PLUS 20 MINUTES SOAKING TIME
COOKING TIME: 1 HOUR
SERVES: 4

* Put the mushrooms into a bowl, cover with cold water, and soak for at least 20 minutes, or until softened. Remove the mushrooms, squeeze dry, and discard the stems.
* Pat the fish dry with paper towels. Heat the oil in a large skillet (frying pan) over medium heat, add the fish, and cook for 3–4 minutes on each side until browned. Transfer the fish to a plate to cool.
* Peel off and discard the fish skin, then separate the flesh from the bones. Transfer the fish flesh to a bowl.
* Combine the fish bones, ginger, and 4¼ cups (34 fl oz/ 1 liter) water in a large saucepan. Bring to a boil over high heat, reduce to medium heat, and simmer for 20 minutes, or until only about 3 cups (25 fl oz/750 ml) liquid remains.
* Strain the broth into another saucepan, add the mushrooms, and bring to a boil. Add the tofu cubes, then return to a boil.
* Combine the water chestnut flour and 2 tablespoons water in a small bowl and stir this mixture into the soup. Bring to a boil, stirring, for about 30 seconds to thicken the soup. Add the salt and white pepper, then adjust the seasoning to taste. Transfer to a tureen, garnish with the cilantro (coriander), and serve.

- 3 DRIED BLACK MUSHROOMS
- 1 (1 LB 2-OZ/500-G) GRASS CARP TAIL OR ANY WHITE FISH, CLEANED
- 2 TABLESPOONS VEGETABLE OIL
- 2 SLICES GINGER
- 9 OZ/250 G FIRM TOFU, DRAINED AND CUT INTO ¾-INCH/2-CM CUBES
- 1 TABLESPOON WATER CHESTNUT FLOUR OR CORNSTARCH (CORNFLOUR)
- ½ TEASPOON SALT, PLUS EXTRA TO TASTE
- ¼ TEASPOON GROUND WHITE PEPPER, PLUS EXTRA TO TASTE
- 1 BUNCH CILANTRO (CORIANDER), CUT INTO ¾-INCH/2-CM LENGTHS

REGION: FUJIAN
PREPARATION TIME: 5 MINUTES
COOKING TIME: 20 MINUTES
SERVES: 4

蟹肉冬茸羹
CRAB MEAT AND WINTER MELON SOUP

- 9 OZ/250 G WINTER MELON, PEELED AND CUT INTO SMALL CHUNKS
- 2 CUPS (16 FL OZ/475 ML) CHICKEN BROTH (STOCK, PAGE 90)
- 3 EGG WHITES, BEATEN
- ⅓ CUP (2½ OZ/60 G) CRAB MEAT
- 1–2 SLICES COOKED HAM, CHOPPED
- ½ TEASPOON SALT, PLUS EXTRA TO TASTE
- 1 TABLESPOON WATER CHESTNUT FLOUR OR CORNSTARCH (CORNFLOUR)

The winter melon is first steamed to reduce its water content rather than being cooked in the soup. Although this is slightly more time-consuming, it minimizes any dilution of the broth and results in a clear, flavorful soup.

* Place the winter melon chunks on a heatproof plate. Put the plate in a collapsible pot or bamboo steamer over a pot of boiling water and steam, covered, for 15 minutes. Discard the water on the plate. Mash the winter melon with a potato masher.
* Bring the chicken broth (stock) to a boil in a saucepan, add the mashed winter melon, stir, and return to a boil.
* Slowly drizzle in the beaten egg white and use chopsticks to stir in one direction, making strands of egg. Add the crab meat, ham, and salt and return to a boil.
* Mix the water chestnut flour with 2 tablespoons water in a small bowl and stir this mixture into the soup. Bring to a boil, stirring, for about 30 seconds to thicken the soup. Season to taste with extra salt, then transfer to a tureen or ladle into individual bowls.

鱔和羹

EEL

SOUP

REGION: SHAANXI
PREPARATION TIME: 10 MINUTES,
    PLUS 20 MINUTES SOAKING TIME
COOKING TIME: 10 MINUTES
SERVES: 4

* Using a sharp knife, cut off and discard the head of the eel. Cut the eel open down the entire length of its body and remove the coarse spine. Rub the eel with the salt, rinse under cold running water, and dry with paper towels.
* Bring a large saucepan of water to a boil, add the eel, and blanch for 30 seconds. Drain and rinse under cold running water. Cut into 1½ × ¾-inch/4 × 2-cm pieces.
* Put the mushrooms into a bowl, cover with cold water, and soak for at least 20 minutes, or until softened. Remove the mushrooms, squeeze dry, and discard the stems. Thinly slice.
* Heat 2 tablespoons oil in a wok or large skillet (frying pan) over medium heat, add the eel, and stir-fry for 1 minute until just about done. Remove the eel and set aside.
* Add ½ tablespoon oil to the wok and reheat over medium heat. Add the ginger, mushrooms, and bamboo shoots and stir-fry for 1–2 minutes. Add the eel, chicken broth (stock), wine, soy sauce, salt, and sugar and bring to a boil. Reduce to low heat and simmer, covered, for 3 minutes.
* Mix the cornstarch (cornflour) with 2 tablespoons water in a small bowl and stir this mixture into the soup. Bring to a boil, stirring, for about 30 seconds to thicken the soup. Season with salt to taste. Ladle the soup into a tureen and add the cilantro (coriander), scallion (spring onion), garlic, and white pepper.
* Heat the remaining ½ tablespoon oil in a clean wok, add the Sichuan peppercorns, and stir-fry for 2–3 minutes until fragrant. Discard the pepper and pour the chili oil over the soup. Serve immediately in the tureen.

- 1 (2-LB/900-G) RICE FIELD EEL
- 1 TEASPOON COARSE SALT
- 4 DRIED BLACK MUSHROOMS
- 3 TABLESPOONS VEGETABLE OIL
- ¾ OZ/20 G GINGER (ABOUT 1-INCH/ 2.5-CM-LENGTH PIECE), SHREDDED
- 10 SLICED BAMBOO SHOOTS
- 2 CUPS (16 FL OZ/475 ML) CHICKEN BROTH (STOCK, PAGE 90)
- 1 TEASPOON RICE WINE
- 1 TEASPOON LIGHT SOY SAUCE
- 1 TEASPOON SALT, PLUS EXTRA TO TASTE
- 1 TEASPOON GRANULATED SUGAR
- 2 TABLESPOONS CORNSTARCH (CORNFLOUR)
- 1 BUNCH CILANTRO (CORIANDER), CUT INTO SECTIONS
- 1 SCALLION (SPRING ONION), CUT INTO 1½-INCH/4-CM LENGTHS
- 1 CLOVE GARLIC, CHOPPED
- ¼ TEASPOON GROUND WHITE PEPPER
- 3 TABLESPOONS SICHUAN PEPPERCORNS

REGION: JIANGSU
PREPARATION TIME: 10 MINUTES
COOKING TIME: 35 MINUTES
SERVES: 4

圆盅鸡

CHICKEN SOUP
IN A CASSEROLE

- 4 BONELESS, SKIN-ON CHICKEN
  THIGHS
- 2 TABLESPOONS SHAOXING WINE
- 3 CUPS (25 FL OZ/750 ML) CHICKEN
  BROTH (STOCK, PAGE 90)
- ½ TEASPOON SALT
- 2 SCALLIONS (SPRING ONIONS),
  SHREDDED
- ⅛ OZ/5 G GINGER (ABOUT ½-INCH/
  1-CM-LENGTH PIECE), SLICED
- STEAMED RICE (PAGE 540), TO SERVE

This is one of those dishes that serves as a soup as well as an accompaniment to rice in a family-style dining experience. The chicken soup is divided equally among the individual bowls and steamed individually. Because the ingredients are undisturbed, you get a very clear soup. This is a popular technique for making soup in southern China.

* Put the chicken into a saucepan, add 4¼ cups (34 fl oz/ 1 liter) water, and bring to a boil over high heat. Remove the chicken immediately and rinse under cold running water. Set aside to cool.
* Cut the chicken into 1-inch/2.5-cm squares and distribute evenly into 4 bowls skin side facing up. To each, add a little of the wine, chicken broth (stock), salt, scallions (spring onions), and ginger, then seal with aluminum foil.
* Place in a collapsible pot or bamboo steamer over a pot of boiling water. Steam, covered, for 30 minutes, or until the chicken is cooked through. Remove the foil, then pick out and discard the scallions and ginger. Serve in the bowls accompanied by rice.

腌笃鲜

YAN DU XIAN
SOUP

REGION: ZHEJIANG
PREPARATION TIME: 20 MINUTES
COOKING TIME: 2 HOURS 30 MINUTES
SERVES: 8

* To prepare the pork belly, scrape the skin clean, then rinse under cold running water.
* Combine the salted pork, pork belly, and enough water to cover it completely in a large saucepan. Bring to a boil over high heat and blanch for 5 minutes. Drain and rinse under cold running water.
* Return the meat to the saucepan, add the ginger, scallions (spring onions), and enough water to cover completely. Bring to a boil, reduce to low heat, and simmer for 1½ hours.
* Meanwhile, in a bowl, combine the tofu knots, baking soda (bicarbonate of soda), and 2 cups (16 fl oz/475 ml) water and soak for 15 minutes. Drain and rinse the tofu knots under cold running water.
* If using fresh bamboo shoots, cut off and discard the base, keeping only the tender tips. Roll cut the bamboo shoots into chunks. Bring a saucepan of water to a boil, add the bamboo shoots, and blanch for 2 minutes. Drain.
* In the same saucepan, bring fresh water to a boil over high heat, add the bok choy, and blanch for 1 minute. Immediately rinse under cold running water.
* Remove the pork and ham from the saucepan, then discard the ginger and scallions. Add the bamboo shoots to the soup, bring to a boil, and reduce to low heat. Simmer for 45 minutes.
* Cut the meat into smaller chunks and return to the pan, add the tofu knots, and cook for another 5 minutes. Add the bok choy, bring to a boil, and season with salt to taste. Transfer to a tureen.

- 1 (11-OZ/300-G) BONELESS, SKIN-ON PORK BELLY
- 9 OZ/250 G SALTED PORK
- 1 OZ/25 G GINGER (ABOUT 2-INCH/ 5-CM-LENGTH PIECE), SLICED
- 2 SCALLIONS (SPRING ONIONS), HALVED
- 4 CUPS (7 OZ/200 G) TOFU KNOTS
- ½ TEASPOON BAKING SODA (BICARBONATE OF SODA)
- 3½ OZ/100 G FRESH BAMBOO SHOOTS OR ⅔ CUP CANNED SLICED BAMBOO SHOOTS
- 5 OZ/150 G GREEN BOK CHOY
- SALT, TO TASTE

REGION: HUBEI
PREPARATION TIME: 15 MINUTES
COOKING TIME: 6 HOURS
SERVES: 6
📷 PAGE 115

排骨煨藕汤
LOTUS ROOT AND
SPARERIB SOUP

- 2¼ LB/1 KG PORK SPARERIBS, CUT INTO
  2-INCH/5-CM CHUNKS
- 1 LB 2 OZ/500 G LOTUS ROOTS, PEELED
  AND ENDS TRIMMED
- 2 TABLESPOONS VEGETABLE OIL
- 3 SCALLIONS (SPRING ONIONS),
  1 CHOPPED AND 2 CUT INTO 1½-INCH/
  4-CM LENGTHS, PLUS EXTRA
  TO GARNISH
- ½ OZ/15 G GINGER (ABOUT 1-INCH/
  2.5-CM-LENGTH PIECE), SLICED
- 1 TEASPOON RICE WINE
- ½ TABLESPOON SALT
- ¼ TEASPOON GROUND WHITE PEPPER

* Put the spareribs into a large saucepan and add enough
  water to cover them completely. Bring to a boil over high
  heat and blanch for 3 minutes. Drain and rinse under cold
  running water.
* Use a chopstick to clean the channels inside the lotus roots
  and rinse thoroughly under cold running water. Cut into
  bite-sized chunks or slice.
* Heat the oil in a large saucepan over medium heat, add
  the spareribs, and pan-fry for about 10 minutes until crispy.
  Add the scallion (spring onion) lengths, ginger, wine, and
  10½ cups (85 fl oz/2.5 liters) water. Bring to a boil, reduce
  to low heat, and simmer, covered, for 1 hour.
* Add the lotus roots and simmer for another 4 hours over
  low heat. Season with the salt, reduce to medium heat, and
  simmer for 30 minutes. (Remove the scallions and ginger,
  if desired.) Pour the soup into a tureen and top with the
  chopped scallions and white pepper.

REGION: HONG KONG
PREPARATION TIME: 10 MINUTES
COOKING TIME: 2 HOURS 15 MINUTES
SERVES: 4

五指毛桃猪腱汤
PORK SHANK AND
HAIRY FIG SOUP

- 1 (14-OZ/400-G) PORK SHANK, RINSED
- ⅛ OZ/5 G GINGER (ABOUT ½-INCH/
  1-CM-LENGTH PIECE), SLICED
- 3½ OZ/100 G HAIRY FIGS, RINSED
- 2 EARS CORN, HUSKS AND SILK
  REMOVED, CUT INTO 1½-INCH/
  4-CM CHUNKS
- 1 CARROT, CUT INTO ¾-INCH/
  2-CM CHUNKS
- 1 TEASPOON SALT, PLUS EXTRA
  TO TASTE

* Put the pork shank into a large saucepan and add enough
  water to cover it completely. Bring to a boil over high heat
  and blanch the pork for 5 minutes. Skim the froth and
  scum off the surface, if needed. Drain and rinse under
  cold running water.
* Bring 6¼ cups (50 fl oz/1.5 liters) water to a boil in a large
  saucepan. Add the pork shank and ginger, cover, and boil
  over high heat for 15 minutes. Add the hairy figs, corn, and
  carrot and bring to a boil. Reduce to medium-low heat and
  cook for 1 hour 45 minutes. Season with the salt, adjust
  to taste, and transfer the soup to a tureen or individual
  serving bowls.

LOTUS ROOT AND SPARERIB SOUP

REGION: HONG KONG
PREPARATION TIME: 20 MINUTES,
   PLUS 30 MINUTES SOAKING TIME
COOKING TIME: 2 HOURS 45 MINUTES
SERVES: 4

莲藕章鱼猪䐍汤
PORK, LOTUS ROOT, AND DRIED OCTOPUS SOUP

- ¼ CUP (2 OZ/50 G) DRIED MUNG BEANS
- 2 OZ/50 G DRIED OCTOPUS
- 1 LB 5 OZ/600 G PORK SHANKS
- 1 LOTUS ROOT (ABOUT 1 LB 5 OZ/ 600 G), PEELED AND ENDS TRIMMED
- ¼ OZ/10 G GINGER (ABOUT ¾-INCH/ 2-CM-LENGTH PIECE), SLICED
- 1 TEASPOON SALT, PLUS EXTRA TO TASTE
- LIGHT SOY SAUCE, TO SERVE

It is customary to stuff the channels of the lotus roots with the mung beans, which would, otherwise, sink to the bottom of the pot. Once cooked, the lotus root, pork, and octopus are served on a separate plate, alongside the broth.

* Combine the mung beans and 1 cup (8 fl oz/250 ml) water in a small bowl and soak for 30 minutes. Drain.
* In a separate bowl, soak the dried octopus in warm water for 30 minutes, then drain. Cut into bite-size pieces and set aside.
* Rinse the pork shank under cold running water. Put the shank in a large saucepan and add enough water to cover it completely. Bring to a boil over high heat and blanch the pork for 1–2 minutes. Drain and rinse under cold running water. Set aside.
* Use a chopstick to clean the channels inside the lotus root and rinse thoroughly under cold running water. Use a chopstick to stuff the lotus root with the mung beans at both ends until it is 80 percent full.
* Bring 8½ cups (68 fl oz/2 liters) water to a boil in a large saucepan. Add the ginger, pork shank, lotus root, and dried octopus. Cover and boil over high heat for 10 minutes, then reduce to low heat, and cook for 2½ hours. Add the salt and adjust to taste.
* Transfer the pork shank and lotus root to a cutting board and when cool enough to handle, cut into large chunks. Transfer to a serving plate, then add the octopus. Ladle the soup into individual bowls and serve with the plate of food. Serve with light soy sauce.

花生煲猪尾
PIG'S TAIL AND
PEANUT SOUP

REGION: GUANGDONG
PREPARATION TIME: 10 MINUTES,
    PLUS 15 MINUTES SOAKING TIME
COOKING TIME: 2 HOURS 20 MINUTES
SERVES: 4-6

* Combine the pig's tail and enough cold water to cover
  it in a bowl and soak for 15 minutes. Drain, then scrape
  the skin clean. Using a sharp knife, cut the pig's tail at
  the joints into small chunks.
* Put the pig's tail chunks in a large saucepan and add
  enough water to cover completely. Bring to a boil over
  high heat and blanch for 5 minutes. Drain and rinse
  under cold running water.
* Put the pig's tail back into the pan, add the peanuts,
  dates, ginger, and 8½ cups (68 fl oz/2 liters) water, and
  cover. Bring to a boil over medium-high heat and cook
  for 10 minutes, then reduce to low heat and simmer for
  another 2 hours. Season with salt to taste.
* Transfer to a tureen or ladle into individual bowls.

- 1 (11-OZ/300-G) PIG'S TAIL
- 1 CUP (5 OZ/150 G) SHELLED RAW
  PEANUTS, RINSED AND DRAINED
- 3 JUJUBE DATES, PITTED AND HALVED
- ¼ OZ/10 G GINGER (ABOUT ¾-INCH/
  2-CM-LENGTH PIECE), SLICED
- SALT, TO TASTE

猪肚白果汤
TRIPE AND GINKGO
SOUP

REGION: CHAOZHOU
PREPARATION TIME: 15 MINUTES,
    PLUS 1 HOUR SOAKING TIME
COOKING TIME: 3 HOURS
SERVES: 4

* Turn the tripe inside out and scrub thoroughly with
  1 tablespoon coarse salt. Rinse under cold running water,
  then rub with 1 tablespoon cornstarch (cornflour). Rinse
  again. Repeat several times until all the grit and film have
  been removed.
* Combine the tripe, vinegar, and 3 cups (25 fl oz/750 ml)
  water in a large bowl and soak for 1 hour.
* Meanwhile, cut away the leaves from the Chaozhou salted
  mustard greens and rinse the stems well. Soak the stems
  in a bowl of cold water for 1 hour.
* Rinse the tripe under cold running water, then transfer to a
  large saucepan. Fill with fresh water and bring to a boil over
  high heat. Reduce to medium heat and blanch the tripe
  for 5 minutes. Drain and rinse, then use kitchen scissors to
  remove all the trimmings and fat from inside the tripe. Cut
  the tripe into long strips and put into a heatproof bowl.
* Drain the mustard greens, squeeze out the excess water,
  and cut into similar-size pieces to the tripe. Add to the bowl
  of tripe.
* Put the ginkgo nuts, white pepper, and chicken broth (stock)
  into the bowl, then put into a collapsible pot or bamboo
  steamer over a pot of boiling water. Steam, covered, for
  3 hours. (Add more water to the pot, if necessary.) Transfer
  to a tureen and serve in individual bowls.

- 1 PORK TRIPE, RINSED
- 3 TABLESPOONS COARSE SALT
- 3 TABLESPOONS CORNSTARCH
  (CORNFLOUR)
- 1 TABLESPOON WHITE VINEGAR
- ¼ HEAD (ABOUT 2 OZ/50 G)
  CHAOZHOU PRESERVED MUSTARD
  GREENS
- ½ CUP (ABOUT 2½ OZ/70 G) SHELLED
  GINKGO NUTS
- 1 TABLESPOON WHITE PEPPERCORNS,
  LIGHTLY CRUSHED
- 2 CUPS (16 FL OZ/475 ML) CHICKEN
  BROTH (STOCK, PAGE 90)

REGION: BEIJING
PREPARATION TIME: 15 MINUTES
COOKING TIME: 20 MINUTES
SERVES: 4

肝糕汤

PORK LIVER
SOUP

- 9 OZ/250 G PORK LIVER
- 1 TEASPOON SALT
- ½ TEASPOON GROUND WHITE PEPPER
- 4¼ CUPS (34 FL OZ/1 LITER) CHICKEN BROTH (STOCK, PAGE 90)
- 1 BONELESS, SKINLESS CHICKEN BREAST

* Place the pork liver in a blender or food processor, add ½ teaspoon salt, the white pepper, and 1 cup (8 fl oz/ 250 ml) chicken broth (stock), and puree. Strain through a sieve (strainer) into a large heatproof bowl.
* Put the pork liver puree into a collapsible pot or bamboo steamer over a pot of boiling water. Steam, covered, for 8 minutes, or until a liver pâté is formed. Remove from the steamer, then cut the pâté in the bowl into small squares. Do not remove the pâté from the bowl (so that it remains intact).
* Put the chicken into the blender or food processor and process into a paste. Mix the blended chicken with 1 cup (8 fl oz/250 ml) chicken broth and puree into a thin paste.
* Pour the remaining generous 2 cups (17 fl oz/500 ml) chicken broth into a large saucepan, add the remaining ½ teaspoon salt, and bring to a boil. Add a third of the chicken paste and stir in one direction as it comes to another boil. Skim off the froth and scum on the surface.
* Repeat with the remaining chicken paste, stir, and return to a boil. Strain the broth and pour into the bowl with the pâté. When ready to serve, place in a collapsible pot or bamboo steamer over a pot of boiling water. Steam, covered, for 5 minutes. Serve.

REGION: HAKKA
PREPARATION TIME: 10 MINUTES, PLUS
    30 MINUTES MARINATING TIME
COOKING TIME: 1 HOUR
SERVES: 4

猪筒骨白菜汤

PORK AND BOK
CHOY SOUP

- 1 (11-OZ/300-G) PORK SHANK, CUT INTO PIECES
- 1 TEASPOON SALT, PLUS EXTRA TO TASTE
- 1 TEASPOON VEGETABLE OIL
- ⅛ OZ/5 G GINGER (ABOUT ½-INCH/ 1-CM-LENGTH PIECE), SLICED
- 1 PORK LEG BONE, HALVED
- 1 LB 5 OZ/600 G BOK CHOY

* Combine the pork shank and ½ teaspoon salt in a bowl and marinate for 30 minutes.
* Heat the oil in a large saucepan over medium-high heat and fry the ginger for 1–2 minutes until fragrant. Pour in 6¼ cups (50 fl oz/1.5 liters) water, bring to a boil over high heat, and put in the pork bone. Reduce to medium heat and simmer for 30 minutes.
* Put in the bok choy, shank, and remaining ½ teaspoon salt and cook for 30 minutes. Season with extra salt to taste. Transfer to a tureen or ladle into bowls.

牛肝菌松茸炖乌鸡

BLACK CHICKEN AND
MUSHROOM SOUP

REGION: YUNNAN
PREPARATION TIME: 15 MINUTES, PLUS
  1 HOUR SOAKING TIME
COOKING TIME: 2 HOURS 5 MINUTES
SERVES: 6

Also known as Silkie chickens, this highly prized black chickens has silky white plumage and black skin (and bones). Commonly found in China and other parts of Asia, it can be substituted with a regular chicken.

* Rinse the mushrooms and soak in 2 cups (16 fl oz/475 ml) cold water for 1 hour. Remove the mushrooms, then strain the mushroom soaking water into a bowl. Set both aside.
* Bring a large saucepan of water to a boil, carefully add the chicken, and blanch for 1 minute. Drain and set aside.
* Fill the same pan with fresh water, bring to a boil, and add the pork. Blanch for 1 minute, then drain.
* Combine the chicken, pork, dates, ginger, and white peppercorns in a large heatproof bowl. Add the mushrooms and the reserved mushroom soaking water. Pour in 4¼ cups (34 fl oz/1 liter) boiling water and seal tightly with aluminum foil. Place in a collapsible pot or bamboo steamer over a pot of boiling water. Steam, covered, for 2 hours, until tender and cooked through. (Add more water to the pot if needed.)
* Season with salt and serve in a tureen.

- ½ OZ/15 G DRIED PORCINI (CEP) MUSHROOMS
- ½ OZ/15 G DRIED MATSUTAKE MUSHROOMS
- 1 (1 LB 8 ½-OZ/700-G) WHOLE BLACK OR REGULAR CHICKEN
- 3½ OZ/100 G LEAN PORK
- 6 JUJUBE DATES, PITTED
- ⅛ OZ/5 G GINGER (ABOUT ½-INCH/ 1-CM-LENGTH PIECE), SLICED
- ½ TABLESPOON WHITE PEPPERCORNS
- SALT, TO TASTE

羊肉泡馍
MUTTON
SOUP

- 1 (1 LB 5-OZ/600-G) LEG OF MUTTON
  OR LAMB, DE-BONED
- ¾ OZ/20 G GINGER (ABOUT
  1-INCH/2.5-CM-LENGTH PIECE),
  CRUSHED
- 6 SCALLIONS (SPRING ONIONS), CUT
  DIAGONALLY INTO ¾-INCH/2-CM
  THICK, 1½-INCH/4-CM-LONG PIECES,
  PLUS EXTRA TO GARNISH
- 4 FLATBREAD (PAGE 54), BROKEN BY
  HAND INTO ¾-INCH/2-CM PIECES,
  TO SERVE
- SALT, TO TASTE

FOR THE SPICE BAG:
- 2 STAR ANISE
- 1 TEASPOON SICHUAN PEPPERCORNS
- 2 BLACK CARDAMOM PODS

This dish is traditionally served with flatbread, which is broken into small pieces by hand and put into the bowls before the soup is poured in. People converse with each other while breaking bread and this convivial ritual has become a regular social event.

* Put the mutton in a large saucepan and add enough water to cover it completely. Bring to a boil over high heat and blanch the mutton for 5 minutes. Skim the froth and scum off the surface, if needed. Drain and rinse under cold running water.
* Put the star anise, Sichuan peppercorns, and cardamom pods into a spice bag.
* Combine the ginger, scallions (spring onions), and spice bag in a large saucepan, add enough water to cover the mutton by ¾ inch/2 cm, and bring to a boil. Reduce to low heat and simmer for 1 hour 15 minutes, or until the meat is tender.
* Pick out and discard the ginger and spice bag. Remove the mutton and set aside to cool. Cut into slices.
* Put the bread into individual serving bowls and put several pieces of mutton into each bowl.
* Bring the soup to a boil and season with salt to taste, then ladle the soup into each bowl and garnish with scallions. (Be sure to ladle generously because some of the soup will be absorbed by the flatbread.) Serve immediately.

杏汁白肺汤
PORK LUNGS AND
APRICOT KERNEL SOUP

REGION: HAKKA
PREPARATION TIME: 10 MINUTES,
   PLUS 1 HOUR SOAKING TIME
COOKING TIME: 3 HOURS
SERVES: 6-8

* Soak the apricot kernels in 2 cups (16 fl oz/475 ml) water for 1 hour. Put the kernels and soaking water into a blender or food processor and puree. Strain through a cheesecloth (muslin) into a bowl. Set aside the juice and discard the dregs.

* Meanwhile, soak the snow fungus in hot water and soak for about 30 minutes. Rinse the snow fungus and trim off the firm part at the base. Tear the fungus into smaller pieces.

* Thoroughly clean the outside and inside of the pork lungs, rinsing them out with cold running water until the lungs turn white. Use a sharp knife to cut away the trachea and bronchus, leaving only the soft part of the lungs. Cut into 1½-inch/4-cm chunks.

* Bring a large saucepan of water to a boil, add the lungs, ginger, and vinegar, and boil for about 5 minutes. Drain, then thoroughly rinse under cold running water until the lungs no longer smell of vinegar.

* In the same saucepan, combine the lungs, snow fungus, pork, and broth (stock) and bring to a boil over high heat. Reduce to low heat, then simmer for about 3 hours. Use a slotted spoon to remove and discard the pork (the pork will have no taste after 3 hours), then stir in the apricot-kernel juice. Season with the salt and white pepper, adjust the seasoning to taste, and transfer the soup to a tureen.

* Serve with soy sauce on the side as a dipping sauce for the lungs.

- 1 CUP (7 OZ/200 G) SWEET APRICOT KERNELS
- 1 DRIED SNOW FUNGUS
- 1 PORK LUNG (ABOUT 2¼ LB/1 KG)
- ⅛ OZ/5 G GINGER (ABOUT ½-INCH/ 1-CM-LENGTH PIECE), SLICED
- 2 TABLESPOONS WHITE VINEGAR
- 14 OZ/400 G LEAN PORK, CUT INTO BITE-SIZE PIECES
- 6¼ CUPS (50 FL OZ/1.5 LITERS) CHICKEN OR PORK BROTH (STOCK, PAGE 90-91)
- 1 TEASPOON SALT, PLUS EXTRA TO TASTE
- ¼ TEASPOON GROUND WHITE PEPPER, PLUS EXTRA TO TASTE
- LIGHT SOY SAUCE, TO SERVE

121

REGION: ZHEJIANG
PREPARATION TIME: 10 MINUTES,
   PLUS 5 MINUTES MARINATING TIME
COOKING TIME: 5 MINUTES
SERVES: 2
📷 PAGE 123

西湖牛肉羹
WEST LAKE
BEEF SOUP

- 5 OZ/150 G GROUND (MINCED) BEEF
- 2 TEASPOONS SWEET POTATO STARCH
  OR CORNSTARCH (CORNFLOUR)
- 2 CUPS (16 FL OZ/475 ML) CHICKEN
  BROTH (STOCK, PAGE 90)
- ½ TEASPOON SALT, PLUS EXTRA
  TO TASTE
- 1 EGG WHITE, BEATEN
- ½ TEASPOON SESAME OIL
- ¼ TEASPOON GROUND WHITE PEPPER
- ¼ CUP (¾ OZ/15 G) CHOPPED
  CILANTRO (CORIANDER), PLUS EXTRA
  TO GARNISH (OPTIONAL)

* Mix the beef with 4 tablespoons water in a bowl and
  set aside for 5 minutes. Stir, then transfer the beef
  to a colander to drain. Return the beef to the bowl
  and mix in 1 teaspoon sweet potato starch.
* Bring the chicken broth (stock) to a boil in a saucepan
  over high heat. Add the beef and salt, stirring continuously
  to separate the beef.
* Mix the remaining 1 teaspoon sweet potato starch with
  1 tablespoon water in a small bowl and stir this mixture
  into the broth. Bring to a boil, stirring, for 30 seconds to
  thicken the soup.
* Slowly drizzle in the beaten egg white and use chopsticks
  to stir in one direction, making strands of egg. Stir in the
  sesame oil, white pepper, and cilantro (coriander), then
  season with extra salt to taste. Transfer the soup to a
  serving bowl or tureen and garnish with cilantro, if using.

REGION: SHANXI
PREPARATION TIME: 10 MINUTES,
   PLUS 15 MINUTES SOAKING TIME
COOKING TIME: 1 HOUR 40 MINUTES
SERVES: 4–6

当归生姜羊肉汤
CHINESE HERBAL
LAMB SOUP

- ¼ OZ/10 G MUNG BEAN VERMICELLI
- 1 LB 2 OZ/500 G BONELESS LEG OF LAMB,
  CUT INTO 2½ × 1¼-INCH/6 × 3-CM SLICES
- 11 OZ/300 G DAIKON RADISH, CUT INTO
  CHUNKS
- ½ CUP (¼ OZ/10 G) DRIED BLACK FUNGUS,
  SOFTENED IN COLD WATER, STEMS
  DISCARDED, AND CAPS TORN INTO PIECES
- 1 TEASPOON SALT

FOR THE MEDICINAL HERBS:
- 2–3 DRIED TANGERINE PEELS
- ¼ OZ/10 G ANGELICA ROOT, SLICED
- 1 OZ/25 G GINGER (ABOUT 2-INCH/
  5-CM-LENGTH PIECE), SLICED
- ¼ OZ/10 G SLICED BAI ZHU
- 7 CLOVES

* Soak the dried tangerine peel in cold water for 15 minutes
  to soften, then drain. Scrape off and discard the white
  membrane from the peel.
* Meanwhile, soak the vermicelli in a bowl of cold water
  for 10 minutes to soften, then drain. Set aside.
* Bring a large saucepan of water to a boil, add the lamb,
  and blanch for 1 minute. Drain and rinse under cold water.
* Combine the lamb and 8 cups (68 fl oz/2 liters) water in
  a large saucepan and bring to a boil over high heat. Skim
  the surface to remove any froth or scum. Put the medicinal
  herbs into a spice bag, add it to the pan, then reduce to low
  heat, and simmer, covered, for about 1 hour. Add the radish
  and simmer for another 30 minutes. Remove and discard
  the spice bag. Stir the black fungus and vermicelli into the
  soup, bring to a boil, and season with the salt. Transfer the
  soup to a tureen or ladle into individual bowls and serve.

WEST LAKE BEEF SOUP

FISH & SEAFOOD

FISH & SEAFOOD

REGION: CHAOZHOU
PREPARATION TIME: 15 MINUTES,
   PLUS 20 MINUTES SOAKING TIME
COOKING TIME: 15 MINUTES
SERVES: 4

潮式古法炊白鯧
CHAOZHOU-STYLE
POMFRET

- 3 DRIED BLACK MUSHROOMS
- 1 (1-LB/450-G) WHITE POMFRET OR
  ANY WHITE FISH, CLEANED AND
  RINSED
- 1 TABLESPOON RICE WINE
- 1½ TEASPOONS SALT
- ¼ OZ/10 G PORK FATBACK, CUT INTO
  THIN STRIPS
- 1 TEASPOON CORNSTARCH
  (CORNFLOUR)
- 4 SCALLIONS (SPRING ONIONS),
  2 STEMS CUT INTO 1½/4-CM SEGMENTS
  AND 2 SHREDDED
- 1 OZ/50 G GINGER (ABOUT 1-INCH/
  2.5-CM-LENGTH PIECE), HALF
  SHREDDED AND HALF SLICED
- 2 TABLESPOONS VEGETABLE OIL
- ¼ OZ/10 G LEAN PORK
- ¼ OZ/10 G PRESERVED MUSTARD
  GREENS, TRIMMED, RINSED, AND
  SLICED
- 1 TOMATO, SEEDED AND CUT INTO
  8 PIECES
- 1 STALK CHINESE CELERY, CUT INTO
  1¼-INCH/3-CM LENGTHS
- ¼ TEASPOON SESAME OIL
- STEAMED RICE (PAGE 540), TO SERVE

* Put the mushrooms into a bowl, cover with cold water, and soak for at least 20 minutes, or until softened. Remove the mushrooms, squeeze dry, and discard the stems. Cut into thin slices.
* Meanwhile, use a sharp knife to make 2–3 slashes on each side of the fish and pat dry. Mix the wine with 1 teaspoon salt in a small bowl, rub all over the fish, inside and out, and marinate for 15 minutes.
* Combine the pork fatback with ½ teaspoon cornstarch (cornflour) in another bowl and mix well. Set aside.
* Line a heatproof plate with the scallion (spring onion) stems and place the fish on top. Put the ginger slices on top of the fish and put into a collapsible pot or bamboo steamer over a pot of boiling water. Steam, covered, for 8–10 minutes, or until cooked through. Carefully remove the plate from the steamer and discard the ginger and scallion stems. Pour the steamed juices from the plate into a bowl and reserve. Sprinkle the fish with the shredded scallions and put on a serving plate.
* Heat the vegetable oil in a wok or large skillet (frying pan). Add the shredded ginger, lean pork, pork fatback, mustard greens, and mushrooms and stir-fry over high heat for 2–3 minutes until fragrant. Add the tomato, Chinese celery, remaining ½ teaspoon salt, and the reserved steamed juices from the fish and stir-fry for another 1 minute, just until the pork is cooked through. Add the sesame oil.
* Mix the remaining ½ teaspoon cornstarch with ½ tablespoon water in a small bowl and stir this mixture into the wok. Bring to a boil, stirring, for 30 seconds to thicken the sauce. Pour over the fish and serve with rice.

鱼饭
FISH
RICE

REGION: CHAOZHOU
PREPARATION TIME: 10 MINUTES,
    PLUS 2 HOURS SALTING TIME
COOKING TIME: 13–15 MINUTES
SERVES: 4

When Chaozhou fishermen went to sea, they carried few supplies other than coarse salt. They relied on the fish they caught as their main source of nourishment. To prepare it, they would salt the fish, steam it, and then set it aside to cool. Served at room temperature, this revered regional dish is widely known as "fish rice" to represent the simple preparation.

* Rub the fish with the sea salt inside and out and marinate in the refrigerator for at least 2 hours.
* Place the fish on a heatproof plate and put into a collapsible pot or bamboo steamer over a pot of boiling water. Steam, covered, for 13–14 minutes until cooked through. Carefully remove the fish and drain the juices from the plate. Set aside to cool completely.
* Meanwhile, make the dipping sauce by combining the bean paste and vinegar in a small bowl.
* When the fish has cooled, use a pair of scissors to cut open the skin along the back of the fish, from head to tail. Lift off and discard the fish skin before serving the fish together with the dipping sauce on the side. Serve with rice.

- 1 (1 LB 5-OZ/600-G) COD, HALIBUT, OR ANY SALTWATER FISH, CLEANED AND RINSED
- 1½ TABLESPOONS SEA SALT
- 2 TABLESPOONS PUNING BEAN PASTE
- 1 TABLESPOON WHITE VINEGAR
- STEAMED RICE (PAGE 540), TO SERVE

REGION: HONG KONG
PREPARATION TIME: 15 MINUTES,
    PLUS 15 MINUTES MARINATING TIME
COOKING TIME: 10 MINUTES
SERVES: 3-4

豉汁蒸盲曹鱼
BARRAMUNDI WITH
BLACK BEAN SAUCE

- ¼ TEASPOON SALT
- 1 (1 LB 2-OZ/500-G) BARRAMUNDI, CLEANED AND RINSED
- 2 TABLESPOONS VEGETABLE OIL
- 1 SCALLION (SPRING ONION), CUT INTO 2-INCH/5-CM LENGTHS, THEN SHREDDED

FOR THE BLACK BEAN PASTE:
- 1 RED CHILE, SEEDED AND FINELY SHREDDED
- 1 TABLESPOON FERMENTED BLACK BEANS, RINSED AND CHOPPED
- 3 CLOVES GARLIC, CHOPPED
- ½ TEASPOON LIGHT SOY SAUCE
- ½ TEASPOON GRANULATED SUGAR

* Rub the salt into the fish, place it into a shallow dish, and set aside for 15 minutes.
* Mix the black bean paste ingredients together into a bowl. Spread the paste evenly over the fish.
* Place the fish in a collapsible pot or bamboo steamer over a pot of boiling water. Steam, covered, for 8 minutes, or until cooked through.
* Heat the oil in a small skillet (frying pan). Transfer the steamed fish to a serving plate, drizzle over the warm oil, then sprinkle over the shredded scallion (spring onion) and serve.

REGION: HONG KONG
PREPARATION TIME: 10 MINUTES
COOKING TIME: 10 MINUTES
SERVES: 4

豆酥鳕鱼
COD WITH
SOYBEAN CRISPS

- 14 OZ/400 G COD OR ANY FIRM WHITE FISH FILLETS
- ½ TEASPOON SALT
- 1 TEASPOON CORNSTARCH (CORNFLOUR)
- 1½ TABLESPOONS VEGETABLE OIL
- 2 SHALLOTS, CHOPPED
- 2 CLOVES GARLIC, CHOPPED
- PINCH OF GROUND WHITE PEPPER
- 1 QUANTITY SOYBEAN CRISPS (PAGE 52)
- STEAMED RICE (PAGE 540), NOODLES, OR BOILED POTATOES, TO SERVE

* Pat the fish fillets dry with paper towels. Combine the fish, salt, and cornstarch (cornflour) in a large bowl and set aside for 5 minutes. Drizzle in ½ tablespoon oil and mix well.
* Place the fish on a heatproof plate and put into a collapsible pot or bamboo steamer over a pot of boiling water. Steam for 8 minutes, or until cooked through. Remove the fish, keep warm, and discard the steamed fish juices from the plate.
* Heat 1 tablespoon oil in a wok or large skillet (frying pan), add the shallots, and stir-fry over medium heat for 1 minute until fragrant. Stir in the garlic and white pepper, add the soybean crisps, and stir-fry briefly. Place over the fish and serve with rice, noodles, or potatoes.

咸鲜青筋鱼
STEAMED SALTED
TILEFISH

REGION: HONG KONG
PREPARATION TIME: 5 MINUTES,
   PLUS 2 HOURS DRAINING TIME
COOKING TIME: 8 MINUTES
SERVES: 4

* Rinse the fish under cold running water, put on a heatproof plate, and top with the ginger. Rub the fish, inside and out, with the salt and place it on a steaming rack on a plate. Set aside for 2 hours to let the water drain from the fish (no need to refrigerate as the salt will preserve the fish).
* Rinse the fish with water, put on a heatproof plate, and top with the ginger. Place the fish in a collapsible pot or bamboo steamer over a pot of boiling water. Steam, covered, for 6–7 minutes, or until cooked through.
* Heat the oil in a small skillet (frying pan) over high heat for 1 minute, or until thoroughly heated. Drizzle over the fish and serve with rice.

* 1 (1 LB 5-OZ/600-G) TILEFISH, CLEANED AND RINSED
* 1 TABLESPOON COARSE SALT
* ¼ OZ/10 G GINGER (ABOUT ¾-INCH/ 2-CM-LENGTH PIECE), SHREDDED
* 2 TABLESPOONS VEGETABLE OIL
* STEAMED RICE (PAGE 540), TO SERVE

清蒸鲳目鱼
STEAMED
FLOUNDER

REGION: SHUNDE
PREPARATION TIME: 15 MINUTES,
   PLUS 20 MINUTES SOAKING TIME
COOKING TIME: 10 MINUTES
SERVES: 4

* Put the mushrooms into a bowl, cover with cold water, and soak for at least 20 minutes, or until softened. Remove the mushrooms, squeeze dry, and discard the stems. Cut into thin slices.
* Put the fish on a plate, rub with the salt, and set aside for 10 minutes. Pour out the water from the plate and pat the fish dry with paper towels.
* Combine the pork, soy sauce, and cornstarch (cornflour) in a bowl and mix well.
* Distribute the chives evenly on a heatproof plate and place the fish on top.
* Mix the mushrooms, ginger, and pork with 1½ teaspoons oil in a bowl, then place on top of the fish. Place the plate on a steaming rack in a wok of boiling water. Steam, covered, for about 8 minutes, or until cooked through.
* Remove from the wok, sprinkle with white pepper, and top with the chopped scallion (spring onion). Heat the remaining 2 tablespoons oil in a small skillet (frying pan) and drizzle over the fish. Serve with rice.

* 4 DRIED BLACK MUSHROOMS
* 1 (1 LB 2-OZ/500-G) FLOUNDER, CLEANED AND RINSED
* ½ TEASPOON SALT
* 2 OZ/50 G LEAN PORK, CUT INTO FINE STRIPS
* ½ TEASPOON LIGHT SOY SAUCE
* ½ TEASPOON CORNSTARCH (CORNFLOUR)
* 3½ OZ/100 G YELLOW CHIVES, CUT INTO 2-INCH/5-CM LENGTHS
* ¼ OZ/10 G GINGER (ABOUT ¾-INCH/ 2-CM-LENGTH PIECE), SHREDDED
* 2½ TABLESPOONS VEGETABLE OIL
* ½ TEASPOON GROUND WHITE PEPPER
* 1 SCALLION (SPRING ONION), CHOPPED
* STEAMED RICE (PAGE 540), TO SERVE

清蒸石斑鱼

STEAMED GROUPER

REGION: HONG KONG
PREPARATION TIME: 5 MINUTES
COOKING TIME: 12 MINUTES
SERVES: 4
📷 PAGE 133

- 1 (1 LB 5-OZ/600-G) QUEENSLAND GROUPER OR ANY FIRM WHITE FISH, CLEANED AND RINSED
- 2 TABLESPOONS VEGETABLE OIL
- ¼ OZ/10 G GINGER (ABOUT ¾-INCH/ 2-CM-LENGTH PIECE), SHREDDED
- 2 SCALLIONS (SPRING ONIONS), SHREDDED
- STEAMED RICE (PAGE 540), TO SERVE

  FOR THE SPECIAL SOY SAUCE:
- 2 TABLESPOONS LIGHT SOY SAUCE
- 2 TEASPOONS FISH SAUCE
- 2 TEASPOONS GRANULATED SUGAR
- ¼ TEASPOON GROUND WHITE PEPPER

* Put the sauce ingredients into a bowl, mix well, and set aside.
* Place the fish on a heatproof plate and put into a bamboo steamer over a pot of boiling water. Steam, covered, for about 9 minutes, or until cooked through. Drain away the steamed fish juices collected on the plate.
* Combine the sauce with 4 tablespoons water in a skillet (frying pan) and bring to a boil, then remove from the heat and pour over the fish.
* Wipe the skillet with paper towels, add the oil, and set over medium heat for 1 minute until thoroughly heated. Stir in the shredded ginger and pour over the fish. Top with the scallions (spring onions) and serve with rice.

焗腌鱼

CHAOZHOU PAN-FRIED FISH

REGION: CHAOZHOU
PREPARATION TIME: 10 MINUTES, PLUS 8 HOURS MARINATING TIME
COOKING TIME: 10 MINUTES
SERVES: 4

- 1 (1 LB 2-OZ/500-G) WHITE CROAKER
- 2 TABLESPOONS DARK SOY SAUCE
- ½ TABLESPOON RICE WINE
- 1 TABLESPOON GINGER JUICE
- 1½ TEASPOONS GRANULATED SUGAR
- ½ TEASPOON SALT
- ¾ OZ/20 G GINGER (ABOUT 1-INCH/ 2.5-CM-LENGTH PIECE), SLICED
- ½ CUP (4 FL OZ/120 ML) VEGETABLE OIL
- STEAMED RICE (PAGE 540), TO SERVE

* Use a sharp knife to make 5–6 deep cuts (to the bone) on each side of the fish, at a 45 degree angle toward the head. (This angled cut allows us to later insert slices of ginger without them falling out.)
* Combine the dark soy sauce, wine, ginger juice, sugar, and salt in a small bowl and mix well.
* Insert a slice of ginger into each cut on the fish on both sides. Transfer the fish to a plate, drizzle the marinade on top, cover with plastic wrap (clingfilm), and place a weighty object (such as a bowl of water) on top. Marinate in the refrigerator for 8 hours, turning the fish over once during marinating.
* Discard the marinade and pat the fish dry with paper towels.
* Heat the oil in a wok over medium-low heat, add the fish, and pan-fry for 5 minutes on each side until brown and crispy. Transfer to a plate and serve with rice.

STEAMED GROUPER

133

冬菜蒸多宝鱼
TURBOT WITH
PRESERVED CABBAGE

- 1 (1 LB 5-OZ/600-G) TURBOT, FLOUNDER, OR ANY FLAT FISH, CLEANED AND RINSED
- ½ TEASPOON SALT
- 2 TABLESPOONS TIANJIN PRESERVED CABBAGE
- 1 TEASPOON GRANULATED SUGAR
- 2½ TABLESPOONS VEGETABLE OIL
- 3 SCALLIONS (SPRING ONIONS), CHOPPED
- STEAMED RICE (PAGE 540), TO SERVE

* Pat the fish dry with paper towels. Salt both sides of the fish and marinate for 5 minutes. Place the fish on a heatproof plate.
* Rinse the preserved cabbage in cold water, squeeze dry, and chop. Combine the preserved cabbage, sugar, and ½ tablespoon oil in a bowl, mix well, and put on top of the fish. Place the fish into a collapsible pot or bamboo steamer over a pot of boiling water. Steam, covered, for 7–8 minutes, or until cooked through. Carefully remove the plate from the steamer and sprinkle over the chopped scallions (spring onions).
* Heat the remaining 2 tablespoons oil in a small skillet (frying pan) over high heat. Pour the hot oil over the fish and serve immediately with rice.

醋香带鱼
RIBBONFISH
WITH VINEGAR

- 1 (1 LB 5-OZ/600-G) RIBBONFISH, CLEANED AND RINSED
- 1 TEASPOON SALT
- ½ TEASPOON GROUND WHITE PEPPER
- 1 TEASPOON CORNSTARCH (CORNFLOUR)
- 1 CUP (8 FL OZ/250 ML) VEGETABLE OIL
- ⅛ OZ/5 G GINGER (ABOUT ½-INCH/ 1-CM-LENGTH PIECE), SHREDDED
- 2 CLOVES GARLIC, SLICED
- 2 SCALLIONS (SPRING ONIONS), SHREDDED
- 3 TABLESPOONS ZHENJIANG OR BALSAMIC VINEGAR
- 2 TEASPOONS GRANULATED SUGAR
- 1 TABLESPOON LIGHT SOY SAUCE
- 1 TEASPOON SHAOXING WINE
- ½ TEASPOON SICHUAN PEPPER OIL
- ½ TEASPOON SESAME OIL
- STEAMED RICE (PAGE 540), TO SERVE

* Remove and discard the head and tail of the fish. Using a sharp knife, cut the fish into 4-inch/10-cm-long pieces and make 2 slashes on each side of each piece. Transfer the fish to a bowl, add the salt and white pepper, and marinate for about 30 minutes. Pat dry with paper towels and dredge lightly with the cornstarch (cornflour).
* Heat the vegetable oil in a wok or large skillet (frying pan) to 340°F/170°C, or until a cube of bread browns in 45 seconds. Add the fish and deep-fry for 3 minutes until golden brown, flip over, and deep-fry for another 3 minutes until cooked through. Use a slotted spoon to carefully remove the fish from the oil and drain on paper towels.
* Pour out most of the oil, leaving about 1 tablespoon in the wok. Add the ginger and garlic and stir-fry over medium heat for 1 minute until fragrant. Add the fish, scallions (spring onions), vinegar, sugar, soy sauce, Shaoxing wine, and Sichuan pepper oil and sauté for 1 minute until the sauce thickens. Remove to a plate and drizzle over the sesame oil. Serve with rice.

冬菇烩花胶
FISH MAW WITH
BLACK MUSHROOMS

REGION: HONG KONG
PREPARATION TIME: 30 MINUTES,
  PLUS 8½ HOURS SOAKING TIME
COOKING TIME: 25 MINUTES
SERVES: 4-6

* Soak the dried fish maw in a bowl of warm water for about 30 minutes until soft. Rinse well under cold running water.
* Fill a large saucepan with cold water, add the fish maw and half the ginger, and bring to a boil. Boil for 10 minutes. Cover and turn off the heat. Soak overnight for at least 8 hours. If the fish maw is not sufficiently soft, repeat the above steps.
* Drain the fish maw and remove any brown spots.
* Put the mushrooms into a bowl, cover with cold water, and soak for at least 20 minutes, or until softened. Remove the mushrooms, squeeze dry, and discard the stems. Combine the mushrooms with 1 tablespoon vegetable oil. Reserve the liquid.
* Heat 1 tablespoon vegetable oil in a wok or large skillet (frying pan) over medium-high heat, add the remaining ginger, and stir-fry for 1 minute. Add the mushrooms, rice wine, chicken broth (stock), reserved mushroom water, oyster sauce, salt, and sugar and bring to a boil.
* Add the fish maw, reduce to low heat, and simmer, covered, for 5 minutes. Uncover the wok and increase to high heat, then simmer for another 5 minutes to reduce the sauce. Add the scallions (spring onions) and sesame oil. Season to taste, mix well, and transfer to a plate. Serve with rice.

• 4 OZ/120 G DRIED FISH MAW
• 2 OZ/50 G GINGER (ABOUT 3-INCH/ 7.5-CM-LENGTH PIECE), SLICED
• 8-10 DRIED BLACK MUSHROOMS
• 2 TABLESPOONS VEGETABLE OIL
• 1 TABLESPOON RICE WINE
• 1 CUP (8 FL OZ/250 ML) CHICKEN BROTH (STOCK, PAGE 90)
• 2 TABLESPOONS OYSTER SAUCE
• 1 TEASPOON SALT, PLUS EXTRA TO TASTE
• 1 TEASPOON GRANULATED SUGAR
• 3 SCALLIONS (SPRING ONIONS), CUT INTO 1½-INCH/4-CM LENGTHS
• 1 TEASPOON SESAME OIL
• STEAMED RICE (PAGE 540), TO SERVE

酥煎带鱼
PAN-FRIED
RIBBONFISH

REGION: CHAOZHOU
PREPARATION TIME: 5 MINUTES,
  PLUS 30 MINUTES STANDING TIME
COOKING TIME: 10 MINUTES
SERVES: 4

* Using a sharp knife, cut the fish into 2¼-inch/6-cm-long pieces and make 2 slashes on each side of each piece of fish. Combine the fish and salt in a bowl and set aside for 30 minutes. Pat dry with paper towels and dredge lightly with the cornstarch (cornflour).
* Heat the oil in a large skillet (frying pan) over high heat, add the fish, and fry for about 10 seconds. Reduce to low heat and cook for 5-6 minutes on each side until browned. Transfer to a plate and serve with rice.

• 1 (14-OZ/400-G) RIBBONFISH, CLEANED AND RINSED
• 1 TEASPOON SALT
• 2 TABLESPOONS CORNSTARCH (CORNFLOUR)
• 2 TABLESPOONS VEGETABLE OIL
• STEAMED RICE (PAGE 540), TO SERVE

PREPARATION TIME: 10 MINUTES,
   PLUS 30 MINUTES SOAKING TIME
COOKING TIME: 30 MINUTES
SERVES: 4

大白菜炆鱼鳔
FISH MAW
WITH CABBAGE

- ¼ OZ/10 G GINGER (ABOUT ¾-INCH/
  2-CM-LENGTH PIECE), SLICED
- 1 OZ/25 G PUFFED FISH MAW, RINSED
- 1 TABLESPOON DRIED SHRIMP
- 4 DRIED BLACK MUSHROOMS
- 1 TABLESPOON VEGETABLE OIL
- 3 CLOVES GARLIC, PEELED
- ⅓ CARROT, SLICED
- ¼ SMALL NAPA CABBAGE, CUT INTO
  2-INCH/5-CM LENGTHS
- 1 TEASPOON FISH SAUCE
- ½ TEASPOON GRANULATED SUGAR
- ½ CUP (4 FL OZ/120 ML) CHICKEN
  BROTH (STOCK, PAGE 90)
- 1 STALK CHINESE CELERY, LEAVES
  REMOVED AND CUT INTO 1¼-INCH/
  3-CM LENGTHS
- ½ TEASPOON CORNSTARCH
  (CORNFLOUR)
- SALT, TO TASTE

* Bring 4¼ cups (34 fl oz/1 liter) water to a boil, add the
  ginger, and boil for 10 minutes. Add the fish maw, bring
  to another boil, cover, and turn off the heat. Let stand for
  30 minutes. Drain and rinse the fish maw, squeeze dry, and
  cut into 2-inch/5-cm lengths.
* Meanwhile, soak the dried shrimp in a small bowl of cold
  water for 5 minutes to soften.
* Put the mushrooms into a bowl, cover with cold water, and
  soak for at least 20 minutes, or until softened. Remove the
  mushrooms, squeeze dry, and discard the stems. Cut each
  mushroom in half and set aside.
* Heat the oil in a wok or large skillet (frying pan), add the
  garlic, fish maw, dried shrimp, mushrooms, carrot, Napa
  cabbage, fish sauce, sugar, and chicken broth (stock), and
  bring to a boil. Reduce to low heat and simmer, covered, for
  15 minutes. Stir in the Chinese celery and cook for another
  1 minute. Mix the cornstarch (cornflour) with ½ tablespoon
  water in a small bowl and stir it into the wok. Bring to a
  boil, stirring, for 30 seconds to thicken the sauce. Season
  with salt, then transfer to a serving plate.

REGION: CHAOZHOU
PREPARATION TIME: 10 MINUTES,
   PLUS 15 MINUTES SALTING TIME
COOKING TIME: 30 MINUTES
SERVES: 2

白萝卜丝煮鱼
SEA BREAM
WITH RADISH

- 1 (14-OZ/400-G) SEA BREAM, CLEANED
- ½ TEASPOON SALT
- 4 TABLESPOONS VEGETABLE OIL
- 1 TABLESPOON CORNSTARCH
  (CORNFLOUR)
- ¼ OZ/10 G GINGER (ABOUT ¾-INCH/
  2-CM-LENGTH PIECE), SLICED
- 7 OZ/200 G DAIKON RADISH, CUT INTO
  2-INCH/5-CM SLICES
- ½ TEASPOON GRANULATED SUGAR
- 1 TEASPOON FISH SAUCE
- 1 CUP (8 FL OZ/250 ML) CHICKEN
  BROTH (STOCK, PAGE 90)
- 1 RED CHILE, SEEDED AND CUT
  INTO STRIPS
- 1 STALK CHINESE CELERY, TRIMMED
  AND CUT INTO 2-INCH/5-CM SLICES

* Rub the fish all over with salt and set aside for 15 minutes.
  Pat dry with paper towels.
* Heat 2 tablespoons oil in a large skillet (frying pan).
  Lightly dredge the fish with cornstarch (cornflour) and add
  to the skillet. Pan-fry over low heat on each side for about
  5 minutes until golden brown. Transfer to a plate.
* Heat the remaining 2 tablespoons oil in the skillet over high
  heat and stir-fry the ginger for 1 minute until fragrant. Stir
  in the Daikon radish, sugar, and fish sauce and pour in the
  chicken broth (stock). Bring to a boil, reduce to medium
  heat, and cook for about 15 minutes, or until the radish
  is cooked. Add the fish, chile, and Chinese celery, and cook
  for another 2 minutes. Transfer to a serving plate.

干烧红鲉
SAUTÉED
RED SNAPPER

REGION: HONG KONG
PREPARATION TIME: 10 MINUTES,
 PLUS 20 MINUTES SOAKING TIME
COOKING TIME: 20 MINUTES
SERVES: 4

* Put the mushrooms into a bowl, cover with cold water, and soak for at least 20 minutes, or until softened. Remove the mushrooms, squeeze dry, and discard the stems. Dice, then set aside.
* Use a sharp knife to make 1 shallow cut on each side of the fish, rub in the salt, and set aside for 10 minutes. Pat the fish dry inside and out with paper towels.
* Heat the oil in a wok or large skillet (frying pan) to 300°F/150°C, or until a cube of bread browns in 1½ minutes. Add the fish and deep-fry for 8–10 minutes until cooked through and golden brown. Use a slotted spoon to carefully remove the fish from the oil and drain on paper towels.
* Pour out most of the oil, leaving about 1 tablespoon in the wok. Heat over medium heat, add the pork fatback, garlic, ginger, and scallions (spring onions) and stir-fry for 1 minute until fragrant. Add the fresh and dried chiles, preserved mustard, and mushrooms and stir-fry for 1 minute. Put in the soy sauces, sugar, and 4 tablespoons water, bring to a boil, and cook for 3 minutes, or until the sauce begins to thicken. Add the vinegar and toss well. Season with salt.
* Put the fish into the sauce and cook for 1 minute, then flip over and cook for another 1 minute until the sauce thickens. Transfer the fish to a plate and pour over the sauce. Serve with rice.

- 4 DRIED BLACK MUSHROOMS
- 1 (1 LB 5-OZ/600-G) MANGROVE RED SNAPPER, CLEANED AND RINSED
- ½ TEASPOON SALT, PLUS EXTRA TO TASTE
- 1 CUP (8 FL OZ/250 ML) VEGETABLE OIL
- ¾ OZ/20 G PORK FATBACK, CUT INTO ½-INCH/1-CM DICE
- 2 CLOVES GARLIC, GRATED
- 4 TEASPOONS GRATED GINGER
- 3 SCALLIONS (SPRING ONIONS), FINELY CHOPPED
- 2 RED CHILES, SEEDED AND CHOPPED
- 2 DRIED RED CHILES, CUT INTO ½-INCH/1-CM PIECES
- 2 OZ/50 G SICHUAN PRESERVED MUSTARD GREENS, TRIMMED, RINSED, AND CHOPPED
- 1 TEASPOON LIGHT SOY SAUCE
- 1 TEASPOON DARK SOY SAUCE
- 1 TEASPOON GRANULATED SUGAR
- 1 TEASPOON ZHENJIANG OR BALSAMIC VINEGAR
- STEAMED RICE (PAGE 540), TO SERVE

REGION: GUANGDONG
PREPARATION TIME: 15 MINUTES, PLUS
  20 MINUTES SOAKING TIME
COOKING TIME: 15 MINUTES
SERVES: 4

生炆斑球

GROUPER WITH BLACK MUSHROOMS AND SCALLIONS

- 1 (1 LB 5-OZ/600-G) GROUPER, CUT INTO 1¼-INCH/3-CM CUBES
- 5 DRIED BLACK MUSHROOMS
- 1 DRIED TANGERINE PEEL
- ½ CUP (4 FL OZ/120 ML) VEGETABLE OIL
- 4 CLOVES GARLIC, PEELED
- 1 OZ/25 G GINGER (ABOUT 2-INCH/ 5-CM-LENGTH PIECE), SHREDDED
- 3 SCALLIONS (SPRING ONIONS), CUT INTO 1½-INCH/4-CM LENGTHS
- 9 OZ/250 G ROAST PORK BELLY, CUT INTO ½-INCH/1-CM DICE
- ½ CARROT, SLICED
- 1 TEASPOON LIGHT SOY SAUCE
- 1 TABLESPOON OYSTER SAUCE
- 1 TEASPOON GRANULATED SUGAR
- ½ CUP (4 FL OZ/120 ML) CHICKEN BROTH (STOCK, PAGE 90)
- 1 TEASPOON CORNSTARCH (CORNFLOUR)
- 2 BUNCHES CILANTRO (CORIANDER), CHOPPED
- SALT, TO TASTE
- STEAMED RICE (PAGE 540), TO SERVE

* Rinse the fish and pat dry with paper towels.
* Soak the mushrooms and dried tangerine peel in 2 separate small bowls of cold water for 20 minutes until softened. Remove and discard the stems from the mushrooms, and slice both the mushrooms and tangerine peel.
* Heat the oil over medium heat in a wok or large skillet (frying pan), add the garlic, and stir-fry for 1–2 minutes until fragrant. Remove the garlic and set aside.
* Reheat the oil over medium-high heat, carefully add the fish, and fry for 5 minutes until just cooked through. Remove the fish and transfer to a colander to drain.
* Pour out most of the oil, leaving about 1 tablespoon in the wok. Add the garlic, ginger, scallions (spring onions), pork belly, dried tangerine peel, mushrooms, and carrot and stir-fry over high heat for 2–3 minutes. Add the fried fish, soy and oyster sauces, sugar, and chicken broth (stock), and bring to a boil. Reduce to low heat and simmer, uncovered, for 5 minutes.
* Mix the cornstarch (cornflour) with 1 tablespoon water in a small bowl and stir this mixture into the wok. Bring to a boil, stirring, for 30 seconds to thicken the sauce. Season with salt to taste. Transfer to a plate and garnish with cilantro (coriander). Serve with rice.

REGION: SHUNDE
PREPARATION TIME: 5 MINUTES,
  PLUS 20 MINUTES SOAKING TIME
COOKING TIME: 5 MINUTES
SERVES: 4

冬菇烩鱼腐

MUSHROOMS WITH FISH PUFFS

- 12 DRIED BLACK MUSHROOMS
- 1 TABLESPOON VEGETABLE OIL
- ⅛ OZ/5 G GINGER (ABOUT ½-INCH/ 1-CM-LENGTH PIECE), SLICED
- 12 SHUNDE FISH PUFFS (PAGE 72)
- ½ TABLESPOON OYSTER SAUCE
- ½ TEASPOON CORNSTARCH (CORNFLOUR)
- ¼ TEASPOON SESAME OIL

* Put the mushrooms into a bowl, cover with cold water, and soak for at least 20 minutes, or until softened. Remove the mushrooms, squeeze dry, and discard the stems.
* Heat the vegetable oil in a wok or large skillet (frying pan) over medium heat, add the ginger, and stir-fry for about 1 minute until fragrant. Add the mushrooms and stir-fry for a few seconds, then add the fish puffs and oyster sauce, and stir well. Add 4 tablespoons water and bring to a boil. Reduce to low heat, cover, and simmer for about 3 minutes. Mix the cornstarch (cornflour) with ½ tablespoon water in a small bowl and stir this mixture into the wok. Bring to a boil, stirring, for 30 seconds to thicken the sauce.
* Stir in the sesame oil, then transfer to a plate.

FISH & SEAFOOD

砂锅鱼头

STEWED FISH
HEAD

REGION: ZHEJIANG
PREPARATION TIME: 10 MINUTES,
  PLUS 20 MINUTES SOAKING TIME
COOKING TIME: 45 MINUTES
SERVES: 4

* Put the mushrooms into a bowl, cover with cold water, and soak for at least 20 minutes, or until softened. Remove the mushrooms, squeeze dry, and discard the stems. Cut into thin slices and set aside.
* Meanwhile, use a sharp knife to slice the fish head down the center in half, then rinse. Combine the fish, 1 teaspoon salt, the ginger juice, and white pepper in a bowl and mix well. Marinate for 15 minutes.
* Heat the vegetable oil in a wok or deep saucepan to 340°F/170°C, or until a cube of bread browns in 45 seconds. Lightly dust the fish with 2 tablespoons cornstarch (cornflour) and add to the hot oil. Deep-fry for 6–7 minutes until golden brown. Use a slotted spoon to carefully remove the fish from the oil and drain on paper towels.
* Add the whole garlic cloves to the oil in the wok and deep-fry over low heat for 2 minutes until light brown. Remove from the oil and set aside. Next, add the tofu and deep-fry for 3–4 minutes until lightly browned. Remove and set aside.
* Bring a large saucepan of water to a boil over high heat. Add the cabbage and blanch for 2 minutes. Drain and set aside.
* Combine the pork, the remaining ¼ teaspoon salt, ¼ teaspoon cornstarch, and 1 teaspoon oil in a bowl.
* Heat the remaining 1 tablespoon oil in a Dutch oven (casserole) over medium heat, add the ginger slices, mushrooms, garlic, pork, and chili bean paste, and stir-fry for 4–5 minutes. Add the chicken broth (stock) and cabbage, place the fish head on top of the cabbage, then add the wine and soy sauce. Bring to a boil and cook over high heat for 10 minutes. Add the tofu, mung bean sheets, and scallions (spring onions) and reduce to medium heat. Simmer, covered, for 6–8 minutes. Stir in the sesame oil and serve in the Dutch oven with rice.

- 4 DRIED BLACK MUSHROOMS
- 1 (1-LB/450-G) SALTWATER FISH HEAD
- 1¼ TEASPOONS SALT
- 1 TABLESPOON GINGER JUICE
- ¼ TEASPOON GROUND WHITE PEPPER
- 2 CUPS (16 FL OZ/475 ML) PLUS 4 TEASPOONS VEGETABLE OIL
- 2 TABLESPOONS CORNSTARCH (CORNFLOUR), PLUS ¼ TEASPOON
- 5 CLOVES GARLIC
- 9 OZ/250 G FIRM TOFU, DRAINED AND DICED
- ½ SMALL NAPA CABBAGE, SLICED
- 1 OZ/30 G SHREDDED PORK
- ⅛ OZ/5 G GINGER (ABOUT ½-INCH/ 1-CM-LENGTH PIECE), SLICED
- 2 TABLESPOONS CHILI BEAN PASTE
- 1 CUP (8 FL OZ/250 ML) CHICKEN BROTH (STOCK, PAGE 90)
- 1 TABLESPOON SHAOXING WINE
- 1 TEASPOON LIGHT SOY SAUCE
- 5 OZ/150 G DRIED MUNG BEAN STARCH SHEETS, SOAKED IN WATER TO SOFTEN
- 3 SCALLIONS (SPRING ONIONS), CUT INTO 1½-INCH/4-CM LENGTHS
- ½ TEASPOON SESAME OIL
- STEAMED RICE (PAGE 540), TO SERVE

REGION: HONG KONG
PREPARATION TIME: 15 MINUTES, PLUS
  20 MINUTES MARINATING TIME
COOKING TIME: 25 MINUTES
SERVES: 4-6

红炆斑尾
BRAISED
GROUPER TAIL

- 5 DRIED BLACK MUSHROOMS
- 1 (1 LB 11-OZ/750-G) GROUPER TAIL,
  CLEANED AND RINSED
- 1 TEASPOON SALT
- ¼ TEASPOON GROUND WHITE PEPPER
- 1 EGG, BEATEN
- 1 TABLESPOON CORNSTARCH
  (CORNFLOUR)
- 4 TABLESPOONS VEGETABLE OIL
- ¾ OZ/20 G GINGER (ABOUT 1-INCH/
  2.5-CM-LENGTH PIECE), SLICED
- 4 CLOVES GARLIC, CRUSHED
- 4 SHALLOTS, QUARTERED
- 2¾ OZ/75 G LEAN PORK, CUT
  INTO STRIPS
- 1 TABLESPOON SHAOXING WINE
- 2 TABLESPOONS OYSTER SAUCE
- 1 TEASPOON LIGHT SOY SAUCE
- 1 TEASPOON GRANULATED SUGAR
- 2 CUPS (16 FL OZ/475 ML) CHICKEN
  BROTH (STOCK, PAGE 90)
- 3 SCALLIONS (SPRING ONIONS),
  STEMS ONLY, CUT INTO
  1½-CM/4-CM LENGTHS
- 1½ TABLESPOONS CORNSTARCH
  (CORNFLOUR)
- ½ TEASPOON SESAME OIL
- STEAMED RICE (PAGE 540), TO SERVE

* Put the mushrooms into a bowl, cover with cold water, and soak for at least 20 minutes, or until softened. Remove the mushrooms, squeeze dry, and discard the stems. Cut into strips and set aside.
* Use a large sharp knife to make a deep cut down one side of the spine of the fish. Rub with salt and white pepper on both sides of the fish tail. Brush each side of the tail with the beaten egg, then lightly dredge with cornstarch (cornflour).
* Heat 3 tablespoons oil in a wok or large skillet (frying pan) to 300°F/150°C, or until a cube of bread browns in 1½ minutes. Add the fish and fry for 5 minutes on each side until golden brown and cooked through. Use a slotted spoon to carefully remove the fish tail from the oil and drain on paper towels.
* Heat the remaining 1 tablespoon oil in the wok or large skillet (frying pan) over medium heat, add the ginger, garlic, and shallots, and stir-fry for 1–2 minutes until fragrant. Add the pork and mushrooms and toss. Sprinkle in the wine and stir-fry for another 1 minute. Add the oyster sauce, soy sauce, sugar, and chicken broth (stock) and bring to a boil. Put the fish tail into the wok, reduce to medium heat, and simmer, covered, for 5 minutes on each side. Transfer the fish tail to a serving plate and leave the sauce in the wok.
* Stir the scallions (spring onions) into the sauce, increase to medium-high heat, and simmer for 5 minutes until reduced to about 1 cup (8 fl oz/250 ml).
* Mix the cornstarch (cornflour) with 4 tablespoons water in a small bowl and stir the mixture into the sauce. Add the sesame oil. Bring to a boil, stirring, for 30 seconds to thicken the sauce. Season to taste. Pour the sauce on top of the fish and serve with rice.

雪菜马头鱼
TILE FISH WITH PRESERVED MUSTARD GREENS

REGION: FUJIAN
PREPARATION TIME: 10 MINUTES,
   PLUS 15 MINUTES MARINATING TIME
COOKING TIME: 15 MINUTES
SERVES: 4

* Combine the pork, soy sauce, and sugar in a bowl and marinate for 15 minutes. Mix in ½ teaspoon cornstarch (cornflour) and set aside.
* Meanwhile, rub the fish inside and outside with the salt and set aside for 15 minutes. Pat dry with paper towels.
* Heat 2 tablespoons oil in a wok or large skillet (frying pan) over medium heat. Brush the fish with a thin layer of cornstarch, add it to the wok, and cook for 4–5 minutes. Turn over and cook for another 4–5 minutes, or until browned and cooked through. Transfer the fish to a plate and set aside.
* Wipe the wok clean with paper towels and put over medium heat. Add the remaining 1 tablespoon oil, ginger, garlic, pork, preserved mustard greens, and ½ cup (4 fl oz/ 120 ml) water and cook for 2 minutes. Put the fish into the sauce and simmer, uncovered, for about 1 minute, then transfer the fish to a plate.
* Mix the remaining ½ teaspoon cornstarch with ½ tablespoon water in a small bowl and stir this mixture into the wok. Bring to a boil, stirring, for 30 seconds to thicken the sauce. Stir in the chile and pour the sauce over the fish. Serve with rice.

- 2 OZ/50 G GROUND (MINCED) PORK
- 1 TEASPOON LIGHT SOY SAUCE
- ½ TEASPOON GRANULATED SUGAR
- 1 TEASPOON CORNSTARCH (CORNFLOUR), PLUS EXTRA FOR BRUSHING
- 1 (14-OZ/400-G) TILEHEAD OR TILAPIA FISH, CLEANED AND RINSED
- ½ TEASPOON SALT
- 3 TABLESPOONS VEGETABLE OIL
- 1 TEASPOON SHREDDED GINGER
- 1 CLOVE GARLIC, FINELY CHOPPED
- 5 OZ/150 G PRESERVED MUSTARD GREENS, TRIMMED, RINSED, AND CHOPPED
- 1 RED CHILE, SEEDED AND CHOPPED
- STEAMED RICE (PAGE 540), TO SERVE

番茄鲈鱼
SEA BASS WITH TOMATOES

- 1 TEASPOON SALT
- PINCH OF GROUND WHITE PEPPER
- 4 SEA BASS FILLETS, CLEANED
- 2 LARGE TOMATOES
- 3 TABLESPOONS VEGETABLE OIL
- ¼ OZ/10 G GINGER (ABOUT ¾-INCH/ 2-CM-LENGTH PIECE), FINELY SHREDDED
- ½ ONION, THINLY SLICED
- 1 TABLESPOON GRANULATED SUGAR
- ½ TEASPOON CORNSTARCH (CORNFLOUR)
- 3 SCALLIONS (SPRING ONIONS), FINELY SHREDDED
- STEAMED RICE (PAGE 540), TO SERVE

* Rub ½ teaspoon salt and the white pepper over the fish and set aside for 5 minutes. Pat dry with paper towels.
* Score the base of the tomatoes. Bring a small saucepan of water to a boil, add the tomatoes, and heat for 1–2 minutes. Immediately transfer to a bowl of ice water. When the tomatoes are cool enough to handle, peel away the skin and chop each tomato into 6 pieces.
* Heat 2 tablespoons oil in a wok or skillet (frying pan) over medium-high heat, add the fish, and pan-fry for 2–3 minutes on each side until golden brown and cooked through. Transfer to a plate.
* Heat the remaining 1 tablespoon oil in the wok over medium heat, add the ginger, and stir-fry for 1 minute until fragrant. Add the onion, tomatoes, sugar, and the remaining ½ teaspoon salt and stir-fry for 2 minutes. Put in the fish, cover, and cook for 2 minutes over high heat. Transfer the fish to a plate.
* Mix the cornstarch (cornflour) with ½ tablespoon water in a small bowl and stir this mixture into the wok. Bring to a boil, stirring, for about 30 seconds to thicken the sauce. Transfer the sauce and fish to a bowl and top with the shredded scallions (spring onions). Serve with rice.

NOTE:
Traditionally, this dish is prepared with whole fish but fillets may be used instead. If using fillets, reduce the cooking time by 1–2 minutes on each side.

SEA BASS WITH TOMATOES

官烧目鱼
FLOUNDER WITH MUSHROOMS
AND BAMBOO SHOOTS

- 4 DRIED BLACK MUSHROOMS
- 9 OZ/250 G FLOUNDER FILLETS,
  CUT INTO 2-INCH/5-CM STRIPS
- 1 TABLESPOON GINGER JUICE
- 1 TABLESPOON RICE WINE
- 1 EGG, BEATEN
- 2½ TABLESPOONS CORNSTARCH
  (CORNFLOUR)
- ½ TEASPOON SALT, PLUS EXTRA
  TO TASTE
- 3 CUPS (25 FL OZ/750 ML) PLUS
  1 TEASPOON VEGETABLE OIL
- ½ CUP (2 OZ/6 G) SLICED BAMBOO
  SHOOTS, DRAINED AND CUT INTO
  STRIPS
- ¾ OZ/20 G CUCUMBER,
  CUT INTO BATONS
- 1 SCALLION (SPRING ONION),
  SHREDDED
- ⅛ OZ/5 G GINGER (ABOUT ½-INCH/
  1-CM-LENGTH PIECE), SHREDDED
- 1 CLOVE GARLIC, SLICED
- 2 TABLESPOONS WHITE VINEGAR
- 5 TABLESPOONS CHICKEN BROTH
  (STOCK, PAGE 90)
- 2 TABLESPOONS GRANULATED SUGAR
- 2 TEASPOONS SICHUAN PEPPER OIL
- STEAMED RICE (PAGE 540), TO SERVE

* Put the mushrooms into a bowl, cover with cold water, and soak for at least 20 minutes, or until softened. Remove the mushrooms, squeeze dry, and discard the stems. Cut into thin slices.
* Combine the fish, ½ tablespoon ginger juice, and 1 teaspoon wine in a bowl. Marinate for 5 minutes.
* In a small bowl, mix half the egg (save the other half for another recipe), 1 tablespoon cornstarch (cornflour), ¼ teaspoon salt, and 1 teaspoon vegetable oil into a paste. Add the mixture to the fish and mix well.
* Heat 3 cups (25 fl oz/750 ml) vegetable oil in a wok or deep saucepan to 340°F/170°C, or until a cube of bread browns in 45 seconds. Add the fish and deep-fry for 4–5 minutes until golden brown and cooked through. Use a slotted spoon to carefully remove the fish from the oil and drain on paper towels.
* Add the mushrooms, bamboo shoots, and cucumber to the oil in the wok and deep-fry for about 2 minutes. Use a slotted spoon to carefully remove the vegetables from the oil and drain on paper towels. Set aside.
* Pour out most of the oil, leaving about 1 tablespoon in the wok. Add the scallion (spring onion), ginger, and garlic and stir-fry over medium heat for 1 minute until fragrant. Add the remaining ginger juice, the wine, vinegar, chicken broth (stock), sugar, and remaining ¼ teaspoon salt and bring to a boil over high heat.
* Mix the remaining 1½ tablespoons cornstarch with 3 tablespoons water in a small bowl and stir this mixture into the wok. Bring to a boil, stirring, for about 30 seconds to thicken the sauce. Add the fish, mushrooms, bamboo shoots, and cucumber, stir, and add the Sichuan pepper oil. Adjust the seasoning to taste and transfer to a plate. Serve with rice.

糟熘鱼片
FISH IN DISTILLED GRAIN SAUCE

REGION: SHANGHAI
PREPARATION TIME: 10 MINUTES,
 PLUS 20 MINUTES SOAKING TIME
COOKING TIME: 10 MINUTES
SERVES: 4

* Put the mushrooms into a bowl, cover with cold water, and soak for at least 20 minutes, or until softened. Remove the mushrooms, squeeze dry, and discard the stems. Tear into small pieces.
* Meanwhile, combine the fish, egg whites, and ½ tablespoon cornstarch (cornflour) and marinate for 10 minutes.
* Put the distilled grain sauce into a blender or food processor and blend into a thick sauce.
* Bring a saucepan of water to a boil, add the bamboo shoots, and blanch for 1 minute. Drain and rinse under cold running water.
* Heat the oil in a wok or deep saucepan to 300°F/150°C, or until a cube of bread browns in 1½ minutes. Add the fish slices, using chopsticks to disperse the pieces rapidly to prevent sticking, and deep-fry for 1 minute until nearly cooked through. Use a slotted spoon to carefully remove the fish from the oil and drain on paper towels.
* Pour out most of the oil, leaving about 1 tablespoon in the wok. Add the black fungus and bamboo and stir-fry over high heat for 2 minutes. Add the wine, ginger juice, salt, sugar, distilled grain sauce, and chicken broth (stock) and bring to a boil. Put in the deep-fried fish slices and stir rapidly for 1 minute.
* Mix the remaining ½ tablespoon cornstarch with 1½ tablespoons water in a small bowl and stir this mixture into the wok. Bring to a boil, stirring, for 30 seconds to thicken the sauce. Transfer to a plate and serve with rice.

* ¼ CUP (⅛ OZ/5 G) DRIED BLACK FUNGUS
* 9 OZ/250 G GREEN WRASSE OR ANY WHITE FISH FILLETS, CUT INTO THICK SLICES
* 2 EGG WHITES, LIGHTLY BEATEN
* 1 TABLESPOON CORNSTARCH (CORNFLOUR)
* 3 TABLESPOONS DISTILLED WHITE GRAIN SAUCE
* ¼ CUP (¾ OZ/20 G) SLICED BAMBOO SHOOTS, DRAINED
* 1 CUP (8 FL OZ/250 ML) VEGETABLE OIL
* 1 TABLESPOON SHAOXING WINE
* 1 TABLESPOON GINGER JUICE
* ½ TEASPOON SALT
* 2 TEASPOONS GRANULATED SUGAR
* ½ CUP (4 FL OZ/120 ML) CHICKEN BROTH (STOCK, PAGE 90)
* STEAMED RICE (PAGE 540), TO SERVE

REGION: HONG KONG
PREPARATION TIME: 15 MINUTES,
    PLUS 2 HOURS MARINATING TIME
COOKING TIME: 15 MINUTES
SERVES: 4
📷 PAGE 147

酥骨鲳鱼
POMFRET WITH
CRISPY BONES

- 1 (14-OZ/400-G) WHITE POMFRET, CLEANED AND RINSED
- 1 EGG WHITE
- 3 CUPS (25 FL OZ/750 ML) VEGETABLE OIL
- ¼ OZ/10 G GINGER (ABOUT ¾-INCH/ 2-CM-LENGTH PIECE), SLICED
- 3 CLOVES GARLIC, SLICED
- 6 STRAW MUSHROOMS, RINSED AND HALVED (OPTIONAL)
- 2 STALKS CHINESE CELERY, CUT INTO 1¼-INCH/3-CM LENGTHS
- ½ RED CAYENNE PEPPER, SLICED
- 1 TEASPOON FISH SAUCE
- ½ TEASPOON GRANULATED SUGAR
- 1 TEASPOON RICE WINE
- ½ TEASPOON CORNSTARCH (CORNFLOUR)
- PINCH OF GROUND WHITE PEPPER
- STEAMED RICE (PAGE 540), TO SERVE

  FOR THE BATTER:
- 3 TABLESPOONS ALL-PURPOSE (PLAIN) FLOUR
- 1 TABLESPOON CORNSTARCH (CORNFLOUR)
- ¼ TEASPOON BAKING POWDER
- ½ TEASPOON SALT
- ½ TABLESPOON VEGETABLE OIL

* First, fillet the fish. Remove the head and outline the fillet by cutting through the skin top, bottom, and over the tail. Cut the fish, following the center line from head to tail, into 2 parts. Insert your knife into the center line and fillet one part. Turn the fish around and fillet the other part. Flip the fish over and repeat. Set aside the bones.
* Slice the fillets into 1¼-inch/3-cm pieces and cut the fish bone horizontally into 3 equal sections. Combine the fish with the egg white and marinate in the refrigerator for 2 hours.
* Heat the oil in a wok or large skillet (frying pan) to 265°F/130°C. Add the fish and deep-fry for 2–3 minutes, using chopsticks to gently separate the fish slices, until white in color. Use a slotted spoon to carefully remove the fish from the oil and drain on paper towels.
* To make the batter, combine the flour, cornstarch (cornflour), baking powder, salt, and 4 tablespoons water in a bowl. Add the oil and blend well to form a batter.
* Reheat the oil in the wok to 300°F/150°C, or until a cube of bread browns in 1½ minutes. Dip the fish bones into the batter and deep-fry for 4–5 minutes until crispy. Arrange the fried fish bones into a fish shape on a plate.
* Pour out most of the oil, leaving about 1 tablespoon oil in the wok. Heat the oil over medium-high heat, add the ginger and garlic, and stir-fry for 1 minute until fragrant. Add the mushrooms, if using, Chinese celery, cayenne pepper, fish sauce, and sugar, and stir-fry for 1 minute. Add the fish and wine.
* Mix the cornstarch with ½ tablespoon water in a small bowl and stir this mixture into the wok. Bring to a boil, stirring, for about 30 seconds to thicken the sauce. Season with white pepper.
* Place the fish on top of the crispy fish bones on the plate. Serve with rice.

POMFRET WITH CRISPY BONES

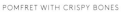

REGION: GUANGDONG
PREPARATION TIME: 10 MINUTES,
   PLUS 20 MINUTES MARINATING TIME
COOKING TIME: 5 MINUTES
SERVES: 4

煎封鲳鱼
SAUTÉED
POMFRET

- 1 (14-OZ/400-G) POMFRET, CLEANED AND RINSED
- ½ TEASPOON SALT
- ¼ TEASPOON GROUND WHITE PEPPER
- 3 TABLESPOONS VEGETABLE OIL
- ¼ OZ/10 G GINGER (ABOUT ¾-INCH/ 2-CM-LENGTH PIECE), SHREDDED
- 2 TEASPOONS GRANULATED SUGAR
- 1 TEASPOON DARK SOY SAUCE
- 1 TABLESPOON KETCHUP
- 1 TABLESPOON WORCESTERSHIRE SAUCE
- ½ CUP (4 FL OZ/120 ML) CHICKEN BROTH (STOCK, PAGE 90)
- 1 SMALL HOT RED CHILE, CUT INTO FINE STRIPS
- 3 SCALLIONS (SPRING ONIONS), STEMS ONLY, SHREDDED
- STEAMED RICE (PAGE 540), TO SERVE

* Use a sharp knife to make 3 slashes on each side of the fish. Rub over the salt and pepper and set aside for 20 minutes. Pat dry with paper towels.
* Heat 2 tablespoons oil in a wok or large skillet (frying pan) over high heat. Add the fish, reduce to medium heat, and fry for 4–5 minutes until browned. Flip over and fry for another 4–5 minutes until brown and cooked through. Remove to a plate.
* Heat the remaining 1 tablespoon oil over medium heat, add the ginger, and stir-fry for 1 minute until fragrant. Add the sugar, soy sauce, ketchup, Worcestershire sauce, and chicken broth (stock) and bring to a boil.
* Add the fish and cook over medium heat for 1 minute on each side. Increase to high heat and cook for 1–2 minutes until the sauce thickens.
* Transfer to a plate and top with the red chile and scallions (spring onions). Serve with rice.

REGION: HONG KONG
PREPARATION TIME: 10 MINUTES,
   PLUS 15 MINUTES MARINATING TIME
COOKING TIME: 10 MINUTES
SERVES: 4

三豉蒸三文鱼头
SALMON FISH HEAD WITH
BLACK BEANS AND
PRESERVED BLACK OLIVES

- ½ TEASPOON SALT
- 2 TEASPOONS RICE WINE
- 1 (ABOUT 14-OZ/400-G) SALMON FISH HEAD, RINSED
- 1 TABLESPOON BEAN PASTE
- 1 TABLESPOON FERMENTED BLACK BEANS, RINSED AND CHOPPED
- 6 PRESERVED BLACK OLIVES, FINELY CHOPPED
- 3 CLOVES GARLIC, CHOPPED
- 1 TEASPOON GRANULATED SUGAR
- 1 TABLESPOON VEGETABLE OIL
- 1 SCALLION (SPRING ONION), CHOPPED, TO GARNISH
- STEAMED RICE (PAGE 540), TO SERVE

* Sprinkle the salt and wine over the fish head and marinate for 15 minutes.
* Use a fork to mash the bean paste. Transfer the paste to a bowl, then add the chopped black beans, preserved black olives, garlic, sugar, and oil. Combine into a paste and spread over the fish head to cover evenly. Place on a heatproof plate and put into a collapsible pot or bamboo steamer over a pot of boiling water. Steam, covered, for 10 minutes until cooked through. Garnish with the chopped scallion (spring onion) and serve with rice.

糖醋鱼块
SWEET AND
SOUR FISH

REGION: ZHEJIANG
PREPARATION TIME: 5 MINUTES,
   PLUS 15 MINUTES MARINATING TIME
COOKING TIME: 10 MINUTES
SERVES: 4

* Combine the fish and salt in a bowl and set aside for 15 minutes. Add the cornstarch (cornflour) and 4 tablespoons of water and mix well.
* Heat the oil in a wok or deep saucepan to 300°F/150°C, or until a cube of bread browns in 1½ minutes. Carefully add the fish fillets and deep-fry for 3–4 minutes until crispy and cooked through. Use a slotted spoon to carefully remove the fillets from the oil and drain on paper towels.
* Combine the sugar and vinegar in a small bowl and mix.
* Drain all but 1 tablespoon of oil from the wok and heat over medium heat. Add the sugar and vinegar mixture, then stir in the fish. Add the peppers and pineapple and stir-fry for 2 minutes until the sauce thickens.
* Transfer to a plate and serve with rice.

- 1 LB/450 G CHICKEN GRUNT OR MONKISH FILLETS, CUT INTO CHUNKS
- 1 TEASPOON SALT
- 2 TABLESPOONS CORNSTARCH (CORNFLOUR)
- 2 CUPS (16 FL OZ/475 ML) VEGETABLE OIL
- 4 TABLESPOONS BROWN SUGAR
- 4 TABLESPOONS RED VINEGAR
- ½ GREEN BELL PEPPER, SEEDED AND DICED
- ½ RED BELL PEPPER, SEEDED AND DICED
- 1 (8-OZ/225-G) CAN PINEAPPLE CHUNKS, DRAINED
- STEAMED RICE (PAGE 540), TO SERVE

五香燻魚
SPICED SMOKE
FISH

REGION: JIANGSU
PREPARATION TIME: 5 MINUTES,
   PLUS 1 HOUR MARINATING TIME
COOKING TIME: 10 MINUTES
SERVES: 4

While the title of this dish is "smoke fish," it does not actually involve any smoking. The name is derived from the color of the fish once it's cooked.

* Combine the scallions (spring onions), ginger, salt, and 2 teaspoons wine in a large bowl and mix well. Add the fish, mix, and marinate in the refrigerator for 1 hour.
* Remove the fish from the bowl and pat dry with paper towels. Reserve the marinade and set aside.
* Heat the oil in a wok or deep saucepan to 300°F/150°C, or until a cube of bread browns in 1½ minutes. Add the fish and deep-fry for 3–4 minutes until light brown and cooked through. Use a slotted spoon to carefully remove the fish from the oil and drain on paper towels.
* Combine the remaining 2 teaspoons wine, the soy sauce, five-spice powder, vinegar, sugar, 1 tablespoon water, and the marinade in a small saucepan. Heat over low heat for 2–3 minutes until the sugar has dissolved, then pour into a large bowl.
* Dip a fish into the sauce so it's well coated. Transfer to a cutting board, brush with sesame oil, and then cut into sections when cooled. Transfer to a serving plate. Repeat with the remaining fish.

- 4 (4-OZ/120-G) JAPANESE MACKEREL OR ANY FRESHWATER FISH FILLETS, RINSED AND PATTED DRY
- 4 SCALLIONS (SPRING ONIONS), STEMS ONLY, CUT INTO 1½-INCH/ 4-CM LENGTHS AND SMASHED
- 1 TABLESPOON GRATED GINGER
- ½ TEASPOON SALT
- 4 TEASPOONS SHAOXING WINE
- 4¼ CUPS (34 FL OZ/1 LITER) VEGETABLE OIL
- 1 TABLESPOON LIGHT SOY SAUCE
- 1 TEASPOON FIVE-SPICE POWDER
- 1 TABLESPOON ZHENJIANG OR BALSAMIC VINEGAR
- 2 OZ/50 G BROWN SUGAR BAR
- 1 TABLESPOON SESAME OIL

REGION: JIANGXI
PREPARATION TIME: 10 MINUTES,
  PLUS 20 MINUTES MARINATING TIME
COOKING TIME: 15 MINUTES
SERVES: 2–4

兴国米粉鱼
FISH WITH
VERMICELLI

- 1 (1-LB/450-G) GRASS CARP BELLY, CUT INTO ¾-INCH/2-CM CHUNKS
- 1 TABLESPOON LIGHT SOY SAUCE
- 1 TEASPOON GINGER JUICE
- 1 TEASPOON CHILI SAUCE
- 1 TEASPOON RICE WINE
- 1 TEASPOON CORNSTARCH (CORNFLOUR)
- 2 TABLESPOONS VEGETABLE OIL
- 7 OZ/200 G JIANGXI RICE VERMICELLI, CRUSHED
- ½ TEASPOON SALT
- ½ TEASPOON FIVE-SPICE POWDER
- ½ TEASPOON GROUND WHITE PEPPER
- 1 SCALLION (SPRING ONION), CHOPPED
- STEAMED RICE (PAGE 540), TO SERVE

This dish is prepared with a local rice vermicelli and as a substitute, we recommend using a Guangxi, Guizhou, or Yunnan variety, which all have a similar cooking time.

* Combine the fish, soy sauce, ginger juice, chili sauce, and wine in a large bowl and marinate for 20 minutes. Mix in the cornstarch (cornflour). Just before cooking, stir in the oil.
* Bring a large saucepan of water to a boil over high heat. Add the vermicelli to the pan and cook for 8 minutes until loose and nearly al dente. Drain well, then combine with the salt and five-spice powder. Place in a heatproof bowl.
* Put the fish on top of the vermicelli and place in a collapsible bowl or bamboo steamer over a pot of boiling water. Steam, covered, for 6 minutes, or until fish is cooked through. Remove from the steamer, sprinkle with pepper, and top with the chopped scallion (spring onion). Serve with rice.

REGION: CHAOZHOU
PREPARATION TIME: 10 MINUTES, PLUS
  10 MINUTES SALTING TIME
COOKING TIME: 10 MINUTES
SERVES: 4

咸柠檬蒸乌头
GREY MULLET WITH
PRESERVED LEMONS

- 1 (1 LB 5-OZ/600-G) GREY MULLET, CLEANED AND RINSED
- ½ TEASPOON SALT, PLUS EXTRA TO TASTE
- 2 SALTED PRESERVED LEMONS (PREFERABLY CHAOZHOU), SEEDED AND THINLY SLICED
- ½ TEASPOON GRANULATED SUGAR
- 1 LEMON, SLICED
- 2 TABLESPOONS VEGETABLE OIL
- STEAMED RICE (PAGE 540), TO SERVE

* Rub the fish with salt and set aside on a heatproof plate for 10 minutes. Pour out any water from the plate.
* Combine the preserved lemon and sugar in a small bowl and place on top of the fish.
* Arrange the fresh lemon slices on top and place in a collapsible pot or bamboo steamer over a pot of boiling water. Steam, covered, for about 8 minutes, or until cooked through.
* Heat the oil in a small skillet (frying pan) and drizzle over the fish. Season with salt to taste. Serve with rice.

板蒸鲩鱼腩
CARP BELLY
OVER TOFU

REGION: SHUNDE
PREPARATION TIME: 20 MINUTES,
   PLUS 15 MINUTES SOAKING TIME
COOKING TIME: 12 MINUTES
SERVES: 4

* Cut the fish into ¾-inch/2-cm pieces along the bones.
  Drain off any excess water and set aside.
* Cut the block of tofu horizontally into 3 equal slices, then
  cut the block vertically 3 times to divide each slice into
  4 sections. Put the tofu pieces into a bowl. Add the salt,
  cover with water, and soak for 15 minutes. Rinse and drain
  the tofu, pat it dry with paper towels, and arrange across
  a heatproof plate so that it lines the bottom.
* Put the black beans, garlic, sugar, and soy sauce into
  a bowl and mix into a sauce.
* Mix the fish with the sauce, then place it over the tofu.
  Arrange the shredded chile on top and put the plate into
  a collapsible pot or bamboo steamer over a pot of boiling
  water. Steam, covered, for 10 minutes until cooked through.
* Heat the oil in a small saucepan over high heat, add the
  ginger, and stir for about 30 seconds. Pour the mixture
  over the fish and serve with rice.

• 1 (11-OZ/300-G) GRASS CARP BELLY
  OR ANY FRESHWATER FISH, BLACK
  MEMBRANE SCRAPED OFF AND RINSED
• 9 OZ/250 G FIRM TOFU, DRAINED
• 1 TEASPOON SALT
• 2 TABLESPOONS FERMENTED BLACK
  BEANS, RINSED AND CHOPPED
• 2 CLOVES GARLIC, CHOPPED
• 1 TEASPOON GRANULATED SUGAR
• 1 TEASPOON LIGHT SOY SAUCE
• 1 RED CHILE, SEEDED AND SHREDDED
• 2 TABLESPOONS VEGETABLE OIL
• ¾ OZ/20 G GINGER (ABOUT 1-INCH/
  2.5-CM-LENGTH PIECE), SHREDDED
• STEAMED RICE (PAGE 540), TO SERVE

鲜柠檬蒸乌头
GREY MULLET
WITH LEMON

REGION: HONG KONG
PREPARATION TIME: 5 MINUTES
COOKING TIME: 10 MINUTES
SERVES: 4

* Salt the fish inside and out. Do not rinse.
* Arrange half the lemon slices on a heatproof plate.
  Place the fish over the lemon and arrange the remaining
  lemon slices on top to cover the fish. Place the plate
  in a collapsible bowl or bamboo steamer over a pot of
  boiling water. Steam, covered, for about 8 minutes,
  or until cooked through.
* Heat the oil in a saucepan over low heat until hot, then
  pour it over the fish. Serve with rice.

• 1 TEASPOON SALT
• 1 (1 LB 5-OZ/600-G) GREY MULLET,
  CLEANED AND RINSED
• 1 LEMON, SLICED
• 1 TABLESPOON VEGETABLE OIL
• STEAMED RICE (PAGE 540), TO SERVE

REGION: HUBEI
PREPARATION TIME: 15 MINUTES,
   PLUS 20 MINUTES SOAKING TIME
COOKING TIME: 20 MINUTES
SERVES: 4
📷 PAGE 153

清蒸鯿鱼

FISH WITH CHINESE CELERY AND BAMBOO SHOOTS

- 2 DRIED BLACK MUSHROOMS
- 1 TABLESPOON SALT
- 1 SCALLION (SPRING ONION), CUT INTO 2-INCH/5-CM LENGTHS
- 1 TABLESPOON GINGER JUICE
- 1 (1 LB 10½-OZ/750-G) SEA BREAM OR TILAPIA, CLEANED AND RINSED
- ⅓ CUP (2 OZ/50 G) SLICED BAMBOO SHOOTS
- ⅛ OZ/5 G GINGER (ABOUT ½-INCH/ 1-CM-LENGTH PIECE), SLICED
- 1 STALK CHINESE CELERY, CUT INTO 2-INCH/5-CM LENGTHS
- 4 TABLESPOONS CHICKEN BROTH (STOCK, PAGE 90)
- ? TABLESPOONS LARD
- STEAMED RICE (PAGE 540), TO SERVE

* Put the mushrooms into a bowl, cover with cold water, and soak for at least 20 minutes, or until softened. Remove the mushrooms, squeeze dry, and discard the stems. Cut the mushrooms into thin slices.
* Mix 2 teaspoons salt, the scallion (spring onion), and the ginger juice in a shallow dish. Marinate the fish in the mixture for 10 minutes. Rinse and drain the fish.
* Bring a saucepan of water to a boil, add the bamboo shoots, and blanch for 1 minute. Drain and rinse under cold running water.
* Put the fish on a heatproof serving plate. Sprinkle over the remaining 1 teaspoon salt, the ginger, celery, bamboo shoots, mushrooms, and chicken broth (stock). Put the plate in a collapsible pot or bamboo steamer over a pot of boiling water. Steam, covered, for 15 minutes, or until the fish is cooked through. Pick out and discard the ginger.
* Put the lard into a small saucepan and heat it gently over low heat until melted. Drizzle the lard over the fish. Serve with rice.

REGION: ZHEJIANG
PREPARATION TIME: 5 MINUTES
COOKING TIME: 15 MINUTES
SERVES: 4

西湖醋鱼

WEST LAKE-STYLE FISH

- 1 (1 LB 2-OZ/500-G) GRASS CARP, CLEANED AND SCALED
- 1 OZ/25 G GINGER (ABOUT 2-INCH/ 5-CM-LENGTH PIECE), HALF SLICED AND HALF SHREDDED
- 1 TEASPOON SALT
- 3 TABLESPOONS ZHENJIANG OR BALSAMIC VINEGAR
- 2 TEASPOONS BROWN SUGAR
- 1 TEASPOON CORNSTARCH (CORNFLOUR)
- STEAMED RICE (PAGE 540), TO SERVE

* Use a small knife to scrape the black membrane from inside the fish and rinse well.
* Put the sliced ginger and ½ teaspoon salt into a large saucepan, add 3 cups (25 fl oz/750 ml) water to cover the fish, and bring to a boil. Turn off the heat, place the fish into a metal colander, and lower the fish, skin side up, into the water. Cover and let sit for 10 minutes, or until cooked through.
* Carefully transfer the fish onto a serving plate and keep warm. Strain 1 cup (8 fl oz/250 ml) of the cooking liquid and pour it into a small saucepan. Add the vinegar, shredded ginger, remaining ½ teaspoon salt, and sugar.
* Mix the cornstarch (cornflour) with 1 tablespoon water in a small bowl and stir this mixture into the sauce. Bring to a boil, stirring, for 30 seconds to thicken the sauce. Pour over the fish and serve with rice.

FISH WITH CHINESE CELERY AND BAMBOO SHOOTS

REGION: HONG KONG
PREPARATION TIME: 10 MINUTES
COOKING TIME: 10 MINUTES
SERVES: 4

榄角蒸鳊鱼
SEA BREAM WITH PRESERVED BLACK OLIVES

- 1 (1 LB 5-OZ/600-G) SEA BREAM, RINSED AND CLEANED
- 1 TEASPOON SALT
- ¼ OZ/10 G GINGER (ABOUT ¾-INCH/ 2-CM-LENGTH PIECE), SHREDDED
- 1 TABLESPOON CHINESE OLIVE VEGETABLE
- 12 PRESERVED BLACK OLIVES, HALVED
- 2 TABLESPOONS OLIVE OIL
- STEAMED RICE (PAGE 540), TO SERVE

* Sprinkle the fish, inside and out, with the salt and put it on a heatproof plate. Top with the shredded ginger, Chinese olive vegetable, and preserved black olives. Drizzle with olive oil.
* Place the fish in a collapsible pot or bamboo steamer over a pot of boiling water. Steam, covered, for about 10 minutes, or until cooked through. Serve with rice.

REGION: GUANGDONG
PREPARATION TIME: 15 MINUTES, PLUS
  15 MINUTES MARINATING TIME
COOKING TIME: 15 MINUTES
SERVES: 2

番茄煮红衫鱼
GOLDEN THREAD WITH TOMATOES

- 1 (14-OZ/400-G) GOLDEN THREAD FISH OR SEA BREAM, CLEANED AND FILLETED
- 1 TEASPOON SALT
- PINCH OF GROUND WHITE PEPPER
- 2 TOMATOES
- 3 TABLESPOONS VEGETABLE OIL
- ¼ OZ/10 G GINGER (ABOUT ¾-INCH/ 2-CM-LENGTH PIECE), FINELY SHREDDED
- ½ ONION, THINLY SLICED
- 1 TABLESPOON GRANULATED SUGAR
- 1 TEASPOON CORNSTARCH (CORNFLOUR)
- 3 SCALLIONS (SPRING ONIONS), SHREDDED
- STEAMED RICE (PAGE 540), TO SERVE

* Combine the fish, ½ teaspoon salt, and white pepper in a bowl and marinate for 15 minutes. Pat the fish dry with paper towels.
* Score the base of the tomatoes. Bring a small saucepan of water to a boil, add the tomatoes, and heat for 1–2 minutes. Immediately transfer to a bowl of ice water. When the tomatoes are cool enough to handle, peel away the skin and cut each tomato into 6 pieces.
* Heat 2 tablespoons oil in a large skillet (frying pan) over high heat, add the fish, and pan-fry for about 3–4 minutes on each side until golden brown and cooked through. Transfer to a plate.
* Heat the remaining 1 tablespoon oil in the skillet over medium heat and stir-fry the ginger for 1 minute until fragrant. Add the onions and stir-fry for another minute. Stir in the tomatoes, sugar, and remaining ½ teaspoon salt and stir-fry for another 2 minutes. Add the fish to the skillet, spoon over the sauce to cover, and cook, covered, for 2 minutes.
* Use a slotted spoon to transfer the fish to a serving dish. Mix the cornstarch (cornflour) with 1 tablespoon water in a small bowl and stir this mixture into the skillet. Bring to a boil, stirring, for 30 seconds to thicken the sauce. Pour the sauce over the fish and sprinkle over the shredded scallions (spring onions). Serve with rice.

荷叶蒸辣子鱼
STEAMED FISH IN
LOTUS LEAVES

REGION: YUNNAN
PREPARATION TIME: 20 MINUTES,
   PLUS 45 MINUTES SOAKING TIME
COOKING TIME: 15 MINUTES
SERVES: 4

* Soak the lotus leaves in cold water for 45 minutes, or until softened.
* Meanwhile, rub the coarse salt all over the fish. Rinse, drain, and cut into 1-inch/2.5-cm chunks. Combine the fish, cilantro (coriander), ginger, scallions (spring onions), garlic, basil, mint, fennel, lemongrass, and cayenne pepper in a large bowl. Stir well. Add the wine, salt, white pepper, and lard to the bowl and mix well. Marinate in the refrigerator for 30 minutes.
* Drain the lotus leaves and pat dry with paper towels. Using a sharp knife, cut out the stiff veins from the lotus leaves near the stem and then lay the leaves, one on top of the other, on a cutting board, making sure any gaps in one leaf is covered by the other leaf.
* Arrange the fish mixture in the center of the leaves, fold in the sides, and wrap into a bundle. Place the leaves on a steaming rack in a collapsible pot or bamboo steamer over a pot of boiling water. Steam, covered, for 15 minutes, or until cooked through. Carefully transfer the bundle to a plate, unwrap the lotus leaves, and serve with rice. (The lotus leaves are not to be consumed.)

- 2 DRIED LOTUS LEAVES
- 1 TEASPOON COARSE SALT
- 1 (11-OZ/300-G) CATFISH, CLEANED AND RINSED
- 4 STALKS CILANTRO (CORIANDER), FINELY CHOPPED
- 2 OZ/50 G GINGER (ABOUT 3-INCH/7.5-CM-LENGTH PIECE), FINELY CHOPPED
- 2 SCALLIONS (SPRING ONIONS), FINELY CHOPPED
- 4 CLOVES GARLIC, FINELY CHOPPED
- 1 CUP (2 OZ/50 G) BASIL LEAVES, FINELY CHOPPED
- 1 CUP (2 OZ/50 G) MINT LEAVES, FINELY CHOPPED
- ¼ FENNEL BULB, FINELY CHOPPED
- 2 LEMONGRASS STALKS, FINELY CHOPPED
- 1 CAYENNE PEPPER, FINELY CHOPPED
- 2 TABLESPOONS RICE WINE
- ½ TABLESPOON SALT
- 1 TEASPOON GROUND WHITE PEPPER
- 2 TABLESPOONS LARD
- STEAMED RICE (PAGE 540), TO SERVE

豉汁蒸黄骨鱼
CATFISH IN BLACK BEAN SAUCE

- 9 OZ/250 G FIRM TOFU, DRAINED AND CUT INTO 6 EQUAL PIECES
- 1 (1 LB 5-OZ/600-G) CATFISH, CLEANED AND RINSED
- 2 TABLESPOONS FERMENTED BLACK BEANS, RINSED AND CHOPPED
- 2 CLOVES GARLIC, CHOPPED
- 1 RED CHILE, SEEDED AND CHOPPED
- 1 TEASPOON GRANULATED SUGAR
- 1 TEASPOON LIGHT SOY SAUCE
- 3 TABLESPOONS VEGETABLE OIL
- ¾ OZ/20 G GINGER (ABOUT 1-INCH/ 2.5-CM-LENGTH PIECE), SHREDDED
- 2 SCALLIONS (SPRING ONIONS), SHREDDED
- STEAMED RICE (PAGE 540), TO SERVE

* Arrange the tofu in two rows on a large heatproof plate. Place the fish on top of the tofu.
* Combine the black beans, garlic, chile, sugar, soy sauce, and 1 tablespoon oil in a bowl. Spread the sauce evenly onto the fish.
* Place the fish in a collapsible pot or bamboo steamer over a pot of boiling water. Steam, covered, for 8 minutes, or until cooked through.
* Heat the remaining 2 tablespoons oil in a small skillet (frying pan), until heated through.
* Place the ginger and scallions (spring onions) on top of the fish, pour over the hot oil, and serve with rice.

剁椒鱼头
FISH HEAD IN CHILI SAUCE

- 1 (1 LB ¼-OZ/750-G) BIGHEAD CARP, GRASS CARP, OR SALMON HEAD, HALVED
- 2 TABLESPOONS WHITE VINEGAR
- 2 TABLESPOONS GINGER JUICE
- ½ TABLESPOON SALT, PLUS EXTRA TO TASTE
- 2 TABLESPOONS CORNSTARCH (CORNFLOUR)
- ½ HEAD GARLIC, CLOVES SEPARATED AND CHOPPED
- 2 OZ/50 G GINGER (ABOUT 3-INCH/ 7.5-CM-LENGTH PIECE), GRATED
- 2 SCALLIONS (SPRING ONIONS), CHOPPED
- 20 PICKLED RED CHILES, CHOPPED
- 1 RED CHILE, CHOPPED
- 3 TABLESPOONS VEGETABLE OIL
- STEAMED RICE (PAGE 540), TO SERVE

* Place the fish head in a large bowl, add the vinegar, ginger juice, and 4¼ cups (34 fl oz/1 liter) water, and wash to remove any lingering blood or fish scent. Rinse thoroughly and drain. Rub the fish head with the salt and lightly dredge with the cornstarch (cornflour). Place the fish head on a large heatproof plate, skin facing upward.
* Mix the garlic, ginger, scallions (spring onions), both chiles, and 1 tablespoon oil in a bowl and sprinkle over the dish. Place the dish in a collapsible pot or bamboo steamer over a pot of boiling water. Steam, covered, for 12 minutes, or until the fish is cooked through.
* Heat the remaining 2 tablespoons oil in a small saucepan and drizzle over the fish head. Season with extra salt and serve with rice.

烟鲳鱼

WOK-SMOKED
POMFRET

REGION: CHAOZHOU
PREPARATION TIME: 10 MINUTES,
   PLUS 2 HOURS MARINATING TIME
COOKING TIME: 20 MINUTES
SERVES: 4

Most home cooks believe you need a barbecue or special equipment for smoking, when in fact, all you need is a wok and aluminum foil. Lining the wok with the foil prevents your smoking ingredients from sticking to the wok (and causing a sticky mess).

* Use a sharp knife to make 2 shallow slashes on each side of the fish. Transfer to a bowl.
* Combine the marinade ingredients in a shallow bowl, pour over the fish, and marinate for 2 hours (no need to refrigerate).
* Preheat the oven to 450°F/230°C/Gas Mark 8. Line a baking sheet with parchment (baking) paper.
* Use your hands to wipe the fish clean of the marinade. Place it on the prepared baking sheet and bake for 5 minutes. Turn the fish over on the baking sheet and bake in the over for another 5 minutes.
* Use 2 sheets of aluminum foil to line a wok, following the wok's curvature, and fold the edges of the foil over the rim of the wok to seal its inner surface completely.
* Mix the tea leaves, sugar, and flour together in a heatproof bowl and put the mixture into the prepared wok. Brush a steaming rack with oil and put it into the wok over the smoking ingredients. Ensure you use a steaming rack that is tall enough to leave 1 inch/2.5 cm between the fish and smoking ingredients. Cover the wok and heat the smoking ingredients over high heat until smoke begins to rise, about 2–3 minutes.
* Uncover, put the fish on the rack, re-cover, and then reduce to low heat and smoke the fish for about 5 minutes, or until cooked through. Transfer the fish to a serving plate and serve with mayonnaise on the side.

- 1 (1 LB 2-OZ/500-G) POMFRET, CLEANED AND RINSED
- 1 TABLESPOON TEA LEAVES
- 1 TABLESPOON GRANULATED SUGAR
- 1 TABLESPOON ALL-PURPOSE (PLAIN) FLOUR
- VEGETABLE OIL, FOR BRUSHING
- MAYONNAISE, TO SERVE

FOR THE MARINADE:
- 1 TABLESPOON GINGER JUICE
- 1 SCALLION (SPRING ONION), CHOPPED
- 1 TABLESPOON GRANULATED SUGAR
- 1 TABLESPOON DARK SOY SAUCE
- 1 TABLESPOON MALTOSE
- 1 TABLESPOON SHAOXING WINE

白萝卜煮鱼松
DACE WITH DAIKON RADISH

- 1 (9-OZ/250-G) DACE, FILLETED AND MINCED
- ½ TEASPOON SALT
- ¼ TEASPOON GROUND WHITE PEPPER
- 2 TABLESPOONS VEGETABLE OIL
- ¼ OZ/10 G GINGER (ABOUT ¾-INCH/ 2-CM-LENGTH PIECE), SLICED
- 1 LB 5 OZ/600 G DAIKON RADISH, CUT INTO CHUNKS
- 4 STALKS CHINESE CELERY, CUT INTO 2-INCH/5-CM LENGTHS
- 1 SCALLION (SPRING ONION), CUT INTO 2-INCH/5-CM LENGTHS
- STEAMED RICE (PAGE 540), TO SERVE

* Combine the dace, ¼ teaspoon salt, and white pepper.
* Heat the oil in a large skillet (frying pan) over low heat, add the fish, and press down, with a spatula (fish slice), to make a ¼-inch/5-mm-thick patty. Fry the patty for 2–3 minutes, or until golden brown. Turn, then fry for another 2–3 minutes.
* Use the spatula to break the patty into small pieces, then add the ginger. Increase the heat to high and add 1 cup (8 fl oz/250 ml) boiling water. Add the radish and Chinese celery and bring to a boil. Reduce the heat to low and simmer, covered, for 15 minutes. Add the remaining ¼ teaspoon salt and the scallion (spring onion), adjust the seasoning to taste, then transfer to a plate and serve with rice.

醋椒鱼
FISH IN SPICY
VINEGAR SAUCE

- 1 (1-LB/450-G) MANDARIN FISH, CLEANED AND RINSED
- 3 TABLESPOONS LARD OR VEGETABLE OIL
- 1 SCALLION (SPRING ONION), STEMS ONLY, CUT INTO 1½-INCH/4-CM STRIPS AND GREEN PART CHOPPED
- 1 TEASPOON CHOPPED GINGER
- ½ TEASPOON GROUND WHITE PEPPER
- 2 CUPS (16 FL OZ/475 ML) CHICKEN BROTH (STOCK, PAGE 90)
- 1 TEASPOON GINGER JUICE
- 1 TEASPOON RICE WINE
- ½ TEASPOON SALT, PLUS EXTRA TO TASTE
- 2 BUNCHES CILANTRO (CORIANDER), CUT INTO ¾-INCH/2-CM LENGTHS
- 2 TABLESPOONS BLACK VINEGAR
- 1 TEASPOON SESAME OIL
- STEAMED RICE (PAGE 540), TO SERVE

* Use a sharp knife to make 3 slashes on each side of the fish.
* Bring a large saucepan of water to a boil, add the fish, and simmer for about 10 seconds. Drain and set aside.
* Heat the lard in a wok over high heat, add the chopped green scallion (spring onion), ginger, and white pepper, and stir-fry for 1–2 minutes until fragrant. Add the chicken broth (stock), ginger juice, wine, and salt. Bring to a boil, add the fish, and return to a boil. Lower the heat, cover, and simmer for about 10 minutes. Add the remaining scallion, the cilantro (coriander), and vinegar and stir in the sesame oil. Season with extra salt to taste.
* Transfer the fish to a plate and pour over the sauce. Serve with rice.

白汤鲫鱼
CRUCIAN CARP IN SOUP

REGION: JIANGSU
PREPARATION TIME: 10 MINUTES
COOKING TIME: 20 MINUTES
SERVES: 4

* Use a sharp knife to make slashes in a crisscross pattern on both sides of each fish.
* Put the mushrooms into a bowl, cover with cold water, and soak for at least 20 minutes, or until softened. Thinly slice the mushrooms.
* Bring a saucepan of water to a boil, add the bamboo shoots, and blanch for 1 minute. Drain and rinse under cold running water.
* Heat the oil in a wok over high heat, add the fish, and pan-fry the fish for about 1 minute, then turn over both and fry for another minute. Add the wine, knotted scallion (spring onion), ginger, and 3 cups (25 fl oz/750 ml) water and bring to a boil. Cover, and simmer over low heat for 10 minutes, or until the fish is cooked through.
* Add the bacon, bamboo, mushrooms, and salt, and cook over high heat for about 2 minutes. Remove and discard the scallion and ginger.
* Put the lard in a small pan and heat it gently over low heat until melted.
* Transfer the fish with all the ingredients and the soup to a serving bowl. Drizzle over the heated lard and serve.

- 2 (9-OZ/250-G) CRUCIAN CARP, CLEANED AND RINSED
- 2 DRIED BLACK MUSHROOMS
- ⅔ CUP (2 OZ/50 G) SLICED BAMBOO SHOOTS
- 3 TABLESPOONS VEGETABLE OIL
- 3 TABLESPOONS SHAOXING WINE
- 1 SCALLION (SPRING ONION), KNOTTED
- ⅛ OZ/5 G GINGER (ABOUT ½-INCH/ 1-CM-LENGTH PIECE), SLICED
- 1 OZ/25 G CHINESE CURED BACON, SLICED
- 1 TEASPOON SALT
- 1 TABLESPOON LARD

清焖荷包鲤
BRAISED
CARP

REGION: JIANGXI
PREPARATION TIME: 15 MINUTES,
  PLUS 20 MINUTES SOAKING TIME
COOKING TIME: 20 MINUTES
SERVES: 4

* Put the mushrooms into a bowl, cover with cold water, and soak for at least 20 minutes, or until softened. Remove the mushrooms, squeeze dry, and discard the stems. Dice, then set aside.
* Meanwhile, pat the fish dry with paper towels. Use a sharp knife to make 3 slashes on each side of the fish. Combine the salt and wine in a small bowl and brush the mixture on both sides of the fish. Marinate for 10 minutes.
* Heat the oil in a wok or large skillet (frying pan) over medium-high heat, add the ginger, scallion (spring onion), and mushrooms, and stir-fry for 1–2 minutes until fragrant. Add the fish along with the broth (stock) and bring to a boil. Reduce to low heat and simmer, covered, for 10 minutes. Flip the fish over and simmer for another 10 minutes. Add the cilantro (coriander) and transfer to a plate. Serve with rice.

- 3 DRIED BLACK MUSHROOMS
- 1 (1 LB 2-OZ/500-G) CARP, CLEANED AND RINSED
- 1 TEASPOON SALT
- 1 TABLESPOON RICE WINE
- 2 TABLESPOONS VEGETABLE OIL
- 2 TEASPOONS FINELY CHOPPED GINGER
- 1 SCALLION (SPRING ONION), CHOPPED
- 1 CUP (8 FL OZ/250 ML) CHICKEN BROTH (STOCK, PAGE 90)
- 3 STALKS CILANTRO (CORIANDER), CUT INTO ¾-INCH/2-CM LENGTHS
- STEAMED RICE (PAGE 540), TO SERVE

REGION: SICHUAN
PREPARATION TIME: 15 MINUTES, PLUS
  10 MINUTES MARINATING TIME
COOKING TIME: 10 MINUTES
SERVES: 4

糖醋脆皮鱼

CARP WITH SWEET
AND SOUR SAUCE

- 1 (1 LB 8½-OZ/700-G) CARP, CLEANED AND RINSED
- 3 TEASPOONS SALT
- 1 TABLESPOON SHAOXING WINE
- 5 TABLESPOONS CORNSTARCH (CORNFLOUR)
- 5 TABLESPOONS GRANULATED SUGAR
- 1 CUP (8 FL OZ/250 ML) CHICKEN BROTH (STOCK, PAGE 90)
- 2 CUPS (16 FL OZ/475 ML) VEGETABLE OIL
- 2 TEASPOONS FINELY CHOPPED GINGER
- 4 CLOVES GARLIC, CHOPPED
- 3 TABLESPOONS BLACK OR BALSAMIC VINEGAR
- ½ TABLESPOON SESAME OIL
- 2 SCALLIONS (SPRING ONIONS), 1 CHOPPED AND 1 SHREDDED
- ¼ OZ/10 G PICKLED CHILES, SHREDDED
- 1 BUNCH CILANTRO (CORIANDER), ROUGHLY CHOPPED
- STEAMED RICE (PAGE 540), TO SERVE

* Use a sharp knife to make 3–4 deep cuts (to the bone) on each side of the fish, at a 45 degree angle toward the head.
* Combine 2 teaspoons salt and the wine in a small bowl, then brush the mixture on both sides of the fish. Marinate for 10 minutes.
* Mix 3 tablespoons cornstarch (cornflour) with 3 tablespoons cold water in a large shallow bowl. Set aside for 5 minutes, or until the starch settles at the bottom of the bowl, then pour out the water to leave a wet starch.
* Mix the remaining 1 teaspoon salt and 2 tablespoons cornstarch, the sugar, and broth (stock) in a bowl and set aside.
* Heat the vegetable oil in a wok or large skillet (frying pan) to 340°F/170°C, or until a cube of bread browns in 45 seconds. Dip the fish into the wet starch, then holding it by the tail, carefully slide it, head first, into the hot oil. Deep-fry the fish for 5 minutes until golden brown and cooked through. Use a slotted spoon to carefully remove the fish from the oil and drain on paper towels. Transfer to a serving plate and keep warm.
* Pour out most of the oil, leaving about 1 tablespoon in the wok. Add the ginger and garlic and stir-fry over high heat for 1–2 minutes until fragrant. Add the broth and cornstarch mixture and stir-fry for another minute over high heat to thicken. Stir in the vinegar, sesame oil, and chopped scallion (spring onion) and pour over the fish. Top with the pickled chiles, shredded scallion (spring onion), and cilantro (coriander). Serve with rice.

干烧石头鱼
BRAISED
CATFISH

REGION: HUBEI
PREPARATION TIME: 10 MINUTES,
    PLUS 10 MINUTES MARINATING TIME
COOKING TIME: 20 MINUTES
SERVES: 4

Milky white, tender, and without scales, Longnose catfish is a freshwater fish from the Han River and this traditional dish is a specialty of Jingmen City in Hubei Province. Since this fish is not particularly bony, the head and tail are served as part of the dish.

* Cut the fish body into 1¼-inch/3-cm-thick chunks. Mix ½ teaspoon salt and 1 tablespoon wine in a shallow dish. Marinate the fish head, tail, and body pieces in this mixture for 10 minutes.
* Heat the oil in a wok or deep saucepan to 340°F/170°C, or until a cube of bread browns in 45 seconds. Add the fish and deep-fry for about 4–5 minutes until brown. Use a slotted spoon to carefully remove the fish from the oil and drain on paper towels.
* Pour out most of the oil, leaving about 1 tablespoon in the wok. Heat over medium-high heat, add the ginger and longer scallion (spring onion) pieces, and stir-fry for about 1 minute until fragrant. Add the chili sauce, pork, and remaining 1 tablespoon wine and toss over high heat for 1 minute. Add the chicken broth (stock) and bring to a boil.
* Put the fish, bamboo shoots, the remaining ½ teaspoon salt, the sugar, and soy sauce into the wok and return to a boil. Reduce to low heat, cover with a lid, and simmer for about 10 minutes, or until the sauce thickens and the fish is cooked through. Stir in the vinegar, white pepper, and chopped scallion.
* Arrange the fish head and tail at either end of a plate, with the fish pieces in the middle. Pour over the sauce from the wok. Serve with rice.

- 1 (1 LB 10½-OZ/750-G) LONGNOSE OR ANY CATFISH, CLEANED AND HEAD AND TAIL RESERVED
- 1 TEASPOON SALT
- 2 TABLESPOONS RICE WINE
- 2 CUPS (16 FL OZ/475 ML) VEGETABLE OIL
- ½ OZ/15 G GINGER (ABOUT ¾-INCH/ 2-CM-LENGTH PIECE), CHOPPED
- 2 SCALLIONS (SPRING ONIONS), 1 CUT INTO 2-INCH/5-CM LENGTHS, 1 CHOPPED
- 2 TABLESPOONS CHILI SAUCE
- 2¾ OZ/75 G PORK SHOULDER, CUT INTO ½-INCH/1-CM CUBES
- ½ CUP (4 FL OZ/120 ML) CHICKEN BROTH (STOCK, PAGE 90)
- ⅓ CUP (2 OZ/50 G) BAMBOO SHOOTS, CUT INTO ½-INCH/1-CM CUBES
- 1 TABLESPOON GRANULATED SUGAR
- 1 TABLESPOON LIGHT SOY SAUCE
- 1 TABLESPOON WHITE VINEGAR
- ¼ TEASPOON GROUND WHITE PEPPER
- STEAMED RICE (PAGE 540), TO SERVE

REGION: JIANGSU
PREPARATION TIME: 15 MINUTES, PLUS
  20 MINUTES SOAKING TIME
COOKING TIME: 15 MINUTES
SERVES: 4

清烩鲈鱼片

BRAISED
PERCH

- ¼ CUP (¼ OZ/5 G) DRIED BLACK
  FUNGUS
- 1 (1 LB 5-OZ/600-G) PERCH, FILLETED,
  BONES RESERVED
- 2 SLICES GINGER, PLUS ½ TEASPOON
  GRATED GINGER
- 1 TEASPOON SALT
- 1 EGG WHITE
- 1 TABLESPOON CORNSTARCH
  (CORNFLOUR)
- 2 TABLESPOONS VEGETABLE OIL
- 1 SCALLION (SPRING ONION),
  CHOPPED
- 2 OZ/50 G YELLOW CHIVES, CUT INTO
  2-INCH/5-CM LENGTHS
- 4 WATER CHESTNUTS, SLICED
- 3 TABLESPOONS SHAOXING WINE
- 1 TABLESPOON SESAME OIL
- ¼ TEASPOON GROUND WHITE PEPPER
- 1 BUNCH CILANTRO (CORIANDER),
  CHOPPED
- 3 TABLESPOONS BLACK OR BALSAMIC
  VINEGAR

* Put the black fungus in a bowl, cover with cold water, and soak for at least 20 minutes, or until softened. Remove the mushrooms, squeeze dry, and discard the stems.
* Put the fish bones and ginger slices into a large pot. Pour in enough water to cover completely. Bring to a boil over high heat. Reduce to low heat and simmer for 5 minutes, or until about 1 cup (8 fl oz/250 ml) of liquid remains. Skim the froth and scum off the surface, if needed. Strain through a strainer (sieve) into a bowl, discard the bones and ginger, and reserve the broth.
* Cut the fish fillets into 2 × 1 × ¼-inch/5 × 2.5 × 0.5-cm pieces. Combine the fish pieces in a bowl with ½ teaspoon salt. Beat the egg white and add to the fish along with ½ tablespoon cornstarch (cornflour), then mix well.
* Heat the vegetable oil in a wok or large skillet (frying pan) over medium-high heat, add the scallion (spring onion) and grated ginger, and stir-fry for 1 minute until fragrant. Add the black fungus, yellow chives, water chestnuts, reserved fish broth, wine, and remaining ½ teaspoon salt and bring to a boil. Reduce to low heat, add the fish, and return to a boil and cook for 2–3 minutes until cooked through
* Mix the remaining ½ tablespoon cornstarch with 1½ tablespoons water in a small bowl and stir this mixture into the wok. Bring to a boil, stirring, for 30 seconds to thicken the sauce.
* Drizzle in the sesame oil and transfer to a large bowl. Top with the white pepper and cilantro (coriander). Serve with the vinegar on the side.

FISH & SEAFOOD

荷包鲫鱼
STUFFED CRUCIAN CARP

REGION: JIANGSU
PREPARATION TIME: 25 MINUTES
COOKING TIME: 30 MINUTES
SERVES: 4

* Fillet one side of the fish with the fillet linked to the fish at the stomach. To remove the spine, cut the spine at both ends and insert a knife to lift it from the fish. The result will be a hollow fish connected at the stomach. Rub both sides of the fish with ½ tablespoon soy sauce.
* To make the filling, combine the pork and bamboo shoots in a large bowl, add 1 teaspoon wine, ½ tablespoon soy sauce, ½ teaspoon sugar, ¼ teaspoon salt, and ½ teaspoon cornstarch (cornflour), and mix well.
* Lift the fillet and spread the filling evenly into the fish. Gently press the sides of the fish together to restore the fish to its original shape. Tie the fish with kitchen string to hold the fillet and filling in place. The fish will look fat at this point.
* Heat the oil in a wok or large skillet (frying pan) over medium-high heat, add the fish, and pan-fry on one side for 4–5 minutes until golden brown. Use a slotted spoon to carefully remove the fish from the oil and drain on paper towels.
* Add the pork fatback, ginger, and scallion (spring onion) to the wok and stir-fry for 1–2 minutes until fragrant. Return the fish to the wok, browned side facing up. Add the remaining 2 teaspoons wine, 2 tablespoons soy sauce, 1½ teaspoons sugar, ¼ teaspoon salt, the bamboo shoot slices, and scant ½ cup (3½ fl oz/100 ml) water, then bring to a boil.
* Cover, reduce to low heat, and simmer for 20 minutes. Increase to high heat and cook, uncovered, to reduce the sauce by half.
* Transfer the fish and bamboo shoots to a plate. Remove the kitchen string. Mix the remaining 1 teaspoon cornstarch with 1 tablespoon water in a small bowl and stir this mixture into the wok. Bring to a boil, stirring, for 30 seconds to thicken the sauce. Pour the sauce over the fish and serve immediately with rice.

• 1 (12-OZ/350-G) CRUCIAN CARP OR PERCH, CLEANED AND RINSED
• 3 TABLESPOONS LIGHT SOY SAUCE
• 4 OZ/120 G MINCED (GROUND) PORK
• 1¼ CUP (5 OZ/150 G) SLICED BAMBOO SHOOTS, ABOUT 1 CUP (4 OZ/120 G) DICED
• 1 TABLESPOON SHAOXING WINE
• 2 TEASPOONS GRANULATED SUGAR
• ½ TEASPOON SALT
• 1½ TEASPOONS CORNSTARCH (CORNFLOUR)
• 3 TABLESPOONS VEGETABLE OIL
• 1 OZ/25 G PORK FATBACK, CUT INTO ¼-INCH/5-MM DICE
• 2 OZ/50 G GINGER (ABOUT 3-INCH/ 7.5-CM-LENGTH PIECE), SLICED
• 1 SCALLION (SPRING ONION), CHOPPED
• STEAMED RICE (PAGE 540), TO SERVE

REGION: SICHUAN
PREPARATION TIME: 10 MINUTES,
    PLUS 1 HOUR MARINATING TIME
COOKING TIME: 1 HOUR 20 MINUTES
SERVES: 4

豆豉鲫鱼
CARP WITH
BLACK BEANS

- 1 (1 LB 2-OZ/500-G) CRUCIAN CARP OR PERCH, CLEANED AND RINSED
- 1 TEASPOON SALT
- 3 TABLESPOONS RICE WINE
- 1 TEASPOON CORNSTARCH (CORNFLOUR)
- 5 TABLESPOONS VEGETABLE OIL
- 1 TABLESPOON GRANULATED SUGAR
- 3½ OZ/100 G GROUND (MINCED) PORK
- 3 TABLESPOONS FERMENTED BLACK BEANS, RINSED AND CHOPPED
- 2 CUPS (16 FL OZ/475 ML) CHICKEN BROTH (STOCK, PAGE 90)
- 2 TEASPOONS SESAME OIL
- STEAMED RICE (PAGE 540), TO SERVE

* Use a sharp knife, make 3–4 slashes on each side of the fish, then rub the fish with ½ teaspoon salt and 1 tablespoon wine. Marinate for 1 hour.
* Lightly dredge the fish in the cornstarch (cornflour).
* Heat 1 tablespoon vegetable oil in a small saucepan over low heat, add 2 teaspoons sugar, and cook for 2 minutes until the sugar has dissolved and the mixture is caramel in color. Stir in 2 tablespoons water and simmer for another 2 minutes, stirring, until the consistency of syrup. Remove from the heat and set aside.
* Heat 2 tablespoons vegetable oil in a wok or large skillet (frying pan), add the fish, and pan-fry for 5 minutes on each side until golden brown and cooked through. Transfer the fish to a plate.
* Add the remaining 2 tablespoons vegetable oil to the wok and heat over medium heat. Add the pork and stir-fry for 3 minutes. Add the black beans and stir-fry for another minute until fragrant. Pour in the chicken broth (stock), the remaining ½ teaspoon salt, 2 tablespoons wine, 1 teaspoon sugar, and the syrup, and bring to a boil.
* Return the fish to the wok, reduce to low heat, and simmer, uncovered, for about 1 hour, or until almost all of the sauce is evaporated. Drizzle the sesame oil over the fish and transfer to a plate. Serve with rice.

REGION: JIANGSU
PREPARATION TIME: 5 MINUTES
COOKING TIME: 10 MINUTES
SERVES: 4

老烧鱼
BRAISED FISH BELLY

- 4 TABLESPOONS LARD
- 1 SCALLION (SPRING ONION), CHOPPED
- 1 TEASPOON GRATED GINGER
- 1 LB 2 OZ/500 G FRESH FISH BELLY, PREFERABLY GRASS CARP
- 3 TABLESPOONS SHAOXING WINE
- 5 TABLESPOONS LIGHT SOY SAUCE
- 3 TABLESPOONS GRANULATED SUGAR
- 1 TEASPOON CORNSTARCH (FLOUR)
- 1 TEASPOON SESAME OIL
- STEAMED RICE (PAGE 540), TO SERVE

* Heat the lard in a Dutch oven (casserole) over medium heat, add the scallion (spring onion) and ginger, and stir-fry for 1 minute until fragrant. Add the fish belly and pan-fry over low heat until slightly brown on both sides. Add the wine, soy sauce, sugar, and 1 cup (8 fl oz/250 ml) water and bring to a boil. Reduce to low heat and simmer, uncovered, for 10 minutes until the sauce thickens or until cooked through.
* Mix the cornstarch (cornflour) with 1 tablespoon water in a small bowl and stir this mixture into the sauce. Bring to a boil to thicken the sauce and toss until the fish belly slices are well coated in sauce. Stir in the sesame oil and transfer to a plate. Serve with rice.

FISH & SEAFOOD

冬瓜炆釀豆卜
STUFFED TOFU PUFFS
WITH WINTER MELON

REGION: HONG KONG
PREPARATION TIME: 15 MINUTES, PLUS
  15 MINUTES SOAKING TIME
COOKING TIME: 20 MINUTES
SERVES: 4

* To make the filling, soak the mushrooms and dried shrimp in separate bowls of hot water for 15 minutes, or until softened. Remove and discard the mushroom stems, and chop both the mushrooms and shrimp.
* Put the dace into a large bowl. Add the salt and white pepper and stir with chopsticks in one direction until the dace becomes elastic and gummy. Add the mushrooms, shrimp, and cornstarch (cornflour) and mix well. Use a spoon to stuff each tofu puff half with the dace filling.
* Heat 1 tablespoon oil in a wok or large skillet (frying pan) over low heat. Place stuffed tofu puff, filling side facing down, in the wok, and pan-fry for 3–4 minutes until golden brown. Transfer the tofu puff to a plate.
* Heat the remaining 1 tablespoon oil in the wok, add the winter melon, salt, and 6 tablespoons water, and bring to a boil. Reduce to medium heat and simmer, covered, for 10–12 minutes until the winter melon becomes translucent.
* Add the tofu puffs and simmer, uncovered, for 3 minutes. Mix the cornstarch with 1 tablespoon water in a small bowl and stir this mixture, along with the scallions, into the wok. Bring to a boil, stirring, for 30 seconds to thicken the sauce. Serve with rice.

- 5 OZ/150 G TOFU PUFFS, HALVED
- 2 TABLESPOONS VEGETABLE OIL
- 1 LB/450 G WINTER MELON, PEELED AND CUT INTO CHUNKS
- 1 TEASPOON SALT
- 1 TEASPOON CORNSTARCH (CORNFLOUR)
- 2 SCALLIONS (SPRING ONIONS), CUT INTO 2-INCH/5-CM LENGTHS
- STEAMED RICE (PAGE 540), TO SERVE

  FOR THE DACE FILLING:
- 2 DRIED SHIITAKE MUSHROOMS
- 6 DRIED SHRIMP
- 5 OZ/150 G UNSALTED DACE FISH OR UNCOOKED SHRIMP (PRAWNS), FINELY CHOPPED
- ¼ TEASPOON SALT
- ¼ TEASPOON GROUND WHITE PEPPER
- ½ TEASPOON CORNSTARCH (CORNFLOUR)

红糟鱼
FISH IN RED DISTILLED GRAIN SAUCE

- 1 (1 LB 5-OZ/600-G) GRASS CARP OR ANY WHITE FISH, CLEANED, FILLETED, AND CUT INTO ¾-INCH/2-CM SLICES
- 3 TABLESPOONS VEGETABLE OIL
- 1 TEASPOON FINELY CHOPPED GINGER
- 2 DRIED CHILES
- 2 TABLESPOONS RED DISTILLED GRAIN SAUCE
- 1 TEASPOON FISH SAUCE
- 1 TABLESPOON SHAOXING WINE
- 1 TABLESPOON GRANULATED SUGAR
- STEAMED RICE (PAGE 540), TO SERVE

* Pat the fish dry with paper towels.
* Heat the oil in a large skillet (frying pan) over high heat, add the fish, and fry for about 10 seconds. Reduce to medium heat and cook for another 3–4 minutes until the fish is browned on both sides. Transfer to a shallow bowl.
* Pour out most of the oil, leaving about 1 tablespoon in the wok. Add the ginger and dried chiles and stir-fry over medium-high heat for 1 minute until fragrant. Add the distilled grain and fish sauces, wine, sugar, and about 2 cups (16 fl oz/475 ml) water and bring to a boil. Reduce to low heat and simmer for 10–15 minutes until the sauce has reduced by half. Pour over the fish, making sure each piece of fish is coated generously with the sauce. Cover and seal with plastic wrap (clingfilm) and marinate in the refrigerator for 8 hours.
* When ready to serve, place the fish on a heatproof plate and put into a collapsible pot or bamboo steamer over a pot of boiling water. Steam, covered, for 5–6 minutes, or until cooked through. Serve with rice.

干煎鱼
PAN-FRIED MANDARIN FISH

- 1 (1-LB/450-G) MANDARIN FISH, CLEANED AND RINSED
- ½ TEASPOON SALT
- 1 CHINESE CHIVE, CUT INTO ¾-INCH/1.5-CM LENGTHS
- 1 TABLESPOON PICKLED WINE SAUCE
- 1 TEASPOON SHAOXING WINE
- ½ TEASPOON GRANULATED SUGAR
- 1 TABLESPOON CORNSTARCH (CORNFLOUR)
- 1 EGG, LIGHTLY BEATEN
- 4 TABLESPOONS VEGETABLE OIL
- STEAMED RICE (PAGE 540), TO SERVE

* Pat the fish dry with paper towels. Use a sharp knife to score both sides of the fish and rub the salt evenly into the cuts. Marinate for 30 minutes.
* Combine the chives, pickled wine sauce, wine, and sugar in a bowl and mix well. Set aside.
* Lightly dredge the fish with the cornstarch (cornflour) and brush with the beaten egg.
* Heat the oil in a large skillet (frying pan) over high heat, add the fish, and pan-fry for about 30 seconds. Reduce to low heat and pan-fry for 5 minutes on each side until golden brown and cooked through.
* Pour in the sauce, increase the high heat, and cook for about 15 seconds. Turn the fish over and cook for another 15 seconds until the fish is coated with sauce on both sides. Transfer the fish to a serving plate and serve with rice.

鱼咬羊

LAMB-STUFFED
FISH

REGION: ANHUI
PREPARATION TIME: 20 MINUTES,
   PLUS 10 MINUTES MARINATING TIME
COOKING TIME: 50 MINUTES
SERVES: 4

The Chinese character for "fresh" (鲜) means both fresh and tasty. It is a combination of two separate characters: the left is "fish" (鱼) and the right is "lamb" (羊). Ancient Chinese believed that combining fish and lamb was the ultimate combination in taste.

* Make a ½-inch/1-cm-deep cut across the vent to sever the intestines. Remove the intestines by inserting two chopsticks through the fish's mouth and grabbing the intestinal matter with the tips of the chopsticks. Twist the chopsticks and, keeping a tight grip, pull the intestinal tract out through the fish's mouth. Rinse thoroughly with cold water.
* Combine the ginger juice, soy sauce, and 1 teaspoon sugar in a bowl. Add the lamb and marinate for 10 minutes.
* Heat 1 tablespoon oil in a wok over high heat, add the lamb, and stir-fry for about 1 minute. Add a third of the ginger slices, ½ teaspoon salt, 1 tablespoon wine, and 1 cup (8 fl oz/250 ml) water and bring to a boil. Reduce to low heat and simmer, covered, for 15 minutes. Turn off the heat. Use chopsticks to stuff the strips of lamb into the fish belly through the mouth. Reserve the sauce.
* Heat the remaining 2 tablespoons oil in a clean wok, add the fish, and pan-fry for 4–5 minutes on each until golden brown and cooked through.
* Transfer the fish to a Dutch oven (casserole), add the remaining ginger, scallion (spring onion), the star anise, the remaining 2 teaspoons sugar, 2½ teaspoons salt, 1 tablespoon wine, the chicken broth (stock), and the reserved sauce, and bring to a boil. Reduce to low heat and simmer for about 30 minutes, or until the sauce thickens and the fish is cooked through. Discard the star anise, ginger, and scallion. Serve with rice.

NOTE:
This recipe can be made with ground (minced) lamb and we recommend using a spoon, rather than chopsticks, to stuff it.

- 1 (14-OZ/400-G) MANDARIN FISH, SCALED AND GILLS REMOVED, BUT NOT GUTTED
- 1 TEASPOON GINGER JUICE
- 1 TABLESPOON LIGHT SOY SAUCE
- 1 TABLESPOON GRANULATED SUGAR
- 1 (7-OZ/200-G) LEG OF LAMB, CUT INTO ½ × ¾ × 1½-INCH/1 × 2 × 4-CM STRIPS (SEE NOTE)
- 3 TABLESPOONS VEGETABLE OIL
- ½ OZ/15 G GINGER (ABOUT 1-INCH/ 2.5-CM-LENGTH PIECE), SLICED
- 1 TABLESPOON SALT
- 2 TABLESPOONS SHAOXING WINE
- 1 SCALLION (SPRING ONION), KNOTTED
- 1 STAR ANISE
- 2 CUPS (16 FL OZ/475 ML) CHICKEN BROTH (STOCK, PAGE 90)
- STEAMED RICE (PAGE 540), TO SERVE

REGION: CHAOZHOU
PREPARATION TIME: 10 MINUTES,
  PLUS 15–20 MINUTES MARINATING TIME
COOKING TIME: 8–10 MINUTES
SERVES: 4

银鱼烙
NOODLEFISH
PANCAKE

- 9 OZ/250 G NOODLEFISH OR
  WHITEBAIT, CLEANED AND RINSED
- 1 TEASPOON SALT
- 4 TEASPOONS CORNSTARCH
  (CORNFLOUR)
- 4 EGGS, BEATEN
- ¼ TEASPOON GROUND WHITE PEPPER
- ¼ TEASPOON SESAME OIL
- 2¾ OZ/75 G YELLOW CHIVES, CUT INTO
  ½-INCH/1-CM LENGTHS
- 2 TABLESPOONS VEGETABLE OIL
- STEAMED RICE (PAGE 540), TO SERVE

* Combine the fish and ½ teaspoon salt in a small bowl, stir, and marinate for 15–20 minutes.
* Mix the cornstarch (cornflour) with 2 tablespoons water in another bowl. Set aside for 5 minutes, or until the starch settles at the bottom of the bowl, then pour out the water to leave a wet starch.
* Combine the eggs, white pepper, remaining ½ teaspoon salt, sesame oil, and wet starch in a large bowl. Stir in the fish and yellow chives to form a batter.
* Heat the vegetable oil in a nonstick flat skillet (frying pan) over medium heat, add the batter, and fry for 4–5 minutes on each side until golden brown and cooked through. Transfer to a plate and serve with rice.

REGION: JIANGXI
PREPARATION TIME: 10 MINUTES
COOKING TIME: 5 MINUTES
SERVES: 4

葱白鱼卷
SAUTÉED FISH ROLLS

- 1 (1-LB/500-G) STRIPED SNAKEHEAD
  FISH OR SOLE, CLEANED AND FILLETED
- 1 EGG WHITE, BEATEN
- 2 TEASPOONS CORNSTARCH
  (CORNFLOUR)
- ½ TEASPOON SALT
- 2 CUPS (16 FL OZ/475 ML)
- VEGETABLE OIL
- ¼ OZ/10 G GINGER (ABOUT ¾-INCH/
  2-CM-LENGTH PIECE), CHOPPED
- 4 SCALLIONS (SPRING ONIONS), CUT
  INTO 2-INCH/5-CM LENGTHS
- 1 TEASPOON GRANULATED SUGAR
- 1 TABLESPOON SHAOXING WINE
- 2 TABLESPOONS CHICKEN BROTH
  (STOCK, PAGE 90)
- 1 TEASPOON WHITE VINEGAR
- ¼ TEASPOON GROUND WHITE PEPPER
- STEAMED RICE (PAGE 540), TO SERVE

* Place the fish on a cutting board, skin side facing down. Use a sharp knife to make slashes in a crisscross pattern, cutting two-thirds of the way into the fillet and spacing the slashes ¼ inch/5 mm apart. Cut the fish into 1¼ × 2-inch/ 3 × 5-cm pieces and put them into a bowl.
* Combine the egg white, 1 teaspoon cornstarch (cornflour) and ¼ teaspoon salt. Mix well and add to the bowl.
* Heat the oil in a wok to 265°F/130°C. Add the fish pieces, disperse them using chopsticks, and fry for about 1 minute until they begin to curl. Use a slotted spoon to remove the fish from the oil and drain on paper towels.
* Pour out most of the oil, leaving about 1 tablespoon in the wok. Heat the oil over high heat, add the ginger and scallions (spring onions), and stir-fry for 30 seconds until fragrant. Add the remaining ¼ teaspoon salt, the sugar, wine, and chicken broth (stock) and bring to a boil. Mix the remaining 1 teaspoon cornstarch with 1 tablespoon water, then stir this mixture into the wok. Bring to a boil, stirring, for about 30 seconds to thicken the sauce.
* Add the fish to the sauce, stir in the vinegar and white pepper, and toss for about 30 seconds. Transfer to a serving plate and serve with rice.

醋溜鲤鱼
FISH IN SWEET AND SOUR SAUCE

REGION: SHANDONG
PREPARATION TIME: 10 MINUTES
COOKING TIME: 15 MINUTES
SERVES: 4–6

* Use a sharp knife to make 3–4 deep cuts (to the bone) on each side of the fish, at a 45 degree angle toward the head.
* Combine the cornstarch (cornflour) with 4 tablespoons water in a large shallow plate and mix well.
* Rub the salt into the fish. Stir the cornstarch mixture, then dip the fish into it and coat it entirely.
* Heat 3 cups (25 fl oz/750 ml) oil in a wok or deep saucepan over to 300°F/150°C, or until a cube of bread browns in 1½ minutes. Hold the fish by the tail and carefully slide it, head first, into the hot oil. Deep-fry the fish for 10 minutes until slightly brown and crispy on the outside and cooked through. Use a slotted spoon and carefully transfer the fish to a serving plate. Keep warm.
* Heat the remaining 2 tablespoons oil in a clean wok, add the garlic, ginger, and scallions (spring onions), and stir-fry over medium heat for about 30 seconds. Add the sauce ingredients and ½ cup (4 fl oz/120 ml) water, then bring to a boil. Cook the sauce for about 1 minute until thickened. Pour the sauce over the fish and serve with rice.

- 1 (1 LB 10½-OZ/750-G) CARP, CLEANED AND RINSED
- 4 TABLESPOONS CORNSTARCH (CORNFLOUR)
- ½ TEASPOON SALT
- 3 CUPS (25 FL OZ/750 ML) PLUS 2 TABLESPOONS VEGETABLE OIL
- 2 CLOVES GARLIC, CHOPPED
- ⅛ OZ/5 G GINGER (ABOUT ½-INCH/ 1-CM-LENGTH PIECE), CHOPPED
- 2 SCALLIONS (SPRING ONIONS), CHOPPED
- STEAMED RICE (PAGE 540), TO SERVE

FOR THE SWEET AND SOUR SAUCE:
- 6 TABLESPOONS GRANULATED SUGAR
- 4 TABLESPOONS WHITE VINEGAR
- 2 TABLESPOONS KETCHUP
- 1 TABLESPOON SHAOXING WINE
- 1 TABLESPOON LIGHT SOY SAUCE
- 2 TABLESPOONS CORNSTARCH (CORNFLOUR)

REGION: SICHUAN
PREPARATION TIME: 15 MINUTES,
    PLUS 20 MINUTES SOAKING TIME
COOKING TIME: 25 MINUTES
SERVES: 4
📷 PAGE 171

大千干烧鱼
FISH IN CHILI
SAUCE

- 3 DRIED BLACK MUSHROOMS
- 1 DRIED BLACK FUNGUS
- 1 (1¾-LB/800-G) CARP, CLEANED AND RINSED
- 1 TEASPOON SALT, PLUS EXTRA TO TASTE
- 1 TABLESPOON CORNSTARCH (CORNFLOUR)
- 4¼ CUPS (34 FL OZ/1 LITER) VEGETABLE OIL
- 2 CLOVES GARLIC, CHOPPED
- 2 TEASPOONS GRATED GINGER
- 5 OZ/150 G GROUND (MINCED) PORK
- 1 TABLESPOON RICE WINE
- 10 PICKLED RED CHILES, CHOPPED
- 2 TABLESPOONS PIXIAN CHILI BEAN PASTE, CHOPPED
- 1 TABLESPOON LIGHT SOY SAUCE
- 2 TEASPOONS GRANULATED SUGAR
- ½-1 TABLESPOON BLACK OR BALSAMIC VINEGAR
- ½ TEASPOON GROUND WHITE PEPPER, PLUS EXTRA TO TASTE
- 4 SCALLIONS (SPRING ONIONS), CHOPPED
- 1 RED CHILE, SLICED, TO GARNISH (OPTIONAL)
- 1 TEASPOON SESAME OIL

* Put the mushrooms and black fungus in 2 separate bowls and soak in cold water for at least 20 minutes, or until softened. Remove the mushrooms, squeeze dry, and discard the stems. Dice, then set aside. Tear the black fungus into small pieces.
* Meanwhile, use a sharp knife to make 5–6 slashes on each side of the fish. Pat the fish dry using paper towels and sprinkle with the salt. Marinate for 10 minutes. Lightly dredge both sides of the fish with cornstarch (cornflour).
* Heat the 4¼ cups (34 fl oz/1 liter) oil in a wok or large skillet (frying pan) to 350°F/180°C, or until a cube of bread browns in 30 seconds. Add the fish and deep-fry for 4–5 minutes until golden brown and crispy. Use a slotted spoon to carefully remove the fish from the oil and drain on paper towels.
* Add the garlic and ginger to the remaining oil in the wok, add pork, and stir-fry over medium heat for 1 minute until fragrant. Sprinkle in the wine, then stir in the pickled chiles, chili bean paste, mushrooms, fungus, soy sauce, and sugar. Add 1½ cups (12 fl oz/350 ml) boiling water and bring to a boil. Add the fish, reduce to medium heat, cover, and simmer for about 5 minutes until cooked through. Flip over and cook for another 5 minutes until cooked through. Transfer the fish to a serving plate.
* Bring the sauce in the wok to a boil. Simmer over medium heat, uncovered, for 2–3 minutes until the sauce has reduced. Finally, stir in the vinegar, white pepper, scallions (spring onions), and sesame oil. Pour the sauce over the fish, garnish with scallions and red chile, if using.

FISH IN CHILI SAUCE

REGION: SHUNDE
PREPARATION TIME: 40 MINUTES,
   PLUS 25 MINUTES MARINATING TIME
COOKING TIME: 30 MINUTES
SERVES: 4

煎酿鲮鱼
STUFFED
DACE

- 3 DRIED BLACK MUSHROOMS
- 1 TABLESPOON DRIED SHRIMP
- 1 (14-OZ/400-G) DACE FISH,
  CLEANED AND RINSED
- ½ TEASPOON SALT
- ½ TEASPOON GRANULATED SUGAR
- ¼ TEASPOON GROUND WHITE PEPPER
- 1 OZ/25 G PORK FATBACK,
  FINELY CHOPPED
- 1 STALK CILANTRO (CORIANDER),
  FINELY CHOPPED
- 2 SCALLIONS (SPRING ONIONS),
  FINELY CHOPPED
- 2 TEASPOONS CORNSTARCH
  (CORNFLOUR)
- 1 TEASPOON SESAME OIL
- 3 TABLESPOONS VEGETABLE OiL
- STEAMED RICE (PAGE 540), TO SERVE

* Put the mushrooms and dried shrimp in 2 separate bowls, cover with cold water, and soak for 20 minutes, or until softened. Remove and discard the stems of the mushrooms and cut into small pieces. Finely chop the shrimp and set them aside with the mushrooms.

* Use a sharp knife to make a cut along the fish's stomach from the head to the tail. Insert your fingers in between the fish skin and meat and slowly work inward to separate the flesh from the skin of the entire fish. Use a pair of scissors to cut one end of the fish flesh and bone from the head, then repeat with the tail.

* Taking care not to tear the skins, turn the fish skin inside out and cut along the back to separate the flesh completely from the skin. The fish head and tail should still be attached to the skin. Fillet the fish and discard the bone.

* Put the fish fillets into a food processor and process until completely pulverized. (The thinner the slices, the finer the bones will be so it is essential to cut as fine as possible.)

* To make the filling, put the dace paste in a large bowl, add the salt, sugar, white pepper, and 4 teaspoons water, and stir with chopsticks in one direction until gluey. Pick up the dace patty and smash it against the bottom of the bowl 5–6 times to increase its gumminess.

* Add the pork fatback, mushrooms, dried shrimp, cilantro (coriander), scallions (spring onions), and 1 teaspoon cornstarch (cornflour) and stir in one direction until fully blended. Add the sesame oil and 1 tablespoon vegetable oil, and mix well.

* Place the fish skin on a plate, spread open the skin, and use kitchen shears to trim the sharp bones protruding from the back inside the skin. Dry the inside of the skin with paper towels and dredge with ½ teaspoon cornstarch (cornflour).

* Use your hands to stuff the fish skin with the filling and smooth out with your fingers.

* Pull the 2 sides of the fish toward the center and press gently to restore the fish's original shape. Dredge the skin of the fish with the remaining ½ teaspoon cornstarch.

* Heat the remaining 2 tablespoons oil in a wok or large skillet (frying pan) over low heat. Add the fish, stomach facing down, and fry for 3–4 minutes until golden brown. Use a slotted spoon to carefully remove the fish from the oil and put on a cutting board. Cut the fish into thick chunks crosswise and return them to the skillet. Fry for 2 minutes, flip them over, and fry for another 2 minutes until golden brown and cooked through. Transfer to a plate and serve with rice.

五柳鱼
SWEET AND SOUR
FISH BELLY

REGION: HAKKA
PREPARATION TIME: 10 MINUTES
COOKING TIME: 15 MINUTES
SERVES: 4

* Rinse the fish belly in cold water and remove the black membrane on the flesh.
* Fill a wok or large skillet (frying pan) with water, add the ginger slices, wine, and ½ teaspoon salt, and bring to a boil over high heat. Turn off the heat, gently lower the fish, skin side facing up, into the hot water, cover the wok, and stand for about 10 minutes until the fish is cooked through. Use a slotted spoon to carefully remove the fish from the oil and drain on paper towels. Keep warm.
* Wipe the wok with paper towels. Add ½ tablespoon oil, the pickled vegetables, vinegar, fish sauce, sugar, and the remaining ½ teaspoon salt and bring to a boil.
* Mix the cornstarch (cornflour) with 1 tablespoon water in a small bowl and stir this mixture into the wok. Bring to a boil, stirring, for 30 seconds to thicken the sauce. Stir in the sesame oil, pour the sauce over the fish, then top with scallions (spring onions), and chile.
* Heat 2 tablespoons oil in a skillet (frying pan) over high heat. Drizzle the hot oil over the fish and serve with rice.

- 1 (1 LB 5-OZ/600-G) GRASS CARP BELLY OR ANY FRESHWATER FISH
- 3 SLICES GINGER, PLUS ¾ OZ/20 G (ABOUT 1-INCH/2.5-CM-LENGTH PIECE), SHREDDED
- 1 TABLESPOON RICE WINE
- 1 TEASPOON SALT
- 2½ TABLESPOONS VEGETABLE OIL
- ⅔ CUP (7 OZ/200 G) PICKLED VEGETABLES, SHREDDED
- 2 TABLESPOONS RED VINEGAR
- 2 TEASPOONS FISH SAUCE
- 1 TEASPOON GRANULATED SUGAR
- 1 TEASPOON CORNSTARCH (CORNFLOUR)
- 1 RED CHILE, SHREDDED
- ¼ TEASPOON SESAME OIL
- 4 SCALLIONS (SPRING ONIONS), SHREDDED

蒜子炆鲶鱼
CATFISH WITH GARLIC

REGION: GUANGDONG
PREPARATION TIME: 15 MINUTES
COOKING TIME: 15 MINUTES
SERVES: 6

* Put the fish, ginger and wine in a bowl and marinate for 10 minutes. Mix in the cornstarch (cornflour).
* Heat the oil in a wok or deep saucepan to 285°F/140°C, or until a cube of bread turns golden in 2 minutes. Add the garlic and deep-fry for 2–3 minutes, or until golden brown. Use a slotted spoon to carefully remove the garlic from the oil and drain on paper towels.
* Heat oil again to 300°F/150°C, or until a cube of bread browns in 1½ minutes. Add the fish, in batches, and deep-fry for 3 minutes until golden brown. Use a slotted spoon to carefully remove the fish and drain on paper towels.
* Pour out most of the oil, leaving about 2 tablespoons in the wok. Add the ginger and bean paste, stir in the roast pork, soy sauce, salt, sugar, and 1 cup (8 fl oz/250 ml) water, then bring to a boil over high heat. Add the fish, bring back to a boil, reduce the heat to low and simmer for 8 minutes, or until the sauce thickens. Stir in the scallions (spring onions) and drizzle over the sesame oil. Transfer to a plate and serve with rice.

- 1 (2-LB/900-G) CATFISH, FILLETED AND CUT INTO 1¼-INCH/3-CM CHUNKS
- 1 TABLESPOON GINGER JUICE
- 1 TABLESPOON RICE WINE
- 2 TABLESPOONS CORNSTARCH (CORNFLOUR)
- 2 CUPS (16 FL OZ/475 ML) VEGETABLE OIL
- 5 OZ/150 G ROAST PORK, CUT INTO ½-INCH/1.5-CM SLICES
- 1 BULB GARLIC, PEELED
- ¾ OZ/20 G GINGER (ABOUT 1-INCH/ 2.5-CM-LENGTH PIECE), SLICED
- 1 TABLESPOON BEAN PASTE
- 1 TABLESPOON LIGHT SOY SAUCE
- 1 TEASPOON SALT
- ½ TABLESPOON GRANULATED SUGAR
- 2 SCALLIONS (SPRING ONIONS), CUT INTO LENGTHS
- ½ TEASPOON SESAME OIL
- STEAMED RICE (PAGE 540), TO SERVE

REGION: SHANGHAI
PREPARATION TIME: 5 MINUTES,
  PLUS 15 MINUTES MARINATING TIME
COOKING TIME: 25 MINUTES
SERVES: 4
📷 PAGE 175

葱燔黄鱼
CORVINA WITH SCALLIONS

- 4 CORVINA (YELLOW CROAKER) OR SEA BASS FILLETS, CLEANED AND RINSED
- 1 TEASPOON GRANULATED SUGAR
- 2 TABLESPOONS LIGHT SOY SAUCE
- 1 TABLESPOON GINGER JUICE
- 4 TABLESPOONS VEGETABLE OIL
- 6 SCALLIONS (SPRING ONIONS), CUT INTO 2-INCH/5-CM LENGTHS AND STEMS FLATTENED
- ⅛ OZ/5 G GINGER (ABOUT ½-INCH/ 1-CM-LENGTH PIECE), SHREDDED
- 1 TABLESPOON SHAOXING WINE
- ½ TEASPOON SESAME OIL
- CILANTRO (CORIANDER), TO GARNISH (OPTIONAL)
- STEAMED RICE (PAGE 540), TO SERVE

* Use a sharp knife to make 3 slashes on each side of the fish. Combine the sugar, soy sauce, and ginger juice in a small bowl, add the fish, and marinate for 15 minutes.
* Pat the fish dry with paper towels and set the marinade aside.
* Heat 3 tablespoons vegetable oil in a wok or large skillet (frying pan) over medium-high heat, add the fish, and fry over low heat for 5 minutes. Flip over and fry for another 5 minutes until both sides are golden. Transfer to a plate.
* Heat remaining 1 tablespoon oil in the wok over medium heat. Add the scallions (spring onions), shredded ginger, and fish, then sprinkle the wine along the inside of the wok. Add the marinade sauce and ⅔ cup (5 fl oz/150 ml) water, cover, and bring to a boil. Reduce to low heat and simmer for 5 minutes. Flip the fish over and simmer, covered, for another 5 minutes, or until cooked through. Remove the lid, drizzle over the sesame oil, and increase to high heat. Simmer for 2-3 minutes, uncovered, to reduce the sauce. Transfer to a plate, garnish with cilantro (coriander), if using, and serve with rice.

酒煎鱼
PAN-FRIED FISH IN WINE

- 1 (1 LB 10½-OZ/750-G) CARP, CLEANED AND RINSED
- 2 TEASPOONS SALT
- 4 TABLESPOONS LARD
- 1 OZ/25 G GINGER (ABOUT 2-INCH/ 5-CM-LENGTH PIECE), SLICED
- 4 SCALLIONS (SPRING ONIONS), CUT INTO 2-INCH/5-CM LENGTHS
- 1 TEASPOON LIGHT SOY SAUCE
- ¼ TEASPOON GROUND WHITE PEPPER
- 6 TABLESPOONS SHAOXING WINE
- 1 TEASPOON CORNSTARCH (CORNFLOUR)
- STEAMED RICE (PAGE 540), TO SERVE

* Use a sharp knife to make 3-4 shallow cuts on each side of the fish. Rub the salt into the fish, then place it in a dish and marinate for 10 minutes. Rinse, drain, and pat dry with paper towels.
* Heat the lard in a wok over medium heat, add the fish, and cook for 4-5 minutes on each side, or until lightly browned. Add the ginger, scallions (spring onions), soy sauce, white pepper, and 4 tablespoons wine and bring to a boil. Reduce to low heat, cover, and simmer for 5 minutes. Turn the fish over and simmer for another 5 minutes, or until cooked through. Transfer the fish to a serving plate, leaving the sauce in the wok.
* Mix the cornstarch (cornflour) with the remaining 2 tablespoons wine, then stir the mixture into the wok. Bring to a boil, stirring, for about 30 seconds to thicken the sauce. Drizzle the sauce over the fish. Serve with rice.

CORVINA WITH SCALLIONS

芋丝鲮鱼球
DACE BALLS
WITH TARO

- 1 DRIED TANGERINE PEEL
- 3 DRIED BLACK MUSHROOMS
- 1 (1 LB 5-OZ/600-G) FRESH DACE FISH, CLEANED, SKINNED, AND FILLETED
- ½ TEASPOON SALT
- ¼ TEASPOON GROUND WHITE PEPPER
- 2 BUNCHES CILANTRO (CORIANDER), CHOPPED
- 7 OZ/200 G TARO, SHREDDED
- 2 TABLESPOONS CORNSTARCH (CORNFLOUR)
- 3 CUPS (25 FL OZ/750 ML) VEGETABLE OIL

Fish paste—made with a small fish known as dace—is used extensively in Asian cooking. I've provided a recipe below for making it but if you're pressed for time, ready-made fish paste can be purchased from specialty Asian shops. You'll need about 1 lb 2 oz/500 g.

* Soak the dried tangerine peel in warm water for 1 hour to rehydrate.
* Meanwhile, put the mushrooms into a bowl, cover with cold water, and soak for at least 20 minutes, or until softened. Remove the mushrooms, squeeze dry, and discard the stems. Finely chop.
* Put the fish into a food processor and pulverize into a paste. Transfer the fish paste to a large bowl, add the salt, white pepper, and 2 tablespoons water, then stir with chopsticks in one direction until gummy.
* Drain, slice, and chop finely the tangerine peel. Stir the mushrooms, dried tangerine peel, and cilantro (coriander) into the fish paste.
* Mix the taro, the cornstarch (cornflour), and 6 tablespoons water in a separate bowl. Using wet hands, form the fish mixture into golf-ball-size balls, then roll them in the taro mixture. Set aside.
* Heat the oil in a wok or deep saucepan to 285°F/140°C, or until a cube of bread turns golden in 2 minutes. Add the dace balls, in batches if needed, and deep-fry for about 3–4 minutes, or until golden brown and cooked through. Use a slotted spoon to carefully remove the dace balls from the oil and drain on paper towels.

刘公香鲤鱼
DEEP-FRIED CARP

REGION: ANHUI
PREPARATION TIME: 10 MINUTES,
    PLUS 1 HOUR MARINATING TIME
COOKING TIME: 5 MINUTES
SERVES: 4

The scales on a carp are both soft and rich in fat. It can even be consumed together with the skin and flesh after it's been deep-fried.

* Pat the fish dry with paper towels, if necessary.
* Mix the salt, chili powder, cumin, cilantro (coriander), and wine in a shallow dish. Rub the fish with this mixture, marinate for 1 hour (no need to refrigerate). Drain the marinade from the dish and pat dry with paper towels.
* Heat the oil in a wok or large skillet (frying pan) over medium-high heat to 340°F/170°C, or until a cube of bread browns in 45 seconds. Hold the fish by the tail and carefully slide it, head first, into the hot oil. Deep-fry for about 5 minutes, or until the skin is golden brown and crispy and the fish is cooked through. Use a slotted spoon to carefully remove the fish from the oil and drain on paper towels.
* Transfer the fish to a serving plate. Serve with the scallions (spring onions) and the Tianmianjiang on the side.

- 1 (1 LB 2-OZ/500-G) CARP, CLEANED BUT NOT SCALED
- ½ TEASPOON SALT
- ½ TEASPOON CHILI POWDER
- ¼ TEASPOON GROUND CUMIN
- 1 STALK CILANTRO (CORIANDER), CHOPPED
- 1 TABLESPOON SHAOXING WINE
- 3 CUPS (25 FL OZ/750 ML) VEGETABLE OIL
- 2 SCALLIONS (SPRING ONIONS), CUT INTO 2-INCH/5-CM LENGTHS AND SHREDDED
- 2 TABLESPOONS TIANMIANJIANG

喜洲鱼
XIZHOU-STYLE BRAISED FISH

REGION: YUNNAN
PREPARATION TIME: 10 MINUTES,
    PLUS 20 MINUTES MARINATING TIME
COOKING TIME: 30 MINUTES
SERVES: 4

* Pat the fish dry with paper towels and transfer to a dish. Combine the soy sauce, wine, salt, fennel seeds, and star anise in a bowl, pour over the fish, and marinate for 20 minutes.
* Meanwhile, Put the mushrooms into a bowl, cover with cold water, and soak for at least 20 minutes, or until softened. Remove the mushrooms, squeeze dry, and discard the stems. Slice and set aside.
* Heat the oil in a wok or large skillet (frying pan), add the garlic and stir-fry over medium heat for 1–2 minutes until lightly brown and fragrant. Stir in the ginger, ham, and mushrooms. Add the chicken broth (stock) and bring to a boil. Add the fish together with its marinade, return to a boil, reduce to medium-low heat and simmer, covered, for 20 minutes, or until the fish is cooked through. Transfer to a plate, sprinkle with the white pepper, and drizzle over the Sichuan chili oil. Adjust the seasoning to taste.

- 1 (2¼-LB/1-KG) CARP, CLEANED AND RINSED
- 1 TABLESPOON LIGHT SOY SAUCE
- 2 TEASPOONS RICE WINE
- 1 TEASPOON SALT, PLUS EXTRA TO TASTE
- ½ TEASPOON GROUND FENNEL SEEDS
- ½ TEASPOON GROUND STAR ANISE
- 4 DRIED BLACK MUSHROOMS
- 2 TABLESPOONS VEGETABLE OIL
- 6 CLOVES GARLIC
- 1 OZ/25 G GINGER (ABOUT 2-INCH/ 5-CM-LENGTH PIECE), SLICED
- 2 OZ/50 G YUNNAN CURED HAM, CUT INTO 1½ × ¾-INCH/4 × 2-CM SLICES
- 2 CUPS (16 FL OZ/475 ML) CHICKEN BROTH (STOCK, PAGE 90)
- ¼ TEASPOON GROUND WHITE PEPPER
- 2 TABLESPOONS SICHUAN CHILI OIL

双豉蒸金钱鳝
EEL WITH BEAN SAUCE

- 1 (1-LB/450-G) FRESHWATER EEL
- 1 TEASPOON SALT
- 1 TEASPOONS CORNSTARCH (CORNFLOUR)
- 1 DRIED TANGERINE PEEL
- 1 TABLESPOON FERMENTED BLACK BEAN, RINSED AND CHOPPED
- 3 CLOVES GARLIC, FINELY CHOPPED
- 1 TEASPOON GRANULATED SUGAR
- ½ TABLESPOON LIGHT SOY SAUCE
- ½ TABLESPOON BEAN PASTE
- ½ TABLESPOON SHAOXING WINE
- ½ TABLESPOON GINGER JUICE
- 3 TABLESPOONS VEGETABLE OIL
- 2 RED CHILES, SEEDED AND CHOPPED
- 3 TABLESPOONS CHOPPED SCALLIONS (SPRING ONIONS)
- STEAMED RICE (PAGE 540), TO SERVE

* Using a sharp knife, cut off and discard the head of the eel. Cut the eel open down the entire length and remove the spine. Sprinkle with the salt and the cornstarch (cornflour) and rub off the mucus from the skin. Rinse under cold running water and drain. Dry and refrigerate for 1 hour.
* Meanwhile, soak the dried tangerine peel in cold water for 10 minutes to soften, then drain and chop.
* In a separate bowl, combine the dried tangerine peel, black beans, garlic, sugar, soy sauce, bean paste, wine, ginger juice, and 1 tablespoon oil into a paste. Set aside.
* Wrap a cloth towel around one end of the eel to prevent it from slipping and cut it into ½-inch/1-cm-thick slices. Spread the eel on a heatproof plate and spread the paste evenly on each piece. Top with the chiles. Place the plate in a collapsible pot or bamboo steamer over a pot of boiling water. Steam, covered, for 10–12 minutes, or until cooked through.
* Heat 2 tablespoons remaining oil in a small frying pan and drizzle it over the eel. Garnish with chopped scallions (spring onions) and serve with rice.

豉椒黄鳝片
EEL IN BLACK BEAN SAUCE

- 1 (1 LB 5-OZ/600-G) RICE FIELD EEL
- 1½ TEASPOONS SALT
- 1 TEASPOON CORNSTARCH (CORNFLOUR)
- 1½ TABLESPOONS FERMENTED BLACK BEANS, RINSED AND CHOPPED
- 3 CLOVES GARLIC, CHOPPED
- 1 TEASPOON GRANULATED SUGAR
- 2 TABLESPOONS VEGETABLE OIL
- 1 RED CHILE, SEEDED AND SHREDDED
- ½ RED BELL PEPPER, SEEDED AND CHOPPED
- ½ GREEN BELL PEPPER, SEEDED AND CHOPPED
- 1 TEASPOON SHAOXING WINE
- 1 TABLESPOON LIGHT SOY SAUCE
- 1 TABLESPOON SESAME OIL
- ¼ TEASPOON GROUND WHITE PEPPER
- STEAMED RICE (PAGE 540), TO SERVE

* Using a sharp knife, cut off and discard the head of the eel. Cut the eel open down the entire length and remove the spine. Sprinkle with 1 teaspoon salt and the cornstarch (cornflour) and rub off the mucus from the skin. Rinse under cold running water and drain. Cut the eel lengthwise into 2 pieces, then cut each into 2-inch/5-cm-long pieces.
* Bring a large saucepan of water to a boil. Add the eel and disperse the pieces with chopsticks, then boil for 10 seconds. Turn off the heat. Drain and rinse.
* Combine the black beans, garlic, and sugar in a small bowl.
* Heat the vegetable oil in a wok or large skillet (frying pan), add the chile and black bean sauce and stir-fry over high heat for 30 seconds. Add the peppers and eel and stir-fry for another minute until the eel looks dry. Add the wine, soy sauce, and remaining ½ teaspoon salt and stir-fry rapidly for another 30 seconds until the eel pieces are fully cooked. Stir in the sesame oil and white pepper. Transfer to a plate and serve with rice.

燴鱔

SAUTÉED
EEL

REGION: JIANGSU
PREPARATION TIME: 10 MINUTES
COOKING TIME: 10 MINUTES
SERVES: 4

* Using a sharp knife, cut off and discard the head of the eel. Cut the eel open down the entire length and remove the spine. Sprinkle with the salt and 1 teaspoon cornstarch (cornflour) and rub off the mucus from the skin. Rinse under cold running water and drain. Cut the eel, on the diagonal, into 2-inch/5-cm pieces.
* Heat the vegetable oil in a wok or deep saucepan to 340°F/170°C, or until a cube of bread browns in 45 seconds. Add the garlic and deep-fry for 1–2 minutes until golden brown and crispy. Use a slotted spoon to carefully remove the garlic from the oil and drain on paper towels.
* Carefully add the eel to the hot oil and deep-fry for about 2 minutes, then remove and pour out the oil.
* Put the wok back over medium-high heat, put in the eel and garlic, then add the wine, soy sauce, sugar, ginger, scallions (spring onions), and ½ cup (4 fl oz/120 ml) water. Bring to a boil over high heat. Reduce to low heat and stir-fry for 3–4 minutes until the sauce starts to thicken and the eel is cooked through. Discard the ginger and scallions.
* Mix the remaining 1 teaspoon cornstarch (cornflour) with 1 tablespoon water in a small bowl and stir this mixture into the wok. Bring to a boil, stirring, for about 30 seconds to thicken the sauce. Drizzle in the sesame oil and toss, then transfer to a plate. Season with salt and the white pepper and serve with rice.

- 1 (1 LB 2-OZ/500-G) RICE FIELD EEL
- ½ TEASPOON SALT, PLUS EXTRA TO TASTE
- 2 TEASPOONS CORNSTARCH (CORNFLOUR)
- 2 CUPS (16 FL OZ/475 ML) VEGETABLE OIL
- 2–3 HEADS GARLIC, PEELED
- 3 TABLESPOONS SHAOXING WINE
- 1½ TABLESPOONS LIGHT SOY SAUCE
- 1 TABLESPOON GRANULATED SUGAR
- ¼ OZ/10 G GINGER (ABOUT ¾-INCH/2-CM-LENGTH PIECE), SLICED
- 2 SCALLIONS (SPRING ONIONS), CUT INTO LENGTHS
- 1 TABLESPOON SESAME OIL
- ¼ TEASPOON GROUND WHITE PEPPER
- STEAMED RICE (PAGE 540), TO SERVE

红烧河鳗
BRAISED RIVER
EEL

- 1 (1 LB 5-OZ/600-G) RIVER EEL
- 1 TABLESPOON SALT
- 1 TEASPOON CORNSTARCH
  (CORNFLOUR)
- 4 TABLESPOONS LARD
- 2 OZ/50 G GINGER (ABOUT
  3-INCH/7.5-CM-LENGTH PIECE),
  SLICED
- 4 SCALLIONS (SPRING ONIONS), CUT
  INTO 1 ½-INCH/4-CM LENGTHS
- 2 TABLESPOONS SHAOXING WINE
- 2 TABLESPOONS GRANULATED SUGAR
- 1 TABLESPOON LIGHT SOY SAUCE
- 2 TABLESPOONS DARK SOY SAUCE

* Soak the eel in 2 cups (16 fl oz/475 ml) boiling water mixed with 1 cup (8 fl oz/250 ml) cold water, in a bowl, for 3 minutes.
* Using a sharp knife, cut off and discard the head of the eel. Cut the eel open down the entire length and remove the spine. Sprinkle with the salt and 1 teaspoon cornstarch (cornflour) and rub off the mucus from the skin. Rinse under cold running water and drain.
* Render 2 tablespoons of lard in a wok or large skillet (frying pan) over low heat. Add the ginger and scallions (spring onions) and stir-fry over medium heat for 2 minutes until fragrant. Add the eel and wine and stir-fry for another 1–2 minutes.
* Add 2 cups (16 fl oz/475 ml) water and bring to a boil over high heat. Stir in the sugar and soy sauces. Reduce to low heat and add 1½ tablespoons lard, ½ tablespoon at a time. Simmer, covered, for about 45 minutes, or until the eel is very tender.
* Increase to high heat and boil, uncovered, for about 5 minutes until the sauce has reduced. Stir in the remaining ½ tablespoon lard. Serve.

FISH & SEAFOOD

晚香玉炒虾片
SHRIMP WITH
TUBEROSE

REGION: TIANJIN
PREPARATION TIME: 15 MINUTES
COOKING TIME: 5 MINUTES
SERVES: 4

* Use paper towels to gently pat dry the tuberose and to remove as much water as possible.
* Use a sharp knife to halve each shrimp (prawn) along its back. Combine the shrimp, ¼ teaspoon salt, the egg white, and cornstarch (cornflour) in a bowl and mix well.
* Heat the oil in a wok or deep saucepan to 300°F/150°C, or until a cube of bread browns in 1½ minutes. Gently lower the shrimp into the oil, using chopsticks to disperse the pieces rapidly to prevent sticking, and deep-fry for 2 minutes, or until the shrimp are pink and cooked through. Add the tuberose, stir, then use a slotted spoon to carefully remove both the tuberose and shrimp from the oil and drain in a colander.
* Pour out most of the oil, leaving about 1 tablespoon in the wok. Heat the oil over medium-high heat, add the ginger and scallion (spring onion), and stir-fry for 1 minute until fragrant. Add the shrimp, tuberose, wine, sugar, and remaining ¼ teaspoon salt, increase to high heat, and stir-fry for another minute. Transfer to a plate and serve with rice.

• ½ CUP (3½ OZ/100 G) TUBEROSE, RINSED
• 1 LB 2 OZ/500 G LARGE UNCOOKED SHRIMP (PRAWNS), SHELLED AND DEVEINED
• ½ TEASPOON SALT
• 1 EGG WHITE
• 1 TABLESPOON CORNSTARCH (CORNFLOUR)
• 2 CUPS (16 FL OZ/475 ML) VEGETABLE OIL
• 1 TEASPOON FINELY CHOPPED GINGER
• 1 TEASPOON FINELY CHOPPED SCALLION (SPRING ONION)
• 2 TEASPOONS RICE WINE
• ½ TEASPOON GRANULATED SUGAR
• STEAMED RICE (PAGE 540), TO SERVE

榄菜焗虾
SHRIMP WITH CHINESE
OLIVE VEGETABLES

REGION: CHAOZHOU
PREPARATION TIME: 10 MINUTES
COOKING TIME: 10 MINUTES
SERVES: 4

* Using scissors, trim the sharp claws and the legs from the shrimp (prawns). At the back, cut open the shell from the tail toward the head, remove the vein, and then rinse and pat dry with paper towels.
* Heat the oil in a wok or large skillet (frying pan) to 340°F/170°C, or until a cube of bread browns in 45 seconds. Gently lower a handful of the shrimp into the oil and once the bubbles in the oil begin to subside, transfer them to a plate. Reheat the oil, then return the shrimp to the pan. Repeat the process 3 times for each batch of shrimp until all have been fried.
* Pour out most of the oil, leaving about 1 tablespoon in the wok. Add the shrimp, sugar, Chinese olive vegetables, and fish sauce and stir-fry over medium heat for 1 minute until combined, being careful not to overcook the shrimp. Transfer to a plate and serve with rice.

• 14 OZ/400 G UNCOOKED SHRIMP (PRAWNS), WITH SHELLS
• 5 TABLESPOONS VEGETABLE OIL
• 1 TABLESPOON GRANULATED SUGAR
• 3 TABLESPOONS CHINESE OLIVE VEGETABLES
• 1 TABLESPOON FISH SAUCE
• STEAMED RICE (PAGE 540), TO SERVE

REGION: GUANGDONG
PREPARATION TIME: 20 MINUTES,
  PLUS 2 HOURS CHILLING TIME
COOKING TIME: 10 MINUTES
SERVES: 6

百花釀鮮菇
SHRIMP-STUFFED MUSHROOMS

- 6 PORTOBELLO MUSHROOMS, STEMS REMOVED
- ½ TEASPOON LIGHT SOY SAUCE
- CORNSTARCH (CORNFLOUR), FOR BRUSHING

FOR THE SHRIMP PATTY:
- 11 OZ/300 G UNCOOKED SHRIMP (PRAWNS), SHELLED AND DEVEINED
- 1¼ TEASPOONS SALT
- ½ TEASPOON GRANULATED SUGAR
- 1 EGG WHITE
- ½ TABLESPOON CORNSTARCH (CORNFLOUR)
- ¾ OZ/20 G PORK FATBACK, FINELY CHOPPED
- ½ TEASPOON GROUND WHITE PEPPER
- 2 TABLESPOONS VEGETABLE OIL
- STEAMED RICE (PAGE 540), TO SERVE

* Put the shrimp (prawns) into a colander, add 1 teaspoon salt, and use your hands to rub the salt into the shrimp. Rinse under cold running water, drain, and wrap in a clean dish towel. Refrigerate for 2 hours.
* Transfer the shrimp to a clean and dry cutting board. Use a large meat cleaver to flatten and then, using the blunt end, coarsely chop the shrimp. Put them into a large bowl, add the sugar and remaining ¼ teaspoon salt, and marinate for 2 minutes.
* Add the egg white and cornstarch (cornflour). Using chopsticks, stir in one direction until the shrimp becomes gluey. Using one hand, take the shrimp patty mixture and smash it against the bowl repeatedly for 1–2 minutes to increase its gumminess. Mix in the pork fatback and white pepper until thoroughly combined.
* Combine the mushrooms and soy sauce in a medium bowl. Spread a thin layer of cornstarch on the underside of each mushroom and then stuff the underside of each mushroom with the shrimp mixture. Dampen your fingers with a little water and use them to smooth out the surface of the patty. Place the stuffed mushrooms on a heatproof plate, shrimp side facing up, and put into a collapsible pot or bamboo steamer over a pot of boiling water. Steam, covered, for 8 minutes, or until the shrimp is cooked through.
* Heat the oil in a small skillet (frying pan). Pour the hot oil over the mushrooms and serve with rice.

鱼香旱蒸虾

STEAMED SHRIMP IN A FRAGRANT SAUCE

REGION: SICHUAN
PREPARATION TIME: 15 MINUTES,
  PLUS 5 MINUTES MARINATING TIME
COOKING TIME: 10 MINUTES
SERVES: 4

* Make 3–4 horizontal cuts along the stomach between the first and fifth abdominal segments on each shrimp (prawn). Each cut should be about half the thickness of the shrimp in order to sever the abdominal muscles, so that the shrimp will not curl when cooked. Cut open the shrimp from the stomach side so that the shrimp can be spread open. Hold each side of a shrimp and bend it backward toward the back to crack the shell.
* Mix ½ teaspoon salt, the sliced ginger, scallion (spring onions), and wine in a bowl. Marinate the shrimp in the mixture for 5 minutes.
* Place the shrimp on a heatproof plate and spread open each shrimp. Place the plate in a collapsible pot or bamboo steamer over a pot of boiling water. Steam, covered, for 5–6 minutes until the shrimp are cooked through. Remove from heat. Drain the water on the plate and discard the ginger and scallion.
* Combine the remaining ½ teaspoon salt, sugar, vinegar, chicken broth (stock), and cornstarch (cornflour) in a bowl and mix into a sauce.
* Heat the oil in a wok or skillet (frying pan). Add the pickled chiles, chopped ginger, and chopped garlic and stir-fry for 1–2 minutes until fragrant. Stir in the sauce and bring to a boil. Drizzle the sauce over the shrimp and garnish with extra chopped scallion.

* 1 LB 2 OZ/500 G (ABOUT 8) UNCOOKED JUMBO SHRIMP (KING PRAWNS), WITH SHELLS, DEVEINED AND HEAD AND LEGS REMOVED
* 1 TEASPOON SALT
* ½ OZ/20 G GINGER (ABOUT ½-INCH/ 1-CM-LENGTH PIECE), HALF SLICED AND HALF CHOPPED
* 1 SCALLION (SPRING ONION), CUT INTO 2-INCH/5-CM LENGTHS, PLUS EXTRA TO GARNISH
* 2 TABLESPOONS SHAOXING WINE
* 1½ TABLESPOONS GRANULATED SUGAR
* 1½ TABLESPOONS BLACK OR BALSAMIC VINEGAR
* ⅔ CUP (5 FL OZ/150 ML) CHICKEN BROTH (STOCK, PAGE 90)
* ½ TABLESPOON CORNSTARCH (CORNFLOUR)
* 2 TABLESPOONS VEGETABLE OIL
* 1¾ OZ/30 G PICKLED CHILES, CHOPPED
* 5 CLOVES GARLIC, CHOPPED

辣虾粉丝
SHRIMP WITH VERMICELLI

- 3 TABLESPOONS VEGETABLE OIL
- 14 OZ/400 G UNCOOKED SHRIMP (PRAWNS), SHELLED, DEVEINED, AND TAILS INTACT
- 4 TABLESPOONS GRATED GINGER
- 4 SCALLIONS (SPRING ONIONS), CHOPPED
- ½ HEAD GARLIC, CHOPPED
- 1 TABLESPOON CHILI SAUCE
- 1 TABLESPOON SHAOXING WINE
- 1 TEASPOON DARK SOY SAUCE
- 1 TEASPOON LIGHT SOY SAUCE
- 1 TABLESPOON GRANULATED SUGAR
- ⅔ CUP (5 OZ/150 G) KETCHUP
- 5 OZ/150 G MUNG BEAN VERMICELLI
- ½ TEASPOON SESAME OIL
- STEAMED RICE (PAGE 540), TO SERVE (OPTIONAL)

In Hong Kong, the dish is prepared with the shrimp (prawn) heads and shells on.

* Heat the vegetable oil in a wok or large skillet (frying pan) over medium heat, add the shrimp, and pan-fry for 2–3 minutes. Transfer to a plate.
* Add the ginger, scallions (spring onions), and garlic to the wok, then stir-fry for 1–2 minutes until fragrant. Stir in the chili sauce, wine, soy sauces, and sugar, and stir-fry over high heat for 1–2 minutes. Add the ketchup and 2 cups (16 fl oz/475 ml) water and bring to a boil. Add the shrimp and sauté for about 1 minute.
* Add the vermicelli, reduce to low heat, and simmer for 5 minutes until the sauce is completely absorbed by the vermicelli. Stir in the sesame oil.
* Transfer the vermicelli to a serving dish and arrange the shrimp on top. Serve with rice, if desired.

青瓜肉碎煮中虾
SHRIMP AND CUCUMBER

- 14 OZ/400 G UNCOOKED SHRIMP (PRAWNS), HEADS REMOVED, SHELLED, DEVEINED, AND TAILS INTACT
- 1½ TEASPOONS SALT, PLUS EXTRA TO TASTE
- 1 EGG WHITE
- 1 OZ/25 G GROUND (MINCED) PORK
- 1 TEASPOON CORNSTARCH (CORNFLOUR)
- 1 TABLESPOON VEGETABLE OIL
- 4 CLOVES GARLIC
- 1 TEASPOON FISH SAUCE
- 1 CUCUMBER, SLICED
- STEAMED RICE (PAGE 540), TO SERVE

* Combine the shrimp (prawns) with ½ teaspoon salt in a bowl. Rinse the shrimp under cold running water and drain. Mix with the egg white and refrigerate for 1 hour.
* Meanwhile, combine the pork with ½ teaspoon salt and stand for 15 minutes. Add ½ teaspoon cornstarch (cornflour) and mix well.
* Heat the oil in a skillet (frying pan) over medium heat, add the garlic, and stir-fry for 2 minutes until golden. Stir in the pork, add the remaining ½ teaspoon salt, the fish sauce, and ½ cup (4 fl oz/120 ml) water, and bring to a boil.
* Add the shrimp and cucumber, toss well, and sauté over high heat for about 1 minute until the shrimp are pink and cooked through.
* Mix the remaining ½ teaspoon cornstarch with ½ tablespoon water in a small bowl and stir this mixture into the pan. Bring to a boil, stirring, for about 30 seconds to thicken the sauce. Season with extra salt to taste, transfer to a platter, and serve with steamed rice.

SHRIMP WITH VERMICELLI

REGION: SICHUAN
PREPARATION TIME: 15 MINUTES
COOKING TIME: 10 MINUTES
SERVES: 4

椒盐虾饼
SHRIMP PATTIES

- 2 EGG WHITES
- 2 TABLESPOONS CORNSTARCH
  (CORNFLOUR)
- 9 OZ/250 G UNCOOKED SHRIMP
  (PRAWNS), SHELLED, DEVEINED, AND
  RINSED
- 2 OZ/50 G HAM, FINELY CHOPPED
- 2 OZ/50 G PORK FATBACK, FINELY
  CHOPPED
- 7 WATER CHESTNUTS, FINELY CHOPPED
- ⅓ CUP (2 OZ/50 G) PEAS
- 1 TABLESPOON RICE WINE
- 1 TEASPOON SALT
- ½ TEASPOON GROUND WHITE PEPPER
- 2 TABLESPOONS VEGETABLE OIL
- 1 TABLESPOON SESAME OIL

  FOR THE SPICED SALT:
- 1 TEASPOON SALT
- ¼ TEASPOON GROUND SICHUAN
  PEPPER
- ¼ TEASPOON SHAJIANG POWDER

* To make the spiced salt, heat the salt in a skillet (frying pan) over low heat until warmed through. Remove from the heat. Add the ground Sichuan pepper and Shajiang powder and mix thoroughly. Set aside.
* Beat the egg whites in a small bowl until foamy. Mix in the cornstarch (cornflour) to make an egg-white batter.
* Put the shrimp, ham, and pork fatback in a large bowl, add the water chestnuts, peas, wine, salt, white pepper, and egg batter and mix well. Form into 10–12 shrimp patties, each about 1½ inch/4 cm in diameter and ½ inches/1 cm thick.
* Heat the vegetable oil in a large skillet over medium heat, add the shrimp patties, in batches, and fry for 2–3 minutes. Flip over and cook for another 1–2 minutes until the patties are browned and cooked through. Transfer to a plate and drizzle with the sesame oil. Serve immediately with the spiced salt on the side.

REGION: SHANGHAI
PREPARATION TIME: 10 MINUTES,
  PLUS 4 HOURS MARINATING TIME
COOKING TIME: 20 MINUTES
SERVES: 6-8

杞子醉虾
SHRIMP AND WOLFBERRIES
IN WINE SAUCE

- 1 LB 5 OZ/600 G UNCOOKED SHRIMP
  (PRAWNS), UNSHELLED
- ⅛ OZ/3 G ANGELICA ROOT, SLICED
- 20 DRIED WOLFBERRIES
- 10 DRIED LONGANS
- ⅛ OZ/5 G GINGER (ABOUT ½-INCH/
  1-CM-LENGTH PIECE), SLICED
- ½ TEASPOON SALT
- ¾ OZ/20 G ROCK SUGAR
- 1 CUP (8 FL OZ/250 ML) SHAOXING
  WINE

* Rinse the shrimp (prawns) under cold running water and pat dry with paper towels.
* Bring a saucepan of water to a boil over high heat. Add the shrimp and blanch for 2 minutes, or until cooked through. Drain and rinse under cold running water. Set aside to cool.
* In the same saucepan, bring 2 cups (16 fl oz/475 ml) water to a boil. Add the angelica root, wolfberries, longans, ginger, salt, and sugar and simmer over low heat for 15 minutes. Remove the pan from the heat and cool completely. Stir in the wine and add the shrimp, making sure they are submerged. Marinate in the refrigerator for 4 hours.
* Drain, transfer to a platter, and serve at room temperature.

FISH & SEAFOOD

豉油皇煎虾
SHRIMP WITH SOY SAUCE

REGION: HONG KONG
PREPARATION TIME: 10 MINUTES
COOKING TIME: 5 MINUTES
SERVES: 4

* Using scissors, trim the sharp claws and the legs from the shrimp (prawns). At the back, cut open the shell from the tail toward the head, remove the vein, and then rinse and pat dry with paper towels.
* Combine all the sauce ingredients in a small bowl and set aside.
* Heat the vegetable oil in a wok or large skillet (frying pan) over medium heat, add the shrimp, and fry for 2–3 minutes, or until they turn pink. Stir in the ginger, scallions (spring onions), wine, and sauce and stir-fry for 1–2 minutes until the sauce thickens. Add the sesame oil and transfer to a plate. Serve with rice.

• 14 OZ/400 G UNCOOKED JUMBO SHRIMP (KING PRAWNS), WITH SHELLS
• 2 TABLESPOONS VEGETABLE OIL
• ¾ OZ/20 G GINGER (ABOUT 1-INCH/ 2.5-CM-LENGTH PIECE), GRATED
• 2 SCALLIONS (SPRING ONIONS), CHOPPED
• 1 TABLESPOON SHAOXING WINE
• 1 TEASPOON SESAME OIL
• STEAMED RICE (PAGE 540), TO SERVE

  FOR THE SAUCE:
• 1½ TABLESPOONS LIGHT SOY SAUCE
• ½ TEASPOON DARK SOY SAUCE
• 1 TABLESPOON GRANULATED SUGAR

醋烹大虾
TIGER PRAWNS IN VINEGAR

REGION: SHANDONG
PREPARATION TIME: 10 MINUTES
COOKING TIME: 5 MINUTES
SERVES: 4

* Devein each prawn by inserting a toothpick (cocktail stick) behind the second abdominal segment to pick out the vein. Cut off the antennae and legs using scissors. Insert the scissors into the head and cut open the shell, from head to tail, along the abdomen of each prawn. Using a sharp knife, cut open the body from the tail to the head. Hold the 2 sides of the body of a prawn and bend them backward toward the back to crack the shell.
* Heat the oil in a wok or deep saucepan to 300°F/150°C, or until a cube of bread browns in 1½ minutes. Gently lower the prawns into the oil and deep-fry for 1 minute, or until the prawns are half cooked. Use a slotted spoon to carefully remove the prawns from the oil and drain on paper towels.
* Pour out most of the oil, leaving about 2 tablespoons in the wok. Heat over medium-high heat, add the ginger and scallions (spring onions), and stir-fry for 1 minute until fragrant. Add the chicken broth (stock), wine, vinegar, and salt, increase to high heat, and bring to a boil. Add the prawns and sauté for about 1 minute until pink and cooked through. Mix the cornstarch (cornflour) with 1 tablespoon water, then stir the mixture into the wok. Bring to a boil, stirring, for about 30 seconds to thicken the sauce. Transfer to a plate and serve with rice.

• 8 UNCOOKED TIGER PRAWNS, WITH SHELLS
• 2 CUPS (16 FL OZ/475 ML) VEGETABLE OIL
• ¼ OZ/10 G GINGER (ABOUT ¾-INCH/ 2-CM-LENGTH PIECE), SHREDDED
• 3 SCALLIONS (SPRING ONIONS), SHREDDED
• 4 TABLESPOONS CHICKEN BROTH (STOCK, PAGE 90)
• 1 TABLESPOON SHAOXING WINE
• 1 TABLESPOON BLACK OR BALSAMIC VINEGAR
• ½ TEASPOON SALT
• 1 TEASPOON CORNSTARCH (CORNFLOUR)
• STEAMED RICE (PAGE 540), TO SERVE

REGION: ZHEJIANG
PREPARATION TIME: 10 MINUTES,
  PLUS 1 HOUR CHILLING TIME
COOKING TIME: 5 MINUTES
SERVES: 4

龙井虾仁
SHRIMP WITH
LONGJING TEA

- 1 LB 5 OZ /600 G UNCOOKED FRESHWATER SHRIMP (PRAWNS), SHELLED AND DEVEINED
- ½ TEASPOON SALT, PLUS EXTRA TO TASTE
- ½ EGG WHITE
- 1 TEASPOON CORNSTARCH (CORNFLOUR)
- 1 TABLESPOON LONGJING TEA
- 2 CUPS (16 FL OZ/475 ML) VEGETABLE OIL
- 1 TABLESPOON SHAOXING WINE
- STEAMED RICE (PAGE 540), TO SERVE

Longjing tea—also known by its literal translation as Dragon Well tea—is a variety of green tea from Zhejiang that dates back 1,500 years. Prized for its quality, it was revered during the Tang Dynasty and became very popular in the Song Dynasty. Legend has it that during the Qing Dynasty, Emperor Qianlong (1711–1799) visited the Longjing plantations in Zhejiang on four separate occasions. He liked the tea so much that he designated 18 tea plants in front of the Hugong Temple near West Lake in Zhejiang as imperial tea plants. Teas from these plants were picked and processed and brought to Beijing annually for the consumption of the imperial court.

* Rub the shrimp (prawns) with ¼ teaspoon salt and let stand for about 30 seconds. Rinse under cold running water, then place the shrimp onto paper towels to absorb excess moisture. Wrap in a clean dish towel and refrigerate for 1 hour.
* Combine the shrimp, the remaining ¼ teaspoon salt, and the egg white in a bowl. Stir in the cornstarch (cornflour) and set aside.
* Put the tea leaves into a cup, add 4 tablespoons boiling water, and steep for about 1 minute. Strain the tea and reserve the leaves.
* Heat the oil in a wok or deep saucepan to 245°F/120°C. Gently lower the shrimp into the oil, using chopsticks to disperse the pieces rapidly to prevent sticking, and deep-fry for 30 seconds until the shrimp turn pink. Use a slotted spoon to carefully remove the shrimp from the oil and drain in a colander.
* Pour out most of the oil, leaving about 2 teaspoons in the wok. Heat the oil over high heat, add the shrimp, and stir-fry for 1 minute until cooked through. Add the reserved tea leaves, sprinkle over the wine, and toss until the wine has evaporated. Adjust the seasoning to taste, transfer the shrimp to a plate, and serve with rice.

宫保大虾
GONGBAO-STYLE SHRIMP
IN CHILI SAUCE

REGION: SICHUAN
PREPARATION TIME: 15 MINUTES, PLUS
  10 MINUTES STANDING TIME
COOKING TIME: 10 MINUTES
SERVES: 4

* Rinse the shrimp (prawns) under cold running water, drain, and place in a bowl. Add the salt and let stand for 10 minutes. Rinse the shrimp under cold running water, drain, and mix in a bowl with the egg white.
* To make the sauce, combine all the ingredients, mix well, and set aside.
* Put the peanuts in a wok or large skillet (frying pan), add the vegetable oil, and stir-fry the peanuts over low heat for 4–5 minutes until crispy. Use a slotted spoon to remove the peanuts and drain on paper towels.
* Reheat the oil, add the shrimp, and stir-fry over high heat for 1–2 minutes until half cooked. Remove and set aside. Heat the remaining oil over medium-high heat, add the garlic, chiles, and Sichuan peppercorns and stir-fry for 1–2 minutes until fragrant. Return the shrimp to the wok along with the scallions (spring onions) and stir-fry for another minute. Pour the sauce into a wok and bring to a boil over high heat. Simmer over medium heat, uncovered, for 1–2 minutes until the sauce is thickened and reduced and the shrimp are cooked through.
* Drizzle in the sesame oil, add the peanuts, and toss. Transfer to a plate and serve with rice.

- 14 OZ/400 G UNCOOKED SHRIMP (PRAWNS), SHELLED AND DEVEINED
- ½ TEASPOON SALT
- 1 EGG WHITE, BEATEN
- ⅓ CUP (2 OZ/50 G) PEANUTS
- 4 TABLESPOONS VEGETABLE OIL
- 2 CLOVES GARLIC, SLICED
- 10 DRIED RED CHILES, HALVED
- 20 SICHUAN PEPPERCORNS
- 2 SCALLIONS (SPRING ONIONS), CHOPPED
- 1 TABLESPOON SESAME OIL
- STEAMED RICE (PAGE 540), TO SERVE

  FOR THE SAUCE:
- 2 TABLESPOONS SHAOXING WINE
- 2 TABLESPOONS CHICKEN BROTH (STOCK, PAGE 90)
- 1 TABLESPOON LIGHT SOY SAUCE
- 2 TEASPOONS WHITE VINEGAR
- 1½ TEASPOONS CORNSTARCH (CORNFLOUR)
- 1½ TEASPOONS GRANULATED SUGAR
- ½ TEASPOON SALT

脆皮大虾

SWEET AND SOUR
SHRIMP

- 1 LB 2 OZ/500 G LARGE UNCOOKED
  SHRIMP (PRAWNS), SHELLED,
  DEVEINED, AND TAIL INTACT
- 2 EGG WHITES, LIGHTLY BEATEN
- ½ TEASPOON SALT
- 1 TABLESPOON SHAOXING WINE
- 3 TABLESPOONS CORNSTARCH
  (CORNFLOUR)
- 1½ TABLESPOONS LIGHT SOY SAUCE
- 2 TABLESPOONS GRANULATED SUGAR
- 2 TABLESPOONS WHITE VINEGAR
- 1 CUP (8 FL OZ/250 ML) CHICKEN
  BROTH (STOCK)
- 2 CUPS (16 FL OZ/475 ML)
  VEGETABLE OIL
- 2 CUPS (5 OZ/150 G) DRIED
  BREADCRUMBS
- 2 TEASPOONS GRATED GINGER
- 3 CLOVES GARLIC, FINELY CHOPPED
- 2 PICKLED CHILES, SEEDED
- 2 SCALLIONS (SPRING ONIONS),
  SHREDDED
- 1 BUNCH CILANTRO (CORIANDER),
  CUT INTO 1-INCH/2.5-CM LENGTHS
- STEAMED RICE (PAGE 540), TO SERVE

* Use a sharp knife to make an insertion on the back of a shrimp (prawn) through to the abdomen, then insert the tail through the opening to make a knot. Repeat with the remaining shrimp.
* Combine the egg whites, salt, 1 teaspoon wine, and 2 tablespoons cornstarch (cornflour) in a large bowl and mix well to make a batter. Add the shrimp and mix until well coated.
* In a small bowl, combine the soy sauce, sugar, the remaining 2 teaspoons wine, white vinegar, the remaining 1 tablespoon cornstarch, and chicken broth (stock) and mix into a sauce.
* Heat the oil in a wok or deep saucepan to 300°F/150°C, or until a cube of bread browns in 1½ minutes. Coat the shrimp in the breadcrumbs, then carefully drop into the hot oil. Deep-fry, in batches, for 2–3 minutes until light brown. Use a slotted spoon to carefully remove the shrimp from the oil and transfer to a plate.
* Heat the oil to about 340°F/170°C, or until a cube of bread browns in 45 seconds. Return all the shrimp to the hot oil and deep-fry for 1–2 minutes until golden brown. Use a slotted spoon to remove the shrimp from the oil and drain on paper towels.
* Pour out most of the oil, leaving about 1 tablespoon in the wok. Heat the oil over medium-high heat, add the ginger, garlic, and sauce, and stir-fry for 2–3 minutes until the sauce thickens. Pour the sauce over the shrimp and garnish with the pickled chiles, scallions (spring onions), and cilantro (coriander). Serve with rice.

翡翠虾仁
SHRIMP WITH
PEAS

REGION: SICHUAN
PREPARATION TIME: 10 MINUTES,
   PLUS 1 HOUR CHILLING TIME
COOKING TIME: 5 MINUTES
SERVES: 4

* Rub the shrimp (prawns) with 1 teaspoon salt and let stand for about 30 seconds. Rinse under cold running water, drain, and then pat with paper towels to absorb excess moisture. Wrap the shrimp in a clean dish towel and refrigerate for 1 hour.
* Combine the shrimp, egg white, and ¼ teaspoon salt in a small bowl.
* In a separate bowl, combine the wine, white pepper, ¼ teaspoon salt, cornstarch (cornflour), and chicken broth (stock) and mix well.
* Heat the oil in a wok or deep saucepan to 265°F/130°C. Gently lower the shrimp into the oil, use chopsticks to stir, and deep-fry for 30 seconds, or until the shrimp turn pink. Use a slotted spoon to carefully remove the shrimp and drain in a colander.
* Pour out the oil and return the shrimp to the wok. Add the peas and the sauce, and sauté over high heat for 2 minutes until the sauce has evaporated and the shrimp are cooked through. Transfer to a serving plate and serve with rice.

- 9 OZ/250 G UNCOOKED SHRIMP (PRAWNS), SHELLED AND DEVEINED
- 1½ TEASPOONS SALT
- 1 EGG WHITE, BEATEN
- 2 TEASPOONS RICE WINE
- ¼ TEASPOON GROUND WHITE PEPPER
- 1 TEASPOON CORNSTARCH (CORNFLOUR)
- 3 TABLESPOONS CHICKEN BROTH (STOCK, PAGE 90)
- 2 CUPS (16 FL OZ/475 ML) VEGETABLE OIL
- 3½ OZ/100 G SUGAR SNAPS, PEAS ONLY AND HALVED
- STEAMED RICE (PAGE 540), TO SERVE

虾多士
SHRIMP ON TOAST

REGION: HONG KONG
PREPARATION TIME: 20 MINUTES
COOKING TIME: 5 MINUTES
SERVE: 2

* Bring a saucepan of water to a boil. Add 8 shrimp (prawns) and blanch for 2 minutes until pink, then drain.
* Put the uncooked shrimp on a cutting board and use the back of a heavy knife to flatten each one repeatedly to make a paste (or process in a food processor). Combine the shrimp paste, salt, sugar, and white pepper in a bowl, and use chopsticks to stir in one direction until the mixture is gummy. Pick up some of the mixture by hand and slap it against the bottom of the bowl for 3–5 minutes to increase the gumminess.
* Stir the ham and cornstarch (cornflour) into the shrimp mixture. Cut the bread into 8 equal-size squares. Spread the shrimp mixture evenly over each piece of bread and press 1 blanched shrimp on top of each.
* Heat the oil in a wok or deep saucepan to 350°F/180°C, or until a cube of bread browns in 30 seconds. Gently lower the squares into the oil and deep-fry for 2 minutes until golden brown and crisp. Use a slotted spoon to carefully remove the toasts from the oil and drain on paper towels.

- 14 OZ/400 G (ABOUT 24) UNCOOKED SHRIMP (PRAWNS), SHELLED AND DEVEINED
- ½ TEASPOON SALT
- ½ TEASPOON GRANULATED SUGAR
- ¼ TEASPOON GROUND WHITE PEPPER
- ¾ OZ/20 G HAM, CHOPPED
- 1 TABLESPOON CORNSTARCH (CORNFLOUR)
- 2 SLICES WHITE BREAD
- 2 CUPS (16 FL OZ/475 ML) VEGETABLE OIL

REGION: HUNAN
PREPARATION TIME: 20 MINUTES,
   PLUS 1 HOUR CHILLING TIME
COOKING TIME: 15 MINUTES
SERVES: 4
📷 PAGE 193

雀巢虾仁
SHRIMP IN
A NEST

- 14 OZ/400 G UNCOOKED SHRIMP (PRAWNS), SHELLED AND DEVEINED
- 1 TEASPOON SALT
- ⅔ CUP (3½ OZ/100 G) SNOW PEAS (MANGETOUT), SLICED
- 2 EGGS, PLUS 1 EGG WHITE
- 4 TABLESPOONS CORNSTARCH (CORNFLOUR)
- 2 TABLESPOONS ALL-PURPOSE (PLAIN) FLOUR
- 2 POTATOES, SHREDDED
- 4 TABLESPOONS CHICKEN BROTH (STOCK, PAGE 90)
- 1 TEASPOON SESAME OIL
- 2 CUPS (16 FL OZ/475 ML) VEGETABLE OIL
- 1 OZ/25 G HAM, DICED
- 1 BUNCH CILANTRO (CORIANDER), LEAVES PICKED, TO GARNISH
- STEAMED RICE (PAGE 540), TO SERVE (OPTIONAL)

* Put the shrimp (prawns) in a colander, sprinkle with ½ teaspoon salt, and use your hands to rub the salt all over the shrimp. Rinse under cold running water and drain. Wrap in a clean dish towel and refrigerate for 1 hour.
* Bring a small saucepan of water to a boil, add the snow peas (mangetout), and blanch for 1 minute. Drain and set aside.
* Beat the egg white in a bowl, stir in 1 tablespoon cornstarch (cornflour), and add the shrimp. Mix well.
* Beat the 2 eggs in a bowl, then add the flour, 2 tablespoons cornstarch, and ¼ teaspoon salt. Add the potatoes and mix well.
* In a small bowl, mix the chicken broth (stock), sesame oil, the remaining 1 tablespoon cornstarch, and ¼ teaspoon salt into a sauce.
* Heat the vegetable oil in a wok or deep saucepan to 250°F/130°C. Gently lower the shrimp into the oil, using chopsticks to disperse, and deep-fry for 1 minute until the shrimp are pink. Use a slotted spoon to carefully remove the shrimp from the oil and drain on paper towels.
* Arrange the potatoes in a hand-held strainer (sieve) and shape into a bird's nest. Bring the oil in the wok to 340°F/170°C, or until a cube of bread browns in 45 seconds. Gently lower the strainer, with the potatoes, into the oil and deep-fry for 2–3 minutes until golden brown. Remove the strainer from the oil and transfer the potato "nest" onto a plate.
* Pour out most of the oil, leaving about 1 tablespoon in the wok. Heat the oil over medium-high heat, add the ham and snow peas, and stir-fry for 1 minute. Stir in the shrimp and sauce, heat until it thickens, then pour the contents of the wok on top of the potato nest. Garnish with cilantro (coriander) and serve with rice, if using.

SHRIMP IN A NEST

REGION: SICHUAN
PREPARATION TIME: 10 MINUTES,
  PLUS 1 HOUR CHILLING TIME
COOKING TIME: 10 MINUTES
SERVES: 6

干烧大虾
SHRIMP WITH
SPICY SAUCE

- 6 UNCOOKED JUMBO SHRIMP (KING PRAWNS, ABOUT 1 LB/450 G), SHELLED AND DEVEINED
- 1 TABLESPOON SHAOXING WINE
- ½ TEASPOON SALT, PLUS EXTRA TO TASTE
- 3 TABLESPOONS VEGETABLE OIL
- 1 OZ/25 G GROUND (MINCED) LEAN PORK
- 1 TEASPOON GRATED GINGER
- ¼ OZ/10 G SICHUAN PRESERVED MUSTARD GREENS, TRIMMED, RINSED, AND CHOPPED
- 2 SCALLIONS (SPRING ONIONS), STEMS ONLY, CUT INTO 1½-INCH/ 4-CM LENGTHS
- 4–5 PICKLED RED CHILES, SEEDED AND HALVED
- 5 TABLESPOONS CHICKEN BROTH (STOCK, PAGE 90)
- 1 TEASPOON LIGHT SOY SAUCE
- PINCH OF GROUND WHITE PEPPER
- 1 TABLESPOON SESAME OIL
- STEAMED RICE (PAGE 540) OR COOKED NOODLES, TO SERVE

* Wrap the shrimp (prawns) in a clean dish towel and refrigerate for 1 hour.
* Mix 1 teaspoon wine with ¼ teaspoon salt in a small bowl.
* Heat the vegetable oil in a wok over medium heat, add the shrimp, and pan-fry for 3–4 minutes until just pink. Transfer to a plate.
* Add the pork to the wok and stir in the ginger, Sichuan preserved mustard, scallions (spring onions), and pickled chiles. Add the chicken broth (stock), the remaining ¼ teaspoon salt, soy sauce, and the remaining 2 teaspoons wine and bring to a boil. Increase to medium-high heat and stir-fry for 2–3 minutes until the sauce is reduced by half.
* Toss in the shrimp, stir, and increase to high heat. Cook for another 1 minute until the sauce is reduced by half. Sprinkle in the sesame oil, season with extra salt to taste, and transfer to a plate. Serve with rice or noodles.

黄金虾
GOLDEN PRAWNS

REGION: HONG KONG
PREPARATION TIME: 10 MINUTES
COOKING TIME: 30 MINUTES
SERVES: 4

* Preheat the oven to 300°F/150°C/Gas Mark 2.
* Devein each prawn by inserting a toothpick (cocktail stick) behind the second abdominal segment to pick out the vein. Cut off the antennae and legs using scissors. Sever the heads from the body behind the first abdominal segment on each prawn. Reserve the heads. Using a sharp knife, cut open the body of each prawn along the abdomen from the tail to the head. Hold 2 sides of the body of a prawn and bend them backward toward the back to crack the shell.
* Put the egg yolks in a heatproof bowl and bake in the oven for 20 minutes. Remove from the oven and crush the egg yolks with a fork. Mix in the sugar.
* To make the crispy garlic, heat the oil in a wok or deep saucepan over low heat to 265°F/130°C, add the garlic, and deep-fry for 1–2 minutes until lightly brown. Use a slotted spoon to carefully remove the garlic from the oil and drain on paper towels. Set aside.
* Reheat the oil over medium-high heat to 340°F/170°C. Add the prawn heads and bodies and deep-fry for 2–3 minutes until they turn pink and the flesh is white and opaque. Use a slotted spoon to carefully remove the prawns from the oil and drain on paper towels. Set aside.
* Heat the butter in a clean wok over medium-low heat. Add the crushed egg yolks. Press them with the spatula (fish slice) to break up the yolks even further and stir–fry for 1 minute. Add the prawns and stir to mix through. Transfer the mixture to a plate and top with the crispy garlic. Serve with rice or potatoes.

* 8 UNCOOKED TIGER PRAWNS
* 6 SALTED DUCK YOLKS
* 1 TEASPOON GRANULATED SUGAR
* 4 TABLESPOONS BUTTER
* STEAMED RICE (PAGE 540) OR POTATOES, TO SERVE

FOR THE CRISPY GARLIC:
* 2 CUPS (16 FL OZ/475 ML) VEGETABLE OIL
* 2 HEADS GARLIC, CHOPPED

REGION: JIANGSU
PREPARATION TIME: 15 MINUTES,
  PLUS 10 MINUTES MARINATING TIME
COOKING TIME: 5 MINUTES
SERVES: 4
📷 PAGE 197

凤尾大虾
FAN-TAILED
SHRIMP

- 8 UNCOOKED JUMBO SHRIMP (KING PRAWNS), HEADS REMOVED, SHELLED, AND TAILS INTACT
- 2 SCALLIONS (SPRING ONIONS), CUT INTO 1½-INCH/4-CM LENGTHS
- 1 TABLESPOON GINGER JUICE
- 1 TEASPOON SHAOXING WINE
- ½ TEASPOON SALT
- ¼ TEASPOON GROUND WHITE PEPPER
- ¼ TEASPOON GROUND SICHUAN PEPPER
- 2 EGGS
- 2 TEASPOONS CORNSTARCH (CORNFLOUR)
- 4¼ CUPS (34 FL OZ/1 LITER) VEGETABLE OIL
- STEAMED RICE (PAGE 540), TO SERVE (OPTIONAL)

FOR THE SICHUAN PEPPER SALT:
- ½ TEASPOON SALT
- ¼ TEASPOON GROUND SICHUAN PEPPER

* Take a shrimp and using a small sharp knife, cut it open from the abdomen to the back (without cutting all the way through) into 2 linked halves. Devein, then spread out the 2 halves and press them down flat on the cutting board. Repeat with the remaining shrimp.
* Put them into a bowl with the scallions (spring onions), ginger juice, wine, salt, and white pepper. Mix well and marinate for at least 10 minutes.
* Discard the scallions and pat the shrimp with paper towels to absorb excess moisture.
* For the Sichuan pepper salt, mix the salt with the ground Sichuan pepper in a small bowl. Set aside.
* Beat the eggs in a separate bowl and mix in the cornstarch (cornflour) to create a smooth batter.
* Heat the oil in a wok or deep saucepan to 325°F/160°C, or until a cube of bread browns in 1 minute. Holding each shrimp by the tail, dip it into the egg batter and gently lower it into the hot oil. Deep-fry the shrimp, in batches, for 1–2 minutes, or until the batter is golden brown and the shrimp are cooked through. Use a slotted spoon to carefully remove the shrimp from the oil and drain on paper towels.
* Transfer to a serving plate and sprinkle with the spiced salt. Serve with rice, if desired.

FAN-TAILED SHRIMP

REGION: HONG KONG
PREPARATION TIME: 5 MINUTES
COOKING TIME: 10 MINUTES
SERVES: 4
📷 PAGE 199

椒盐中虾
SHRIMP WITH
SPICED SALT

- 1 LB 5 OZ/600 G UNCOOKED SHRIMP (PRAWNS), WITH SHELLS
- 2 CUPS (16 FL OZ/475 ML) VEGETABLE OIL
- 2 TABLESPOONS CORNSTARCH (CORNFLOUR)
- 1 RED CHILE, SEEDED AND SHREDDED
- 2 CLOVES GARLIC, CHOPPED
- 2 SCALLIONS (SPRING ONIONS), STEMS ONLY, CUT INTO 1½-INCH/4-CM LENGTHS
- 1 TABLESPOON SHAOXING WINE
- STEAMED RICE (PAGE 540) OR POTATOES, TO SERVE

FOR THE SPICED SALT:
- 1 TEASPOON SALT
- 1 TEASPOON SHAJIANG POWDER
- ½ TEASPOON FIVE-SPICE POWDER
- ½ TEASPOON CHILI POWDER

* To make the spiced salt, heat the salt in a pan over low heat for 1–2 minutes, then transfer to a small bowl. Add the remaining ingredients and mix well. Set aside.
* Using scissors, trim the sharp claws and the legs from the shrimp (prawns). At the back, cut open the shell from the tail toward the head, remove the vein, and then rinse and pat dry with paper towels.
* Heat the oil in a wok or deep saucepan to 300°F/150°C, or until a cube of bread browns in 1½ minutes. Dredge the shrimp in cornstarch (cornflour), gently lower into the oil, using chopsticks to disperse the pieces rapidly to prevent sticking, and deep-fry for 2–3 minutes until golden brown, crispy, and cooked through. Use a slotted spoon to carefully remove the shrimp from the oil and drain on paper towels.
* Pour out most of the oil, leaving about 1 tablespoon in the wok. Heat the oil over medium heat, add the chile, garlic, scallions (spring onions), and shrimp, and stir-fry for 1 minute. Sprinkle in the wine, turn off the heat, and mix in the spiced salt. Serve with rice or potatoes.

REGION: HONG KONG
PREPARATION TIME: 10 MINUTES
COOKING TIME: 5 MINUTES
SERVES: 4

黑胡椒罗勒焗虾
SHRIMP WITH BLACK
PEPPER AND BASIL

- 1 LB/450 G UNCOOKED SHRIMP (PRAWNS), WITH SHELLS
- 1 TABLESPOON BUTTER
- 3 SHALLOTS, SLICED
- 2 CLOVES GARLIC, FINELY CHOPPED
- 1 TEASPOON SALT
- ½ TEASPOON GRANULATED SUGAR
- 2 TEASPOONS COARSELY GROUND BLACK PEPPER
- 1 TABLESPOON SHAOXING WINE
- 1 CUP (2 OZ/50 G) BASIL LEAVES

* Using scissors, trim the sharp claws and the legs from the shrimp (prawns). At the back, cut open the shell from the tail toward the head, remove the vein, and then rinse and pat dry with paper towels.
* Melt the butter in a Dutch oven (casserole) over medium heat, add the shallots, and stir-fry for 1 minute until fragrant. Add the garlic, salt, sugar, and shrimp, and fry for 2–3 until the shrimp turn pink. Stir in the black pepper, sprinkle in the wine, toss through the basil leaves, and cover for 30 seconds. Turn off the heat.
* Serve in the Dutch oven.

FISH & SEAFOOD

SHRIMP WITH SPICED SALT

REGION: HONG KONG
PREPARATION TIME: 10 MINUTES,
    PLUS 1 HOUR CHILLING TIME
COOKING TIME: 10 MINUTES
SERVES: 6

茄汁煎虾碌
PAN-FRIED SHRIMP
IN SAUCE

- 1 LB/450 G UNCOOKED JUMBO SHRIMP (KING PRAWNS), WITH SHELLS
- 3 TABLESPOONS KETCHUP
- 1 TABLESPOON GRANULATED SUGAR
- 2 TEASPOONS ZHENJIANG OR BALSAMIC VINEGAR
- 1 TEASPOON LIGHT SOY SAUCE
- ½ TEASPOON GROUND WHITE PEPPER
- 3 TABLESPOONS VEGETABLE OIL
- 1 TABLESPOON CORNSTARCH (CORNFLOUR)
- 2 SHALLOTS, CHOPPED
- 1 TABLESPOON CHOPPED GARLIC
- ¼ TEASPOON SESAME OIL
- STEAMED RICE (PAGE 540), TO SERVE

* Using scissors, trim the sharp claws and the legs from the shrimp (prawns). At the back, cut open the shell from the tail toward the head, remove the vein, and then rinse and pat dry with paper towels. Cut each shrimp into 2 at the first abdominal segment. Wrap the shrimp in a clean dish towel and refrigerate for 1 hour.
* Combine the ketchup, sugar, vinegar, soy sauce, and white pepper in a bowl and set aside.
* Heat the vegetable oil in a wok or large skillet (frying pan). Lightly dredge the shrimp with the cornstarch (cornflour) and add them to the wok. Pan-fry over medium heat for 3–4 minutes until cooked through. Use your spatula (fish slice) to push the shrimp to the side of the wok, add the shallots and garlic to the center of the wok, and stir-fry for another minute until fragrant. Toss well with the shrimp, add the sauce, and stir-fry for another 1–2 minutes to reduce the sauce. Drizzle in the sesame oil, transfer to a serving plate, and serve with rice.

REGION: HONG KONG
PREPARATION TIME: 10 MINUTES,
    PLUS 10 MINUTES FREEZING TIME
COOKING TIME: 35 MINUTES
SERVES: 3

盐焗奄仔蟹
CRABS BAKED
IN SALT

- 3 (5-OZ/150-G) FRESH VIRGIN CRABS
- 3 CUPS (1 LB 5 OZ/600 G) COARSE SALT
- 1 TABLESPOON FIVE-SPICE POWDER

Virgin crabs are small, female crabs. The crabs are frozen numb for 10 minute prior to cooking, which is more humane.

* Rinse the crabs under cold running water and pat dry with paper towels. Freeze for 10 minutes.
* Stir-fry the salt for 5–6 minutes in a dry wok or large skillet (frying pan) over high heat until very hot. Stir in the five-spice powder and carefully bury the crabs inside the hot salt with their stomachs facing up. Cover, reduce to medium heat, and cook for 5 minutes. Reduce to low heat and cook for another 20–25 minutes, or until the crabs are cooked through.
* Use tongs to remove the crabs from the salt. Brush off the excess salt, then remove the carapace of each crab, and cut each crab down the middle into 2 halves. Transfer to a plate and serve.

FISH & SEAFOOD

粉丝蟹煲

CRAB AND MUNG BEAN VERMICELLI CASSEROLE

REGION: HONG KONG
PREPARATION TIME: 15 MINUTES
COOKING TIME: 25 MINUTES
SERVES: 4

* Lift off and discard each crab's abdomen, brush the underside clean, lift the carapace, remove the stomach and gills, and rinse under cold running water. Cut each crab into 2 halves and each half into 3–4 pieces. Use the back of a heavy knife to lightly crush the claws.
* Soak the vermicelli in a bowl of hot water for 3 minutes to soften. Drain.
* Combine the oyster sauce, salt, sugar, and 4 tablespoons chicken broth (stock) in a bowl and mix well.
* Put the cornstarch (cornflour) in a large bowl, add the crab pieces, and lightly dredge.
* Heat 2 cups (16 fl oz/475 ml) vegetable oil in a wok or deep saucepan to 340°F/170°C, or until a cube of bread browns in 45 seconds. Gently lower the crab pieces into the oil, in batches, and deep-fry for 2–3 minutes. Use a slotted spoon to carefully remove the pieces from the oil and drain on paper towels.
* Pour out most of the oil, leaving 2 tablespoons oil in the wok. Heat the oil over medium-high heat, add the ginger and garlic, and stir-fry for 1–2 minutes. Stir in the shallots and stir-fry for another 30 seconds, then add the crab, wine, and oyster sauce mixture and toss to mix thoroughly. Turn off the heat.
* Heat 1 tablespoon vegetable oil in a Dutch oven (casserole) over high heat. Add the cabbage and stir-fry for 2–3 minutes until almost cooked. Add the vermicelli and stir-fry until well coated in oil. Combine the soy sauce with the remaining chicken broth in a small bowl and gradually stir into the vermicelli. Put in the crab, sauce, and scallions (spring onions), cover, and simmer for 10 minutes over medium-low heat. Mix in the sesame oil, transfer to a serving plate, and serve with steamed rice.

- 2 (1¾-LB/800-G) FRESH CRABS
- 5 OZ/150 G MUNG BEAN VERMICELLI
- 1 TABLESPOON OYSTER SAUCE
- 1 TEASPOON SALT
- 1 TEASPOON GRANULATED SUGAR
- ⅔ CUP (5 FL OZ/150 ML) CHICKEN BROTH (STOCK, PAGE 90)
- 4 TABLESPOONS CORNSTARCH (CORNFLOUR)
- 2 CUPS (16 FL OZ/475 ML) PLUS 1 TABLESPOON VEGETABLE OIL
- ¼ OZ/10 G GINGER (ABOUT ¾-INCH/ 2-CM-LENGTH PIECE), SLICED
- 2 CLOVES GARLIC, SLICED
- 4 SHALLOTS, CHOPPED
- 1 TABLESPOON SHAOXING WINE
- ⅓ (ABOUT 11 OZ/300 G) HEAD CABBAGE, SHREDDED
- 1 TABLESPOON LIGHT SOY SAUCE
- 3 SCALLIONS (SPRING ONIONS), STEMS ONLY, CUT INTO 2-INCH/5-CM LENGTHS
- 1 TEASPOON SESAME OIL
- STEAMED RICE (PAGE 540), TO SERVE

REGION: FUJIAN
PREPARATION TIME: 15 MINUTES,
   PLUS 1 HOUR SOAKING TIME
COOKING TIME: 1 HOUR 10 MINUTES
SERVES: 4–6
📷 PAGE 203

- 1¼ CUPS (9 OZ/250 G) GLUTINOUS RICE, RINSED
- ½ TEASPOON SALT
- 1 DRIED LOTUS LEAF
- 1 (1-LB/450-G) FRESH CRAB, FEMALE WITH ROE OR OTHER MEATY CRAB
- 3 MEDIUM DRIED SCALLOPS
- 8 DRIED BLACK MUSHROOMS
- 2 TABLESPOONS VEGETABLE OIL
- 1 TABLESPOON GRATED GINGER, PLUS 1 TABLESPOON SHREDDED GINGER
- 3 SHALLOTS, CHOPPED
- 7 OZ/200 G GROUND (MINCED) PORK
- 1 TABLESPOON LIGHT SOY SAUCE
- 1 TABLESPOON CHOPPED SCALLIONS (SPRING ONIONS)

红蟳米糕
STEAMED CRAB OVER GLUTINOUS RICE

Many Taiwanese have ancestors from Fujian, which has inevitably influenced some of the culinary culture. This dish is a perfect example: it is a popular Taiwanese dish but its roots are grounded in Fujian cuisine.

* Put the rice and salt into a large bowl and add enough boiling water to cover. Soak for 1 hour, then rinse thoroughly and drain.
* Meanwhile, soak the lotus leaves in cold water for 45 minutes, or until softened. Drain, rinse, and pat dry with a dish towel.
* Lift off and discard the crab's abdomen, brush the underside clean, lift the carapace, remove the stomach and gills, and rinse under cold running water. Cut the crab into 6–8 pieces.
* Put the dried scallops and ½ cup (4 fl oz/120 ml) cold water in a small bowl and soak for 15 minutes. Drain and reserve the scallop water for later use. Remove the small hard muscle from the scallops, then shred the scallops.
* Put the mushrooms into a bowl, add 1 cup (8 fl oz/ 250 ml) cold water, and soak for at least 20 minutes, or until softened. Remove the mushrooms and squeeze dry, then discard the stems and chop. Reserve the liquid.
* Heat the oil in a wok or large skillet (frying pan) over medium heat, add the grated ginger and shallots, and stir-fry for 1 minute until fragrant. Add the pork, mushrooms, dried scallops, and soy sauce and stir-fry for another minute. Transfer the mixture to a bowl with the drained glutinous rice and add the reserved scallop and mushroom water. Mix well.
* Line a steaming rack or heatproof plate with the lotus leaf and spread out the rice in the center of the leaf. Fold over the leaf. Place in a collapsible pot or bamboo steamer over a pot of boiling water. Steam, covered, for 45 minutes.
* Remove the lid, place the crab pieces on top of the rice, then add the shredded ginger on top. Steam for another 20 minutes, or until the rice and crab are thoroughly cooked. Sprinkle over the scallions (spring onions) and serve. (The lotus leaf is not to be consumed.)

STEAMED CRAB OVER GLUTINOUS RICE

豆酱焗蟹
CRAB IN PUNING
BEAN PASTE

- 1 (2-LB/900-G) FRESH CRAB
- 3 CUPS (25 FL OZ/750 ML) VEGETABLE OIL
- 6 TABLESPOONS CORNSTARCH (CORNFLOUR)
- 3 TABLESPOONS PUNING BEAN PASTE, CHOPPED
- 2 TABLESPOONS SESAME PASTE
- 1 TEASPOON GRANULATED SUGAR
- 1 TABLESPOON SHAOXING WINE
- 3½ OZ/100 G PORK FATBACK, CUT INTO ¼-INCH/5-MM CUBES
- ¾ OZ/20 G GINGER (ABOUT 1-INCH/2.5-CM-LENGTH PIECE), SLICED
- ½ CUP (4 FL OZ/120 ML) CHICKEN BROTH (STOCK, PAGE 90)
- 2 SCALLIONS (SPRING ONIONS), CUT INTO 1½-INCH/4-CM LENGTHS
- SALT, TO TASTE
- STEAMED RICE (PAGE 540), TO SERVE

* Lift off and discard each crab's abdomen, brush the underside clean, lift the carapace, remove the stomach and tear out the gills, and rinse with water. Cut the crab into 2 halves and each half into 3–4 pieces. Put into a colander to drain.
* Heat the oil in a wok or deep saucepan to 350°F/180°C, or until a cube of bread browns in 30 seconds. Dredge the crab pieces in cornstarch (cornflour), and carefully lower the pieces into the hot oil. Deep-fry for 3–4 minutes until golden brown. Transfer to a colander to drain any excess oil.
* Combine the Puning bean paste, sesame paste, sugar, and ½ tablespoon wine in a small bowl. Set aside.
* Heat a skillet and fry the pork fatback over low heat for 1–2 minutes until the pork is crisp and the fat is rendered. Use a slotted spoon to remove the crispy pork and drain on paper towels. Set aside.
* Pour out most of the oil, leaving about 2 tablespoons in the wok. Heat the oil over high heat, add the ginger, and stir-fry for 1–2 minutes until fragrant. Put in the crab and puning bean paste, then sprinkle in the remaining ½ tablespoon wine. Stir-fry for another 1 minute, then pour in the chicken broth (stock) and bring to a boil.
* Reduce to low heat and simmer, covered, for 10 minutes. Remove the lid, add the pork crisps and scallions (spring onions), and toss well. Season to taste.
* Transfer to a serving plate and serve with rice.

襄烧蟹

CRAB CAKES

REGION: JIANGSU
PREPARATION TIME: 15 MINUTES
COOKING TIME: 15 MINUTES
SERVES: 4-6

Tomalley, also known as crab fat, is not actually fat but the crab's hepatopancreas, a main component of the crab's digestive system. It's widely eaten in many cultures and often considered a delicacy, when eating steamed or boiled crab. It should be consumed in moderation (as with the livers of other animals), because it may contain high levels of chemical contaminants.

* Combine the scallion and ginger together, then squeeze over a bowl to extract their juices. Combine the juices in a small bowl, the egg white, wine, cornstarch (cornflour), and salt and mix well. Add the chopped fish, pork fatback, crab meat and tomalley, and stir thoroughly.
* Oil a rectangular or square baking pan large enough to let the mixture spread to a thickness of about ¼ inch/5 mm. Put in the crab cake mixture and spread evenly. Place the pan on a steaming rack in a wok of boiling water. Steam, covered, for 5 minutes. Cut the mixture into ¾ × 1½-inch/ 2 × 4-cm pieces.
* Beat 2 eggs in a bowl, then add the flour and mix to an egg batter that drips slowly and smoothly from a spoon. Add a little water if the batter is too thick.
* Heat the oil in a wok or large skillet (frying pan) to 300°F/150°C, or until a cube of bread browns in 1½ minutes. Dip the crab cakes into the egg batter, then shallow-fry, in batches, for about 3–4 minutes until they are golden brown. Use a slotted spoon to remove the crab from the oil and drain on paper towels. Transfer to a clean plate.
* For the Sichuan pepper salt, mix the salt with the ground Sichuan pepper in a small bowl. Sprinkle the Sichuan pepper salt and white pepper over the crab cakes and serve.

- 1 SCALLION (SPRING ONION), FINELY GRATED
- ¼ OZ/10 G GINGER (ABOUT ¾-INCH/ 2-CM-LENGTH PIECE), FINELY GRATED
- 2 EGGS, PLUS 1 EGG WHITE
- 2 TABLESPOONS SHAOXING WINE
- ½ TABLESPOON CORNSTARCH (CORNFLOUR)
- ¼ TEASPOON SALT
- 3½ OZ/100 G WHITE FISH FILLETS, CHOPPED
- 1 OZ/25 G PORK FATBACK, CHOPPED
- ⅔ CUP (5 OZ/150 G) CRAB MEAT AND TOMALLEY
- 1 CUP (8 FL OZ/250 ML) VEGETABLE OIL, PLUS EXTRA FOR GREASING
- 2 TABLESPOONS ALL-PURPOSE (PLAIN) FLOUR
- ¼ TEASPOON GROUND WHITE PEPPER

- FOR THE SICHUAN PEPPER SALT:
- ½ TEASPOON SALT
- ¼ TEASPOON GROUND SICHUAN PEPPER

REGION: GUANGDONG
PREPARATION TIME: 15 MINUTES
COOKING TIME: 15 MINUTES
SERVES: 4

姜葱炒蟹
CRAB WITH GINGER
AND SCALLIONS

- 1 TABLESPOON OYSTER SAUCE
- 1½ TEASPOONS LIGHT SOY SAUCE
- 1 TEASPOON GRANULATED SUGAR
- 1 (2-LB/900-G) FRESH CRAB
- 2 TABLESPOONS CORNSTARCH
  (CORNFLOUR)
- 2 CUPS (16 FL OZ/475 ML)
  VEGETABLE OIL
- 2 OZ/50 G GINGER (ABOUT 3-INCH/
  7.5-CM-LENGTH PIECE), SLICED
- 1 OZ/25 G PORK FATBACK,
  FINELY CHOPPED
- 2 CLOVES GARLIC, SLICED
- 6 SCALLIONS (SPRING ONIONS),
  CUT INTO LENGTHS
- 1 TEASPOON SHAOXING WINE
- 2 EGGS, BEATEN
- STEAMED RICE (PAGE 540), TO SERVE

* Combine the oyster sauce, soy sauce, sugar, and 2 table-spoons water in a bowl and set aside.
* Lift off and discard the crab's abdomen, brush the underside clean, lift the carapace, remove the stomach and gills, and rinse under cold running water. Cut the crab into 2 halves and each half into 3–4 pieces. Crush the claws with the back of the knife. Lightly dredge the crab pieces and carapace in the cornstarch (cornflour).
* Heat the oil in a wok or deep saucepan to 340°F/170°C, or until a cube of bread browns in 45 seconds. Gently lower the ginger, crab pieces, and carapace into the oil and deep-fry for 5 minutes, or until golden. Use a slotted spoon to carefully remove the ginger and crab from the oil and drain in a colander.
* Pour off most of the oil, leaving about 1 tablespoon in the wok. Heat the oil over high heat, add the pork fatback, and stir-fry for 1 minute. Add the garlic and half of the scallions (spring onions), and stir-fry for another minute. Add the fried crab and ginger, toss, and then sprinkle in the wine and oyster sauce mixture. Toss again, cover, and cook over medium-high heat for 2 minutes, or until the crab is cooked through. Remove the lid, stir in the remaining scallions, pour in the egg batter, and toss until the sauce thickens.
* Transfer to a platter and serve immediately with rice.

避风塘炒蟹

CRAB IN SPICY GARLIC SAUCE

REGION: HONG KONG
PREPARATION TIME: 10 MINUTES
COOKING TIME: 15 MINUTES
SERVES: 4

* Lift off and discard the crab's abdomen, brush the underside clean, lift the carapace, remove the stomach and gills, and rinse under cold running water. Cut the crab into 2 halves and each half into 3–4 pieces.
* Heat the salt, 1 teaspoon sugar, and soybean crisps in a small pan over low heat for 2 minutes. Set aside.
* Heat the oil in a wok or deep saucepan to 340°F/170°C, or until a cube of bread browns in 45 seconds. Gently lower the crab into the oil and deep-fry for 5 minutes until golden brown. Use a slotted spoon to carefully remove the crab from the oil and drain on paper towels. Set aside.
* Pour off most of the oil, leaving about 2 tablespoons in the wok. Heat the oil over medium heat, add the shallots, and stir-fry for 1–2 minutes until fragrant. Add the dried and fresh chiles, black beans, Sichuan peppercorns, crispy garlic, crispy soybean mixture, soy sauce, and remaining 1 teaspoon sugar, and stir-fry over high heat for 2 minutes. Stir in the crab pieces, add the scallions (spring onions), and toss thoroughly. Transfer to a serving plate and serve with rice.

- 1 (1 LB 5-OZ/600-G) FRESH CRAB
- 1 TEASPOON SALT
- 2 TEASPOONS GRANULATED SUGAR
- 4 TABLESPOONS SOYBEAN CRISPS (PAGE 22)
- 2 TABLESPOONS CORNSTARCH (CORNFLOUR)
- 2 CUPS (16 FL OZ/475 ML) VEGETABLE OIL
- 4 SHALLOTS, CHOPPED
- 16 DRIED CHILES, CHOPPED
- 4 RED CHILES, CUT INTO LENGTHS
- ½ TABLESPOON FERMENTED BLACK BEANS, RINSED
- ½ TEASPOON SICHUAN PEPPERCORNS, CRUSHED
- 2 SCALLIONS (SPRING ONIONS), CHOPPED
- 1 QUANTITY CRISPY GARLIC (PAGE 52)
- 2 TABLESPOONS LIGHT SOY SAUCE
- STEAMED RICE (PAGE 540), TO SERVE

冻蟹

CHILLED CRAB WITH GINGER SAUCE

REGION: CHAOZHOU
PREPARATION TIME: 10 MINUTES,
  PLUS 30 MINUTES FREEZING TIME
COOKING TIME: 20–25 MINUTES
SERVES: 4

* Put the crabs in a plastic bag, then freeze for 30 minutes.
* Remove the crabs from freezer, tear off the abdomen of each crab, brush, and rinse under cold running water. Put the crabs on a plate with the carapace facing down. Sprinkle over the salt and place in a collapsible pot or bamboo steamer over a pot of boiling water. Steam, covered, for 20–25 minutes until cooked through. Remove the crabs and set aside on a plate to cool.
* Lift off the carapace, cut the body of each crab in half, then cut each half into 3–4 chunks. On a serving plate, arrange the parts into the shape of a crab.
* Combine the ginger and vinegar in a small bowl to make a dipping sauce.
* Serve the crabs with the dipping sauce on the side.

- 2 (1 LB 2-OZ/500-G) FRESH CRABS
- 1 TEASPOON SALT
- 2 TEASPOONS FINELY CHOPPED GINGER
- 3 TABLESPOONS RED VINEGAR

豉汁龙虾
LOBSTER IN BLACK BEAN SAUCE

- 1 (2-LB/900-G) LIVE LOBSTER, COOLED IN FREEZER FOR 15 MINUTES IF LIVE
- 4 TABLESPOONS CORNSTARCH (CORNFLOUR)
- 3 CUPS (25 FL OZ/750 ML) VEGETABLE OIL
- ¼ OZ/10 G GINGER (ABOUT ¾-INCH/ 2-CM-LENGTH PIECE), SLICED
- 1 TABLESPOON LIGHT SOY SAUCE
- 1 TABLESPOON SHAOXING WINE
- 4 TABLESPOONS CHICKEN BROTH (STOCK, PAGE 90)
- 2 SCALLIONS (SPRING ONIONS), CUT INTO 2-INCH/5-CM LENGTHS
- 2 EGGS
- 1 TEASPOON SESAME OIL
- STEAMED RICE (PAGE 540), TO SERVE

FOR THE BLACK BEAN SAUCE:
- 2 TABLESPOONS FERMENTED BLACK BEANS, RINSED AND CHOPPED
- 2 CLOVES GARLIC, CHOPPED
- 1 TABLESPOON GRANULATED SUGAR
- 1 TABLESPOON VEGETABLE OIL

Because lobsters are cold-blooded, their body temperature will adapt to the surrounding temperature. Freezing them will slow down their heart rate, metabolism, and neural functioning and it also prevents the lobster from moving around. We've provided instructions for preparing a live lobster, but you can ask your fishmonger to prepare this for you or purchase a frozen one.

* Insert a sharp knife between the head and body and sever the head. Cut the body lengthwise into two, then cut each half into 1¼-inch/3-cm pieces. Remove and crack the claws from the head. Discard the head. Rinse the pieces and set aside.
* Combine the lobster pieces and cornstarch (cornflour) in a large bowl.
* To make the black bean sauce, combine all the ingredients in a bowl and mix well.
* Heat the vegetable oil in a wok or deep saucepan to 340°F/170°C, or until a cube of bread browns in 45 seconds. Gently lower the lobster pieces into the oil and deep-fry for 3–4 minutes until light brown. Use a slotted spoon to carefully remove the lobster from the oil and drain on paper towels.
* Pour out most of the oil, leaving about 2 tablespoons in the wok. Heat the oil, add the ginger slices and stir-fry over medium heat for 1 minute until fragrant. Stir in the black bean sauce. Put in the lobster, increase to high heat, and toss to mix. Add the soy sauce, wine, and chicken broth (stock) and bring to a boil. Sauté the lobster for about 30 seconds, until cooked through. Add the scallions (spring onions), crack in the eggs, and toss to coat the lobster. Add the sesame oil, stir, and transfer to a plate. Serve with rice.

LOBSTER IN BLACK BEAN SAUCE

REGION: TAIWAN
PREPARATION TIME: 10 MINUTES,
    PLUS 1 HOUR SOAKING AND 5 HOURS
    MARINATING TIME
COOKING TIME: 10-15 MINUTES
SERVES: 4-6

蒜香腌蚬仔

BABY CLAMS MARINATED
IN GARLIC SAUCE

- 4 LB/1.8 KG BABY CLAMS
- 2 HEADS (ABOUT 2¼ OZ/60 G) GARLIC, CLOVES SEPARATED
- 1 CUP (8 FL OZ/250 ML) LIGHT SOY SAUCE
- ⅔ CUP (5 FL OZ/150 ML) DARK SOY SAUCE
- 2 TABLESPOONS RICE WINE
- 4 TABLESPOONS GRANULATED SUGAR
- ½ CUP (4 FL OZ/120 ML) BLACK OR BALSAMIC VINEGAR

* Soak the clams in a bowl of cold water for 1 hour until any sand is regurgitated. Drain.
* Put 2 cups (16 fl oz/475 ml) water into the bottom part of a double boiler. Place the clams and 6¼ cups (50 fl oz/1.5 liters) water in the top part. Do not cover.
* Place the double boiler over high heat and, when the temperature of the clam water reaches 130°F/55°C (use a thermometer), stir it once to keep the temperature even throughout the water. When the water temperature reaches 140°F/60°C, turn off the heat. Use a slotted spoon to carefully remove the clams from the water and drain on paper towels. Discard any unopened clams. Strain the clam juice.
* Pour 5¾ cups (45 fl oz/1.3 liters) of the strained clam juice into a saucepan, bring to a boil over high heat, and turn off the heat. Put the saucepan into a baking pan of cold water to reduce the clam juice temperature to 122°F/50°C. Stir in the garlic, soy sauces, rice wine, sugar, and vinegar while keeping the juice temperature between 105–122°F/41–50°C.
* Add the juice to the clams in the bowl and refrigerate for 5 hours. Remove the garlic before serving.

豉椒炒蛏子
RAZOR CLAMS IN
BLACK BEAN SAUCE

REGION: HONG KONG
PREPARATION TIME: 15 MINUTES,
   PLUS 1 HOUR SOAKING TIME
COOKING TIME: 10 MINUTES
SERVES: 4

* Immerse the clams in a bowl of cold water for 1 hour until any sand is regurgitated. Drain.
* Bring a large saucepan of water to a boil, add the clams, and return to a boil. Remove immediately from the heat. Drain and discard any unopened clams. Rinse under cold water, then transfer to a colander. Open up each clam, discard half of each shell, rinse, and remove the intestines.
* Combine the black beans, bean paste, garlic, and sugar and mix into a sauce.
* Heat the vegetable oil in a wok or large skillet (frying pan). Add the ginger and sauce and stir-fry over high heat for 30 seconds until fragrant. Add the chiles and clams and stir-fry for 1 minute. Sprinkle in the wine and soy sauce and stir-fry for another 30 seconds.
* Mix the cornstarch (cornflour) with 1 tablespoon water in a small bowl and stir this mixture into the wok along with the scallions (spring onions). Bring to a boil, stirring, for 30 seconds to thicken the sauce. Drizzle over the sesame oil and transfer to a plate. Serve with rice.

* 1 LB 5 OZ/600 G RAZOR OR ANY TYPE OF CLAMS
* 1½ TABLESPOONS FERMENTED BLACK BEANS, RINSED AND CHOPPED
* 1 TABLESPOON BEAN PASTE
* 2 CLOVES GARLIC, CHOPPED
* 1 TEASPOON GRANULATED SUGAR
* 2 TABLESPOONS VEGETABLE OIL
* ⅛ OZ/5 G GINGER (ABOUT ½-INCH/ 1-CM-LENGTH PIECE), SLICED
* 3 RED CHILES, SEEDED AND SHREDDED
* 1 TABLESPOON SHAOXING WINE
* ½ TABLESPOON LIGHT SOY SAUCE
* 1 TEASPOON CORNSTARCH (CORNFLOUR)
* 2 SCALLIONS (SPRING ONIONS), CUT INTO 1½-INCH/4-CM SECTIONS
* ½ TEASPOON SESAME OIL
* STEAMED RICE (PAGE 540), TO SERVE

蒜茸蒸竹蚌
RAZOR CLAMS WITH
GARLIC SAUCE

REGION: HONG KONG
PREPARATION TIME: 15 MINUTES
COOKING TIME: 4 MINUTES
SERVES: 4

* Bring a large saucepan of water to a boil, add the clams, and return to a boil. Remove immediately from the heat. Drain and discard any unopened clams. Rinse under cold water, then transfer to a colander and drain.
* Open up each clam, discard half of each shell, rinse, and remove the intestines. Slice each piece of meat, lengthwise, in half. Rinse and drain the meat, then place a piece of meat on each side of each shell. Transfer the shells to a heatproof plate.
* Mix the grated garlic, salt, and oil in a bowl. Put about ½ teaspoon of this mixture on each side of each shell. Place the plate in a collapsible pot or bamboo steamer over a pot of boiling water. Steam, covered, for 3–4 minutes.
* Serve immediately.

* 8 LARGE RAZOR CLAMS, RINSED
* 1 HEAD GARLIC, GRATED
* ½ TEASPOON SALT
* 3 TABLESPOONS VEGETABLE OIL

豉椒炒蚬

CLAMS IN BLACK
BEAN SAUCE

- 1 LB 5 OZ/600 G CLAMS
- 1 TABLESPOON HOISIN SAUCE
- 1 TABLESPOON LIGHT SOY SAUCE
- 1 TEASPOON GRANULATED SUGAR
- ½ TEASPOON SALT
- 2 TABLESPOONS VEGETABLE OIL
- ⅛ OZ/5 G GINGER (ABOUT ½-INCH/ 1-CM-LENGTH PIECE), SLICED
- 4 CLOVES GARLIC, CRUSHED
- 2 RED CHILES, SEEDED AND CHOPPED
- 1 TABLESPOON FERMENTED BLACK BEANS, RINSED AND CHOPPED
- 1 TABLESPOON SHAOXING WINE
- 1 TABLESPOON CORNSTARCH (CORNFLOUR)
- 2 SCALLIONS (SPRING ONIONS), CHOPPED, PLUS EXTRA TO GARNISH
- 1 TEASPOON SESAME OIL
- STEAMED RICE (PAGE 540), TO SERVE (OPTIONAL)

* Immerse the clams in a bowl of cold water for 1 hour until any sand is regurgitated. Rinse, then put into a colander to drain.
* Bring a large saucepan of water to a boil, add the clams, and return to a boil. Remove from the heat immediately, drain, and discard any unopened clams.
* Mix the hoisin sauce, soy sauce, sugar, and salt in a small bowl. Set aside.
* Heat the vegetable oil in a wok or large skillet (frying pan) over medium-high heat and add the ginger, garlic, and chiles. Stir-fry for 1–2 minutes until fragrant. Stir in the black beans and clams, sprinkle in the wine, and toss. Add the hoisin sauce mixture and stir.
* Mix the cornstarch (cornflour) with 2 tablespoons water in a small bowl and stir the mixture into the wok. Bring to a boil, stirring, for 30 seconds to thicken the sauce.
* Finally, toss in the scallions (spring onions) and sesame oil. Garnish with extra scallions and serve with rice or as a snack accompanied with beer.

油盐水粉丝浸花甲

CLAMS WITH VERMICELLI

- 1 LB 5 OZ/600 G MANILA OR SHORT NECK CLAMS
- 1 TEASPOON SALT, PLUS EXTRA TO TASTE
- 1 DRIED TANGERINE PEEL
- 1 TABLESPOON VEGETABLE OIL
- 4 CLOVES GARLIC, PEELED
- ¼ OZ/10 G SALTED RUTABAGA, SHREDDED
- 1 RED CHILE, SEEDED AND CHOPPED
- PINCH OF GROUND WHITE PEPPER, PLUS EXTRA TO TASTE
- ¾ OZ/20 G MUNG BEAN VERMICELLI
- 1 STALK CILANTRO (CORIANDER), CUT INTO 2-INCH/5-CM LENGTHS

* Immerse the clams in a bowl of cold water, add the salt, and soak for 1 hour until any sand is regurgitated. Rinse, then put into a colander to drain.
* Meanwhile, soak the tangerine peel in cold water for 10 minutes to soften. Drain and cut into thin strips. Set aside.
* Heat the oil in a wok or large skillet (frying pan), add the garlic, and fry over low heat for 1–2 minutes until fragrant and lightly browned. Put in 3 cups (25 fl oz/750 ml) water, the salted rutabaga, dried tangerine peel, chile, and white pepper. Bring to a boil over medium heat and cook for 2 minutes. Add the clams and mung bean vermicelli and cook for about 2 minutes until the clam shells open. Stir in the cilantro (coriander) and turn off the heat. Adjust the seasoning to taste. Discard any clams that are unopened. Serve the clams with the vermicelli and broth.

CLAMS IN BLACK BEAN SAUCE

炒西施舌
SAUTÉED
CLAMS

- 2 DRIED BLACK MUSHROOMS
- 3¼ LB/1.5 KG CHERRYSTONE CLAMS
- 1½ TABLESPOONS SHAOXING WINE
- 2 TABLESPOONS VEGETABLE OIL
- 2 CLOVES GARLIC, CHOPPED
- ½ CUP (2¾ OZ/75 G) SLICED
  BAMBOO SHOOTS, DRAINED
- STEAMED RICE (PAGE 540),
  TO SERVE

FOR THE SAUCE:
- 1 SCALLION (SPRING ONION),
  CHOPPED
- 3 TABLESPOONS CHICKEN BROTH
  (STOCK, PAGE 90)
- ½ TEASPOON SALT
- 1 TEASPOON GRANULATED SUGAR
- 1 TABLESPOON LIGHT SOY SAUCE
- ½ TEASPOON SESAME OIL
- ½ TEASPOON CORNSTARCH
  (CORNFLOUR)

* Put the mushrooms into a bowl, cover with cold water, and soak for at least 20 minutes, or until softened. Remove the mushrooms, squeeze dry, and discard the stems. Cut into thin slices and set aside.
* Using a clam knife (or a short, dull knife), hold the clam firmly in your hand and insert the knife between the top and bottom shell. Carefully work the knife around to cut through the hinge muscle and pry open the shell. Remove the intestines and slice each piece of meat, lengthwise, into half.
* Bring a small saucepan of water to a boil, then set aside to cool for 5 minutes. Add the clam slices and sit for about 30 seconds. Drain.
* Remove any ligaments and viscera from each clam. Transfer the clams to a bowl and mix with 1 tablespoon wine, then drain.
* To make the sauce, combine the ingredients in a small bowl and mix well. Set aside.
* Heat the vegetable oil in a wok or large skillet (frying pan) over medium-high heat, add the garlic, and stir-fry for 1 minute until fragrant. Add the mushrooms, bamboo shoots, and remaining ½ tablespoon wine, then pour in the sauce and bring to a boil. Simmer for 4 minutes, or until the sauce thickens, then put in the clams and stir rapidly to combine. Transfer to a plate and serve with rice.

花雕蛋白蒸花蛤
CLAMS WITH EGGS AND
SHAOXING WINE

REGION: HONG KONG
PREPARATION TIME: 15 MINUTES
COOKING TIME: 15 MINUTES
SERVES: 4

* Bring a large saucepan of water to a boil, add the clams, and return to a boil. Remove immediately from the heat. Drain and discard any unopened clams. Rinse under cold water, then transfer to a colander. Open up each clam, discard half of each shell, rinse, and remove the intestines.
* Strain the egg whites through a strainer (sieve) into a shallow heatproof bowl, add the chicken broth (stock) and ½ teaspoon salt, and mix well. Cover and seal with aluminum foil and place in a collapsible pot or bamboo steamer over a pot of boiling water. Steam, covered, for 12 minutes. Remove the foil, place the clams in their half shells in the bowl, re-cover and steam for another 3 minutes.
* Meanwhile, heat the oil in a small skillet (frying pan) over low heat. Add the garlic and the remaining ¼ teaspoon salt and stir-fry for 2 minutes until fragrant. Spoon the garlic oil over each clam.
* Combine the wine and sugar in another bowl, mix, and drizzle lightly over the clams. Top with the chopped scallion (spring onion) and serve immediately.

- 1 LB 5 OZ/600 G MANILA CLAMS, BRUSHED AND RINSED
- 6 EGG WHITES, LIGHTLY BEATEN
- 1 CUP (8 FL OZ/250 ML) CHICKEN BROTH (STOCK, PAGE 90)
- ¾ TEASPOON SALT
- 2 TABLESPOONS VEGETABLE OIL
- 6 CLOVES GARLIC, CHOPPED
- 2 TABLESPOONS SHAOXING WINE
- ½ TEASPOON GRANULATED SUGAR
- 1 SCALLION (SPRING ONION), CHOPPED

三丝炒蛏子
CLAMS WITH HAM,
MUSHROOMS, AND PEPPERS

REGION: ZHEJIANG
PREPARATION TIME: 15 MINUTES,
   PLUS 20 MINUTES SOAKING TIME
COOKING TIME: 5 MINUTES
SERVES: 4

* Put the mushrooms into a bowl, cover with cold water, and soak for at least 20 minutes, or until softened. Remove the mushrooms, squeeze dry, and discard the stems. Cut into thin slices and set aside.
* Bring a large saucepan of water to a boil. Add the clams and blanch for 1 minute until the clams open up. Drain, discard any unopened shells, and set aside to cool briefly. Remove the clam meat from the shells, remove the intestines, rinse, and set aside.
* Heat the vegetable oil in a wok or large skillet (frying pan) over medium heat, add the ginger, and stir-fry for 1 minute until fragrant. Put in the mushrooms and ham and stir-fry for another minute. Add the clams and cayenne peppers, and stir-fry over high heat for another 30 seconds. Stir in the vinegar, soy sauce, salt, and sugar. Mix in the sesame oil and transfer to a plate. Serve with rice.

- 4 DRIED BLACK MUSHROOMS
- 1 LB 5 OZ/600 G RAZOR CLAMS, RINSED
- 2 TABLESPOONS VEGETABLE OIL
- ⅛ OZ/5 G GINGER (ABOUT ½-INCH/ 1-CM-LENGTH PIECE), SLICED
- 1 OZ/25 G JINHUA OR SMITHFIELD HAM, CUT INTO STRIPS
- 2 RED OR GREEN CAYENNE PEPPERS, SEEDED AND CUT INTO STRIPS
- 1 TEASPOON WHITE VINEGAR
- ½ TABLESPOON LIGHT SOY SAUCE
- ¼ TEASPOON SALT
- ½ TEASPOON GRANULATED SUGAR
- ½ TEASPOON SESAME OIL
- STEAMED RICE (PAGE 540), TO SERVE

REGION: CHAOZHOU
PREPARATION TIME: 5 MINUTES,
  PLUS 1 HOUR SOAKING TIME
COOKING TIME: 5 MINUTES
SERVES: 4
🖼 PAGE 217

韭菜炒蚬
CLAMS WITH
CHIVES

- 11 OZ/300 G CLAMS, RINSED
- 2 TABLESPOONS VEGETABLE OIL
- ½ OZ/15 G GINGER (ABOUT
  1-INCH/2.5-CM-LENGTH PIECE),
  CHOPPED
- 1 CLOVE GARLIC, FINELY CHOPPED
- 1 RED CHILE, SEEDED AND
  THINLY SLICED
- ½ TEASPOON GRANULATED SUGAR
- 5 OZ/150 G CHINESE CHIVES, CUT
  INTO ½-INCH/1-CM SECTIONS
- ½ TEASPOON FISH SAUCE
- PINCH OF GROUND WHITE PEPPER

* Immerse the clams in a bowl of cold water, add the salt, and soak for 1 hour until any sand is regurgitated. Rinse, then put into a colander to drain.
* Put the clams into a saucepan and add enough water to cover them completely. Bring to a boil over high heat and blanch for 30 seconds. Drain.
* Heat the oil in a wok or large skillet (frying pan) over high heat. Add the ginger, garlic, and chile and stir-fry for 30 seconds until fragrant. Add the clams, sugar, chives, and fish sauce and stir-fry for 1 minute, or until the clams are cooked through. Add the white pepper, toss, and transfer to a plate. Serve with rice.

金不换炒薄壳
MUSSELS WITH
BASIL

- 1 LB 5 OZ/600 G FRESH MUSSELS,
  CLEANED AND RINSED
- 1 TEASPOON SALT
- 1 TEASPOON GRANULATED SUGAR
- 2 TABLESPOONS SHA CHA SAUCE
- 2 TABLESPOONS VEGETABLE OIL
- 4 CLOVES GARLIC, CHOPPED
- 2 SMALL RED CHILES, SLICED
- 1 TEASPOON WHITE WINE VINEGAR
- 1 TEASPOON LIGHT SOY SAUCE
- 1½ CUPS (2¾ OZ/75 G) BASIL
  LEAVES
- STEAMED RICE (PAGE 540), TO SERVE

The Asian mussel, also known as the Asian date mussel or bag mussel, is a small olive-green mussel with pale purple stripes radiating from the center of growth. This is a classic Chaozhou dish but if Asian mussels are not available, any type of mussel can be used with acceptable results.

* Place the mussels in a large pot with enough cold water to cover, add the salt, and soak for 1 hour. Rinse the mussels under cold running water a few times until the water runs clear and there is no trace of sand. Drain.
* Combine the sugar, sha cha sauce, and 2 tablespoons water in a small bowl and mix well.
* Heat the oil in a wok or large skillet (frying pan) over medium-high heat, add the garlic, and stir-fry over high heat for 1 minute until fragrant. Add the sha cha sauce mixture, chiles, vinegar, and soy sauce and stir. Add the mussels and stir-fry for 1–2 minutes, or until the shells open, then toss in the basil. Discard any unopened shell. Transfer to a plate and serve with rice.

CLAMS WITH CHIVES

REGION: HONG KONG
PREPARATION TIME: 5 MINUTES
COOKING TIME: 25 MINUTES
SERVES: 3–4

蜜汁金蠔
SEMI-DRIED OYSTERS
IN SAUCE

- 12 SEMI-DRIED OYSTERS
- 1½ TABLESPOONS GINGER JUICE
- 2 TABLESPOONS GRANULATED SUGAR
- 1 TABLESPOON SHAOXING WINE
- 1 TABLESPOON OYSTER SAUCE
- ½ TEASPOON GROUND WHITE PEPPER
- 1 TEASPOON SESAME OIL
- STEAMED RICE (PAGE 540), TO SERVE

  FOR THE PUFFED VERMICELLI
  (OPTIONAL):
- 2 TABLESPOONS VEGETABLE OIL
- ¼ OZ/5 G MUNG BEAN VERMICELLI

This recipe uses semi-dried oysters, which should not be confused with the dried oysters used in some of the other recipes in the book. Semi-dried oysters are oysters that have been dried in the open air for less than a week and therefore still retain a lot of their moisture. They are plump and soft to the touch.

* Rinse the oysters thoroughly and pat dry with paper towels.
* In a heatproof bowl, combine the oysters, ginger juice, sugar, wine, oyster sauce, and white pepper and mix well. Place in a collapsible pot or bamboo steamer over a pot of boiling water. Steam, covered, for 10 minutes. Remove and drain the cooking juices into a large bowl. Set aside the oysters.
* To make the puffed vermicelli, heat the vegetable oil in a wok or large skillet (frying pan) over medium-high heat, add the vermicelli, and fry for 1 minute until puffed and crispy. Use a slotted spoon to transfer to a plate and keep warm.
* Add the oysters to the wok and pan-fry over low heat for 5–6 minutes until golden brown. Stir in the reserved oyster cooking juices, increase to medium heat, and simmer, uncovered, for 5–6 minutes until the sauce is reduced and thickened. The sauce should adhere to the oysters at this stage. Use a spatula (fish slice) to turn the oysters once to coat them in the sauce.
* Place the oysters on top of the vermicelli and brush with the sesame oil. Serve with rice.

客家酿蚝豉
DRIED OYSTERS
WRAPPED IN PORK

REGION: HAKKA
PREPARATION TIME: 20 MINUTES,
   PLUS 5 MINUTES SOAKING AND
   10 MINUTES MARINATING TIME
COOKING TIME: 20 MINUTES
SERVES: 4

* Soak the dried oysters in a bowl of cold water for 5 minutes, or until softened. Drain, then combine with the ginger juice, scallion (spring onion), and wine in a small heatproof bowl.
* Place the bowl in a collapsible pot or bamboo steamer over a pot of boiling water. Steam, covered, for 10 minutes. Remove and strain the cooking liquid into a large bowl. Set them both aside.
* Add the pork, soy sauce, ½ teaspoon salt, and the sugar to the oyster cooking liquid. Mix well and marinate for 10 minutes. Stir in the oatmeal, cornstarch (cornflour), and white pepper.
* Wrap an oyster in a heaping tablespoon of the pork mixture, adding more if necessary. Shape into an oval ball, enclosing the oyster completely with the pork. Repeat with the remaining oysters and pork mixture.
* Soak the vermicelli in a bowl of hot water for about 3 minutes to soften.
* Meanwhile, combine the garlic, remaining ½ teaspoon salt, and oil in a small bowl. Drain, then transfer the vermicelli to a heatproof shallow bowl and stir in the garlic oil. Place the wrapped oysters on top of the vermicelli and put into a collapsible pot or bamboo steamer over a pot of boiling water. Steam, covered, for 10 minutes until the pork mixture is cooked through. Carefully remove the bowl from the pot and serve with rice.

- 8 DRIED OYSTERS
- 1 TEASPOON GINGER JUICE
- 1 SCALLION (SPRING ONION), SHREDDED
- 1 TEASPOON RICE WINE
- 7 OZ/200 G GROUND (MINCED) PORK
- 1 TEASPOON LIGHT SOY SAUCE
- 1 TEASPOON SALT
- ½ TEASPOON GRANULATED SUGAR
- 1 TEASPOON OATMEAL, CRUSHED
- 1 TEASPOON CORNSTARCH (CORNFLOUR)
- 2 OZ/50 G MUNG BEAN VERMICELLI
- ¼ TEASPOON GROUND WHITE PEPPER
- 3 CLOVES GARLIC, CHOPPED
- 1 TEASPOON VEGETABLE OIL
- STEAMED RICE (PAGE 540), TO SERVE

REGION: HONG KONG
PREPARATION TIME: 10 MINUTES,
    PLUS 20 MINUTES SOAKING TIME
COOKING TIME: 10 MINUTES
SERVES: 4
📷 PAGE 221

蠔松生菜包
LETTUCE WRAPS WITH
DRIED OYSTERS

- 6 DRIED BLACK MUSHROOM
- 12 LARGE DRIED OYSTERS
- 5 OZ/150 G GROUND (MINCED) PORK
- ¼ TEASPOON SALT
- 1 TEASPOON CORNSTARCH
  (CORNFLOUR)
- 3 TABLESPOONS VEGETABLE OIL
- ¼ OZ/10 G GINGER (ABOUT ¾-INCH/
  2-CM-LENGTH PIECE), FINELY
  CHOPPED
- 2 SHALLOTS, FINELY CHOPPED
- 2 SMALL CARROTS, FINELY CHOPPED
- 1 DUCK LIVER SAUSAGE, FINELY
  CHOPPED
- 1 TABLESPOON BEAN PASTE
- 1 TEASPOON OYSTER SAUCE
- 2 TABLESPOONS GINGER JUICE
- 1 TEASPOON GRANULATED SUGAR
- 6 WATER CHESTNUTS, FINELY CHOPPED
- ½ TEASPOON SESAME OIL
- 1 QUANTITY PUFFED VERMICELLI (PAGE
  218, OPTIONAL)
- 1 HEAD ICEBERG LETTUCE, LEAVES
  SEPARATED

* Put the mushrooms into a bowl, cover with cold water, and soak for at least 20 minutes, or until softened. Remove the mushrooms, squeeze dry, and discard the stems. Drain and finely chop.
* In a bowl, soak the oysters in cold water for 15 minutes, or until softened and thoroughly cleaned. Finely chop.
* Combine the pork, salt, and 2 tablespoons water in a separate bowl and marinate for 10 minutes. Mix in the cornstarch (cornflour).
* Heat 2 tablespoons vegetable oil in a wok or large skillet (frying pan) over medium-high heat, add the pork, and stir-fry for 3–5 minutes, or until cooked through. Transfer to a plate.
* Heat the remaining 1 tablespoon oil in the wok over medium-high heat, add the ginger and shallots, and stir-fry for 1 minute until fragrant. Stir in the oysters, mushrooms, carrots, sausage, bean paste, oyster sauce, ginger juice, sugar, pork, and water chestnuts. Toss well and mix in the sesame oil.
* Transfer the oyster mixture to a platter, garnish with puffed vermicelli, if using, and serve with the lettuce cups.

LETTUCE WRAPS WITH DRIED OYSTERS

酥炸生蠔
DEEP-FRIED
OYSTERS

- 1 LB 5 OZ/600 G OYSTERS, SHUCKED
- 1 TEASPOON SALT
- 2 TABLESPOONS GINGER JUICE
- 1 TABLESPOON RICE WINE
- 1 TABLESPOON LIGHT SOY SAUCE
- ¼ TEASPOON GROUND WHITE PEPPER
- 2 CUPS (16 FL OZ/475 ML)
  VEGETABLE OIL
- WORCESTERSHIRE SAUCE, TO SERVE
- STEAMED RICE (PAGE 540), TO SERVE

  FOR THE BATTER:
- 3 TABLESPOONS ALL-PURPOSE
  (PLAIN) FLOUR
- 1 TABLESPOON CORNSTARCH
  (CORNFLOUR)
- ¼ TEASPOON BAKING POWDER
- ½ TEASPOON SALT
- ½ TABLESPOON VEGETABLE OIL

  FOR THE SPICED SALT:
- 1 TEASPOON SALT
- PINCH OF FIVE-SPICE POWDER

* To make the spiced salt, heat the salt in a small dry skillet (frying pan) over medium-high heat. Remove from the heat, allow to cool, and then mix in the five-spice powder. Set aside.
* Use a soft brush to clean the oysters, then rub them gently with the salt. Rinse under cold running water and drain.
* Bring a large saucepan of water to a boil, add the oysters, and blanch for 30 seconds.
* Combine the ginger juice, wine, soy sauce, and white pepper in a small bowl and mix well. Add the oysters and marinate for 10 minutes, then drain.
* Combine all the batter ingredients and 4 tablespoons water in a large bowl.
* Heat the oil in a wok or deep saucepan to 300°F/150°C, or until a cube of bread browns in 1½ minutes. Dip the oysters into the batter, one at a time, and then gently lower into the hot oil and deep-fry, in batches, for 2 minutes until golden brown. Use a slotted spoon to carefully remove the oysters from the oil and drain on paper towels.
* Serve the oysters with the spiced salt and Worcestershire sauce, alongside steamed rice.

蚝烙
OYSTER PANCAKE

REGION: CHAOZHOU
PREPARATION TIME: 10 MINUTES
COOKING TIME: 15 MINUTES
SERVES: 4

* Rub the oysters with the cornstarch (cornflour) and pick out any fragments of shell. Rinse under cold running water.
* Bring a saucepan of water to a boil over high heat, add the oysters, and blanch for about 30 seconds. Drain.
* In a large bowl, combine the sweet potato starch, cilantro (coriander), salt, white pepper, and ½ cup (4 fl oz/120 ml) water. Add the oysters and combine well.
* Heat 2 tablespoons oil in a wok or large skillet (frying pan) over medium heat, add the scallions (spring onions), and stir-fry for 1 minute until fragrant. Pour in the oyster batter, smoothing it out evenly on the surface of the wok to form a round pancake. Pour the eggs on top and fry for 4–5 minutes until lightly browned.
* When the pancake is about half cooked, use a spatula (fish slice) to flip it over. Add the remaining 1 tablespoon oil along the inside of the wok and fry for another 4–5 minutes until the edges of the pancake become crispy. Transfer to a plate and serve with the fish sauce as a dip.

* 11 OZ/300 G PEARL OYSTERS OR SMALL OYSTERS, SHUCKED
* 1 TABLESPOON CORNSTARCH (CORNFLOUR)
* ⅓ CUP (2 OZ/50 G) SWEET POTATO STARCH
* 2 BUNCHES CILANTRO (CORIANDER), CUT INTO ½-INCH/1-CM LENGTHS
* ½ TEASPOON SALT
* ½ TEASPOON GROUND WHITE PEPPER
* 3 TABLESPOONS VEGETABLE OIL
* 2 SCALLIONS (SPRING ONIONS), STEM ONLY, CHOPPED INTO ½-INCH/1-CM PIECES
* 3 DUCK EGGS, BEATEN
* FISH SAUCE, TO SERVE

荫豉煮鲜蚵
OYSTERS WITH BLACK BEANS

REGION: TAIWAN
PREPARATION TIME: 5 MINUTES
COOKING TIME: 5 MINUTES
SERVES: 4

* Rub the oysters with the cornstarch (cornflour) and pick out any fragments of shell. Rinse well under cold running water. Set aside.
* Bring a saucepan of water to a boil over high heat, add the oysters, and blanch for about 30 seconds. Drain.
* Heat the vegetable oil in a wok or large frying pan (skillet) over medium heat, add the scallions (spring onions), and stir-fry for 1 minute until slightly brown. Add the garlic and stir-fry for another minute until fragrant. Stir in the chile and black beans and cook for 30 seconds until fragrant, then add the wine, chicken broth (stock), soy sauce, sugar, and salt and bring to a boil. Add the oysters, stir, and remove from the heat. Stir in the sesame oil and transfer to a serving plate. Serve with rice.

* 11 OZ/300 G PEARL OYSTER OR ANY SMALL OYSTER MEAT, RINSED
* 1 TABLESPOON CORNSTARCH (CORNFLOUR)
* 1 TABLESPOON VEGETABLE OIL
* 4 SCALLIONS (SPRING ONIONS), CUT INTO ¾-INCH/2-CM LENGTHS
* 3 CLOVES GARLIC, CHOPPED
* ½ RED CHILE, SEEDED AND SLICED
* 1 TABLESPOON FERMENTED BLACK BEANS, RINSED AND CHOPPED
* 2 TABLESPOONS RICE WINE
* 1¼ CUPS (10 FL OZ/300 ML) CHICKEN BROTH (STOCK, PAGE 90)
* 1 TABLESPOON DARK SOY SAUCE
* ½ TEASPOON GRANULATED SUGAR
* ¼ TEASPOON SALT
* 1 TEASPOON SESAME OIL
* STEAMED RICE (PAGE 540), TO SERVE

REGION: ANHUI
PREPARATION TIME: 20 MINUTES
COOKING TIME: 1 HOUR
SERVES: 4

干贝萝卜
STEAMED DAIKON RADISH
WITH DRIED SCALLOP

- 2 MEDIUM DRIED SCALLOPS
- 1 TEASPOON GINGER JUICE
- 1 TABLESPOON SHAOXING WINE
- 2½ TABLESPOONS VEGETABLE OIL
- 1 LB 2 OZ/500 G DAIKON RADISH,
  CUT INTO ½-INCH/1-CM SLICES
- ½ OZ/15 G JINHUA OR SMITHFIELD
  HAM, CUT INTO 2-INCH/5-CM STRIPS
- ⅔ CUP (5 FL OZ/150 ML) CHICKEN
  BROTH (STOCK, PAGE 90)
- 1 TEASPOON SALT
- ¼ TEASPOON GRANULATED SUGAR
- 2 TEASPOONS CORNSTARCH
  (CORNFLOUR)
- 1 SCALLION (SPRING ONION),
  CHOPPED, TO GARNISH
- STEAMED RICE (PAGE 540), TO SERVE

* Put the dried scallops, ginger juice, wine, and 4 tablespoons water into a heatproof bowl and place in a collapsible pot or bamboo steamer over a pot of boiling water. Steam, covered, for 15 minutes. Set aside.
* Use your fingers to shred the scallops into thin strands. Pour the juices from the steamed scallops through a strainer (sieve) into a bowl and reserve for later use.
* Heat 2 tablespoons oil in a skillet (frying pan), add the Daikon, and cook over low heat for 5 minutes, or until softened. Remove from the skillet and set aside.
* Place the scallops in the bottom of a heatproof bowl, surround with the ham, and top with the Daikon radish. Add the chicken broth (stock), the reserved scallop juices, salt, and sugar and seal the bowl with aluminum foil. Place the bowl in a collapsible pot or bamboo steamer over a pot of boiling water. Steam, covered, for 45 minutes until the scallops are tender. Remove from the heat and leave to cool slightly.
* When the bowl is cool enough to handle, carefully remove the foil. Drain the sauce into a wok. Cover the bowl of Daikon radishes with a shallow dish and, using dish towels, invert the contents into the dish. (Alternatively, use tongs to transfer the everything.)
* Heat the sauce in the wok over high heat. Mix the cornstarch (cornflour) with 2 tablespoons water in a small bowl and stir this mixture into the wok. Bring to a boil, stirring, for 30 seconds to thicken the sauce. Add the remaining ½ tablespoon oil, stir, then pour the sauce over the scallop dish. Garnish with the scallion (spring onion) and serve with rice.

干贝明珠
DRIED SCALLOPS WITH
QUAIL EGGS

REGION: YUNNAN
PREPARATION TIME: 15 MINUTES,
  PLUS 20 MINUTES SOAKING TIME
COOKING TIME: 1 HOUR 10 MINUTES
SERVES: 4

* Put the mushrooms into a bowl, cover with cold water, and soak for at least 20 minutes, or until softened. Remove the mushrooms, squeeze dry, and discard the stems. Cut into thin slices.
* Meanwhile, in a small bowl, soak the dried scallops in ½ cup (4 fl oz/120 ml) cold water for 15 minutes. Drain and remove the tough muscle.
* Bring a small saucepan of water to a boil over high heat, add the pea shoots, and blanch for 1 minute. Drain and set aside to cool.
* Combine the chicken with ¼ teaspoon salt in a small bowl.
* Line the bottom of a heatproof bowl with the scallops, then add the chicken, mushrooms, bamboo shoots, and ham. Place in a collapsible pot or bamboo steamer over a pot of boiling water. Steam, covered, for 1 hour. (Add more water to the pot if needed.)
* Drain the steamed juices from the bowl into a wok or skillet (frying pan). Cover the bowl of scallops with a serving plate and, using dish towels, invert the contents onto the plate. (Alternatively, use tongs to transfer the scallops.) Surround the scallops with pea shoots and the quail eggs.
* Add the remaining ¾ teaspoon salt and the white pepper to the wok. Mix the cornstarch (cornflour) with 1 tablespoon water in a small bowl and stir this mixture into the wok. Bring to a boil, stirring, for 30 seconds to thicken the sauce. Stir in the sesame oil. Pour the sauce over the scallops. Serve with rice.

- 3 DRIED BLACK MUSHROOMS
- 2 OZ/50 G DRIED SCALLOPS
- 3½ OZ/100 G PEA SHOOTS
- 1 BONELESS, SKINLESS CHICKEN BREAST, FINELY CHOPPED
- 1 TEASPOON SALT
- ¼ CUP (1½ OZ/40 G) SLICED BAMBOO SHOOTS
- 1 OZ/25 G YUNNAN OR ANY DRY-CURED HAM, SLICED
- 12 HARD-BOILED QUAIL EGGS
- ¼ TEASPOON GROUND WHITE PEPPER
- 1 TEASPOON CORNSTARCH (CORNFLOUR)
- ½ TEASPOON SESAME OIL
- STEAMED RICE (PAGE 540), TO SERVE

REGION: HONG KONG
PREPARATION TIME: 15 MINUTES
COOKING TIME: 10 MINUTES
SERVES: 4
PAGE 227

蒜蓉粉丝蒸扇贝
STEAMED SCALLOPS
WITH GARLIC

- 8 SEA SCALLOPS
- ¾ OZ/20 G MUNG BEAN VERMICELLI
- 4 TABLESPOONS VEGETABLE OIL
- 16 CLOVES GARLIC, CHOPPED
- ½ TEASPOON SEA SALT
- 2 TABLESPOONS CHOPPED SCALLIONS
  (SPRING ONIONS)
- 1 RED CHILE, SLICED (OPTIONAL)

* Clean the scallop shells with a brush and pat dry with paper towels. Separate the 2 sides of the shells and discard the side unattached to the adductor muscles. Remove the muscles from the shell and discard the intestines, then rinse under cold running water. Set the scallops aside in a bowl and reserve 8 shells. Soak the vermicelli in a bowl of hot water for about 3 minutes to soften. Drain, then cut the vermicelli into 2-inch/5-cm lengths. Divide the vermicelli among the shells and place the scallops on top.
* Heat 3 tablespoons oil in a wok or large skillet (frying pan), add half the chopped garlic and stir-fry over low heat for 1 minute until lightly golden and crisp. Use a slotted spoon to remove the garlic, and drain on paper towels. Set aside.
* Combine the remaining chopped garlic, the salt, and remaining 1 tablespoon oil in a bowl and mix well. Drizzle over the scallops. Transfer to a collapsible pot or bamboo steamer over a pot of boiling water. Steam, covered, for 5–6 minutes until the scallops are cooked through.
* Top with the garlic, scallions (spring onions), and chile, if using.

REGION: HUBEI
PREPARATION TIME: 10 MINUTES
COOKING TIME: 15 MINUTES
SERVES: 4

桂花干贝
DRIED SCALLOPS
WITH EGGS

- 10 MEDIUM DRIED SCALLOPS
- 1 EGG
- 5 EGG YOLKS
- ½ TEASPOON SALT
- 4 TABLESPOONS LARD
- STEAMED RICE (PAGE 540), TO SERVE

* Put the dried scallops and ½ cup (4 fl oz/120 ml) cold water in a small bowl and soak for 5 minutes. Drain, then remove the small hard muscle. Put the scallops into a heatproof bowl and place in a collapsible pot or bamboo steamer over a pot of boiling water. Steam, covered, for 10 minutes. Drain the juices from the bowl and shred the scallops into thin fibers.
* Combine the egg and egg yolks in a bowl and beat. Stir in the shredded scallops and salt.
* Heat the lard in a wok or large skillet (frying pan) over medium heat. Add the scallop and egg mixture and use the back of a spatula (fish slice) to scramble until the eggs cling to the scallops. Transfer to a plate and serve with rice.

FISH & SEAFOOD

STEAMED SCALLOPS WITH GARLIC

REGION: HONG KONG
PREPARATION TIME: 10 MINUTES
COOKING TIME: 15 MINUTES
SERVES: 4
📷 PAGE 229

虾酱带子炒芦笋
SCALLOPS AND ASPARAGUS

- 11 OZ/300 G ASPARAGUS, TRIMMED
- 11 OZ/300 G FROZEN SEA SCALLOPS, DEFROSTED AND RINSED
- 2 TABLESPOONS VEGETABLE OIL
- 3 CLOVES GARLIC, 1 SLICED AND 2 FINELY CHOPPED
- ½ CARROT, CUT INTO ¼-INCH/ 5-MM-THICK SLICES
- ¼ TEASPOON SALT
- 2 TEASPOONS SHAOXING WINE
- 1 TEASPOON GRANULATED SUGAR
- ½ TEASPOON SHRIMP PASTE
- 4 SCALLIONS (SPRING ONIONS), CUT INTO 1½-INCH/4-CM LENGTHS
- ½ TEASPOON CORNSTARCH (CORNFLOUR)
- ½ TEASPOON SESAME OIL
- STEAMED RICE (PAGE 540), TO SERVE

* Cut the asparagus stems, at an angle, into 1½-inch/4-cm-long pieces, about ½-inch/1-cm thick.
* Bring a saucepan of water to a boil over high heat. Add the scallops and blanch for 1 minute. Remove the scallops with a slotted spoon and drain.
* Heat 1 tablespoon vegetable oil in a wok, add the sliced garlic and stir-fry over high heat for 1 minute until fragrant. Add the asparagus, carrot, and salt and stir-fry rapidly for 1 minute. Remove the asparagus and carrot from the wok.
* Heat the remaining 1 tablespoon oil in a clean wok over medium heat. Add the chopped garlic, wine, sugar, shrimp paste, scallops, asparagus, carrot, and scallions (spring onions) and stir-fry rapidly for about 30 seconds.
* Mix the cornstarch (cornflour) with ½ tablespoon water in a small bowl, then stir this mixture into the wok. Bring to a boil, stirring, for about 30 seconds to thicken the sauce. Stir in the sesame oil and transfer to a serving plate. Serve with rice.

REGION: SHUNDE
PREPARATION TIME: 5 MINUTES, PLUS 15 MINUTES MARINATING TIME
COOKING TIME: 5 MINUTES
SERVES: 4

荷芹炒田鸡
FROG LEGS WITH SNOW PEAS AND CELERY

- 8 FROG LEGS, RINSED AND DRAINED
- 1 TABLESPOON GINGER JUICE
- 1 TEASPOON LIGHT SOY SAUCE
- 2 TEASPOONS CORNSTARCH (CORNFLOUR)
- 2 TABLESPOONS VEGETABLE OIL
- ¼ OZ/10 G GINGER (ABOUT ¾-INCH/ 2-CM-LENGTH PIECE), SLICED
- 1¼ CUPS (3½ OZ/100 G) SNOW PEAS (MANGETOUT), STRINGY PART REMOVED AND TRIMMED
- 2 STALKS CELERY, CUT DIAGONALLY INTO ¼-INCH/5-MM-THICK SLICES
- ½ CARROT, THINLY SLICED
- ½ TEASPOON SALT, PLUS EXTRA TO TASTE
- 1 TABLESPOON RICE WINE
- STEAMED RICE (PAGE 540), TO SERVE

* Combine the frog legs, ginger juice, and soy sauce in a bowl and marinate for 15 minutes. Mix in the cornstarch (cornflour).
* Heat 1 tablespoon oil in a wok or large skillet (frying pan) over medium-high, add the sliced ginger, snow peas (mangetout), celery, carrot, and ½ teaspoon salt and stir-fry for about 30 seconds. Transfer the ingredients to a plate and set aside.
* Heat the remaining 1 tablespoon oil in the wok over high heat, add the frog legs, and stir-fry for 1–2 minutes until cooked through. Sprinkle in the wine and stir in the snow peas, celery, and carrots. Toss thoroughly and season with salt to taste. Serve with rice.

SCALLOPS AND ASPARAGUS

REGION: HONG KONG
PREPARATION TIME: 30 MINUTES
COOKING TIME: 10 MINUTES
SERVES: 6
📷 PAGE 231

清蒸鲍鱼
STEAMED ABALONES

- 6 FRESH ABALONES IN THE SHELL, (ABOUT 2 OZ/50 G EACH)
- ¼ TEASPOON SALT
- ⅛ OZ/5 G GINGER (ABOUT ½-INCH/ 1-CM-LENGTH PIECE), SHREDDED
- 3 CLOVES GARLIC, GRATED
- 1 TABLESPOON VEGETABLE OIL
- 1 SCALLION (SPRING ONION), SHREDDED
- 1 RED CHILE, SLICED, TO GARNISH (OPTIONAL)
- STEAMED RICE (PAGE 540), TO SERVE

* Brush the abalone shells and rinse thoroughly. Bring a large saucepan of water to a boil, add the abalone, and blanch for 1 minute. Drain and rinse under cold water.
* Using a small knife, separate the abalone meat from each shell and remove the internal organs. Clean the feet (the flat side) of the abalones by scraping it lightly with a knife and brush the sides clean. Rinse the abalones thoroughly.
* Put the abalones back in the shells and place on a heatproof plate with the shells facing down. Mix the salt, ginger, garlic, and oil in a small bowl and drizzle on top of the abalones. Place in a collapsible pot or bamboo steamer over a pot of boiling water. Steam, covered, for 7–10 minutes until cooked through. Do not overcook. Transfer the abalones to a serving plate and top with the shredded scallion (spring onion) and chile. Serve with rice.

REGION: HONG KONG
PREPARATION TIME: 15 MINUTES
COOKING TIME: 5 MINUTES
SERVES: 4

椒盐鲍鱼
ABALONES WITH SPICED SALT

- 8 FRESH ABALONE IN THE SHELL
- 2 CUPS (16 FL OZ/475 ML) VEGETABLE OIL
- 2 TABLESPOONS CORNSTARCH (CORNFLOUR)

FOR THE SPICED SALT:
- 1 TEASPOON SALT
- 1 TEASPOON SHAJIANG POWDER
- ½ TEASPOON FIVE-SPICE POWDER
- ½ TEASPOON CHILI POWDER

* To make the spiced salt, heat the salt in a small dry skillet (frying pan) over low heat, then remove from the heat. Add the remaining ingredients and mix well. Put the spiced salt into a salt shaker and set aside.
* Brush the abalone shells and rinse thoroughly. Bring a large saucepan of water to a boil, add the abalone, and blanch for 1 minute. Drain and rinse under cold water.
* Using a small knife, separate the abalone meat from each shell and remove the internal organs. Clean the feet (the flat side) of the abalones by scraping lightly with a knife and brush the sides with a brush. Rinse the abalones thoroughly. Score the foot of each abalone in a crisscross pattern. The cuts should be deep but not cutting through the sides. Set aside the shells.
* Heat the oil in a wok or deep saucepan to 350°F/180°C, or until a cube of bread browns in 30 seconds. Lightly dredge the abalone in the cornstarch (cornflour), gently lower into the oil, one at a time, and deep-fry for 30 seconds.
* Sprinkle both sides of each abalone with the spiced salt and put them back into their shells. Serve immediately, whole or sliced.

STEAMED ABALONES

REGION: SHANDONG
PREPARATION TIME: 20 MINUTES
COOKING TIME: 10 MINUTES
SERVES: 4

扒原壳鲍鱼
SAUTÉED
ABALONES

- 8 FRESH ABALONE IN THE SHELL
  (ABOUT 4 OZ/120 G EACH), BRUSHED
  AND RINSED
- 1¼ OZ/30 G CHINESE CURED BACON
- 1½ CUPS (2¼ OZ/60 G) SLICED
  BAMBOO SHOOTS
- 1 TABLESPOON LARD
- ½ CUP (4 FL OZ/120 ML) CHICKEN
  BROTH (STOCK, PAGE 90)
- ¼ TEASPOON SALT
- 1 TABLESPOON SHAOXING WINE
- 1 TEASPOON CORNSTARCH
  (CORNFLOUR)
- STEAMED RICE (PAGE 540), TO SERVE

* Brush the abalone shells and rinse thoroughly. Bring a large saucepan of water to a boil, add the abalone, and blanch for 1 minute. Remove the abalones with a slotted spoon, leaving the remaining water in the wok. Rinse the abalone and drain.
* Using a small knife, separate the abalone meat from each shell and remove the internal organs. Clean the feet (the flat side) of the abalones by scraping it lightly with a knife and brush the sides clean. Rinse the abalones thoroughly. Cut into ¼-inch/5-mm-thick slices and set aside.
* Return the abalone shells to the wok and blanch for about 1 minute over high heat, then place the shells on a plate, with the insides of the shells facing upward, ready to act as serving dishes for the abalone. Set aside.
* Put the cured bacon in a collapsible pot or bamboo steamer over a pot of boiling water. Steam, covered, for 5 minutes. Cut the bacon into thin slices. Set aside.
* If using fresh bamboo shoots, bring a saucepan of water to a boil, add the bamboo shoots, and blanch for 1 minute. Drain and rinse under cold running water.
* Heat the lard in a wok or frying pan (skillet) over medium heat, add the chicken broth (stock), salt, and wine, and bring to a boil. Put in the cured bacon, bamboo shoots, and abalones and sauté for 30 seconds. Distribute the abalone, cured bacon, and bamboo evenly among the shells.
* Increase to high heat and reduce the sauce left in the wok by half. Mix the cornstarch (cornflour) with 1 tablespoon water in a small bowl, then stir this mixture into the wok. Bring to a boil, stirring, for about 30 seconds to thicken the sauce.
* Drizzle the sauce over the abalones in the shells. Serve with steamed rice.

香荽三杯小卷
SQUID WITH CHILES
AND CILANTRO

REGION: TAIWAN
PREPARATION TIME: 15 MINUTES
COOKING TIME: 5 MINUTES
SERVES: 4

* Bring a saucepan of water to a boil over high heat. Add the squid and blanch for 10 seconds. Drain immediately and rinse under cold running water. Cut the squid into ¾-inch/ 2-cm rings. Set aside.
* Heat the sesame oil in a wok or large skillet (frying pan) over medium heat, add the garlic, ginger, and scallions (spring onions), and stir-fry for 1 minute until fragrant. Add the wine, soy sauce, and rock sugar.
* Increase to high heat, add the squid rings, and stir-fry for 1–2 minutes, or until the squid rings are cooked. Stir in the chiles and cilantro (coriander), season with salt to taste, and then transfer to a plate.

• 2 LB/900 G SQUID, CLEANED
• ½ CUP (4 FL OZ/120 ML) SESAME OIL
• 8 CLOVES GARLIC, SLICED
• ¾ OZ/20 G GINGER (ABOUT 1-INCH/ 2.5-CM-LENGTH PIECE), CHOPPED
• 3 SCALLIONS (SPRING ONIONS), STEM ONLY, CHOPPED
• ½ CUP (4 FL OZ/120 ML) RICE WINE
• ½ CUP (4 FL OZ/120 ML) LIGHT SOY SAUCE
• 1 OZ/25 G ROCK SUGAR, CRUSHED
• 4 RED CHILES, SEEDED AND DICED
• 4 BUNCHES CILANTRO (CORIANDER), CHOPPED
• SALT, TO TASTE

酥炸鱿鱼须
SQUID WITH SPICED SALT

REGION: HONG KONG
PREPARATION TIME: 10 MINUTES
COOKING TIME: 5 MINUTES
SERVES: 4

* To make the spiced salt, heat a small skillet (frying pan) over medium-high heat and add the salt. Stir for 30 seconds, just to warm, and remove from the heat. Transfer to a small bowl and cool slightly. Stir in the remaining ingredients and mix well.
* Bring a large saucepan of water to a boil, add the tentacles, and cook for 30 seconds, or until the tentacles start to curl. Drain, then pat dry with paper towels. Put the tentacles into a bowl and mix in the cornstarch (cornflour).
* Combine all the batter ingredients and ¾ cup (6 fl oz/175 ml) cold water in a large bowl. Add the tentacles and mix well so that each piece is coated in batter.
* Heat the oil in a wok or deep saucepan to 350°F/180°C, or until a cube of bread browns in 30 seconds. Gently lower the tentacles into the oil, using chopsticks to separate the pieces, and deep-fry for 1–2 minutes until light brown. Use a slotted spoon to carefully remove the tentacles.
* Reheat the oil to 350°F/180°C and deep-fry for another minute until golden brown. Remove and drain the excess oil on paper towels.
* Put the tentacles on a plate and sprinkle with the spiced salt. Serve immediately.

• 1 LB/450 G SQUID TENTACLES, RINSED AND CUT IN HALF LENGTHWISE
• 2 TABLESPOONS CORNSTARCH (CORNFLOUR)
• 3 CUPS (25 FL OZ/750 ML) VEGETABLE OIL

FOR THE BATTER:
• 6 TABLESPOONS ALL-PURPOSE (PLAIN) FLOUR
• 2 TABLESPOONS CORNSTARCH
• ½ EGG
• 2 TEASPOONS BAKING POWDER
• ½ TEASPOON SALT
• 2 TABLESPOONS VEGETABLE OIL

FOR THE SPICED SALT:
• 1 TEASPOON SALT
• ¼ TEASPOON FIVE-SPICE POWDER
• ½ TEASPOON SHAJIANG POWDER
• ½ TEASPOON RED CHILI POWDER

韭菜花炒鲜鱿
SQUID WITH
CHINESE CHIVES

- 11 OZ/300 G CHINESE CHIVES, RINSED, DRAINED, AND CUT INTO 3¼-INCH/ 8-CM LENGTHS
- 1 LB 2 OZ/500 G FRESH SQUID, CLEANED, OR 1 LB/450 G CALAMARI TUBES
- 2 TABLESPOONS VEGETABLE OIL
- 4 CLOVES GARLIC, CHOPPED
- 2 SHALLOTS, QUARTERED
- 1 TEASPOON SALT
- 1 TEASPOON RICE WINE
- ½ TEASPOON GRANULATED SUGAR
- ½ TEASPOON CORNSTARCH (CORNFLOUR)
- ¼ TEASPOON SESAME OIL
- STEAMED RICE (PAGE 540), TO SERVE (OPTIONAL)

In this dish, the squid is scored in a crisscross pattern to create a "flowering" effect—the markings are not only decorative and great for carrying sauces but flowers are regarded as lucky in Chinese culture. We will always prefer fresh seafood, but if it's unavailable, we suggest replacing fresh squid with 1 lb/450 g of calamari tubes.

* Bring a saucepan of water to a boil over high heat, add the chives, and blanch for 30 seconds. Drain and rinse under cold running water.
* Pull out the squid tentacles from the main body, cut below the eye, and discard the innards. Discard the beak from the head and peel off the membrane. Remove the quill, then use the back of a knife to remove the innards. Open it out flat, rinse, and trim. Lightly and finely score the squid, then cut into 1½ × 2-inch/4 × 6-cm pieces.
* Fill a wok or large skillet (frying pan) with water and bring to a boil. Place the squid in a hand-held metal strainer (sieve) and lower into the boiling water. Turn off the heat immediately and use chopsticks to disperse the squid pieces in the water. Steep in the water for 5 seconds, then remove with the strainer, drain, and transfer the squid to a bowl of ice-cold water. Set aside to cool. Drain and pat the squid dry with paper towels.
* Heat the vegetable oil in the wok or large skillet over medium-high heat, add the garlic and shallots, and stir-fry for 1 minute until fragrant. Increase to high heat, put in the squid, and stir-fry for another 30 seconds until half cooked. Add the salt, wine, sugar, and chives and stir-fry rapidly for another 30 seconds, until the squid is cooked through.
* Mix the cornstarch (cornflour) with ½ tablespoon water in a small bowl and stir this mixture into the wok. Bring to a boil, stirring, for 30 seconds to thicken the sauce. Stir in the sesame oil and transfer to a serving plate. Serve with rice, if using.

SQUID WITH CHINESE CHIVES

葱烧海参
SEA CUCUMBERS WITH BEIJING SCALLIONS

- 1 LB 5 OZ/600 G PRE-SOAKED SEA CUCUMBERS
- 3 TABLESPOONS GINGER JUICE
- 2 TABLESPOONS VEGETABLE OIL
- 3 BEIJING SCALLIONS OR 9 SCALLIONS (SPRING ONIONS), CUT INTO 2-INCH/5-CM LENGTHS
- 1 CUP (8 FL OZ/250 ML) CHICKEN BROTH (STOCK, PAGE 90)
- ⅛ OZ/5 G GINGER (ABOUT ½-INCH/ 1-CM-LENGTH PIECE), SLICED
- 2 TABLESPOONS OYSTER SAUCE
- 1 TEASPOON SESAME OIL
- STEAMED RICE (PAGE 540), TO SERVE

The sea cucumber is a sea animal with a leathery skin and elongated body. Revered in Chinese cuisine since ancient times, it is often served alongside abalone or shark's fin soup in Chinese banquets. Sea cucumbers are often sold dried: choose those which are firm and rubbery in feel with a mild salty fish. Pre-soaked sea cucumbers are available frozen in Asian supermarkets.

* Clean the sea cucumbers under cold running water, using your fingers to remove any sand particles inside. Slice the sea cucumbers into 2-inch/5-cm lengths.
* Bring a large saucepan of water to a boil over high heat. Add the ginger juice and the sea cucumbers and blanch for 1 minute. Drain and rinse under cold running water.
* Heat the vegetable oil in a wok or large skillet (frying pan) over medium heat and pan-fry the Beijing scallions for 4 minutes, or until golden brown. Discard the scallion greens and reserve the scallion whites.
* In the saucepan used to blanch the sea cucumbers, add the chicken broth (stock) and ginger slices. Bring to a boil over medium heat, add the sea cucumbers, and return to a boil. Stir in the oyster sauce, reduce to low heat, and simmer for about 5 minutes. Add the reserved scallions and another simmer for 5 minutes until the sauce thickens. Finally, stir in the sesame oil. Serve with rice.

鸡焖甲鱼

SOFTSHELL TURTLE
WITH CHICKEN

REGION: SHANDONG
PREPARATION TIME: 30 MINUTES
COOKING TIME: 1 HOUR 30 MINUTES
SERVES: 6

Softshell turtle, a delicacy in Chinese cuisine, is renowned for its nutritional and medicinal value but due to rising demand and hunting many species of turtles are now listed as threatened or endangered. We advise to prepare this dish only when turtles are sustainable.

* Put the chicken and ginger slices into a large saucepan and add enough water to cover. Bring to a boil, reduce to low heat, and simmer for about 20 minutes, or until the chicken pieces are cooked through. Remove the chicken breast, thighs, and legs, and leave the rest of the chicken to simmer, uncovered, until as scant 1 cup (7 fl oz/200 ml) chicken broth remains. Strain the chicken broth and reserve.
* Remove the chicken meat from the bones, tear into pieces, and set aside. Discard the bones.
* Put the turtle into a large bowl, then pour over 7½ cups (60 fl oz/1.75 liters) hot water (about 140°F/60°C). Use a scouring pad, brush the shell to remove the dark film on the surface.
* Fill a separate bowl with cold water. Cut the turtle into smaller pieces and soak in the water for 15 minutes to clean. Drain, put the turtle pieces back into the bowl, and then pour enough boiling water to cover. Set aside for 1 minute, then drain.
* Heat the vegetable oil in a wok or large skillet (frying pan), add the Sichuan peppercorns, and stir-fry for 2–3 minutes until fragrant. Using a slotted spoon, remove the Sichuan peppercorns, leaving the flavored oil behind.
* Add the ginger and scallions (spring onions) to the wok and stir-fry over medium heat for 1–2 minutes until fragrant. Add the turtle, star anise, and ⅔ cups (5 fl oz/150 ml) reserved chicken broth and bring to a boil. Reduce to low heat and simmer, covered, for 30 minutes, or until cooked through. Using a slotted spoon to discard the star anise. Place the chicken in the wok, add the wine, soy sauce, and rock sugar, and simmer for 3 minutes. Drizzle over the sesame oil.
* Transfer to a serving platter and serve with rice.

- 1 (2¼-LB/1-KG) WHOLE CHICKEN, CUT INTO LARGE PIECES (BREAST, THIGHS, LEGS, WINGS, BACK)
- 2 OZ/50 G GINGER (ABOUT 3-INCH/ 7.5-CM-LENGTH PIECE), HALF SLICED AND HALF SHREDDED
- 1 (1 LB 5-OZ/600-G) SOFTSHELL TURTLE
- 2 TABLESPOONS VEGETABLE OIL
- 1 TABLESPOON SICHUAN PEPPERCORNS
- 5 SCALLIONS (SPRING ONIONS), CUT INTO 1½-INCH/4-CM LENGTHS
- 2 STAR ANISE
- 2 TABLESPOONS RICE WINE
- 2 TABLESPOONS DARK SOY SAUCE
- ¼ OZ/10 G ROCK SUGAR
- 1 TEASPOON SESAME OIL
- STEAMED RICE (PAGE 540), TO SERVE

POULTRY

POULTRY

PREPARATION TIME: 10 MINUTES,
  PLUS 1 HOUR MARINATING TIME
COOKING TIME: 30 MINUTES
SERVES: 4

怪味鸡

SPICY CHICKEN WITH SICHUAN PEPPERCORNS

- 1 (2¼-LB/1-KG) WHOLE CHICKEN
- 1 TABLESPOON RICE WINE
- 1 TABLESPOON SALT
- 1 TEASPOON SICHUAN PEPPERCORNS, CRUSHED
- 1 TEASPOON SESAME OIL
- 1 TABLESPOON PEANUT BUTTER
- 1 TABLESPOON SESAME PASTE
- 1 TABLESPOON CHILI OIL
- 1 TEASPOON GRANULATED SUGAR
- 1 TABLESPOON BLACK OR BALSAMIC VINEGAR
- 1 TABLESPOON LIGHT SOY SAUCE
- ¼ OZ/10 G GINGER (ABOUT ¾-INCH/ 2-CM-LENGTH PIECE), SHREDDED
- 1 SCALLION (SPRING ONION), SHREDDED
- STEAMED RICE (PAGE 540), TO SERVE

* Put the chicken into a heatproof bowl and rub with wine and salt. Cover and marinate for 1 hour.
* Place the bowl of chicken into a collapsible pot or bamboo steamer over a pot of boiling water. Steam, covered, for 20–25 minutes, or until cooked through. Take off the heat and stand for 5 minutes. Remove the chicken and let cool. Strain the steamed chicken juice into a bowl and reserve for later use.
* Toast the Sichuan peppercorns in a small skillet (frying pan) over medium-high heat for 2–3 minutes. Set aside.
* Combine the sesame oil, peanut butter, sesame paste, chili oil, sugar, vinegar, soy sauce, and toasted Sichuan peppercorns in a bowl. Stir in about ½ cup (4 fl oz/120 ml) of the reserved chicken juices to make a sauce. (Top up with more water or chicken juices, if needed.) Cut the chicken into chunks and arrange on a plate. Pour over the sauce and top with the ginger and the scallion (spring onion). Serve with rice.

PREPARATION TIME: 5 MINUTES
COOKING TIME: 1 HOUR 45 MINUTES
SERVES: 4

海南椰奶鸡

HAINANESE CHICKEN WITH COCONUT MILK

- 1 (2½-LB/1.2-KG) WHOLE CHICKEN
- 1 CUP (8 FL OZ/250 ML) CHICKEN BROTH (STOCK, PAGE 90)
- ¼ OZ/10 G GINGER (ABOUT ¾-INCH/ 2-CM-LENGTH PIECE), SLICED
- 2 SCALLIONS (SPRING ONIONS), EACH KNOTTED
- 1 TABLESPOON RICE WINE
- SCANT ½ CUP (3½ FL OZ/100 ML) MILK
- SCANT ½ CUP (3½ FL OZ/100 ML) COCONUT MILK
- 1 TEASPOON SALT, PLUS EXTRA TO TASTE
- 1 TEASPOON GRANULATED SUGAR
- 1 TABLESPOON CORNSTARCH (CORNFLOUR)
- STEAMED RICE (PAGE 540), TO SERVE

* Put the chicken into a large saucepan and add enough water to cover it completely. Bring to a boil over high heat and blanch for 5 minutes. Drain and rinse under cold running water.
* In a large heatproof bowl, combine the chicken, chicken broth (stock), ginger, scallions (spring onions), and wine. Seal the bowl with aluminum foil and place it in a collapsible pot or bamboo steamer over a pot of boiling water. Steam, covered, for 1 hour 30 minutes, or until cooked through. (Add more water to the pot if needed.)
* Transfer the chicken to a deep plate, then strain the sauce into a saucepan. Discard the ginger and scallions.
* Add the milk, coconut milk, salt, and sugar to the saucepan and bring to a boil. Mix the cornstarch (cornflour) with 2 tablespoons water and add to the pan. Bring to a boil, stirring, for about 30 seconds to thicken the sauce. Season with salt. Pour the sauce over the chicken. Serve with rice.

荷叶蒸滑鸡

CHICKEN IN
LOTUS LEAF

REGION: SHUNDE
PREPARATION TIME: 15 MINUTES,
  PLUS 45 MINUTES SOAKING TIME
COOKING TIME: 25 MINUTES
SERVES: 4

* Soak the lotus leaf in cold water for 45 minutes, or until softened.
* Meanwhile, put the mushrooms in a bowl, cover with cold water, and soak for at least 20 minutes, or until softened. Mix well with ½ teaspoon soy sauce.
* Put the chicken into a large bowl, add salt, sugar, oyster sauce, and the remaining 1 teaspoon soy sauce and set aside to marinate for 15 minutes.
* Mix the ginger juice, wine, white pepper, and cornstarch (cornflour) into the chicken, then add the sesame and vegetable oils. Add Chinese sausage, mushrooms, and jujube dates and mix well.
* Drain the lotus leaf and use paper towels to pat dry. Using a sharp knife, cut out the stiff veins near the stem and then lay the leaf on a steaming rack. Cover with multiple layers if necessary. Place the chicken mixture on the leaf and fold in the sides to create a parcel that covers the ingredients completely. Put the rack in a collapsible pot or bamboo steamer over a pot of boiling water. Steam, covered, for 25–30 minutes, or until cooked through.
* Once done, unwrap the lotus leaf, scatter over the shredded scallions (spring onions), and serve with rice. (The lotus leaf is not to be consumed.)

- 1–2 DRIED LOTUS LEAVES
- 5 DRIED BLACK MUSHROOMS
- 1½ TEASPOONS LIGHT SOY SAUCE
- 2¼ LB/1 KG CHICKEN PIECES
- ½ TEASPOON SALT
- ½ TEASPOON GRANULATED SUGAR
- 1 TEASPOON OYSTER SAUCE
- 1 TABLESPOON GINGER JUICE
- 1 TEASPOON SHAOXING WINE
- ¼ TEASPOON GROUND WHITE PEPPER
- 1 TABLESPOON CORNSTARCH (CORNFLOUR)
- ½ TEASPOON SESAME OIL
- 1 TABLESPOON VEGETABLE OIL
- 1 CHINESE SAUSAGE, CUT DIAGONALLY INTO THICK SLICES
- 4 JUJUBE DATES, PITTED AND HALVED
- 2 SCALLIONS (SPRING ONIONS), STEMS ONLY, SHREDDED
- STEAMED RICE (PAGE 540), TO SERVE

REGION: HUBEI
PREPARATION TIME: 1 HOUR
COOKING TIME: 1 HOUR 15 MINUTES
SERVES: 4–6

糯米全鸡
CHICKEN STUFFED WITH GLUTINOUS RICE

- 1 (2¼-LB/1-KG) WHOLE CHICKEN
- 2 CUPS (16 FL OZ/475 ML) PLUS 2 TABLESPOONS VEGETABLE OIL
- ¾ OZ/20 G GINGER (ABOUT 1-INCH/ 2.5-CM-LENGTH PIECE), CHOPPED
- 1 SCALLION (SPRING ONION), CHOPPED
- 2 OZ/50 G PORK FATBACK, DICED
- 1 TEASPOON SALT
- 1 TEASPOON GRANULATED SUGAR
- 1 TEASPOON LIGHT SOY SAUCE
- 2 TEASPOON SHAOXING WINE
- ¾ OZ/20 G BAMBOO SHOOTS, DICED
- ½ OZ/15 G HAM, DICED
- 2 OZ/50 G TIANJIN PRESERVED CABBAGE, RINSED AND CHOPPED
- 2 CUPS (14 OZ/400 G) COOKED GLUTINOUS RICE
- 2 TABLESPOONS CORNSTARCH (CORNFLOUR)

Stuffed fowl is a Cantonese, Shanghainese, and Beijing specialty. The fowl, duck, or chicken is de-boned and the meat is removed, then filled with various ingredients. Such dishes are considered gourmet dishes.

* Make a small cut on the chicken skin directly on the breast bone near the tail end. Insert your fingers between the skin and flesh to separate them. Start at the breast and work your way to the back, then down along the thighs and legs, carefully separating the flesh and skin as you go. Ensuring you do not break the skin, slowly pull the skin off one leg and then the other. Slowly pull the skin up to the neck and cut the joint between the wing and the body under the skin so that the wing is still connected to the rest of the skin. Repeat the process with the other wing. Pull the skin over the stub of the neck. The skin of the whole chicken, together with the wings, should now be off the carcass. Trim the excess fat off the skin. Tie the ends of the skin of the legs with kitchen string.
* Remove all the meat from the chicken carcass and dice.
* Heat 2 tablespoons oil in a wok or large skillet (frying pan), add the ginger, scallion (spring onion), and pork fatback and stir-fry over medium heat for about 2 minutes. Add the diced chicken, salt, sugar, soy sauce, and wine and stir-fry over high heat for 3–4 minutes until cooked through.
* Add the bamboo shoots, ham, and preserved cabbage, stir, then add the cooked rice. Mix well.
* Place the chicken skin on a cutting board, breast side facing upward. Through the opening at the tail end, stuff the rice filling into the chicken skin, starting with the legs, then working into the rest of the body (there should be enough filling to re-create the chicken). Sew up the opening using a needle and thread.
* Transfer the chicken to a heatproof plate. Place in a collapsible pot or bamboo steamer over a pot of boiling water. Steam, covered, for 1 hour, or until cooked through. (Add more water to the pot if needed.) Remove the chicken and dust with a thin layer of cornstarch (cornflour).
* Heat the remaining 2 cups (16 fl oz/475 ml) vegetable oil in a wok or deep saucepan to 300°F/150°C, or until a cube of bread browns in 1½ minutes. Gently lower the chicken into the oil and deep-fry for 4 minutes, turning occasionally, until golden brown. Use a slotted spoon to carefully remove the chicken from the oil and drain on paper towels.
* Remove the thread and string. Cut the stuffed chicken into smaller pieces, about ¾ × 2-inch/2 × 5-cm, and serve.

贵妃鸡
GUIFEI
CHICKEN

REGION: GUANGDONG
PREPARATION TIME: 10 MINUTES,
    PLUS 1 HOUR SOAKING TIME
COOKING TIME: 55 MINUTES
SERVES: 4

"Guifei" is the term used for one of the wives (not the empress) of the emperor. The use of the term in this recipe is to indicate the chicken is as tender and smooth as the wife of the emperor. By soaking the chicken in saturated salt water, the chicken will be more tender and the flavor enhanced.

* Combine the chicken, salt, and 12½ cups (100 fl oz/3 liters) water in a large saucepan and soak for 1 hour to tenderize the chicken. Use a large slotted spoon to remove the chicken and set aside.
* Place all the spice bag ingredients into a spice bag. Add the spice bag to the salted water and bring to a boil over high heat. Reduce to low heat and simmer for 15 minutes. Put the chicken back into the water, breast facing up, and bring to a boil. Reduce to low heat, cover and gently simmer for 25–30 minutes. Remove the lid, turn the chicken over, breast-side down, and re-cover. Turn off the heat and let stand for 5 minutes.
* Meanwhile, prepare a large bowl of ice water.
* Carefully transfer the chicken into the bowl of ice water (this will firm up the chicken skin and flesh). Remove and drain the chicken. Brush the chicken skin with sesame oil. Cut the chicken into chunks and transfer to a serving plate. Serve with rice.

- 1 (2½-LB/1.2-KG) WHOLE CHICKEN
- SCANT 1 CUP (9 OZ/250 G) TABLE SALT
- SESAME OIL, FOR BRUSHING
- STEAMED RICE (PAGE 540), TO SERVE

FOR THE SPICE BAG:
- 4 STAR ANISE
- 1 DRIED TANGERINE PEEL
- ½ STICK CINNAMON
- ⅛ DRIED LOHAN FRUIT
- 2 OZ/50 G SHAJIANG
- ¼ OZ/8 G LICORICE ROOT
- ½ TABLESPOON SICHUAN PEPPERCORNS
- ½ TABLESPOON CUMIN SEEDS
- ½ TEASPOON CLOVES

REGION: HONG KONG
PREPARATION TIME: 30 MINUTES, PLUS
  2 HOURS MARINATING TIME
COOKING TIME: 35 MINUTES
SERVES: 4
📷 PAGE 247

金华玉树鸡
CHICKEN WITH CHINESE HAM

- 1 (2½-LB/1.2-KG) WHOLE CORN-FED CHICKEN, FAT TRIMMED AND RESERVED
- 2 TABLESPOONS GINGER JUICE
- ½ TABLESPOON SHAOXING WINE
- ½ TABLESPOON SALT
- 7 OZ/200 G JINHUA OR SMITHFIELD HAM
- 1 TABLESPOON CORNSTARCH (CORNFLOUR)
- 1 TEASPOON GRANULATED SUGAR
- 1 TEASPOON VEGETABLE OIL
- 11 OZ/300 G CHINESE BROCCOLI, TRIMMED
- ½ TEASPOON SESAME OIL
- ¼ TEASPOON GROUND WHITE PEPPER
- STEAMED RICE (PAGE 540), TO SERVE

This dish was created in 1959 for a banquet to welcome Prince Philip from England to Hong Kong. It was created with the consideration that the prince might not have known how to handle the bony chicken pieces with chopsticks.

* Put the chicken into a large bowl and rub it inside and out with ginger juice, wine, and salt. Cover and marinate in the refrigerator for 2 hours.
* Wrap the chicken in aluminum foil and place on a heatproof plate, then place in a collapsible pot or bamboo steamer over a pot of boiling water. Steam, covered, for 23–25 minutes, or until cooked through. Remove the chicken and set aside to cool. Strain the steamed chicken juices into a bowl and reserve.
* Steam the ham for 3 minutes, then cut into thin slices and set aside.
* Heat a small skillet (frying pan) over medium-low heat, add the reserved chicken fat, and cook for 2–3 minutes until the fat renders. Set aside and discard any solids.
* When the chicken has cooled, remove the bones, taking care to keep the meat with skin intact (particularly from the breast and legs). Discard the rest. Cut the chicken breast lengthwise into 2 long pieces, then cut widthwise into ¾-inch/2-cm pieces. Cut the chicken legs into similar-size pieces to the chicken breast.
* Mix the cornstarch (cornflour) with 3 tablespoons water in a small bowl. Set aside for 5 minutes, or until the starch settles at the bottom, then pour out the water to leave a wet starch. Set aside.
* Lay out the chicken in 2 columns on an oval heatproof plate with the skin side facing up. Insert the ham slices in between and among the chicken pieces. Place the plate in a collapsible pot or bamboo steamer over a pot of boiling water. Steam, covered, for 3 minutes.
* Meanwhile, bring a large pot of water to a boil, add the sugar, vegetable oil, and broccoli, and blanch for 2 minutes, then drain. Arrange the steamed broccoli around the chicken.
* Heat the chicken oil in a wok or skillet, add the reserved steamed chicken juices, sesame oil, and white pepper. Bring to a boil and pour the wet starch slowly into the wok, stirring constantly for 30 seconds to make a gravy. Pour over the chicken and broccoli. Serve with rice.

CHICKEN WITH CHINESE HAM

REGION: GUANGDONG
PREPARATION TIME: 20 MINUTES, PLUS
  20 MINUTES MARINATING TIME
COOKING TIME: 15 MINUTES
SERVES: 4

鱼肚棉花鸡
CHICKEN WITH
FISH MAW

- 1 OZ/40 G FISH MAW PUFF, RINSED
- ¼ OZ/10 G GINGER (ABOUT ¾-INCH/
  2-CM-LENGTH PIECE), SLICED
- 4 DRIED BLACK MUSHROOMS
- 1 TEASPOON OYSTER SAUCE
- 2½ TABLESPOONS VEGETABLE OIL
- 8 BONELESS CHICKEN THIGHS,
  CUT INTO BITE-SIZE PIECES
- 1 TABLESPOON LIGHT SOY SAUCE
- ½ TABLESPOON RICE WINE
- ½ TEASPOON GRANULATED SUGAR
- 3 CLOVES GARLIC, CHOPPED
- 1 TABLESPOON CORNSTARCH
  (CORNFLOUR)
- STEAMED RICE (PAGE 540), TO SERVE

* Put the fish maw, ginger, and 4¼ cups (34 fl oz/1 liter) water into a large saucepan. Bring to a boil over high heat and blanch for 3 minutes. Cover, turn off the heat, and let stand for 30 minutes.
* Meanwhile, put the mushrooms in a bowl, cover with cold water, and soak for at least 20 minutes, or until softened. Cut each mushroom in half. Squeeze out excess water, put in a bowl, and mix with the oyster sauce and 1 tablespoon oil.
* Transfer the fish maw to a colander and rinse with cold water. Squeeze the excess water and cut into 2-inch/5-cm sections.
* Combine the chicken, soy sauce, wine, sugar, and garlic in a large bowl and marinate for 10 minutes. Mix in the cornstarch (cornflour). Add the fish maw, mushrooms, and the remaining 1½ tablespoons oil, mix well, and place on a heatproof plate. Put into a collapsible pot or bamboo steamer over a pot of boiling water. Steam, covered, for 10 minutes until cooked through. Serve with rice.

REGION: GUANGXI
PREPARATION TIME: 15 MINUTES, PLUS
  1 HOUR MARINATING TIME
COOKING TIME: 30 MINUTES
SERVES: 4

五味手撕鸡
CHICKEN IN AN
AROMATIC SAUCE

- ½ TABLESPOON SESAME SEEDS
- 1 (2½-LB/1.2-KG) WHOLE CHICKEN
- 1 TEASPOON SALT
- 2 TABLESPOONS PICKLED VEGETABLES,
  SHREDDED
- ¾ OZ/20 G PICKLED GINGER
  (PAGE 296)
- 3 STALKS CILANTRO (CORIANDER),
  CHOPPED
- STEAMED RICE (PAGE 540), TO SERVE

  FOR THE SAUCE:
- 1 TABLESPOON LIGHT SOY SAUCE
- 1 TABLESPOON GRANULATED SUGAR
- 1 TEASPOON RED VINEGAR
- 1 TEASPOON ENGLISH MUSTARD
- 1 TEASPOON SESAME OIL
- ½ TEASPOON CHILI OIL

* Toast the sesame seeds over medium heat in a small pan and shake occasionally for 3–5 minutes or until golden brown. Set aside.
* Put the chicken into a heatproof bowl and rub it with the salt. Cover and marinate in the refrigerator for 1 hour.
* Place the chicken in the bowl in a collapsible pot or bamboo steamer over a pot of boiling water. Steam, covered, for 23 minutes. Turn off the heat and let stand for 5 minutes. Remove the chicken and set aside until cool enough to handle.
* De-bone the chicken, tearing the skin and flesh into long strips. Combine the chicken, pickled vegetables, and pickled ginger in a bowl, then transfer to a serving plate.
* Combine all the sauce ingredients in a small bowl. Pour the sauce over the chicken and top with the sesame seeds and cilantro (coriander). Serve at room temperature with rice.

雪花丁香鸡
CHICKEN
WITH CLOVES

REGION: ANHUI
PREPARATION TIME: 15 MINUTES,
  PLUS 1 HOUR DRYING TIME
COOKING TIME: 20 MINUTES
SERVES: 4–6

* Place the chicken in a large bowl, pour boiling water over the skin of the chicken, then drain. Rub the skin with 2 teaspoons soy sauce. Air-dry the chicken in the refrigerator for 1 hour.

* Place the chicken in a large heatproof bowl. Heat the oil in a wok or deep saucepan to 340°F/170°C, or until a cube of bread browns in 45 seconds. Ladle the heated oil over the chicken until golden brown, then carefully transfer the chicken to a plate lined with paper towels. Cut the chicken into small chunks and place in a large heatproof bowl, skin-side down. Add the scallions (spring onions) and ginger.

* Combine the salt, sugar, wine, remaining 1 teaspoon soy sauce, and the spices in a small bowl and pour over the chicken. Place the chicken in a collapsible pot or bamboo steamer over a pot of boiling water. Steam, covered, for about 15 minutes, or until cooked through. Remove and drain the steamed chicken juices into a saucepan. Cover the bowl with a large plate and, using dish towels, invert the chicken onto the plate. (Alternatively, use tongs to transfer the chicken). Discard the scallions, ginger, and whole spices.

* Heat the steamed chicken juices in a saucepan over high heat. Mix the cornstarch (cornflour) with ½ tablespoon water in a small bowl and stir this mixture into the wok. Bring to a boil, stirring, for 30 seconds to thicken the sauce. Pour the sauce over the chicken.

* Beat the egg whites in a small bowl until foamy. Wipe the wok and place over medium heat. Add 4 tablespoons water, bring to a boil, and add the egg whites. Stir until combined—the egg whites should appear snow-like in texture. Spoon the cooked egg whites on top of the chicken. Serve with rice.

- 1 (2½-LB/1.2-KG) WHOLE CHICKEN
- 3 TEASPOONS LIGHT SOY SAUCE
- 1 CUP (8 FL OZ/250 ML) VEGETABLE OIL
- 2 SCALLIONS (SPRING ONIONS), CUT INTO 2-INCH/5-CM LENGTHS
- ¼ OZ/10 G GINGER (ABOUT ¾-INCH/ 2-CM-LENGTH PIECE), SLICED
- 2 TEASPOONS SALT
- 1 TEASPOON GRANULATED SUGAR
- 1 TABLESPOON SHAOXING WINE
- 2 TEASPOONS CLOVES
- 1 STAR ANISE
- ¼ TEASPOON GROUND CINNAMON
- ¼ TEASPOON GROUND CUMIN
- ½ TEASPOON CORNSTARCH (CORNFLOUR)
- 3 EGG WHITES
- STEAMED RICE (PAGE 540), TO SERVE

REGION: GUANGDONG
PREPARATION TIME: 10 MINUTES, PLUS
    1 HOUR DRYING AND 2 HOURS
    MARINATING TIME
COOKING TIME: 30 MINUTES
SERVES: 4–6

白切鸡
STEAMED CHICKEN

- 1 (2½-LB/1.2-KG) WHOLE CHICKEN
- 1 TABLESPOON SALT
- 1 TABLESPOON GINGER JUICE
- 1 TABLESPOON SHAOXING WINE
- 2 TEASPOONS GRATED GINGER
- 2 SCALLIONS (SPRING ONIONS), CHOPPED
- 2 TABLESPOONS VEGETABLE OIL
- 1 TEASPOON SESAME OIL
- STEAMED RICE (PAGE 540), TO SERVE

* Allow the chicken to air dry for 1 hour in the refrigerator. Rub the chicken, inside and out, with the salt, ginger juice, and wine. Marinate for at least 2 hours. Turn the chicken over once or twice during this time.

* Wrap the chicken in aluminum foil but leave an opening at the tail. Place on a heatproof plate, then put in a collapsible pot or bamboo steamer over a pot of boiling water. Steam over high heat, covered, for about 25 minutes, or until cooked through. Turn off the heat and stand for 5 minutes. Remove the chicken and set aside to cool.

* Strain the steamed chicken juices and reserve for future use (see Note).

* To make the sauce, combine the grated ginger, scallions (spring onions), and 1 teaspoon of the reserved chicken juices in a small bowl. Heat the vegetable oil in a small saucepan over medium-high heat, then pour the hot oil over the sauce and mix well.

* When the chicken has cooled, remove the foil and brush with sesame oil. Cut the chicken into pieces and serve at room temperature together with the dip and rice.

NOTE:
The salty chicken juices can be used for enhancing dishes such as Hainan Chicken Rice (page 542). It can also be used as a seasoning for fried rice or vegetables. Store in the refrigerator for up to 3 days.

口水鸡

STEAMED CHICKEN
WITH SPICY SAUCE

REGION: SICHUAN
PREPARATION TIME: 10 MINUTES,
   PLUS 1 HOUR MARINATING TIME
COOKING TIME: 45 MINUTES
SERVES: 4

* Put the chicken into a heatproof bowl and rub it with the wine and salt. Cover and marinate in the refrigerator for 1 hour.
* Place the chicken in the bowl in a collapsible pot or bamboo steamer over a pot of boiling water. Steam over high heat, covered, for about 23–25 minutes, or until cooked through. Turn off the heat and let stand for 5 minutes. Remove the chicken and set aside to cool. Strain the steamed chicken juices into a bowl and reserve.
* Meanwhile, roast the Sichuan peppercorns in a small skillet (frying pan) over medium-low heat for 2–3 minutes, then transfer to a mortar and pestle and crush lightly. Set aside.
* Toast the peanuts in the same pan until light brown, then cool slightly. Remove the husks, crush lightly, and set aside.
* Cut the chicken into smaller pieces and arrange the pieces on a serving plate.
* To make the sauce, combine the sesame oil, chili oil, and peanut butter in a bowl. Add the toasted Sichuan peppercorns, garlic, vinegar, chili paste, sugar, and ½ cup (4 fl oz/120 ml) of the reserved chicken juices. Heat the vegetable oil in a pan over medium-high heat, add the chili sauce, and stir-fry for 1 minute until fragrant.
* Pour the sauce over the chicken and sprinkle with the sesame seeds, peanuts, and cilantro (coriander). Serve with rice.

- 1 (2¼-LB/1.5-KG) WHOLE CHICKEN
- 1 TABLESPOON RICE WINE
- ½ TEASPOON SALT
- ½ TABLESPOON SICHUAN PEPPERCORNS
- 1 TABLESPOON RAW PEANUTS
- ½ TABLESPOON SESAME OIL
- 2 TABLESPOONS CHILI OIL
- 1 TABLESPOON PEANUT BUTTER
- 4 CLOVES GARLIC, CHOPPED
- 2 TABLESPOONS BLACK OR BALSAMIC VINEGAR
- 1 TABLESPOON PIXIAN CHILI BEAN PASTE, CHOPPED
- 1 TEASPOON GRANULATED SUGAR
- 1 TEASPOON VEGETABLE OIL
- 1 TABLESPOON TOASTED WHITE SESAME SEEDS
- 1 BUNCH CILANTRO (CORIANDER), CHOPPED
- STEAMED RICE (PAGE 540), TO SERVE

PREPARATION TIME: 10 MINUTES, PLUS
  10 MINUTES MARINATING TIME
COOKING TIME: 10 MINUTES
SERVES: 4
📷 PAGE 253

豆豉鸡
CHICKEN IN BLACK
BEAN SAUCE

- 1 LB/450 G CHICKEN PIECES
- ½ TABLESPOON LIGHT SOY SAUCE
- ½ TEASPOON GRANULATED SUGAR
- 1 TEASPOON SHAOXING WINE
- 2 TABLESPOON VEGETABLE OIL
- ¼ TEASPOON CORNSTARCH
  (CORNFLOUR)
- ¼ TEASPOON SALT
- ½ TABLESPOON FERMENTED BLACK
  BEANS, RINSED AND CHOPPED
- 1 CLOVE GARLIC, CHOPPED
- 6 SHALLOTS, HALVED
- 1 LARGE RED CHILE, ROUGHLY
  CHOPPED
- 1 GREEN CHILE, ROUGHLY CHOPPED
- 4 SCALLIONS (SPRING ONIONS),
  STEMS ONLY, CUT INTO 1½-INCH/4-CM
  LENGTHS, PLUS EXTRA TO GARNISH
- ¼ TEASPOON SESAME OIL
- STEAMED RICE (PAGE 540), TO SERVE

* Rinse the chicken in cold water and cut it into bite-size
  chunks. Combine the chicken, soy sauce, ¼ teaspoon sugar,
  ½ teaspoon wine, ½ tablespoon vegetable oil, cornstarch
  (cornflour), and salt in a large bowl. Set aside and marinate
  for 10 minutes.
* Combine the black beans, garlic, ¼ teaspoon sugar, and
  ½ tablespoon vegetable oil in a bowl and mix well.
* Heat the remaining 1 tablespoon vegetable oil in a wok
  or large skillet (frying pan) over medium-high heat, add
  the shallots, and fry for 1–2 minutes until fragrant. Add the
  chicken and stir-fry over medium heat for 3 minutes until
  half cooked. Put the black bean mixture and the chiles on
  top of chicken.
  Do not stir. Sprinkle the remaining ½ teaspoon wine along
  the inside of the wok, reduce to low heat, cover, and
  simmer for 2 minutes.
* Remove the lid, increase to high heat, and stir-fry the
  ingredients in the wok until the chicken is fully cooked.
  Toss in the scallions (spring onions) and sesame oil.
  Transfer to a serving plate, garnish with more scallions,
  and serve with rice.

REGION: HUBEI
PREPARATION TIME: 15 MINUTES
COOKING TIME: 5 MINUTES
SERVES: 2

玉米鸡茸
STEWED CHICKEN AND CORN

- 2 BONELESS, SKINLESS CHICKEN BREASTS, FINELY CHOPPED
- 5 EGG WHITES
- 2 TEASPOONS CORNSTARCH (CORNFLOUR)
- 1 TEASPOON FINELY CHOPPED SCALLION (SPRING ONION)
- 1 TEASPOON FINELY CHOPPED GINGER
- ½ TEASPOON SALT, PLUS EXTRA TO TASTE
- ⅔ CUP (5 FL OZ/150 ML) CHICKEN BROTH (STOCK, PAGE 90)
- 1 EAR OF CORN, KERNELS ONLY
- ⅔ CUP (5 OZ/150 G) LARD
- 1 SLICE COOKED HAM, DICED
- STEAMED RICE (PAGE 540), TO SERVE

* In a food processor, combine the chicken breasts, egg whites, cornstarch (cornflour), scallion (spring onion), ginger, salt, and chicken broth (stock) and process to a puree. Transfer to a bowl and set aside.
* Clean the food processor, then add the corn kernels and 2 tablespoons water and process to a puree. Line a strainer (sieve) with cheesecloth (muslin). Strain the corn puree into a bowl, pressing down to extract as much corn juice as possible. Pour the strained corn juice into the chicken purée.
* Heat the lard in a wok or large skillet (frying pan) over medium high heat. Carefully spoon in the chicken and corn puree, then use a spatula (fish slice) to stir for 4–5 minutes until the puree thickens. Season with extra salt to taste.
* Transfer to a serving plate and top with the diced ham. Serve with rice.

REGION: GUANGDONG
PREPARATION TIME: 10 MINUTES, PLUS 20 MINUTES SOAKING TIME
COOKING TIME: 25 MINUTES
SERVES: 4

金针云耳蒸滑鸡
CHICKEN WITH ORANGE DAYLILY

- ½ OZ/15 G DRIED ORANGE DAYLILY
- ½ CUP (¼ OZ/10 G) DRIED BLACK FUNGUS
- 1 LB 8½ OZ/700 G CHICKEN PIECES, CHOPPED INTO 1½-INCH/4-CM PIECES
- 1 TEASPOON LIGHT SOY SAUCE
- ½ TEASPOON SALT
- ½ TEASPOON GRANULATED SUGAR
- 1 TABLESPOON GINGER JUICE
- 1 TEASPOON SHAOXING WINE
- 1 TABLESPOON CORNSTARCH (CORNFLOUR)
- ¾ OZ/20 G SALTED RUTABAGA, CUT INTO THICK MATCHSTICKS
- 4 JUJUBE DATES, PITTED
- 3 SCALLIONS (SPRING ONIONS), STEMS ONLY, CHOPPED
- 1 TEASPOON OYSTER SAUCE
- ¼ TEASPOON GROUND WHITE PEPPER
- 2 TABLESPOONS VEGETABLE OIL
- STEAMED RICE (PAGE 540), TO SERVE

* Fill a small bowl with cold water, and soak the orange daylily along with the black fungus for 20 minutes until soft. Drain, then cut the orange daylily into 2½-inch/6-cm sections and the black fungus into smaller pieces. Set aside.
* Meanwhile, in a large heatproof bowl, combine the chicken pieces, soy sauce, salt, and sugar and marinate for 15 minutes. Add the ginger juice, wine, and cornstarch (cornflour) and mix well.
* Add the orange daylily, black fungus, rutabaga, jujube dates, and scallions to the chicken pieces, then mix in the oyster sauce, white pepper, and oil. Place the bowl in a collapsible pot or bamboo steamer over a pot of boiling water. Steam, covered, for 25 minutes, or until cooked through. Serve with rice.

安东子鸡
ANDONG

CHICKEN

REGION: HUNAN
PREPARATION TIME: 10 MINUTES
COOKING TIME: 20 MINUTES
SERVES: 4

This revered dish hails from the city of Andong in Hunan. Dating back to the Tang Dynasty, more than 1,200 years ago, it's one of the best-known Hunan dishes.

* Bring a large saucepan of water to a boil, add the chicken, then reduce to low heat and cook the chicken for 10 minutes. Set aside and when cool enough to handle, cut the meat into 2-inch/5-cm strips.
* Heat the lard in a wok or skillet (frying pan) over medium-high heat.
* Add the ginger and chiles and stir-fry for 1 minute until fragrant. Add the chicken strips, vinegar, wine, salt, Sichuan peppercorns, and chicken broth (stock) and bring to a boil. Cover, reduce the heat, and simmer for about 2 minutes. Remove the lid, increase to high heat, and cook for 1–2 minutes to reduce the sauce to 4 tablespoons.
* Mix the cornstarch (cornflour) with ½ tablespoon water in a small bowl, then stir this mixture into the wok. Bring to a boil, stirring, for about 30 seconds to thicken the sauce. Stir in the scallions (spring onions), season with salt to taste, and transfer to a serving plate. Serve with rice.

- 1 LB 5 OZ/600 G BONELESS CHICKEN
- 4 TABLESPOONS LARD
- ¾ OZ/20 G GINGER (ABOUT ¾-INCH/ 2-CM-LENGTH PIECE), SHREDDED
- 14 DRIED CHILES, CHOPPED
- 3 TABLESPOONS WHITE VINEGAR
- 2 TABLESPOONS SHAOXING WINE
- 1 TEASPOON SALT, PLUS EXTRA TO TASTE
- ¼ TEASPOON SICHUAN PEPPERCORNS, CRUSHED
- 4 TABLESPOONS CHICKEN BROTH (STOCK, PAGE 90)
- ½ TEASPOON CORNSTARCH (CORNFLOUR)
- ½ TEASPOON SESAME OIL
- 2 SCALLIONS (SPRING ONIONS), CUT INTO 1½-INCH/4-CM LENGTHS
- STEAMED RICE (PAGE 540), TO SERVE

客家娘酒鸡
CHICKEN IN WINE

REGION: HAKKA
PREPARATION TIME: 10 MINUTES
COOKING TIME: 30 MINUTES
SERVES: 4

This Hakka dish is traditionally served to women who have just given birth. It is believed that it will help with blood circulation and fortify the immune system and contribute to the restoration of health.

* Clean the chicken and cut it into 2 × ¾-inch/5 × 2-cm pieces (bone-in).
* Heat the oil in a saucepan over high heat, add the ginger, and stir-fry for 1–2 minutes until browned. Add the chicken and stir-fry for about 5 minutes, or until golden brown. Add the wine and bring to a boil.
* Reduce to low heat, cover, and simmer for 20 minutes, or until the chicken is cooked through. Transfer to a serving bowl and serve immediately.

- 1 (2¼-LB/1-KG) WHOLE CHICKEN
- 1 TABLESPOON VEGETABLE OIL
- 2 OZ/50 G GINGER (ABOUT 3-INCH/7.5-CM-LENGTH PIECE), SLICED
- 4¼ CUPS (34 FL OZ/1 LITER) GLUTINOUS RICE WINE

家乡梅菜鸡

CHICKEN WITH SWEET MUSTARD GREENS

- 1 (3¼-LB/1.5-KG) WHOLE CHICKEN
- ½ TEASPOON SALT
- 1 TABLESPOON SHAOXING WINE
- 2 TEASPOONS DARK SOY SAUCE
- 11 OZ/300 G SWEET MUSTARD GREENS
- 1 TABLESPOON GRANULATED SUGAR
- 2 TABLESPOONS GINGER JUICE
- 2 CUPS (16 FL OZ/475 ML) VEGETABLE OIL
- ½ TEASPOON CORNSTARCH (CORNFLOUR)
- STEAMED RICE (PAGE 540), TO SERVE

* Place the chicken in a large heatproof bowl, pour boiling water over the skin of the chicken, then drain. Rub the chicken cavity with salt, then rub the skin with the wine and soy sauce. Air dry for 1 hour in the refrigerator.
* Soak the sweet mustard greens in a small bowl of cold water for 3 minutes. Drain and squeeze out any excess water. Trim off the stems, return to the bowl, and add the sugar and ginger juice. Set aside.
* Heat the oil in a wok or deep saucepan to 300°F/150°C, or until a cube of bread browns in 1½ minutes. Carefully add the chicken and use a slotted spoon to gently roll it in the hot oil for 3–4 minutes until the skin is golden. Carefully remove the chicken from the oil and drain in a colander.
* Place the chicken on a heatproof plate and stuff it with two-thirds of the mustard green mixture. Put the remaining mustard greens on top of the chicken and transfer the plate to a bamboo steamer over a pot of boiling water. Steam, covered, for 25 minutes, or until cooked through. Remove from the heat and let stand for 10 minutes. Remove the chicken and reserve any steamed chicken juices. Spoon the mustard greens from the top of the chicken and inside the cavity into a shallow bowl. Cut the chicken into bite-size pieces and lay them on top of the mustard greens.
* To make the sauce, pour the steamed chicken juices into a small saucepan and bring to a boil. Mix the cornstarch (cornflour) with ½ tablespoon water in a small bowl and stir this mixture into the pan. Bring to a boil, stirring, for 30 seconds to thicken the sauce, then drizzle over the chicken. Serve with rice.

柱侯鸡
CHICKEN IN ZHUHOU SAUCE

REGION: SHUNDE
PREPARATION TIME: 10 MINUTES, PLUS
  15 MINUTES MARINATING TIME
COOKING TIME: 18 MINUTES
SERVES: 4

* Cut the chicken into 1 × 2-inch/2.5 × 5-cm pieces (bone-in).
* Combine the chicken, ginger juice, salt, white pepper, and cornstarch (cornflour) in a bowl and marinate for 15 minutes.
* Heat the vegetable oil in a wok or large skillet (frying pan) over medium heat, add the chicken, and stir-fry for 5 minutes until browned. Remove the chicken from the wok and transfer to a plate.
* Add the ginger, shallots, and garlic to the oil remaining in the wok and stir-fry over medium heat for about 30 seconds. Add the zhuhou sauce, soy sauce, sugar, and chicken pieces and sprinkle in the wine. Mix well.
* Add ½ cup (4 fl oz/120 ml) water to the wok and bring to a boil, then reduce to medium-low heat and simmer for 5 minutes, or until the sauce thickens and the chicken is cooked through. Add the scallions (spring onions) and sesame oil and toss well.
* Transfer to a serving plate and serve with rice.

- 1 (2¼-LB/1-KG) WHOLE CHICKEN
- 1 TABLESPOON GINGER JUICE
- ½ TEASPOON SALT
- PINCH OF GROUND WHITE PEPPER
- 2 TABLESPOONS CORNSTARCH (CORNFLOUR)
- 2 TABLESPOONS VEGETABLE OIL
- ¼ OZ/10 G GINGER (ABOUT ¾-INCH/ 2-CM-LENGTH PIECE), SLICED
- 4 SHALLOTS, QUARTERED
- 4 CLOVES GARLIC, CHOPPED
- 2 TABLESPOONS ZHUHOU SAUCE
- 1 TEASPOON LIGHT SOY SAUCE
- 1 TEASPOON GRANULATED SUGAR
- 1 TABLESPOON SHAOXING WINE
- 4 SCALLIONS (SPRING ONIONS), CUT INTO 2-INCH/5-CM LENGTHS
- ½ TEASPOON SESAME OIL
- STEAMED RICE (PAGE 540), TO SERVE

茶树菇干锅鸡
CHICKEN WITH BLACK POPLAR MUSHROOMS

REGION: HUNAN
PREPARATION TIME: 10 MINUTES
COOKING TIME: 10 MINUTES
SERVES: 4

This recipe showcases a popular cooking style from southwest China. Traditionally, the food is served in a wok over a portable kitchen range during the entire course of the meal—it is similar to a hot pot, but without the soup.

* Trim the ends of the mushrooms and separate the mushrooms into stems. Rinse briefly, then drain.
* Heat the oil in a small wok or skillet (frying pan) over medium heat. Stir in the chili bean paste and stir-fry for 1 minute until fragrant. Add the chicken and stir-fry for 1–2 minutes until it is browned.
* Add the garlic sprouts and mushrooms, then the salt, soy sauce, and ½ cup (4 fl oz/120 ml) water. Sauté over medium-high heat for 2–3 minutes until the chicken is cooked through and most of the water has evaporated.
* Reduce to low heat and transfer to a serving plate. Serve with rice.

- 9 OZ/250 G BLACK POPLAR, ENOKI (STEMS SEPARATED), OR MATSUTAKE MUSHROOMS
- 2 TABLESPOONS VEGETABLE OIL
- 1 TABLESPOON CHILI BEAN PASTE
- 6 BONELESS, SKINLESS CHICKEN THIGHS, CUT INTO ¾-INCH/2-CM- THICK PIECES
- 1 BUNCH (ABOUT 25 STALKS) GARLIC SPROUTS, CUT INTO 2-INCH/5-CM LENGTHS
- ½ TEASPOON SALT
- 1 TEASPOON LIGHT SOY SAUCE
- STEAMED RICE (PAGE 540), TO SERVE

REGION: GUANGDONG
PREPARATION TIME: 5 MINUTES, PLUS
  10 MINUTES MARINATING TIME
COOKING TIME: 15 MINUTES
SERVES: 4
[📷] PAGE 259

腰果鸡球

CHICKEN WITH
CASHEW NUTS

- 5 BONELESS CHICKEN LEGS, CUT INTO
  ¾-INCH/2-CM CUBES
- 1 CLOVE GARLIC, CHOPPED
- ½ TEASPOON SALT
- 1 TEASPOON SHAOXING WINE
- 1½ TEASPOONS CORNSTARCH
  (CORNFLOUR)
- 1 TABLESPOON VEGETABLE OIL, PLUS
  EXTRA FOR DEEP-FRYING
- ¾ CUP (3/½ OZ/100 G) CASHEW NUTS
- 6 SHALLOTS, QUARTERED
- 1 RED BELL PEPPER, SEEDED AND
  COARSELY CHOPPED
- 1 TEASPOON LIGHT SOY SAUCE
- 2 SCALLIONS (SPRING ONIONS),
  STEMS ONLY, CUT INTO 2-INCH/5-CM
  LENGTHS
- ½ TEASPOON SESAME OIL
- COARSELY CHOPPED CILANTRO
  (CORIANDER) LEAVES, TO GARNISH
  (OPTIONAL)
- STEAMED RICE (PAGE 540), TO SERVE

* Combine the chicken, garlic, salt, wine, and 1 teaspoon
  cornstarch (cornflour) in a large bowl, then add the oil and
  marinate for 10 minutes.
* Put the cashew nuts into a wok or large skillet (frying pan)
  and add enough oil to cover them completely. Heat the oil
  to 285°F/140°C, or until a cube of bread turns golden in
  2 minutes. Deep fry the nuts for 2-3 minutes, or until
  crunchy. Use a slotted spoon to carefully remove the
  nuts from the oil and drain on paper towels.
* Pour out most of the oil leaving 1 tablespoon in the wok
  and heat over medium heat. Add the shallots and stir-fry
  for 1–2 minutes until fragrant. Put in the chicken, increase
  to high heat, and toss rapidly for 2 minutes until browned.
  Add the bell pepper and soy sauce and stir-fry for another
  minute, or until the chicken is cooked through. Stir in the
  scallions (spring onions).
* Mix the remaining ½ teaspoon cornstarch with 1 teaspoon
  water in a small bowl and stir this mixture into the wok.
  Bring to a boil, stirring, for about 30 seconds to thicken
  the sauce. Add the sesame oil and garnish with cilantro
  (coriander), if using. Serve with rice.

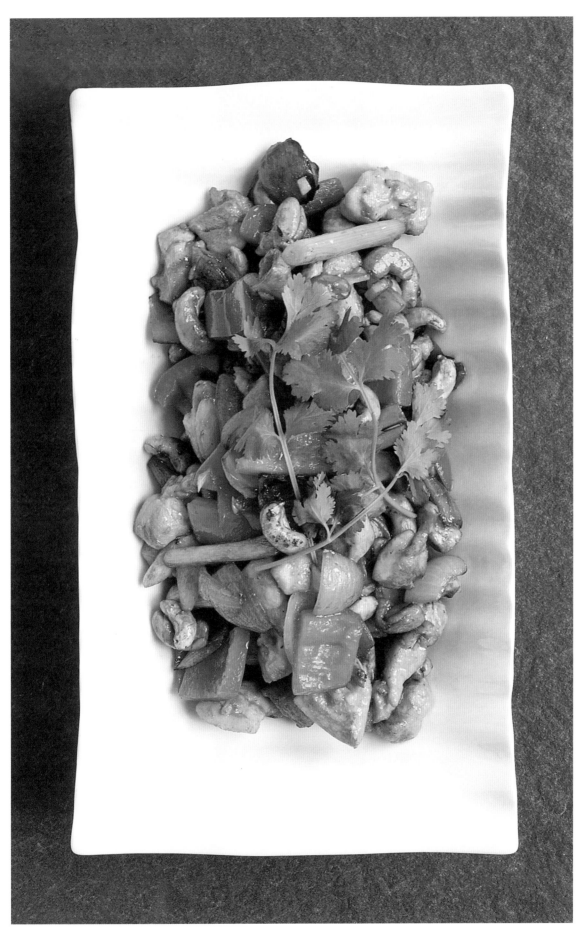

CHICKEN WITH CASHEW NUTS

核桃虾球

CHICKEN WITH WALNUTS

- 2 DRIED BLACK MUSHROOMS
- ½ CUP (2 OZ/50 G) WALNUTS
- 4 BONELESS, SKINLESS CHICKEN BREASTS, CUT INTO BITE-SIZE PIECES
- 1 CUP (8 FL OZ/250 ML) VEGETABLE OIL
- 2 CLOVES GARLIC, CRUSHED
- ⅛ OZ/5 G GINGER (ABOUT ½-INCH/ 1-CM-LENGTH PIECE), SLICED
- 1 TEASPOON SHAOXING WINE
- ½ TABLESPOON OYSTER SAUCE
- ¼ TEASPOON GROUND WHITE PEPPER
- ½ TEASPOON SESAME OIL
- ½ TEASPOON CORNSTARCH (CORNFLOUR)
- 3 BUNCHES CILANTRO (CORIANDER), CHOPPED, TO GARNISH
- STEAMED RICE (PAGE 540), TO SERVE

* Put the mushrooms in a bowl, cover with cold water, and soak for at least 20 minutes, or until softened. Slice into strips and set aside.
* Meanwhile, soak the walnuts in a bowl of warm water for 15 minutes. Drain, then rub them between 2 clean dish towels to remove the skins. Set aside.
* Heat the vegetable oil in a wok or deep saucepan to 250°F/130°C. Gently lower the walnuts into the oil and deep-fry for 4–5 minutes until crispy. Use a slotted spoon to carefully remove the walnuts from the oil and drain on paper towels.
* Reheat the oil to 250°F/130°C, add the chicken, stir, and cook for about 30 seconds until opaque. Use a slotted spoon to remove the chicken from the oil and drain on paper towels.
* Pour out most of the oil, leaving about 1 tablespoon in the wok. Heat the oil over medium-high heat, add the garlic and ginger, and stir-fry for 1 minute until fragrant. Add the chicken and toss for 1–2 minutes over high heat, until cooked through. Sprinkle in the wine.
* Add the walnuts and oyster sauce, toss, and stir in the white pepper and sesame oil.
* Mix the cornstarch (cornflour) with ½ tablespoon water in a small bowl and stir this mixture into the wok. Bring to a boil, stirring, for 30 seconds to thicken the sauce.
* Transfer to a serving plate, garnish with the chopped cilantro (coriander), and serve with rice.

鸡茸炒银耳
CHICKEN WITH
SNOW FUNGUS

REGION: BEIJING
PREPARATION TIME: 5 MINUTES, PLUS
    30 MINUTES SOAKING TIME
COOKING TIME: 15 MINUTES
SERVES: 4

* Cover the snow fungus in hot water and soak for about
  30 minutes. Rinse the snow fungus, squeeze dry, and
  trim off the firm part at the base. Tear the fungus into
  smaller pieces.
* Soak the chicken in a bowl of cold water for 20 minutes.
* Using a large sharp knife, chop the chicken until very finely
  ground. Mix in 2 teaspoons milk, then continue to chop to
  blend the chicken and milk completely. Transfer to a bowl.
* Combine the snow fungus, 1 teaspoon rice wine, and
  ½ teaspoon ginger juice in a bowl and let stand for
  1 minute. Wrap in a clean dish towel and squeeze to
  remove excess fluid. Add the snow fungus to the chicken
  and combine well.
* Beat the egg whites in a small bowl until foamy, then stir
  gradually into the mixture until completely incorporated.
* Bring 8½ cups (68 fl oz/2 liters) water to a boil. Immediately
  turn off the heat. Using your hands, shape the chicken
  mixture into 3 × 1½ × ¼-inch/7.5 × 3 × 0.5-cm rectangular
  pieces and carefully place them in the hot water after each
  piece is made. Bring the water to just below boiling, reduce
  to low heat, and simmer for about 1 minute until cooked
  through. Use a slotted spoon to carefully remove the slices
  from the water and transfer to a plate.
* Heat the oil in a wok or large skillet (frying pan) over
  medium-high heat, add the scallion (spring onion), and
  stir-fry for 1 minute until fragrant. Put in the remaining
  1 teaspoon wine and remove the scallion. Add the chicken
  broth (stock), then gently slide the chicken pieces into the
  broth, add the salt, and bring to a boil.
* Add the remaining milk and the remaining ½ teaspoon
  ginger juice, and return to a boil. Mix the cornstarch
  (cornflour) with 1 tablespoon water in a small bowl and
  stir this mixture into the wok. Bring to a boil, stirring, for
  30 seconds to thicken the sauce.
* Transfer to a large bowl and serve with rice.

* ¾ OZ/20 G SNOW FUNGUS
* 1 BONELESS SKINLESS CHICKEN
  BREAST, THIN MEMBRANE REMOVED
* ⅔ CUP (5 FL OZ/150 ML) MILK
* 2 TEASPOONS RICE WINE
* 1 TEASPOON GINGER JUICE
* 4 EGG WHITES
* 2 TABLESPOONS VEGETABLE OIL
* 1 SCALLION (SPRING ONION), CUT
  INTO 1½-INCH/4-CM SECTIONS AND
  SHREDDED
* ⅓ CUP (2½ FL OZ/75 ML) CHICKEN
  BROTH (STOCK, PAGE 90)
* ½ TEASPOON SALT
* 1 TEASPOON CORNSTARCH
  (CORNFLOUR)
* STEAMED RICE (PAGE 540), TO SERVE

REGION: YUNNAN
PREPARATION TIME: 10 MINUTES,
 PLUS 15 MINUTES SOAKING
COOKING TIME: 4 HOURS
SERVES: 4–6

汽锅鸡

CHICKEN IN A
STEAM CASSEROLE

- 1 (4½-LB/2-KG) WHOLE CHICKEN, CUT INTO 1½-INCH/4-CM DICE
- 1¼ OZ/30 G GINGER, SLICED
- 2 SCALLIONS (SPRING ONIONS), CUT INTO 1½-INCH/4-CM LENGTHS
- 2 TEASPOONS SALT
- ½ TEASPOON GROUND WHITE PEPPER
- STEAMED RICE (PAGE 540), TO SERVE

A steam casserole is a special cookware from Yunnan. It cooks by letting a small amount of steam through a small hole in the casserole to cook the food together with its natural juice. No water is added to the casserole, only to the steaming pan below.

* Soak the chicken pieces in cold water for 15 minutes, then drain.
* Put the chicken into a Yunnan steam casserole, top with the ginger and scallions (spring onions), and cover the casserole. Fill the steamer pan with water and bring to a boil over high heat. Place the steam casserole on top of the steamer pan and seal any gap between the casserole and the steamer pan with damp dish cloths to prevent steam from escaping. Steam for about 4 hours. Add water to the steamer pan during this time if necessary.
* Discard the ginger and scallions, then season the soup with salt and ground white pepper. Serve in the steam casserole with rice.

REGION: CHAOZHOU
PREPARATION TIME: 15 MINUTES
COOKING TIME: 15 MINUTES
SERVES: 4
📷 PAGE 263

豆酱鸡翼

CHICKEN WINGS
IN BEAN SAUCE

- 1 LB /450 G CHICKEN WINGETTES
- 2 TABLESPOONS PUNING BEAN PASTE, MASHED
- 2 TABLESPOONS GINGER JUICE
- ½ TABLESPOON RICE WINE
- ½ TABLESPOON SESAME PASTE
- ½ TEASPOON GRANULATED SUGAR
- 1 TABLESPOON VEGETABLE OIL
- ¼ OZ/10 G PORK FATBACK, FINELY CHOPPED
- 2 SHALLOTS, CHOPPED
- SHREDDED CHILE AND SCALLIONS (SPRING ONION), TO GARNISH (OPTIONAL)
- STEAMED RICE (PAGE 540), TO SERVE

* Bring a large saucepan of water to a boil, add the wingettes, and blanch for 1 minute. Drain and rinse under cold running water.
* Combine the bean paste, ginger juice, rice wine, sesame paste, and sugar in a small bowl and mix well. Set aside.
* Heat the oil in a wok or large skillet (frying pan), add the pork fatback, and stir-fry over medium heat for 2 minutes until slightly brown. Add the shallots and stir-fry until fragrant. Add the sauce and wingettes and sauté for another minute, then pour in ½ cup (4 fl oz/120 ml) water and bring to a boil over high heat. Cook for 3 minutes until the sauce thickens and the wingettes are cooked through.
* Transfer to a serving plate, garnish with chile and scallions (spring onions), if using, and serve with rice.

CHICKEN WINGS IN BEAN SAUCE

REGION: SICHUAN
PREPARATION TIME: 10 MINUTES
COOKING TIME: 5 MINUTES
SERVES: 4

辣子鸡丁
CHICKEN IN SPICY SAUCE

- 2 LARGE BONELESS, SKINLESS CHICKEN BREASTS, CUT INTO ¾-INCH/2-CM CUBES
- 2 TEASPOONS CORNSTARCH (CORNFLOUR)
- ½ TEASPOON SALT
- 2 TEASPOONS RICE WINE
- 2 TEASPOONS LIGHT SOY SAUCE
- ½ TEASPOON GRANULATED SUGAR
- 1 TEASPOON BLACK OR BALSAMIC VINEGAR
- 2 TABLESPOONS CHICKEN BROTH (STOCK, PAGE 90)
- 3 TABLESPOONS VEGETABLE OIL
- 4 CLOVES GARLIC, SLICED
- ¼ OZ/10 G GINGER (ABOUT ¾-INCH/ 2-CM-LENGTH PIECE), SLICED
- 4 PICKLED RED CHILES, CHOPPED
- 6 WATER CHESTNUTS, CUT INTO ½-INCH/1-CM CUBES
- 2 SCALLIONS (SPRING ONIONS), CUT INTO ½-INCH/1-CM LENGTHS
- 1 TEASPOON SESAME OIL

* Combine the chicken, 1 teaspoon cornstarch (cornflour), the salt, and 1 teaspoon wine in a large bowl, mix well, and set aside.
* In a separate bowl, combine the soy sauce, sugar, vinegar, chicken broth (stock), remaining 1 teaspoon wine and 1 teaspoon cornstarch and mix into a sauce. Set aside.
* Stir 1 tablespoon oil into the chicken. Heat the remaining 2 tablespoons in a wok or large skillet (frying pan) over medium-high heat, add the garlic and ginger, and stir-fry for 1 minute until fragrant. Add the chicken and stir-fry for 2 minutes until browned. Add the pickled chiles and water chestnuts and stir-fry for another minute until the chicken is fully cooked. Stir in the scallions (spring onions) and the sauce, then toss thoroughly.
* Stir in the sesame oil, transfer to a serving plate.

REGION: HONG KONG
PREPARATION TIME: 10 MINUTES, PLUS
  30 MINUTES MARINATING TIME
COOKING TIME: 15 MINUTES
SERVES: 4

南乳炸鸡
CHICKEN WITH RED
BEAN CURD SAUCE

- 2 CUBES RED BEAN CURD
- 1 TABLESPOON RED BEAN CURD JUICE
- 10–12 BONELESS CHICKEN THIGHS, CUT INTO BITE-SIZE PIECES
- 1 TABLESPOON RICE WINE
- ½ TEASPOON SALT
- ½ TEASPOON GROUND WHITE PEPPER
- 2 TABLESPOONS CORNSTARCH (CORNFLOUR)
- 1 EGG WHITE, BEATEN
- ⅔ CUP (5 OZ/150 G) BREADCRUMBS
- 4¼ CUPS (34 FL OZ/1 LITER) VEGETABLE OIL
- STEAMED RICE (PAGE 540), TO SERVE

* Mash the bean curd in a small bowl, then add the bean curd juice and stir. Set aside.
* Place the chicken in a large bowl, add the bean curd sauce, wine, salt, and white pepper and marinate for 30 minutes in the refrigerator. Stir in the cornstarch (cornflour). Add the egg white and mix thoroughly. Coat the chicken pieces in breadcrumbs and shake off the excess.
* Heat the oil in a wok or deep saucepan to 300°F/150°C, or until a cube of bread browns in 1½ minutes. Add the chicken, in batches, and deep-fry for 3–4 minutes until golden brown and cooked through. Use a slotted spoon to carefully transfer the chicken to a colander and drain.
* Reheat the oil to 300°F/150°C, return the chicken to the wok, and fry for 1–2 minutes until crispy. Drain on paper towels, then serve with rice.

贵妃鸡翅
CHICKEN WINGS
IN WINE SAUCE

REGION: SICHUAN
PREPARATION TIME: 5 MINUTES
COOKING TIME: 40 MINUTES
SERVES: 3-4

* Put the wingettes into a saucepan and add enough water to cover them completely. Bring to a boil over high heat and blanch the chicken for 1 minute. Drain.
* Put the Sichuan peppercorns into a spice bag. Heat the vegetable oil in a saucepan over medium heat, add the ginger and scallion (spring onion), and stir-fry for about 1 minute until fragrant. Add the wingettes, salt, rock sugar, spice bag, red wine, and 1 cup (8 fl oz/250 ml) water, and bring to a boil. Reduce to low heat and simmer for 30 minutes.
* Add the carrots and simmer for about 5 minutes, or until the sauce thickens. Add the sesame oil and white pepper, season with extra salt to taste, then transfer the chicken wings and carrots to a serving plate.

- 12 CHICKEN WINGETTES
- 1 TEASPOON SICHUAN PEPPERCORNS
- 1 TABLESPOON VEGETABLE OIL
- ⅛ OZ/5 G GINGER (ABOUT ½-INCH/ 1-CM-LENGTH PIECE), SLICED
- 1 SCALLION (SPRING ONION), CUT INTO 2-INCH/5-CM LENGTHS
- ½ TEASPOON SALT, PLUS EXTRA TO TASTE
- ¾ OZ/20 G ROCK SUGAR, CRUSHED
- ⅓ CUP (2½ FL OZ/75 ML) RED WINE
- 1 LARGE CARROT, THINLY SLICED
- 1 TEASPOON SESAME OIL
- PINCH OF GROUND WHITE PEPPER

酥炸鸡软骨
DEEP-FRIED CHICKEN
CARTILAGE

REGION: HONG KONG
PREPARATION TIME: 10 MINUTES, PLUS
   20 MINUTES MARINATING TIME
COOKING TIME: 15 MINUTES
SERVES: 4

The Chinese enjoy the springy yet crunchy texture of cartilage, which is also believed to rebuild collagen and alleviate arthritis symptoms. You may be able to purchase it frozen at your local Asian supermarket or order it from your butcher.

* Combine the chicken cartilage, soy sauce, wine, sugar, salt, and white pepper in a bowl and marinate in the refrigerator for 20 minutes. Stir in the cornstarch (cornflour) and mix in the egg white.
* Dip the chicken cartilage into the breadcrumbs and shake off the excess. Heat the oil in a wok or deep saucepan to 340°F/170°C, or until a cube of bread browns in 45 seconds. Gently lower the chicken cartilage, in batches, and deep-fry for 2-3 minutes until golden brown. Use a slotted spoon to carefully remove the chicken from the oil and drain in a colander.
* Reheat the oil to 340°F/170°C, return the chicken to the wok, and deep-fry for 1 minute until crispy. Use a slotted spoon to carefully remove the cartilage and drain on paper towels. Serve immediately, accompanied by cold beer.

- 1 LB 2 OZ/500 G CHICKEN CARTILAGE
- 1 TABLESPOON LIGHT SOY SAUCE
- 1 TEASPOON RICE WINE
- 1 TEASPOON GRANULATED SUGAR
- ½ TEASPOON SALT
- ½ TEASPOON GROUND WHITE PEPPER
- 1 TABLESPOON CORNSTARCH (CORNFLOUR)
- 1 EGG WHITE, BEATEN
- 5 TABLESPOONS BREADCRUMBS
- 3 CUPS (25 FL OZ/750 ML) VEGETABLE OIL

REGION: HUNAN
PREPARATION TIME: 10 MINUTES, PLUS
30 MINUTES MARINATING TIME
COOKING TIME: 10 MINUTES
SERVES: 6
📷 PAGE 267

左宗棠鸡

GENERAL TSO'S CHICKEN

- 6 BONELESS SKINLESS CHICKEN THIGHS, CUT INTO BITE-SIZE CHUNKS
- 1 TEASPOON SALT
- ½ TABLESPOON LIGHT SOY SAUCE
- 1 TEASPOON WINE
- ½ TEASPOON GRANULATED SUGAR
- 1 EGG, BEATEN
- 4 TABLESPOONS ALL-PURPOSE (PLAIN) FLOUR
- 1 CUP (8 FL OZ/250 ML) VEGETABLE OIL
- 2 CLOVES GARLIC, SLICED
- 4 RED CHILES, SLICED
- ½ ONION, CUT INTO CHUNKS
- ½ GREEN BELL PEPPER, SEEDED AND CUT INTO CHUNKS
- STEAMED RICE (PAGE 540), TO SERVE

FOR THE SWEET AND SOUR SAUCE:
- 4 TABLESPOONS RED VINEGAR
- 2 TABLESPOONS BROWN SUGAR

General Tso Tsong-T'ang was a famous general in the Qing Dynasty and known for his fondness of spicy hot food. This dish, however, was the creation of a restaurant in Taiwan and had nothing to do with the General—his name was only used to reflect the spiciness of the dish.

* Combine the chicken, salt, and 4 tablespoons water in a bowl and marinate for 15 minutes. Pour out any excess water. Add the soy sauce, wine, and sugar and set aside for 15 minutes. Stir in the beaten egg and flour and mix well.
* To make the sauce, mix the ingredients in a bowl. Set aside.
* Heat the oil in a wok or deep saucepan to 300°F/150°C, or until a cube of bread browns in 1½ minutes. Add the chicken, in batches, and deep-fry for 4–5 minutes until golden brown, crispy, and cooked through. Use a slotted spoon to remove from the oil and drain on paper towel.
* Pour out most of the oil, leaving 1 tablespoon in the wok. Heat the oil over medium heat, add the garlic and chiles, and stir-fry for 1 minute until fragrant. Stir in the onions and pepper.
* Add the sweet and sour sauce and sauté for 1 minute until the sauce thickens. Add the chicken and toss thoroughly until they are well coated. Transfer the chicken to a serving plate and serve with rice.

REGION: ANHUI
PREPARATION TIME: 15 MINUTES
COOKING TIME: 5 MINUTES
SERVES: 4

纸包鸡

CRISPY CHICKEN BUNDLES

- 2 BONELESS, SKINLESS CHICKEN BREASTS, CUT INTO 16 SLICES
- 1 SCALLION (SPRING ONION), CHOPPED
- 1 TEASPOON CHOPPED GINGER
- ½ TEASPOON SALT
- 1 TABLESPOON SHAOXING WINE
- 2 TEASPOONS SESAME OIL
- 4 SHEETS RICE PAPER, CUT INTO 8 (7-INCH/18-CM) SQUARES
- 2 OZ/50 G JINHUA OR SMITHFIELD HAM, CUT INTO 8 SLICES
- STEAMED RICE (PAGE 540), TO SERVE

* Combine the chicken, scallion (spring onion), ginger, salt, wine, and sesame oil in a large bowl.
* Put a square of rice paper on a cutting board, add 1 slice of chicken and 1 slice of ham, and then sandwich with another slice of chicken. Fold over the rice paper and enclose the chicken and ham to form a rectangular bundle. Tuck the loose end into the bundle. Repeat with the remaining chicken, ham, and rice paper to make 8 bundles.
* Heat the oil in a wok or deep saucepan to 300°F/150°C, or until a cube of bread browns in 1½ minutes. Gently lower the bundles, in batches, and deep-fry for about 1 minute or until the chicken is cooked through. Use a slotted spoon to carefully remove the bundles from the oil and drain on paper towels. Transfer to a plate and serve with rice.

REGION: HAKKA
PREPARATION TIME: 10 MINUTES, PLUS
  10 MINUTES MARINATING TIME
COOKING TIME: 10 MINUTES
SERVES: 4

沙葛鸡球
CHICKEN WITH
JICAMA

- 1 LB 5 OZ/600 G CHICKEN PIECES, CUT INTO 1½ × 1¼-INCH/4 × 3-CM CHUNKS (BONE-IN)
- ½ TEASPOON DARK SOY SAUCE
- ½ TEASPOON SALT
- 2 JUJUBE DATES, PITTED AND HALVED
- 1 TABLESPOON VEGETABLE OIL
- ¼ OZ/10 G GINGER (ABOUT ¾-INCH/ 2-CM-LENGTH PIECE), SLICED
- ½ TEASPOON LIGHT SOY SAUCE
- 3 TABLESPOONS GLUTINOUS RICE WINE
- 1 JICAMA, PEELED AND CUT INTO 1-INCH/2.5-CM CHUNKS
- ½ TEASPOON BROWN SUGAR
- ¼ TEASPOON WHITE VINEGAR
- STEAMED RICE (PAGE 540), TO SERVE

* Put the chicken into a large saucepan and add enough water to cover them completely. Bring to a boil over high heat and blanch for about 1 minute. Drain.
* Combine the chicken, dark soy sauce, and salt in a large bowl and marinate for 10 minutes.
* Meanwhile, cover the jujube dates in cold water and soak for at least 10 minutes until soft.
* Heat the oil in a wok or large skillet (frying pan) over medium-high heat, add the ginger, and stir-fry for 1 minute until slightly brown. Add the chicken and jujube dates and stir-fry over high heat for about 30 seconds. Stir in the light soy sauce and 2 tablespoons wine and cook for 2 minutes, or until the chicken is almost cooked through.
* Add the jicama, brown sugar, vinegar, and the remaining 1 tablespoon wine. Sauté the chicken for about 1–2 minutes, or until the chicken is fully cooked and the sauce has thickened.
* Transfer to a serving plate and serve with rice.

REGION: BEIJING
PREPARATION TIME: 5 MINUTES, PLUS
  10 MINUTES SOAKING TIME
COOKING TIME: 5 MINUTES
SERVES: 4

夜来香炒鸡丝
CHICKEN WITH
TUBEROSE

- 4 BONELESS, SKINLESS CHICKEN BREASTS
- 3½ OZ/100 G TUBEROSE, RINSED
- 1 TEASPOON SALT
- 1 TABLESPOON SHAOXING WINE
- 2 TEASPOONS CORNSTARCH (CORNFLOUR)
- 2 TABLESPOONS CHICKEN BROTH (STOCK, PAGE 90)
- 1 TEASPOON GRANULATED SUGAR
- 1 TABLESPOON VEGETABLE OIL
- 1 TEASPOON SESAME OIL
- STEAMED RICE (PAGE 540), TO SERVE

* Soak the chicken in a bowl of cold water for 10 minutes. Drain, then cut into thin strips and put into a bowl.
* Bring a saucepan of water to a boil over high heat, add the tuberose, and blanch for 30 seconds. Drain and set aside.
* Mix ½ teaspoon salt, the wine, and 1 teaspoon cornstarch (cornflour) with the chicken.
* In another bowl, combine the chicken broth (stock), sugar, the remaining ½ teaspoon salt, and 1 teaspoon cornstarch. Set aside.
* Heat the vegetable oil in a wok or large skillet (frying pan) over high heat, add the chicken, and stir-fry 2 minutes until opaque. Add the tuberose and chicken broth mixture and cook for another minute, or until the chicken is cooked through. Drizzle with sesame oil and transfer to a serving plate. Serve with rice.

鸡里蹦

CHICKEN WITH
SHRIMP

REGION: HEBEI
PREPARATION TIME: 10 MINUTES, PLUS
  10 MINUTES MARINATING TIME
COOKING TIME: 10 MINUTES
SERVES: 4

* Combine the chicken, ¼ teaspoon salt, and ½ tablespoon wine in a bowl and marinate for 10 minutes. Stir in 1 tablespoon cornstarch (cornflour) and 1 tablespoon water.
* Meanwhile, combine the shrimp (prawns), remaining ¼ teaspoon salt and ½ tablespoon wine, and white pepper in a separate bowl and marinate for 10 minutes. Stir in 1 tablespoon cornstarch and 1 tablespoon water.
* Mix the soy sauce, white vinegar, sugar, remaining ½ tablespoon cornstarch, and 2 tablespoons water in a small bowl. Set aside.
* Heat the oil in a wok or deep saucepan over medium-low heat to 265°F/130°C. Gently lower the chicken and deep-fry for 2 minute until the chicken is almost cooked through. Use a slotted spoon to remove the chicken and drain on paper towels.
* Reheat the oil to 265°F/130°C, carefully add the shrimp, and deep-fry for 30 seconds. Drain on paper towels.
* Pour out most of the oil, leaving 2 tablespoons in the wok. Heat the oil over medium heat, add the Sichuan peppercorns, and stir-fry for 1 minute until fragrant. Remove the peppercorns, then add the ginger and dry chiles to the wok and stir-fry until fragrant. Add the bell peppers, increase to high heat, toss a few times, then stir in the chicken and shrimp.
* Beat the sauce in the bowl, add to the wok, and sauté for 2 minutes until the chicken and shrimp are fully cooked. Stir in the chopped scallion (spring onion) and transfer to a serving plate. Serve with rice.

* 4 BONELESS, SKINLESS CHICKEN THIGHS, CUT INTO ¾-INCH/ 2-CM CUBES
* ½ TEASPOON SALT
* 1 TABLESPOON RICE WINE
* 2½ TABLESPOONS CORNSTARCH (CORNFLOUR)
* 11 OZ/300 G UNCOOKED SHRIMP (PRAWNS), SHELLED AND DEVEINED
* PINCH OF GROUND WHITE PEPPER
* 1 TEASPOON LIGHT SOY SAUCE
* 1 TABLESPOON WHITE VINEGAR
* 1 TABLESPOON GRANULATED SUGAR
* 1 CUP (8 FL OZ/250 ML) VEGETABLE OIL
* 1 TABLESPOON SICHUAN PEPPERCORNS
* ⅛ OZ/5 G GINGER (ABOUT ½-INCH/ 1-CM-LENGTH PIECE), SLICED
* 4 DRIED CHILES
* 1 GREEN BELL PEPPER, SEEDED AND CUT INTO ¾-INCH/2-CM SQUARES
* 1 RED BELL PEPPER, SEEDED AND CUT INTO ¾-INCH/2-CM SQUARES
* 1 SCALLION (SPRING ONION), CHOPPED, TO GARNISH
* STEAMED RICE (PAGE 540), TO SERVE

REGION: SICHUAN
PREPARATION TIME: 15 MINUTES,
  PLUS 15 MINUTES SOAKING TIME
COOKING TIME: 15 MINUTES
SERVES: 4
📷 PAGE 271

宫保鸡丁
GONGBAO
CHICKEN

- 6 BONELESS, SKINLESS CHICKEN THIGHS, CUT INTO ¾-INCH/2-CM CUBES
- ½ TEASPOON SALT
- 1 TEASPOON CORNSTARCH (CORNFLOUR)
- ⅔ CUP (3½ OZ/100 G) RAW PEANUTS
- 1 TEASPOON VEGETABLE OIL, PLUS EXTRA FOR DEEP-FRYING
- 1 TABLESPOON SICHUAN PEPPERCORNS
- 3 DRIED CHILES, HALVED
- 4 CLOVES GARLIC, SLICED
- ¼ OZ/10 G GINGER (ABOUT ¾-INCH/ 2-CM-LENGTH PIECE), SLICED
- 1 TABLESPOON CHILI OIL
- 1 TABLESPOON CHILI BEAN PASTE
- 2 OZ/50 G BAMBOO SHOOTS, CUT INTO ½-INCH/1-CM DICE (OR ⅓ CUP SLICED)
- 1 TABLESPOON SHAOXING WINE
- 1 TABLESPOON BLACK OR BALSAMIC VINEGAR
- 1 TEASPOON LIGHT SOY SAUCE
- 1 TEASPOON GRANULATED SUGAR
- 4 SCALLIONS (SPRING ONIONS) STEMS ONLY, CUT INTO ¼-INCH/5-MM LENGTHS
- ½ TEASPOON SESAME OIL
- STEAMED RICE (PAGE 540), TO SERVE

* Combine the chicken, salt, and 3 tablespoons water in a bowl and soak for 15 minutes. Drain away any excess water. Add the cornstarch (cornflour) to the chicken and mix thoroughly.
* Put the peanuts into a wok or deep saucepan and add enough oil to cover. Heat the oil over medium heat and deep-fry the peanuts for 3–4 minutes until light brown and crunchy. Use a slotted spoon to remove the peanuts and drain them on paper towels.
* Pour out most of the oil, leaving about 2 tablespoons in the wok, heat over low heat, add the Sichuan peppercorns, and stir-fry for 1 minute until fragrant. Remove and discard the peppercorns, then add the dried chiles, garlic, ginger, chili oil, and chili bean paste, and stir-fry for 1 minute until fragrant.
* Stir 1 teaspoon vegetable oil into the bowl of chicken. Add the chicken, bamboo shoots, and wine to the wok, increase to high heat, and stir-fry for about 3 minutes, or until the chicken is nearly cooked through. Stir in the vinegar, soy sauce, and sugar, then add the scallions (spring onions) and sesame oil. Scatter over the peanuts and toss well.
* Transfer to a serving plate and serve with rice.

GONGBAO CHICKEN

REGION: ANHUI
PREPARATION TIME: 15 MINUTES,
    PLUS 35–40 MINUTES DRYING TIME
COOKING TIME: 2 HOURS 15 MINUTES
SERVES: 4

符离集烧鸡
FULIJI BRAISED CHICKEN

- 1 (2½-LB/1.2-KG) WHOLE CHICKEN
- 1 TABLESPOON MALTOSE SYRUP
- 2 CUPS (16 FL OZ/475 ML) VEGETABLE OIL
- 4 TABLESPOONS SALT
- 1 TABLESPOON GRANULATED SUGAR
- STEAMED RICE (PAGE 540), TO SERVE

FOR THE SPICE BAG:
- 4 CLOVES
- 2 STAR ANISE
- 1 BLACK CARDAMOM POD
- 1 DRIED TANGERINE PEEL
- ¾ OZ/20 G GINGER (ABOUT 1-INCH/ 2.5-CM-LENGTH PIECE), SLICED
- 1 TEASPOON SICHUAN PEPPERCORNS
- ½ TEASPOON SHAJIANG POWDER
- ½ TEASPOON GROUND CUMIN
- ½ TEASPOON GRATED NUTMEG

Fuli, a town in Anhui Province, is home to this famed dish. It was first documented when archaeologists excavated a tomb and unearthed an urn marked "Office of the Fuli" filled with a complete set of well-preserved chicken bones. The dish is said to have originated 2000 years ago.

* Air-dry the chicken in the refrigerator for 30 minutes.
* Mix the maltose with 2 tablespoons hot water in a small bowl and brush onto the skin of the chicken. Set aside for 2–3 minutes. Brush another coat on and let dry for another 2–3 minutes.
* Heat the oil in a wok or large saucepan to 300°F/150°C, or until a cube of bread browns in 1½ minutes. Carefully add the chicken and use a slotted spoon to gently roll it in the hot oil for 3–4 minutes until the skin is golden. Carefully remove the chicken from the oil and drain in a colander.
* Put the spices into a spice bag. Put the chicken, salt, and sugar in a large saucepan and add enough water to cover it completely. Bring to a boil over high heat and add the spice bag. Reduce to low heat, cover, and simmer for about 2 hours, until chicken is cooked through and tender. Transfer the chicken (without the broth, which is too spicy) to a serving plate and serve with rice.

REGION: SHANDONG
PREPARATION TIME: 10 MINUTES
COOKING TIME: 25 MINUTES
SERVES: 4

黄焖鸡块
CHICKEN IN TIANMIANJIANG

- 2 TABLESPOONS VEGETABLE OIL
- 2 TABLESPOONS GRANULATED SUGAR
- 2 TABLESPOONS TIANMIANJIANG
- ¼ OZ/10 G GINGER (ABOUT ¾-INCH/ 2-CM-LENGTH PIECE), SLICED
- 2 SCALLIONS (SPRING ONIONS), CUT INTO 2-INCH/5-CM LENGTHS
- 2¼ LB/1 KG CHICKEN LEGS, CUT INTO 1¼ × 1½-INCH/3 × 4-CM PIECES
- 1 TEASPOON SALT
- 1 CUP (8 FL OZ/250 ML) CHICKEN BROTH (STOCK, PAGE 90)
- 1 TABLESPOON SHAOXING WINE
- 1 TEASPOON SESAME OIL
- STEAMED RICE (PAGE 540), TO SERVE

* Heat the vegetable oil in a saucepan over low heat, add the sugar, and cook gently for 1–2 minutes until the sugar is caramelized. Add the tianmianjiang, ginger, and scallions (spring onions) and stir-fry for 1–2 minutes until fragrant.
* Put the chicken, salt, and chicken broth (stock) into the pan and bring to a boil. Cover, reduce to low heat, and simmer for 15 minutes.
* Add the wine, increase to medium heat, and simmer for about 5 minutes, or until the sauce thickens and the chicken is cooked through. Stir in the sesame oil and transfer to a serving plate. Serve with rice.

捶烩鸡片
CHICKEN WITH MUSHROOMS
AND BAMBOO

REGION: SHANDONG
PREPARATION TIME: 10 MINUTES,
  PLUS 20 MINUTES SOAKING TIME
COOKING TIME: 10 MINUTES
SERVES: 4

* Put the mushrooms in a bowl, cover with cold water, and soak for at least 20 minutes, or until softened. Cut the caps into slices at an angle (so that it creates a larger surface area). Set aside.
* Put the chicken into a bowl and mix with 1½ tablespoons cornstarch (cornflour). Put a few pieces of chicken on a sheet of plastic wrap (clingfilm), fold the film to cover the chicken, and use a rolling pin to bash the chicken until paper thin (about 1/12 inch/2 mm thick). Repeat with the remaining chicken pieces.
* Heat the oil in a wok or deep saucepan over medium-low heat, add the chicken, and deep fry for 30 seconds until cooked through. Use a slotted spoon to remove the chicken and drain on paper towels.
* Pour out most of the oil, leaving about 2 tablespoons in the wok. Heat the oil over medium heat, add the scallions (spring onions), and stir-fry for 2 minutes until brown and fragrant. Use a slotted spoon to remove and discard the scallions.
* Add the bamboo shoots and the mushrooms to the wok and stir-fry for 2 minutes. Sprinkle in the wine, then add the chicken broth (stock), salt, sugar, and ham and bring to a boil. Add the chicken and return to a boil.
* Combine the remaining ½ tablespoon cornstarch with 2 tablespoons water in a small bowl and stir this into the wok. Bring to a boil, stirring, for about 30 seconds to thicken the sauce. Drizzle over the sesame oil, stir, and transfer to a serving plate. Serve with rice.

- 6 DRIED BLACK MUSHROOMS
- 3 SKINLESS CHICKEN BREASTS, CUT INTO ¾-INCH/2-CM-SQUARE PIECES, ABOUT ¼ INCH/5 MM THICK
- 2 TABLESPOONS CORNSTARCH (CORNFLOUR)
- 2 CUPS (16 FL OZ/475 ML) VEGETABLE OIL
- 2 SCALLIONS (SPRING ONIONS), CUT INTO 1½-INCH/4-CM LENGTHS
- ⅓ CUP (2 OZ/50 G) SLICED BAMBOO SHOOT, DRAINED
- 1 TABLESPOON RICE WINE
- 2 CUPS (16 FL OZ/475 ML) CHICKEN BROTH (STOCK, PAGE 90)
- ½ TEASPOON SALT
- ½ TEASPOON GRANULATED SUGAR
- 2 OZ/50 G JINHUA OR SMITHFIELD HAM, THINLY SLICED
- ½ TEASPOON SESAME OIL
- STEAMED RICE (PAGE 540), TO SERVE

REGION: YUNNAN
PREPARATION TIME: 5 MINUTES, PLUS
   30 MINUTES MARINATING TIME
COOKING TIME: 25 MINUTES
SERVES: 4
📷 PAGE 275

酱汁鸡腿

DRUMSTICKS
IN SAUCE

- 8 CHICKEN DRUMSTICKS
- 2 CUPS (16 FL OZ/475 ML)
  VEGETABLE OIL
- 1 TABLESPOON TIANMIANJIANG
- 1 TABLESPOON GRANULATED SUGAR
- 1 TABLESPOON LIGHT SOY SAUCE
- 4 TABLESPOONS CHICKEN BROTH
  (STOCK, PAGE 90)
- STEAMED RICE (PAGE 540), TO SERVE

  FOR THE MARINADE:
- 1 TABLESPOON GINGER JUICE
- 2 SCALLIONS (SPRING ONIONS), CUT
  INTO 2-INCH/5-CM LENGTHS
- ½ TEASPOON SALT
- 1 TEASPOON LIGHT SOY SAUCE
- 1 TEASPOON DARK SOY SAUCE
- 1 TABLESPOON RICE WINE
- 1 TEASPOON FIVE-SPICE POWDER

* Combine the chicken and marinade ingredients in a
  large bowl and marinate for 30 minutes.
* Heat the oil in a wok or deep saucepan over medium heat
  to 300°F/150°C, or until a cube of bread turns brown
  in 1½ minutes. Gently lower the drumsticks into the oil
  and deep-fry for 2–3 minutes until golden brown. Use
  a slotted spoon to carefully remove the drumsticks
  from the oil and drain on paper towels.
* Pour out most of the oil, leaving 1 tablespoon in the wok.
  Heat the oil over medium heat, add the tianmianjiang,
  and stir-fry for 1 minute until fragrant. Add the sugar,
  soy sauce, and chicken broth (stock) and bring to a boil.
* Transfer the chicken to a shallow heatproof bowl, pour
  the sauce over the chicken, and place in a collapsible pot
  or bamboo steamer over a pot of boiling water. Steam,
  covered, for 15 minutes, or until cooked through.
* Remove the chicken from the steamer and carefully drain
  the sauce into the wok. Reduce the sauce over medium
  heat to about half, or until thickened. Drizzle the sauce
  over the chicken, then serve with rice.

DRUMSTICKS IN SAUCE

REGION: TAIWAN
PREPARATION TIME: 10 MINUTES
COOKING TIME: 25 MINUTES
SERVES: 2

三杯鸡

CHICKEN WITH SESAME OIL, SOY SAUCE, AND WINE

- 1 LB/450 G CHICKEN DRUMSTICKS, CUT INTO ¾-INCH/2-CM PIECES
- 2 TABLESPOONS SESAME OIL
- 2 OZ/50 G GINGER (ABOUT 3-INCH/7.5-CM-LENGTH PIECE), THINLY SLICED
- 6 CLOVES GARLIC, PEELED
- 1 TABLESPOON GRANULATED SUGAR
- 1 RED CHILE, SEEDED
- 2 TABLESPOONS LIGHT SOY SAUCE
- 2 TABLESPOONS RICE WINE
- 1 CUP (2 OZ/50 G) BASIL LEAVES
- STEAMED RICE (PAGE 540), TO SERVE

* Put the drumsticks into a saucepan and add enough water to cover them completely. Bring to a boil and blanch for 2 minutes. Drain and rinse under cold running water.
* Heat the oil in a Dutch oven (casserole) over medium-high heat, add the ginger, and fry for 1 minute until golden. Add the garlic and fry for another 30 seconds. Put in the chicken and stir-fry for 2 minutes until slightly brown. Add the sugar and cook for another 2–3 minutes until light caramel in color. Add the chile, soy sauce, and wine and stir to mix thoroughly. Bring to a boil, reduce to low heat, and simmer, covered, for 10 minutes, or until the sauce thickens and the chicken is cooked through.
* Add the basil leaves, cover, then turn off the heat and stand for 1 minute until the leaves are slightly wilted. Serve in the Dutch oven together with rice.

REGION: SICHUAN
PREPARATION TIME: 10 MINUTES, PLUS 30 MINUTES MARINATING TIME
COOKING TIME: 25 MINUTES
SERVES: 4–6

热窝姜汁鸡

CHICKEN AND GINGER CASSEROLE

- 1 (2¼-LB/1-KG) WHOLE CHICKEN
- 1 TABLESPOON SALT
- 1 TABLESPOON RICE WINE
- 2 TABLESPOONS VEGETABLE OIL
- SCANT ½ CUP (3½ OZ/100 G) CHOPPED GINGER
- 3 SCALLIONS (SPRING ONIONS), CUT INTO 1½-INCH/4-CM LENGTHS
- 3 SHALLOTS, QUARTERED
- 1 TEASPOON GRANULATED SUGAR
- 1 TABLESPOON CORNSTARCH (CORNFLOUR)
- 2 TABLESPOONS BLACK OR BALSAMIC VINEGAR
- 1 TEASPOON SESAME OIL

* Put the chicken in a large heatproof bowl, rub with the salt and wine, and marinate in the refrigerator for 30 minutes.
* Place the bowl of chicken in a collapsible pot or bamboo steamer over a pot of boiling water. Steam, covered, for 15 minutes. Carefully transfer the chicken to a plate and set aside to cool. Reserve the chicken juices in a bowl.
* Once the chicken is cool enough to handle, chop it into ¾ × 1½-inch/2 × 4-cm pieces. (At this time, the chicken is only partially cooked so don't worry if it is a little pink.)
* Heat the oil in a Dutch oven (casserole) over medium heat. Add the ginger and stir-fry for 1 minute until fragrant, then add the scallions (spring onions) and shallots. Increase to high heat, add the chicken and sugar, and stir-fry for 3–4 minutes until cooked through.
* Mix the cornstarch (cornflour) with 3 tablespoons of the reserved steamed chicken juices in a small bowl and stir this mixture into the Dutch oven. Bring to a boil, stirring, for about 30 seconds to thicken the sauce. Add the vinegar and sesame oil and boil for another 20 seconds. Serve in the Dutch oven.

POULTRY

司马怀府鸡

CHICKEN WITH
WILD YAMS

REGION: HENAN
PREPARATION TIME: 15 MINUTES, PLUS
  10 MINUTES MARINATING TIME
COOKING TIME: 25 MINUTES
SERVES: 4–6

* Combine the chicken pieces, salt, and pepper in a large bowl and marinate for 10 minutes. Add the cornstarch (cornflour) and mix well.
* Heat the vegetable oil in a wok or deep saucepan to 350°F/180°C, or until a cube of bread browns in 30 seconds. Gently lower the chicken into the hot oil and deep-fry for 3–4 minutes until lightly golden and half cooked. Use a slotted spoon to carefully transfer the chicken to a heatproof bowl.
* Drain the wild yams and pat dry with paper towels. Reheat the oil to 350°F/180°C and deep-fry for 4–5 minutes until golden brown. Use a slotted spoon to carefully transfer the yams to the bowl of chicken.
* In a separate bowl, mix together the soy sauces, sugar, wine, star anise, ginger, scallions (spring onions), and chicken broth (stock). Pour over the yams and the chicken.
* Place the bowl of yams and chicken in a collapsible pot or bamboo steamer over a pot of boiling water. Steam, covered, for 12 minutes until the yams and chicken are cooked through.
* Carefully pour the sauce from the bowl into a wok or skillet (frying pan) and bring to a boil over high heat. Continue to boil until it's reduced by two-thirds. Stir in the sesame oil and pour the sauce over the dish. Serve with rice.

- 2¼-LB/1-KG CHICKEN PIECES, CUT INTO 1 × 2-INCH/2.5 × 5-CM CHUNKS (BONE-IN)
- 1 TEASPOON SALT
- ¼ TEASPOON GROUND WHITE PEPPER
- 1 TABLESPOON CORNSTARCH (CORNFLOUR)
- 2 CUPS (16 FL OZ/475 ML) VEGETABLE OIL
- 1½ (ABOUT 1 LB 5 OZ/600 G) WILD YAMS, PEELED, CUT INTO SMALL CHUNKS, AND SOAKED IN ICE-COLD WATER
- 2 TEASPOONS LIGHT SOY SAUCE
- 1 TEASPOON DARK SOY SAUCE
- ½ TEASPOON GRANULATED SUGAR
- 1 TEASPOON RICE WINE
- 2 STAR ANISE
- ¼ OZ/10 G GINGER (ABOUT ¾-INCH/ 2-CM-LENGTH PIECE), SLICED
- 3 SCALLIONS (SPRING ONIONS), CUT INTO 1½-INCH/4-CM LENGTHS
- ½ CUP (4 FL OZ/120 ML) CHICKEN BROTH (STOCK, PAGE 90)
- 1 TEASPOON SESAME OIL
- STEAMED RICE (PAGE 540), TO SERVE

REGION: GUANGDONG

PREPARATION TIME: 15 MINUTES,
  PLUS 20 MINUTES SOAKING TIME
COOKING TIME: 45 MINUTES
SERVES: 4
📷 PAGE 279

栗子焖鸡
CHICKEN WITH CHESTNUTS

- 15 SHELLED CHESTNUTS
- 4 DRIED BLACK MUSHROOMS
- ½ CUP (4 FL OZ/120 ML) PLUS
  2½ TABLESPOONS VEGETABLE OIL
- 1 LB 8½ OZ/700 G CHICKEN PIECES,
  CUT INTO CHUNKS (BONE-IN)
- ½ TEASPOON SALT
- ¼ TEASPOON GROUND WHITE PEPPER
- 1 TABLESPOON SHAOXING WINE
- 1 TABLESPOON CORNSTARCH
  (CORNFLOUR)
- 3 SHALLOTS, QUARTERED
- 2 CLOVES GARLIC, SLICED
- ⅛ OZ/5 G GINGER (ABOUT ½-INCH/
  1-CM-LENGTH PIECE), SLICED
- 1 TEASPOON GRANULATED SUGAR
- 1 TABLESPOON LIGHT SOY SAUCE
- 1 TABLESPOON OYSTER SAUCE
- 3 SCALLIONS (SPRING ONIONS), CUT
  INTO 2½-INCH/6-CM LENGTHS
- ½ TEASPOON SESAME OIL

* Place the chestnuts on a heatproof plate and put into a collapsible pot or bamboo steamer over a pot of boiling water. Steam, covered, for 15 minutes. Set aside.
* Put the mushrooms in a bowl, cover with cold water, and soak for at least 20 minutes, or until softened. Drain, return to the bowl, and add ½ tablespoon vegetable oil. Mix well.
* Combine the chicken, salt, white pepper, wine, and cornstarch (cornflour) in a bowl. Marinate for 15 minutes.
* Heat ½ cup (4 fl oz/120 ml) oil in a wok or large skillet (frying pan) to 300°F/150°C, or until a cube of bread browns in 1½ minutes. Carefully add the chicken pieces and pan-fry for 3–4 minutes until light brown. Transfer the chicken to a plate lined with paper towels.
* Heat the remaining 2 tablespoons oil in a Dutch oven (casserole), add the shallots, garlic, ginger, and mushrooms, and stir-fry over high heat for 2 minutes until fragrant. Add the chicken, chestnuts, sugar, soy and oyster sauces, scallions (spring onions), and ½ cup (4 fl oz/120 ml) water, then bring to a boil. Reduce to medium heat and braise, covered, for 20 minutes. Stir in the sesame oil and serve in the Dutch oven.

REGION: YUNNAN
PREPARATION TIME: 10 MINUTES, PLUS
  15 MINUTES MARINATING TIME
COOKING TIME: 30 MINUTES
SERVES: 4–6

番木瓜焖鸡
CHICKEN WITH PAPAYA

- 2½-LB/1.2-KG BONE-IN CHICKEN
  PIECES
- 1 TABLESPOON SALT
- 2 TABLESPOONS BAIJIU OR VODKA
- 1 TABLESPOON CORNSTARCH
  (CORNFLOUR)
- 2 TABLESPOONS VEGETABLE OIL
- ¼ OZ/10 G GINGER (ABOUT ¾-INCH/
  2-CM-LENGTH PIECE), SLICED
- 1 SCALLION (SPRING ONION), CUT
  INTO 1½-INCH/4-CM LENGTHS
- 1 PAPAYA, PEELED, SEEDED, AND CUT
  INTO CHUNKS
- 2 TABLESPOONS GRANULATED SUGAR
- STEAMED RICE (PAGE 540), TO SERVE

* Put the chicken into a large bowl and rub with the salt, 1 tablespoon baijiu, and the cornstarch (cornflour). Marinade for 15 minutes.
* Heat the oil in a wok or large saucepan over medium-high heat, add the ginger and scallion (spring onion), and stir-fry for 1 minute until fragrant. Increase to high heat, add the chicken, and cook for 4–5 minutes. Add the papaya, sugar, remaining 1 tablespoon baijiu, and enough water to cover the chicken. Bring to a boil, reduce to medium heat, and simmer, covered, for 20 minutes, or until cooked. Transfer to a serving bowl and serve with rice.

CHICKEN WITH CHESTNUTS

大盘鸡
XINJIANG-STYLE CHICKEN

- 1 LB 8½ OZ/700 G CHICKEN BREAST AND LEGS, CUT INTO ¾ × 1½-INCH/ 2 × 4-CM PIECES
- 1 STAR ANISE
- 1 TEASPOON SICHUAN PEPPERCORNS
- ½ SMALL CINNAMON STICK
- 2 TABLESPOONS VEGETABLE OIL
- 1 TABLESPOON GRANULATED SUGAR
- 1 TABLESPOON PIXIAN CHILI BEAN PASTE
- 4 DRIED CHILES, HALVED
- 2 RED CHILES, HALVED
- ⅛ OZ/5 G GINGER (ABOUT ½-INCH/ 1-CM-LENGTH PIECE), SLICED
- 2 CLOVES GARLIC, SLICED
- ½ TEASPOON SALT
- 1 TABLESPOON LIGHT SOY SAUCE
- 1 TABLESPOON RICE WINE
- 2 POTATOES, CUT INTO ¾-INCH/2-CM DICE
- 3 CARROTS, CUT INTO ¾-INCH/2-CM DICE
- 1 RED BELL PEPPER, SEEDED AND CUT INTO ¾-INCH/2-CM SQUARES
- COOKED WHEAT NOODLES, TO SERVE

* Put the chicken pieces into a large saucepan and add enough water to cover them completely. Bring to a boil over high heat and blanch for 1 minute. Drain and rinse under cold running water. Drain again.
* Put the star anise, Sichuan peppercorns, and cinnamon stick into a spice bag.
* Heat the oil in a wok or large skillet (frying pan) over low heat, add the sugar, and stir for 1–2 minutes until the sugar is caramelized.
* Put in the chicken pieces and stir until they are fully coated in the caramel. Add the Pixian chili bean paste, dried and fresh chiles, ginger, and garlic and stir-fry over medium-high heat for 1 minute until fragrant. Add the salt, soy sauce, wine, spice bag, and enough water to cover the chicken completely. Bring to a boil.
* Put in the potatoes and carrots, cover with a lid, reduce to low heat, and simmer for about 15 minutes until the chicken is cooked through and the vegetables are softened. Stir frequently to prevent burning and add water, if necessary.
* Add the bell pepper, discard the spice bag, and stir. Increase to high heat and cook until the sauce has reduced to ½ cup (4 fl oz/120 ml).
* Transfer to a serving plate and serve with the cooked noodles.

鲍鱼鸡煲
CHICKEN AND ABALONE CASSEROLE

REGION: HONG KONG
PREPARATION TIME: 15 MINUTES,
  PLUS 20 MINUTES SOAKING TIME
COOKING TIME: 20 MINUTES
SERVES: 4

* Put the mushrooms in a bowl, cover with cold water, and soak for at least 20 minutes, or until softened. Set aside.
* Meanwhile, put the chicken into a bowl and rub with the salt and 1 teaspoon sugar. Marinate for 10 minutes. Mix in 1 tablespoon cornstarch (cornflour).
* Bring a large saucepan of water to a boil over high heat and add the abalone. Remove immediately after 1 minute, drain, and rinse under cold running water.
* Using a small knife, separate the abalone meat from each shell and remove the internal organs. Clean the feet (the flat side) of the abalones by scraping lightly with a knife and brush the sides with a brush. Rinse the abalones thoroughly. Score the foot of each abalone in a crisscross pattern.
* Lightly dredge the abalones in the remaining 1 tablespoon cornstarch. Heat the oil in a Dutch oven (casserole) over medium-high and add the abalone. Fry one side of the abalone for 1 minute until slightly browned. Flip over and fry for another minute. Transfer to a plate and set aside.
* Add the shallots and ginger to the Dutch oven and stir-fry for 1 minute until fragrant. Add the chicken and stir-fry for another 2–3 minutes until golden brown. Sprinkle in the wine and stir in the mushrooms, soy and oyster sauces, and remaining 1 teaspoon sugar. Pour in ½ cup (4 fl oz/ 120 ml) water and bring to a boil over high heat, then cook, uncovered, for 2–3 minutes to reduce and thicken the sauce. Add the abalones, bell pepper, and scallions (spring onions) and toss well. Reduce to low heat and simmer, covered, for 2–3 minutes, or until the chicken is cooked through.
* Garnish with the cilantro (coriander) and serve with rice.

* 4 DRIED BLACK MUSHROOMS
* 11 OZ/300 G BONE-IN CHICKEN PIECES (BREASTS AND LEGS)
* ½ TEASPOON SALT
* 2 TEASPOONS GRANULATED SUGAR
* 2 TABLESPOONS CORNSTARCH (CORNFLOUR)
* 8 (2½-OZ/75-G) FRESH ABALONE
* 2 TABLESPOONS VEGETABLE OIL
* 10 SHALLOTS, PEELED
* 2 OZ/50 G GINGER (ABOUT 3-INCH/ 7.5-CM-LENGTH PIECE), SLICED
* 2 TABLESPOONS SHAOXING WINE
* 1 TEASPOON LIGHT SOY SAUCE
* 1 TABLESPOON OYSTER SAUCE
* ½ RED BELL PEPPER, SEEDED AND CUT INTO CHUNKS
* 3 SCALLIONS (SPRING ONIONS), STEMS ONLY, CUT INTO LENGTHS
* CILANTRO (CORIANDER), CHOPPED, TO GARNISH
* STEAMED RICE (PAGE 540), TO SERVE

SOY SAUCE CHICKEN

REGION: HONG KONG
PREPARATION TIME: 10 MINUTES, PLUS
  1½ HOURS DRYING TIME
COOKING TIME: 1 HOUR
SERVES: 4
📷 PAGE 283

- 1 (3¼-LB/1.5-KG) WHOLE CHICKEN
- 1 TABLESPOON DARK SOY SAUCE
- 2 CUPS (16 FL OZ/475 ML)
  VEGETABLE OIL
- ½ CUP (4 FL OZ/120 ML) LIGHT SOY
  SAUCE
- 4 OZ/120 G ROCK SUGAR
- 2 STAR ANISE
- ¾ OZ/20 G GINGER (ABOUT 1-INCH/
  2.5-CM-LENGTH PIECE), SLICED
- STEAMED RICE (PAGE 540), TO SERVE

* Air-dry the chicken in the refrigerator for 30 minutes. Rub the dark soy sauce all over the chicken and air-dry for another hour.
* Heat the oil in a wok or large saucepan to 300°F/150°C, or until a cube of bread browns in 1½ minutes. Carefully add the chicken and use a slotted spoon to gently roll it in the hot oil for 3–4 minutes until the skin is golden. Carefully remove the chicken from the oil and drain in a colander.
* Pour out most of the oil, leaving about 2 tablespoons in the wok. Add the light soy sauce, rock sugar, star anise, ginger, and 3 cups (25 fl oz/750 ml) water. Bring to a boil over high heat, reduce to low heat, and simmer. Put the chicken, side down, into the wok and cook for 18 minutes, basting with the sauce as it cooks. Turn the chicken over, cook for another 18 minutes, and baste occasionally. Turn chicken again with the breast facing down and cook for another 5 minutes, or until cooked through.
* Carefully transfer the chicken to a colander to drain and set aside to cool. Cut into pieces.
* Heat the sauce in the wok over high heat and boil for 3–4 minutes until reduced to ½ cup (4 fl oz/120 ml). Pour the sauce over the chicken, then serve with rice.

椰子砂锅鸡

DAI CHICKEN WITH COCONUT

REGION: YUNNAN
PREPARATION TIME: 15 MINUTES
COOKING TIME: 2 HOURS 15 MINUTES
SERVES: 4

- 2 OZ/50 G YUNNAN OR OTHER CURED
  HAM
- 1 (2½-LB/1.2-KG) WHOLE CHICKEN,
  BUTTERFLIED
- 1 RIPE COCONUT
- ⅛ OZ/5 G GINGER (ABOUT ½-INCH/
  1-CM-LENGTH PIECE), SLICED
- 1 TEASPOON SALT
- STEAMED RICE (PAGE 540), TO SERVE

* Place the ham in a collapsible pot or bamboo steamer over a pot of boiling water. Steam, covered, for 5 minutes. Remove and allow to cool. When cooled, slice the ham and set aside.
* Spread the chicken in a Dutch oven (casserole) with the skin facing upward.
* Crack open the coconut and pour the coconut juice into the Dutch oven. Cut the coconut flesh into small pieces and add to the chicken, then sprinkle over the ham and ginger, and pour in enough water to cover. Season with the salt.
* Cover and bring to a boil over high heat, then skim the scum and froth off the surface, and reduce to low heat. Simmer for 2 hours. Serve in the Dutch oven with rice.

POULTRY

SOY SAUCE CHICKEN

REGION: HONG KONG
PREPARATION TIME: 15 MINUTES,
  PLUS 30 MINUTES SOAKING
  AND MARINATING TIME
COOKING TIME: 25 MINUTES
SERVES: 4

啫啫猪肝滑鸡煲

CHICKEN AND PORK LIVER CASSEROLE

- 5 OZ/150 G PORK LIVER, CUT INTO ¼-INCH/5-MM-THICK PIECES
- 1 TEASPOON WHITE VINEGAR
- 4 DRIED BLACK MUSHROOMS
- 1½ TEASPOONS LIGHT SOY SAUCE
- 2 TEASPOONS CORNSTARCH (CORNFLOUR)
- 3 TABLESPOONS VEGETABLE OIL
- 1 LB 2 OZ/500 G CHICKEN PIECES, BONE-IN, CUT INTO 2 × 1-INCH/ 5 × 2.5-CM PIECES
- ½ TEASPOON SALT
- 1 TEASPOON GRANULATED SUGAR
- 2 TABLESPOONS RICE WINE
- 2 OZ/50 G GINGER (ABOUT 3-INCH/ 7.5-CM-LENGTH PIECE), SLICED
- 6 SHALLOTS, PEELED
- 4 CLOVES GARLIC, CRUSHED
- 1 TABLESPOON GROUND BEAN PASTE
- 1 LARGE CARROT, SLICED
- 3 SCALLIONS (SPRING ONIONS), CUT INTO 2-INCH/5-CM LENGTHS
- STEAMED RICE (PAGE 540), TO SERVE

* Combine the pork liver pieces, vinegar, and 2 cups (16 fl oz/ 475 ml) water in a large bowl and soak for 30 minutes. Rinse under cold running water to remove the smell of vinegar and drain.
* Meanwhile, put the mushrooms in a bowl, cover with cold water, and soak for at least 20 minutes, or until softened.
* In a small heatproof bowl, combine the mushrooms, ½ teaspoon soy sauce, ½ teaspoon cornstarch (cornflour), and 1 teaspoon oil and mix well. Place the bowl in a collapsible pot or bamboo steamer over a pot of boiling water. Steam, covered, for 10 minutes. Set aside to cool slightly, then cut each mushroom in half.
* Mix the chicken pieces, salt, sugar, ½ tablespoon wine, and the remaining 1 teaspoon soy sauce. Stir in the remaining 1½ teaspoons cornstarch and marinate for 15 minutes.
* Mix 2 teaspoons oil into the chicken. Heat 1 tablespoon oil in a Dutch oven (casserole), add the chicken pieces, and stir-fry over high heat for about 4 minutes until golden. Remove the chicken and set aside.
* Add the remaining 1 tablespoon oil in the Dutch oven. Heat over medium-high heat, add the ginger, shallots, and garlic, and stir-fry for 1 minute until fragrant. Add the bean paste, carrot slices, and mushrooms and mix well.
* Increase to high heat, add the pork liver and stir–fry for about 1 minute. Sprinkle in the remaining 1½ tablespoons wine and add the chicken pieces. Stir to mix well. Cover, cook for about 3 minutes, then add the scallions (spring onions). Re-cover, turn off the heat, and let stand for another 1 minute. Serve with rice.

鸡豆花
CHICKEN "TOFU"

REGION: SICHUAN
PREPARATION TIME: 20 MINUTES,
  PLUS 15 MINUTES SOAKING TIME
COOKING TIME: 45 MINUTES
SERVES: 4

This classic Sichuan dish is a light and satisfying addition
to any family meal. The chicken will resemble tofu once
cooked—the key is to cook it in a hot, but not boiling, broth.

* 1 (2¼-LB/1-KG) WHOLE CHICKEN
* ½ TEASPOON SALT
* ¼ OZ/10 G GINGER (ABOUT ¾-INCH/
  2-CM-LENGTH PIECE), SLICED
* 2 TABLESPOONS CORNSTARCH
  (CORNFLOUR)
* 2 EGG WHITES

* Tear off and discard the chicken skin. Fillet the chicken
  breast, remove any membrane and ligaments, and
  set aside.
* Soak the chicken breast in a bowl of cold water for
  15 minutes. Drain, then thinly slice the chicken and pound
  repeatedly with the back of a knife until it turns to a paste.
  Transfer the paste to a bowl and add ¼ teaspoon salt.
* Meanwhile, put the carcass and the remainder of the
  chicken into a large saucepan, add the ginger and 4¼ cups
  (34 fl oz/1 liter) water, and bring to a boil over high heat.
  Reduce to medium heat and cook for 30 minutes, or until
  2 cups (16 fl oz/475 ml) chicken broth (stock) remains. Line
  a strainer (sieve) with cheesecloth (muslin) and strain the
  broth into a bowl. Season with the remaining ¼ teaspoon
  salt and set aside.
* Mix the cornstarch (cornflour) with 4 tablespoons water
  in a small bowl. Use chopsticks to gradually stir this
  cornstarch mixture in one direction into the chicken paste.
  Add another 4 tablespoons water and continue to stir to
  form a runny chicken paste.
* Beat the egg whites until foamy, then gradually add them
  to the paste, following one single direction, until fully
  blended.
* Heat the chicken broth in a saucepan over medium-high
  heat (about 194°F/90°C) but do not bring it to a boil. Add
  the chicken paste, 1 tablespoonful at a time. Reduce to
  low heat, cover, and simmer for 2–3 minutes until cooked
  through. Transfer to a soup tureen.

REGION: NORTHEAST
PREPARATION TIME: 10 MINUTES,
   PLUS 20 MINUTES SOAKING TIME
COOKING TIME: 40 MINUTES
SERVES: 4–6
[📷] PAGE 287

小鸡炖蘑菇
BRAISED CHICKEN
WITH MUSHROOMS

- 2¾ OZ/75 G DRIED HAZEL OR BLACK
  MUSHROOMS
- 2¼ LB/1 KG CHICKEN BREASTS AND
  DRUMSTICKS, BONE-IN
- 2 TABLESPOONS VEGETABLE OIL
- 2 SCALLIONS (SPRING ONIONS),
  CUT INTO 1½-INCH/4-CM SECTIONS
- ¼ OZ/10 G GINGER (ABOUT ¾-INCH/
  2-CM-LENGTH PIECE), SLICED
- 1 DRIED RED CHILE, CUT IN HALF
  LENGTHWISE
- 1 TABLESPOON RICE WINE
- 2 STAR ANISE
- 1 TABLESPOON LIGHT SOY SAUCE
- 1 TEASPOON SALT, PLUS EXTRA TO
  TASTE
- 1 TEASPOON GRANULATED SUGAR
- STEAMED RICE (PAGE 540), TO SERVE

Northeast China is cold most of the year, with temperature sometimes as low as -40°F/-40°C so to no surprise, braised meat dishes in savory sauces are often prepared both at homes and in restaurants. This dish in particular takes advantage of the wild mushrooms that are abundant in this heavy wooded region.

* Rinse the mushrooms, put in a small bowl of water, and soak for 20 minutes until softened. Remove the mushrooms, squeeze dry, and discard the stems. Slice in half. Strain the soaking water into a bowl. Set both aside separately.
* Put the chicken pieces into a large saucepan and add enough water to cover them completely. Bring to a boil over high heat and blanch for 2 minutes. Drain and rinse under cold running water.
* Heat the oil in a wok or large skillet (frying pan) over high heat, add the scallions (spring onions), ginger, and chile, and stir-fry for 1 minute until fragrant. Add the chicken and stir-fry for another minute. Sprinkle in the wine, add the star anise, soy sauce, salt, sugar, and mushrooms along with the soaking water. Pour in enough water to cover the chicken and bring to a boil. Reduce to low heat and simmer, covered, for 30 minutes. Season with extra salt to taste, transfer to a serving bowl, and serve with rice.

BRAISED CHICKEN WITH MUSHROOMS

REGION: HONG KONG
PREPARATION TIME: 10 MINUTES,
  PLUS 1 HOUR DRYING TIME
COOKING TIME: 30 MINUTES
SERVES: 4

瓦罉葱油鸡
CHICKEN, SCALLION, AND SHALLOT CASSEROLE

- 1 (2½-LB/1.2-KG) WHOLE CHICKEN
- 1 TABLESPOON DARK SOY SAUCE
- 2 TABLESPOONS VEGETABLE OIL
- ¼ OZ/10 G GINGER (ABOUT ¾-INCH/
  2-CM-LENGTH PIECE), SLICED
- 4 CLOVES GARLIC, GRATED
- 8 SHALLOTS, CHOPPED
- 2 TABLESPOONS BEAN PASTE
- 5 TABLESPOONS SHAOXING WINE
- 1 TABLESPOON OYSTER SAUCE
- 1 TEASPOON GRANULATED SUGAR
- 1½ TEASPOONS SALT
- ⅔ CUP (5 FL OZ/150 ML) CHICKEN
  BROTH (STOCK, PAGE 90)
- 1 TEASPOON CORNSTARCH
  (CORNFLOUR)
- 6 SCALLIONS (SPRING ONIONS),
  CHOPPED
- STEAMED RICE (PAGE 540), TO SERVE

When preparing some poultry dishes, we air-dry the chicken or duck to drain out any moisture and dry the skin. This process helps the bird take on sauces better and aids deep-frying. Drying just with paper towels is not good enough as moisture continues to be released to the surface of the skin.

* Rub the chicken skin with the soy sauce, then air-dry the chicken in the refrigerator for 1 hour.
* Heat 1 tablespoon oil in a Dutch oven (casserole) over high heat, add the ginger, garlic, shallots, and bean paste, and stir-fry for 1 minute until fragrant. Place the chicken in the Dutch oven, on its side, add the wine, oyster sauce, sugar, salt, and chicken broth (stock). Cover and bring to a boil. Reduce to low heat and simmer for 10 minutes. Turn the chicken over, cover, and simmer for another 10 minutes, until cooked through.
* Transfer the chicken to a cutting board and set aside to cool. Pour the sauce with the garlic and shallots into another saucepan and set aside.
* When cool enough to handle, cut the chicken into bite-size pieces and return to the Dutch oven.
* Heat the sauce over medium-high heat. Mix the cornstarch (cornflour) with 1 tablespoon water in a small bowl and stir this mixture into the sauce. Bring to a boil, stirring, for 30 seconds to thicken the sauce to a light gravy. Pour the gravy over the chicken in the Dutch oven, cover, bring to a boil, then turn off the heat. Set aside until ready to serve. Before serving, reheat the chicken on the stove.
* Heat the remaining 1 tablespoon oil in a small skillet (frying pan) over medium-high heat, add the scallions (spring onions), and stir-fry for 1 minute until fragrant. Pour over the chicken. Serve with rice.

道口烧鸡
DAOKOU-STYLE
STEWED CHICKEN

REGION: HEBEI
PREPARATION TIME: 10 MINUTES
COOKING TIME: 1 HOUR 15 MINUTES
SERVES: 4

* Fold the wings backward next to the back of the chicken.
  Use kitchen string to tie the 2 legs together.
* Combine the honey and 2–3 tablespoons hot water to
  make a thin sauce, then rub it over the chicken skin.
* Heat the oil in a wok or large saucepan to 300°F/150°C, or
  until a cube of bread browns in 1½ minutes. Carefully add
  the chicken and use a slotted spoon to gently roll it in the
  hot oil for 3–4 minutes until the skin is golden. Carefully
  remove the chicken from the oil and drain in a colander.
* Put all the spices into a spice bag. Put the ginger, salt,
  sugar, wine, and spice bag into a large saucepan. Add
  8½ cups (68 fl oz/2 liters) water and bring to a boil.
  Reduce to low heat and simmer for 15 minutes.
* Put in the chicken, return to a boil, and simmer over
  low heat for 45 minutes until cooked through. Use a wire
  strainer to carefully remove the chicken and transfer
  it to a serving plate. Cut and remove the kitchen string.
  Serve with rice.

* 1 (2½-LB/1.2-KG) WHOLE CHICKEN
* 3 TABLESPOONS HONEY
* 2 CUPS (16 FL OZ/475 ML) VEGETABLE OIL
* ¼ OZ/10 G GINGER (ABOUT ¾-INCH/
  2-CM-LENGTH PIECE), SLICED
* 6 TABLESPOONS SALT
* 2 OZ/50 G ROCK SUGAR
* 4 TABLESPOONS SHAOXING WINE
* STEAMED RICE (PAGE 540), TO SERVE

FOR THE SPICE BAG:
* 10 GREEN CARDAMOM PODS
* 2 BLACK CARDAMOM PODS
* 2 STAR ANISE
* 1 DRIED TANGERINE PEEL
* 2 OZ/50 G SHAJIANG
* ¼ OZ/8 G LICORICE ROOT
* ½ TABLESPOON SICHUAN
  PEPPERCORNS
* ½ TABLESPOON GROUND CUMIN
* ½ SMALL CINNAMON STICK
* ½ TEASPOON CLOVES

烤红糟鸡
ROAST CHICKEN IN RED
DISTILLED GRAIN SAUCE

REGION: TAIWAN
PREPARATION TIME: 10 MINUTES,
  PLUS 10 MINUTES MARINATING TIME
COOKING TIME: 18 MINUTES
SERVES: 2

* Combine the chopped garlic, white pepper, sugar, kaoliang
  wine, and distilled grain sauce in a bowl. Add the chicken
  and rub in the mixture for about 2 minutes, then marinate
  for 10 minutes.
* Preheat the oven to 350°F/180°C/Gas Mark 4.
* Heat the oil in a skillet (frying pan) over medium heat, add
  the remaining garlic, and cook for 1 minute until browned.
* Put the chicken pieces and the marinade in a roasting pan
  (tin). Top with the whole garlic and drizzle over some of the
  oil. Roast in the oven for 8 minutes, turn over the chicken
  pieces, and roast for another 7 minutes until cooked
  through.
* Transfer the chicken to a serving plate and serve with rice.

* 20 CLOVES GARLIC, HALF CHOPPED
  AND HALF LEFT WHOLE
* ¼ TEASPOON GROUND WHITE PEPPER
* ½ TEASPOON GRANULATED SUGAR
* 1 TABLESPOON KAOLIANG WINE
* 3 TABLESPOONS RED DISTILLED GRAIN
  SAUCE
* 12 OZ/350 G BONELESS CHICKEN,
  CUT INTO 1-INCH/2.5-CM CHUNKS
* 2 TABLESPOONS SESAME OIL
* STEAMED RICE (PAGE 540), TO SERVE

SALT-BAKED
CHICKEN

REGION: HAKKA
PREPARATION TIME: 20 MINUTES,
   PLUS 1 HOUR DRYING TIME
COOKING TIME: 1 HOUR 15 MINUTES
SERVES: 4

- 1 (2½-LB/1.2-KG) WHOLE CHICKEN,
  BUTTERFLIED
- 1 TEASPOON SALT
- ¾ OZ/20 G FRESH SHAJIANG OR
  ½ TABLESPOON SHAJIANG POWDER
- 1 TEASPOON VEGETABLE OIL
- STEAMED RICE (PAGE 540) OR BOILED
  POTATOES, TO SERVE

FOR THE FIVE-SPICE SALT:
- 4 CUPS (1 LB 5 OZ/600 G) COARSE
  SEA SALT
- 1 TEASPOON FIVE-SPICE POWDER

The Hakka method of baking chicken in salt dates back centuries ago to an area southeast of Guangdong, which had been densely populated with Hakkas and was the center for the salt trade. Traditionally, the chicken was wrapped in a sheet of paper and buried in a large wok of salt heated to a high temperature; the flavors of the salt and five-spice powder would be infused through the paper without the salt ever coming into contact with the chicken.

* Air-dry the chicken in the refrigerator for 1 hour. Pat the inside dry with paper towels. Rub the chicken inside and out with the salt and shajiang, leaving the shajiang inside the chicken. Rub the skin with the oil.
* Preheat the oven to 425°F/220°C/Gas Mark 7.
* To make the five-spice salt, combine the ingredients and mix well.
* Wrap a large sheet of parchment (baking) paper around the chicken to cover it completely—making sure there are no gaps—and secure and tie with kitchen string. Put the chicken bundle on a long piece of aluminum foil and wrap the foil around it very loosely, closing only one end. Put the spiced salt in the tube of foil through the open side and shake the tube to distribute the salt evenly. Fold and seal the open end.
* Place the chicken in a roasting pan and bake for 1 hour 15 minutes, or until cooked through (for a very well done chicken, add an extra 10–15 minutes, if desired). Remove the chicken from the oven and let rest for 15 minutes.
* Unwrap the foil tube and discard, then brush the salt off the chicken bundle. Cut the kitchen string and transfer the chicken to a cutting board. Cut the chicken into several pieces and serve with rice or potatoes.

山东烧鸡
SHANDONG
ROAST CHICKEN

REGION: SHANDONG
PREPARATION TIME: 15 MINUTES,
  PLUS 1 HOUR DRYING TIME
COOKING TIME: 30 MINUTES
SERVES: 4

* Put the chicken into a large bowl, rub all over with the soy sauce and marinate for 15 minutes, turning it over several times to obtain an even color on the skin. Air-dry the chicken in the refrigerator for 1 hour.
* Heat the oil in a wok or large saucepan to 300°F/150°C, or until a cube of bread browns in 1½ minutes. Carefully add the chicken and use a slotted spoon to gently roll it in the hot oil for 3–4 minutes until the skin is golden. Carefully remove the chicken from the oil and drain in a colander.
* Toast the Sichuan peppercorns in a small dry skillet (frying pan) over medium-low heat for 2–3 minutes until fragrant, then transfer to a mortar and pestle, and crush lightly. Set aside.
* Place the chicken in a deep heatproof plate, put the ginger, scallions (spring onions), and crushed Sichuan peppercorns on top. Place in a collapsible pot or bamboo steamer over a pot of boiling water. Steam, covered, for 25 minutes, or until the chicken has cooked through.
* Transfer the chicken to a cutting board and set aside to cool. Strain the steamed chicken juices into a bowl and reserve. Once cool, separate the wings, legs, breast, and back from
  the chicken. De-bone the chicken legs and breast and pick out as much meat as possible from the back. Cut the chicken meat into pieces.
* Arrange the cucumber on a serving plate, then arrange the chicken on top of the cucumber. Put the chicken wings on the side.
* To make the sauce, combine all the ingredients and ¼ cup (2 fl oz/60 ml) reserved steamed chicken juices. Drizzle over the chicken, then serve with rice.

- 1 (2¼-LB/1-KG) WHOLE CHICKEN
- 3 TABLESPOONS LIGHT SOY SAUCE
- 2 CUPS (16 FL OZ/475 ML) VEGETABLE OIL
- 1 TABLESPOON SICHUAN PEPPERCORNS
- 2 TEASPOONS CHOPPED GINGER
- 2 SCALLIONS (SPRING ONIONS), CHOPPED
- 1 CUCUMBER, CUT INTO 1¼-INCH/ 3-CM PIECES
- STEAMED RICE (PAGE 540), TO SERVE

FOR THE SAUCE:
- 2 TABLESPOONS CHOPPED GARLIC
- 2 TABLESPOONS CHOPPED CILANTRO (CORIANDER)
- 2 TABLESPOONS LIGHT SOY SAUCE
- 2 TABLESPOONS BLACK OR BALSAMIC VINEGAR
- 1 TABLESPOON SESAME OIL
- ½ TABLESPOON SALT
- 1 TEASPOON GRANULATED SUGAR

包烧鸡
ROAST CHICKEN WITH PRESERVED MUSTARD

- 1 (2½-LB/1.2-KG) WHOLE CHICKEN
- 2 TABLESPOONS VEGETABLE OIL
- ¼ OZ/10 G GINGER (ABOUT ¾-INCH/ 2-CM-LENGTH PIECE), CHOPPED
- 2 OZ/50 G GROUND (MINCED) PORK
- 7 OZ/200 G SICHUAN PRESERVED MUSTARD GREENS, TRIMMED, RINSED, AND CHOPPED
- 2 OZ/50 G PICKLED CHILES, CHOPPED
- 2 TABLESPOONS GRANULATED SUGAR
- STEAMED RICE (PAGE 540), TO SERVE

* Fold the chicken wings backward next to the back.
* Preheat the oven to 375°F/190°C/Gas Mark 5.
* Heat the oil in a wok or large skillet (frying pan), add the ginger, and stir-fry over medium heat for 1 minute until fragrant. Add the pork, increase to high heat, and stir-fry for about 1 minute until cooked through. Add the mustard greens, chiles, and sugar and stir-fry for about 2 minutes. Transfer the filling to a bowl.
* Using a spoon, stuff the chicken with the filling. Tie the legs together with kitchen string. Place the stuffed chicken in a roasting pan and roast for 45 minutes until cooked through. Remove the chicken, cut off the kitchen string, and remove the thread.
* Empty the filling from the chicken cavity onto a plate. Cut the chicken into 1½ × ¾-inch/4 × 2-cm pieces and arrange these on top of filling. Serve with rice.

清炖硕鸭
DUCK WITH MUSHROOMS AND HAM

- 1 (3¼-LB/1.5-KG) WHOLE DUCK
- 4 DRIED BLACK MUSHROOMS
- 4¼ CUPS (34 FL OZ/1 LITER) CHICKEN BROTH (STOCK, PAGE 90)
- 3½ OZ/100 G JINHUA OR SMITHFIELD HAM, SLICED
- 2 TEASPOONS SALT
- SCANT ½ CUP (3½ FL OZ/100 ML) SHAOXING WINE
- ¼ OZ/10 G GINGER (ABOUT ¾-INCH/ 2-CM-LENGTH PIECE), SLICED
- 2 SCALLIONS (SPRING ONIONS), KNOTTED
- STEAMED RICE (PAGE 540), TO SERVE

* Put the duck into a large saucepan and add enough water to cover it completely. Bring to a boil over high heat, then remove the duck. Drain, rinse under cold running water, then drain again.
* Put the mushrooms in a bowl, cover with cold water, and soak for at least 20 minutes, or until softened. Set aside.
* Put the duck into a Dutch oven (casserole), add the chicken broth (stock), ham, mushrooms, salt, wine, ginger, and scallions (spring onions), and bring to a boil. Reduce to low heat and simmer, covered, for 2 hours, until tender and cooked through. Discard the ginger and scallions.
* Serve in the Dutch oven with rice.

香酥鸭片

SLICED CRISPY DUCK

REGION: SICHUAN
PREPARATION TIME: 5 MINUTES,
    PLUS 1 HOUR MARINATING TIME
COOKING TIME: 20 MINUTES
SERVES: 4–6

* Combine the wine, ginger juice, salt, ground Sichuan pepper, and five-spice powder in a large bowl. Add the duck, toss to coat, and set aside to marinate for 1 hour.
* Transfer the duck to a heatproof plate and top with the scallions (spring onions). Place in a collapsible pot or bamboo steamer over a pot of boiling water. Steam, covered, for 15 minutes until cooked through. Transfer the duck breasts to a colander to drain and discard the scallions.
* Heat the vegetable oil in a wok or deep saucepan to 340°F/170°C, or until a cube of bread browns in 45 seconds. Gently lower the duck and deep-fry for 2–3 minutes until the skin turns golden brown. Use a slotted spoon to carefully remove the duck from the oil and drain. Brush the skin with sesame oil, then cut into slices. Transfer to a serving plate and serve with rice.

* 2 TABLESPOONS SHAOXING WINE
* 1 TABLESPOON GINGER JUICE
* ½ TABLESPOON SALT
* 1 TEASPOON GROUND SICHUAN PEPPER
* ¼ TEASPOON FIVE-SPICE POWDER
* 4 (6-OZ/175-G) BONELESS, SKIN-ON DUCK BREASTS
* 2 SCALLIONS (SPRING ONIONS), CUT INTO 1½-INCH/4-CM LENGTHS
* 2 CUPS (16 FL OZ/475 ML) VEGETABLE OIL
* ½ TABLESPOON SESAME OIL
* STEAMED RICE (PAGE 540), TO SERVE

生焖鸭

JIANGXI-STYLE DUCK

REGION: JIANGXI
PREPARATION TIME: 10 MINUTES
COOKING TIME: 1 HOUR 15 MINUTES
SERVES: 4–6

* Put the duck pieces into a large saucepan and add enough water to cover them completely. Add 1 tablespoon wine, bring to a boil over high heat, and blanch the duck for 1 minute. Drain and rinse under cold running water.
* Heat 2 tablespoons vegetable oil in a wok or large skillet (frying pan) over medium-low heat, add the sugar, and cook for 2 minutes to caramelize. Add the duck and stir-fry over medium heat for 2–3 minutes until the duck takes on a dark amber color. Remove the duck and set aside.
* In the same wok, heat the remaining 2 tablespoons oil over low heat and add the garlic. Fry for 1–2 minutes until browned, then remove the garlic and reserve. Add the chili sauce and ginger to the wok and stir-fry over medium heat for 1 minute until fragrant. Add the duck, salt, and soy sauce, and remaining 1 tablespoon wine.
* Add 2 cups (16 fl oz/475 ml) boiling water and bring to a boil. Reduce to low heat and simmer, covered, for 1 hour, or until tender and cooked through. Stir in the garlic and chiles and simmer for another 3 minutes, then increase to high heat to reduce the sauce by a third.
* Stir in the sesame oil and transfer to a serving bowl. Serve with rice.

* 1 (3¼-LB/1.5-KG) DUCK, CUT INTO 1¼-INCH/3-CM CHUNKS (BONE-IN)
* 2 TABLESPOONS RICE WINE
* 4 TABLESPOONS VEGETABLE OIL
* 2 TABLESPOONS GRANULATED SUGAR
* 1 HEAD GARLIC, CLOVES SEPARATED
* 1 TABLESPOON CHILI SAUCE
* 3½ OZ/100 G GINGER (ABOUT 6-INCH/ 15-CM-LENGTH PIECE), THINLY SLICED
* 1 TEASPOON SALT
* 1 TABLESPOON LIGHT SOY SAUCE
* 4 RED CHILES, SEEDED AND CHOPPED
* 1 TEASPOON SESAME OIL
* STEAMED RICE (PAGE 540), TO SERVE

REGION: SICHUAN
PREPARATION TIME: 10 MINUTES, PLUS
  30 MINUTES MARINATING TIME
COOKING TIME: 1 HOUR
SERVES: 4

豆渣鸭脯
DUCK WITH
SOYBEAN CRISPS

- 4 (6-OZ/175-G) DUCK BREASTS
- 1 TEASPOON SALT
- 3 TABLESPOONS RICE WINE
- ½ OZ/20 G GINGER (ABOUT
  1-INCH/2.5-CM-LENGTH PIECE),
  GRATED
- 1 SCALLION (SPRING ONION),
  CHOPPED
- 2 TABLESPOONS VEGETABLE OIL
- 1 QUANTITY SOYBEAN CRISPS
  (PAGE 52)
- GROUND WHITE PEPPER, TO TASTE
- STEAMED RICE (PAGE 540), TO SERVE

* Place the duck breasts in a shallow heatproof bowl, add
  ½ teaspoon salt, the wine, ginger, and scallion (spring
  onion) and marinate in the refrigerator for 30 minutes.
* Add enough water to just cover the duck, then place in a
  collapsible pot or bamboo steamer over a pot of boiling
  water. Steam, covered, for 15 minutes until cooked through.
  Remove and set aside to cool. Drain the juices into a bowl.
* Slice the duck and put into a heatproof bowl, skin side
  facing down. Cover with aluminum foil and steam over
  high heat for 30 minutes. Remove and set aside.
* Meanwhile, heat the oil in a wok or large skillet (frying
  pan), add the soybean crisps, and stir-fry over high heat
  for 1 minute until fragrant. Stir in 5 tablespoons duck juice,
  ½ teaspoon salt, and the white pepper and bring to a boil.
* Remove the foil from the bowl of duck, cover with a plate,
  and, using dish towels, invert the duck onto the plate.
  (Alternatively, use tongs to transfer the duck.) Pour the
  sauce over the duck and serve with rice.

REGION: JIANGXI
PREPARATION TIME: 10 MINUTES
COOKING TIME: 2 HOURS 30 MINUTES
SERVES: 4–6

丁香烩鸭
DUCK WITH CLOVES

- 2½ TEASPOONS CLOVES
- 1 (1-INCH/2.5-CM) CINNAMON STICK
- ¾ OZ/20 G GINGER (ABOUT
  1-INCH/2.5-CM-LENGTH PIECE),
  CRUSHED
- 2 SCALLIONS (SPRING ONIONS),
  KNOTTED
- 1 (3¼-LB/1.5-KG) WHOLE DUCK
- 2 TEASPOONS SALT
- 1 TABLESPOON DARK SOY SAUCE
- 2 TEASPOONS GRANULATED SUGAR
- ¼ TEASPOON GROUND WHITE PEPPER
- 2 TABLESPOONS SHAOXING WINE
- 1 TEASPOON SESAME OIL
- STEAMED RICE (PAGE 540), TO SERVE

* Put the cloves, cinnamon, ginger, and scallion (spring
  onions) into the cavity of the duck. Put the duck into a
  large heatproof bowl, then add the salt and enough water
  to cover the duck. Seal with aluminum foil, then place in
  a collapsible pot over a pot of boiling water. Steam for
  2 hours. (Add more water to the pot if needed.)
* Remove the duck and discard the cloves, cinnamon, ginger,
  and scallions. Drain the sauce into a wok or saucepan.
* Add the soy sauce, sugar, and white pepper to the wok and
  cook over medium heat until the sauce has reduced by half.
  Stir in the wine.
* Put the duck into the sauce and simmer for about
  5–10 minutes until the sauce thickens. Baste the duck
  with the sauce until the duck takes on a uniform color.
* Transfer the duck to a cutting board and cut it into
  ¾ × 2-inch/2 × 5-cm pieces. Transfer to a serving plate.
* Mix the sesame oil into the sauce in the wok, then drizzle
  the sauce over the duck. Serve with rice.

洋葱鸭
DUCK WITH
ONIONS

REGION: JIANGSU
PREPARATION TIME: 15 MINUTES,
 PLUS 1 HOUR DRYING TIME
COOKING TIME: 2 HOURS 15 MINUTES
SERVES: 6–8

* Air-dry the duck in the refrigerator for 1 hour. Pat dry with kitchen towels.
* Heat 1 cup (8 fl oz/250 ml) oil in a wok or deep saucepan to 300°F/150°C, or until a cube of bread browns in 1½ minutes. Gently lower the pork and deep-fry for 4–5 minutes until light brown. Use a slotted spoon to carefully remove the pork from the oil and drain on paper towels.
* Reheat the oil to 300°F/150°C. Carefully add the duck and use a slotted spoon to gently roll it in the hot oil for 3–4 minutes until the skin is golden. Carefully remove the duck from the oil and drain in a colander.
* Heat 2 tablespoons oil in a large skillet (frying pan) over medium-high heat, add the ginger, and stir-fry for 1 minute until fragrant. Add the onions and stir-fry for 2 minutes until lightly browned. Add the soy sauces, salt, sugar, star anise, and beer and bring to a boil over high heat. Add the pork, then the duck, with the breast facing downward. Cook, covered, over medium-low heat for 45 minutes. Turn the duck over and cook for another 45 minutes until cooked through and tender.
* Transfer the pork to a cutting board. Turn the duck again in the wok and cook for another 30 minutes.
* Transfer the duck to a large serving plate. Cut the pork into chunks and place next to the duck.
* Mix the cornstarch (cornflour) with 3 tablespoons water in a small bowl and stir this mixture into the wok. Bring to a boil, stirring, for 30 seconds to thicken the sauce, then pour over the duck and pork. Serve with steamed rice.

* 1 (3¼-LB/1.5-KG) WHOLE DUCK, FAT TRIMMED
* 1 CUP (8 FL OZ/250 ML) PLUS 2 TABLESPOONS VEGETABLE OIL
* 1 (9-OZ/250-G) BONELESS, SKIN-ON PORK BELLY
* 2 OZ/50 G GINGER (ABOUT 3-INCH/7.5-CM-LENGTH PIECE), SLICED
* 6 LARGE ONIONS, CUT INTO WEDGES
* 1 TABLESPOON DARK SOY SAUCE
* 4 TABLESPOONS LIGHT SOY SAUCE
* 2 TEASPOONS SALT
* 2 TABLESPOONS ROCK SUGAR
* 1 STAR ANISE
* 1½ CUPS (12 FL OZ/350 ML) BEER
* 1 TABLESPOON CORNSTARCH (CORNFLOUR)
* STEAMED RICE (PAGE 540), TO SERVE

REGION: HONG KONG
PREPARATION TIME: 15 MINUTES,
  PLUS 9 HOURS PICKLING TIME
COOKING TIME: 10 MINUTES
SERVES: 4
📷 PAGE 297

子萝鸭片
DUCK WITH SPRING GINGER
AND PINEAPPLE

- 2 (8-OZ/225-G) DUCK BREASTS, SLICED
- 1 TEASPOON LIGHT SOY SAUCE
- 1 TEASPOON CORNSTARCH (CORNFLOUR)
- 2½ TABLESPOONS VEGETABLE OIL
- 4 SHALLOTS, HALVED
- 1 RED BELL PEPPER, SEEDED AND DICED
- ½ GREEN BELL PEPPER, SEEDED AND DICED
- 1 TABLESPOON SHAOXING WINE
- ¼ TEASPOON SALT, PLUS EXTRA TO TASTE
- ¼ FRESH PINEAPPLE, DICED, OR 1 (8-OZ/225-G) CAN PINEAPPLE CHUNKS, STRAINED
- CILANTRO (CORIANDER) AND SPRING ONION (SCALLIONS), TO GARNISH (OPTIONAL)
- STEAMED RICE (PAGE 540), TO SERVE

FOR THE PICKLED GINGER:
- 4 OZ/100 G GINGER (ABOUT 6-INCH/15-CM-LENGTH PIECE), CUT INTO SMALL CHUNKS
- ¼ TEASPOON SALT
- 2 TEASPOONS GRANULATED SUGAR
- 2 TEASPOONS WHITE VINEGAR

* To make the pickled ginger, combine the ginger and salt in a bowl and set aside for 1 hour. Rinse the ginger, then drain. Add the sugar and vinegar to the ginger and stand for 8 hours.
* Combine the duck, soy sauce, and ½ teaspoon cornstarch (cornflour) in a large bowl and marinate for 10 minutes. Mix in ½ tablespoon oil.
* Heat 1 tablespoon oil in a wok or large skillet (frying pan) over medium-high heat, add the shallots, and stir-fry for 1–2 minute until fragrant. Put in the pickled ginger and bell peppers and stir-fry for another minute until the peppers are half done. Transfer to a plate and set aside.
* Add the remaining 1 tablespoon oil to the wok and heat over high heat, then add the duck and stir-fry for 2 minutes, or until the duck is just about cooked. Sprinkle in the wine and stir in the reserved peppers and shallots. Add the salt, then adjust the seasoning to taste.
* Mix the remaining ½ teaspoon cornstarch with ½ tablespoon water in a small bowl and stir this mixture into the wok. Bring to a boil, stirring, for 30 seconds to thicken the sauce. Stir in the pineapple and transfer to a serving plate. Garnish with cilantro (coriander) and spring onions (scallions), if using. Serve with rice.

DUCK WITH SPRING GINGER AND PINEAPPLE

REGION: SICHUAN
PREPARATION TIME: 15 MINUTES,
    PLUS 1 HOUR DRYING TIME
COOKING TIME: 2 HOURS 50 MINUTES
SERVES: 4

神仙鸭子
SICHUAN-STYLE
BRAISED DUCK

- 1 (3¼-LB/1.5-KG) WHOLE DUCK, WINGS TUCKED
- 4 LARGE DRIED BLACK MUSHROOMS
- 2 CUPS (16 FL OZ/475 ML) VEGETABLE OIL
- 3½ OZ/100 G CURED HAM, SLICED
- ⅔ CUP (3½ OZ/100 G) SLICED BAMBOO SHOOTS
- 1 OZ/25 G GINGER (ABOUT 2-INCH/ 5-CM-LENGTH PIECE), CRUSHED
- 2 SCALLIONS (SPRING ONIONS), KNOTTED
- 2 TABLESPOONS SHAOXING WINE
- 1½ TABLESPOONS LIGHT SOY SAUCE
- 1 TEASPOON SALT
- 8½ CUPS (68 FL OZ/2 LITERS) CHICKEN BROTH (STOCK, PAGE 90)
- 2 TABLESPOONS SESAME OIL
- STEAMED RICE (PAGE 540), TO SERVE

This classic duck dish requires some time but the results will be worth your while. The duck is wrapped and braised in a cheesecloth so it can be transferred to a serving plate without destroying its shape or preventing the meat from falling off the bone.

* Put the duck into a large saucepan and add enough water to cover it completely. Bring the water to a boil and blanch for 5 minutes. Drain and rinse under cold running water. Air-dry the duck in the refrigerator for 1 hour. Pat dry the cavity with paper towels.
* Put the mushrooms in a bowl, cover with cold water, and soak for at least 20 minutes, or until softened. Cut into slices.
* Heat the vegetable oil in a wok or deep saucepan to 300°F/150°C, or until a cube of bread browns in 1½ minutes. Carefully add the duck and use a slotted spoon to gently roll it in the hot oil for 3–4 minutes until the skin is golden. Carefully remove the duck from the oil and drain in a colander.
* Line a large bowl with cheesecloth (muslin) with plenty of overhang. Arrange slices of ham, mushrooms, and the bamboo shoots on the cheesecloth, then place the duck on top, breast side facing down. Tuck the reserved duck feet down the side of the duck's body. Using the overhanging ends of the cheesecloth, tie it into a bundle, then transfer the bundle to a large pan. Add the ginger, scallions (spring onions), wine, soy sauce, salt, and chicken broth (stock). Bring to a boil over medium-high heat and cook for 20 minutes. Reduce to low heat and simmer for 2 hours.
* Carefully transfer the bundle to a large plate. Carefully, untie the cheesecloth (watch out as the steam will be hot) and lift one of the edges up to roll the duck onto the plate so that the duck breast faces up. Pick out and discard the ginger and scallions.
* Bring the pan of broth to a boil over high heat. Reduce to medium-high heat and simmer, uncovered, for about 25 minutes until the broth has reduced to 1 cup (8 fl oz/ 250 ml). Add the sesame oil and pour the thickened broth over the duck. Serve with rice.

湘西风味鸭
DUCK CASSEROLE

REGION: HUNAN
PREPARATION TIME: 10 MINUTES
COOKING TIME: 1 HOUR 15 MINUTES
SERVES: 4–6

* Put the star anise and Sichuan peppercorns in a spice bag.
* Heat the oil in a Dutch oven (casserole) over low heat, add the garlic, and cook for about 2 minutes until brown. Stir in the chili bean paste and cook for 1 minute until fragrant.
* Increase to high heat and add the duck. Stir for about 1 minute until the duck is well coated. Add the cayenne peppers, spice bag, salt, soy sauce, wine, tianmianjiang, and enough water to cover the duck. Bring to a boil, cover, then reduce to low heat and simmer for 1 hour.
* Uncover, increase to high heat, and cook until the sauce has reduced to about ½ cup (4 fl oz/120 ml). Mix the cornstarch (cornflour) with 1 tablespoon water and stir the mixture into the Dutch oven. Bring to a boil, stirring, for about 30 seconds to thicken the sauce.
* Serve in the Dutch oven with rice.

• 2 TABLESPOONS VEGETABLE OIL
• 4 CLOVES GARLIC
• 1 TABLESPOON CHILI BEAN PASTE
• ½ DUCK, CUT INTO ¾-INCH/2-CM-THICK PIECES
• 1 GREEN CAYENNE PEPPER, CUT INTO ¾-INCH/2-CM PIECES
• 1 RED CAYENNE PEPPER, CUT INTO ¾-INCH/2-CM PIECES
• 1 TEASPOON SALT
• 1 TABLESPOON LIGHT SOY SAUCE
• 2 TABLESPOONS RICE WINE
• 1 TABLESPOON TIANMIANJIANG
• 1 TEASPOON CORNSTARCH (CORNFLOUR)
• STEAMED RICE (PAGE 540), TO SERVE

FOR THE SPICE BAG:
• 2 STAR ANISE
• 1 TABLESPOON SICHUAN PEPPERCORNS

油爆鸭丁
SAUTÉED DUCK

REGION: BEIJING
PREPARATION TIME: 15 MINUTES
COOKING TIME: 10 MINUTES
SERVES: 2

* Combine the duck, ½ teaspoon salt, 3 tablespoons chicken broth (stock), and 1 tablespoon cornstarch (cornflour) in a large saucepan. Add the egg whites and mix.
* Heat the oil in a wok or a deep saucepan to 265°F/130°C. Gently add the duck, using chopsticks to separate the pieces, and deep-fry for 30 seconds until golden brown and crispy. Use a slotted spoon to remove the duck and drain in a colander.
* Leave 2 tablespoons of oil in the wok and heat over medium-high heat. Add the ginger and garlic and stir-fry for 1 minute until fragrant. Add the duck and stir-fry for 2 minutes over high heat. Add the wine, the remaining ½ teaspoon salt, and chicken broth and simmer 1–2 minutes until duck is cooked through.
* In a small bowl, mix the remaining 1 tablespoon cornstarch with 1 tablespoon water and stir this mixture into the wok. Bring to a boil, stirring, for 30 seconds to thicken the sauce.
* Add the scallions (spring onions) and toss well. Transfer to a serving plate and serve with rice.

• 2 DUCK BREASTS, CUT INTO ¾-INCH/2-CM CUBES
• 1 TEASPOON SALT
• ½ CUP (4 FL OZ/120 ML) CHICKEN BROTH (STOCK, PAGE 90)
• 2 TABLESPOONS CORNSTARCH (CORNFLOUR)
• 2 EGG WHITES, BEATEN
• 2 CUPS (16 FL OZ/475 ML) VEGETABLE OIL
• ¼ OZ/10 G GINGER (ABOUT ¾-INCH/2-CM-LENGTH PIECE), SLICED
• 2 CLOVES GARLIC
• 1 TABLESPOON SHAOXING WINE
• 2 SCALLIONS (SPRING ONIONS), SHREDDED
• STEAMED RICE (PAGE 540), TO SERVE

炒鸭松
STIR-FRIED
DUCK

- 2 TABLESPOONS VEGETABLE OIL
- 3½ OZ/100 G STRING (GREEN) BEANS, CHOPPED
- 1 TABLESPOON GRATED GINGER
- 2 DUCK BREASTS, MEMBRANE REMOVED AND FINELY CHOPPED
- 1 DUCK LIVER SAUSAGE, CHOPPED
- 2 OZ/50 G PRESERVED MUSTARD GREENS, TRIMMED, RINSED, AND FINELY CHOPPED
- 1 TEASPOON GRANULATED SUGAR
- 2 TABLESPOONS BEAN PASTE
- ½ TEASPOON SESAME OIL
- 1 HEAD ICEBERG LETTUCE, LEAVES SEPARATED AND TRIMMED INTO CUPS
- CILANTRO (CORIANDER), TO GARNISH (OPTIONAL)
- 2 TABLESPOONS HOISIN SAUCE, TO SERVE

* Heat 1 tablespoon vegetable oil in a wok or skillet (frying pan) over medium heat, add the string beans, and stir-fry for about 30 seconds. Remove the string beans from the wok and set aside.
* Add the remaining 1 tablespoon oil to the wok and stir-fry the ginger for 30 seconds, until fragrant.
* Add the duck, sausage, preserved mustard greens, and sugar and stir-fry over high heat for about 3 minutes until the duck is cooked. Stir in the bean paste and string beans, then stir-fry until all the ingredients are well combined. Mix in the sesame oil and transfer to a serving plate. Garnish with cilantro (coriander), if using.
* Serve with the lettuce cups as wraps and accompany with the hoisin sauce.

REGION: JIANGSU
PREPARATION TIME: 15 MINUTES,
    PLUS 1 HOUR DRYING AND 6
    HOURS STANDING TIME
COOKING TIME: 1½ HOURS
SERVES: 8

南京盐水鸭
NANJING
DUCK

- 1 (3¼-LB/1.5-KG) WHOLE DUCK
- ½ CUP (5 OZ/150 G) PLUS 3 TABLESPOONS SALT
- 1 TEASPOON SICHUAN PEPPERCORNS, CRUSHED
- 6 CLOVES
- 6 BAY LEAVES
- 2 STAR ANISE
- 1 DRIED TANGERINE PEEL
- 1 TEASPOON LICORICE ROOT POWDER
- 1 TEASPOON WHITE PEPPERCORNS, CRUSHED
- ¾ OZ/20 G GINGER (ABOUT 1-INCH/2.5-CM-LENGTH PIECE), SLICED
- 3 TABLESPOONS SHAOXING WINE
- STEAMED RICE (PAGE 540), TO SERVE

* Air-dry the duck in the refrigerator for 1 hour.
* Heat 3 tablespoons salt in a skillet (frying pan) until warmed. Put in a bowl and mix in the Sichuan peppercorns. Rub the duck inside and out with the mixture and let stand for 6 hours.
* Put the cloves, bay leaves, star anise, tangerine peel, licorice root powder, and white peppercorns into a spice bag, then place into a large saucepan. Add the ginger and 9 cups (76 fl oz/2.25 liters) water. Bring to a boil over high heat, reduce to low heat, and simmer for 20 minutes.
* Add the salt and wine to the brine and stir until the salt dissolves. Put the duck into the brine, breast facing down, and return to a boil. Reduce to low heat and allow to simmer for 30 minutes. Use tongs to turn the duck over so the breast faces up and simmer for another 30 minutes, or until cooked through. Transfer the duck to a cutting board and set aside to cool. Slice and transfer to a plate.

STIR-FRIED DUCK

301

芋头焖鸭
DUCK WITH
TARO

- 1 (1 LB 10½ OZ/750 G) WHOLE DUCK
- 1 TABLESPOON DARK SOY SAUCE
- 1 LB 5 OZ/600 G TARO, CUT INTO
  1-INCH/2.5-CM CHUNKS
- 1 DRIED TANGERINE PEEL
- 1 CUP (8 FL OZ/250 ML)
  VEGETABLE OIL
- ⅛ OZ/5 G GINGER (ABOUT ½-INCH/
  1-CM-LENGTH PIECE), SLICED
- 4 SHALLOTS, SLICED
- 3 CLOVES GARLIC, CHOPPED
- 2 TABLESPOONS ZHUHOU SAUCE
- ⅛ OZ/5 G ROCK SUGAR, CRUSHED
- 1 TABLESPOON OYSTER SAUCE
- 1 TABLESPOON RICE WINE
- 1 CUP (8 FL OZ/250 ML) CHICKEN
  BROTH (STOCK, PAGE 90)
- 2 CILANTRO (CORIANDER) STALKS,
  CUT INTO 2-INCH/5-CM LENGTHS
  TO GARNISH
- STEAMED RICE (PAGE 540), TO SERVE

* Rub the duck all over with the soy sauce and air-dry in the refrigerator for 1 hour.
* Place the taro in a collapsible pot or bamboo steamer over a pot of boiling water. Steam, covered, for 10 minutes until tender. Carefully remove and set aside.
* Soak the dried tangerine peel in cold water for 10 minutes to soften, then drain and shred. Set aside.
* Heat the oil to 300°F/150°C, or until a cube of bread browns in 1½ minutes. Carefully add the duck and use a slotted spoon to gently roll it in the hot oil for 3–4 minutes until the skin is golden. Carefully remove the duck from the oil and drain in a colander.
* Pour out most of the oil, leaving about 1 tablespoon in the wok. Heat the oil over medium-high heat, add the ginger slices, and stir-fry for 1 minute until fragrant. Add the tangerine peel, shallots, garlic, and zhuhou sauce and stir-fry for another minute. Stir in the sugar, oyster sauce, wine, chicken broth (stock), and 1 cup (8 fl oz/250 ml) water and bring to a boil. Add the duck and return to a boil. Cover, reduce to low heat, and simmer for 1½ hours, until cooked through. Halfway through the cooking time, use tongs to turn the duck over. Add the taro to the sauce in the wok and simmer for another 15 minutes.
* Transfer the taro to a serving plate. Carefully transfer the duck to the cutting board and, when cool enough to handle, cut into 1-inch/2.5-cm chunks and arrange on top of the taro. Ladle the sauce over the duck and taro, then garnish with the cilantro (coriander). Serve with rice.

冬菜大酿鸭

DUCK WITH PRESERVED

MUSTARD HEARTS

REGION: SICHUAN
PREPARATION TIME: 20 MINUTES, PLUS
  15 MINUTES MARINATING TIME
COOKING TIME: 3 HOURS 30 MINUTES
SERVES: 4

* Put the pork belly into a bowl, add the soy sauce and sugar, and marinate for 15 minutes.
* Meanwhile, soak the preserved mustard hearts in a bowl of cold water for about 2 minutes. Squeeze out the excess water and set aside.
* Heat the oil in a wok or large skillet (frying pan) over medium-high heat. Add the garlic and stir-fry for 1 minute until fragrant. Put in the ginger, pork, and preserved mustard hearts and stir-fry for 1 minute. Pour in the chicken broth (stock) and bring to a boil over high heat. Reduce to low heat and simmer for about 20 minutes. Strain the soup into a large heatproof bowl and put the strained ingredients in a separate bowl. Set both aside.
* Stuff the strained ingredients into the duck, then carefully add the duck to the soup and seal with aluminum foil. Place in a collapsible pot or bamboo steamer over a pot of boiling water. Steam, covered, for 3 hours until tender and cooked through. (Add more water to the pot if needed.)
* Remove the foil and strain the soup into a saucepan. Carefully transfer the duck to a cutting board and scoop out the contents from inside the duck to a large serving plate. Cut the duck into smaller pieces and place on top.
* Heat the soup over medium heat and season with the salt. Mix the cornstarch (cornflour) with 1 tablespoon water in a small bowl and stir this mixture into the pan. Bring to a boil, stirring, for 30 seconds to thicken the soup. Pour the soup over duck. Serve with rice.

- 1 (5-OZ/150-G) PORK BELLY, CUT INTO ½-INCH/1-CM SLICES
- 1 TEASPOON DARK SOY SAUCE
- 1 TEASPOON GRANULATED SUGAR
- 7 OZ/200 G SICHUAN PRESERVED MUSTARD HEARTS, RINSED
- 1 TABLESPOON VEGETABLE OIL
- 4 CLOVES GARLIC, PEELED
- 2 SLICES GINGER
- 1 CUP (8 FL OZ/250 ML) CHICKEN BROTH (STOCK, PAGE 90)
- 1 (3¼-LB/1.5-KG) WHOLE DUCK
- 1 TEASPOON SALT
- 1 TEASPOON CORNSTARCH (CORNFLOUR)
- STEAMED RICE (PAGE 540), TO SERVE

当归鸭

DUCK WITH ANGELICA ROOT

REGION: TAIWAN
PREPARATION TIME: 10 MINUTES, PLUS
  30 MINUTES MARINATING TIME
COOKING TIME: 1 HOUR
SERVES: 4
📷 PAGE 305

- 1 (3¼-LB/1.5-KG) WHOLE DUCK, CUT INTO LARGE PIECES, BONE-IN
- 1 TABLESPOON SALT
- 1 TABLESPOON GINGER JUICE
- ¼ OZ/10 G ANGELICA ROOT, SLICED
- ⅛ OZ/5 G SICHUAN LOVAGE ROOT
- 2 TABLESPOONS RICE WINE
- 2 STALKS CILANTRO (CORIANDER), CUT INTO 1½-INCH/4-CM LENGTHS, TO GARNISH
- STEAMED RICE (PAGE 540), TO SERVE

* Put the duck into a heatproof bowl and rub with the salt and ginger juice. Marinate in the refrigerator for 30 minutes.
* Add the angelica and lovage roots to the bowl and seal with aluminum foil. Place in a collapsible pot or bamboo steamer over a pot of boiling water. Steam, covered, for 30 minutes. Reduce to low heat and steam for another 30 minutes. Remove the foil and discard the angelica and lovage roots.
* Drizzle the duck with the wine and garnish with the cilantro (coriander). Serve with rice.

馄饨鸭

BRAISED DUCK WITH WONTONS

REGION: JIANGSU
PREPARATION TIME: 20 MINUTES
COOKING TIME: 3 HOURS 15 MINUTES
SERVES: 8

- 9 OZ/250 G GROUND (MINCED) PORK BELLY OR GROUND PORK
- 2 TABLESPOONS LIGHT SOY SAUCE
- 1 TABLESPOON GRANULATED SUGAR
- 2 TABLESPOONS SESAME OIL
- 24 LARGE WONTON WRAPPERS
- 1 (4½-LB/2-KG) WHOLE DUCK
- 2 SCALLIONS (SPRING ONIONS)
- ¾ OZ/20 G GINGER (ABOUT 1-INCH/2.5-CM-LENGTH PIECE), SLICED
- 4 TABLESPOONS SHAOXING WINE
- ⅔ CUP (3½ OZ/100 G) SLICED BAMBOO SHOOTS
- ½ TABLESPOON SALT

* Combine the pork, soy sauce, sugar, and sesame oil in a bowl and mix well. Divide it into 24 portions.
* Place a portion of filling on one corner of a wonton wrapper, fold the wrapper over the filling, and roll halfway until the filling is completely enclosed by the wrapper. Fold the 2 ends of the wrapper into the center, one on top of another, brush a little water in between the layers, and press tight on the layers to seal into a wonton. Repeat with the remaining wrappers and filling.
* Put the duck into a large saucepan of cold water and bring to a boil. Remove the duck, then rinse with cold running water.
* Place the duck in a large oval-shaped Dutch oven (casserole), breast facing downward. Add the scallions (spring onions), ginger, wine, and enough water to cover the duck. Bring to a boil and skim the surface to remove any froth and scum. Cover, reduce to low heat, and simmer for 3 hours, or until the duck is cooked through and tender.
* Uncover, turn over the duck so that breast faces upward, add the bamboo shoots and salt, and bring to a boil.
* Meanwhile, bring 4¼ cups (1¾ pints/1 liter) water to a boil in a saucepan, add the wontons, and boil for 3 minutes until they float to the surface. Drain, then add them to the Dutch oven and serve.

DUCK WITH ANGELICA ROOT

REGION: HAKKA
PREPARATION TIME: 15 MINUTES,
  PLUS 12 HOURS STANDING TIME
COOKING TIME: 1 HOUR
SERVES: 8

蒸咸鹅

STEAMED SALTED GOOSE

- 1 (5½-LB/2.5-KG) GOOSE
- 3 TABLESPOONS SALT
- ½ TEASPOON FIVE-SPICE POWDER
- 3 TABLESPOONS GINGER JUICE
- 3 TABLESPOONS GLUTINOUS
  RICE WINE
- ¼ OZ/5 G ANGELICA ROOT, SLICED
- 2 CLOVES GARLIC, CHOPPED
- 2 TABLESPOONS WHITE VINEGAR
- STEAMED RICE (PAGE 540), TO SERVE

Goose is an all-time favorite among the southern Chinese and popular dishes include Cantonese roast goose, Chaozhou goose in brine, Jiangsu wind-dried goose, and the Hakka salted goose—just to name a few. A goose will often require a long marinating time for flavors to penetrate.

* Put the goose into a large bowl and rub the inside and outside with the salt and five-spice powder and let marinate for 4 hours. Rub the ginger juice and wine all over the goose, inside and out, and marinate in the refrigerator for 8 hours. Turn the goose over once or twice.
* Put the angelica root inside the goose cavity. Transfer to a plate and place in a heatproof collapsible pot or bamboo steamer over a pot of boiling water. Steam, covered, for about 1 hour, or until cooked through. (Add more water to the pot if needed.) Carefully remove the goose and discard the angelica root. Put the goose on a cutting board and when cool enough to handle, cut into small chunks. Transfer to a serving plate.
* Combine the garlic and vinegar in a small bowl to make a dipping sauce. Serve with the sauce and rice on the side.

REGION: TAIWAN
PREPARATION TIME: 5 MINUTES, PLUS
  15 MINUTES SOAKING TIME
COOKING TIME: 2 MINUTES
SERVES: 6

卤味鹅肠

GOOSE INTESTINES IN SOY SAUCE

- 11 OZ/300 G GOOSE INTESTINES
- 2 CUPS (16 FL OZ/475 ML) CHICKEN
  BROTH (STOCK, PAGE 90)
- ⅔ CUP (5 FL OZ/150 ML) LIGHT SOY
  SAUCE
- 2½ TABLESPOONS GRANULATED SUGAR
- 5 OZ/150 G FLOWERING CHIVES

* Put the goose intestines into a large saucepan and add enough water to cover them completely. Bring to a boil over high heat and blanch for 5 seconds. Drain.
* Put the chicken broth (stock), soy sauce, and sugar into a saucepan, bring to a boil, and pour the mixture into a heatproof bowl. Add the intestines and soak for 15 minutes.
* Bring a saucepan of water to a boil, add the flowering chives, and blanch for 1 minute. Drain, rinse, and pat dry with paper towels. Cut into 1½-inch/4 cm-lengths. Line the bottom of a serving plate with the chives.
* Cut the goose intestines to 2-inch/5-cm lengths and arrange on top of the flowering chives.

POULTRY

玫瑰醉鸽煲

SQUAB AND ROSE
WINE CASSEROLE

REGION: HONG KONG
PREPARATION TIME: 5 MINUTES
COOKING TIME: 30 MINUTES
SERVES: 4

Chinese rose wine is created by adding roses to sorghum or other grains in the distilling process, resulting in a heavy rose-scented liquor. It is often used to enhance the flavor of meats in Cantonese cuisine.

* Bring 10 cups (85 fl oz/2.5 liters) water to a boil in a large saucepan. Using tongs, carefully hold the squabs by the heads and submerge them in the hot water for 30 seconds to let the hot water flow into the body cavities. Transfer the squabs to a colander, and then drain. Bring the water to another boil, put the squabs into the hot water entirely, cover, and turn off the heat. (We dip the squabs into hot water to fill the cavity so the inside and outside temperature of the squabs are the same and therefore cook more evenly.)
* Steep the squabs in the hot water for about 15 minutes. Remove the squabs and set aside to cool. When cooled, cut each squab into 6 pieces.
* Heat the oil in a Dutch oven (casserole) over medium-high heat, add the scallions (spring onions) and ginger, and stir-fry for 1 minute until fragrant. Add the jujube dates, both wines, soy sauce, salt, sugar, and chicken broth (stock) and bring to a boil. Carefully, arrange the squab pieces in the Dutch oven, then reduce the heat, cover, and simmer for 12 minutes until cooked through. Transfer the squabs to a serving plate.
* Mix the cornstarch (cornflour) with 1 tablespoon water in a small bowl and stir this mixture into the Dutch oven. Bring to a boil, stirring, for 30 seconds to thicken the sauce. Add the sesame oil and pour the sauce over the squabs. Serve with rice.

- 2 (9-OZ/250-G) SQUABS
- 2 TABLESPOONS VEGETABLE OIL
- 4 SCALLIONS (SPRING ONIONS), STEMS ONLY, CUT INTO 1½-INCH/ 4-CM LENGTHS
- ¼ OZ/10 G GINGER (ABOUT ¾-INCH/ 2-CM-LENGTH PIECE), SLICED
- 4 JUJUBE DATES, PITTED
- 4 TABLESPOONS SHAOXING WINE
- 2 TABLESPOONS CHINESE ROSE WINE
- 1 TABLESPOON DARK SOY SAUCE
- 1 TEASPOON SALT
- 1 TEASPOON GRANULATED SUGAR
- ½ CUP (4 FL OZ/120 ML) CHICKEN BROTH (STOCK, PAGE 90)
- 1 TEASPOON CORNSTARCH (CORNFLOUR)
- ½ TEASPOON SESAME OIL
- STEAMED RICE (PAGE 540), TO SERVE

REGION: GUANGDONG
PREPARATION TIME: 15 MINUTES, PLUS
    1½ HOURS DRYING TIME
COOKING TIME: 45 MINUTES
SERVES: 4
📷 PAGE 309

脆皮鸽

DEEP-FRIED
SQUAB

- 2 (9-OZ/250-G) SQUABS
- 6 TABLESPOONS SALT
- 2 CUPS (16 FL OZ/475 ML)
  VEGETABLE OIL
- STEAMED RICE (PAGE 540), TO SERVE

FOR THE GLAZE:
- 3 TABLESPOONS MALTOSE
- 1 TABLESPOON CORNSTARCH
  (CORNFLOUR)
- 2 TEASPOONS VINEGAR
- 2 TEASPOONS RICE WINE

FOR THE SPICE BAG:
- 2 STAR ANISE
- 1 DRIED TANGERINE PEEL
- 1 SMALL CINNAMON STICK
- 2 OZ/50 G SHAJIANG
- ⅛ DRIED LOHAN FRUIT
- ¼ OZ/8 G LICORICE ROOT
- ½ TABLESPOON SICHUAN
  PEPPERCORNS
- ½ TABLESPOON GROUND CUMIN
- ½ TEASPOON CLOVES

FOR THE SPICED SALT:
- 1 TEASPOON SALT
- ½ TEASPOON FIVE-SPICE POWDER

Squabs are typically young domestic pigeon, under four weeks old. When deep-fried or roasted, the skin turns crispy and glossy, while the meat remains tender and juicy. It's a popular dish to have at Chinese restaurants and often served during special occasions such as birthdays or weddings.

* Bring a large saucepan of water to a boil, add the squabs and blanch for about 1 minute. Drain and set aside.
* Combine the spice bag ingredients and place in the saucepan. Add the salt and 6¼ cups (50 fl oz/1.5 liters) water, and bring to a boil over high heat. Reduce to low heat and simmer for 15 minutes or until the flavors are extracted from the spice bag.
* Add the squabs and bring the water to another boil. Cover, turn off the heat, and stand in the hot water for 12 minutes. Carefully transfer the squabs to a colander and rinse the skin with boiling water. Air-dry the squabs in the refrigerator for 30 minutes.
* To make the glaze, stir the maltose and 3 tablespoons boiling water together in small bowl until the maltose has melted. Add the remaining glaze ingredients and mix well.
* Brush the squabs with the glaze and air-dry for another 30 minutes. Repeat again.
* To make the spiced salt, heat the salt in a small dry skillet (frying pan) over medium heat for 1 minute. Turn off the heat and let cool. Stir in the five-spice powder.
* Heat the oil in a wok or deep saucepan to 300°F/150°C, or until a cube of bread browns in 1½ minutes. Carefully add the squab and use a slotted spoon to gently roll it in the hot oil for 3–4 minutes until the skin turns a deep red. Carefully remove the squab from the oil and drain in a colander. Repeat with the remaining squab.
* When ready to serve, halve each squab and transfer to a serving plate. Serve with the spiced salt and steamed rice.

DEEP-FRIED SQUAB

REGION: JIANGSU
PREPARATION TIME: 10 MINUTES
COOKING TIME: 5 MINUTES
SERVES: 4

三丝炒鸽松
STIR-FRIED PIGEON

- 4–5 BONELESS PIGEON BREASTS (ABOUT 11 OZ/300 G), FINELY CHOPPED
- ½ TEASPOON SALT
- 1 EGG WHITE
- 1½ TEASPOONS CORNSTARCH (CORNFLOUR)
- 2 TABLESPOONS SESAME OIL
- 3 TABLESPOONS LARD
- ¼ OZ/10 G GINGER (ABOUT ¾-INCH/ 2-CM-LENGTH PIECE), SHREDDED
- 1 SCALLION (SPRING ONION), SHREDDED
- 1 RED CAYENNE PEPPER, SLICED
- 1 TABLESPOON SHAOXING WINE
- 2 TABLESPOONS LIGHT SOY SAUCE
- 1 TEASPOON GRANULATED SUGAR
- ½ TEASPOON WHITE VINEGAR
- STEAMED RICE (PAGE 540), TO SERVE

* Combine the pigeon, salt, egg white, and 1 teaspoon cornstarch (cornflour) in a large bowl and mix well. Stir in 1 tablespoon sesame oil.
* Heat 2 tablespoons lard in a wok or large skillet (frying pan) over medium heat, add the pigeon, and stir-fry rapidly for 30 seconds. Transfer the pigeon to a plate.
* Heat the remaining 1 tablespoon lard in the wok over medium-high heat, add the ginger, scallion (spring onion), and cayenne pepper, and stir-fry for 1 minute until fragrant. Add the wine, soy sauce, and sugar and toss well.
* Mix the remaining ½ teaspoon cornstarch with ½ tablespoon water in a small bowl and stir this mixture into the wok. Bring to a boil, stirring, for about 30 seconds to thicken the sauce. Return the pigeon into the wok, toss, and stir in the vinegar and the remaining 1 tablespoon sesame oil. Transfer to a serving plate and serve with rice.

REGION: SICHUAN
PREPARATION TIME: 5 MINUTES
COOKING TIME: 45 MINUTES
SERVES: 2

熏五香鸽
SMOKED PIGEON

- 2 (9-OZ/250-G) WHOLE PIGEONS
- ¼ OZ/10 G GINGER (ABOUT ¾-INCH/ 2-CM-LENGTH PIECE), SLICED
- 2 TABLESPOONS DARK SOY SAUCE
- 6 TABLESPOONS SALT
- 2 OZ/50 G ROCK SUGAR
- 4 TABLESPOONS SHAOXING WINE
- 2 TABLESPOONS JASMINE TEA LEAVES
- STEAMED RICE (PAGE 540), TO SERVE

  FOR THE SPICE BAG:
- 2 STAR ANISE
- 1 DRIED TANGERINE PEEL
- 2 OZ/50 G SHAJIANG
- ¼ OZ/8 G LICORICE ROOT
- ½ SMALL CINNAMON STICK
- ½ TABLESPOON SICHUAN PEPPERCORNS
- ½ TABLESPOON GROUND CUMIN
- ½ TEASPOON CLOVES

* Put the pigeons into a large saucepan and add enough water to cover them completely. Bring to a boil over high heat and blanch for 1 minute. Drain.
* Put the spices in a spice bag. Put 17 cups (36 fl oz/4 liters) water into a large saucepan. Add the ginger, soy sauce, salt, sugar, wine, and spice bag and bring to a boil. Reduce to low heat and simmer for 15 minutes.
* Bring the sauce to a boil and add the pigeons. Return to a boil, cover, and then turn off the heat and let stand for another 12 minutes. Transfer the pigeons to a colander to drain. Discard the liquid.
* Heat a dry wok over high heat, add the tea leaves, and place a metal steaming rack in the wok over the leaves. Arrange the pigeons on the rack, cover, and then reduce to low heat. Smoke for about 10 minutes.
* Transfer the pigeons to a cutting board and when cool enough to handle, cut each in half. Transfer to a serving plate and serve with rice.

干收鹌鹑
BRAISED QUAIL

REGION: SICHUAN
PREPARATION TIME: 10 MINUTES,
  PLUS 1 HOUR MARINATING TIME
COOKING TIME: 1 HOUR 15 MINUTES
SERVES: 4

* Combine the quails, soy sauce, wine, and ½ teaspoon salt in a large bowl and marinate for 1 hour.
* Heat 2 cups (16 fl oz/475 ml) oil in a wok or deep saucepan over medium-high heat to about 340°F/170°C, or until a cube of bread browns in 45 seconds. Gently lower the quail into the oil and deep-fry for 3–4 minutes until golden. Transfer the quails to a plate lined with paper towels to drain and pour out the oil.
* Heat 1 tablespoon oil in a clean wok over high heat, add the ginger and scallions (spring onions), and stir-fry for 1 minute until fragrant. Add the chicken broth (stock) and bring to a boil. Put in the quails, sugar, and remaining ½ teaspoon salt and simmer over medium heat for about 1 hour or until all the sauce has been absorbed by the quails. Turn over the quails several times during braising.
* Discard the ginger and scallions, transfer the quails to a serving plate, and brush with the sesame oil. Serve with rice.

- 4 (7-OZ/200-G) QUAILS
- 1 TABLESPOON LIGHT SOY SAUCE
- 1 TABLESPOON SHAOXING WINE
- 1 TEASPOON SALT
- 2 CUPS (16 FL OZ/475 ML) PLUS 1 TABLESPOON VEGETABLE OIL
- ¼ OZ/10 G GINGER (ABOUT ¾-INCH/ 2-CM-LENGTH PIECE), CRUSHED
- 2 SCALLIONS (SPRING ONIONS), CUT INTO 1½-INCH/4-CM LENGTHS
- 2 CUPS (16 FL OZ/475 ML) CHICKEN BROTH (STOCK, PAGE 90)
- 2 TEASPOONS GRANULATED SUGAR
- 2 TEASPOONS SESAME OIL
- STEAMED RICE (PAGE 540), TO SERVE

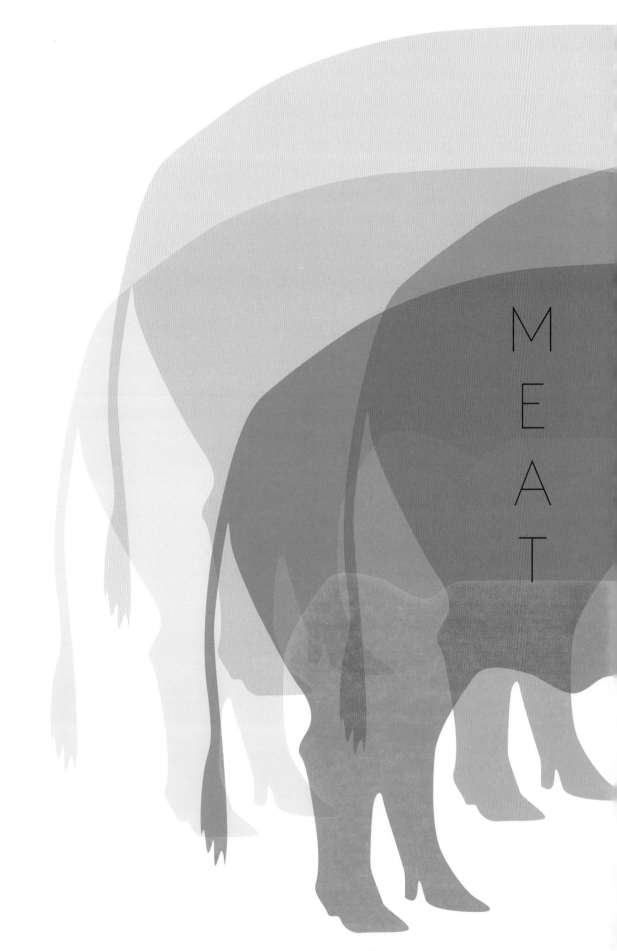

MEAT

MEAT

REGION: TAIWAN
PREPARATION TIME: 1 HOUR,
  PLUS 3 HOURS MARINATING TIME
COOKING TIME: 30 MINUTES
SERVES: 6–8

粉肝

COLD PORK
LIVER

- 2¼ LB/1 KG PORK LIVERS
- 1 TABLESPOON WHITE PEPPERCORNS
- 2 OZ/50 G GINGER (ABOUT 3-INCH/
  7.5-CM-LENGTH PIECE), SHREDDED,
  TO SERVE

FOR THE SAUCE:
- 4 TABLESPOONS LIGHT SOY SAUCE
- 4 TABLESPOONS SHAOXING WINE
- 1 TABLESPOON GRANULATED SUGAR
- 1 TABLESPOON GINGER JUICE
- 1 TABLESPOON SALT

* To make the sauce, combine all the ingredients and 2 cups
  (16 fl oz/475 ml) cold water in a large bowl and refrigerate.
* Rinse the livers under cold running water. Fill the liver with
  water, allowing it to run through the openings, then press
  down on the liver to release the water and blood from
  inside. Repeat rinsing and pressing, until most of the blood
  inside the liver has been drained and the liver becomes light
  pink in color.
* Place the livers on a nonmetallic heatproof plate and put
  into a large saucepan. Add the white peppercorns and
  enough water to completely cover the livers. Heat the
  water to 150°F/70°C and steep for 30 minutes. (You need to
  maintain the water temperature by using a thermometer
  and adding a little hot water.) Remove and immediately
  dunk the livers into the cold sauce. Marinate the livers in
  the sauce for at least 3 hours.
* Drain the sauce. Use a sharp knife to shave off the
  hardened skin of the livers, then slice the livers and transfer
  to a serving plate. Serve together with the shredded ginger.

REGION: ZHEJIANG
PREPARATION TIME: 5 MINUTES,
  PLUS 2 DAYS SOAKING TIME
COOKING TIME: 2 HOURS 10 MINUTES
SERVES: 4

醉猪手

DRUNKEN
TROTTERS

- 2¼ LB / 1 KG PIG'S TROTTER, CLEANED
- 1¼ OZ/30 G GINGER (ABOUT 2-INCH/
  5-CM-LENGTH PIECE), SLICED
- 1 TABLESPOON SICHUAN
  PEPPERCORNS
- 1 CUP (8 FL OZ/250 ML) PICKLED WINE
  SAUCE
- ½ CUP (4 FL OZ/120 ML) SHAOXING
  WINE
- 1 TEASPOON GRANULATED SUGAR
- ½ TEASPOON SALT

* Put the trotters into a large saucepan and add enough
  water to cover them completely. Bring to a boil over high
  heat and blanch for 5 minutes. Skim the froth and scum
  off the surface, if needed. Drain, then rinse under cold
  running water.
* Return the trotters to the pan and add the ginger and
  Sichuan peppercorns. Pour enough water to cover and
  bring to a boil over high heat, then reduce to low heat
  and simmer for 2 hours. Drain and discard the ginger and
  peppercorns. Immerse the trotters in cold water until cold,
  then drain.
* In a large nonmetallic bowl, combine the pickled wine
  sauce, wine, sugar, salt, and 1 cup (8 fl oz/250 ml) cold
  water. Put the trotters into the bowl and immerse. Let
  soak for 2 days in the refrigerator.
* Serve chilled without the sauce.

MEAT

粉蒸肉
PORK BELLY WITH
CRUSHED RICE

REGION: HUBEI
PREPARATION TIME: 30 MINUTES,
  PLUS 10 MINUTES MARINATING TIME
COOKING TIME: 1 HOUR 15 MINUTES
SERVES: 6

* For the pork belly, scrape the skin clean, then rinse the pork under cold running water.
* Put the pork into a large saucepan and add enough water to cover it completely. Bring to a boil over high heat and blanch the pork for 10 minutes. Drain and rinse under cold running water until cooled.
* Meanwhile, in a small skillet (frying pan), dry roast the rice over low heat for 3–4 minutes until slightly brown. Add the salt, star anise, Sichuan peppercorns, cloves, and cinnamon and roast the spices over medium-low heat for about 3 minutes. Transfer the contents to a grinder (or mortar and pestle) and grind to the texture of coarse breadcrumbs. Set aside.
* Cut the pork into 1½ × 1 × ½-inch/4 × 2.5 × 1-cm pieces, then put into a large bowl and add the marinade ingredients. Marinate for 10 minutes.
* Meanwhile, use a chopstick to clean the channels inside the lotus root and rinse thoroughly under cold running water. Cut the lotus root into 1¼-inch/3-cm-wide slices. Place in a bowl and mix with 1 tablespoon spiced ground rice.
* Add the remaining spiced ground rice to the bowl with the pork and combine well.
* Line the bottom of a heatproof bowl with the pork, skin-side down, and put the lotus root slices on top. Place the bowl in a collapsible pot or bamboo steamer over a pot of boiling water. Steam, covered, for 1 hour. (Add more water to the pot if needed.) Carefully remove the bowl from the steamer.
* Using dish towels, cover the bowl with a plate, and invert to transfer the pork and lotus root mixture onto the plate. (Alternatively, use tongs to transfer the contents.)
* Garnish with the scallions (spring onions), then serve with rice.

- 1 (1-LB 2-OZ/500-G) BONELESS, SKIN-ON PORK BELLY
- SCANT ½ CUP (2¾ OZ/75 G) LONG-GRAIN RICE
- 1 TEASPOON SALT
- 2 STAR ANISE
- 1 TABLESPOON SICHUAN PEPPERCORNS
- ¾ TEASPOON CLOVES
- ½ TEASPOON GROUND CINNAMON
- 5 OZ/150 G LOTUS ROOT, PEELED
- 1 TABLESPOON CHOPPED SCALLIONS (SPRING ONIONS) TO GARNISH
- STEAMED RICE (PAGE 540), TO SERVE

FOR THE MARINADE:
- 1 TABLESPOON GINGER JUICE
- 1 TABLESPOON RED BEAN CURD JUICE
- 1 TABLESPOON TIANMIANJIANG
- 1 TEASPOON RICE WINE
- 1 TEASPOON GRANULATED SUGAR
- ¼ TEASPOON GROUND WHITE PEPPER

REGION: ZHEJIANG
PREPARATION TIME: 10 MINUTES,
    PLUS 30 MINUTES MARINATING TIME
COOKING TIME: 20 MINUTES
SERVES: 6

虾酱蒸五花腩
STEAMED PORK WITH
SHRIMP PASTE

- 1 (11-OZ/300-G) BONELESS, SKIN-ON PORK BELLY
- 2 OZ/50 G SHELLED UNCOOKED SHRIMP (PRAWNS), DEVEINED
- ¼ OZ/10 G PORK FATBACK, CHOPPED
- 1½ TABLESPOONS SHRIMP PASTE
- 1 TABLESPOON GRANULATED SUGAR
- 1 TABLESPOON SHAOXING WINE
- 1 TABLESPOON GINGER JUICE
- 1 TABLESPOON CORNSTARCH (CORNFLOUR)
- 10 TOFU PUFFS, HALVED
- 1 TABLESPOON CHOPPED SCALLIONS (SPRING ONIONS), TO GARNISH
- STEAMED RICE (PAGE 540), TO SERVE

* For the pork belly, scrape the skin clean, then rinse the pork under cold running water. Cut into ¼-inch/5-mm-thick slices. Set aside.
* Finely chop the shrimp (prawns) until ground (minced). In a bowl, combine the ground shrimp, pork fatback, shrimp paste, sugar, wine, ginger juice, and cornstarch (cornflour) into a sauce and add the pork. Marinate for 30 minutes.
* Line the bottom of a heatproof plate with the tofu puffs, then put the marinated pork slices on top. Pour the marinade sauce over the pork and place in a collapsible pot or bamboo steamer over a pot of boiling water. Steam, covered, for 20 minutes. Garnish with scallions (spring onions), then serve with rice.

REGION: GUANGXI
PREPARATION TIME: 15 MINUTES,
    PLUS 15 MINUTES MARINATING TIME
COOKING TIME: 3 HOURS 30 MINUTES
SERVES: 4-6

芋头扣肉
PORK BELLY
WITH TARO

- 1 (14-OZ/400-G) BONELESS, SKIN-ON PORK BELLY, ABOUT 3¼ INCHES/8 CM WIDE
- 3 CUBES RED BEAN CURD, MASHED
- 2 TABLESPOONS RICE WINE
- 2 TABLESPOONS GRANULATED SUGAR
- 1 TABLESPOON GINGER JUICE
- 1 LB 5 OZ/600 G TARO, PEELED
- STEAMED RICE (PAGE 540), TO SERVE

* For the pork belly, scrape the skin clean, then rinse the pork under cold running water.
* Put the pork into a large saucepan and add enough water to cover it. Bring to a boil over high heat and blanch for 15 minutes. Skim the froth and scum off the surface, if needed. Drain and rinse under cold running water. Set aside to cool.
* Combine the red bean curd, wine, sugar, and ginger juice and mix into a sauce.
* Cut the pork into 12 equal slices. Combine the slices with the sauce and marinate for 15 minutes.
* Cut the taro into 12 equal slices, similar in size to the pork slices. Put the taro slices into a collapsible or bamboo steamer over a pot of boiling water. Steam, covered, for 15 minutes. Carefully remove from the steamer.
* Remove the pork from the sauce and transfer to a bowl. Dip the taro slices into the sauce to coat.
* On a deep heatproof plate, arrange alternate layers of pork and taro slices, then pour over the remaining sauce. Seal the plate tightly with aluminum foil, place in the steamer, and steam over high heat for 3 hours. (Add more water to the pot, if needed). Serve with rice.

夹心扣肉
PORK WITH YAMS

REGION: JIANGXI
PREPARATION TIME: 20 MINUTES
COOKING TIME: 2 HOURS 30 MINUTES
SERVES: 4

* For the pork belly, scrape the skin clean, then rinse the pork under cold running water.
* Put the pork into a large saucepan, then add the ginger, knotted scallion (spring onion), and enough water to cover them completely. Bring to a boil over high heat, reduce to low heat, and cook for 20 minutes. Transfer the pork to a colander to drain and reserve about 2 tablespoons cooking broth (stock).
* Place the pork belly in a bowl and rub with the dark soy sauce and wine.
* Heat the oil in a wok or deep saucepan to 340°F/170°C, or until a cube of bread browns in 45 seconds. Use paper towels to pat the pork belly dry and gently lower into the oil. Deep-fry for 2–3 minutes until golden brown. Use a slotted spoon to carefully remove the pork from the oil and drain on paper towels. Set aside to cool. Cut into ½-inch/1-cm-thick slices and set aside.
* Reheat the oil to 340°F/170°C and deep-fry the yams for 3–4 minutes until golden brown. Use a slotted spoon to carefully remove the yams from the oil and drain on paper towels.
* Line the sides and bottom of a large heatproof bowl with pork, skin facing down, and yam slices, interlacing them as you go.
* Combine the light soy sauce, sugar, salt, and reserved cooking broth in a small bowl. Pour over the pork and yams, then seal tightly with aluminum foil, and place in a collapsible pot or bamboo steamer over a pot of boiling water. Steam, covered, for 2 hours. (Add more water to the pot if needed.)
* Carefully remove the foil, then strain the sauce into a saucepan. Cover the bowl with a serving plate and, using dish towels, invert the contents onto the plate (alternatively, use tongs to transfer the contents to a serving plate).
* Heat the sauce over medium-high heat.
* Mix the cornstarch (cornflour) with 1 tablespoon water in a small bowl and stir this mixture into the pan. Bring to a boil, stirring, for 30 seconds to thicken the sauce. Pour over the pork and yams and serve with rice.

- 1 (12-OZ/350-G) BONELESS, SKIN-ON PORK BELLY
- ¼ OZ/10 G GINGER (ABOUT ¾-INCH/2-CM-LENGTH PIECE), SLICED
- 1 SCALLION (SPRING ONION), KNOTTED
- 1 TABLESPOON DARK SOY SAUCE
- 1 TABLESPOON RICE WINE
- 1 CUP (8 FL OZ/250 ML) VEGETABLE OIL
- 11 OZ/300 G YAMS, CUT INTO ½-INCH/1-CM-THICK SLICES
- 2 TABLESPOONS LIGHT SOY SAUCE
- 1 TEASPOON GRANULATED SUGAR
- ½ TEASPOON SALT
- 1 TEASPOON CORNSTARCH (CORNFLOUR)
- STEAMED RICE (PAGE 540), TO SERVE

REGION: HAKKA
PREPARATION TIME: 15 MINUTES,
  PLUS 30 MINUTES MARINATING TIME
COOKING TIME: 4 HOURS 15 MINUTES
SERVES: 4–6

梅菜扣肉
PORK WITH PRESERVED MUSTARD GREENS

- 11 OZ/300 G SWEET PRESERVED MUSTARD GREENS, TRIMMED, RINSED, AND FINELY CHOPPED
- 3 TABLESPOONS GRANULATED SUGAR
- 1 TABLESPOON LIGHT SOY SAUCE
- 1 TABLESPOON RICE WINE
- 1 (1 LB 5-OZ/600-G) BONELESS, SKIN-ON PORK BELLY
- 1 TABLESPOON DARK SOY SAUCE
- 4 TABLESPOONS VEGETABLE OIL
- ¼ OZ/10 G GINGER (ABOUT ¾-INCH/ 2-CM-LENGTH PIECE), SLICED
- STEAMED RICE (PAGE 540), TO SERVE

* Put the mustard greens in a bowl, add the sugar, light soy sauce, and wine, and marinate for 30 minutes.
* Meanwhile, for the pork belly, scrape the skin clean, then rinse the pork under cold running water.
* Put the pork into a large saucepan and add enough water to cover it completely. Bring to a boil over high heat and blanch the pork for 10 minutes. Drain and rinse under cold running water until cooled. Pat dry with paper towels, then rub the skin with the dark soy sauce.
* Heat 2 tablespoons oil in a wok or large skillet (frying pan) over medium heat, add the pork, skin-side down, and pan-fry for about 2 minutes until blisters form on the skin. Transfer to a cutting board to cool. Cut into ½-inch/ 1-cm-thick slices.
* Heat a small skillet over medium heat and add the mustard greens. Dry-fry for 3 minutes to remove some of the moisture. Add the remaining 2 tablespoons oil and mix thoroughly.
* Line the sides and bottom of a large heatproof bowl with the pork slices, skin facing down, and fill the center with the mustard greens. Put the ginger on top, seal tightly with aluminum foil, and place in a collapsible pot or bamboo steamer over a pot of boiling water. Steam, covered, for 4 hours. (Add more water to the pot if needed.) Carefully remove the foil and discard the ginger.
* Strain the sauce into another bowl. Cover the bowl of pork with a serving plate and, using dish towels, carefully invert the contents onto the plate. The pork will then lay on a bed of the greens. Pour the reserved sauce over the pork and serve with rice.

大头菜蒸肉饼
STEAMED PORK WITH PRESERVED KOHLRABI

REGION: HAKKA
PREPARATION TIME: 10 MINUTES,
    PLUS 30 MINUTES FREEZING TIME
COOKING TIME: 10 MINUTES
SERVES: 4

* Put the pork fatback in the freezer for 30 minutes to firm up. Remove and finely chop while still frozen. Set aside.
* Meanwhile, combine the soy sauce, sugar, salt, and 4 tablespoons water in a large bowl and mix well. Marinate for 15 minutes.
* Using chopsticks, stir the pork in a single direction for about 1 minute, or until gummy in consistency. Pick up the pork with one hand and slap it against the bowl about 5 times; this will cause the patty to become sticky and elastic. Add the crushed oatmeal and pork fatback, and mix well with your hands. Incorporate the preserved kohlrabi, garlic, cornstarch (cornflour), vegetable oil, and sesame oil.
* Shape the pork patty into a flat disk on a shallow heatproof bowl, cover with aluminum foil, and place in a collapsible or bamboo steamer over a pot of water. Bring to a boil and steam, covered, for 8–10 minutes until cooked. (Pierce the patty with a fork or spoon and separate the meat to see if it's fully cooked.) Serve with rice.

- 3½ OZ/100 G PORK FATBACK
- 7 OZ/200 G GROUND (MINCED) LEAN PORK, FINELY CHOPPED
- 1 TEASPOON LIGHT SOY SAUCE
- 1 TEASPOON GRANULATED SUGAR
- ½ TEASPOON SALT
- 2 TABLESPOONS OATMEAL, CRUSHED
- 2 OZ/50 G PRESERVED KOHLRABI, CHOPPED
- 2 CLOVES GARLIC, CHOPPED
- 1 TABLESPOON CORNSTARCH (CORNFLOUR)
- 1 TABLESPOON VEGETABLE OIL
- ½ TEASPOON SESAME OIL
- STEAMED RICE (PAGE 540), TO SERVE

葱爆肉
PORK WITH BEIJING SCALLIONS

REGION: SHANDONG
PREPARATION TIME: 10 MINUTES
COOKING TIME: 10 MINUTES
SERVES: 4

* Combine the pork with cornstarch (cornflour) in a bowl, then stir in 1 tablespoon oil.
* Heat the remaining 2 tablespoons oil in a wok or large skillet (frying pan). Add the pork and stir-fry over medium-low heat for 2–3 minutes until cooked. Transfer the pork to a plate and set aside.
* Put the scallions into the wok and stir-fry over medium-high heat for 1–2 minutes until fragrant. Add the Tianmianjiang, soy sauce, wine, salt, and the pork, and stir-fry over high heat for another minute. Season with salt to taste.
* Transfer to a serving plate and serve with rice.

- 1 (11-OZ/300-G) PORK BELLY, SLICED
- 1 TABLESPOON CORNSTARCH (CORNFLOUR)
- 3 TABLESPOONS VEGETABLE OIL
- 2 BEIJING SCALLIONS OR 6 SCALLIONS (SPRING ONIONS), CUT INTO 1¼-INCH/3-CM LENGTHS
- 1 TABLESPOON TIANMIANJIANG
- 1 TEASPOON LIGHT SOY SAUCE
- 1 TABLESPOON RICE WINE
- ½ TEASPOON SALT, PLUS EXTRA TO TASTE
- STEAMED RICE (PAGE 540), TO SERVE

REGION: HONG KONG
PREPARATION TIME: 20 MINUTES, PLUS
   30 MINUTES FREEZING TIME
COOKING TIME: 10-12 MINUTES
SERVES: 4

咸鱼瑶柱蒸肉饼
STEAMED PORK WITH SALTED FISH

- 3½ OZ/100 G PORK FATBACK
- ¾ CUP (2¾ OZ/75 G) DRIED SCALLOPS
- 9 OZ/250 G GROUND (MINCED) LEAN PORK, FINELY CHOPPED
- 1 TEASPOON GRANULATED SUGAR
- ½ TEASPOON LIGHT SOY SAUCE
- ½ TEASPOON SALT
- 2 TABLESPOONS OATMEAL, CRUSHED
- 1 TABLESPOON CORNSTARCH (CORNFLOUR)
- ½ TEASPOON SESAME OIL
- 1 TABLESPOON VEGETABLE OIL, PLUS EXTRA FOR FRYING
- 2¾ OZ/75 G CHINESE SALTED FISH
- ½ TEASPOON SHREDDED GINGER, TO GARNISH
- STEAMED RICE (PAGE 540), TO SERVE

* Put the pork fatback in the freezer for 30 minutes to firm up. Remove and finely chop while still frozen. Set aside.
* Meanwhile, combine the dried scallops and 4 tablespoons cold water in a small bowl and soak for 15 minutes. Drain, then remove the small hard muscle. Shred the scallops, then strain the soaking water and reserve.
* Combine the ground (minced) pork, sugar, soy sauce, salt, and scallop soaking water in a large bowl. Marinate for 15 minutes.
* Using chopsticks, stir the pork in one direction for about 1 minute, or until gummy in consistency. Pick up the pork with one hand and slap it against the bowl about 5 times; this will cause the patty to become sticky and elastic. Add the crushed oatmeal and pork fatback, and mix well with your hands. Incorporate the dried scallops, cornstarch (cornflour), sesame oil, and vegetable oil.
* Shape the pork patty into a flat disk and place in a shallow heatproof bowl. Cover with aluminum foil and place in a collapsible pot or bamboo steamer over a pot of boiling water. Steam, covered, for 10–12 minutes until cooked through. (Pierce the patty with a fork and separate the meat to see if it's cooked.)
* Meanwhile, heat a little vegetable oil in a small skillet (frying pan) over low heat, add the salted fish, and pan-fry for 1–2 minutes on each side until slightly browned. Remove from the heat and put the salted fish on top of the steamed pork, then sprinkle over the shredded ginger. Serve with steamed rice.

咸蛋蒸肉饼
STEAMED PORK WITH
SALTED DUCK EGGS

REGION: GUANGDONG
PREPARATION TIME: 10 MINUTES,
    PLUS 30 MINUTES FREEZING TIME
COOKING TIME: 10 MINUTES
SERVES: 4

* Put the pork fatback in the freezer 30 minutes to firm up. Remove and finely chop while still frozen. Set aside.
* Meanwhile, combine the ground (minced) pork, salt, sugar, and 4 tablespoons water in a bowl and marinate for 15 minutes. Mix in the pork fatback. Using chopsticks, stir the meat in 1 direction for 1 minute, or until gummy.
* Add the oatmeal, cornstarch (cornflour), and oil to the pork mixture. Mix well.
* Chop the duck yolks into small pieces, and add both the whites and yolks to the beaten egg.
* Shape the pork patty into a flat disk and place in a shallow heatproof bowl. Cover with aluminum foil and place in a collapsible pot or bamboo steamer over a pot of boiling water. Steam, covered, for 10–12 minutes until cooked through. (Pierce the patty with a fork and separate the meat to see if it's cooked.)

- 3 OZ/80 G PORK FATBACK
- 7 OZ/200 G GROUND (MINCED) PORK
- ½ TEASPOON SALT
- 1 TEASPOON GRANULATED SUGAR
- 3 TABLESPOONS OATMEAL, CRUSHED
- 2 TEASPOONS CORNSTARCH (CORNFLOUR)
- 1 TABLESPOON VEGETABLE OIL
- 2 SALTED DUCK EGGS, PEELED, HALVED LENGTHWISE, AND SEPARATED
- 1 EGG, BEATEN
- STEAMED RICE (PAGE 540), TO SERVE

土鱿蒸肉饼
STEAMED PORK WITH
DRIED SQUID

REGION: HONG KONG
PREPARATION TIME: 10 MINUTES,
    PLUS 30 MINUTES SOAKING TIME
COOKING TIME: 10 MINUTES
SERVES: 4

* Put the squid into a saucepan, cover with warm water, and soak for 30 minutes. Using your hands, remove the membrane and cartilage and finely chop.
* Meanwhile, put the pork fatback in the freezer 30 minutes to firm up. Remove and finely chop while still frozen. Set aside.
* Combine the ground (minced) pork, 2 tablespoons water, the soy sauce, salt, and sugar in a bowl, then marinate for 10 minutes. Stir with chopsticks in one direction for about 1 minute, or until gummy in texture. Pick up the pork with one hand and slap it against the bowl about 5 times; this will cause the patty to become sticky and elastic. Mix in the squid and pork fatback.
* Drain the water chestnuts and add to the pork, along with the garlic, cornstarch (cornflour), and white pepper. Combine well, then add the oatmeal and sesame oil. Use your fingers to gently press the pork mixture to form a meat patty. Place in a collapsible pot or bamboo steamer over a pot of boiling water. Steam, covered, for 10 minutes until cooked. Serve with rice.

- 2 OZ/50 G DRIED SQUID, RINSED
- 2¾ OZ/75 G PORK FATBACK
- 7 OZ/200 G GROUND (MINCED) PORK, FINELY CHOPPED
- ½ TABLESPOON LIGHT SOY SAUCE
- ½ TEASPOON SALT
- ½ TEASPOON GRANULATED SUGAR
- 2 WATER CHESTNUTS, DICED AND SOAKED IN COLD WATER
- 1 CLOVE GARLIC, CHOPPED
- 1 TABLESPOON CORNSTARCH (CORNFLOUR)
- ½ TEASPOON GROUND WHITE PEPPER
- 1 TABLESPOON OATMEAL, CRUSHED
- 1 TEASPOON SESAME OIL
- STEAMED RICE (PAGE 540), TO SERVE

REGION: JIANGSU
PREPARATION TIME: 30 MINUTES,
    PLUS 30 MINUTES FREEZING TIME
COOKING TIME: 2 HOURS
SERVES: 3
📷 PAGE 325

清汤狮子头
LION'S HEAD
MEATBALLS

- 7 OZ/200 G PORK FATBACK
- 11 OZ/300 G GROUND (MINCED) LEAN PORK
- 3½ OZ/100 G UNCOOKED SHRIMP (PRAWNS), SHELLED AND MINCED
- 1 TABLESPOON GINGER JUICE
- 1 TEASPOON SALT
- ¼ TEASPOON GRANULATED SUGAR
- ¼ TEASPOON GROUND WHITE PEPPER
- 1½ TABLESPOONS CORNSTARCH (CORNFLOUR)
- 1 TABLESPOON OATMEAL, CRUSHED TO A POWDER
- 4¼ CUPS (34 FL OZ/1 LITER) CHICKEN BROTH (STOCK, PAGE 90)
- SCALLIONS (SPRING ONIONS), TO GARNISH (OPTIONAL)

* Put the pork fatback in the freezer 30 minutes to firm up. Remove and finely chop while still frozen. Set aside.
* Divide the ground (minced) pork in half. Take one portion and finely chop.
* Combine both portions of the pork, the fatback, and shrimp (prawns) in a large bowl and add the ginger juice, salt, sugar, white pepper, cornstarch (cornflour), and oatmeal. Use your hands to mix well.
* With wet hands, form the mixture into 6 large meatballs, then put them into 6 separate heatproof bowls deep enough to hold the meatball and broth. Pour in enough chicken broth (stock) to cover the meatballs. Cover the bowls with aluminum foil and place in a collapsible pot or bamboo steamer over a pot of boiling water. Steam, covered, for 2 hours. (Add more water to the pot if needed.) Season with extra salt to taste, garnish with scallions (spring onions), if using, and serve.

REGION: ANHUI
PREPARATION TIME: 25 MINUTES
COOKING TIME: 30 MINUTES
SERVES: 6

笼仔粉砣
AROMATIC MEATBALLS

- 1 STAR ANISE
- 1 TEASPOON SICHUAN PEPPERCORNS
- 1 TOFU SHEET
- 2 OZ/50 G SWEET POTATO VERMICELLI
- 11 OZ/300 G GROUND (MINCED) PORK
- 1 TABLESPOON GINGER JUICE
- 1 TEASPOON SALT
- 4 TABLESPOONS LOTUS ROOT FLOUR, SWEET POTATO STARCH, OR CORNSTARCH (CORNFLOUR)
- 2 EGGS, BEATEN

* In a small skillet (frying pan), toast the star anise and Sichuan peppercorns over medium-low heat for 2–3 minutes, or until fragrant. Grind using a mortar and pestle. Set aside.
* Use a clean, damp dish towel to gently brush the tofu sheet and soften. Cut into pieces to line a steaming rack.
* Bring a large saucepan of water to a boil and add the sweet potato vermicelli. Reduce to medium heat and cook for 3–4 minutes until soft. Drain and cut into 4-inch/10-cm lengths. Put into a bowl and set aside.
* In a separate bowl, combine the pork, ginger juice, salt, ground star anise and peppercorns, and lotus root flour. Form into 6 meatballs, roll them in the beaten eggs, and transfer to a plate.
* Pour any leftover egg into a hot skillet and fry over medium heat for 2–3 minutes, then cut into long, thin strips. Wrap the meatballs with the egg strips and vermicelli and place on top of the tofu sheet on the steaming rack. Put the rack in a collapsible pot or bamboo steamer over a pot of boiling water. Steam, covered, for about 18 minutes. Serve.

LION'S HEAD MEATBALLS

荷叶肉
PORK WRAPPED
IN LOTUS LEAVES

- 1 (1-LB/450-G) BONELESS, SKIN-ON PORK BELLY
- 1 TABLESPOON GRATED GINGER
- 1 TABLESPOON CHOPPED SCALLIONS (SPRING ONIONS)
- 1 TABLESPOON TIANMIANJIANG
- 2 TABLESPOONS LIGHT SOY SAUCE
- 1 TABLESPOON SHAOXING WINE
- 4 TABLESPOONS LONG-GRAIN RICE
- 10 SICHUAN PEPPERCORNS
- 2 STAR ANISE
- ½ TEASPOON GROUND CINNAMON
- 3 DRIED LOTUS LEAVES, SOAKED IN WATER UNTIL SOFTENED AND CUT INTO 3¼-INCH/8-CM SQUARES
- STEAMED RICE (PAGE 540), TO SERVE

* For the pork belly, scrape the skin clean, then rinse the pork under cold running water.
* Put the pork into a large saucepan and add enough water to cover it completely. Bring to a boil over high heat and blanch the pork for 15 minutes. Drain and rinse under cold running water until cooled. Cut the pork into 2 × 1¼ × ¼-inch/5 × 3 × 0.5-cm slices.
* In a large bowl, combine the ginger, scallions (spring onions), tianmianjiang, soy sauce, and wine. Marinate for 30 minutes.
* Meanwhile, put the rice in a small dry pan and toast over low heat for 4–5 minutes until brown. Add the Sichuan peppercorns and star anise and toast for 2–3 minutes over medium-low heat until fragrant. Remove from the heat, then set aside to cool. Using a pestle and mortar, grind to a coarse powder. Stir in the cinnamon, add 4 tablespoons boiling water, and blend into a paste.
* Coat the pork with the rice paste, place each piece in a lotus leaf square, and wrap into small bundles. Place the bundles onto a heatproof plate or steam rack in a collapsible pot or bamboo steamer over a pot of boiling water. Steam, covered, for 30 minutes.
* Transfer the bundles to a serving plate and serve with rice. Each person takes a bundle and unwraps it. (The lotus leaf is not to be consumed.)

榄角虾干蒸猪肉
PORK WITH PRESERVED
OLIVES AND DRIED SHRIMP

- 2 TABLESPOONS DRIED SHRIMP
- 11 OZ/300 G PORK SHOULDER OR TENDERLOIN, THINLY SLICED
- 1½ TEASPOONS LIGHT SOY SAUCE
- 1 TEASPOON GRANULATED SUGAR
- 1 TEASPOON CORNSTARCH (CORNFLOUR)
- 12 PRESERVED BLACK OLIVES, CHOPPED
- 1 TEASPOON GINGER JUICE
- 1 TABLESPOON VEGETABLE OIL
- STEAMED RICE (PAGE 540), TO SERVE

* Rinse the dried shrimp, put in a bowl of cold water, and soak for 15 minutes. Drain and reserve the soaking water.
* Meanwhile, combine the pork, soy sauce, ½ teaspoon sugar, and 2 tablespoons reserved shrimp water in a bowl. Marinate for 10 minutes, then mix in the cornstarch (cornflour).
* In a heatproof bowl, combine the preserved black olives, ginger juice, and remaining ½ teaspoon sugar. Place in a collapsible pot or bamboo steamer over a pot of boiling water. Steam, covered, for 10 minutes. Carefully remove the bowl from the steamer, mix in the pork and dried shrimp, and stir in the oil. Steam again for 10 minutes, or until cooked through. Serve with rice.

MEAT

萝卜干南瓜蒸肉片
PORK WITH DRIED
TURNIPS AND PUMPKIN

REGION: HONG KONG
PREPARATION TIME: 10 MINUTES
COOKING TIME: 10 MINUTES
SERVES: 4

* Combine the pork, salt, sugar, soy sauce, cornstarch (cornflour), and oil in a bowl and mix well. Add the preserved turnips and stir.
* Place the pumpkin on a heatproof plate, then top with the preserved turnips and pork mixture. Transfer to a collapsible pot or bamboo steamer over a pot of boiling water. Steam, covered, for 10 minutes until cooked through. Serve with rice.

- 11 OZ/300 G SKIN-ON PORK SHOULDER, CUT INTO ¼-INCH/5-MM SLICES
- ½ TEASPOON SALT
- ½ TEASPOON GRANULATED SUGAR
- 1 TEASPOON LIGHT SOY SAUCE
- 1 TEASPOON CORNSTARCH (CORNFLOUR)
- 1 TABLESPOON VEGETABLE OIL
- 2 OZ/50 G PRESERVED TURNIPS, RINSED AND CUT DIAGONALLY INTO THIN SLICES
- 3½ OZ/100 G PUMPKIN, CUT INTO ½-INCH/1-CM-THICK SLICES
- STEAMED RICE (PAGE 540), TO SERVE

客家腐乳肉
PORK WITH FERMENTED
BEAN CURD

REGION: HAKKA
PREPARATION TIME: 10 MINUTES,
   PLUS COOLING TIME
COOKING TIME: 40 MINUTES
SERVES: 4

* Put the pork into a large saucepan and add enough water to cover it completely. Bring to a boil over high heat and blanch the pork for 10 minutes. Skim the froth and scum off the surface, if needed. Drain and rinse under cold running water until cooled. Cut the pork into ½-inch/1-cm-thick slices.
* In a large bowl, combine the fermented bean curd, garlic, bean paste, soy sauce, wine, and sugar to form a paste. Add the pork slices to the bowl and mix well.
* Put the tofu strips on a heatproof plate.
* Place the marinated pork slices on top of the tofu strips, pour the remaining paste mix on top, and put into a collapsible pot or bamboo steamer over a pot of boiling water. Steam, covered, for 30 minutes. Serve with rice.

NOTE:
Deep-fried bean curd sticks can be purchased at Asian food markets. If unavailable, it can be made at home. Heat 2 cups (8 fl oz/475 ml) vegetable oil to 285°F/140°C in a deep saucepan and deep-fry dried bean curd sticks for 2–3 minutes until they puff up.

- 1 (1 LB 2-OZ/500-G) SKIN-ON PORK SHOULDER
- 3 FERMENTED BEAN CURD, MASHED
- 3 CLOVES GARLIC, CHOPPED
- 2 TABLESPOONS BEAN PASTE, MASHED
- 1 TABLESPOON LIGHT SOY SAUCE
- 2 TABLESPOONS GLUTINOUS RICE WINE
- 1 TABLESPOON ROCK SUGAR, CRUSHED
- 7 OZ/200 G DEEP-FRIED BEAN CURD STICKS, RINSED AND CUT INTO 2-INCH/5-CM LENGTHS (SEE NOTE)
- STEAMED RICE (PAGE 540), TO SERVE

PORK AND SPICED RICE ROLLS OVER TOFU SKIN

REGION: ANHUI
PREPARATION TIME: 20 MINUTES,
   PLUS 1 HOUR MARINATING TIME
COOKING TIME: 2 HOURS
SERVES: 4

- 1 (1-LB/450-G) SKIN-ON PORK SHOULDER, TRIMMED INTO A RECTANGLE
- 4 TABLESPOONS LIGHT SOY SAUCE
- 3 TABLESPOONS SHAOXING WINE
- 2 TABLESPOONS GRANULATED SUGAR
- SCANT ½ CUP (4 OZ/120 G) LONG-GRAIN RICE, RINSED AND DRAINED
- 2 STAR ANISE
- 1 CLOVE
- ½ SMALL CINNAMON STICK
- 1 DRIED TOFU SHEET, SOAKED IN WATER UNTIL SOFT AND DRAINED
- STEAMED RICE (PAGE 540), TO SERVE

* Cut the pork into 4-inch/10-cm-wide slices, about ⅛-inch/3-mm thick. Each slice should contain both skin and meat.
* Combine the soy sauce, wine, and sugar in a large bowl, add the pork slices, and marinate for 1 hour.
* Meanwhile, put the rice on a plate lined with paper towels to absorb any excess moisture. Transfer to a dry skillet (frying pan), add the star anise, clove, and cinnamon, and toast over low heat for 4–5 minutes until the rice becomes aromatic and crunchy. Remove and set aside to cool.
* Put the spices and rice into a food processor and pulse until you have coarse crumbs. Add the ground rice to the pork mixture and mix well.
* Spread the softened tofu sheet on a heatproof plate. Roll each piece of pork into a roll and arrange on top of the tofu sheet, skin facing up. Place the plate in a collapsible pot or bamboo steamer over a pot of boiling water. Steam, covered, for 2 hours, or until the pork rolls are cooked through. (Add more water to the pot if needed.) Serve with rice.

PORK JOWLS WITH SHRIMP PASTE

REGION: GUANGDONG
PREPARATION TIME: 10 MINUTES
COOKING TIME: 10 MINUTES
SERVES: 4

- 14 OZ/400 G PORK JOWLS, CUT INTO ½-INCH/1-CM CUBES
- 1½ TABLESPOONS SHRIMP PASTE
- 1 TABLESPOON GRANULATED SUGAR
- 1 OZ/25 G GINGER (ABOUT 2-INCH/5-CM-LENGTH PIECE), GRATED
- 1 TABLESPOON SHAOXING WINE
- 1½ TEASPOONS CORNSTARCH (CORNFLOUR)
- 1 SCALLION (SPRING ONION), SHREDDED, TO GARNISH
- STEAMED RICE (PAGE 540), TO SERVE

Shrimp paste is an ingredient popular in the coastal regions of China as well as in Southeast Asia where it is called by many names such as "belacan" in Malay and "kapi" in Thai. It is made with fermented ground (minced) shrimp and salt and lends a pungent odor and distinctive taste to dishes.

* In a heatproof bowl, combine the pork, shrimp paste, sugar, ginger, wine, and cornstarch (cornflour) and mix well.
* Place the bowl in a collapsible pot or bamboo steamer over a pot of boiling water. Steam, covered, for 10 minutes until cooked through. Carefully remove from the steamer and garnish with the scallions (spring onions). Serve with rice.

梅子蒸猪颈肉
PORK JOWLS WITH
PLUM SAUCE

REGION: HONG KONG
PREPARATION TIME: 10 MINUTES
COOKING TIME: 12 MINUTES
SERVES: 4

* Combine the pork, ginger juice, and cornstarch (cornflour) in a bowl and mix well.
* In a heatproof bowl, combine the salted plums, chile, plum sauce, and the pork. Place in a collapsible pot or bamboo steamer over a pot of boiling water. Steam, covered, for 12 minutes until cooked through. Serve in the bowl with rice.

- 14 OZ/400 G PORK JOWLS, CUT INTO ½-INCH/1-CM CUBES
- 2 TABLESPOONS GINGER JUICE
- 1 TABLESPOON CORNSTARCH (CORNFLOUR)
- 2 SALTED PLUMS, PITTED AND CRUSHED
- 1 RED CHILE, SEEDED AND SLICED
- 2 TABLESPOONS PLUM SAUCE
- STEAMED RICE (PAGE 540), TO SERVE

白菜肉卷
PORK AND
CABBAGE ROLLS

REGION: ANHUI
PREPARATION TIME: 20 MINUTES,
   PLUS 20 MINUTES SOAKING TIME
COOKING TIME: 30 MINUTES
SERVES: 4 (MAKES 8 ROLLS)

* Put the mushrooms in a bowl, cover with cold water, and soak for at least 20 minutes, or until softened.
* Meanwhile, combine the pork, ¼ teaspoon salt, sugar, white pepper, and 2 tablespoons water in a large bowl. Marinate for 15 minutes, then mix in 1 teaspoon cornstarch (cornflour).
* Remove the mushrooms, squeeze dry, and discard the stems. Chop, then add to the pork mixture and mix well. Divide the filling into 8 portions.
* Bring a saucepan of water to a boil, add the cabbage leaves, and blanch for 2–3 minutes until soft. Drain.
* Take a cabbage leaf and lightly dredge one side with a thin layer of cornstarch, then add a portion of filling and roll up, tucking in the ends. Repeat with the remaining leaves, 1 teaspoon cornstarch, and filling.
* Place the rolls on a heatproof plate and put into a collapsible pot or bamboo steamer over a pot of boiling water. Steam, covered, for 20 minutes until cooked through. Drain the water from the plate.
* Pour the chicken broth (stock) into a small saucepan, add the remaining ¼ teaspoon salt, and bring to a boil. Mix the remaining 1 teaspoon cornstarch with 1 tablespoon water in a small bowl and stir this mixture into the pan. Bring to a boil, stirring, for 30 seconds to thicken the sauce. Pour the sauce over the pork and cabbage rolls. Serve with rice.

- 2 DRIED BLACK MUSHROOMS
- 7 OZ/200 G GROUND (MINCED) PORK
- ½ TEASPOON SALT
- ½ TEASPOON GRANULATED SUGAR
- ¼ TEASPOON GROUND WHITE PEPPER
- 1 TABLESPOON CORNSTARCH (CORNFLOUR)
- 8 LARGE NAPA CABBAGE LEAVES
- 4 TABLESPOONS CHICKEN BROTH (STOCK, PAGE 90)
- STEAMED RICE (PAGE 540), TO SERVE

PREPARATION TIME: 20 MINUTES,
    PLUS 2 HOURS 10 MINUTES
    SOAKING TIME
COOKING TIME: 15 MINUTES
SERVES: 4
📷 PAGE 331

珍珠圆子
MEATBALLS WITH GLUTINOUS RICE

- ½ CUP (3½ OZ/100 G) GLUTINOUS RICE, RINSED
- 14 OZ/400 G LEAN PORK, FINELY CHOPPED
- 1 TEASPOON SALT
- 1 TEASPOON GROUND WHITE PEPPER
- 3½ OZ/100 G PORK FATBACK, FINELY CHOPPED
- 4 WATER CHESTNUTS, FINELY CHOPPED
- 1 TEASPOON CHOPPED GINGER
- 2 TABLESPOONS CORNSTARCH (CORNFLOUR)
- STEAMED RICE (PAGE 540), TO SERVE

* Soak the glutinous rice in a large bowl of cold water for 2 hours. Drain and put the rice back into the bowl.
* In a separate bowl, combine the lean pork, salt, white pepper, and 6 tablespoons water. Soak for 10 minutes. Mix in the pork fatback, water chestnuts, ginger, and cornstarch (cornflour).
* Using your hands, form the pork mixture into 1¼-inch/3-cm diameter balls and roll in the glutinous rice to coat. Place the meatballs in a collapsible pot or bamboo steamer over a pot of boiling water. Steam, covered, for 15 minutes until cooked through. Transfer to a serving plate and serve with rice.

REGION: SHANDONG
PREPARATION TIME: 20 MINUTES,
    PLUS 20 MINUTES SOAKING TIME
COOKING TIME: 10 MINUTES
SERVES: 4

蒸白菜肉丸
PORK AND CABBAGE MEATBALLS

- ¼ CUP (¼ OZ/5 G) DRIED BLACK FUNGUS
- 1 TABLESPOON DRIED SHRIMP
- 11 OZ/300 G GROUND (MINCED) PORK
- ½ TEASPOON SALT
- 2-3 NAPA CABBAGE LEAVES, CHOPPED
- 2 BUNCHES CILANTRO (CORIANDER), HALF CHOPPED AND HALF CUT INTO 2-INCH/5-CM LENGTHS
- 1 SCALLION (SPRING ONION), SHREDDED
- 1 EGG WHITE
- ½ TABLESPOON RICE WINE
- ½ TABLESPOON CORNSTARCH (CORNFLOUR)
- ½ TEASPOON GRATED GINGER
- ½ TEASPOON GROUND WHITE PEPPER
- 1 TABLESPOON LIGHT SOY SAUCE
- 1 TABLESPOON WHITE VINEGAR
- ½ TABLESPOON SESAME OIL
- STEAMED RICE (PAGE 540), TO SERVE

* Soak the black fungus in a small bowl of cold water for 20 minutes, or until softened. Remove the fungus, discard the stems, and tear the caps into small pieces.
* Meanwhile, soak the dried shrimp in a bowl of cold water for 5 minutes. Drain, chop, and then set aside.
* Combine the pork and salt in a large bowl and mix thoroughly. Add the shrimp, fungus, cabbage, and chopped cilantro (coriander) and mix well, then add the scallion (spring onion), egg white, wine, cornstarch (cornflour), ginger, and ¼ teaspoon white pepper. Form into 1-inch/2.5-cm meatballs and place on a heatproof plate in a collapsible pot or bamboo steamer over a pot of boiling water. Steam, covered, for 8 minutes until cooked through. Transfer the meatballs to a serving dish.
* Pour the steamed juices into a wok or saucepan, add the soy sauce, vinegar, remaining ¼ teaspoon white pepper, and a scant 1 cup (7 fl oz/200 ml) water and bring to a boil. Stir in the remaining cilantro and sesame oil and pour the sauce over the meatballs. Serve with rice.

MEATBALLS WITH GLUTINOUS RICE

REGION: ZHEJIANG
PREPARATION TIME: 15 MINUTES
COOKING TIME: 1 HOUR 55 MINUTES
SERVES: 4

南乳肉
PORK BELLY WITH
RED BEAN CURD

- 1 (14-OZ/400-G) BONELESS, SKIN-ON PORK BELLY
- ½ TEASPOON RED YEAST RICE OR CHERRY JUICE
- ⅛ OZ/5 G GINGER (ABOUT ½-INCH/1-CM-LENGTH PIECE), SLICED
- 1 SCALLION (SPRING ONION), CUT INTO 2-INCH/5-CM LENGTHS
- 1 TABLESPOON GRANULATED SUGAR
- 1 TABLESPOON SHAOXING WINE
- 2 TEASPOONS LIGHT SOY SAUCE
- 1 CUBE RED BEAN CURD
- ½ TEASPOON SALT
- STEAMED RICE (PAGE 540), TO SERVE

* For the pork belly, scrape the skin clean, then rinse the pork under cold running water.
* Put the pork into a large saucepan and add enough water to cover it completely. Bring to a boil over high heat and blanch the pork for 10 minutes. Skim the froth and scum off the surface, if needed. Drain and rinse under cold running water until cooled. Cut the pork into 1¼-inch/3-cm squares.
* Put the red yeast rice into a small saucepan, add ½ cup (4 fl oz/120 ml) water, and bring to a boil. Reduce to low heat and simmer for about 5 minutes. Strain the mixture through a strainer (sieve) and set aside.
* Mix the ginger, scallion (spring onion), sugar, wine, soy sauce, red bean curd, and salt in a large bowl. Use a large spoon to mash the bean curd. Add the red yeast rice water and 2 tablespoons water and blend all the ingredients. Add the pork and mix until each piece is coated in the sauce.
* Put the coated pork belly pieces into a heatproof bowl, skin facing down. Seal the bowl with aluminum foil, place it in a collapsible pot or bamboo steamer over a pot of boiling water. Steam, covered, for 1 hour 30 minutes. (Add more water to the pot if needed.)
* Transfer to a serving plate and serve with rice.

REGION: YUNNAN
PREPARATION TIME: 10 MINUTES,
  PLUS 20 MINUTES SOAKING TIME
COOKING TIME: 1 HOUR 5 MINUTES
SERVES: 4

蜜汁云腿
YUNNAN HAM IN
HONEYED SAUCE

- 11 OZ/300 G YUNNAN HAM, CUT INTO THIN 2 × 1-INCH/5 × 2.5-CM SLICES
- 2 TABLESPOONS GRANULATED SUGAR
- 4 OZ/100 G ROCK SUGAR, CRUSHED
- 2 PEARS, CORED AND SLICED
- 1½ TABLESPOONS HONEY
- STEAMED RICE (PAGE 540), TO SERVE

* In a heatproof bowl, combine the ham and granulated sugar and add enough boiling water to cover. Soak for 20 minutes, then drain the water.
* Add half of the rock sugar and enough water to cover the ham. Place in a collapsible pot or bamboo steamer over a pot of boiling water. Steam, covered, for 1 hour. Add more water to the pot if needed. Carefully remove the bowl and drain away the water.
* Line the bottom of a heatproof plate with the pear slices and top with the ham. Steam for 5 minutes, then drain away the juices from the plate.
* Meanwhile, in a small saucepan, heat the honey and remaining half of the rock sugar over low heat, stirring frequently to dissolve the sugar. Pour over the ham, then serve with rice.

蜜汁白果火腿
GINKGO NUTS
AND HAM

REGION: HUNAN
PREPARATION TIME: 15 MINUTES
COOKING TIME: 2 HOURS 20 MINUTES
SERVES: 4–6

* Bring a saucepan of water to a boil, add the ginkgo nuts, and blanch for about 15 minutes. Drain and rinse under cold running water. Rub each nut to remove the skin.
* Put the ginkgo nuts in a heatproof bowl and add enough water to cover them completely. Place the bowl in a collapsible pot or bamboo steamer over a pot of water. Steam, covered, over high heat for about 1 hour. (Add more water to the pot if needed.) Drain the ginkgo nuts.
* Meanwhile, line the bottom of a heatproof bowl with the ham slices. Add 2 oz/50 g crushed rock sugar, 1 tablespoon wine, and enough water to cover the ham completely. Place the bowl in a collapsible pot or bamboo steamer over a pot of water. Bring to a boil and steam, covered, for about 1 hour. Drain the sauce, leaving the ham in the bowl.
* Put the ginkgo nuts on top of ham slices in the bowl. Add 2¾ oz/75 g crushed rock sugar and the remaining 2 tablespoons wine. Place the bowl in a collapsible pot or bamboo steamer over a pot of water. Steam, covered, over high heat for 1 hour. (Add more water to the pot if needed.)
* Carefully remove the bowl and drain the liquid. Cover the bowl with a serving plate and, using dish towels, invert the contents onto the plate (alternatively, use tongs to transfer the contents to a serving plate).
* Put the rose sugar, if using, and the remaining 2¾ oz/75 g rock sugar in a wok with 2 tablespoons water and heat over low heat until the sugar dissolves. Mix the cornstarch (cornflour) with 1 tablespoon water and stir the mixture into the wok. Bring to the boil, stirring, for about 30 seconds to thicken the sauce. Drizzle the sauce over the ham and ginkgo nuts to serve.

* 1 CUP (5 OZ/150 G) SHELLED GINKGO NUTS
* 11 OZ/300 G CURED HAM, CUT INTO 1¼ × ½-INCH/3 × 1-CM SLICES
* 7 OZ/200 G ROCK SUGAR, CRUSHED
* 3 TABLESPOONS SHAOXING WINE
* ½ TEASPOON ROSE SUGAR (OPTIONAL)
* 1 TEASPOON CORNSTARCH (CORNFLOUR)

REGION: SHANDONG
PREPARATION TIME: 20 MINUTES,
    PLUS 15 MINUTES MARINATING TIME
COOKING TIME: 1 HOUR 10 MINUTES
SERVES: 4

冬菜五花肉

PORK BELLY WITH PRESERVED CABBAGE

- 1 (1-LB 2-OZ/500-G) SKIN-ON PORK BELLY, CUT INTO 4 × 2-INCH/ 10 × 5-CM SLICES
- 2 TABLESPOONS RICE WINE
- 2 TEASPOONS LIGHT SOY SAUCE
- 2 SCALLIONS (SPRING ONIONS), 1 SHREDDED AND 1 CUT INTO 1½-INCH/4-CM LENGTHS
- 1 TABLESPOON GINGER JUICE
- 3 TABLESPOONS TIANJIN PRESERVED CABBAGE, FINELY CHOPPED
- 2 TABLESPOONS VEGETABLE OIL
- 1 TABLESPOON GRANULATED SUGAR
- SCANT ½ CUP (3½ FL OZ/100 ML) PORK BROTH (STOCK, PAGE 91)
- ½ TEASPOON SALT
- ⅛ OZ/5 G GINGER (ABOUT ½-INCH/ 1-CM-LENGTH PIECE), SLICED
- 1 TEASPOON CORNSTARCH (CORNFLOUR)
- 1 TABLESPOON SICHUAN CHILI OIL
- STEAMED RICE (PAGE 540), TO SERVE

* Combine the pork, 1 tablespoon wine, 1 teaspoon soy sauce, the shredded scallion (spring onion), and ginger juice in a large bowl and marinate for 15 minutes.
* In another bowl, mix the preserved cabbage and 1 tablespoon vegetable oil.
* Heat the remaining 1 tablespoon vegetable oil in a saucepan over medium-low heat, stir in the sugar, and cook 2 minutes until caramelized. Add the broth (stock), salt, the remaining 1 tablespoon wine and 1 teaspoon soy sauce and bring to a boil.
* Lay a slice of pork on a cutting board. Spread the preserved cabbage along the entire length of the pork, then roll the pork slice into a cylinder shape, enclosing the cabbage completely. Repeat with all the pork slices and cabbage. Arrange the pork rolls vertically in a heatproof bowl, skin-side down, drizzle over the sauce, and top with the remaining scallion and ginger slices.
* Seal with aluminum foil and place in a collapsible pot or bamboo steamer over a pot of boiling water. Steam, covered, for 1 hour. (Add more water to the pot if needed.)
* Carefully remove the aluminum foil and drain the sauce into a wok or large skillet (frying pan). Cover the bowl of pork with a serving plate and, using dish towels, invert the pork rolls onto the plate. (Alternatively, use tongs to transfer the content.)
* Bring the sauce in the wok to a boil. Mix the cornstarch (cornflour) with 1 tablespoon water in a small bowl and stir this mixture into the wok. Bring to a boil, stirring, for 30 seconds to thicken the sauce. Stir in the Sichuan chili oil, then pour the sauce over the pork rolls. Serve with rice.

爆糟排骨
SPARERIBS WITH RED DISTILLED GRAIN SAUCE

REGION: FUJIAN
PREPARATION TIME: 5 MINUTES
COOKING TIME: 10 MINUTES
SERVES: 4

* Heat the vegetable oil in a wok or large skillet (frying pan) over medium-low heat, add the garlic, and stir-fry for 1–2 minutes until golden. Remove the garlic with a slotted spoon and set aside.
* Heat the oil remaining in the wok, add the spareribs, and stir-fry over medium heat for 2 minutes until cooked. Transfer the spareribs to a plate and set aside.
* Add the ginger to the wok and stir-fry for 1 minute until fragrant. Add the red distilled grain sauce, fish sauce, salt, wine, five-spice powder, the reserved garlic, and spareribs. Stir-fry over high heat for about 1 minute, then add the broth (stock) and bring to a boil over high heat. Simmer to reduce the sauce for 3–4 minutes.
* Mix the cornstarch (cornflour) with ½ tablespoon water in a small bowl and stir this mixture into the wok. Bring to a boil, stirring, for 30 seconds to thicken the sauce. Stir in the sesame oil, transfer to a serving plate, and serve with rice.

- 3 TABLESPOONS VEGETABLE OIL
- 6 CLOVES GARLIC
- 1 LB 2 OZ/500 G PORK SPARERIBS, CUT INTO 1-INCH/2.5-CM PIECES
- ½ TEASPOON CHOPPED GINGER
- 3 TABLESPOONS RED DISTILLED GRAIN SAUCE
- 2 TABLESPOONS FISH SAUCE
- 2 TABLESPOONS SALT
- 1 TABLESPOON GLUTINOUS WINE
- ¼ TEASPOON FIVE-SPICE POWDER
- 1 CUP (8 FL OZ/250 ML) CHICKEN OR PORK BROTH (STOCK, PAGES 90–91)
- ½ TEASPOON CORNSTARCH (CORNFLOUR)
- ¼ TEASPOON SESAME OIL
- STEAMED RICE (PAGE 540), TO SERVE

梅子蒸排骨
SPARERIBS WITH SALTED PLUMS

REGION: GUANGDONG
PREPARATION TIME: 10 MINUTES, PLUS 10 MINUTES SOAKING TIME
COOKING TIME: 10 MINUTES
SERVES: 4

* Combine the spareribs, salt, and 2 tablespoons water in a large bowl and soak for 10 minutes.
* In another bowl, combine the sour plums, bean paste, garlic, and sugar and use a fork to mash it into a paste.
* Add the paste to the spareribs, then mix with the cornstarch (cornflour) and stir in the vegetable oil. Arrange the spareribs on a heatproof plate and top with the pickled ginger and chile. Place the bowl into a collapsible pot or bamboo steamer over a pot of boiling water. Steam, covered, for 10 minutes until cooked through. Serve immediately with rice.

- 14 OZ/400 G PORK SPARERIBS, CUT INTO SMALL PIECES
- 1 TEASPOON SALT
- 3 SALTED PLUMS, PITTED
- 2 TEASPOONS BEAN PASTE
- 2 CLOVES GARLIC, CHOPPED
- 1 TEASPOON GRANULATED SUGAR
- 1 TEASPOON CORNSTARCH (CORNFLOUR)
- 1 TABLESPOON VEGETABLE OIL
- 8 SLICES PICKLED GINGER (PAGE 296)
- 1 RED CHILE, SEEDED AND FINELY SHREDDED
- STEAMED RICE (PAGE 540), TO SERVE

REGION: HONG KONG
PREPARATION TIME: 5 MINUTES,
   PLUS 30 MINUTES SOAKING TIME
COOKING TIME: 20 MINUTES
SERVES: 4
📷 PAGE 337

京都排骨
JINGDU
SPARERIBS

- 2 TEASPOONS SALT
- 4 (8-OZ/200-G) BONE-IN PORK
  SHOULDER CHOPS, RINSED
- 2 TABLESPOONS RED VINEGAR
- 2 TABLESPOONS KETCHUP
- 1 TABLESPOON GRANULATED SUGAR
- 1 TEASPOON WORCESTERSHIRE SAUCE
- 1 TEASPOON LIGHT SOY SAUCE
- 2 TABLESPOONS VEGETABLE OIL
- ¼ OZ/10 G GINGER (ABOUT ¾-INCH/
  2-CM-LENGTH PIECE), SLICED
- 3 TABLESPOONS SHAOXING WINE
- 2 SCALLIONS (SPRING ONIONS),
  SHREDDED, TO GARNISH (OPTIONAL)
- CILANTRO (CORIANDER), TO GARNISH
  TO GARNISH
- STEAMED RICE (PAGE 540), NOODLES,
  OR POTATOES, TO SERVE

* Mix the salt and 2 cups (16 fl oz/475 ml) water in a bowl
  and add the pork. Soak for 30 minutes. Drain and rinse.
* Put the pork into a large saucepan and add enough water
  to cover it completely. Bring to a boil over high heat and
  blanch the pork for 1 minute. Drain and rinse under cold
  running water.
* Combine the vinegar, ketchup, sugar, Worcestershire sauce,
  and soy sauce in a small bowl to make a sauce. Set aside.
* Heat the oil in a wok or large skillet (frying pan) over
  medium-high heat, add the ginger, and stir-fry for 1 minute
  until fragrant. Add the pork and pan-fry for 3–4 minutes
  until golden brown on both sides. Sprinkle the wine in along
  the inside of the wok, stir in the sauce, and add just enough
  water to cover the pork. Bring to a boil, then reduce to
  medium-high heat and cook for about 5 minutes. Reduce
  to medium-low heat and simmer for another 3–4 minutes
  until the sauce thickens and the pork is cooked through.
  Transfer to a serving plate, garnish with scallions (spring
  onions) and cilantro (coriander), if using, and serve with
  rice, noodles, or potatoes.

REGION: SHANDONG
PREPARATION TIME: 5 MINUTES
COOKING TIME: 15 MINUTES
SERVES: 4

茶香排骨
SPARERIBS IN TEA

- 11 OZ/300 G PORK SPARERIBS,
  CUT INTO 1½-INCH/4-CM PIECES
- 2½ TABLESPOONS JASMINE TEA LEAVES
- 1 TABLESPOON VEGETABLE OIL
- 1 TEASPOON CHOPPED GINGER
- 1 SCALLION (SPRING ONION),
  CHOPPED
- 2 TABLESPOONS LIGHT SOY SAUCE
- 1 TEASPOON SHAOXING WINE
- ½ TEASPOON SALT
- 1 TABLESPOON SICHUAN CHILI OIL
- STEAMED RICE (PAGE 540), TO SERVE

* Put the spareribs into a large saucepan and add enough
  water to cover them completely. Bring to a boil over high
  heat and blanch for 5 minutes. Drain and rinse under cold
  running water.
* Meanwhile, combine the tea leaves and 1 cup (8 fl oz/
  250 ml) boiling water and steep for 5 minutes.
* Heat the vegetable oil in a Dutch oven (casserole) over
  medium-high heat, add the ginger and scallion (spring
  onion), and stir-fry for 1 minute until fragrant. Add the
  spareribs, soy sauce, wine, and stir-fry for about 2 minutes.
  Pour in the jasmine tea, reserving the tea leaves, bring to a
  boil, and cook for about 5 minutes until the pork is cooked
  through. Stir in the tea leaves and drizzle in the Sichuan
  chili oil. Transfer to a serving dish and serve with rice.

MEAT

JINGDU SPARERIBS

茶烧肉
SAUTÉED PORK
WITH TEA LEAVES

- 1 (11-OZ/300-G) BONELESS, SKIN-ON PORK BELLY
- 3 TABLESPOONS JASMINE TEA LEAVES
- 2 TABLESPOONS VEGETABLE OIL
- 1 TEASPOON CHOPPED GINGER
- ½ SCALLION (SPRING ONION), CHOPPED
- 1 TABLESPOON RICE WINE
- 1 TABLESPOON LIGHT SOY SAUCE
- ½ TEASPOON GRANULATED SUGAR
- ½ TEASPOON SALT
- 1 TABLESPOON SICHUAN CHILI OIL
- STEAMED RICE (PAGE 540), TO SERVE

* For the pork belly, scrape the skin clean, then rinse the pork under cold running water.
* Put the pork into a large saucepan and add enough water to cover it completely. Bring to a boil over high heat and blanch the pork for 5 minutes. Drain. Rinse under cold running water until cooled. Cut the pork into 1¼-inch/ 3-cm chunks.
* Put the tea in a teapot and add boiling water. Pour out the tea and reserve the tea leaves.
* Heat the vegetable oil in a wok or large skillet (frying pan), add the ginger and scallion (spring onion), and stir-fry over medium-high heat for 1 minute until fragrant. Put in the pork and stir. Add the wine, soy sauce, sugar, and salt and mix thoroughly. Reduce to low heat and stir-fry for another 5 minutes until the pork is cooked. Add the reserved tea leaves and chili oil, toss, and transfer to a serving plate. Serve with rice.

酸菜炖排骨
PICKLED VEGETABLE AND
SPARERIB CASSEROLE

- 2 OZ/50 G DRIED MUNG BEAN STARCH STRIPS
- 9 OZ/250 G PORK SPARERIBS, CUT INTO 1-INCH/2.5-CM PIECES
- 2 POTATOES, CUT INTO CHUNKS
- 1 BEIJING SCALLION OR 3 SCALLIONS (SPRING ONIONS), CUT INTO 2-INCH/5-CM LENGTHS
- ⅛ OZ/5 G GINGER (ABOUT ½-INCH/ 1-CM-LENGTH PIECE), SLICED
- ½ TEASPOON SALT
- 1 TABLESPOON RICE WINE
- 2 TABLESPOONS VEGETABLE OIL
- 5 OZ/150 G PICKLED NAPA CABBAGE, RINSED AND CUT INTO THIN STRIPS
- STEAMED RICE (PAGE 540), TO SERVE

* Soak the mung bean starch strips in a bowl of cold water for 30 minutes until soft. Drain and set aside.
* Meanwhile, in a medium saucepan, add the spareribs and enough water to cover them completely. Bring to a boil over high heat and blanch for 2 minutes. Drain and rinse under cold running water.
* Put 4¼ cups (34 fl oz/1 liter) water in a Dutch oven (casserole), add the spareribs, potatoes, Beijing scallion, ginger, salt, and wine, and bring to a boil over high heat. Reduce to low heat and simmer, covered, for 1 hour.
* Heat the oil in a wok or large skillet (frying pan), add the pickled cabbage and stir-fry over medium heat for 1 minute. Transfer the pickled cabbage to the Dutch oven and cook for another 20 minutes. Add the mung bean starch strips and cook for another 5 minutes. Serve in the Dutch oven with rice.

南煎丸子
PAN-FRIED MEATBALLS

REGION: SHANDONG
PREPARATION TIME: 20 MINUTES
COOKING TIME: 10 MINUTES
SERVES: 4

* Combine the pork, egg whites, salt, and cornstarch (cornflour) in a large bowl. Using chopsticks, stir in one direction until the ingredients are well combined and gluey. Mix in the water chestnuts and ham. Use your hands to form 1-inch/2.5-cm-diameter meatballs. Set aside.
* Combine the chicken broth (stock), wine, sugar, and soy sauce in a small bowl to make a sauce. Set aside.
* Heat 2 tablespoons vegetable oil in a wok or large skillet (frying pan), add the meatballs, and use a spatula (fish slice) to flatten them slightly into patties. (Work in batches if necessary.) Pan-fry the patties for 2 minutes over medium heat until browned. Flip over and pan-fry for another 2 minutes until cooked through. Remove from the pan.
* Heat the remaining 1 tablespoon vegetable oil in the wok over medium-high heat and stir-fry the ginger and scallion (spring onion) for 1 minute until fragrant. Add the meatballs, sauce, and sesame oil and cook over high heat for 2 minutes until the sauce is reduced. Transfer the meatballs to a serving plate and serve as a snack on their own or with rice for a more substantial meal.

* 7 OZ/200 G GROUND (MINCED) PORK
* 2 EGG WHITES
* ½ TEASPOON SALT
* 2 TABLESPOONS CORNSTARCH (CORNFLOUR)
* 5 WATER CHESTNUTS, COARSELY CHOPPED
* ¾ OZ/20 G JINHUA OR SMITHFIELD HAM, CHOPPED
* 2 TABLESPOONS CHICKEN BROTH (STOCK, PAGE 90)
* 1 TABLESPOONS RICE WINE
* 1 TEASPOON GRANULATED SUGAR
* 2 TEASPOON LIGHT SOY SAUCE
* 3 TABLESPOONS VEGETABLE OIL
* 2 TEASPOONS CHOPPED GINGER
* 1 SCALLION (SPRING ONION), CHOPPED
* 1 TEASPOON SESAME OIL
* STEAMED RICE (PAGE 540), TO SERVE (OPTIONAL)

浏阳合蒸
LIUYANG-STYLE MEATBALLS

REGION: HUNAN
PREPARATION TIME: 15 MINUTES, PLUS 1 HOUR STANDING TIME
COOKING TIME: 40 MINUTES
SERVES: 4

Liuyang is a city in the province of Hunan where they like to steam their foods. It's common to see several plates of food cooked in a steamer or wok at the same time.

* In a bowl, combine the pork and salt and let stand for 1 hour.
* Rinse the preserved fish with warm water and place it on a heatproof plate. Put the plate into a collapsible pot or bamboo steamer over a pot of boiling water. Steam, covered, for 10 minutes. Scale the fish and cut into pieces similar in size to the pork.
* In a small bowl, combine the sugar and garlic. Line the bottom of a heatproof bowl with the pickled string (green) beans, followed by the fish and pork. Top with the fermented black beans and chiles, then steam for 30 minutes until the pork is cooked through. Serve with rice.

* 1 (11-OZ/300-G) BONELESS, SKIN-ON PORK BELLY, CUT INTO 1½ × ¼-INCH/ 4 × 0.5-CM STRIPS
* 1 TEASPOON SALT
* 7 OZ/200 G PRESERVED FISH
* 1½ TABLESPOONS GRANULATED SUGAR
* 3 CLOVES GARLIC, CHOPPED
* 7 OZ/200 G PICKLED STRING (GREEN) BEANS, CUT INTO SECTIONS
* 1½ TABLESPOONS FERMENTED BLACK BEANS, RINSED AND CHOPPED
* 4 RED CHILES, SLICED DIAGONALLY
* STEAMED RICE (PAGE 540), TO SERVE

REGION: FUJIAN
PREPARATION TIME: 10 MINUTES,
  PLUS 15 MINUTES SOAKING TIME
COOKING TIME: 10 MINUTES
MAKES: 18
📷 PAGE 341

福州荔枝肉
FUZHOU LYCHEE
MEATBALLS

- 9 OZ/250 G GROUND (MINCED) LEAN PORK
- ¾ TEASPOON SALT
- ½ TEASPOON GRANULATED SUGAR
- 1 TABLESPOON CORNSTARCH (CORNFLOUR)
- 3 WATER CHESTNUTS, COARSELY CHOPPED
- 2 CUPS (16 FL OZ/475 ML) VEGETABLE OIL
- 2 CLOVES GARLIC, SLICED
- STEAMED RICE (PAGE 540), TO SERVE

FOR THE SAUCE:
- 1 TABLESPOON RED DISTILLED GRAIN SAUCE
- 2 TABLESPOONS GRANULATED SUGAR
- 3 TABLESPOONS RED VINEGAR

While there are no lychees in the recipe, the meatballs are made to resemble lychees: from the reddish color of the meatballs to the water chestnut, which resemble the fruit.

* Combine the pork, salt, sugar, and 3 tablespoons water in a bowl, stir well, and soak for 15 minutes. Using chopsticks, stir the pork in a single direction for about a minute, or until the mixture becomes elastic and gummy. Add the cornstarch (cornflour) and mix thoroughly. Use your hands to divide the mixture into 18 equal-size rough patties.
* Place 1 or 2 pieces of water chestnuts into the center of a patty and cover with the meat, shaping the pork into a meatball. Repeat with the remaining water chestnuts and meat.
* To make the sauce, combine the ingredients in a mortar and pestle and pound until well mixed. Set aside.
* Heat the oil in a wok or large skillet (frying pan) over low heat, add the meatballs, in batches if needed, and fry for 2–3 minutes until lightly browned. Remove and set aside.
* Pour out most of the oil, leaving about 1 tablespoon in the wok. Heat the oil over medium heat, add the garlic, and stir-fry for 1–2 minutes until fragrant. Discard the garlic and stir in the sauce. Add the meatballs and sauté. Increase to high heat and cook, uncovered, for another minute to thicken the sauce. Serve with rice.

FUZHOU LYCHEE MEATBALLS

REGION: CHAOZHOU
PREPARATION TIME: 10 MINUTES,
    PLUS 8 HOURS DRYING TIME
COOKING TIME: 30 MINUTES
SERVES: 4

脆姜鱼露炒猪肉

PORK WITH CRISPY GINGER

- 2 OZ/50 G GINGER (ABOUT 3-INCH/7.5-CM-LENGTH PIECE), UNPEELED AND CUT INTO VERY THIN SLICES
- 1½ TEASPOONS BROWN SUGAR
- 1 (14-OZ/400-G) BONELESS, SKIN-ON PORK BELLY
- ½ CUP (4 FL OZ/120 ML) VEGETABLE OIL
- 1½ TABLESPOONS FISH SAUCE
- 2 TABLESPOONS SHAOXING WINE
- STEAMED RICE (PAGE 540), TO SERVE

* In a shallow bowl, combine the ginger with 1 teaspoon brown sugar. Spread the ginger in a single layer on a tray and leave to dry for 8 hours.
* For the pork belly, scrape the skin clean, then rinse the pork under cold running water. Put the pork into a large saucepan and add enough water to cover it completely. Bring to a boil over high heat and blanch the pork for 20 minutes. Drain and rinse under cold water. Cut the pork into ¼-inch/5-mm-thick slices and set aside.
* Heat the oil in a wok or deep saucepan to 340°F/170°C, or until a cube of bread browns in 45 seconds. Gently lower the ginger into the oil and deep-fry for 1–2 minutes until crispy. Use a slotted spoon to carefully remove the ginger and drain on paper towels.
* Pour out most of the oil, leaving about 2 tablespoons in the wok. Heat the oil over medium heat, add the pork and half the amount of crispy ginger, and stir-fry for 1–2 minutes. Stir in the fish sauce and 1 tablespoon wine and stir-fry for 1 minute until the liquid has evaporated. Add the remaining 1 tablespoon wine and ½ teaspoon brown sugar and stir-fry for a few seconds, then stir in the crispy ginger. Transfer to a serving plate and serve with rice.

REGION: GUIZHOU
PREPARATION TIME: 15 MINUTES
COOKING TIME: 10 MINUTES
SERVES: 4

炸酥肉

PORK WITH SPICED SALT

- 3 TABLESPOONS ALL-PURPOSE (PLAIN) FLOUR
- 1 TABLESPOON CORNSTARCH (CORNFLOUR)
- 1½ TEASPOONS SALT
- ¼ TEASPOON BAKING SODA (BICARBONATE OF SODA)
- 2 CUPS (16 FL OZ/475 ML) PLUS ½ TABLESPOON VEGETABLE OIL
- 7 OZ/200 G PORK TENDERLOIN, CUT INTO 1¼-INCH/3-CM-THICK SLICES
- ¼ TEASPOON GROUND SICHUAN PEPPER

* To make the batter, combine the flour, cornstarch (cornflour), ½ teaspoon salt, baking soda (bicarbonate of soda), and 4 tablespoons water in a bowl. Set aside for 10 minutes, then stir in the oil.
* Meanwhile, use a meat mallet or heavy cleaver to pound the pork tenderloin slices repeatedly until very thin.
* To make the spiced salt, heat 1 teaspoon salt in a skillet (frying pan) over low heat, then remove from the heat. Add the ground Sichuan pepper and mix thoroughly. Set aside.
* Heat the oil in a wok or deep saucepan to 340°F/170°C, or until a cube of bread browns in 45 seconds. Dip the pork tenderloin into the batter, then gently lower into the hot oil. Deep-fry for 2–3 minutes until golden brown and cooked through. Use a slotted spoon to carefully remove the pork from the oil and drain on paper towels. Transfer to a serving plate and sprinkle with the spiced salt.

MEAT

酱爆肉条

STIR-FRIED PORK TENDERLOIN

REGION: BEIJING
PREPARATION TIME: 10 MINUTES
COOKING TIME: 10 MINUTES
SERVES: 4

* Combine the pork slices, half the egg white, 1 tablespoon cornstarch (cornflour), and 2 tablespoons water in a bowl. (Discard the remaining egg white or save for another recipe.) Set aside.
* Bring a saucepan of water to a boil over high heat. Add the bamboo shoots and blanch for 1 minute. Drain and rinse under cold running water.
* In a small bowl, combine the chicken broth (stock), the remaining ½ tablespoon cornstarch, the fermented bean curd, sugar, salt, and soy sauce into a sauce.
* Heat the oil in a wok or deep saucepan to 340°F/170°C, or until a cube of bread browns in 45 seconds. Gently lower the pork into the oil, using chopsticks to disperse the pieces rapidly to prevent sticking, and deep-fry for 1 minute until the pork turns white. Use a slotted spoon to carefully transfer the pork and drain in a colander.
* Pour out most of the oil, leaving about 2 tablespoons in the wok. Heat the oil over high heat, add the scallion (spring onion), ginger, and garlic, and stir-fry for a minute until fragrant. Add the bamboo shoots, cucumber, and pork and stir-fry for another 2 minutes until the pork is fully cooked. Pour in the sauce and stir-fry for 1–2 minutes until the sauce thickens. Transfer to a serving plate and serve with rice.

- 7 OZ/200 G PORK TENDERLOIN, CUT INTO 2½ × ¼-INCH/6 × 0.5-CM STRIPS
- 1 EGG WHITE, BEATEN
- 1½ TABLESPOONS CORNSTARCH (CORNFLOUR)
- ⅓ CUP (2 OZ/50 G) SLICED BAMBOO SHOOTS, DRAINED
- 2 TABLESPOONS CHICKEN BROTH (STOCK, PAGE 90)
- 1 CUBE FERMENTED BEAN CURD, MASHED
- 1½ TEASPOONS GRANULATED SUGAR
- ½ TEASPOON SALT
- 2 TEASPOONS LIGHT SOY SAUCE
- 2 CUPS (16 FL OZ/475 ML) VEGETABLE OIL
- 1 SCALLION (SPRING ONION), SHREDDED
- 1 TEASPOON CHOPPED GINGER
- 2 CLOVES GARLIC, CHOPPED
- 1 CUCUMBER, CUT INTO STRIPS
- STEAMED RICE (PAGE 540), TO SERVE

REGION: SICHUAN
PREPARATION TIME: 10 MINUTES,
  PLUS 20 MINUTES SOAKING TIME
COOKING TIME: 10 MINUTES
SERVES: 4

鱼香肉丝
PORK IN
GARLIC SAUCE

- ½ CUP (¼ OZ/10 G) DRIED BLACK FUNGUS
- 9 OZ/250 G PORK TENDERLOIN, CUT INTO FINE STRIPS
- ½ TABLESPOON LIGHT SOY SAUCE
- 2 TABLESPOONS VEGETABLE OIL
- ½ TEASPOON CHOPPED GINGER
- 3 CLOVES GARLIC, CHOPPED
- 1 OZ/25 G PICKLED CHILES, CHOPPED
- 1 TABLESPOON RICE WINE
- ½ TABLESPOON GRANULATED SUGAR
- ½ TEASPOON SALT
- 1 TABLESPOON BLACK OR BALSAMIC VINEGAR
- ¼ CUP (1 OZ/25 G) SLICED BAMBOO SHOOTS, DRAINED
- 1 TEASPOON CORNSTARCH (CORNFLOUR)
- ½ TEASPOON SESAME OIL
- STEAMED RICE (PAGE 540), TO SERVE

* Soak the black fungus in a large bowl of cold water for 15 minutes, or until softened.
* Bring a saucepan of water to a boil over high heat, add the black fungus, and blanch for 3 minutes. Drain and rinse under cold running water, then cut into fine strips.
* Meanwhile, in a bowl, combine the pork, soy sauce, and 1 tablespoon water and marinate for 15 minutes.
* Heat the vegetable oil in a wok or large skillet (frying pan), add the ginger, garlic, and chiles, and stir-fry over medium-high heat for 1 minute until fragrant. Put in the pork and stir-fry for another 2 minutes until just cooked through. Stir in the wine, sugar, salt, vinegar, and 2 tablespoons water and bring to a boil. Add the black fungus and bamboo shoots and cook for another minute. Mix the cornstarch (cornflour) with 1 tablespoon water in a small bowl and stir this mixture into the wok. Bring to a boil, stirring, for 30 seconds to thicken the sauce.
* Stir in the sesame oil and transfer to a serving plate. Serve with rice.

REGION: SHAANXI
PREPARATION TIME: 10 MINUTES
COOKING TIME: 5 MINUTES
SERVES: 4

姜芽肉丝
PORK WITH SPRING GINGER

- 7 OZ/200 G PORK TENDERLOIN, CUT INTO 1½-INCH/4-CM-LONG STRIPS
- 2 TEASPOONS SHAOXING WINE
- 1 TABLESPOON LIGHT SOY SAUCE
- 1 TEASPOON CORNSTARCH (CORNFLOUR)
- 1 CUP (8 FL OZ/250 ML) VEGETABLE OIL
- 3½ OZ/100 G YOUNG GINGER (ABOUT 6-INCH/15-CM-LENGTH PIECE), SHREDDED INTO ½-INCH/4-CM-LONG STRIPS
- 2 SCALLIONS (SPRING ONIONS), SHREDDED INTO ½-INCH/4-CM-LONG STRIPS
- ⅓ TEASPOON SALT, PLUS EXTRA TO TASTE
- STEAMED RICE (PAGE 540), TO SERVE

Fresh ginger is aromatic, zesty, and ubiquitous in Chinese cuisine, while spring ginger is fresh, juicy, and mild in taste. The skin is translucent and can be rubbed, rather than peeled, off.

* Combine the pork, 1 teaspoon wine, 1 teaspoon soy sauce, and the cornstarch (cornflour) in a bowl and set aside.
* Heat the oil in a wok or deep saucepan to 325°C/160°C, or until a cube of bread browns in 1 minute. Stir in the pork strips and cook for 3–4 minutes until the pork begins to brown. Transfer to a plate lined with paper towels.
* Pour out most of the oil, leaving 2 tablespoons in the wok. Add the ginger and scallions (spring onions) and stir-fry over high heat for 1 minute until fragrant. Add the pork, salt, the remaining 1 teaspoon wine, and 2 teaspoons soy sauce and toss to mix all the ingredients. Season with salt to taste. Transfer to a serving plate and serve with rice.

芙蓉肉丝
SHANDONG
PORK

REGION: SHANDONG
PREPARATION TIME: 15 MINUTES,
   PLUS 20 MINUTES SOAKING TIME
COOKING TIME: 10 MINUTES
SERVES: 4

* Soak the black fungus in a small bowl of cold water for 20 minutes, or until softened. Remove the fungus, discard the stems, and cut into thin slices.
* Meanwhile, soak the pork in a bowl of cold water for 10 minutes. Drain and mix with ½ teaspoon salt.
* Bring a saucepan of water to a boil over high heat. Add the bamboo shoots, black fungus, and peas and blanch for 2 minutes. Drain and rinse under cold running water.
* Beat the egg white in a bowl until foamy, add the cornstarch (cornflour), and mix into an egg white batter. Add the pork and mix well.
* Heat the oil in a wok or deep saucepan to 275°F/140°C, or until a cube of bread turns golden in 2 minutes. Gently lower the pork into the oil, using chopsticks to disperse the pieces rapidly to prevent sticking, and deep-fry for 2–3 minutes until golden brown and cooked through. Use a slotted spoon to carefully remove the pork from the oil and drain on paper towels.
* Pour out most of the oil, leaving about 1 tablespoon in the wok. Add the scallion (spring onion) and ginger and stir-fry for 1 minute over medium-high heat until fragrant. Add the bamboo shoots, black fungus, peas, pork, ham, chicken broth (stock), wine, and the remaining ½ teaspoon salt and stir-fry for 1–2 minutes over high heat. Transfer to a serving plate and serve with rice.

- ¼ CUP (⅛ OZ/5 G) DRIED BLACK FUNGUS
- 5 OZ/150 G PORK TENDERLOIN, CUT INTO THIN 2¾-INCH/7-CM-LONG STRIPS
- 1 TEASPOON SALT
- ¼ CUP (1 OZ/25 G) SLICED BAMBOO SHOOTS, DRAINED
- 2 TABLESPOONS PEAS
- 1 EGG WHITE
- 1 TEASPOON CORNSTARCH (CORNFLOUR)
- 1 CUP (8 FL OZ/250 ML) VEGETABLE OIL
- ½ SCALLION (SPRING ONION), SHREDDED
- ⅛ OZ/5 G GINGER (ABOUT ½-INCH/ 1-CM-LENGTH PIECE), SHREDDED
- 1 OZ/30 G COOKED HAM, CUT INTO THIN STRIPS
- 3 TABLESPOONS CHICKEN BROTH (STOCK, PAGE 90)
- 1 TABLESPOON RICE WINE
- STEAMED RICE (PAGE 540), TO SERVE

REGION: BEIJING
PREPARATION TIME: 10 MINUTES,
    PLUS 30 MINUTES SOAKING TIME
COOKING TIME: 5 MINUTES
SERVES: 4
📷 PAGE 347

芫爆里脊
PORK TENDERLOIN
WITH CILANTRO

- 9 OZ/250 G PORK TENDERLOIN,
  CUT ON THE DIAGONAL INTO THIN
  1½ × 1-INCH/4 × 2.5-CM SLICES
- 1 TABLESPOON SHAOXING WINE
- ½ TEASPOON SALT
- ½ EGG WHITE
- 1 TEASPOON CORNSTARCH
  (CORNFLOUR)
- 4 BUNCHES CILANTRO (CORIANDER),
  CUT INTO 1½-INCH/4-CM LENGTHS
- 2 SCALLIONS (SPRING ONIONS),
  SHREDDED
- 4 CLOVES GARLIC, SLICED
- 2 TEASPOONS GINGER JUICE
- 1 TEASPOON WHITE VINEGAR
- ¼ TEASPOON GROUND WHITE PEPPER
- 3 TABLESPOONS VEGETABLE OIL
- 1 TABLESPOON SESAME OIL
- STEAMED RICE (PAGE 540), TO SERVE

* Soak the pork in a large bowl of cold water for about
  30 minutes until the meat begins to turn white. Squeeze
  the water out of the pork, then mix in 1 teaspoon wine,
  ¼ teaspoon salt, the egg white, and cornstarch (cornflour).
* In another bowl, combine the cilantro (coriander), scallions
  (spring onions), garlic, remaining 2 teaspoons wine and
  ¼ teaspoon salt, the ginger juice, vinegar, and white pepper
  and mix into a sauce.
* Heat the vegetable oil in a wok or large skillet (frying pan),
  add the pork, and stir-fry over high heat for 2–3 minutes
  until the pork is just cooked through. Transfer to a plate.
  Add the sauce to the wok, then bring to a boil. Return the
  pork to the wok and stir-fry for another 2 minutes over
  high heat until the sauce is reduced and the pork is fully
  cooked. Add the sesame oil and toss thoroughly. Transfer
  to a serving plate and serve with rice.

茄子火腩煲
EGGPLANT WITH ROAST PORK

- 2 CUPS (16 FL OZ/475 ML) VEGETABLE
  OIL, PLUS 1 TABLESPOON
- 1 LB 5 OZ/600 G (ABOUT 2 MEDIUM)
  EGGPLANTS (AUBERGINES), STEMS
  REMOVED AND CUT INTO BITE-SIZE
  CHUNKS
- 1½ OZ/40 G GINGER (ABOUT 2½-INCH/
  6-CM-LENGTH PIECE), SLICED
- 2 CLOVES GARLIC, SLICED
- 2 SHALLOTS, SLICED
- ½ TABLESPOONS BEAN PASTE
- 11 OZ/300 G ROAST PORK, CHOPPED
- 1 TABLESPOON RICE WINE
- ½ TEASPOON GRANULATED SUGAR
- 1 TEASPOON LIGHT SOY SAUCE
- 3 SCALLIONS (SPRING ONIONS), CUT
  INTO 1½-INCH/4-CM PIECES

* Heat the oil in a wok or deep fryer to 340°F/170°C, or
  until a cube of bread browns in 45 seconds. Gently lower
  the eggplants (aubergines) into the oil and deep-fry for
  2 minutes until they are just about half done. Use a slotted
  spoon to carefully remove the eggplants from the oil and
  drain on paper towels.
* Heat 1 tablespoon oil in a Dutch oven (casserole), add the
  ginger, garlic, and shallots, and stir-fry over high heat for
  1 minute until fragrant. Stir in the bean paste and roast
  pork, sprinkle in the wine, and stir-fry rapidly for another
  30 seconds. Add the eggplants, sugar, soy sauce, scallions
  (spring onions), and 3 tablespoons boiling water. Stir,
  cover, and cook for about 2 minutes until the eggplants
  are tender. Turn off the heat and serve in the Dutch oven.

PORK TENDERLOIN WITH CILANTRO

糖醋里脊

PORK TENDERLOIN WITH SWEET AND SOUR SAUCE

- 11 OZ/300 G PORK TENDERLOIN, CUT INTO ¾-INCH/2-CM CUBES
- ½ TABLESPOON LIGHT SOY SAUCE
- 3 TABLESPOONS CORNSTARCH (CORNFLOUR)
- 3 CUPS (25 FL OZ/750 ML) VEGETABLE OIL
- 2 SCALLIONS (SPRING ONIONS), CUT INTO 1½-INCH/4-CM LENGTHS
- 1 TEASPOON SESAME OIL
- STEAMED RICE (PAGE 540), TO SERVE

  FOR THE SWEET AND SOUR SAUCE:
- 2 TABLESPOONS GRANULATED SUGAR
- 2 TABLESPOONS ZHENJIANG OR BALSAMIC VINEGAR
- 2 TABLESPOONS CORNSTARCH (CORNFLOUR)
- 1 TABLESPOON LIGHT SOY SAUCE
- 1 TABLESPOON GINGER JUICE
- 1 TEASPOON SALT

* In a large bowl, combine the pork, ½ tablespoon soy sauce, and 4 tablespoons water and marinate for 10 minutes. Stir in 3 tablespoons cornstarch (cornflour).
* To make the sweet and sour sauce, combine all the ingredients in a small bowl and mix well. Set aside.
* Heat the vegetable oil in a wok or deep saucepan to 340°F/170°C, or until a cube of bread browns in 45 seconds. Gently lower the pork into the oil, using chopsticks to disperse the pieces rapidly to prevent sticking, and deep-fry for 1 minute. Use a slotted spoon to carefully remove the pork from the oil and drain on paper towels. Reheat the oil to 340°F/170°C, return the pork to the wok, and deep-fry for 2–3 minutes until golden brown and cooked through. Remove to a colander to drain.
* Pour out most of the oil, leaving about 1 tablespoon in the wok.
* Heat the oil over medium-high heat, add the scallions (spring onions), and stir-fry for 1 minute until fragrant.
* Add the pork and sweet and sour sauce and toss over high heat until the sauce thickens. Stir in the sesame oil and transfer to a serving plate. Serve with rice.

过油肉
PORK WITH
VINEGAR SAUCE

REGION: SHAANXI
PREPARATION TIME: 15 MINUTES,
  PLUS 20 MINUTES SOAKING TIME
COOKING TIME: 10 MINUTES
SERVES: 4

* Combine the pork, the egg yolk and 1 teaspoon cornstarch (cornflour) in a bowl, mix well, and set aside.
* Soak the black fungus in a small bowl of cold water for 20 minutes, or until softened. Remove the fungus, discard the stems, and tear into small pieces.
* Heat the vegetable oil in a wok or deep saucepan to 300°F/150°C, or until a cube of bread browns in 1½ minutes. Gently lower the pork into the oil, using chopsticks to disperse the pieces rapidly to prevent sticking, and shallow-fry for 2 minutes until golden brown and cooked through. Use a slotted spoon to carefully remove the pork from the oil and drain on paper towels.
* Pour out most of the oil, leaving 1 tablespoon in the wok. Heat the oil over medium-high heat, add the garlic, ginger, and scallion (spring onion), and stir-fry for 1 minute until fragrant. Add the black fungus and bamboo shoots and stir-fry for another minute.
* Return the pork to the wok and add the soy sauce and wine. Mix the remaining ½ teaspoon cornstarch with 1 tablespoon water in a small bowl and stir this mixture into the wok. Bring to a boil, stirring, for 30 seconds to thicken the sauce. Stir in the vinegar, drizzle in the sesame oil, then transfer to a serving plate. Serve with rice.

- 5 OZ/150 G PORK TENDERLOIN, THINLY SLICED
- 1 EGG YOLK
- 1½ TEASPOONS CORNSTARCH (CORNFLOUR)
- ¼ CUP (⅛ OZ/5 G) DRIED BLACK FUNGUS
- 1 CUP (8 FL OZ/250 ML) VEGETABLE OIL
- 2 CLOVES GARLIC, SLICED
- ½ TABLESPOON GRATED GINGER
- 1 TABLESPOON FINELY CHOPPED SCALLION (SPRING ONION)
- ¼ CUP (1 OZ/25 G) SLICED BAMBOO SHOOTS, DRAINED
- 1 TEASPOON LIGHT SOY SAUCE
- 1 TABLESPOON RICE WINE
- 1 TEASPOON BLACK OR BALSAMIC VINEGAR
- 1 TEASPOON SESAME OIL
- STEAMED RICE (PAGE 540), TO SERVE

REGION: NORTHEAST
PREPARATION TIME: 15 MINUTES,
  PLUS 20 MINUTES SOAKING TIME
COOKING TIME: 10 MINUTES
SERVES: 2
📷 PAGE 351

木须肉

MUXU

PORK

- ¼ CUP (⅛ OZ/5 G) DRIED BLACK FUNGUS
- 5 OZ/150 G LEAN PORK, CUT INTO THIN STRIPS
- ½ TEASPOON LIGHT SOY SAUCE
- 1 TEASPOON CORNSTARCH (CORNFLOUR)
- 2 TABLESPOONS PLUS 1 TEASPOON VEGETABLE OIL
- 3 EGGS, BEATEN
- ⅛ OZ/5 G GINGER (ABOUT ½-INCH/ 1-CM-LENGTH PIECE), SLICED
- ¼ CUP (1 OZ/25 G) SLICED BAMBOO SHOOT, DRAINED
- ½ SMALL CARROT, CUT INTO MATCHSTICKS
- ⅓ SMALL CUCUMBER, CUT INTO MATCHSTICKS
- ½ TEASPOON SALT
- PANCAKES (PAGE 53), TO SERVE

* Soak the black fungus in a small bowl of cold water for about 20 minutes until softened, then rinse. Bring a saucepan of water to a boil over high heat, add the black fungus, and blanch for 1–2 minutes. Drain and rinse under cold running water. Set aside.
* Combine the pork, soy sauce, and cornstarch (cornflour) in a bowl. Stir in 1 teaspoon oil and set aside to marinate.
* Heat 1 tablespoon oil in a wok or large skillet (frying pan) over medium-high heat until heated through. Reduce to low heat, then immediately add the eggs, stirring gently for about 45 seconds, until the eggs are very softly scrambled. Remove and set aside on a plate. Wipe the wok clean.
* Heat the remaining 1 tablespoon oil in the wok over medium-high heat, add the ginger, and stir-fry for 1 minute until fragrant. Add the pork, increase to high heat, and cook for 2 minutes until cooked through. Add the black fungus, bamboo shoots, carrot, cucumber, and salt and toss for another minute. Add the scrambled eggs and stir-fry for another minute, or until the eggs are fully cooked. Transfer to a serving plate and serve with pancakes.

REGION: GUANGDONG
PREPARATION TIME: 10 MINUTES,
  PLUS 20 MINUTES SOAKING TIME
COOKING TIME: 3 MINUTES
SERVES: 4

榨菜炒肉丝

PORK WITH PRESERVED

MUSTARD

- 6 DRIED BLACK MUSHROOMS
- 2 TABLESPOONS PLUS 2 TEASPOONS VEGETABLE OIL
- 5 OZ/150 G PORK SHOULDER, CUT INTO THIN STRIPS
- 1 TEASPOON LIGHT SOY SAUCE
- 2 TEASPOONS GRANULATED SUGAR
- 1 TEASPOON CORNSTARCH (CORNFLOUR)
- 2 OZ/50 G SICHUAN PRESERVED MUSTARD HEARTS, RINSED
- 1 RED CHILE, SEEDED AND CUT INTO STRIPS

* Put the mushrooms in a bowl, cover with cold water, and soak for at least 20 minutes, or until softened. Remove the mushrooms, squeeze dry, and discard the stems. Cut the mushrooms into thin strips and mix with 1 teaspoon oil.
* Meanwhile, combine the pork, soy sauce, and 1 teaspoon sugar and marinate for 10 minutes. Mix in the cornstarch (cornflour). Mix in 1 teaspoon oil just prior to cooking.
* Cut the preserved mustard hearts into thin strips. Soak in a bowl of cold water for 5 minutes, then drain.
* Heat the remaining 2 tablespoons oil in a wok or large skillet/frying pan over high heat, add the pork, and stir-fry for about 1 minute. Add the mushrooms and stir-fry for another minute. Add the preserved mustard hearts, chile, remaining 1 teaspoon sugar, and 1 tablespoon water and sauté for another minute until the pork is cooked through. Transfer to a serving plate and serve.

MEAT

REGION: SHUNDE
PREPARATION TIME: 10 MINUTES,
  PLUS 20 MINUTES SOAKING TIME
COOKING TIME: 5 MINUTES
SERVES: 4

凤城生菜包
PORK LETTUCE
WRAPS

- 3 DRIED BLACK MUSHROOMS
- 3½ OZ/100 G GROUND (MINCED) PORK
- ½ TEASPOON SALT
- 1 TEASPOON CORNSTARCH
  (CORNFLOUR)
- 1 HEAD ICEBERG LETTUCE, LEAVES
  SEPARATED
- 1 TABLESPOON VEGETABLE OIL
- 2 CLOVES GARLIC, CHOPPED
- 1 CHINESE LIVER SAUSAGE, RINSED
  AND CUT INTO ¼-INCH/5-MM DICE
- 1 CARROT, FINELY CHOPPED
- 1 TABLESPOON PRESERVED KOHLRABI,
  CHOPPED
- 1 TABLESPOON OYSTER SAUCE
- 6 WATER CHESTNUTS, FINELY CHOPPED
- ⅜ CUP (2 OZ/50 G) PINE NUTS
- 2 TABLESPOONS HOISIN SAUCE,
  TO SERVE

* Put the mushrooms in a bowl, cover with cold water, and soak for at least 20 minutes, or until softened. Remove the mushrooms, squeeze dry, and discard the stems.
* Meanwhile, in a bowl combine the pork, salt, and 1 tablespoon water and let stand for 15 minutes. Mix in the cornstarch (cornflour).
* Trim each lettuce leaf into a cup-like shape.
* Heat the oil in a wok or large skillet (frying pan), add the garlic, and stir-fry over medium-high heat for 1 minute until fragrant. Add the pork, increase to high heat, and stir-fry for about 2 minutes until cooked through, breaking up any lumps in the process.
* Stir in the sausage, carrot, mushrooms, and kohlrabi, add the oyster sauce, and toss the mixture thoroughly. Mix in the water chestnuts and pine nuts.
* Transfer to a serving plate and serve the hoisin sauce and lettuce wrappers on the side.

REGION: FUJIAN
PREPARATION TIME: 10 MINUTES, PLUS
  10 MINUTES MARINATING TIME
COOKING TIME: 10 MINUTES
SERVES: 2-4

丁香鱼炒肉丝
PORK WITH
ANCHOVIES

- 7 OZ/200 G PORK TENDERLOIN, CUT
  INTO 1½-INCH/4-CM-LONG STRIPS
- 1 TABLESPOON LIGHT SOY SAUCE
- ½ TEASPOON GRANULATED SUGAR
- 1 TEASPOON CORNSTARCH
  (CORNFLOUR)
- 2 TABLESPOONS PLUS 1 TEASPOON
  VEGETABLE OIL
- 1 CUP (2 OZ/50 G) DRIED ANCHOVIES
- 2 CLOVES GARLIC, SLICED
- 4 SHALLOTS, SLICED
- 1 RED CHILE, SEEDED AND SLICED
- 1 TABLESPOON FERMENTED BLACK
  BEANS, RINSED AND CHOPPED
- 1 TABLESPOON SHAOXING WINE
- ½ TEASPOON SESAME OIL
- STEAMED RICE (PAGE 540), TO SERVE

* Combine the pork, soy sauce, sugar, and 2 tablespoons water in a bowl and marinate for 10 minutes. Mix in the cornstarch (cornflour) and 1 teaspoon vegetable oil.
* Meanwhile, soak the dried anchovies in cold water for 5 minutes. Drain.
* Heat 1 tablespoon vegetable oil in a wok or large skillet (frying pan) over low heat, add the pork, and stir-fry for about 2–3 minutes until cooked through. Transfer the pork to a plate.
* Add the remaining 1 tablespoon vegetable oil to the wok. Add the garlic, shallots, and chile and stir-fry over medium-high heat for 1 minute until fragrant. Add the anchovies and stir-fry for another minute, then stir in the black beans and pork. Toss over high heat for 30 seconds.
* Drizzle the wine along the inside of the wok and stir in the sesame oil. Transfer to a serving plate and serve with rice.

MEAT

椒酱肉
PORK WITH
CHILI SAUCE

REGION: CHAOZHOU
PREPARATION TIME: 15 MINUTES,
  PLUS 20 MINUTES SOAKING TIME
COOKING TIME: 10 MINUTES
SERVES: 6–8

* Put the mushrooms in a bowl, cover with cold water, and soak for at least 20 minutes, or until softened. Remove the mushrooms, squeeze dry, and discard the stems. Dice and set aside.
* In a wok or skillet (frying pan) over low heat, combine 3 tablespoons vegetable oil and the peanuts and stir-fry for 3–4 minutes until the peanuts are crunchy. Remove the peanuts and set aside to cool.
* Pour out most of the oil, leaving about 1 tablespoon. Add 1 tablespoon bean paste, preserved turnips, mushrooms, dried bean curd, and dried shrimp and stir-fry over medium heat for 1 minute until fragrant. Remove all the ingredients and set aside.
* Heat 1 tablespoon vegetable oil in the wok over high heat and stir-fry the garlic and 1 teaspoon bean paste for about 1 minute. Add the pork and stir-fry for another 2 minutes until the pork is fully cooked. Stir in the bell pepper, chile, and bean-curd-and-shrimp mixture, then add the soy sauce, sugar, and sesame oil. Stir-fry for 1 minute until the sauce thickens. Mix in the peanuts and transfer to a serving plate. Serve with rice.

* 6 DRIED BLACK MUSHROOMS
* 4 TABLESPOONS VEGETABLE OIL
* ¾ CUP (3 OZ/80 G) RAW PEANUTS, SHELLED
* 1 TABLESPOON PLUS 1 TEASPOON BEAN PASTE
* 3 TABLESPOONS PRESERVED TURNIPS, DICED
* 1 SEMI-DRIED TOFU, CUT INTO ½-INCH/1-CM CUBES
* 2 TABLESPOONS DRIED SHRIMP
* 1 TABLESPOON GARLIC GRATED
* 7 OZ/200 G PORK TENDERLOIN, CUT INTO ½-INCH/1-CM CUBES
* ½ GREEN BELL PEPPER, SEEDED AND DICED INTO ½-INCH/1-CM CUBES
* 1 RED CHILE, FINELY CHOPPED
* 1 TEASPOON DARK SOY SAUCE
* 2 TEASPOONS GRANULATED SUGAR
* 1 TEASPOON SESAME OIL
* STEAMED RICE (PAGE 540), TO SERVE

红糟五花肉
PORK BELLY WITH RED
DISTILLED GRAIN SAUCE

REGION: TAIWAN
PREPARATION TIME: 5 MINUTES, PLUS
  8 HOURS MARINATING TIME
COOKING TIME: 10 MINUTES
SERVES: 4

* In a bowl, combine the pork strips with the red distilled grain sauce, sugar, and wine and marinate for 8 hours.
* Mix the pork strips with the coarse sweet potato starch.
* Heat the oil in a wok or deep saucepan over medium-high heat to 340°F/170°C, or until a cube of bread browns in 45 seconds. Gently lower in the pork strips and immediately reduce to low heat. Deep-fry the pork for about 5 minutes. Increase to medium heat and deep-fry for another 2–3 minutes until golden and cooked through. Use a slotted spoon to carefully remove the pork from the oil and drain on paper towels. Transfer to a serving plate and serve with rice.

* 1 (5-OZ/150-G) PORK BELLY, CUT INTO ¾-INCH/2-CM THICK STRIPS
* 1 TABLESPOON RED DISTILLED GRAIN SAUCE
* ½ TEASPOON GRANULATED SUGAR
* 1 TABLESPOON KAOLIANG WINE
* 3 TABLESPOONS COARSE SWEET POTATO STARCH
* 2 CUPS (16 FL OZ/475 ML) VEGETABLE OIL
* STEAMED RICE (PAGE 540), TO SERVE

PREPARATION TIME: 15 MINUTES,
   PLUS 4 HOURS MARINATING TIME
COOKING TIME: 40 MINUTES
SERVES: 4
📷 PAGE 355

回锅肉
PORK WITH
GARLIC SPROUTS

- 1 TABLESPOON SALT
- 1 (7-OZ/200-G) SKIN-ON PORK
  SHOULDER
- 3 TABLESPOONS VEGETABLE OIL
- ¼ HEAD CABBAGE, COARSELY
  CHOPPED
- 3 GARLIC SPROUTS, GREEN PARTS
  ONLY, CUT INTO 1½-INCH/4-CM
  LENGTHS
- 4 CLOVES GARLIC, MINCED
- 1 TABLESPOON TIANMIANJIANG
- 1½ TABLESPOONS PIXIAN CHILI BEAN
  PASTE, CHOPPED
- 6 DRIED CHILES
- 2 RED CHILES
- ½ RED BELL PEPPER, SEEDED AND CUT
  INTO SMALL CHUNKS
- 1 TEASPOON SHAOXING WINE
- ½ TEASPOON GRANULATED SUGAR
- 1 TEASPOON LIGHT SOY SAUCE
- ½ TEASPOON SESAME OIL

* Rub the salt all over the pork and marinate for
  4 hours. Rinse under cold running water, then drain.
* Put the pork into a large saucepan and add enough water
  to cover it completely. Bring to a boil over high heat, then
  reduce to medium-low heat, just below boiling. Cook the
  pork for 15 minutes, then turn off the heat, cover, and
  stand for 15 minutes. Drain and rinse under cold running
  water until cooled. Cut the pork into very thin slices.
* Heat 2 tablespoons vegetable oil in a wok or large skillet
  (frying pan), add the cabbage and garlic sprouts, and
  stir-fry over high heat for 2 minutes until soft. Remove
  the cabbage and garlic sprouts and set aside on a plate.
  Add the remaining 1 tablespoon vegetable oil to the wok
  and stir-fry the pork slices over high heat for 2 minutes
  until sizzling and beginning to curl. Put in the garlic,
  tianmianjiang, chili bean paste, dried and fresh chiles and
  stir-fry for 2 minutes. Stir in the bell pepper, garlic sprouts,
  and cabbage, then add the wine, sugar, and soy sauce.
  Drizzle over the sesame oil and toss thoroughly. Transfer
  to a serving dish and serve.

REGION: HUBEI
PREPARATION TIME: 10 MINUTES
COOKING TIME: 5 MINUTES
SERVES: 4

红菜苔炒腊肉
PURPLE BRASSICA
WITH CURED PORK

- 2 TABLESPOONS LARD
- 1 TEASPOON CHOPPED GINGER
- 7 OZ/200 G CHINESE CURED BACON,
  RINSED AND THINLY SLICED
- 1 LB 2 OZ/500 G PURPLE BRASSICA OR
  CHOY SUM, CUT INTO 1½-INCH/4-CM
  LENGTHS
- ½ TEASPOON SALT
- STEAMED RICE (PAGE 540), TO SERVE

Purple brassica is a leafy vegetable found in central China.
Purple in color and very sweet, it is best used in stir-fries.
If unavailable, choy sum can be used as a substitute.

* Heat the lard in a wok or large skillet (frying pan) over
  medium-high heat, add the ginger, and stir-fry for 1 minute
  until fragrant. Put in the cured bacon and stir-fry for
  another 1–2 minutes until the bacon is cooked. Transfer
  to a plate.
* Put the purple brassica in the wok, add the salt, and
  stir-fry for 2 minutes over high heat until cooked but still
  crispy. Return the bacon to the wok, stir, and mix with the
  brassica. Transfer to a plate and serve with rice.

PORK WITH GARLIC SPROUTS

REGION: HUBEI
PREPARATION TIME: 10 MINUTES
COOKING TIME: 45 MINUTES
SERVES: 4

桃仁酱汁肉
PORK BELLY WITH
CRISPY WALNUTS

- 1 (1-LB 2-OZ/500-G) BONELESS, SKIN-ON PORK BELLY
- 1 CUP (8 FL OZ/250 ML) VEGETABLE OIL
- 1 CUP (3½ OZ/100 G) WALNUTS
- 2 OZ/50 G GINGER (ABOUT 3-INCH/7.5-CM-LENGTH PIECE), SLICED
- 2 SCALLIONS (SPRING ONIONS), CUT INTO 1½-INCH/4-CM LENGTHS
- 3 TABLESPOONS GRANULATED SUGAR
- ½ TABLESPOON TIANMIANJIANG
- 1 TEASPOON SALT, PLUS EXTRA TO TASTE
- 1 TABLESPOON GLUTINOUS RICE WINE
- STEAMED RICE (PAGE 540), TO SERVE

* For the pork belly, scrape the skin clean, then rinse the pork under cold running water.
* Put the pork into a large saucepan and add enough water to cover it completely. Bring to a boil over high heat and blanch the pork for 10 minutes. Drain and rinse under cold running water until cooled. Cut the pork into ¾-inch/2-cm cubes.
* Heat the oil in a wok or deep saucepan to 270°F/130°C. Gently lower the walnuts into the oil and deep-fry for 4–5 minutes until golden brown. Use a slotted spoon to carefully remove the walnuts from the oil and drain on paper towels.
* Pour out most of the oil, leaving about 2 tablespoons in the wok. Heat over medium heat, add the ginger and scallions (spring onions), and stir-fry for 1 minute until fragrant. Add the sugar and stir-fry for 2 minutes until caramelized.
* Stir in the tianmianjiang, add the pork, and stir-fry over high heat for 2 minutes. Add the salt, wine, and enough water to cover, and bring to a boil. Reduce to low heat and simmer for 12–15 minutes until the sauce thickens and the pork is cooked. Stir in the crispy walnuts and toss. Season with extra salt to taste, then transfer to a serving dish. Serve with rice.

REGION: HAKKA
PREPARATION TIME: 10 MINUTES
COOKING TIME: 20 MINUTES
SERVES: 4

爆炒猪舌
STIR-FRIED PIG'S TONGUE

- 1 PIG'S TONGUE
- 2 TABLESPOONS VEGETABLE OIL
- 2 OZ/50 G GINGER (ABOUT 3-INCH/7.5-CM-LENGTH PIECE), SLICED
- 3 CLOVES GARLIC, SLICED
- 1 TABLESPOON BEAN PASTE
- ½ TEASPOON GRANULATED SUGAR
- 1 TEASPOON RICE WINE
- 5 OZ/150 G YELLOW CHIVES, CUT INTO 2-INCH/5-CM PIECES
- 1 RED BELL PEPPER, SEEDED AND CUT INTO STRIPS
- STEAMED RICE (PAGE 540), TO SERVE

* Put the pig's tongue into a large saucepan and add enough water to cover it completely. Bring to a boil over high heat and cook the pig's tongue for 15 minutes until cooked through. Skim the froth and scum off the surface, if needed. Drain and rinse under cold running water.
* Scrape the skin off the surface of the tongue with a knife and remove any bones. Cut the tongue into halves lengthwise, then horizontally into ¼-inch/5-mm slices.
* Heat the oil in a wok or large skillet (frying pan), add the ginger and garlic, and stir-fry over medium-high heat for 1 minute until fragrant. Add the bean paste, sugar, and pig's tongue, and stir-fry for another minute. Add the wine, chives, and bell pepper, and toss for another minute.
* Transfer to a serving plate and serve with rice.

MEAT

葱爆猪心
PIG'S HEART WITH SCALLIONS

REGION: TAIWAN
PREPARATION TIME: 10 MINUTES,
    PLUS 15 MINUTES SOAKING TIME
COOKING TIME: 2 MINUTES
SERVES: 2–4

* Cut open the pig's heart and remove the blood vessels and membranes. Cut the heart into ⅛-inch/3-mm-thick slices.
* In a large bowl, combine 2 cups (16 fl oz/475 ml) water with the vinegar, add the pig's heart slices, and soak for 15 minutes. Rinse under cold running water and drain.
* Heat the vegetable oil in a wok or large skillet (frying pan) over high heat, add the scallion (spring onion) stems and cayenne pepper, and stir-fry for about 30 seconds. Add the pig's heart slices, scallion greens, rice wine, soy sauce, and 1 tablespoon water and toss rapidly for about 30 seconds. Season to taste with salt, then stir in the sesame oil. Transfer to a serving plate and serve with rice.

- 1 PIG'S HEART
- 1 TEASPOON WHITE VINEGAR
- 3 TABLESPOONS VEGETABLE OIL
- 2 SCALLIONS (SPRING ONIONS), WHITE AND GREEN PARTS CHOPPED SEPARATELY
- 1 RED CAYENNE PEPPER, SEEDED AND CUT DIAGONALLY INTO ½-INCH/1-CM SLICES
- 1 TABLESPOON RICE WINE
- 1 TEASPOON LIGHT SOY SAUCE
- SALT, TO TASTE
- 1 TEASPOON SESAME OIL
- STEAMED RICE (PAGE 540), TO SERVE

白云猪手
PICKLED PIG'S TROTTER

REGION: GUANGDONG
PREPARATION TIME: 10 MINUTES,
    PLUS 8 HOURS SOAKING TIME
COOKING TIME: 2 HOURS
SERVES: 6

* Put the trotter into a large saucepan and add enough water to cover it completely. Bring to a boil over high heat and blanch for 5 minutes. Skim the froth and scum off the surface, if needed. Drain and rinse under cold running water.
* Put the trotter pieces back into the pan with half the ginger, add enough water to cover, and bring to a boil. Reduce to low heat and simmer, uncovered, for about 30 minutes. Drain and discard the ginger. Rinse the trotter pieces under cold running water until cool and soak in a large bucket of ice water for 1 hour. Remove the trotter pieces and return to the pan, add the remaining ginger, and cover with water. Bring to a boil, then reduce the heat, and simmer for 30 minutes. Drain and discard the ginger, and soak in ice water once more for another hour.
* Put the trotter pieces back into the pan, add water to cover, and bring to a boil. Reduce to low heat and simmer, uncovered, for about 20 minutes. Turn off the heat, cover, and let the trotter pieces continue to cook in the residual heat for 30 minutes. Remove from the pan.
* Combine the vinegar, sugar, and salt in a saucepan and bring to a boil, then reduce to low heat and cook for 3–4 minutes until the sugar and salt are dissolved. Strain the mixture into a large bowl. Add the lemon zest and bay leaves and let cool.
* Add the trotter pieces and soak for 6 hours. Remove the pieces, drain, and transfer to a plate.

- 1 (1 LB 5-OZ/600-G) PIG'S TROTTER, CLEANED, RINSED, AND CHOPPED INTO 1-OZ/25-G PIECES
- ¾ OZ/20 G GINGER (ABOUT 1-INCH/ 2.5-CM-LENGTH PIECE), SLICED
- 2½ CUPS (20 FL OZ/600 ML) WHITE VINEGAR
- 1½ CUPS (12 OZ/350 G) GRANULATED SUGAR
- 2 TEASPOONS SALT
- SHREDDED ZEST OF 1 LEMON
- 3 BAY LEAVES

REGION: FUJIAN
PREPARATION TIME: 10 MINUTES, PLUS
    30 MINUTES SOAKING TIME AND
    15 MINUTES MARINATING TIME
COOKING TIME: 3 MINUTES
SERVES: 4

南煎肝

SAUTÉED
PORK LIVER

- 1 LB 2 OZ/500 G PORK LIVER, THINLY
  SLICED
- 1 TEASPOON WHITE VINEGAR
- 2 TEASPOONS LIGHT SOY SAUCE
- 1 TABLESPOON RICE WINE
- ¼ TEASPOON GROUND WHITE PEPPER
- ½ TABLESPOON CORNSTARCH
  (CORNFLOUR)
- 1 TEASPOON GRANULATED SUGAR
- 2 CUPS (16 FL OZ/475 ML)
  VEGETABLE OIL
- 1 TABLESPOON GRATED GINGER
- 1 TABLESPOON CHOPPED SCALLION
  (SPRING ONION)
- STEAMED RICE (PAGE 540), TO SERVE

* Combine the pork liver, vinegar, and 2 cups (16 fl oz/475
  ml) water in a large bowl and soak for 30 minutes, then
  drain. Return the liver to the bowl, add 1 teaspoon soy
  sauce, ½ tablespoon wine, the white pepper, and cornstarch
  (cornflour) and marinate for 15 minutes.
* Combine the remaining ½ tablespoon wine, 1 teaspoon soy
  sauce, and the sugar in a small bowl. Set aside.
* Heat the oil in a wok or deep saucepan to 265°F/130°C.
  Gently lower the liver into the oil, using chopsticks to
  disperse the pieces rapidly to prevent sticking, and deep-fry
  for about 1 minute until golden brown. Use a slotted spoon
  to remove the liver from the oil and drain on paper towels.
* Pour out most of the oil, leaving about 1 tablespoon in
  the wok. Heat the oil over medium-high heat, add the
  ginger and scallion (spring onion), and stir-fry for 1 minute
  until fragrant. Add the liver and the reserved sauce and
  stir-fry for 30 seconds until the sauce thickens and coats
  the liver. Transfer to a serving plate and serve with rice.

韭菜腊味炒猪肝
PORK LIVER WITH CURED MEAT AND CHIVES

REGION: HAKKA
PREPARATION TIME: 10 MINUTES,
  PLUS 30 MINUTES SOAKING TIME
COOKING TIME: 10 MINUTES
SERVES: 4

* Remove the veins and outer membrane of the pork liver, then cut the liver into ¼-inch/5-mm-thick slices. Combine the pork liver, vinegar, and 2 cups (16 oz/475 ml) water in a large bowl and soak for 30 minutes, then rinse thoroughly to remove the vinegar. Drain.
* Meanwhile, place the cured bacon and the Chinese sausage in a collapsible pot or bamboo steamer over a pot of boiling water. Steam, covered, for 5 minutes. Cut the bacon and sausage into ¼-inch/5-mm-thick slices.
* Place the liver in a bowl and mix with the ginger, wine, white pepper, and 1 teaspoon vegetable oil.
* Heat the remaining 2 tablespoons vegetable oil in a wok or large skillet (frying pan) over medium-high heat, add the garlic, and stir-fry for 1 minute until fragrant. Add the liver and stir-fry quickly over high heat for 1 minute. Add the cured bacon, Chinese sausage, chives, sugar, salt, and soy sauce and stir-fry for another 1–2 minutes—do not overcook the liver. Stir in the sesame oil, transfer to a plate, and serve with rice.

- 11 OZ/300 G PORK LIVER
- 1 TEASPOON WHITE VINEGAR
- 3½ OZ/100 G CHINESE CURED BACON, SKIN REMOVED AND RINSED
- 1 CHINESE SAUSAGE
- ¼ OZ/10 G GINGER (ABOUT ¾-INCH/ 2-CM-LENGTH PIECE), SHREDDED
- 1 TEASPOON RICE WINE
- PINCH OF GROUND WHITE PEPPER
- 2 TABLESPOONS PLUS 1 TEASPOON VEGETABLE OIL
- 2 CLOVES GARLIC, SLICED
- 7 OZ/200 G CHIVES, CUT INTO 2¼-INCH/6-CM LENGTHS
- 1 TEASPOON GRANULATED SUGAR
- 1 TEASPOON SALT
- 1 TEASPOON LIGHT SOY SAUCE
- 1 TEASPOON SESAME OIL
- STEAMED RICE (PAGE 540), TO SERVE

腊肉炒豆干
CHINESE CURED BACON
WITH SEMI-DRIED TOFU

- 2 OZ/50 G CHINESE CURED BACON
- 1 TABLESPOON VEGETABLE OIL
- 2 CLOVES GARLIC, SLICED
- 2 RED CHILES, SEEDED AND CHOPPED
- 2 CHINESE CELERY, STALKS CHOPPED
  AND LEAVES DISCARDED
- 1 FIVE-SPICE TOFU, THINLY SLICED
- ½ TEASPOON LIGHT SOY SAUCE
- ½ TEASPOON SALT, PLUS EXTRA
  TO TASTE
- STEAMED RICE (PAGE 540), TO SERVE

* Place the cured bacon in a collapsible pot or bamboo
  steamer over a pot of boiling water. Steam, covered, for
  5 minutes until soft and cooked. Cut the pork into $1/12$-inch/
  2-mm slices.
* Heat the oil in a wok or large skillet (frying pan), add the
  garlic and chiles, and stir-fry over medium heat for 1 minute
  until fragrant. Put in the bacon, celery, tofu, soy sauce, and
  salt and stir-fry for another 2 minutes until the celery is just
  tender. Season with extra salt to taste. Transfer to a serving
  plate and serve with rice.

鲜炖咸
STEAMED PORK BELLY
WITH SALTED PORK

- 1 (11-OZ/300-G) BONELESS, SKIN-ON
  PORK BELLY, CUT INTO ¾-INCH/2-CM
  CUBES
- ¾ CUP (3½ OZ/100 G) SLICED BAMBOO
  SHOOTS, DRAINED
- ¼ TEASPOON SALT
- 9 OZ/250 G SALTED PORK, CUT INTO
  ¾-INCH/2-CM CUBES
- SCANT 1 CUP (7 FL OZ/200 ML)
  CHICKEN BROTH (STOCK, PAGE 90)
- 2 TABLESPOONS RICE WINE
- 2 SCALLIONS (SPRING ONIONS),
  CUT INTO 2-INCH/5-CM LENGTHS
- 1 OZ/25 G GINGER (ABOUT 2-INCH/
  5-CM-LENGTH PIECE), SLICED
- ¼ TEASPOON GROUND WHITE PEPPER
- STEAMED RICE (PAGE 540), TO SERVE

* Put the pork belly into a large saucepan and add enough
  water to cover it completely. Bring to a boil over high
  heat and blanch for 5 minutes. Drain and rinse under
  cold running water until cooled.
* Arrange both the pork belly and salted pork, skin-side
  down, in a heatproof bowl by interlacing them. Place the
  bamboo shoots on top of the pork. Pour over the chicken
  broth (stock), wine, scallions (spring onions), and ginger.
  Seal tightly with aluminum foil and place in a collapsible
  pot or bamboo steamer over a pot of boiling water.
  Steam over high heat, covered, for 2 hours.
* Carefully remove the foil, discard the ginger, then strain
  the sauce into a saucepan. Cover the bowl of pork with
  a serving plate and, using dish towels, invert the contents
  onto the plate. (Alternatively, use tongs to transfer the
  pork.) Keep warm.
* Heat the sauce over medium-high heat and cook for
  15 minutes until reduced by half. Pour the sauce over the
  pork, sprinkle with the white pepper, and serve with rice.

CHINESE CURED BACON WITH SEMI-DRIED TOFU

REGION: HONG KONG
PREPARATION TIME: 20 MINUTES
COOKING TIME: 1 HOUR 45 MINUTES
SERVES: 4

大豆芽菜炒猪肠

CHITTERLINGS WITH

SOYBEAN SPROUTS

- 4 LARGE CHITTERLINGS (PIG INTESTINES)
- 4 TEASPOONS SALT
- 2 CUPS (5 OZ/150 G) SOYBEAN SPROUTS
- 1 TABLESPOON WHITE VINEGAR
- 2 OZ/50 G GINGER (ABOUT 3-INCH/7.5-CM-LENGTH PIECE), SLICED
- 2 TABLESPOONS VEGETABLE OIL
- 1 RED CHILE, DICED
- 2 TABLESPOONS BEAN PASTE
- 1 TABLESPOON LIGHT SOY SAUCE
- ½ TEASPOON GRANULATED SUGAR
- 2 TABLESPOONS RICE WINE
- STEAMED RICE (PAGE 540), TO SERVE

* Cut off and discard the thinner section of the intestines, keeping only the thick part.
* Tie the narrow end of 1 intestine with kitchen string and, using a chopstick, push against the knot into the intestine. Use your free hand to pull the intestine over onto the
* chopstick to turn the intestine inside out. Rub the intestine with 1 teaspoon salt and rinse under cold running water.
* Turn the intestine outside in so that the skin is on the outside again, then untie the string. Repeat with the remaining intestines.
* Bring a large saucepan of water to a boil over high heat. Add the intestines and cook for about 5 minutes. Remove, drain, and rinse under cold running water. Connect one end of each intestine to the faucet and rinse the inside with water.
* In a small dry skillet (frying pan), roast the soybean sprouts over low heat for 2–3 minutes, or until most of the external moisture has evaporated. Set aside.
* Bring 8½ cups (68 fl oz/2 liters) water to a boil in a large pot, add the intestines, vinegar, and a quarter of the ginger, and return to a boil. Skim the surface to remove any froth and scum, reduce to low heat, and simmer for 1½ hours. Drain the intestines and rinse well under cold running water until cool. Discard the ginger.
  Cut the intestines diagonally into ¾-inch/2-cm-thick pieces.
* Heat the oil in a wok or large skillet (frying pan) over medium-high heat and add the chile and remaining ginger. Stir-fry for 1 minute until fragrant. Add the bean paste and stir-fry for another 15 seconds. Increase to high heat, add the intestines, soy sauce, and sugar, then sprinkle the wine along the inside of the wok. Stir-fry for another minute, then add the sprouts and toss thoroughly until well mixed and heated through. Serve with rice.

爆炒腰花

STIR-FRIED
PORK KIDNEYS

REGION: SHANDONG
PREPARATION TIME: 15 MINUTES,
    PLUS 30 MINUTES SOAKING TIME
COOKING TIME: 5 MINUTES
SERVES: 4

* Slice each kidney horizontally into halves and remove all the white glands and any dark red areas. Put the kidneys into a bowl, add the vinegar and 2 cups (16 fl oz/475 ml) water, and soak for about 30 minutes.
* Meanwhile, soak the black fungus in a small bowl of cold water for 20 minutes, or until softened. Remove the fungus, discard the stems, and tear the caps into small pieces. Set aside.
* Rinse the kidneys thoroughly under cold running water. Score the surface of the kidneys in a crisscross pattern with each cut about a third of the thickness of the kidneys. Cut the kidneys crosswise into 1¼-inch/3-cm slices and soak in water until ready to cook. Change the water a couple times if necessary.
* Heat the vegetable oil in a wok or large skillet (frying pan), add the garlic, and stir-fry over high heat for about 30 seconds until fragrant. Add the kidneys and stir-fry for another minute. Sprinkle the wine along the inside of the wok. Add the bamboo shoots and black fungus, stir in the soy sauce, salt, and 2 tablespoons water, and mix well. Stir-fry for 1–2 minutes until all the water has evaporated. Season with extra salt to taste. Add the sesame oil and the chopped scallion (spring onion) and toss thoroughly. Transfer to a serving plate and serve with rice.

- 2 PORK KIDNEYS
- 1 TABLESPOON WHITE VINEGAR
- ½ CUP (¼ OZ/10 G) DRIED BLACK FUNGUS
- 2 TABLESPOONS VEGETABLE OIL
- 2 CLOVES GARLIC, CHOPPED
- 1 TABLESPOON SHAOXING WINE
- ¼ CUP (1 OZ/25 G) SLICED BAMBOO SHOOTS, DRAINED
- ½ TABLESPOON LIGHT SOY SAUCE
- ½ TEASPOON SALT, PLUS EXTRA TO TASTE
- 1 TEASPOON SESAME OIL
- 1 SCALLION (SPRING ONION), CHOPPED
- STEAMED RICE (PAGE 540), TO SERVE

锅巴肘子
CRISPY PORK KNUCKLE

- 1 (1-LB 5-OZ/600-G) PORK KNUCKLE, DE-BONED AND SKIN SCRAPED CLEAN
- ¼ OZ/10 G GINGER (ABOUT ¾-INCH/ 2-CM-LENGTH PIECE), SLICED
- 2 SCALLIONS (SPRING ONIONS), KNOTTED
- 2 TABLESPOONS SALT
- 5 TABLESPOONS CORNSTARCH (CORNFLOUR)
- 2 CUPS (16 FL OZ/475 ML) VEGETABLE OIL
- STEAMED RICE (PAGE 540), TO SERVE

FOR THE SPICE BAG:
- 1 TABLESPOON SICHUAN PEPPERCORNS
- 2 STAR ANISE

FOR THE SPICED SALT:
- 1 TABLESPOON SALT
- ½ TEASPOON FIVE-SPICE POWDER

* In a large saucepan, add the pork knuckle and enough water to cover it completely. Bring to a boil over high heat and blanch the pork for 5 minutes. Skim the froth and scum off the surface, if needed. Drain and rinse under cold running water.
* Put the Sichuan peppercorns and star anise into a spice bag. Bring 6¼ cups (50 fl oz/1.5 liters) water to a boil in a large saucepan over high heat. Add the pork knuckle, ginger, scallions (spring onions), salt, and spice bag and return to a boil. Reduce to low heat and simmer for 1 hour. Remove the pork, rinse, and drain.
* Heat the salt for the spiced salt in a dry skillet (frying pan) over medium heat for about 1 minute. Set aside to cool for about 1 minute, then mix in the five-spice powder.
* Mix the cornstarch (cornflour) with 4 tablespoons water. Brush the pork knuckle with the mixture.
* Heat the oil in a skillet over medium-high heat to 340°F/ 170°C, or until a cube of bread browns in 45 seconds. Gently lower the pork knuckle and deep-fry for 3–4 minutes until the skin is golden and crispy. Carefully remove and transfer to a cutting board, then cut into ½-inch/1-cm-thick slices. Sprinkle over the spiced salt and serve with rice.

梅膏骨
PLUM
SPARERIBS

- 1 LB 5 OZ/600 G PORK SPARERIBS, CUT INTO 2-INCH/5-CM PIECES
- ½ TEASPOON SALT
- 2 CUPS (16 FL OZ/475 ML) VEGETABLE OIL
- ¼ OZ/10 G GINGER (ABOUT ¾-INCH/ 2-CM-LENGTH PIECE), SLICED
- ½ CUP (4 FL OZ/120 ML) RICE WINE
- 3 TABLESPOONS CHAOZHOU PLUM PASTE OR PLUM SAUCE
- 1 TEASPOON ZHENJIANG OR BALSAMIC VINEGAR
- 1 TABLESPOON LIGHT SOY SAUCE
- 1 TEASPOON GRANULATED SUGAR
- ½ TEASPOON SESAME OIL
- STEAMED RICE (PAGE 540), TO SERVE

* Sprinkle the spareribs with salt and let stand for 1 hour. Rinse under cold running water and pat dry with paper towels.
* Heat the vegetable oil in a wok or deep saucepan to 340°F/170°C, or until a cube of bread browns in 45 seconds. Gently lower the spareribs into the oil and deep-fry for 3 minutes until golden brown. Use a slotted spoon to carefully remove the spareribs from the oil and drain on paper towels.
* Pour out most of the oil, leaving about 1 tablespoon in the wok. Heat the oil over medium heat, add the spareribs, ginger, wine, plum paste, vinegar, soy sauce, and sugar, and stir-fry for 10 minutes until the sauce thickens and the spareribs are cooked through. Add the sesame oil and transfer to a serving plate. Serve with rice.

紫酥肉

CRISPY PORK
BELLY

REGION: HENAN
PREPARATION TIME: 10 MINUTES, PLUS
  30 MINUTES MARINATING TIME
COOKING TIME: 1 HOUR
SERVES: 4-6

* For the pork belly, scrape the skin clean, then rinse the pork under cold running water.
* In a large bowl, combine the pork belly, ginger, chopped scallions (spring onions), Sichuan peppercorns, soy sauce, and salt and marinate for 30 minutes.
* Put the pork on a heatproof plate and place in a collapsible pot or bamboo steamer over a pot of boiling water. Steam and cover for 30 minutes. Carefully drain the water from the plate and discard the ginger and scallions. Set the pork aside to cool.
* Heat the oil in a wok or deep saucepan to 275°F/140°C, or until a cube of bread turns golden in 2 minutes. Gently lower the pork into the oil and deep-fry for 10 minutes. Carefully remove the pork from the hot oil and drain on paper towels.
* Heat the oil to 340°F/170°C, or until a cube of bread browns in 45 seconds. Brush the vinegar over the pork skin and deep-fry for 1 minute until the skin turns brown. Remove the pork from the oil to drain. Reheat the oil and repeat this process twice more. Remove the pork from the oil, drain, and slice.
* Quarter each remaining scallion length. Serve the pork belly with the pancakes, the scallion stems and hoisin sauce on the side.

- 1 (1-LB 2-OZ/500-G) BONELESS, SKIN-ON PORK BELLY
- ¼ OZ/10 G GINGER (ABOUT ¾-INCH/ 2-CM-LENGTH PIECE), CHOPPED
- 4 SCALLIONS (SPRING ONIONS), 2 CHOPPED AND 2, STEMS ONLY, CUT INTO 2-INCH/5-CM SECTIONS
- 1 TEASPOON SICHUAN PEPPERCORNS
- 1 TABLESPOON LIGHT SOY SAUCE
- 1 TABLESPOON SALT
- 3 CUPS (25 FL OZ / 750 ML) VEGETABLE OIL
- 3 TABLESPOONS WHITE VINEGAR
- 2 TABLESPOONS HOISIN SAUCE, TO SERVE
- 12 PANCAKES (PAGE 53), TO SERVE

REGION: GUANGDONG
PREPARATION TIME: 10 MINUTES, PLUS
  10 MINUTES SOAKING AND
  15 MINUTES MARINATING TIME
COOKING TIME: 15 MINUTES
SERVES: 4
📷 PAGE 367

甜酸排骨
SWEET AND SOUR
SPARERIBS

- 11 OZ/300 G PORK SPARERIBS,
  CUT INTO SMALL CHUNKS
- 2 CLOVES GARLIC, CHOPPED
- ½ TEASPOON SALT
- ½ TEASPOON BROWN SUGAR
- ½ TEASPOON RICE WINE
- ¼ TABLESPOON LIGHT SOY SAUCE
- 1 EGG, BEATEN
- 4 TABLESPOONS GLUTEN-FREE FLOUR
- 1 CUP (8 FL OZ/250 ML)
  VEGETABLE OIL
- ½ ONION, CUT INTO WEDGES
- ½ GREEN BELL PEPPER, SEEDED AND
  CUT INTO WEDGES
- ½ RED BELL PEPPER, SEEDED AND CUT
  INTO WEDGES
- 1 (8-OZ/225-G) CAN PINEAPPLE,
  DRAINED AND CUT INTO CHUNKS
- CILANTRO (CORIANDER), TO GARNISH
  (OPTIONAL)
- STEAMED RICE (PAGE 540), TO SERVE

  FOR THE SWEET AND SOUR SAUCE:
- 4 TABLESPOONS RED VINEGAR
- 4 TABLESPOONS BROWN SUGAR

* Soak the spareribs in a large bowl of cold water for
  10 minutes, then drain.
* Combine the spareribs, garlic, salt, brown sugar, wine,
  and soy sauce in a large bowl and marinate for 15 minutes.
  Stir in the egg, add the flour, and mix well so that each
  sparerib is coated in flour.
* To make the sauce, combine all the ingredients and mix
  until the sugar is dissolved. Set aside.
* Heat the oil in a wok or deep saucepan to 350°F/180°C,
  or until a cube of bread browns in 30 seconds. Gently
  lower the spareribs into the oil, in batches, and deep-fry
  for 3–4 minutes until golden brown and cooked through.
  Use a slotted spoon to carefully remove the spareribs
  from the oil and drain on paper towels.
* Pour out most of the oil, leaving only 1 tablespoon in the
  wok. Heat the oil over medium-high heat, add the onion
  and stir-fry for about 1–2 minutes until slightly soft. Toss in
  the bell peppers and the sauce and simmer for 2–3 minutes
  until the sauce thickens.
* Add the spareribs and toss quickly until each piece is fully
  coated with the sauce. Stir in the pineapple and heat
  through, then transfer to a serving plate and garnish
  with cilantro (coriander), if using. Serve with rice.

SWEET AND SOUR SPARERIBS

REGION: ANHUI
PREPARATION TIME: 20 MINUTES
COOKING TIME: 10 MINUTES
SERVES: 4

寸金肉
CRISPY PORK ROLLS

- 1 (7-OZ/200-G) PORK TENDERLOIN
- 2 TABLESPOONS GINGER JUICE
- ¼ TEASPOON GROUND WHITE PEPPER
- 1 TEASPOON RICE WINE
- ½ TEASPOON SALT
- 1 EGG
- 1 TABLESPOON PLUS ½ TEASPOON CORNSTARCH (CORNFLOUR)
- 1 OZ/25 G BREAKFAST HAM, CHOPPED
- 2 SCALLIONS (SPRING ONIONS), CHOPPED
- ⅓ CUP (2 OZ/50 G) WHITE SESAME SEEDS
- 2 CUPS (16 FL OZ/475 ML) VEGETABLE OIL
- STEAMED RICE (PAGE 540), TO SERVE (OPTIONAL)

* Remove any membrane and sinew from the pork tenderloin and cut the meat in half to create a long sheet. Using the back of a cleaver or meat mallet, pound the pork repeatedly to flatten it.
* Combine the ginger juice, white pepper, wine, and salt in a small bowl, pour over the pork, and then rub in. Let stand for 10 minutes.
* In another bowl, beat the egg, add 1 tablespoon cornstarch (cornflour), and mix to form an egg batter.
* Combine the ham, the remaining ½ teaspoon cornstarch, and the scallions (spring onions) in a bowl.
* Put the pork flat on a cutting board and brush with some of the egg batter. Put the ham mixture on top and firmly roll the pork into a long meat roll. Brush with the remaining egg batter and sprinkle with the sesame seeds.
* Heat the oil in a wok or deep saucepan to 260°F/130°C. Gently lower the pork roll into the oil and deep-fry for 3–4 minutes until slightly brown. Use a slotted spoon to carefully remove the roll from the oil and set aside to cool. Cut the pork into 4-inch/10-cm-long rolls. Reheat the oil to 300°F/150°C, or until a cube of bread browns in 1½ minutes, return the pork rolls to the wok, and deep-fry for another 1–2 minutes until golden brown and cooked through. Carefully remove the rolls from the oil, then cut each roll into 3 sections, and transfer to a serving plate. Serve with rice or as a snack.

溜核桃肉

PORK AND WALNUT ROLLS IN A SWEET AND SOUR SAUCE

REGION: ANHUI
PREPARATION TIME: 15 MINUTES,
    PLUS 15 MINUTES SOAKING TIME
COOKING TIME: 15 MINUTES
SERVES: 4

* Soak the walnuts in a bowl of boiling water for 15 minutes. Drain.
* Meanwhile, combine the pork with the salt in a bowl and stand for 10 minutes.
* Mix 1 tablespoon cornstarch (cornflour) with 2 teaspoons water in a small bowl and set aside for 5 minutes, or until the cornstarch settles at the bottom of the bowl. Pour out the water to leave a wet starch.
* In another small bowl, beat the egg whites and mix in the wet starch to form a batter. Set aside.
* Heat the oil in a wok or deep saucepan to 270°F/130°C. Add the walnuts and deep-fry for 4–5 minutes until golden brown. Use a slotted spoon to carefully remove the walnuts from the oil and drain on paper towels.
* Put a piece of pork on a cutting board, brush over a coat of egg batter, and place 1-2 pieces walnuts along one edge of the pork slice. Roll up, tucking the ends in, then dip the roll into the batter. Repeat with the remaining pork, walnuts, and batter.
* Reheat the oil to 300°F/150°C, or until a cube of bread browns in 1½ minutes, add the pork and walnut rolls and deep-fry for 3–4 minutes until golden brown. Use a slotted spoon to carefully remove the rolls and drain on paper towels.
* Pour out most of the oil, leaving about 1 teaspoon in the wok. Heat the oil over medium heat, add the chile, and stir-fry for 1–2 minutes until fragrant. Stir in the sugar, soy sauce, vinegar, and 4 tablespoons water, then bring to a boil.
* Mix the remaining 1 teaspoon cornstarch with 1 tablespoon water in a small bowl and stir this mixture into the wok. Bring to a boil, stirring, for 30 seconds to thicken the sauce. Add the pork and walnut rolls, stir to coat, and transfer to a serving plate. Serve with rice.

• 1 CUP (3½ OZ/100 G) SHELLED WALNUTS
• 7 OZ/200 G PORK TENDERLOIN, CUT INTO THIN 2 × 1-INCH/5 × 2.5-CM SLICES
• ¼ TEASPOON SALT
• 1 TABLESPOON PLUS 1 TEASPOON CORNSTARCH (CORNFLOUR)
• 2 EGG WHITES
• 2 CUPS (16 FL OZ/475 ML) VEGETABLE OIL
• 1 RED CHILE, SLICED
• 3 TABLESPOONS GRANULATED SUGAR
• ½ TABLESPOON LIGHT SOY SAUCE
• 1½ TABLESPOONS ZHENJIANG OR BALSAMIC VINEGAR
• STEAMED RICE (PAGE 540), TO SERVE

PREPARATION TIME: 20 MINUTES, PLUS
  10 MINUTES MARINATING TIME
COOKING TIME: 20 MINUTES
SERVES: 4

芝麻金钱肉
PORK WITH
SESAME SEEDS

- 5 OZ/150 G PORK FATBACK
- 7 OZ/200 G PORK TENDERLOIN,
  SLICED INTO BITE-SIZE PIECES
- 2 TEASPOONS CHOPPED GINGER
- 1 SCALLION (SPRING ONION),
  CHOPPED
- 1 TEASPOON SALT
- 1 TEASPOON RICE WINE
- ¾ CUP (3½ OZ/100 G) ALL-PURPOSE
  (PLAIN) FLOUR
- 2 EGGS, LIGHTLY BEATEN
- 2½ TABLESPOONS WHITE SESAME
  SEEDS
- 4¼ CUPS (34 FL OZ/1 LITER)
  VEGETABLE OIL
- 1 TABLESPOON SESAME OIL
- 1-2 SPRIGS CILANTRO (CORIANDER),
  TO GARNISH
- 2 TABLESPOONS KETCHUP, TO SERVE
- BAMBOO SKEWERS

  FOR THE SPICED SALT:
- 1 TEASPOON SALT
- ¼ TEASPOON GROUND SICHUAN
  PEPPERCORNS

* Soak the bamboo skewers in water for 10 minutes.
* Meanwhile, make the spiced salt. Heat a small dry skillet
  (frying pan) over medium heat and add the salt. Stir for
  1 minute to warm through, then turn off the heat, transfer
  to a small bowl, and set aside to cool slightly. Stir in the
  ground Sichuan peppercorns. Set aside.
* Put the pork fatback into a small saucepan and add
  enough water to cover it completely. Bring to a boil over
  high heat and blanch for 5 minutes. Drain and rinse under
  cold running water. Cut the fatback into pieces similar
  in size to the pork.
* Combine the tenderloin, fatback, ginger, scallion (spring
  onion), and wine in a large bowl and marinate for
  10 minutes. Separate the tenderloin and fatback into
  2 separate bowls.
* Working with the tenderloin, dredge in the flour, and then
  lightly coat in the eggs. Sprinkle with the sesame seeds
  on both sides of the meat and press gently to hold the
  sesame seeds in place. Set aside. Repeat the process with
  the fatback.
* Drain the skewers. Skewer the tenderloin followed by the
  fatback and repeat with the remaining meat.
* Heat the vegetable oil in a wok or deep saucepan to
  300°F/150°C, or until a cube of bread browns in 1½ minutes.
  Carefully add the meat skewers and deep-fry for 3–4
  minutes, or until the meat is cooked through. Use tongs to
  remove them from the oil and drain on paper towels.
* Reheat the oil to 300°F/150°C, return the meat skewers to
  the wok, and deep-fry for 2–3 minutes until golden brown.
  Carefully remove from the oil and drain on paper towels.
  Use a fork to push the meat off the skewers and arrange
  the fried meat on a plate. Brush with the sesame oil and
  garnish with the cilantro (coriander). Serve with the spiced
  salt and ketchup on the side.

洛阳肉片

LUOYANG
PORK

REGION: HENAN
PREPARATION TIME: 15 MINUTES,
  PLUS 20 MINUTES SOAKING TIME
COOKING TIME: 15 MINUTES
SERVES: 4

* Soak the black fungus in a small bowl of cold water for 20 minutes, or until softened. Remove the fungus, discard the stems, and tear the caps into small pieces.
* For the pork belly, scrape the skin clean, then rinse the pork under cold running water.
* Combine the pork with ¼ teaspoon salt, ½ teaspoon soy sauce, and 1 teaspoon cornstarch (cornflour) in a bowl. Mix in half the beaten egg. Reserve the remaining half for future use.
* Heat the oil in a wok or deep saucepan to 300°F/150°C, or until a cube of bread browns in 1½ minutes. Gently lower the pork into the oil, using chopsticks to disperse the pieces rapidly to prevent sticking, and deep-fry for 2 minutes until golden brown and cooked through. Use a slotted spoon to carefully remove the pork from the oil and drain on paper towels.
* Pour out most of the oil, leaving about 1 tablespoon in the wok. Heat the oil over medium-high heat, add the garlic to the wok and stir-fry for 1 minute until fragrant. Stir in the bamboo shoots, black fungus, and peas. Add the chicken broth (stock), wine, remaining 1½ teaspoons soy sauce and ¾ teaspoon salt, and the pork. Bring to a boil.
* Mix the remaining 1 teaspoon cornstarch with 1 tablespoon water in a small bowl and stir this mixture into the wok. Add the vinegar. Bring to a boil, stirring, for 30 seconds to thicken the sauce. Sprinkle over the chopped scallion (spring onion) and white pepper. Transfer to a serving dish and serve with rice.

* ¼ CUP (¼ OZ/5 G) DRIED BLACK FUNGUS
* 1 (7-OZ/200-G) BONELESS, SKIN-ON PORK BELLY, CUT INTO 1½ × ¾ × 1/12-INCH /4 × 2 × ¼-CM SLICES
* 1 TEASPOON SALT
* 2 TEASPOONS LIGHT SOY SAUCE
* 2 TEASPOONS CORNSTARCH (CORNFLOUR)
* 1 EGG, BEATEN
* 2 CUPS (16 FL OZ/475 ML) VEGETABLE OIL
* 1 CLOVE GARLIC, SLICED
* ¼ CUP (1 OZ/25 G) BAMBOO SHOOTS, SLICED
* 2 TABLESPOONS PEAS
* ½ CUP (4 FL OZ/120 ML) CHICKEN BROTH (STOCK, PAGE 90)
* 1 TEASPOON RICE WINE
* 2 TEASPOONS VINEGAR
* 1 SCALLION (SPRING ONION), CHOPPED
* ½ TEASPOON GROUND WHITE PEPPER
* STEAMED RICE (PAGE 540), TO SERVE

REGION: HAKKA
PREPARATION TIME: 10 MINUTES,
   PLUS 15 MINUTES MARINATING TIME
COOKING TIME: 5 MINUTES
SERVES: 4
📷 PAGE 373

唐蒜炒肉片
PORK WITH
CHINESE LEEKS

- 11 OZ/300 G SKINLESS PORK
  SHOULDER, SLICED
- 3 CLOVES GARLIC, CHOPPED
- ½ TEASPOON GRANULATED SUGAR
- ½ TABLESPOON LIGHT SOY SAUCE
- 1 TEASPOON CORNSTARCH
  (CORNFLOUR)
- 2 TABLESPOONS PLUS 1 TEASPOON
  VEGETABLE OIL
- 14 OZ/400 G CHINESE LEEKS, CUT INTO
  2½-INCH/6-CM LENGTHS
- ¼ TEASPOON SALT, PLUS EXTRA
  TO TASTE
- STEAMED RICE (PAGE 540), TO SERVE

* Combine the pork, garlic, sugar, and soy sauce in a bowl,
  mix well, and marinate for 15 minutes. Stir in the cornstarch
  (cornflour) and 1 teaspoon oil.
* Heat 1 tablespoon oil in a wok or large skillet (frying pan)
  over high heat, add the leeks and salt, and stir-fry for
  1 minute. Transfer to a plate.
* Heat the remaining 1 tablespoon oil over high heat, add
  the pork, and stir-fry for 2 minutes until cooked through.
  Add the leeks and stir-fry for another minute. Transfer
  to a serving plate and serve with rice.

话梅猪手
TROTTERS WITH
SALTED PLUMS

- 1 LB/450 G PIG TROTTERS, SCRAPED
  CLEAN, RINSED, AND CUT INTO
  CHUNKS
- 2 TABLESPOONS RICE VINEGAR
- 1 OZ/25 G GINGER (ABOUT 2-INCH/
  5-CM-LENGTH PIECE), SLICED
- 5 LARGE SALTED PLUMS
- 1 TABLESPOON BLACK OR BALSAMIC
  VINEGAR
- ½ TEASPOON DARK SOY SAUCE
- ¼ TEASPOON SALT

* Put the trotters into a large saucepan and add enough
  water to cover them completely. Bring to a boil over high
  heat and blanch for 10 minutes. Skim the froth and scum
  off the surface, if needed. Drain and rinse under cold water.
* In a clean saucepan, combine the trotters, rice vinegar, and
  enough water to cover everything. Cover and bring to a boil
  over high heat. Reduce to low heat and cook for 15 minutes.
  Drain and rinse under cold running water.
* Return the trotters to the saucepan, add the ginger,
  salted plums, vinegar, soy sauce, salt, and enough water
  to cover the trotters. Bring to a boil over high heat, reduce
  to medium heat, cover, and simmer for about 45 minutes.
  Transfer the trotters to a serving bowl.
* Increase to high heat and reduce the sauce by half. Pour
  it over the trotters, then set aside to cool. Serve at room
  temperature.

PORK WITH CHINESE LEEKS

京酱肉丝
PORK WITH
BEIJING SAUCE

- 11 OZ/300 G LEAN PORK, CUT INTO
  THIN STRIPS
- ½ TEASPOON SALT
- ½ TEASPOON LIGHT SOY SAUCE
- 2 TEASPOONS GRANULATED SUGAR
- 1 TABLESPOON CORNSTARCH
  (CORNFLOUR)
- 2 CUPS (16 FL OZ/475 ML) PLUS
  1 TABLESPOON VEGETABLE OIL
- 2 SCALLIONS (SPRING ONIONS),
  STEMS ONLY, SHREDDED
- 1 TABLESPOON TIANMIANJIANG
- ½ TABLESPOON DARK SOY SAUCE
- 1 TEASPOON SESAME OIL
- STEAMED RICE (PAGE 540), TO SERVE

* Combine the pork, salt, light soy sauce, and ½ teaspoon sugar in a bowl, mix well, and marinate for 10 minutes. Mix in the cornstarch (cornflour). Stir in 1 tablespoon vegetable oil just before cooking.
* Line the bottom of a serving plate with the scallions (spring onions). Set aside.
* Heat the remaining vegetable oil in a wok or deep saucepan to 300°F/150°C, or until a cube of bread browns in 1½ minutes. Gently lower the pork into the oil, using chopsticks to disperse the pieces rapidly to prevent sticking, and deep-fry for 1 minute. Use a slotted spoon to carefully remove the pork from the oil and drain on paper towels.
* Pour out most of the oil, leaving about 1 tablespoon in the wok. Heat the oil over high heat, stir in the tianmianjiang, the dark soy sauce, and the remaining 1½ teaspoons sugar, return the pork to the wok, and stir-fry for 1–2 minutes until the pork is cooked through. Add the sesame oil and toss thoroughly. Transfer to the serving plate and serve with rice.

丁香肘子
PORK KNUCKLE WITH CLOVES

- 1 (2¼-LB/1-KG) PORK KNUCKLE,
  SCRAPED CLEAN AND RINSED
- 1 TABLESPOON VEGETABLE OIL
- 3 TABLESPOONS GRANULATED SUGAR
- STEAMED RICE (PAGE 540), TO SERVE

  FOR THE SAUCE:
- 6 CLOVES
- ¼ OZ/10 G GINGER (ABOUT ¾-INCH/
  2-CM-LENGTH PIECE), SLICED
- 2 TABLESPOONS RICE WINE
- 1 TEASPOON SALT
- 2 TABLESPOONS LIGHT SOY SAUCE
- 2 CUPS (16 FL OZ/475 ML) CHICKEN
  BROTH (STOCK, PAGE 90)

* Put the pork knuckle into a large saucepan and add enough water to cover it completely. Bring to a boil over high heat, reduce to low heat, and blanch for 30 minutes. Drain and rinse under cold running water.
* Transfer the pork knuckle to a cutting board and score the skin in a crisscross pattern at 1-inch/2.5-cm intervals.
* Heat the oil in a wok or large skillet (frying pan) over medium-low heat. Add the sugar and cook for 3–4 minutes, or until caramelized. Add the pork knuckle and roll it in the caramelized sugar until the skin is fully coated.
* Transfer the pork knuckle to a heatproof bowl, add the sauce ingredients, and seal the bowl with aluminum foil. Put into a bamboo steamer over a pot of boiling water. Steam, covered, for 2 hours, or until tender. Transfer the knuckle to a shallow bowl, cut open, and remove the bone.
* Pour the sauce into a saucepan and discard the cloves and ginger. Bring to a boil over high heat, reduce to medium heat, and simmer, uncovered, for 25 minutes until the liquid has reduced to half. Pour the sauce over the pork knuckle and serve with rice.

红烧狮子头
BRAISED RED
MEATBALLS

REGION: SHANGHAI
PREPARATION TIME: 20 MINUTES,
  PLUS 20 MINUTES SOAKING TIME
COOKING TIME: 15 MINUTES
SERVES: 6

* Cover the mushrooms in ½ cup (4 fl oz/120 ml) cold water and soak for at least 20 minutes, or until softened. Remove the mushrooms, squeeze dry, and discard the stems. Reserve the soaking water.
* In a large bowl, combine the ground (minced) pork, pork fatback, ginger juice, salt, sugar, white pepper, cornstarch (cornflour), and crushed oatmeal. Pick up the pork with one hand and slap it against the bowl about 5 times; this will cause the patty to become sticky and elastic. Wet your hands and form the mixture into 6 meatballs, then roll in a thin layer of cornstarch.
* Heat the vegetable oil in a wok or deep saucepan to 300°F/150°C, or until a cube of bread browns in 1½ minutes. Carefully add the meatballs and deep-fry for 1–2 minutes until firm, then reduce to low heat and continue deep-frying for another 1–2 minutes until the meatballs are just under done. Use a slotted spoon to carefully remove them from the oil and drain on paper towels.
* Pour out most of the oil, leaving about 1 tablespoon in the wok. To make the sauce, add the ginger and whole mushrooms, and stir-fry over medium heat for 1 minute until fragrant. Add the wine, soy and oyster sauces, and sugar. Add the meatballs, chicken broth (stock), and mushroom soaking water and bring to a boil over high heat. Reduce to low heat and simmer for 2–3 minutes until cooked through. Transfer the meatballs to a plate and keep warm.
* Bring the wok of sauce to a boil and boil, uncovered, for 2–3 minutes until the sauce has reduced by half.
* Mix the cornstarch (cornflour) with 1 tablespoon water in a small bowl and stir this mixture into the wok. Bring to a boil, stirring, for 30 seconds to thicken the sauce.
* Stir in the sesame oil and pour the sauce over the meatballs. Serve with steamed vegetables, if desired.

- 11 OZ/300 G GROUND (MINCED) LEAN PORK, FINELY CHOPPED
- 7 OZ/200 G PORK FATBACK, DICED
- 1 TABLESPOON GINGER JUICE
- ½ TEASPOON SALT
- ½ TEASPOON GRANULATED SUGAR
- ¼ TEASPOON GROUND WHITE PEPPER
- 1 TABLESPOON CORNSTARCH (CORNFLOUR), PLUS EXTRA FOR DUSTING
- 1 TABLESPOON OATMEAL, CRUSHED
- 2 CUPS (16 FL OZ/475 ML) VEGETABLE OIL
- STEAMED VEGETABLES, TO SERVE (OPTIONAL)

FOR THE SAUCE:
- 6 DRIED BLACK MUSHROOMS
- ¼ OZ/10 G GINGER (ABOUT ¾-INCH/ 2-CM-LENGTH PIECE), SLICED
- 1 TABLESPOON SHAOXING WINE
- ½ TEASPOON DARK SOY SAUCE
- 1 TABLESPOON OYSTER SAUCE
- ½ TEASPOON GRANULATED SUGAR ½ CUP (4 FL OZ/120 ML) CHICKEN BROTH (STOCK, PAGE 90) OR WATER
- 1 TEASPOON CORNSTARCH (CORNFLOUR)
- 1 TEASPOON SESAME OIL

REGION: ANHUI
PREPARATION TIME: 10 MINUTES
COOKING TIME: 1 HOUR
SERVES: 2

燴三鮮

ANHUI-STYLE BRAISED MEATS

- 1 (4-OZ/120-G) BONELESS, SKIN-ON PORK BELLY
- 1 BONELESS CHICKEN THIGH
- 4 TABLESPOONS LARD OR VEGETABLE OIL
- 1 (4-OZ/120-G) BLACK CARP OR SEA BASS FILLET, CUT INTO 2-INCH/5-CM CHUNKS
- 1 TEASPOON CORNSTARCH (CORNFLOUR)
- 1 SCALLION (SPRING ONION), CUT INTO 1½-INCH/4-CM LENGTHS
- ⅛ OZ/5 G GINGER (ABOUT ½-INCH/ 1-CM-LENGTH PIECE), SLICED
- 1 STAR ANISE
- 1 TEASPOON SALT
- 1 TEASPOON GRANULATED SUGAR
- 1 TABLESPOON LIGHT SOY SAUCE
- 3 CUPS (25 FL OZ/750 ML) CHICKEN BROTH (STOCK, PAGE 90)
- 1 BUNCH CILANTRO (CORIANDER), CHOPPED, TO GARNISH
- STEAMED RICE (PAGE 540), TO SERVE

* For the pork belly, scrape the skin clean, then rinse the pork under cold running water.
* Put the chicken and pork into a large saucepan and add enough water to cover them completely. Bring to a boil over high heat and blanch for 2 minutes. Drain and rinse under cold running water until cooled, then cut into large chunks (the same size as the fish).
* Heat the lard in a wok or large skillet (frying pan) over medium-high heat. Dredge the fish pieces with the cornstarch (cornflour) and gently lower them into the hot oil, in batches. Fry for 3–4 minutes until golden brown. Use a slotted spoon to carefully remove the fish and drain on paper towels.
* Put the chicken and pork into the wok, add the scallion (spring onion), ginger, star anise, salt, sugar, soy sauce, and chicken broth (stock) and bring to a boil. Reduce to low heat and simmer, uncovered, for about 40 minutes, or until reduced by 75 percent. Add the fish, increase to medium heat, and continue to cook for about 8 minutes, or until the sauce thickens. Discard the scallion (spring onion), ginger, and star anise.
* Transfer to a serving bowl and garnish with the cilantro (coriander). Serve with rice.

木耳炖猪尾
PIG'S TAIL WITH WHITE-BACK WOOD EARS

REGION: HAKKA
PREPARATION TIME: 15 MINUTES,
    PLUS 10 MINUTES SOAKING TIME
COOKING TIME: 3 HOURS
SERVES: 4

* Soak the pig tail in plenty of cold water, then scrape the skin clean. Use a sharp knife to cut the pig tail into small chunks at the joints.
* Put the pig tail pieces into a large saucepan and enough water to cover them completely. Bring to a boil over high heat and blanch for 5 minutes. Drain and rinse under cold running water.
* Soak the wood ears in a bowl of cold water for 10 minutes until softened. Cut into ½-inch/1-cm-wide strips and set aside. In a separate bowl, soak the tangerine peel in cold water for 10 minutes to soften then drain and set aside.
* Toast the black beans in a small skillet (frying pan) over low heat for 3–4 minutes until they burst, then remove and rinse under cold running water.
* Put the pig tail, wood ears, roasted black beans, tangerine peel, jujube dates, ginger, and 4¼ cups (34 fl oz/1 liter) water in a large saucepan. Bring to a boil over high heat, reduce to low heat, and simmer, covered, for 2½ hours. Season with salt to taste, then transfer to a serving bowl. Serve with rice.

- 1 PIG'S TAIL
- 1 CUP (¾ OZ/20 G) WHITE-BACK WOOD EAR FUNGUS
- 1 DRIED TANGERINE PEEL
- 8 JUJUBE DATES, PITTED
- 2 TABLESPOONS DRIED BLACK BEANS
- ⅛ OZ/5 G GINGER (ABOUT ½-INCH/ 1-CM-LENGTH PIECE), SLICED
- SALT, TO TASTE
- STEAMED RICE (PAGE 540), TO SERVE

REGION: GUANGDONG
PREPARATION TIME: 3 DAYS
COOKING TIME: 4 HOURS 15 MINUTES
SERVES: 6

猪脚姜醋
GINGER AND VINEGAR TROTTERS

- 1 LB 5 OZ/600 G GINGER, PEELED, CUT INTO 2-INCH/5-CM PIECES, HALVED, AND CRUSHED
- ½ TABLESPOON SALT
- 6¼ CUPS (50 FL OZ/1.5 LITERS) CANTONESE SWEETENED BLACK VINEGAR
- 1 LB 5 OZ/600 G PIGS' TROTTERS, SCRAPED CLEAN, RINSED, AND CUT INTO SMALL PIECES
- 6 EGGS, AT ROOM TEMPERATURE

This is a favorite Cantonese dish to celebrate the birth of a baby. It is usually prepared in a large batch to share with family members and friends as part of the celebration. Ginger, vinegar, and the collagen from the trotters are thought to benefit a mother's recovery from childbirth.

Day 1
* Combine the ginger and salt in a small bowl and let stand for 30 minutes. Rinse and drain.
* Place the ginger on a heatproof plate in a collapsible pot or bamboo steamer over a pot of boiling water. Steam, covered, for 30 minutes. Drain the water on the plate. Transfer the ginger to a clay pot or stainless-steel saucepan, then add the vinegar. Cover and bring to a boil over high heat, then reduce to low heat, and simmer for 2 hours. Turn off the heat and let stand overnight.

Day 2
* Put the pigs' trotters in a large saucepan and add enough water to cover them completely. Bring to a boil over high heat and blanch for 5 minutes. Drain and rinse thoroughly under cold running water.
* Return the trotters to the pan and fill with cold water. Cover, bring to a boil over high heat, reduce to low heat, and simmer for 45 minutes. Skim the froth and scum off the surface, if needed. Turn off the heat, cover, and stand for another 45 minutes.
* Drain the trotters and rinse under cold running water until completely cold. Put them into the pot with the ginger and vinegar, cover, and bring to a boil over high heat. Reduce to low heat and cook for 45 minutes. Turn off the heat and stand covered overnight.
* Put the whole eggs into a saucepan and add enough cold water to cover completely. Bring to a boil over medium-high heat for 3½ minutes. Remove the eggs immediately, drain, and rinse well under cold running water. When cool enough to handle, peel and add to the trotter mixture.

Day 3
* Transfer the trotters and eggs into a separate container.
* At this stage, you will have a large pot of vinegar and you'll only need to heat your desired serving portion. Pour the vinegar into a large saucepan and bring to a boil over high heat. Reduce the heat, add the trotters and eggs, and heat through. Ladle into individual bowls, then serve.

湖南红烧肉
HUNAN-STYLE PORK BELLY

REGION: HUNAN
PREPARATION TIME: 15 MINUTES
COOKING TIME: 2 HOURS
SERVES: 6

* Place the pork belly, skin facing down, on a cutting board. Trim the meat to an even thickness and scrape the skin clean, then rinse the pork under cold running water.
* Put the pork into a large saucepan and add enough water to cover it completely. Bring to a boil over high heat and blanch the pork for 15 minutes. Skim the froth and scum off the surface. Drain and rinse under cold running water until cooled. Cut the pork into 1¼-inch/3-cm square pieces.
* Heat the oil in a wok or large skillet (frying pan) over medium heat, add the dried chiles, and stir-fry for 1 minute until fragrant. Stir in the fresh chiles, garlic, ginger, and black beans. Add the chili bean paste and red distilled grain sauce and stir-fry for about 1 minute. Put in the pork, increase to high heat, and stir-fry until fragrant. Sprinkle in the wine. Add the Sichuan peppercorns, star anise, and 1 cup (8 fl oz/250 ml) water, and bring to a boil. Reduce to low heat and simmer, covered, for about 45 minutes. Turn the pork over once or twice during cooking.
* Add the soy sauces and rock sugar, stir, and simmer, covered, for about another 45 minutes, or until the pork is very soft. Once ready, transfer the pork to a serving plate and keep warm. Bring the sauce to a boil over high heat, then reduce to medium heat, and simmer uncovered, for 2–3 minutes until slightly thickened. Pour the sauce over the pork. Serve with rice.

- 1 (1 LB 5-OZ/600-G) BONELESS, SKIN-ON PORK BELLY
- 2 TABLESPOONS VEGETABLE OIL
- 4 DRIED CHILES, HALVED
- 3 RED CHILES, HALVED
- 2 CLOVES GARLIC, CHOPPED
- 1 OZ/25 G GINGER (ABOUT 2-INCH/5-CM-LENGTH PIECE), SLICED
- 1 TABLESPOON FERMENTED BLACK BEANS, RINSED AND CHOPPED
- 1½ TABLESPOONS CHILI BEAN PASTE
- 1 TABLESPOON RED DISTILLED GRAIN SAUCE
- 2 TABLESPOONS SHAOXING WINE
- 1 TABLESPOON SICHUAN PEPPERCORNS
- 2 STAR ANISE
- 1 TEASPOON DARK SOY SAUCE
- ½ TEASPOON LIGHT SOY SAUCE
- ¾ OZ/20 G ROCK SUGAR
- STEAMED RICE (PAGE 540), TO SERVE

东坡肉
DONGPO
PORK

- 1 (1-LB 2-OZ/500-G) BONELESS, SKIN-ON PORK BELLY
- 1 TEASPOON VEGETABLE OIL
- 2 TABLESPOONS BROWN SUGAR
- 1 TABLESPOON RED YEAST RICE OR CHERRY JUICE
- ¼ OZ/10 G GINGER (ABOUT ¾-INCH/ 2-CM-LENGTH PIECE), SLICED
- 2 BEIJING SCALLIONS OR 6 SCALLIONS (SPRING ONIONS), CUT INTO 1½-INCH/4-CM LENGTHS
- GENEROUS 1½ CUPS (13 FL OZ/375 ML) SHAOXING WINE
- 1 TABLESPOON ROCK SUGAR
- 3 TABLESPOONS LIGHT SOY SAUCE
- 11 OZ/300 G GREEN BOK CHOY
- CILANTRO (CORIANDER) LEAVES, TO GARNISH (OPTIONAL)
- STEAMED RICE (PAGE 540), TO SERVE

Dongpo Pork is named after Su Dongpo (1037–1101) of the Song Dynasty. Not only was Su a renowned essayist and revered poet, he was also a great gastronome—his poem on how to cook pork was probably one of the earliest writings on slow cooking. Dongpo pork was one of his many creations and a favorite dish throughout China.

* Place the pork belly, skin facing down, on a cutting board. Trim the meat to an even thickness and scrape the skin clean, then rinse the pork under cold running water.
* Put the pork in a large saucepan and add enough water to cover it completely. Bring to a boil over high heat and blanch the pork for 20 minutes. Skim the froth and scum off the surface, if needed. Drain and rinse well under cold running water for 5 minutes until cooled. Place the pork on the cutting board, skin facing down. Cut the lean meat into 4 equal quadrants without cutting through the skin.
* Heat 1 teaspoon oil in a saucepan, add the brown sugar, and cook over low heat for 2–3 minutes until caramelized. Stir in 2 tablespoons water, carefully place the pork into the caramel, skin-side down, and then turn over to ensure the pork is covered in the caramel. Turn off the heat.
* Combine the red yeast rice and 1 cup (8 fl oz/250 ml) water in a small saucepan and bring to a boil. Simmer for 15 minutes, strain into a bowl, and set aside.
* Line the bottom of a Dutch oven (casserole) with the ginger slices and place the pork on top, skin facing down. Surround the pork with the Beijing scallions. Pour over the reserved red yeast rice water, the wine, and enough cold water to completely cover the pork. Bring to a boil, then reduce to low heat, and simmer for 30 minutes. Add the rock sugar and soy sauce and simmer for another hour. Turn the pork over and simmer for another 1 hour.
* Meanwhile, bring a large saucepan of water to a boil, add the boy choy, and blanch for 2 minutes. Transfer the pork to a plate, skin-side up, and surround with the bok choy. Pour over the sauce from the pan, garnish with cilantro (coriander), if using, and serve with rice.

DONGPO PORK

REGION: ZHEJIANG
PREPARATION TIME: 20 MINUTES,
    PLUS 1 HOUR SOAKING TIME
COOKING TIME: 5 HOURS
SERVES: 8

蜜汁火方
DOUBLE-BOILED
CURED HAM

- 1 (1-LB 5-OZ/600-G) JINHUA OR SMITHFIELD HAM
- ¼ CUP (2 OZ/50 G) GRANULATED SUGAR
- 4 TABLESPOONS RED WINE
- 4 OZ/120 G ROCK SUGAR, CRUSHED
- 4 TABLESPOONS SHAOXING WINE
- 3 CUPS (3½ OZ/100 G) DRIED LOTUS SEEDS
- CHINESE BUNS, SUCH AS MANTOU, OR BREAD, TO SERVE

The history of this dish dates back about three hundred years, possibly earlier. Yuan Mei, the famous gourmet in the Qing Dynasty, wrote about this dish in his work, *Suiyuan Shidan*. Traditionally, this dish called for a special cut from the center of a Jinhua ham; however, any good-quality ham can be used as a substitute.

* Scrape the skin of the ham clean of any fat and rinse well with hot water. Trim the ham into a square, then trim so that the total thickness of the ham is about 1½ inch/4 cm, with the skin. The lean ham can be saved for future use.
* Place the ham on a cutting board, skin-side down, and make crisscross cuts on the lean meat. The cuts should only be about two-thirds of the ham's total thickness.
* Place the ham, skin-side down, in a heatproof bowl large enough to hold the ham, add the sugar and fill the bowl with water to cover the ham completely. Seal tightly with aluminum foil.
* Place in a collapsible pot or large bamboo steamer over a pot of boiling water. Steam, covered, for 1 hour. Carefully remove the foil and drain the water from the bowl.
* Add both wines and 3 oz/90 g rock sugar to the bowl and fill with fresh water to cover the ham. Cover tightly with aluminum foil and steam for another 4 hours. Add more water to the wok if needed.
* Meanwhile, soak the dried lotus seeds in a bowl of warm water for about 1 hour. Drain, pick out and discard the heart of the seeds, and rinse.
* Put the lotus seeds into a saucepan, add the remaining 1½ oz/40 g rock sugar and 2 cups (16 fl oz/475 ml) water, and bring to a boil. Reduce to low heat and simmer for 1 hour until the sugar and water become a syrup. Turn off the heat.
* Use tongs to carefully transfer the ham, skin-side up, to a deep plate. Sprinkle the lotus seeds around the ham. Keep warm.
* Pour the sauce from the cooked ham into a small saucepan, bring to a boil over high heat, and reduce to 1 cup (8 fl oz/250 ml) until it becomes a syrup. Pour over the ham. Serve with Chinese buns or other bread of choice.

櫻桃肉

BRAISED CHERRY-COLORED
PORK

REGION: JIANGSU
PREPARATION TIME: 15 MINUTES
COOKING TIME: 2 HOURS
SERVES: 4

Scoring the pork skin creates an interesting textural effect while the red yeast rice, an all-natural coloring ingredient used frequently in Chinese cuisine, gives its signature hue. The result? A bold and dramatic dish that's great for serving to guests.

* Place the pork belly, skin facing down, on a cutting board. Trim the meat to an even thickness and scrape the skin clean, then rinse the pork under cold running water.
* Put the pork into a large saucepan and add enough water to cover it completely. Bring to a boil over high heat and blanch the pork for 10 minutes. Drain and rinse under cold running water until cooled.
* Meanwhile, if using red yeast rice, combine the red yeast rice and ½ cup (4 fl oz/120 ml) water in a saucepan and bring to a boil over high heat. Reduce to medium-low heat and cook for 3–4 minutes until about 2 tablespoons liquid remain in the pot. Pour the liquid through a cheesecloth (muslin)-lined strainer (sieve) into a bowl. Set aside.
* Put the pork on the cutting board, skin-side up, and use a sharp knife to score the pork, in a crisscross pattern, at ½-inch/1-cm intervals. The cuts should be made through the skin and fat but before they reach the first layer of lean meat.
* Place the pork belly in a Dutch oven (casserole), skin-side up, add the chicken broth (stock), scallions (spring onions), ginger, wine, salt, and red yeast rice water or cherry juice, and bring to a boil over high heat. Cover, reduce to medium heat, and simmer for about 45 minutes.
* Add the rock sugar, reduce to low heat, and simmer for about another hour. Increase to medium heat and simmer until the sauce has reduced by half. Discard the scallions and ginger slices. Serve in the Dutch oven with rice.

- 1 (1 LB 2-OZ/500-G) BONELESS, SKIN- ON PORK BELLY
- 2 TABLESPOONS RED YEAST RICE OR CHERRY JUICE
- 3 CUPS (25 FL OZ/750 ML) CHICKEN BROTH (STOCK, PAGE 90)
- 2 SCALLIONS (SPRING ONIONS), KNOTTED
- ⅛ OZ/5 G GINGER (ABOUT ½-INCH/ 1-CM-LENGTH PIECE), SLICED
- 2 TABLESPOONS SHAOXING WINE
- 2 TEASPOONS SALT
- 2 OZ/50 G ROCK SUGAR
- STEAMED RICE (PAGE 540), TO SERVE

虎皮肉

PORK BELLY IN TIGER STRIPES

- 1 (1-LB 2-OZ/500-G) BONELESS, SKIN-ON PORK BELLY
- 1 OZ/25 G PRESERVED MUSTARD GREEN STEMS, TRIMMED, RINSED, AND CUT INTO ¾-INCH/2-CM LENGTHS
- 3 TABLESPOONS OIL
- 2 TEASPOONS LIGHT SOY SAUCE
- 1 TEASPOON DARK SOY SAUCE
- 1 TABLESPOON SHAOXING WINE
- 2 TABLESPOONS GRANULATED SUGAR
- 1 TEASPOON SALT
- 2 SCALLIONS (SPRING ONIONS)
- ¼ OZ/10 G GINGER (ABOUT ¾-INCH/ 2-CM-LENGTH PIECE), SLICED
- 1 STAR ANISE
- STEAMED RICE (PAGE 540), TO SERVE

Legend has it that this dish was created during the Ming Dynasty by a beautiful lady named Dong Xiaowan (1624–1651) who was said to be one of the eight beauties in Nanjing. She was highly intelligent, cultured, and artistic, as well as a great cook. A number of dim sum dishes in Jiangsu today still bear her name.

* Place the pork belly, skin facing down, on a cutting board. Trim the meat to an even thickness and scrape the skin clean, then rinse the pork under cold running water.
* Put the pork into a large saucepan and add enough water to cover it completely. Bring to a boil over high heat and blanch the pork for 5 minutes. Skim the froth and scum off the surface, if needed. Drain and rinse under cold running water until cooled. Using a sharp knife, make horizontal cuts through the skin and fat layer only, at ½-inch/1-cm intervals, to create the "tiger stripes."
* Put the mustard greens on paper towels to absorb any excess water.
* Heat the oil in a large saucepan, add the mustard green stems, and pan-fry over high heat for about 2–3 minutes until brown. Transfer the stems to a plate and set aside.
* Add the pork, skin-side up, and enough water to cover. Add the soy sauces, wine, sugar, salt, scallions (spring onions), ginger, and star anise. Bring to a boil, then reduce to low heat and simmer for about 1 hour. Skim the froth and scum off the surface. Transfer the pork to a heatproof bowl, skin-side down, then top with the mustard greens and pour the broth (stock) on top. Place in a collapsible pot or bamboo steamer over a pot of boiling water. Steam, covered, for 1 hour. (Add more water to the pot, if needed.)
* Drain the sauce into a small saucepan. Cover the bowl of pork with a plate, and using dish towels, invert the contents onto the plate. (Alternatively, use tongs to transfer the contents to a serving plate.)
* Heat the sauce over high heat and boil, uncovered, until thickened and reduced. Pour the sauce over the pork. Serve with rice.

莲藕焖猪肉

PORK BELLY WITH
LOTUS ROOT

REGION: SHUNDE
PREPARATION TIME: 15 MINUTES
COOKING TIME: 1 HOUR 15 MINUTES
SERVES: 4

* Use a chopstick to clean the channels inside the lotus root and rinse thoroughly under cold running water. Cut the lotus root into 3¼ × 2-inch/8 × 5-cm rectangular pieces. Place in a bowl and set aside.
* Place the pork belly, skin facing down, on a cutting board. Trim the meat to an even thickness and scrape the skin clean, then rinse the pork under cold running water.
* Put the pork into a large saucepan and add enough water to cover it completely. Bring to a boil over high heat and blanch the pork for 5 minutes. Drain and rinse under cold running water until cooled. Cut the pork into pieces similar in size to the lotus roots.
* Heat the oil in a wok or large skillet (frying pan), add the ginger, and stir-fry over medium heat for 1 minute until fragrant. Add the red bean curd and bean paste and use your spatula (fish slice) to break it up. Add the pork, increase to high heat, and stir-fry for 1 minute. Sprinkle in the wine, add enough water to cover the pork by about ½ inch/1 cm, and bring to a boil. Reduce to low heat and simmer, covered, for 30 minutes.
* Add the lotus roots, soy sauce, and sugar, then cover and simmer for 30 minutes. Uncover and simmer over high heat for 2–3 minutes until the sauce has reduced slightly. Transfer to a serving plate and serve with rice.

- 1 LB 5 OZ/600 G LOTUS ROOT, PEELED AND ENDS TRIMMED
- 1 (11-OZ/300-G) BONELESS, SKIN-ON PORK BELLY
- 1 TABLESPOON VEGETABLE OIL
- 1 OZ/25 G GINGER (ABOUT 2-INCH/ 5-CM-LENGTH PIECE) SLICED
- 1 CUBE RED BEAN CURD
- 1 TABLESPOON BEAN PASTE
- 1 TABLESPOON RICE WINE
- 1 TEASPOON LIGHT SOY SAUCE
- 1 TEASPOON GRANULATED SUGAR
- STEAMED RICE (PAGE 540), TO SERVE

REGION: HAKKA
PREPARATION TIME: 10 MINUTES
COOKING TIME: 1 HOUR 20 MINUTES
SERVES: 4
PAGE 387

客家焖猪肉

HAKKA STEWED PORK

- 1 (14-OZ/400-G) BONELESS, SKIN-ON PORK BELLY
- 4 TABLESPOONS VEGETABLE OIL
- 1 STAR ANISE
- 1 TEASPOON SICHUAN PEPPERCORNS
- 3 CLOVES GARLIC, SLICED
- ⅛ OZ/5 G GINGER (ABOUT ½-INCH/ 1-CM-LENGTH PIECE), SLICED
- ½ TEASPOON GROUND CINNAMON
- ½ TEASPOON GROUND CUMIN
- 1 TABLESPOON LIGHT SOY SAUCE
- ½ TABLESPOON DARK SOY SAUCE
- ¼ OZ/10 G ROCK SUGAR, CRUSHED
- 1 CUP (8 FL OZ/250 ML) GLUTINOUS RICE WINE
- 6¼ OZ/180 G PRESERVED MUSTARD GREENS, TRIMMED, RINSED, AND CUT INTO ¾-INCH/2-CM PIECES
- STEAMED RICE (PAGE 540), TO SERVE

* Place the pork belly, skin facing down, on a cutting board. Trim the meat to an even thickness and scrape the skin clean, then rinse the pork under cold running water.
* Put the pork into a large saucepan and add enough water to cover it completely. Bring to a boil over high heat and blanch the pork for 5 minutes. Skim the froth and scum off the surface, if needed. Drain and rinse under cold water.
* Heat the oil in a wok or large skillet (frying pan). Add the pork, skin-side down, and brown for 2–3 minutes until golden brown and crispy. Carefully remove the pork from the oil and drain on paper towels.
* Pour out most of the oil, leaving about 1 tablespoon in the wok. Put the star anise and Sichuan peppercorns in a spice bag. Heat the oil in the wok over medium-high heat, add the garlic, and ginger and stir-fry for 1 minute until fragrant. Add 1 cup (8 fl oz/250 ml) water, the spice bag, cinnamon, cumin, soy sauces, and sugar and bring to a boil.
* Add the pork, skin-side down, and pour in the wine. Cover and simmer over medium-low heat for about 40 minutes. Halfway through cooking, turn the pork over. Discard the spice bag, transfer the pork to a cutting board, and leave to cool, slightly, before cutting it into chunks.
* Meanwhile, put the mustard greens into the sauce and add 4 tablespoons water. Bring to a boil, then reduce to medium heat, and simmer for 15 minutes. Add the pork and simmer for another 15 minutes. Transfer to a serving bowl and serve with rice.

HAKKA STEWED PORK

REGION: TAIWAN
PREPARATION TIME: 10 MINUTES, PLUS
  20 MINUTES MARINATING TIME
COOKING TIME: 35 MINUTES
SERVES: 4

香菇卤肉
PORK BELLY WITH MUSHROOMS

- 1 (1-LB 5-OZ/600-G) BONELESS, SKIN-ON PORK BELLY, RINSED AND CUT INTO BITE-SIZE CHUNKS
- 1 TABLESPOON DARK SOY SAUCE
- 8 LARGE DRIED BLACK MUSHROOMS
- 1 STAR ANISE
- 1 TEASPOON SICHUAN PEPPERCORNS
- ¼ CINNAMON STICK
- 2 TABLESPOONS VEGETABLE OIL
- 3 CLOVES GARLIC, SLICED
- 1 TABLESPOON RICE WINE
- 1 TABLESPOON LIGHT SOY SAUCE
- ¾ OZ/20 G ROCK SUGAR
- STEAMED RICE (PAGE 540), TO SERVE

* Combine the pork and dark soy sauce in a bowl and marinate for 20 minutes.
* Meanwhile, cover the mushrooms in cold water and soak for at least 20 minutes, or until softened. Remove the mushrooms, squeeze dry, and discard the stems.
* Put the star anise, Sichuan peppercorns, and cinnamon stick into a spice bag.
* Heat the oil in a Dutch oven (casserole), add the pork, and stir-fry over high heat for 1–2 minutes until golden. Remove the pork and set aside on a plate. Add the garlic and mushrooms to the Dutch oven and stir-fry for 1 minute over medium-high heat until fragrant.
* Return the pork to the Dutch oven, add the wine and light soy sauce, and stir well. Add the rock sugar, spice bag, and 1 cup (8 fl oz/250 ml) water and bring to a boil. Reduce to low heat and simmer, covered, for about 30 minutes, or until the pork is tender. Discard the spice bag. Serve in the Dutch oven with rice.

REGION: TAIWAN
PREPARATION TIME: 5 MINUTES,
  PLUS COOLING TIME
COOKING TIME: 1 HOUR 15 MINUTES
SERVES: 4

卤肉
PORK BELLY IN SOY SAUCE

- 2 CUPS (16 FL OZ/475 ML) VEGETABLE OIL
- 1 (1 LB 5-OZ/600-G) BONELESS, SKIN-ON PORK BELLY, RINSED
- 3 SCALLIONS (SPRING ONIONS), CUT INTO 2-INCH/5-CM LENGTHS
- 6 CLOVES GARLIC
- ½ TEASPOON GROUND WHITE PEPPER
- ⅓ CUP (2½ FL OZ/80 ML) DARK SOY SAUCE
- 1 CUP (8 FL OZ/250 ML) LIGHT SOY SAUCE
- ½ CUP (4 FL OZ/120 ML) RICE WINE
- ½ OZ/15 G ROCK SUGAR, CRUSHED
- STEAMED RICE (PAGE 540), TO SERVE

* Heat the oil in a wok or large skillet (frying pan) over medium-high heat. Add the pork and deep-fry for 4–5 minutes until golden. Transfer to a cutting board. Set aside the wok of oil.
* When cool enough to handle, cut the pork into 1-inch/2.5-cm chunks, then transfer to a large saucepan.
* Reheat the oil in the wok, add the scallions (spring onions) and garlic, and deep-fry over medium heat for 2 minutes until golden. Use a slotted spoon to transfer them to the saucepan, then add the white pepper, soy sauces, wine, sugar, and 4¼ cups (34 fl oz/1 liter) water and bring to a boil. Reduce to low heat and simmer for 1 hour, or until tender. Transfer the pork to a serving bowl and serve with rice.

笋虾焖猪肉

PORK BELLY WITH DRIED
BAMBOO SHOOTS

REGION: HONG KONG
PREPARATION TIME: 15 MINUTES,
    PLUS 24 HOURS SOAKING TIME
COOKING TIME: 1 HOUR 30 MINUTES
SERVES: 8

* Soak the dried bamboo shoots in cold water for 24 hours until soft. Change the water 2–3 times during the soaking time.
* Cover the mushrooms in cold water and soak for at least 20 minutes, or until softened. Remove the mushrooms, squeeze dry, and discard the stems.
* Place the pork belly, skin facing down, on a cutting board. Trim the meat to an even thickness and scrape the skin clean, then rinse the pork under cold running water.
* Put the pork belly in a large saucepan and add enough water to cover it completely. Bring to a boil over high heat and blanch for 15 minutes. Skim the froth and scum off the surface, if needed. Drain and rinse under cold running water until cooled. Cut the pork into ¾-inch/2-cm squares.
* Put the bamboo shoots into a saucepan and add enough water to cover them completely. Bring to a boil over high heat and blanch for 5 minutes. Rinse under cold running water. Repeat the process and blanch the bamboo shoots again. Drain and set aside.
* Heat the oil in a Dutch oven (casserole) over high heat, add the ginger, shallots, and garlic, and stir-fry for 1 minute until fragrant. Add the bean paste and red bean curd. Use a spatula (fish slice) to mash the red bean curd.
* Add the pork belly, wine, bamboo shoots, mushrooms, sugar, salt, and enough water to cover all the ingredients. Bring to a boil, then reduce to low heat, and simmer, covered, for about 1 hour, or until the pork belly is soft enough to pierce through with a chopstick. Serve in the Dutch oven with rice on the side.

- 3½ OZ/100 G DRIED BAMBOO SHOOTS, RINSED
- 8 DRIED BLACK MUSHROOMS
- 1 (1-LB 5-OZ/600-G) BONELESS, SKIN-ON PORK BELLY
- 2 TABLESPOONS VEGETABLE OIL
- 2 OZ/50 G GINGER (ABOUT 3-INCH/7.5-CM-LENGTH PIECE), SLICED
- 4 SHALLOTS, HALVED
- 2 CLOVES GARLIC, CRUSHED
- 1 TABLESPOON GROUND BEAN PASTE
- 1 CUBE RED BEAN CURD
- 2 TABLESPOONS RICE WINE
- 2 TEASPOONS GRANULATED SUGAR
- ½ TEASPOON SALT
- STEAMED RICE (PAGE 540), TO SERVE.

REGION: ANHUI
PREPARATION TIME: 10 MINUTES,
   PLUS 45 MINUTES SOAKING TIME
COOKING TIME: ABOUT 3 HOURS
SERVES: 4

绩溪干锅炖

JIXI

PORK

- 1 DRIED LOTUS LEAF
- 1 (1-LB 5-OZ/600-G) BONELESS,
  SKIN-ON PORK BELLY
- ¼ OZ/10 G GINGER (ABOUT ¾-INCH/
  2-CM-LENGTH PIECE), SLICED
- 2 SCALLIONS (SPRING ONIONS),
  CUT INTO 2-INCH/5-CM LENGTHS
- 2 TABLESPOONS SHAOXING WINE
- 2½ TABLESPOONS LIGHT SOY SAUCE
- 1 TEASPOON SALT
- ⅛ OZ/5 G ROCK SUGAR, CRUSHED
- STEAMED RICE (PAGE 540), TO SERVE

* Soak the dried lotus leaf in cold water for 45 minutes.
* Place the pork belly, skin facing down, on a cutting board. Trim the meat to an even thickness and scrape the skin clean, then rinse the pork under cold running water.
* Put the pork into a large saucepan and add enough water to cover it completely. Bring to a boil over high heat and blanch the pork for 5 minutes. Skim the froth and scum off the surface, if needed. Drain and rinse under cold running water until cooled. Cut the pork into 2 × 1¼-inch/5 × 3-cm slices that are ¾ inch/2 cm thick.
* Rinse the lotus leaf, then use it to line the bottom of a Dutch oven (casserole). (Cut it to size if necessary.) Place the ginger and scallions (spring onions) on the lotus leaf and arrange the pork slices, skin facing up, on top.
* Combine the wine, soy sauce, salt, and sugar, then pour the mixture over the pork. Cover and cook over low heat for 3 hours. Serve in the Dutch oven with rice on the side. (The lotus leaf is not to be consumed.)

REGION: JIANGXI
PREPARATION TIME: 5 MINUTES
COOKING TIME: ABOUT 1 HOUR
SERVES: 4

信丰萝卜干烧排骨

SPARERIBS AND DRIED

TURNIP CASSEROLE

- 2 TABLESPOONS VEGETABLE OIL
- ⅛ OZ/5 G GINGER (ABOUT ½-INCH/
  1-CM-LENGTH PIECE), SLICED
- 12 OZ/350 G PORK SPARERIBS,
  CUT INTO 2-INCH/5-CM PIECES
- 1 TEASPOON GRANULATED SUGAR
- 2 TEASPOONS LIGHT SOY SAUCE
- 1 TEASPOON DARK SOY SAUCE
- 1 TABLESPOON RICE WINE
- 5 OZ/150 G DRIED TURNIP, RINSED
  AND CUT INTO 2-INCH/5-CM LENGTHS
- ½ TEASPOON SALT
- 1 TEASPOON CORNSTARCH
  (CORNFLOUR)
- STEAMED RICE (PAGE 540), TO SERVE

* Heat the oil in a Dutch oven (casserole) over medium-high heat, add the ginger, and stir-fry for 1 minute until fragrant. Add the spareribs, increase to high heat, and stir-fry for another minute. Add the sugar, soy sauces, wine, and enough water to cover the spareribs. Bring to a boil, add the dried turnip, reduce to low heat and simmer, covered, for about 1 hour. Season with the salt.
* In a small bowl, mix the cornstarch (cornflour) with 1 tablespoon water and stir this mixture into the Dutch oven. Bring to a boil, stirring, for 30 seconds to thicken the sauce. Serve in the Dutch oven with rice.

杏仁肉丁
PORK WITH
APRICOT KERNELS

REGION: SHANXI
PREPARATION TIME: 15 MINUTES, PLUS
  10 MINUTES MARINATING TIME
COOKING TIME: 10 MINUTES
SERVES: 4

* Combine the pork, 1 teaspoon soy sauce, ¼ teaspoon salt, and 1 teaspoon wine in a bowl and marinate for 10 minutes. Stir in 1 teaspoon cornstarch (cornflour) and 1 tablespoon oil. Set aside.
* Bring a saucepan of water to a boil. Add the carrots and apricot kernels, reduce to medium heat, and simmer for 5 minutes. Drain and rinse under cold running water.
* Heat the remaining 2 tablespoons oil in a wok or large skillet (frying pan) over medium heat. Add the ginger and scallion (spring onion) and stir-fry for 1 minute until fragrant. Stir in the pork and the remaining wine and stir-fry for another 3–4 minutes until the pork is fully cooked. Add the carrots, apricot kernels, bell pepper, and toss well. Stir in the remaining ¼ teaspoon salt, 1 teaspoon soy sauce, and 3 tablespoons water and stir-fry for 2–3 minutes.
* Mix the remaining 1 teaspoon cornstarch with 1 tablespoon water in a small bowl and stir this mixture into the wok. Bring to a boil, stirring, for about 30 seconds to thicken the sauce. Transfer to a serving plate and serve with rice.

- 7 OZ/200 G LEAN PORK, DICED INTO ¾-INCH/1.5-CM CUBES
- 2 TEASPOONS LIGHT SOY SAUCE
- ½ TEASPOONS SALT
- 1 TABLESPOON SHAOXING WINE
- 2 TEASPOONS CORNSTARCH (CORNFLOUR)
- 3 TABLESPOONS VEGETABLE OIL
- ½ CARROT, DICED INTO ½-INCH/ 1-CM CUBES
- ½ CUP (3½ OZ/100 G) SWEET APRICOT KERNELS OR ALMONDS, RINSED
- 1 TEASPOON FINELY CHOPPED GINGER
- 1 SCALLION (SPRING ONION), CHOPPED
- ¼ GREEN BELL PEPPER, SEEDED AND DICED INTO ½-INCH/1-CM CUBES
- STEAMED RICE (PAGE 540), TO SERVE

节瓜面筋焖火腩
ROAST PORK WITH GLUTEN
AND FUZZY MELON

REGION: HONG KONG
PREPARATION TIME: 15 MINUTES
COOKING TIME: 45 MINUTES
SERVES: 4

* Rinse the melon, then cut them in half lengthwise. Cut each half into 3–4 pieces.
* Heat the oil in a wok or deep saucepan to 300°F/150°C, or until a cube of bread browns in 1½ minutes. Add the gluten and deep-fry for about 1 minute until slightly firm. Use a slotted spoon to remove from the oil and drain on paper towels.
* Pour out most of the oil, leaving about 2 tablespoons in the wok. Add the garlic and stir-fry over medium heat for 1 minute until fragrant. Add the black beans, shrimp paste, salt, sugar, roast pork, and gluten and sprinkle in the wine. Stir-fry for 1 minute, then add 1 cup (8 fl oz/250 ml) water and bring to a boil.
* Add fuzzy melon, reduce to medium heat, cover, and simmer for 30 minutes or until the melon is tender. Mix the cornstarch with 1 tablespoon water, then stir the mixture into the sauce in the wok. Bring to a boil, stirring, for about 30 seconds to thicken the sauce. Transfer to a serving plate.

- 2 FUZZY MELONS, PEELED
- 1 CUP (8 FL OZ/250 ML) VEGETABLE OIL
- 7 OZ/200 G GLUTEN, CUT INTO 1-INCH/2.5-CM SQUARES, ABOUT ½-INCH/1-CM THICK
- 4 CLOVES GARLIC, CRUSHED
- 1 TABLESPOON FERMENTED BLACK BEANS, RINSED AND CHOPPED
- 2 TEASPOONS SHRIMP PASTE
- ½ TEASPOON SALT
- 1 TEASPOON GRANULATED SUGAR
- 7 OZ/200 G ROAST PORK, CUT INTO 1-INCH/2.5-CM CHUNKS
- 1 TABLESPOON SHAOXING WINE
- 1 TEASPOON CORNSTARCH (CORNFLOUR)

REGION: JIANGSU
PREPARATION TIME: 10 MINUTES,
  PLUS 8 HOURS STANDING TIME
COOKING TIME: 2 HOURS 15 MINUTES
SERVES: 4

无锡肉骨头
WUXI-STYLE
SPARERIBS

- 1 LB 5 OZ/600 G PORK SPARERIBS,
  CUT INTO 2½-INCH/6-CM LENGTHS
- 2 TEASPOONS SALT
- 1 STAR ANISE
- 1 TEASPOON RED YEAST RICE OR
  CHERRY JUICE
- ¼ OZ/10 G GINGER (ABOUT ¾-INCH/
  2-CM-LENGTH PIECE), SLICED
- 2 BEIJING SCALLIONS OR 6 SCALLIONS
  (SPRING ONIONS), CUT INTO
  1½-INCH/4-CM LENGTHS
- ½ TEASPOON GROUND CINNAMON
- ½ CUP (4 FL OZ/120 ML) SHAOXING
  WINE
- 1 TABLESPOON DARK SOY SAUCE
- 1½ OZ/40 G ROCK SUGAR
- STEAMED RICE (PAGE 540), TO SERVE

Wuxi is a coastal city located just outside of Shanghai and renowned for its rich, cultural history. This signature dish is one of my favorites: tender and juicy spareribs, coated with a delicious, glossy sauce, will have your guests pining for more.

* Rinse the ribs and pat dry with paper towels. Transfer the ribs to a bowl and rub with the salt, cover with plastic wrap (clingfilm) and stand for 8 hours or overnight.
* Rinse the spareribs under cold running water. Combine the spareribs and enough water to cover them completely in a large saucepan, bring to a boil over high heat, and blanch them for about 2 minutes. Skim the froth and scum off the surface, if needed. Drain and rinse under cold running water.
* Put the star anise and red yeast rice into a spice bag. Line the bottom of a small Dutch oven (casserole) with the ginger slices and Beijing scallions. Add the spareribs, spice bag, ground cinnamon, wine, and enough water to cover the ingredients completely. Bring to a boil over high heat and cook for 5 minutes. Add the soy sauce and rock sugar, reduce to low heat, and simmer, covered, for about 2 hours or until the sauce thickens. Turn off the heat and discard the spice bag.
* Transfer the spareribs, ginger, and Beijing scallions to a serving plate and top with the sauce from the pot. Serve with rice.

蒜香金沙骨

SPARERIBS IN A SWEET SAUCE

REGION: HONG KONG
PREPARATION TIME: 10 MINUTES,
    PLUS 30 MINUTES MARINATING TIME
COOKING TIME: 35 MINUTES
SERVES: 4

* Combine the spareribs and soy sauce in a large bowl and marinate in the refrigerator for 30 minutes. Lightly dredge with the cornstarch (cornflour).
* Heat the oil in a wok or large skillet (frying pan) over medium heat, add the spareribs, and pan-fry for 3–4 minutes until golden brown. Remove the spareribs and set aside.
* Preheat the oven to 375°F/190°C/Gas Mark 5.
* Reheat the oil in the wok over medium-high heat, add the garlic and shallots, and stir-fry for 1 minute until fragrant. Add the spareribs, ketchup, curry powder, sugar, and salt and pour in ½ cup (4 fl oz/120 ml) water. Bring to a boil over high heat, reduce to medium heat, and simmer for about 12 minutes.
* Transfer the mixture to a roasting pan. Brush the spareribs with the melted butter and roast for about 12 minutes. Transfer to a serving plate and serve with rice.

- 11 OZ/300 G PORK SPARERIBS, CUT INTO 2-INCH/5-CM PIECES
- 1 TEASPOON LIGHT SOY SAUCE
- 1 TEASPOON CORNSTARCH (CORNFLOUR)
- 3 TABLESPOONS VEGETABLE OIL
- 2 CLOVES GARLIC, CHOPPED
- 4 SHALLOTS, CHOPPED
- ½ TABLESPOON KETCHUP
- ½ TABLESPOON CURRY POWDER
- 2 TEASPOONS GRANULATED SUGAR
- 1 TEASPOON SALT
- 2 TABLESPOONS BUTTER, MELTED
- STEAMED RICE (PAGE 540), TO SERVE

冬菜牛肉餅

STEAMED BEEF WITH TIANJIN PRESERVED CABBAGE

REGION: HONG KONG
PREPARATION TIME: 10 MINUTES,
    PLUS 15 MINUTES MARINATING TIME
COOKING TIME: 8-10 MINUTES
SERVES: 4

* Rinse the preserved cabbage in cold water, squeeze out any excess water, and coarsely chop the cabbage.
* In a large bowl, combine the beef, soy sauce, sugar, and 4 tablespoons water and marinate for 15 minutes. Add the preserved cabbage and cornstarch (cornflour) and stir well. Pick up the beef with one hand and slap it repeatedly against the bowl about 5 times; this will cause the patty to become sticky and elastic.
* Stir in the oatmeal and oil. Transfer the mixture to a heatproof plate and use your fingers to gently press to form a ½-inch/1-cm-thick patty. Place the patty in a collapsible pot or bamboo steamer over a pot of boiling water. Steam, covered, for 8–10 minutes until cooked through. (Pierce the patty with a fork or spoon and separate the meat to see if it's fully cooked.)
* Sprinkle with the chopped scallions (spring onions) and serve with rice.

- 3 TABLESPOONS TIANJIN PRESERVED CABBAGE
- 9 OZ/250 G GROUND (MINCED) BEEF
- 1 TEASPOON LIGHT SOY SAUCE
- ½ TEASPOON GRANULATED SUGAR
- 1½ TABLESPOONS CORNSTARCH (CORNFLOUR)
- 2 TABLESPOONS OATMEAL, CRUSHED
- 2 TABLESPOONS VEGETABLE OIL
- 1 TABLESPOON CHOPPED SCALLIONS (SPRING ONIONS)
- STEAMED RICE (PAGE 540), TO SERVE

REGION: GUANGDONG
PREPARATION TIME: 20 MINUTES,
  PLUS 30 MINUTES SOAKING AND
  1 HOUR MARINATING TIME
COOKING TIME: 25 MINUTES
SERVES: 2
📷 PAGE 395

蜜汁叉烧
BARBECUE
PORK

- 1 (14-OZ/400-G) SKINLESS PORK
  SHOULDER, CUT INTO ¾-INCH/
  2-CM-WIDE STRIPS
- 1 TABLESPOON SALT
- STEAMED RICE (PAGE 540), TO SERVE

FOR THE MARINADE:
- 6 TABLESPOONS GRANULATED SUGAR
- 2 TABLESPOONS SHAOXING WINE
- 2 TABLESPOONS CHOPPED GARLIC
- 1 SHALLOT, CHOPPED
- 2 TABLESPOONS HOISIN SAUCE
- 1 TABLESPOON GINGER JUICE
- 1 TEASPOON FIVE-SPICE POWDER
- ½ TEASPOON SHAJIANG POWDER
- ½ TEASPOON LIGHT SOY SAUCE

FOR THE GLAZE:
- 3 TABLESPOONS MALTOSE
- 3 TABLESPOONS GRANULATED SUGAR
- 1 TABLESPOON MIRIN

* Combine the pork, salt, and 2 cups (16 fl oz/475 ml) water in a large bowl and soak for 30 minutes. Rinse under cold running water, drain, and pat dry with paper towels.
* Combine all the marinade ingredients in a bowl, add the pork, cover, and marinate for 1 hour, turning 2–3 times. Discard the marinade.
* Preheat the oven to 375°F/190°C/Gas Mark 5. Line a roasting pan with a sheet of aluminum foil and place a wire mesh on top. Transfer the pork on the wire mesh and roast for 15 minutes until slightly brown.
* Heat the honeyed sauce ingredients in a small saucepan over low heat and stir for 1–2 minutes to dissolve. Brush the pork with the glaze. Switch the cooking method to broil (grill), preheat to medium, and broil the pork for 3–5 minutes. Turn the pork over, brush with another coat of glaze, and broil for another 3–5 minutes until caramelized. Transfer the pork to a plate and brush on the remaining glaze. Serve with rice.

REGION: GUANGXI
PREPARATION TIME: 5 MINUTES
COOKING TIME: 1 HOUR 15 MINUTES
SERVES: 4

慈菇焖猪肉

PORK BELLY WITH
ARROWROOT

- 1 (11-OZ/300-G) BONELESS, SKIN-ON PORK BELLY, RINSED
- 11 OZ/300 G ARROWROOT, PEELED AND HALVED
- 2 TABLESPOONS VEGETABLE OIL
- ⅛ OZ/5 G GINGER (ABOUT ½-INCH/ 1-CM-LENGTH PIECE), SLICED
- 1 TABLESPOON BEAN PASTE
- ½ TEASPOON SALT
- 1 TEASPOON GRANULATED SUGAR
- 1 TABLESPOON SHAOXING WINE
- 1 TEASPOON CORNSTARCH (CORNFLOUR)
- STEAMED RICE (PAGE 540), TO SERVE

* Place the pork belly, skin facing down, on a cutting board. Trim the meat to an even thickness and scrape the skin clean, then rinse the pork under cold running water.
* Put the pork belly in a large saucepan and add enough water to cover it completely. Bring to a boil over high heat and blanch for 5 minutes. Drain and rinse under cold running water until cooled. Cut the pork into ½-inch/ 1-cm-thick slices. Set aside.
* Add fresh water to the pot and bring to a boil over high heat. Add the arrowroot and blanch for 1 minute. Drain and set aside.
* Heat the oil in a Dutch oven (casserole) over medium-high heat, add the ginger and stir-fry for 1 minute until fragrant. Add the bean paste, salt, sugar, and pork. Stir, then add the wine and enough water to cover the pork. Bring to a boil over high heat, reduce to low heat, and simmer, covered, for about 45 minutes. Add the arrowroots, cover, and cook for another 5 minutes. Uncover, return to a boil over high heat, then simmer for 15 minutes until the sauce has reduced to about ½ cup (4 fl oz/120 ml).
* Mix the cornstarch (cornflour) with 1 tablespoon water in a small bowl and stir this mixture into the Dutch oven. Bring to a boil, stirring, for 30 seconds to thicken the sauce. Serve in the Dutch oven with rice.

中式牛柳
CHINESE BEEF TENDERLOIN

REGION: HONG KONG
PREPARATION TIME: 5 MINUTES,
    PLUS 10 MINUTES SOAKING TIME
COOKING TIME: 5 MINUTES
SERVES: 4

* Put the beef into a bowl, mix in 2 tablespoons water, and leave to soak for 10 minutes. Add the cornstarch (cornflour) and set aside.
* Heat 2 tablespoons oil in a wok or large skillet (frying pan) over medium heat, add the onion, and stir-fry for 2 minutes until translucent. Remove the onion from the wok.
* To make the sauce, combine all the ingredients in a bowl and mix well.
* Stir the remaining 1 tablespoon oil into the beef mixture, then add to the wok. Stir-fry over high heat for 1–2 minutes until about 60 percent done. Add the sauce and stir-fry for 1 minute until the sauce thickens. Return the onion to the wok, add the crushed black pepper, and toss thoroughly. Transfer to a serving plate and serve with rice.

- 14 OZ/400 G BEEF TENDERLOIN, CUT INTO ½-INCH/1-CM-THICK SLICES
- 1 TEASPOON CORNSTARCH (CORNFLOUR)
- 3 TABLESPOONS VEGETABLE OIL
- 1 ONION, THINLY SLICED
- 1 TEASPOON BLACK PEPPERCORNS, CRUSHED
- STEAMED RICE (PAGE 540), TO SERVE

  FOR THE SAUCE:
- 1 TABLESPOON LIGHT SOY SAUCE
- 1 TABLESPOON WORCESTERSHIRE SAUCE
- 1 TABLESPOON KETCHUP
- 1 TEASPOON FRENCH MUSTARD
- 1 TEASPOON GRANULATED SUGAR
- ¼ TEASPOON SALT

陈皮蒸牛腱
BEEF SHIN WITH JUJUBE DATES

REGION: SHUNDE
PREPARATION TIME: 20 MINUTES,
    PLUS 1 HOUR FREEZING TIME
COOKING TIME: 5 MINUTES
SERVES: 4

* Rinse the beef shin, pat dry with paper towels, and roll up in plastic wrap (clingfilm). Put in the freezer for 1 hour, or until very firm but not hard. Cut into very thin slices.
* Meanwhile, soak the black fungus in a small bowl of cold water for 20 minutes, or until softened. Remove the fungus, discard the stems, and tear the caps in half. Soak the dried tangerine peel in cold water for 10 minutes to soften. Drain and cut into very thin strips. Set both aside.
* Combine the sliced beef, ginger juice, wine, and salt in a bowl, then stir in the dried tangerine peel, jujube dates, and cornstarch (cornflour). Mix in 2 teaspoons oil.
* Mix the black fungus with 1 teaspoon oil and spread evenly on a heatproof plate. Place the sliced beef evenly over the black fungus, making sure each slice lies flat. Place in a collapsible pot or bamboo steamer over a pot of boiling water. Steam, covered, for 5 minutes. Spread the scallions (spring onions) and ginger evenly over the beef and pour 1 tablespoon heated oil on top. Serve with rice.

- 1 (9-OZ/250-G) BEEF SHIN, ANY MEMBRANE TRIMMED OFF
- ½ CUP (¼ OZ/10 G) DRIED BLACK FUNGUS
- 2 DRIED TANGERINE PEELS
- 1 TABLESPOON GINGER JUICE
- ½ TABLESPOON RICE WINE
- ½ TEASPOON SALT
- 4 JUJUBE DATES, PITTED AND CHOPPED
- 1½ TEASPOONS CORNSTARCH (CORNFLOUR)
- 2 TABLESPOONS VEGETABLE OIL
- 2 SCALLIONS (SPRING ONIONS), CHOPPED
- ¾ OZ/20 G GINGER (ABOUT 1-INCH/2.5-CM-LENGTH PIECE), SHREDDED
- STEAMED RICE (PAGE 540), TO SERVE

REGION: SICHUAN
PREPARATION TIME: 5 MINUTES,
   PLUS 15 MINUTES MARINATING TIME
COOKING TIME: 15 MINUTES
SERVES: 4

陈皮牛肉
BEEF AND DRIED TANGERINE PEEL STIR-FRY

- 1 LB/500 G BEEF TENDERLOIN
- ½ TEASPOON SALT
- 1 TABLESPOON GINGER JUICE
- 1 TABLESPOON SHAOXING WINE
- 7–8 DRIED TANGERINE PEELS
- 2 CUPS (16 FL OZ/475 ML) VEGETABLE OIL
- 15 DRIED CHILES, HALVED
- 1 TABLESPOON SICHUAN PEPPERCORNS
- 3 SLICES GINGER
- 1 CUP (8 FL OZ/250 ML) CHICKEN BROTH (STOCK, PAGE 90)
- 2 TEASPOONS GRANULATED SUGAR
- 1 TEASPOON SESAME OIL
- STEAMED RICE (PAGE 540), TO SERVE

* Cut the beef into 2½ x 1½-inch/6 × 4-cm strips, about ¹⁄₁₂ inch/2 mm thick. Combine the strips with the salt, ginger juice, and wine in a bowl and marinate for 15 minutes.
* Meanwhile, soak the dried tangerine peel in cold water for 10 minutes to soften, then drain. Scrape to remove any pith, then chop the peel.
* Heat the vegetable oil in a wok or deep saucepan over medium heat to 300°F/150°C, or until a cube of bread browns in 1½ minutes. Gently lower the beef into the oil, in batches, and deep-fry for 1 minute, or until firm. Use a slotted spoon to carefully remove the beef from the oil.
* Reheat the oil over medium-high heat to 350°F/180°C, or until a cube of bread browns in 30 seconds. Return the beef to the wok again and deep-fry for 1–2 minutes until crispy. Carefully remove the beef and drain on paper towels.
* Pour out most of the oil, leaving about 1 tablespoon in the wok. Add the chiles, Sichuan peppercorns, and tangerine peel and stir-fry over medium heat until fragrant. Add the beef, ginger, and chicken broth (stock) and bring to a boil. Sauté until the sauce is reduced.
* Stir in the sugar and sesame oil, then transfer to a serving plate. Set aside to cool. Serve with rice.

REGION: GUANGDONG
PREPARATION TIME: 5 MINUTES,
   PLUS 10 MINUTES SOAKING TIME
COOKING TIME: 3 MINUTES
SERVES: 2–4

蚝油牛肉
BEEF IN OYSTER SAUCE

- 11 OZ/300 G BEEF FLANK STEAK, CUT INTO THIN 2 × ¾-INCH/5 × 2-CM SLICES
- 2 TEASPOONS CORNSTARCH (CORNFLOUR)
- 3 TABLESPOONS VEGETABLE OIL
- ⅛ OZ/5 G GINGER (ABOUT ½-INCH/ 1-CM-LENGTH PIECE), SLICED
- 2 TABLESPOONS OYSTER SAUCE
- ½ TEASPOON SESAME OIL
- STEAMED RICE (PAGE 540), TO SERVE

* Combine the beef with 2 tablespoons water in a bowl and soak for 10 minutes. Mix in 1 teaspoon cornstarch (cornflour). Stir in 1 tablespoon vegetable oil.
* Heat the remaining 2 tablespoons vegetable oil in a wok or large skillet (frying pan) over medium-high heat, add the ginger, and stir-fry for 1 minute until fragrant. Increase to high heat, add the beef, and stir-fry for 30 seconds. Add the oyster sauce and 2 tablespoons water, stir, and bring to a boil.
* Mix the remaining 1 teaspoon cornstarch with 1 tablespoon water and stir this mixture into the wok to thicken the sauce. Stir-fry for 30 seconds, then drizzle in the sesame oil. Transfer to a serving plate and serve with rice.

兴宁牛对猪
BEEF AND PORK MEATBALLS

REGION: HAKKA
PREPARATION TIME: 15 MINUTES
COOKING TIME: 10 MINUTES
SERVES: 4

* In a large bowl, combine the beef, ground (minced) pork, pork fatback, tapioca flour, ½ teaspoon sugar, and ½ tablespoon soy sauce and mix well. Using your hands, form the mixture into 16 balls.
* Bring a saucepan of water with the salt and ½ tablespoon oil to a boil over high heat. Add the spinach and blanch for 1 minute. Drain and transfer to a serving plate. Keep warm.
* Heat the remaining 2 tablespoons oil in a wok or large skillet (frying pan) over low heat, add the meatballs, and cook for 3–4 minutes until browned. Sprinkle the wine along the inside of the wok, add the remaining ½ tablespoon soy sauce and ½ teaspoon sugar, and fry over medium-high heat for 2 minutes until the meatballs are cooked through.
* Mix the cornstarch (cornflour) with ½ tablespoon water in a small bowl and stir this mixture into the wok. Bring to a boil, stirring, for 30 seconds to thicken the sauce. Transfer the meatballs to the serving plate and serve immediately with rice.

• 5 OZ/150 G RUMP OR CHUCK STEAK, FINELY CHOPPED
• 5 OZ/150 G GROUND (MINCED) PORK
• ¾ OZ/20 G PORK FATBACK, FINELY CHOPPED
• 1 TABLESPOON TAPIOCA FLOUR
• 1 TEASPOON GRANULATED SUGAR
• 1 TABLESPOON LIGHT SOY SAUCE
• ½ TEASPOON SALT
• 8 CUPS (1 LB 2 OZ/500 G) PACKED BABY SPINACH
• 2½ TABLESPOONS VEGETABLE OIL
• 1 TABLESPOON RICE WINE
• ½ TEASPOON CORNSTARCH (CORNFLOUR)
• STEAMED RICE (PAGE 540), TO SERVE

姜葱焗牛腱
BEEF SHIN WITH GINGER AND SCALLIONS

REGION: GUANGDONG
PREPARATION TIME: 10 MINUTES
COOKING TIME: 45 MINUTES
SERVES: 4

* In a large saucepan, add the beef shin and enough water to cover it completely. Bring to a boil over high heat and blanch for 5 minutes. Drain and rinse under cold water until cooled. Cut the beef into ½-inch/1-cm-thick slices.
* Heat the vegetable oil in a Dutch oven (casserole) over medium-high heat, add the ginger and half the scallions (spring onions), and stir-fry for 1 minute until fragrant. Add the beef and enough water to cover everything completely. Bring to a boil over high heat, then reduce to low heat, and simmer, covered, for 30 minutes, or until the beef is tender enough to pierce through with a chopstick. Add more water to keep the beef covered, if necessary.
* Stir in the oyster sauce, sugar, and the remaining scallions. In a small bowl, mix the cornstarch (cornflour) with 1 tablespoon water and stir this mixture into the Dutch oven. Bring to a boil, stirring, for 30 seconds to thicken the sauce. Drizzle in the sesame oil, season with salt to taste, and serve in the Dutch oven with rice.

• 9 OZ/250 G BEEF SHIN
• 2 TABLESPOONS VEGETABLE OIL
• ¾ OZ/20 G GINGER (ABOUT 1-INCH/ 2.5-CM-LENGTH PIECE), SLICED
• 4 SCALLIONS (SPRING ONIONS), CUT INTO 2-INCH/5-CM LENGTHS
• 2 TABLESPOONS OYSTER SAUCE
• 1 TEASPOON GRANULATED SUGAR
• 1 TEASPOON CORNSTARCH (CORNFLOUR)
• 1 TEASPOON SESAME OIL
• SALT, TO TASTE
• STEAMED RICE (PAGE 540), TO SERVE

REGION: SICHUAN
PREPARATION TIME: 20 MINUTES
COOKING TIME: 15 MINUTES
SERVES: 4
📷 PAGE 401

水煮牛肉
BEEF IN CHILI BROTH

- 11 OZ/300 G BEEF TENDERLOIN (FILLET), CUT INTO 1½ × 1-INCH/ 4 × 2.5-CM SLICES
- 1 TABLESPOON CORNSTARCH (CORNFLOUR)
- 5 TABLESPOONS VEGETABLE OIL
- 1½ CUPS (5 OZ/150 G) BEAN SPROUTS
- 2 STALKS CHINESE CHIVES, CUT INTO 2½-INCH/6-CM LENGTHS
- 1 LEEK, CUT INTO 2½-INCH/ 6-CM LENGTHS AND EACH SECTION QUARTERED LENGTHWISE
- 4 CLOVES GARLIC, SLICED
- 1 TEASPOON GRATED GINGER
- 2 OZ/50 G DRIED RED CHILES, TORN IN HALF
- 6 RED CHILES, HALVED LENGTHWISE
- 2½ TEASPOONS SICHUAN PEPPERCORNS, COARSELY CRUSHED
- 2 TABLESPOONS PIXIAN CHILI BEAN PASTE, CHOPPED
- 1 TABLESPOON RICE WINE
- 1 TEASPOON SALT
- 1 TEASPOON GRANULATED SUGAR
- 2 TABLESPOONS SESAME OIL
- ½ TABLESPOON GROUND SICHUAN PEPPERCORNS
- SLICED RED CHILE AND CILANTRO (CORIANDER) LEAVES, TO GARNISH (OPTIONAL)
- STEAMED RICE (PAGE 540), TO SERVE

* Lightly dredge the beef slices in cornstarch (cornflour). Using a cleaver or meat mallet, pound both sides of the beef. Place in a bowl and add 1 tablespoon vegetable oil, then mix well.
* Bring 3 cups (25 fl oz/750 ml) water to a boil in a medium saucepan. Add the bean sprouts and blanch for 30 seconds, or until half cooked. Use a slotted spoon to transfer the sprouts to a large bowl. Bring the water to another boil, add the chives and leek, and blanch for 2 minutes until just tender. Tip both the chives and leek and the cooking water into the bowl with the sprouts.
* Heat the remaining 4 tablespoons vegetable oil in a wok or deep saucepan to 275°F/140°C, or until a cube of bread turns golden in 2 minutes. Gently lower in the beef, in batches, using chopsticks to disperse the pieces rapidly to prevent sticking, and deep-fry for 1 minute until half cooked. Use a slotted spoon to transfer the beef to the sprouts and leek mixture.
* Reheat the oil to 300°F/150°C, or until a cube of bread browns in 1½ minutes, add the garlic, ginger, dried and fresh chiles, and peppercorns, and cook for 1 minute until fragrant. Stir in the bean paste and sprinkle in the wine.
* Add the beef and sprouts mixture and cooking liquid into the wok, add the salt, sugar, and sesame oil, and then stir and cook for 1 minute. Transfer to a serving bowl, sprinkle with ground Sichuan peppercorns, the cilantro (coriander), and chiles, if using, and serve with rice.

NOTE:
This popular dish is fiery and spicy—adjust the number of dried chiles to suit your taste.

BEEF IN CHILI BROTH

袈裟牛肉
BEEF IN EGG'S CLOTHING

- 9 OZ/250 G BEEF TENDERLOIN,
  CUT INTO STRIPS AND CHOPPED
- ¼ TEASPOON GROUND WHITE PEPPER
- ⅛ OZ/5 G GINGER (ABOUT ½-INCH/
  1-CM-LENGTH PIECE), CHOPPED
- 1 BEIJING SCALLION OR 3 SCALLIONS
  (SPRING ONIONS), CHOPPED
- 2 CLOVES GARLIC, CHOPPED
- ½ TEASPOON SALT
- 1 TABLESPOON RICE WINE
- 4 TABLESPOONS CORNSTARCH
  (CORNFLOUR)
- 2 EGGS, BEATEN, PLUS 1 EGG WHITE
- 1 CUP (8 FL OZ/250 ML) PLUS
  2 TEASPOONS VEGETABLE OIL

* Combine the beef, white pepper, ginger, Beijing scallion, garlic, salt, and wine in a large bowl, then mix in the cornstarch (cornflour) and egg white. Blend into a paste.
* Heat 1 teaspoon oil in a skillet (frying pan) over low heat, add half the beaten eggs, tilt the skillet to spread the egg over the bottom, and fry for about 1–2 minutes until you have a thin sheet of cooked egg. Gently transfer the egg sheet, without breaking it, to a cutting board.
* Add 1 teaspoon oil to the skill and heat over low heat, then add the remaining eggs and repeat the process to make a second egg sheet. Turn off the heat as soon as the second egg sheet is formed and set aside.
* Meanwhile, spread the beef paste evenly on the egg sheet on the cutting board, covering the entire surface. Lift the second egg sheet from the skillet and place it over the beef paste to cover. Press gently so that the beef paste sticks to both egg sheets to create a sandwich.
* Cut the sandwich into 1½-inch/4-cm squares.
* Heat the remaining 1 cup (8 fl oz/250 ml) oil in a wok or large skillet over medium heat to 275°F/140°C, or until a cube of bread turns golden in 2 minutes. Gently lower the sandwich pieces into the oil and deep-fry for about 5 minutes until golden brown. Use a slotted spoon to carefully remove the sandwiches from the oil, drain on paper towels, and serve.

干拌牛肉
BEEF WITH SPICY SAUCE

REGION: ANHUI
PREPARATION TIME: 10 MINUTES
COOKING TIME: 35 MINUTES
SERVES: 4

* Put the steak into a large saucepan and add enough water to cover it completely. Bring to a boil over high heat. Reduce to low heat and simmer for 30 minutes. Use tongs to remove the steak from the pan and set aside to cool. Discard the water.
* Toast the peanuts in a small saucepan over medium heat for 2–3 minutes until golden brown. Transfer to a mortar and pestle and coarsely crush. Set aside.
* Combine the chile, salt, sugar, soy sauce, and chili oil in a small bowl and mix well. Set aside.
* Cut the steak into thin slices, then transfer it to a large bowl. Add the scallion (spring onion) and the chile mixture and mix well. Transfer to a serving plate and sprinkle with the crushed peanuts, ground Sichuan peppercorns, and cilantro (coriander). Serve with rice.

- 1 (1-LB/450-G) RUMP STEAK
- 3–4 TABLESPOONS PEANUTS
- 1 RED CHILE, SEEDED AND CUT INTO STRIPS
- ¼ TEASPOON SALT
- ½ TEASPOON GRANULATED SUGAR
- ½ TABLESPOON LIGHT SOY SAUCE
- 1 TABLESPOON CHILI OIL
- 1 SCALLION (SPRING ONION), SHREDDED
- ½ TEASPOON GROUND SICHUAN PEPPERCORNS
- 1 STALK CILANTRO (CORIANDER), COARSELY CHOPPED
- STEAMED RICE (PAGE 540), TO SERVE

清炖牛肉
BRAISED BEEF

REGION: HUNAN
PREPARATION TIME: 10 MINUTES
COOKING TIME: 2 HOURS 15 MINUTES
SERVES: 4

* Put the beef into a large saucepan and add enough water to cover it completely. Bring to a boil over high heat and blanch for 10 minutes. Drain and rinse under cold running water until cooled. Cut the beef into 1½ × ¾ × ½-inch/ 4 × 2 × 1-cm pieces.
* Place the beef into a Dutch oven (casserole). Add the cinnamon, wine, scallions (spring onions), ginger, salt, oil, and 4¼ cups (34 fl oz/1 liter) water. Bring to a boil, reduce to low heat, and simmer, covered, for about 2 hours, or until the beef is tender. Pick out and discard the scallions, ginger, and cinnamon, then stir in the chives and white pepper. Season with extra salt to taste. Serve in the Dutch oven with rice.

- 1 (1 LB 8½-OZ/750-G) BEEF NECK
- ½ SMALL CINNAMON STICK
- 4 TABLESPOONS RICE WINE
- 2 SCALLIONS (SPRING ONIONS), KNOTTED
- ¼ OZ/10 G GINGER (ABOUT ¾-INCH/ 2-CM-LENGTH PIECE), CRUSHED
- 1 TEASPOON SALT, PLUS EXTRA TO TASTE
- 2 TABLESPOONS VEGETABLE OIL
- 2–3 STALKS CHINESE CHIVES, CUT INTO ½-INCH/1-CM LENGTHS
- ¼ TEASPOON GROUND WHITE PEPPER
- STEAMED RICE (PAGE 540), TO SERVE

沙葛炒牛柳丝
SAUTÉED BEEF
WITH JICAMA

- 5 OZ/150 G BEEF TENDERLOIN,
  CUT INTO THICK STRIPS
- 1 TEASPOON CORNSTARCH
  (CORNFLOUR)
- 2½ TABLESPOONS VEGETABLE OIL
- ⅛ OZ/5 G GINGER (ABOUT ½-INCH/
  1-CM-LENGTH PIECE), SLICED
- 1 TEASPOON LIGHT SOY SAUCE
- ½ TEASPOON SALT
- 11 OZ/300 G JÍCAMA, CUT INTO
  1½-INCH/4-CM-LONG STRIPS
- 2 SCALLIONS (SPRING ONIONS),
  STEMS ONLY, CUT INTO 1½-INCH/
  4-CM LENGTHS
- STEAMED RICE (PAGE 540), TO SERVE

* Combine the beef, cornstarch (cornflour), and ½ tablespoon
  oil in a bowl and mix well.
* Heat the remaining 2 tablespoons oil in a wok or large
  skillet (frying pan) over medium heat, add the ginger,
  and stir-fry for 1 minute until fragrant. Add the beef and
  stir-fry for another 1 minute just until half done. Add the
  soy sauce, salt, and 2 tablespoons water, then toss in the
  jicama and scallions (spring onions). Stir-fry for another
  1–2 minutes until the jicama is tender. Transfer to a serving
  plate and serve with rice.

干煸牛肉丝
STIR-FRIED BEEF

- 11 OZ/300 G BEEF TENDERLOIN, CUT
  FOLLOWING THE GRAIN INTO THIN
  SLICES, THEN CUT INTO FINE STRIPS
- 2 TABLESPOONS VEGETABLE OIL
- 1 TABLESPOON PIXIAN CHILI BEAN
  PASTE, CHOPPED
- ¼ OZ/10 G GINGER (ABOUT ¾-INCH/
  2-CM-LENGTH PIECE), SHREDDED
- 1 TEASPOON GRANULATED SUGAR
- ¼ TEASPOON SALT
- 1 TEASPOON RICE WINE
- 1 TABLESPOON DARK SOY SAUCE
- ½ TEASPOON SESAME OIL
- ½ TEASPOON SICHUAN PEPPERCORNS,
  CRUSHED
- STEAMED RICE (PAGE 540), TO SERVE

* Combine the beef with 1 tablespoon vegetable oil
  in a large bowl.
* Heat the remaining 1 tablespoon vegetable oil in a wok
  or large skillet (frying pan) over high heat, add the beef,
  and stir-fry for 2–3 minutes until cooked through. Stir in
  the chili bean paste, then add the ginger, sugar, and salt
  and stir rapidly for another minute. Sprinkle in the wine,
  then add the soy sauce and the sesame oil and toss.
* Transfer to a serving plate, sprinkle with the Sichuan
  peppercorns, and serve with rice.

沙茶牛肉
BEEF IN SHA CHA SAUCE

REGION: CHAOZHOU
PREPARATION TIME: 10 MINUTES,
   PLUS 10 MINUTES MARINATING TIME
COOKING TIME: 5 MINUTES
SERVES: 4

* Use a sharp knife to cut the beef across the grain into slices, then put into a bowl with the pineapple juice. Marinate for 10 minutes, then rinse under cold running water.
* Add the garlic and 1 teaspoon cornstarch (cornflour), then mix in 1 tablespoon vegetable oil.
* Bring a saucepan of water to a boil over high heat. Add the bean sprouts and blanch for 30 seconds. Drain, rinse under cold running water, and transfer to a serving plate.
* Heat the remaining 2 tablespoons vegetable oil in a wok or large skillet (frying pan) over medium heat, add the sha cha sauce, ginger, soy sauce, and sugar, and stir-fry for 1 minute until fragrant. Increase to high heat and stir in the beef. Add 3 tablespoons water and stir-fry for about 1 minute until the beef is nearly cooked through.
* Mix the remaining 1 teaspoon cornstarch with 1 teaspoon water in a small bowl and stir this mixture into the wok. Bring to a boil, stirring, for 30 seconds to thicken the sauce. Stir in the scallions (spring onions) and sesame oil, toss, and pour over the bean sprouts. Serve with rice.

- 11 OZ/300 G FLANK STEAK
- 2 TABLESPOONS PINEAPPLE JUICE
- 3 CLOVES GARLIC, FINELY CHOPPED
- 2 TEASPOONS CORNSTARCH (CORNFLOUR)
- 3 TABLESPOONS VEGETABLE OIL
- 1½ CUPS (5 OZ/150 G) BEAN SPROUTS
- 2 TABLESPOONS SHA CHA SAUCE
- 1 TEASPOON SHREDDED GINGER
- 1 TEASPOON LIGHT SOY SAUCE
- ½ TEASPOON GRANULATED SUGAR
- 2 SCALLIONS (SPRING ONIONS), CUT INTO 1½-INCH/4-CM LENGTHS
- 1 TEASPOON SESAME OIL
- STEAMED RICE (PAGE 540), TO SERVE

味菜牛百页
TRIPE WITH SWEET PICKLED MUSTARD GREENS

REGION: GUANGDONG
PREPARATION TIME: 5 MINUTES
COOKING TIME: 10 MINUTES
SERVES: 4

* Put the tripe into a large saucepan and add enough water to cover it completely. Bring to a boil over high heat and blanch for about 20 seconds. Drain and rinse under cold running water until cooled. Cut the tripe into 1½ × ¾-inch/ 4 × 2-cm slices.
* Heat a wok or large skillet (frying pan) over medium-high heat, add the mustard greens, and dry-fry for 4–5 minutes to remove any moisture. Transfer to a plate and set aside.
* Heat the oil in the wok over medium heat, add the garlic and bean paste and stir-fry for 1 minute until fragrant. Stir in the tripe, mustard greens, soy sauce, sugar, and salt. Mix the cornstarch (cornflour) with 1 tablespoon water in a small bowl and add to the wok. Bring to a boil, stirring, for 30 seconds to thicken the sauce. Transfer to a serving plate and serve with rice.

- 1 LB 5 OZ/600 G TRIPE
- 7 OZ/200 G SWEET PICKLED MUSTARD GREENS, TRIMMED, RINSED AND CUT INTO 1½ × ¾-INCH/4 × 2-CM SLICES
- 2 TABLESPOONS VEGETABLE OIL
- 3 CLOVES GARLIC, FINELY CHOPPED
- 1 TABLESPOON BEAN PASTE
- ½ TABLESPOON LIGHT SOY SAUCE
- 2 TEASPOONS GRANULATED SUGAR
- ¼ TEASPOON SALT
- 1 TEASPOON CORNSTARCH (CORNFLOUR)
- STEAMED RICE (PAGE 540), TO SERVE

REGION: GUANGDONG
PREPARATION TIME: 5 MINUTES,
    PLUS 10 MINUTES MARINATING TIME
COOKING TIME: 3 MINUTES
SERVES: 2
📷 PAGE 407

芥兰炒牛肉
BEEF WITH CHINESE BROCCOLI

- 5 OZ/150 G FLANK STEAK, CUT INTO ⅛-INCH/3-MM-THICK SLICES
- 1 CLOVE GARLIC, CHOPPED
- 1 TEASPOON CORNSTARCH (CORNFLOUR)
- 3 TABLESPOONS VEGETABLE OIL
- 11 OZ/300 G CHINESE BROCCOLI, CUT INTO 4-INCH/10-CM LENGTHS
- 1 TABLESPOON GINGER JUICE
- 1 TABLESPOON SHAOXING WINE
- 1 TEASPOON GRANULATED SUGAR
- 2 TABLESPOONS OYSTER SAUCE
- 1 MILD RED CHILE, SLICED, TO GARNISH (OPTIONAL)
- STEAMED RICE (PAGE 540), TO SERVE

* Mix the beef with the garlic, cornstarch (cornflour), and 1 tablespoon water in a bowl and marinate for 10 minutes. Stir in 1 tablespoon oil just prior to cooking.
* Heat 1 tablespoon oil in a wok or large skillet (frying pan) over high heat, add the broccoli, and stir-fry for about 1 minute. Add the ginger juice, wine, and sugar, and stir-fry for another minute. Transfer the broccoli together with the sauce to a plate. Wipe the wok clean.
* Heat the remaining 1 tablespoon oil over high heat, add the beef, and stir-fry for about 30 seconds. Stir in the oyster sauce, then add the Chinese broccoli and sauce, and toss for about 30 seconds until the beef is just cooked.
* Transfer to a serving plate, garnish with the sliced chile, if using, and serve with rice.

REGION: SICHUAN
PREPARATION TIME: 5 MINUTES,
    PLUS 10 MINUTES SOAKING TIME
COOKING TIME: 10 MINUTES
SERVES: 4

野山椒炒牛柳
BEEF WITH PICKLED CHILES

- 11 OZ/300 G BEEF TENDERLOIN, THINLY SLICED
- 1 TABLESPOON CORNSTARCH (CORNFLOUR)
- 2 TABLESPOONS VEGETABLE OIL
- 1 TEASPOON WHITE SESAME SEEDS
- 2 CLOVES GARLIC, SLICED
- 1 RED CAYENNE PEPPER, SEEDED AND SLICED
- 1 OZ/25 G GREEN PICKLED CHILES
- 1 TABLESPOON OYSTER SAUCE
- ½ TEASPOON SESAME OIL
- ¼ TEASPOON GROUND SICHUAN PEPPERCORNS
- SALT, TO TASTE
- STEAMED RICE (PAGE 540), TO SERVE

* Combine the beef, 3 tablespoons water, the cornstarch (cornflour) in a large bowl and soak for 10 minutes. Stir in 1 tablespoon vegetable oil.
* Toast the sesame seeds in a small pan over medium heat and shake occasionally for 3–5 minutes, or until golden brown. Set aside.
* Heat 1 tablespoon vegetable oil in a wok or large skillet (frying pan) over medium-high heat, add the garlic, and stir-fry for 1 minute until fragrant. Put in the cayenne pepper and toss briefly for about 10 seconds. Add the beef, increase to high heat, and stir in the pickled chiles and oyster sauce. Toss well for another 2–3 minutes until the beef is just cooked. Stir in the sesame oil and ground Sichuan peppercorns. Season with salt to taste. Transfer to a serving plate and serve with rice.

BEEF WITH CHINESE BROCCOLI

红酒炆牛胸
BRAISED BEEF BRISKET
WITH RED WINE

- 1 LB 5 OZ/600 G BEEF BRISKET
- 1½ TABLESPOONS WHITE
  PEPPERCORNS, CRUSHED
- 1 DRIED TANGERINE PEEL
- ¼ OZ/10 G GINGER (ABOUT ¾-INCH/
  2-CM-LENGTH PIECE), SLICED
- 1 TABLESPOON VEGETABLE OIL
- 2 ONIONS, HALVED AND CUT INTO
  WEDGES
- 2 TABLESPOONS BEAN PASTE
- 1 CUP (8 FL OZ/250 ML) RED WINE
- 1 CARROT, CUT INTO CHUNKS
- ¾ OZ/20 G ROCK SUGAR
- SALT, TO TASTE
- STEAMED RICE (PAGE 540) OR BOILED
  POTATOES, TO SERVE

* Soak the brisket in a large bowl of cold water for 1 hour,
  then rinse and drain.
* Put the beef into a large saucepan and add enough water
  to cover it completely. Bring to a boil over high heat and
  blanch for 1–2 minutes. Drain and rinse under cold running
  water. Set aside.
* Put the peppercorns into a spice bag. Put the brisket back
  into the pan, add the tangerine peel, spice bag, and half
  the ginger slices. Cover with enough water to submerge
  the brisket by ¾ inch/2 cm. Bring to a boil, cover, and cook
  over high heat for about 15 minutes. Reduce to low heat
  and simmer for another 45 minutes. Use a slotted spoon
  or pair of tongs to remove the brisket and set aside to cool.
  Transfer the broth (stock) to a bowl and set aside.
* Cut the brisket into bite-size chunks.
* Heat the oil in a large saucepan, add the remaining ginger
  slices and stir-fry over medium-high heat for 1 minute until
  fragrant. Add the onions and stir-fry for 2–3 minutes until
  they are golden brown. Stir in the bean paste and brisket.
  Add the reserved broth, wine, carrot, and sugar, then bring
  to a boil over high heat. Reduce the heat to medium-low
  and simmer, covered, for about 30 minutes, or until the
  beef is sufficiently tender. Add the salt to taste and serve
  with rice or boiled potatoes.

清汤牛腩
BEEF IN CLEAR BROTH

REGION: HONG KONG
PREPARATION TIME: 5 MINUTES
COOKING TIME: 2 HOURS
SERVES: 4

* Put the beef into a large saucepan and add enough water to cover it completely. Bring to a boil over high heat and blanch for 10 minutes. Skim the froth and scum off the surface, if needed. Drain and rinse under cold water.
* Clean the saucepan, fill with water, and bring to a boil. Add the radish and blanch for 1–2 minutes. Drain and set aside.
* To a clean saucepan, add the beef, ginger, star anise, Sichuan peppercorns, white peppercorns, tangerine peel, monkfruit, and enough water to cover the beef completely. Bring to a boil over high heat, reduce to low heat, and simmer, covered, for 1½ hours, or until the beef is tender enough to pierce through with a chopstick. Transfer the beef to a colander, then rinse thoroughly with cold running water until cooled. Discard the remaining contents. Cut the beef into thick slices.
* Bring the chicken broth (stock) to a boil in a Dutch oven (casserole). Add the beef and radish, season with salt to taste, and return to a boil. Reduce to low heat, cover, and simmer for about 15 minutes, or until radish is tender. Serve with rice or noodles.

- 1 (1-LB 5-OZ/600-G) BONELESS BEEF RIBS
- 14 OZ/400 G DAIKON RADISH, CUT INTO CHUNKS
- ¾ OZ/20 G GINGER (ABOUT 1-INCH/ 2.5-CM-LENGTH PIECE), SLICED
- 2 STAR ANISE
- 1 TEASPOON SICHUAN PEPPERCORNS
- 1 TEASPOON WHITE PEPPERCORNS
- 1 DRIED TANGERINE PEEL
- 1 DRIED MONKFRUIT
- 2 CUPS (16 FL OZ/475 ML) CHICKEN BROTH (STOCK, PAGE 90)
- SALT, TO TASTE
- STEAMED RICE (PAGE 540) OR COOKED RICE NOODLES, TO SERVE

瓦罐煨牛肉
BRAISED BEEF
IN A CASSEROLE

REGION: HUBEI
PREPARATION TIME: 10 MINUTES
COOKING TIME: 2 HOURS 30 MINUTES
SERVES: 4

* Put the beef into a large saucepan and add enough water to cover it completely. Bring to a boil over high heat and blanch for about 15 minutes. Drain and rinse under cold running water. Cut the beef into thin slices.
* Heat the oil in a Dutch oven (casserole) over low heat, add the peppercorns and pan-fry for 2–3 minutes until fragrant. Remove and discard the peppercorns. Add the scallions (spring onions) and pan-fry for 2 minutes until golden brown. Remove the scallions and set aside.
* Add the ginger and dried chiles to the Dutch oven and stir-fry over high heat for 1 minute until fragrant. Add the beef and stir-fry for another minute. Sprinkle in the wine, add the soy sauce, sugar, salt, and 3 cups (25 fl oz/750 ml) water, and bring to a boil. Put in the star anise, cinnamon, and scallions, cover, and simmer over low heat for about 2 hours, or until tender.
* To serve, season with white pepper, transfer to a serving bowl, and garnish with cilantro (coriander).

- 1 LB 10½ OZ/750 G BONELESS BEEF RIB
- 4 TABLESPOONS VEGETABLE OIL
- 1¼ TEASPOONS SICHUAN PEPPERCORNS
- 4 SCALLIONS (SPRING ONIONS), CUT INTO 2-INCH/5-CM LENGTHS
- ½ OZ/10 G GINGER (ABOUT ¾-INCH/ 2-CM-LENGTH PIECE), CRUSHED
- 2 DRIED CHILES
- 1 TABLESPOON RICE WINE
- 2 TABLESPOONS LIGHT SOY SAUCE
- ¼ OZ/10 G ROCK SUGAR
- 1 TABLESPOON SALT
- 2 STAR ANISE
- ½ CINNAMON STICK
- ½ TEASPOON GROUND WHITE PEPPER
- 1 TABLESPOON CILANTRO (CORIANDER), CHOPPED, TO GARNISH

REGION: GUANGDONG
PREPARATION TIME: 15 MINUTES,
   PLUS 1 HOUR SOAKING TIME
COOKING TIME: 2 HOURS
SERVES: 4-6
📷 PAGE 411

柱侯牛筋腩
BRAISED RIBS
AND TENDON

- 1 LB 5 OZ/600 G BONELESS BEEF RIBS
- 1 OZ/25 G GINGER(ABOUT 2-INCH/
  5-CM-LENGTH PIECE), SLICED
- 11 OZ/300 G BEEF TENDONS
- 2 TABLESPOONS VEGETABLE OIL
- 3 TABLESPOONS ZHUHOU SAUCE
- 1 DAIKON RADISH, CUT INTO LARGE
  CHUNKS
- 1 DRIED TANGERINE PEEL
- 1 TEASPOON SALT, PLUS EXTRA
  TO TASTE
- 1 TEASPOON GRANULATED SUGAR
- 1 TABLESPOON DARK SOY SAUCE
- 1 TABLESPOON CORNSTARCH
  (CORNFLOUR)
- STEAMED RICE (PAGE 540), TO SERVE
- SHREDDED SCALLION (SPRING
  ONION), TO GARNISH

* Soak the beef ribs in a bowl of cold water for 1 hour, then rinse and drain.
* Put the beef ribs and 5 slices ginger into a large saucepan, add enough water to cover, and bring to a boil. Reduce to low heat and simmer, uncovered, for 1¼–1½ hours, or until the beef ribs is tender enough to pierce through with a chopstick. Do not add water while cooking. Use a slotted spoon or tongs to remove the ribs, drain, and transfer to a bowl. Set the broth (stock) aside.
* Meanwhile, in a separate saucepan, add the beef tendons and enough water to cover them completely. Bring to a boil over high heat and blanch the tendons for 2 minutes. Skim the froth and scum off the surface, if needed. Drain and rinse under cold running water. Place the tendons in a heatproof bowl, then place the bowl in a collapsible pot or bamboo steamer over a pot of boiling water. Steam, covered, for about 1 hour. (Add more water to the pot if needed.) Rinse thoroughly under cold running water until cooled. Cut the tendon into 1-inch/2.5-cm pieces.
* Heat a large skillet (frying pan) over medium heat, add the ribs, and cook for 2–3 minutes until brown. Flip and cook for another 2–3 minutes. Remove and cut into 1¼-inch/3-cm cubes.
* Heat the oil in a saucepan over medium-high heat, add the remaining ginger, and stir-fry for 1 minute until fragrant. Stir in the zhuhou sauce. Add 1 cup (8 fl oz/250 ml) beef rib broth, the radish, dried tangerine peel, salt, sugar, and soy sauce. Bring to a boil, reduce to medium heat, and cook for about 10 minutes, or until the radish is just tender. Add the drained ribs and tendons and cook for 15–20 minutes. Season with extra salt to taste.
* Mix the cornstarch (cornflour) with 2 tablespoons water in a small bowl and stir this mixture into the beef. Bring to a boil, stirring, for about 30 seconds to thicken the sauce. Garnish with scallion (spring onion) and serve with steamed rice.

BRAISED RIBS AND TENDON

REGION: SHAANXI
PREPARATION TIME: 15 MINUTES,
   PLUS 30 MINUTES MARINATING TIME
COOKING TIME: 2 HOURS
SERVES: 4-6

红烧牛尾
OXTAIL
CASSEROLE

- 2¼ LB / 1 KG OXTAIL, CUT AT THE JOINTS INTO SMALLER PIECES AND RINSED
- 3 TABLESPOONS LIGHT SOY SAUCE
- 3 TABLESPOONS RICE WINE
- 1 TEASPOON SALT
- 2 CUPS (16 FL OZ/475 ML) PLUS 2 TABLESPOONS VEGETABLE OIL
- ⅓ CUP (2 OZ/50 G) SLICED BAMBOO SHOOTS, DRAINED
- 12-15 DRIED CHILES, SEEDED
- 2 SCALLIONS (SPRING ONIONS), CUT INTO 1½-INCH/4-CM LENGTHS
- 1 SLICE GINGER, CRUSHED
- 4 STAR ANISE
- ½ OZ/15 G LICORICE ROOT
- 1½ TABLESPOONS GRANULATED SUGAR
- 1 TEASPOON SICHUAN PEPPERCORNS
- ¼ TEASPOON GROUND WHITE PEPPER
- 1 LARGE CARROT, CUT INTO LARGE CHUNKS
- STEAMED RICE (PAGE 540) OR NOODLES, TO SERVE

* Put the oxtail into a large saucepan and add enough water to cover it completely. Bring to a boil over high heat and blanch for about 5 minutes. Skim any froth and scum off the surface. Drain and rinse under cold running water.
* Combine 1 tablespoon soy sauce, 1 tablespoon wine, and ½ teaspoon salt in a large bowl, then add the oxtail. Marinate for 30 minutes.
* Heat the 2 cups (16 fl oz/475 ml) oil in a wok or deep saucepan to 300°F/150°C, or until a cube of bread browns in 1½ minutes. Gently lower the bamboo shoots into the oil and deep-fry for 5-6 minutes until golden brown. Use a slotted spoon to carefully remove the bamboo from the oil and drain on paper towels. Set aside.
* Using paper towels, pat dry the oxtail and deep-fry for 5-6 minutes until brown. Carefully remove and drain on paper towels.
* Heat 2 tablespoons oil in a Dutch oven (casserole) over high heat, add the chiles, and stir-fry for 30 seconds until fragrant. Add the oxtail, scallions (spring onions), ginger, star anise, licorice, sugar, Sichuan peppercorns, white pepper, the remaining ½ teaspoon salt, and 2 tablespoons soy sauce, 2 tablespoons wine, and 3 cups (25 fl oz/750 ml) boiling water. Reduce to low heat and simmer, covered, for about 1½ hours, or until the oxtail is tender.
* Add the carrot and bamboo shoots, then bring to a boil. Reduce to low heat and simmer, covered, for another 15 minutes until the carrot is tender. Serve in the Dutch oven along with rice or noodles.

清炖牛尾
BRAISED OXTAIL IN CLEAR BROTH

REGION: SICHUAN
PREPARATION TIME: 10 MINUTES,
   PLUS 20 MINUTES SOAKING TIME
COOKING TIME: 2 HOURS
SERVES: 6

* Soak the oxtail by each joint in a bowl of cold water for 20 minutes. Drain.
* Combine the ginger and Sichuan peppercorns in a spice bag.
* Bring 8½ cups (68 fl oz/2 liters) water to a boil in a large pot. Put in the oxtail, return to a boil, add the spice bag and wine, and simmer over low heat for 1 hour. Skim the froth and scum off the surface.
* Remove the oxtail, discard the spice bag, and strain the broth into a bowl. Return both the broth and oxtail to the pot, add the salt, and bring to a boil. Reduce to low heat and simmer for another hour, or until the oxtail is tender. Season with extra salt to taste. Transfer the oxtail and broth to a large soup bowl.
* To make the dipping sauce, heat the sesame oil in a small skillet (frying pan) over medium-high heat, add the chili bean paste and sugar, and stir-fry for 1 minute until fragrant. Transfer to a small bowl and mix in the chopped cilantro (coriander). Serve the oxtail and broth with the dipping sauce and rice.

- 1 (2½-LB/1.2-KG) OXTAIL, CUT AT THE JOINTS INTO SMALLER PIECES
- 2 OZ/50 G GINGER (ABOUT 3-INCH/7.5-CM-LENGTH PIECE), CRUSHED
- 1 TEASPOON SICHUAN PEPPERCORNS
- ½ CUP (4 FL OZ/120 ML) SHAOXING WINE
- 2 TEASPOONS SALT, PLUS EXTRA TO TASTE
- STEAMED RICE (PAGE 540) OR NOODLES, TO SERVE

FOR THE DIPPING SAUCE:
- 1½ TABLESPOONS SESAME OIL
- 1½ TABLESPOONS PIXIAN CHILI BEAN PASTE, CHOPPED
- 2 TEASPOONS GRANULATED SUGAR
- ½ BUNCH CILANTRO (CORIANDER), CHOPPED
- STEAMED RICE (PAGE 540), TO SERVE

香酥羊腿
CRISPY LEG
OF LAMB

- 1 (2¼-LB/1-KG) LEG OF LAMB
- 2 TABLESPOONS GINGER JUICE
- 6 CLOVES GARLIC, CHOPPED
- 1 TABLESPOON SICHUAN
  PEPPERCORNS, CRUSHED
- 2 TABLESPOONS RICE WINE
- 3 CUPS (25 FL OZ/750 ML)
  VEGETABLE OIL
- 1 TEASPOON GROUND CUMIN
- FLATBREAD (PAGE 54), BOILED
  POTATOES, OR STEAMED RICE
  (PAGE 540), TO SERVE

* Use a sharp knife to make slashes across the surface of the leg of lamb in a crisscross pattern, about ¼ inch/5 mm deep. Combine the ginger juice, garlic, Sichuan peppercorns, and wine in a bowl, then rub this mixture into the lamb. Marinate for 30 minutes.
* Place the lamb on a rack in a bamboo steamer over a pot of boiling water. Steam, covered, over high heat for about 1 hour, or until cooked through. (Add more water to the pot if needed.) Transfer the lamb to a serving plate.
* Heat the oil in a wok or deep saucepan over medium-high heat to 340°F/170°C, or until a cube of bread browns in 45 seconds. Gently lower the lamb into the oil and deep-fry for 3–4 minutes until the surface is crispy. Roll the lamb in the oil so that it is cooked evenly. Carefully remove the lamb from the oil and return to the serving plate, then sprinkle with the ground cumin.
* Slice the lamb and serve with flatbread, potatoes, or rice.

它似蜜
GOAT WITH TIANMIANJIANG

REGION: BEIJING
PREPARATION TIME: 10 MINUTES
COOKING TIME: 5 MINUTES
SERVES: 4

* Combine the goat belly, tianmianjiang, salt, and 1 tablespoon cornstarch (cornflour) in a bowl. Set aside.
* Combine 3 tablespoons water and 2 tablespoons sugar in a small saucepan and cook over medium heat for 3–4 minutes until caramelized. Transfer to a bowl, then add the soy sauces, ginger juice, vinegar, wine, remaining 2 tablespoons sugar, and 1 tablespoon cornstarch.
* Heat the vegetable oil in a wok or deep saucepan to 340°F/170°C, or until a cube of bread browns in 45 seconds. Gently lower the goat into the oil, using chopsticks to disperse the pieces rapidly to prevent sticking, and deep-fry for 10 seconds until the goat is opaque. Use a slotted spoon to carefully remove the goat from the oil and drain on paper towels.
* Heat 3 tablespoons sesame oil in the wok, add the goat and sauce, and toss rapidly over high heat for 1–2 minutes to coat thoroughly. Stir in the remaining 1 tablespoon sesame oil. Transfer to a serving plate and serve with rice.

- 11 OZ/300 G GOAT BELLY, FINELY SLICED
- ½ TEASPOON TIANMIANJIANG
- ¼ TEASPOON SALT
- 2 TABLESPOONS CORNSTARCH (CORNFLOUR)
- 4 TABLESPOONS GRANULATED SUGAR
- 2 TEASPOONS DARK SOY SAUCE
- 1 TEASPOON LIGHT SOY SAUCE
- 1 TEASPOON GINGER JUICE
- 1 TEASPOON BLACK OR BALSAMIC VINEGAR
- 1 TEASPOON SHAOXING WINE
- 2 CUPS (16 FL OZ/475 ML) VEGETABLE OIL
- 4 TABLESPOONS SESAME OIL
- STEAMED RICE (PAGE 540), TO SERVE

REGION: BEIJING
PREPARATION TIME: 15 MINUTES
COOKING TIME: 5 MINUTES
SERVES: 4

醋熘肉片
SAUTÉED LAMB
IN VINEGAR

- 1 (9-OZ/250-G) BONELESS LEG OF LAMB, THINLY SLICED ACROSS THE GRAIN
- 1½ TEASPOONS CORNSTARCH (CORNFLOUR)
- 2 SCALLIONS (SPRING ONIONS), SHREDDED
- 1 TEASPOON CHOPPED GINGER
- 1 CLOVE GARLIC, CHOPPED
- 1 TABLESPOON BLACK OR BALSAMIC VINEGAR
- 2 TABLESPOONS LIGHT SOY SAUCE
- 1 TABLESPOON RICE WINE
- 2 CUPS (16 FL OZ/475 ML) VEGETABLE OIL
- ⅓ CUP (2 OZ/50 G) SLICED BAMBOO SHOOTS, DRAINED
- 1 TABLESPOON SESAME OIL
- SALT, TO TASTE
- STEAMED RICE (PAGE 540), TO SERVE

* Combine the lamb, ½ teaspoon cornstarch (cornflour), and ½ teaspoon water in a bowl. Mix well and set aside.
* In a separate bowl, combine the scallions (spring onions), ginger, and garlic, then add the vinegar, soy sauce, wine, remaining 1 teaspoon cornstarch (cornflour), and 1 tablespoon water. Mix into a sauce and set aside.
* Heat the vegetable oil in a wok or deep saucepan to 275°F/140°C, or until a cube of bread turns golden in 2 minutes. Gently lower the lamb and bamboo shoots into the oil, using chopsticks to disperse and separate the pieces, and deep-fry for 6–7 seconds. Use a slotted spoon to carefully remove the lamb and bamboo shoots from the oil and drain on paper towels.
* Pour out most of the oil, leaving about 1 tablespoon in the wok. Heat the oil over medium-high heat, add the lamb, bamboo shoots, and sauce, and stir rapidly for 1–2 minutes until the sauce thickens and coats the lamb and bamboo shoots. Stir in the sesame oil and season with salt to taste. Transfer to a serving plate and serve with rice.

香芹羊肉丝
LAMB WITH
CHINESE CELERY

REGION: SICHUAN
PREPARATION TIME: 10 MINUTES,
   PLUS 10 MINUTES MARINATING TIME
COOKING TIME: 5 MINUTES
SERVES: 4

* Combine the lamb, salt, 1 teaspoon soy sauce, 1 tablespoon cornstarch (cornflour), and 2 tablespoons water in a bowl and marinate for 10 minutes. Stir in 1 tablespoon oil.
* Combine the remaining 1 teaspoon soy sauce, the wine, vinegar, the remaining ½ tablespoon cornstarch, and 3 tablespoons water in a small bowl and mix into a sauce. Set aside.
* Heat the remaining 2 tablespoons oil in a wok or large skillet (frying pan), add the ginger, and stir-fry over high heat for 1 minute until fragrant. Put in the lamb and stir-fry over medium heat for another 2–3 minutes until the lamb is just cooked through. Add the chili bean paste, celery, garlic sprouts, and the sauce, then stir-fry for another 1–2 minutes until sauce thickens. Transfer to a serving plate and serve with rice.

• 1 (11-OZ/300-G) BONELESS LEG OF LAMB, CUT INTO THIN STRIPS
• ½ TEASPOON SALT
• 2 TEASPOONS LIGHT SOY SAUCE
• 1½ TABLESPOONS CORNSTARCH (CORNFLOUR)
• 3 TABLESPOONS VEGETABLE OIL
• 1 TABLESPOON RICE WINE
• ½ TEASPOON WHITE VINEGAR
• ½ OZ/15 G GINGER (ABOUT ¾-INCH/ 2-CM-LENGTH PIECE), SHREDDED
• 1½ TABLESPOONS PIXIAN CHILI BEAN PASTE, CHOPPED
• 1 SMALL BUNCH CHINESE CELERY, CUT INTO 1½-INCH/4-CM LENGTHS
• 2 GARLIC SPROUTS, CUT INTO 1½-INCH/4-CM LENGTHS
• STEAMED RICE (PAGE 540), TO SERVE

烤羊肉串
LAMB
KEBABS

REGION: XINJIANG
PREPARATION TIME: 15 MINUTES,
   PLUS 15 MINUTES MARINATING TIME
COOKING TIME: 6 MINUTES
SERVES: 4

* In a large bowl, combine the lamb, onion, ½ teaspoon salt, and 5 tablespoons water and marinate for 15 minutes.
* Meanwhile, soak the bamboo skewers in water for 10 minutes. Drain.
* In a small bowl, mix the ground Sichuan peppercorns, chili powder, and remaining ½ teaspoon salt to make the spiced salt. Set aside.
* Preheat the broiler (grill) to high heat. Thread the lamb pieces onto the skewers, put the skewers under the broiler, and cook for 2–3 minutes. Turn over, brush with the soy sauce, and sprinkle with the spiced salt, then broil for another 2–3 minutes until golden brown and cooked through. Brush with the sesame oil and sprinkle over the cumin. Serve immediately.

• 1 (1 LB 2-OZ/500-G) BONELESS LEG OF LAMB, CUT INTO 2 × 1 × ¼-INCH/5 × 2.5 × 0.5-CM SLICES
• 1 ONION, CHOPPED
• 1 TEASPOON SALT
• ½ TEASPOON GROUND SICHUAN PEPPERCORNS
• ¼ TEASPOON CHILI POWDER
• 4 TABLESPOONS LIGHT SOY SAUCE
• 2 TABLESPOONS SESAME OIL
• 1 TEASPOON GROUND CUMIN
• 8-12 BAMBOO SKEWERS

REGION: TIBET
PREPARATION TIME: 15 MINUTES,
  PLUS 30 MINUTES SOAKING TIME
COOKING TIME: 10 MINUTES
SERVES: 4

赛蜜羊肉
HONEYED
LAMB

- 1 (1 LB 2-OZ/500-G) BONELESS LEG
  OF LAMB, CUT INTO 1¼ × ¾ × ¼-INCH/
  3 × 2 × 0.5-CM SLICES
- 1 EGG YOLK
- 2 TABLESPOONS LIGHT SOY SAUCE
- 2 TEASPOONS CORNSTARCH
  (CORNFLOUR)
- ½ CUP (3½ OZ/100 G) GRANULATED
  SUGAR
- ¼ TEASPOON SALT, PLUS EXTRA
  TO TASTE
- 1 TEASPOON HULLESS BARLEY WINE
- 1 TEASPOON VINEGAR
- 2 TEASPOONS GINGER JUICE
- 4¼ CUPS (34 FL OZ/1 LITER)
  VEGETABLE OIL
- 2 TABLESPOONS YAK BUTTER, GHEE,
  OR BUTTER
- STEAMED RICE (PAGE 540) OR
  POTATOES, TO SERVE

Hulless barley wine is a special wine made in Tibet, Qinghai, and Sichuan. It can be substituted with another liquor that has 40–50 percent alcohol content.

* Put the lamb slices in a bowl of cold water and soak for 30 minutes. Drain.
* Combine the egg yolk, 1 tablespoon soy sauce, 1 teaspoon cornstarch (cornflour), and 1 tablespoon water in a large bowl and mix into a batter. Add the lamb and mix well.
* In a separate bowl, combine the sugar, salt, wine, vinegar, ginger juice, remaining 1 tablespoon soy sauce, 1 teaspoon cornstarch, and 1 tablespoon water and mix into a sauce.
* Heat the oil in a wok or deep saucepan to 300°F/150°C, or until a cube of bread browns in 1½ minutes. Gently lower the lamb into the oil, using chopsticks to disperse the pieces rapidly to prevent sticking, and deep-fry for 3–4 minutes until golden brown and almost cooked. Use a slotted spoon to carefully remove the lamb from the oil and drain on paper towels.
* Pour out most of the oil, leaving about 1 tablespoon in the wok. Heat the oil over high heat, add the lamb and sauce, and stir-fry for 1–2 minutes until the sauce thickens. Stir in the butter and season with extra salt to taste. Serve with rice or potatoes.

羊肉馅饼
LAMB
PIES

REGION: SHAANXI
PREPARATION TIME: 20 MINUTES,
   PLUS 30 MINUTES PROOFING TIME
COOKING TIME: 20 MINUTES
SERVES: 8

* To make the dough, put the flour into a large bowl, gradually add ⅔ cup (5 fl oz/150 ml) warm water (about 160°F/70°C), and stir with chopsticks until thoroughly mixed. The dough may appear a little dry and flaky. Knead for about 3–4 minutes until it is silky and smooth. If the dough seems too sticky, add a little more flour. Cover the bowl with a clean, damp dish towel and proof at room temperature for about 30 minutes.
* Meanwhile, make the filling. In a bowl, combine the lamb, salt, soy sauce, and 2 tablespoons water and marinate for 15 minutes. Stir in the chopped Beijing scallions together with the ginger, wine, and sesame oil. Mix in the cornstarch (cornflour). Divide the filling into 8 portions.
* To put the pie together, dust a clean cutting board with flour. Transfer the dough from the bowl onto the board and knead for 1 minute until smooth. Divide the dough into 8 portions, about 2 oz/50 g each. Using a rolling pin, roll each piece of dough into a flat disk about 4¾ inches/ 12 cm in diameter. Put a portion of filling in the center of the disk and fold the round edges toward the center to form a closed pie. Pinch the top to seal. Repeat with the remaining dough pieces and filling.
* Heat the vegetable oil in a large skillet (frying pan) over low heat, add a few lamb pies, tops facing down, and cook for 3–4 minutes until brown, then flip over to brown the other side. Add more oil if needed. Repeat with the remaining pies and serve hot.

• 2 CUPS (9 OZ/250 G) ALL-PURPOSE (PLAIN) FLOUR, PLUS EXTRA IF NEEDED
• 1 TABLESPOON VEGETABLE OIL

FOR THE LAMB FILLING:
• 9 OZ/250 G GROUND (MINCED) LAMB
• 1 TEASPOON SALT
• 1 TABLESPOON LIGHT SOY SAUCE
• 2 BEIJING SCALLIONS OR 6 SCALLIONS (SPRING ONIONS), STEMS CHOPPED
• 1 TABLESPOON CHOPPED GINGER
• 1 TABLESPOON RICE WINE
• 2 TABLESPOONS SESAME OIL
• 1 TABLESPOON CORNSTARCH (CORNFLOUR)

REGION: ANHUI
PREPARATION TIME: 15 MINUTES, PLUS
  10 MINUTES MARINATING TIME
COOKING TIME: 45 MINUTES
SERVES: 4
📷 PAGE 421

焦炸羊肉

DEEP-FRIED LAMB

- 11 OZ/300 G BONELESS LAMB RIB
- ¼ TEASPOON SICHUAN PEPPERCORNS, TOASTED AND CRUSHED
- 2 TABLESPOONS CHOPPED GINGER
- 1 SCALLION (SPRING ONION), CHOPPED
- 1 TEASPOON SALT
- 1 TEASPOON ALL-PURPOSE (PLAIN) FLOUR
- ¼ TEASPOON GROUND SICHUAN PEPPER
- 6 TABLESPOONS CORNSTARCH (CORNFLOUR)
- 3 EGG WHITES
- 3 TABLESPOONS SESAME OIL
- 3 CUPS (25 FL OZ/750 ML) VEGETABLE OIL
- 1 SCALLION (SPRING ONION), STEM ONLY, CUT INTO 2-INCH/5-CM SECTIONS, TO GARNISH
- 2 TABLESPOONS TIANMIANJIANG, TO SERVE

* In a large saucepan, add the lamb and enough water to cover it completely. Bring to a boil over high heat and cook the lamb for 30 minutes. Skim the froth and scum off the surface, if needed. Drain and rinse under cold running water. Cut the lamb into 2 × ¾ × ¼-inch/5 × 2 x 0.5-cm pieces and put into a bowl.
* Add the Sichuan peppercorns, ginger, scallion (spring onion), and ½ teaspoon salt to the lamb. Mix together well and marinate for 10 minutes. Stir in the flour.
* Mix the remaining ½ teaspoon salt with the ground Sichuan pepper to make a spiced pepper salt and set aside.
* In a small bowl, mix the cornstarch (cornflour) with ⅔ cup (5 fl oz/150 ml) water. Set aside for 5 minutes, or until the starch settles at the bottom of the bowl, then pour out the water to leave a wet starch.
* In a bowl, beat the egg whites, add the sesame oil and wet starch, and mix thoroughly.
* Heat the vegetable oil in a wok or deep saucepan to 300°F/150°C, or until a cube of bread browns in 1½ minutes. Dip pieces of lamb, in batches, into the egg whites and then gently lower into the oil. Deep-fry for 3–4 minutes until slightly brown. Use a slotted spoon to carefully remove the lamb from the oil and put on a plate. Put all of the lamb back into the oil and deep-fry for another 2 minutes until golden brown and cooked through. Carefully remove the lamb from the oil using a slotted spoon, transfer to a plate, and sprinkle with the spiced pepper salt. Garnish with scallions (spring onions) and serve with tianmianjiang.

DEEP-FRIED LAMB

REGION: SICHUAN
PREPARATION TIME: 10 MINUTES
COOKING TIME: 40 MINUTES
SERVES: 4-6

酥脆香辣羊肉
CRISPY LAMB WITH
SPICY DIP

- 1 (1 LB 8½-OZ/750-G) BONELESS LEG OF LAMB, RINSED AND CUT INTO 5-6 PIECES
- ¼ OZ/10 G GINGER (ABOUT ¾-INCH/ 2-CM-LENGTH PIECE), CRUSHED
- 1 SCALLION (SPRING ONION), SLICED INTO 1½-INCH/4-CM LENGTHS
- 2 STAR ANISE, CRUSHED
- 1¼ TEASPOONS SICHUAN PEPPERCORNS, CRUSHED
- 1 TEASPOON GROUND CINNAMON
- 1 TEASPOON LIGHT SOY SAUCE
- 1 TEASPOON DARK SOY SAUCE
- 1 TABLESPOON RICE WINE
- ½ TEASPOON SALT
- 3 EGG WHITES
- 2 TABLESPOONS CORNSTARCH (CORNFLOUR)
- 3 CUPS (25 FL OZ/750 ML) VEGETABLE OIL
- STEAMED RICE (PAGE 540), TO SERVE

  FOR THE DIPPING SAUCE:
- 1 OZ/25 G PICKLED CHILES, CHOPPED
- 2 CLOVES GARLIC, CHOPPED
- 1 SCALLION (SPRING ONION), CHOPPED
- 2 TABLESPOONS GRANULATED SUGAR
- 1 TABLESPOON CORNSTARCH (CORNFLOUR)
- 1 TEASPOON CHOPPED GINGER
- 1 TEASPOON BLACK OR BALSAMIC VINEGAR
- ½ TEASPOON SALT
- SCANT ½ CUP (3½ FL OZ/100 ML) CHICKEN OR BEEF BROTH (STOCK, PAGES 90-91)

* Bring a large saucepan of water to a boil over high heat. Add the lamb and blanch for 10 minutes. Skim the froth and scum off the surface, if needed. Drain and rinse under cold running water.
* In a heatproof bowl, combine the lamb with the ginger, scallion (spring onion), star anise, Sichuan peppercorns, cinnamon, both soy sauces, wine, and the salt. Transfer to a collapsible pot or bamboo steamer over a pot of boiling water. Steam, covered, for 20 minutes.
* In a bowl, beat the egg whites and mix in the cornstarch (cornflour). Heat the oil in a wok or deep fryer to 340°F/170°C, or until a cube of bread browns in 45 seconds. Dip the lamb pieces, in batches, into the egg whites and then gently lower into the oil. Deep-fry for 3–4 minutes until brown and crispy. Use a slotted spoon to carefully remove the lamb from the oil and drain on paper towels. When cool enough to handle, slice into smaller pieces. Keep warm.
* To make the dipping sauce, pour out most of the oil, leaving 2 tablespoons in the wok. Heat the oil over medium-high heat, add the pickled chiles, and stir-fry for 2 minutes until fragrant. Add all the remaining ingredients for the dipping sauce and cook for 1–2 minutes until thickened. Pour the sauce into a small bowl.
* Transfer the lamb to a serving plate and serve with the dipping sauce and rice.

香酥岩羊
CRISPY LAMB WITH SPICED SALT

REGION: QINGHAI
PREPARATION TIME: 15 MINUTES
COOKING TIME: 40 MINUTES
SERVES: 4–6

* Put the lamb in a medium saucepan and add enough water to cover it completely. Bring to a boil over high heat, reduce to a simmer, and blanch for 30 minutes. Drain and rinse under cold water.
* Slice the lamb, transfer to a bowl, add the white pepper, Sichuan pepper, salt, and wine.
* Mix the cornstarch (cornflour) with 3 tablespoons water in a small bowl. Allow the starch to settle at the bottom of the bowl for 5 minutes, then pour out the water to leave a wet starch.
* In another small bowl, beat the egg whites until foamy. Add the egg whites to the wet starch to make a batter.
* Heat the oil in a wok or large skillet (frying pan) to 340°F/170°C, or until a cube of bread browns in 45 seconds. Dip each slice of lamb into the egg white batter, then carefully drop the slices, one at a time, in the hot oil. Use chopsticks to disperse the pieces rapidly to prevent sticking, and deep-fry for 2–3 minutes until crispy. Use a slotted spoon to remove the lamb from the hot oil and drain on paper towels.
* To make the spiced salt, heat a small skillet (frying pan) over medium-high heat and add the salt. Stir for a minute, just to warm, turn off the heat, transfer to a small bowl, and allow the salt to cool slightly. Stir in the ground Sichuan pepper.
* Plate the crispy lamb and serve with spiced salt on the side for sprinkling.

- 1 (1 LB 2-OZ/500-G) LAMB FILLET
- ½ TEASPOON GROUND WHITE PEPPER
- ½ TEASPOON GROUND SICHUAN PEPPER
- 1 TEASPOON SALT
- 2 TABLESPOONS RICE WINE
- 2 TABLESPOONS CORNSTARCH (CORNFLOUR)
- 3 EGG WHITES
- 2 CUPS (16 FL OZ/475 ML) VEGETABLE OIL

FOR THE SPICED SALT:
- 1 TEASPOON SALT
- ½ TEASPOON GROUND SICHUAN PEPPER

REGION: HONG KONG
PREPARATION TIME: 10 MINUTES,
    PLUS 5 MINUTES STANDING TIME
COOKING TIME: 15 MINUTES
SERVES: 4
📷 PAGE 425

避风塘炒羊排

LAMB CHOPS
AND CHILES

- 8 LAMB CHOPS (CUTLETS)
- 1 TEASPOON SALT
- GENEROUS 4 CUPS (1¾ PINTS / 1 LITER) VEGETABLE OIL, FOR FRYING AND DEEP-FRYING
- 2 HEADS GARLIC, PEELED AND COARSELY CHOPPED
- 2 TABLESPOONS CORNSTARCH (CORNFLOUR)
- 4 SHALLOTS, CHOPPED
- 6–12 DRIED CHILES
- 1 RED CHILE, SHREDDED
- 1 TABLESPOON GROUND SICHUAN PEPPERCORNS
- 3 QUANTITIES SOYBEAN CRISPS (PAGE 52)
- 1 TABLESPOON LIGHT SOY SAUCE
- 1 TEASPOON GRANULATED SUGAR
- 2 SCALLIONS (SPRING ONIONS), CUT INTO 2-INCH/5-CM LENGTHS
- STEAMED RICE (PAGE 540), TO SERVE

* Sprinkle the lamb chops with the salt and place in a bowl. Let stand for 5 minutes.
* Heat 2 tablespoons oil in a wok or deep saucepan over low heat, add the garlic, and pan-fry for 20–30 seconds until golden. Use a slotted spoon to remove the garlic from the oil and drain on paper towels.
* Dust the lamb chops with cornstarch (cornflour). Add the remaining 4 cups (32 fl oz/950 ml) oil to the wok and heat to 300°F/150°C, or until a cube of bread browns in 1½ minutes. Gently lower the lamb chops into the oil and deep-fry for 4–5 minutes, or until golden brown and cooked through. Use a slotted spoon to carefully remove the lamb chops from the oil and drain on paper towels.
* Pour out most of the oil, leaving about 2 tablespoons in the wok. Heat over medium heat, add the shallots, and stir-fry for 1–2 minutes until fragrant. Increase to high heat, add the dried chiles, red chile, ground Sichuan peppercorns, crispy garlic, soybean crisps, soy sauce, and sugar. Toss well until all the ingredients are combined. Put in the lamb chops and stir-fry for about 1 minute, then add the scallions (spring onions) and toss. Transfer to a serving plate and serve with rice.

LAMB CHOPS AND CHILES

REGION: HUNAN
PREPARATION TIME: 15 MINUTES
COOKING TIME: 1 HOUR 15 MINUTES
SERVES: 6

酸辣红烧羊肉
HOT AND SOUR
LAMB

- 1 (2-LB/900-G) BONELESS LAMB RIB
- 4 TABLESPOONS VEGETABLE OIL
- 4 TABLESPOONS RICE WINE
- 1 TABLESPOON LIGHT SOY SAUCE
- 1 TABLESPOON DARK SOY SAUCE
- 1 TEASPOON SALT
- 2 SCALLIONS (SPRING ONIONS), CUT INTO 1¼-INCH/4-CM LENGTHS
- ½ OZ/15 G GINGER (ABOUT ¾-INCH/ 2-CM-LENGTH PIECE), SLICED
- 5 DRIED RED CHILES
- 3 TABLESPOONS PICKLED VEGETABLES, RINSED AND CHOPPED
- 1–2 GREEN CHILES, SEEDED AND FINELY CHOPPED
- 1 TEASPOON WHITE VINEGAR
- 1 TABLESPOON CORNSTARCH (CORNFLOUR)
- 1 CHINESE LEEK, CHOPPED
- ½ TEASPOON SESAME OIL
- 4 BUNCHES CILANTRO (CORIANDER), CHOPPED
- STEAMED RICE (PAGE 540), TO SERVE

* Put the lamb into a large pot and add enough water to cover it completely. Bring to a boil over high heat and blanch the lamb for 5 minutes. Skim the froth and scum off the surface, if needed. Drain and rinse under cold running water until cooled. Cut the lamb into 1¼-inch/3-cm cubes.
* Heat 2 tablespoons vegetable oil in a wok or large skillet (frying pan) over high heat, add the lamb, and stir-fry for about 1 minute. Sprinkle in the wine. Add the soy sauces and salt and stir-fry for another minute. Stir in the scallions (spring onions), ginger, and dried red chiles.
* Add 2 cups (16 fl oz/475 ml) water and bring to a boil. Reduce to low heat and simmer, covered, for 1 hour.
* Discard the scallions, ginger, and dried chiles. Using a slotted spoon, transfer the lamb to a shallow bowl and keep warm. Reserve the lamb broth (stock).
* Heat the remaining 2 tablespoons vegetable oil in the wok, add the pickled vegetables and green chiles, and stir-fry for about 1 minute. Pour in the vinegar and the lamb broth and bring to a boil. Mix the cornstarch (cornflour) with 2 tablespoons water in a small bowl and stir this mixture into the wok. Bring to a boil, stirring, for about 30 seconds to thicken the sauce. Add the leek and stir in the sesame oil.
* Pour the sauce over the lamb and sprinkle with the chopped cilantro (coriander). Serve with rice.

支竹羊腩煲

GOAT AND TOFU CASSEROLE

REGION: GUANGDONG
PREPARATION TIME: 15 MINUTES
COOKING TIME: 2 HOURS
SERVES: 4

* In a large saucepan, add the goat belly and enough water to cover it completely. Bring to a boil over high heat and blanch for about 3 minutes. Drain and rinse under cold running water.
* Heat the oil in a wok or deep saucepan to 300°F/150°C, or until a cube of bread browns in 1½ minutes. Carefully add the bean curd sticks and deep-fry for 1 minute until puffed up. Remove and transfer to a bowl of cold water. Soak for 2–3 minutes. Drain and cut the bean curd sticks into about 2½-inch/6-cm lengths. Set aside.
* Peel the water chestnuts and then soak in a small bowl of cold water until ready to use.
* Heat the remaining 2 tablespoons oil in a Dutch oven (casserole) over medium-high heat, add the ginger and garlic, and stir-fry for 30 seconds until fragrant. Put in the goat, wine, cardamom, water chestnuts, jujube dates, and 2 cups (16 fl oz/475 ml) water. Bring to a boil, reduce to low heat, then cover and simmer for about 1 hour.
* Add the soy sauces, salt, sugar, and the bean curd sticks and continue to cook for 30 minutes. Put in the leeks and simmer for another 15 minutes. In a small bowl, mix the cornstarch (cornflour) with 2 tablespoons water and stir this mixture into the Dutch oven. Bring to a boil, stirring, for 30 seconds to thicken the sauce. Stir in the white pepper. Transfer to a serving dish and serve with rice.

• 1 LB 5 OZ/600 G GOAT BELLY, CUT INTO BITE-SIZE PIECES
• 2 CUPS (16 FL OZ/475 ML) PLUS 2 TABLESPOONS VEGETABLE OIL
• 4 DRIED BEAN CURD STICKS
• 6 WATER CHESTNUTS
• 2 OZ/50 G GINGER (ABOUT 3-INCH/7.5-CM-LENGTH PIECE), SLICED
• 4 CLOVES GARLIC, SLICED
• 1 TABLESPOON RICE WINE
• 2 BLACK CARDAMOM PODS
• 3 JUJUBE DATES
• 1 TABLESPOON LIGHT SOY SAUCE
• 1 TABLESPOON DARK SOY SAUCE
• 1 TEASPOON SALT
• 1 TEASPOON GRANULATED SUGAR
• 3 CHINESE LEEKS, CUT INTO 1¼-INCH/4-CM LENGTHS
• 1 TABLESPOON CORNSTARCH (CORNFLOUR)
• ¼ TEASPOON GROUND WHITE PEPPER
• STEAMED RICE (PAGE 540), TO SERVE

REGION: GANSU
PREPARATION TIME: 10 MINUTES,
  PLUS 1 HOUR MARINATING TIME
COOKING TIME: 1 HOUR
SERVES: 4–6
📷 PAGE 429

靖远焖羔羊
BRAISED
LAMB

- 2¼ LB/1 KG STEWING LAMB, CUT INTO
  1½-INCH/4-CM CUBES
- ¼ OZ/10 G GINGER (ABOUT ¾-INCH/
  2-CM-LENGTH PIECE), HALF CHOPPED
  AND HALF SLICED
- 2 SCALLIONS (SPRING ONIONS),
  1 CHOPPED AND 1 KNOTTED, PLUS
  EXTRA TO GARNISH
- ½ TEASPOON SALT
- 1 TABLESPOON RICE WINE
- 1½ TABLESPOONS LIGHT SOY SAUCE
- 2 CUPS (16 FL OZ/475 ML)
  VEGETABLE OIL
- ½ TEASPOON GROUND WHITE PEPPER
- 1 TABLESPOON CORNSTARCH
  (CORNFLOUR)
- 1 TEASPOON SESAME OIL
- STEAMED RICE (PAGE 540), TO SERVE

* In a bowl, combine the lamb, chopped ginger, chopped scallion (spring onion), salt, wine, and ½ tablespoon soy sauce and marinate for 1 hour.
* Heat the vegetable oil in a wok or deep saucepan to 300°F/150°C, or until a cube of bread browns in 1½ minutes. Gently lower in the lamb, using chopsticks to disperse the pieces rapidly to prevent sticking, and deep-fry for 3–4 minutes until golden brown. Use a slotted spoon to carefully remove the lamb from the oil and drain on paper towels. Transfer the lamb to a Dutch oven (casserole) and add enough water to cover the lamb completely. Bring to a boil, add the ginger slices, knotted scallion, white pepper, and remaining 1 tablespoon soy sauce. Reduce to low heat, cover, and simmer for about 40 minutes, until tender.
* In a small bowl, mix the cornstarch (cornflour) with 2 tablespoons water and stir this mixture into the wok. Bring to a boil, stirring, for 30 seconds to thicken the sauce. Drizzle over the sesame oil and transfer to a serving plate. Garnish with scallions, then serve with rice.

REGION: YUNNAN
PREPARATION TIME: 10 MINUTES,
  PLUS 1 HOUR MARINATING AND
  15 MINUTES RESTING TIME
COOKING TIME: 2 HOURS 30 MINUTES
SERVES: 8

丁香烤羊腿
ROAST LAMB
WITH CLOVES

- 1 (6-LB 10-OZ/3-KG) WHOLE LEG OF
  LAMB, BONE-IN
- 2 TABLESPOONS SALT
- ½ TEASPOON GROUND WHITE PEPPER
- 2 TABLESPOONS CHOPPED SCALLIONS
  (SPRING ONIONS)
- 2 TABLESPOONS CHOPPED GINGER
- ½ CUP (4 FL OZ/120 ML)
  VEGETABLE OIL
- 12 CLOVES
- 2 TABLESPOONS SESAME OIL
- 2 TABLESPOONS TIANMIANJIANG
- 4 SCALLIONS (SPRING ONIONS), CUT
  INTO 2-INCH/5-CM LENGTHS
- 24 STEAMED EGG ROLL WRAPPERS

* Take the lamb out of the refrigerator and set aside to warm to room temperature.
* Poke a dozen holes across the surface of the lamb with a skewer. Combine the salt, white pepper, chopped scallions (spring onions) and ginger, and rub the lamb with this mixture. Marinate for 1 hour.
* Preheat the oven to 375°F/190°C/Gas Mark 5.
* Rub the lamb thoroughly with the vegetable oil. Fill each hole you made on the lamb with a clove, then place the lamb in roasting pan. Add ½ cup (4 fl oz/120 ml) water to the roasting pan. Roast for about 2 hours 30 minutes, or until all the water has evaporated and the meat is golden brown. Remove from the oven and brush with sesame oil.
* Let the lamb rest for 15 minutes, then slice. Serve with tianmianjiang, scallion lengths, and egg roll wrappers.

BRAISED LAMB

REGION: SHANXI
PREPARATION TIME: 15 MINUTES,
  PLUS 24 HOURS FREEZING TIME
COOKING TIME: 1 HOUR 50 MINUTES
SERVES: 4

羊肉冻豆腐
BRAISED LAMB
WITH TOFU

- 14 OZ/400 G FIRM TOFU, DRAINED
- 11 OZ/300 G STEWING LAMB
- 1 TEASPOON SALT, PLUS EXTRA
  TO TASTE
- 1 TEASPOON GRATED GINGER
- 1 TABLESPOON DRIED SHRIMP, RINSED,
  DRAINED, AND CHOPPED
- 1 TEASPOON GROUND SICHUAN
  PEPPER
- 3½ OZ/100 G POTATO VERMICELLI
- ½ CUP (3½ OZ/100 G) SPINACH,
  LEAVES SLICED IN HALF
- ¼ OZ/10 G YELLOW CHIVES, CUT INTO
  ½-INCH/1-CM LENGTHS
- 1 BUNCH CILANTRO (CORIANDER),
  CUT INTO ½-INCH/1-CM LENGTHS
- STEAMED RICE (PAGE 540), TO SERVE

This is a delicious recipe favored by locals. When the tofu is frozen, the water inside the tofu crystallizes. When the crystals melt, they leave gaps within the tofu, which absorb the sauce.

* Put the tofu in a freezerproof container, cover, and place in the freezer for 24 hours. Thaw completely before use.
* Put the tofu into a large saucepan and add enough water to cover it completely. Bring to a boil over high heat and blanch for 2 minutes. Drain and rinse under cold running water until cooled. When the tofu is cool enough to handle, squeeze out most of the water inside the tofu. Cut into 1-inch/2.5-cm cubes and set aside.
* Put the lamb into a large saucepan and add enough water to cover it completely. Bring to a boil over high heat and blanch for 5 minutes. Drain and rinse under cold running water until cooled.
* Cut the lamb into 1½-inch/4-cm cubes and return to the saucepan with enough water to cover. Return to a boil, add the salt, ginger, dried shrimp, and ground Sichuan pepper. Reduce to low heat and simmer, covered, for 1½ hours, or until the lamb is sufficiently soft.
* Meanwhile soak the vermicelli in a bowl of hot water for about 3 minutes to soften. Drain and set aside.
* Add the tofu and drained vermicelli to the lamb, bring to a boil, cover, and simmer for another 5 minutes. Stir in the spinach and yellow chives and return to a boil. Transfer to a large serving bowl and garnish with the cilantro (coriander). Serve with rice.

山药炖羊肉
LAMB
WITH WILD YAM

REGION: SHANXI
PREPARATION TIME: 15 MINUTES
COOKING TIME: 2 HOURS 15 MINUTES
SERVES: 4–6

* Place the wild yams in a bowl of ice-cold water and set aside.
* Put the lamb into a large saucepan and enough water to cover it completely. Bring to a boil over high heat and blanch for 10 minutes. Drain and rinse under cold running water. Set aside.
* Put the Sichuan peppercorns and star anise in a spice bag. Heat the oil in a Dutch oven (casserole) over medium-high heat, add the ginger and Beijing scallions, and stir-fry for 1–2 minutes until fragrant. Add the lamb and stir-fry for about 1 minute, then stir in the wine, wolfberries, spice bag, and enough water to cover the lamb by 1½ inches/4 cm.
* Bring to a boil over high heat, reduce to low heat and simmer, covered, for 2 hours, or until the lamb is tender enough to pierce through with a chopstick. Add the wild yams, season with the salt, and simmer for another 5 minutes. Transfer to a serving plate and serve with rice or cooked noodles.

- ¼ (ABOUT 3½ OZ/100 G) WILD YAM OR CASSAVA, PEELED AND CUT INTO ½-INCH/1-CM SLICES
- 11 OZ/300 G STEWING LAMB
- 1 TEASPOON SICHUAN PEPPERCORNS
- 1 STAR ANISE
- 1 TABLESPOON VEGETABLE OIL
- ¼ OZ/10 G GINGER (ABOUT ¾-INCH/ 2-CM-LENGTH PIECE), SLICED
- 2 BEIJING SCALLIONS OR 6 SCALLIONS (SPRING ONIONS), CUT INTO 2-INCH/5-CM LENGTHS
- 1 TABLESPOON RICE WINE
- 1 TABLESPOON DRIED WOLFBERRIES
- 1 TEASPOON SALT
- STEAMED RICE (PAGE 540) OR COOKED NOODLES, TO SERVE

白汁东山羊
GOAT IN A
CASSEROLE

REGION: HAINAN
PREPARATION TIME: 5 MINUTES,
   PLUS 5 MINUTES SOAKING AND
   15 MINUTES MARINATING TIME
COOKING TIME: 1 HOUR 20 MINUTES
SERVES: 4

* In a large saucepan, add the goat and enough water to cover it completely. Bring to a boil over high heat and blanch the goat for 5 minutes. Skim the froth and scum off the surface, if needed. Drain and rinse under cold running water until cooled. Cut the goat into 1½-inch/4-cm squares. Put the goat into a large bowl, cover with warm water, and soak for 5 minutes. Drain.
* In a bowl, combine the goat and marinade ingredients and marinate for 15 minutes.
* Heat the oil in a wok or large skillet (frying pan) over high heat, add the goat, and stir-fry for 2 minutes. Add ½ cup (4 fl oz/120 ml) chicken broth (stock) and bring to a boil, then cover, reduce to medium heat, and simmer for 10 minutes. Transfer to a Dutch oven (casserole).
* Add the salt and the remaining 1½ cups (12 fl oz/350 ml) chicken broth and bring to a boil. Add the tofu, reduce to low heat, and simmer for 1 hour. Season with extra salt to taste. Serve in the Dutch oven with rice.

- 1 (1 LB 8½-OZ/700-G) BONELESS, SKIN-ON GOAT MEAT
- 1 TABLESPOON VEGETABLE OIL
- 2 CUPS (16 FL OZ/475 ML) CHICKEN BROTH (STOCK, PAGE 90)
- ½ TEASPOON SALT, PLUS EXTRA TO TASTE
- 9 OZ/250 G FIRM TOFU, DRAINED AND CUT INTO 1-INCH/2.5-CM CUBES
- STEAMED RICE (PAGE 540), TO SERVE

FOR THE MARINADE:
- 4 CLOVES GARLIC, CHOPPED
- 2 BAY LEAVES
- 1 TABLESPOON RICE WINE
- ¼ OZ/10 G GINGER (ABOUT ¾-INCH/ 2-CM-LENGTH PIECE), SHREDDED
- ¼ TEASPOON GROUND WHITE PEPPER

手抓羊肉
MUTTON
RIBS

- 2¼ LB/1 KG MUTTON OR LAMB RIBS, SEPARATED ALONG THE BONES
- 4 BLACK CARDAMOM PODS
- 2 OZ/50 G GINGER (ABOUT 3-INCH/7.5-CM-LENGTH PIECE), SLICED
- 2 BEIJING SCALLIONS OR 6 SCALLIONS (SPRING ONIONS), CUT INTO 1¼-INCH/4-CM LENGTHS
- 2 TABLESPOONS SALT

FOR THE DIPPING SAUCE:
- 2 CLOVES GARLIC, CHOPPED
- 1 BUNCH CILANTRO (CORIANDER), CHOPPED
- 1 TABLESPOON LIGHT SOY SAUCE
- 1 TABLESPOON BLACK OR BALSAMIC VINEGAR

* Put the mutton ribs in a large saucepan, add enough water to cover completely, and bring to a boil over high heat. Blanch the ribs for 5 minutes, then drain and rinse under cold running water.
* In another large saucepan, bring 8½ cups (68 fl oz/2 liters) water to a boil over high heat. Add the ribs, cardamom, ginger slices, and Beijing scallions. Return to a boil and skim the surface to remove any froth and scum. Reduce to low heat and cook the ribs for another 1 hour 15 minutes, or until tender. Add the salt and continue to cook for another 15 minutes. Transfer the ribs to a serving plate.
* To make the dipping sauce, combine all the ingredients in a small bowl and mix well.
* Serve the ribs with the sauce.

白切羊肉
STEWED
GOAT

- 1 (1-LB 5-OZ/600-G) GOAT BELLY
- 10 SWEET APRICOT KERNELS, CRUSHED
- 20 WHITE PEPPERCORNS
- 1 ¼ OZ/30 G GINGER (ABOUT 2-INCH/5-CM-LENGTH PIECE), SLICED AND CRUSHED
- 2 BEIJING SCALLIONS OR 6 SCALLIONS (SPRING ONIONS), CUT INTO 2-INCH/ 5-CM LENGTHS
- 3 BLACK CARDAMOM PODS
- 1 TEASPOON SALT
- 2 STALKS CILANTRO (CORIANDER), TO GARNISH

FOR THE DIPPING SAUCE:
- 1 TEASPOON CHOPPED GARLIC
- 2 TABLESPOONS ZHENJIANG VINEGAR
- 2 TABLESPOONS LIGHT SOY SAUCE
- ¼ TEASPOON SICHUAN CHILI OIL
- ½ TEASPOON SESAME OIL

* In a large saucepan, add the goat belly and enough water to cover it completely. Bring to a boil over high heat and blanch for 5 minutes. Drain and rinse under cold running water. Set aside.
* Combine the apricot kernels and white peppercorns in a spice bag.
* Return the goat belly to the pan, then add the ginger, Beijing scallions, cardamom, spice bag, and enough water to cover the ingredients. Cover and bring to a boil over high heat, then reduce to low heat, and simmer for 1 hour. Stir in the salt, turn off the heat, and re-cover. Stand for another 30 minutes. Remove the goat side from the pan and set aside on a plate to cool completely.
* Meanwhile, make the dipping sauce. Combine all the ingredients in a small bowl and set aside.
* Slice the goat into strips and serve cold accompanied by the cilantro (coriander) leaves and dipping sauce.

MEAT

麻辣兔丁
RABBIT IN
CHILE SAUCE

REGION: HUNAN
PREPARATION TIME: 10 MINUTES
COOKING TIME: 10 MINUTES
SERVES: 4

* In a large bowl, combine the rabbit, 1 teaspoon soy sauce, ½ teaspoon salt, the wine, and cornstarch (cornflour).
* Heat the vegetable oil in a wok or deep saucepan to 340°F/170°C, or until a cube of bread browns in 45 seconds. Gently lower the rabbit into the oil, using chopsticks to disperse the pieces rapidly to prevent sticking, and deep-fry for 2–3 minutes until light brown. Use a slotted spoon to carefully remove the rabbit from the oil and drain on paper towels.
* Reheat the oil to 340°F/170°C, carefully return the rabbit to the wok, and deep-fry for 2 minutes until golden brown and cooked through. Transfer the rabbit to a colander to drain.
* Pour out most of the oil, leaving about 2 tablespoons in the wok. Heat the oil over high heat, add the chiles and Sichuan peppercorns, and stir-fry for 30 seconds until fragrant. Add the rabbit and the remaining ½ teaspoon salt, toss, and stir-fry briefly. Put in the Chinese leeks, vinegar, and remaining 2 teaspoons soy sauce and stir-fry for another minute.
* Sprinkle over the sesame oil, toss, and transfer to a serving plate. Serve with rice.

* 14 OZ/400 G BONELESS RABBIT, CUT INTO ½-INCH/1-CM CUBES
* 1 TABLESPOON LIGHT SOY SAUCE
* 1 TEASPOON SALT
* 1 TABLESPOON RICE WINE
* 1 TABLESPOON CORNSTARCH (CORNFLOUR)
* 3 CUPS (25 FL OZ/750 ML) VEGETABLE OIL
* 3½ OZ/100 G MEDIUM-HOT RED CHILES, SEEDED AND CHOPPED INTO ½-INCH/1-CM PIECES
* 1 TEASPOON SICHUAN PEPPERCORNS, CRUSHED
* 1 CHINESE LEEK, CUT INTO ¾-INCH/ 2-CM PIECES
* 3 TEASPOONS BLACK OR BALSAMIC VINEGAR
* 1 TEASPOON SESAME OIL
* STEAMED RICE (PAGE 540), TO SERVE

VEGETABLES

TOFU & EGGS

VEGETABLES, TOFU & EGGS

REGION: SICHUAN
PREPARATION TIME: 10 MINUTES
COOKING TIME: 10 MINUTES
SERVES: 4

开水白菜
CABBAGE HEARTS
IN BROTH

- 1 LB/450 G NAPA CABBAGE HEARTS, TRIMMED TO 5-INCH/12.5-CM LENGTH
- 2 TEASPOONS SHAOXING WINE
- ¼ TEASPOON GROUND WHITE PEPPER
- ½ TEASPOON SALT
- 5 CUPS (40 FL OZ/1.2 LITERS) CHICKEN BROTH (STOCK, PAGE 90)

This seemingly simple and easy dish is one of Sichuan's most demanding dishes. The broth, which normally uses chicken, duck, pork, pork bones, and ham, is cooked for at least a day, and then clarified to achieve an absolutely clear soup. For ease, the recipe uses a common chicken broth.

* Bring a large saucepan of water to a boil, add the cabbage hearts, and blanch for 1 minute. Drain, then put in a heatproof bowl.
* Add the wine, white pepper, salt, and 1 cup (8 fl oz/ 250 ml) chicken broth (stock). Place the bowl in a collapsible pot or bamboo steamer over a pot of boiling water. Steam, covered, for 2 minutes. Drain and set aside.
* Heat the remaining 4 cups (32 fl oz/1 liter) broth in the saucepan over high heat and pour over the cabbage.

REGION: SHAANXI
PREPARATION TIME: 5 MINUTES
COOKING TIME: 5 MINUTES
SERVES: 4

金边白菜
SAUTÉED CABBAGE

- 1 LB 2 OZ/500 G NAPA CABBAGE
- 2 TABLESPOONS VEGETABLE OIL
- 20 DRIED CHILES, SEEDED AND HALVED
- 1 TABLESPOON WHITE VINEGAR
- 2 TABLESPOONS GRANULATED SUGAR
- 1 TEASPOON SALT
- 2 TEASPOONS LIGHT SOY SAUCE
- ½ TEASPOON CORNSTARCH (CORNFLOUR)
- 1 TEASPOON SESAME OIL
- STEAMED RICE (PAGE 540), TO SERVE

* Use only the firmer parts of the cabbage. Cut these into 1½ × ¾-inch/4 × 2-cm pieces.
* Heat the vegetable oil in a wok or large skillet (frying pan) over low heat, add the chiles, and stir-fry for 2–3 minutes until fragrant. Add the cabbage and stir-fry over high heat for 4–5 minutes until the edges turn slightly brown.
* Stir in the vinegar, sugar, salt, and soy sauce and toss thoroughly. Mix the cornstarch (cornflour) with ½ tablespoon water, then stir it into the wok. Bring to a boil, stirring, for 30 seconds to thicken the sauce. Mix in the sesame oil and transfer to a plate. Serve with rice.

荷香娃娃菜
YOUNG CABBAGE
OVER LOTUS LEAF

REGION: BUDDHIST VEGETARIAN
PREPARATION TIME: 15 MINUTES,
    PLUS 30 MINUTES SOAKING
COOKING TIME: 10 MINUTES
SERVES: 4

* Cover the lotus leaf in cold water and soak for
  45 minutes.
* Cover the black fungus in cold water and soak for
  15 minutes. Rinse the black fungus, then cut it into
  fine strips.
* Rinse the mustard greens and squeeze to remove excess
  water, trim, then chop and set aside.
* Rinse the lotus leaf and spread it out across a 12-inch/
  30-cm bamboo steamer.
* Cut the cabbage in half down the middle, and each half
  into four equal pieces, ensuring the leaves of each piece
  remain linked at the stem.
* Bring a saucepan of water to a boil, add the cabbage, and
  blanch for 1 minute until softened. Transfer the cabbage
  to a colander to drain, then arrange the cabbage pieces
  on top of the lotus leaf in the bamboo steamer, with
  the stem of each piece pointing toward the center of
  the bamboo steamer.
* Heat the vegetable oil in a wok or large skillet (frying pan)
  over medium heat. Add the mustard greens, black fungus,
  carrots, and red bell pepper and stir-fry for about 1 minute.
  Stir in the soy sauce, sugar, and sesame oil, season with
  salt, and transfer to the bamboo steamer, placing the
  mixture on top of the cabbage. Add the shredded ginger.
  Place the bamboo steamer over a pot of boiling water.
  Steam for 5 minutes. Serve with rice. (The lotus leaf is not
  to be consumed.)

• 1 DRIED LOTUS LEAF
• ½ CUP (¼ OZ/10 G) DRIED BLACK
  FUNGUS
• 2 OZ/50 G PRESERVED MUSTARD
  GREENS
• 1 LB 2 OZ/500 G YOUNG NAPA
  CABBAGE
• 2 TABLESPOONS VEGETABLE OIL
• 2 SMALL CARROTS, SHREDDED
• 1 RED BELL PEPPER, SEEDED AND
  SHREDDED
• 1 TEASPOON LIGHT SOY SAUCE
• ½ TEASPOON GRANULATED SUGAR
• 1 TEASPOON SESAME OIL
• 1 OZ/25 G GINGER (ABOUT 2-INCH/
  5-CM-LENGTH PIECE), SHREDDED
• SALT, TO TASTE
• STEAMED RICE (PAGE 540), TO SERVE

439

REGION: GUANGDONG
PREPARATION TIME: 15 MINUTES
COOKING TIME: 25 MINUTES
SERVES: 4

蟹肉扒西兰花
CRAB MEAT OVER BROCCOLI

- ½ CUP (4 FL OZ/120 ML) CHICKEN BROTH (STOCK, PAGE 90)
- ½ TABLESPOON CORNSTARCH (CORNFLOUR)
- 1 TEASPOON SALT
- 1½ TEASPOONS GRANULATED SUGAR
- PINCH OF GROUND WHITE PEPPER
- 2 TABLESPOONS VEGETABLE OIL
- 1 BROCCOLI, FLORETS ONLY
- 3 CLOVES GARLIC, FINELY CHOPPED
- ¾ CUP (6 OZ/160 G) CRAB MEAT
- 1 EGG WHITE, BEATEN
- ⅛ TEASPOON SESAME OIL
- 3 TABLESPOONS CRAB ROE
- STEAMED RICE (PAGE 540), TO SERVE

* Combine the chicken broth (stock), cornstarch (cornflour), ½ teaspoon salt, ½ teaspoon sugar, and the white pepper in a bowl and mix into a sauce. Set aside.
* Bring 4¼ cups (1¾ pints/1 liter) water to a boil in a large saucepan. Add the remaining ½ teaspoon salt, 1 teaspoon sugar, and 1 tablespoon vegetable oil. Add the broccoli and blanch over high heat for 1 minute, then drain and transfer to a serving plate.
* Heat the remaining 1 tablespoon vegetable oil in a wok or large skillet (frying pan) over medium-high heat. Add the garlic and stir-fry for 1 minute until fragrant. Add the sauce and bring to a boil. Put in the crab meat, stir in the egg white and sesame oil, and turn off the heat once the egg white is cooked. Transfer the mixture to the serving plate and top with crab roe to finish. Serve with rice.

REGION: CHAOZHOU
PREPARATION TIME: 10 MINUTES, PLUS 30 MINUTES FREEZING TIME
COOKING TIME: 5 MINUTES
SERVES: 4
📷 PAGE 441

姜汁鱼露炒芥兰
CHINESE BROCCOLI WITH FISH SAUCE

- 1 OZ/30 G PORK FATBACK
- 1 TABLESPOON GINGER JUICE
- 1 TABLESPOON SHAOXING WINE
- 1 TEASPOON GRANULATED SUGAR
- 2 TABLESPOONS VEGETABLE OIL
- 1 LB 5 OZ/600 G CHINESE BROCCOLI, CUT INTO 2¾-INCH/7-CM PIECES
- 1 TABLESPOON FISH SAUCE
- STEAMED RICE (PAGE 540), TO SERVE

* Put the pork fatback in the freezer for 30 minutes until firm. Cut into thin slices.
* Combine the ginger juice, wine, and sugar in a small bowl.
* Heat the oil in a wok or large skillet (frying pan) over medium heat, add the broccoli, and stir-fry rapidly for 2–3 minutes over high heat, until the broccoli is just about cooked.
* Stir in the ginger juice mixture, add the fish sauce, toss, and transfer to a plate. Serve with rice.

VEGETABLES, TOFU & EGGS

CHINESE BROCCOLI WITH FISH SAUCE

翡翠白玉

CAULIFLOWER
AND PEPPERS

- 1 SMALL HEAD CAULIFLOWER, FLORETS ONLY, CUT INTO ¾-INCH/2-CM PIECES
- 3 TABLESPOONS ALL-PURPOSE (PLAIN) FLOUR
- 1 TEASPOON SALT, PLUS EXTRA TO TASTE
- ½ TEASPOON BAKING POWDER
- 2 CUPS (16 FL OZ/475 ML) PLUS 1 TEASPOON VEGETABLE OIL
- 1 GREEN BELL PEPPER, SEEDED AND CUT INTO ¾-INCH/2-CM CHUNKS
- 1 TEASPOON GRANULATED SUGAR
- 1 TEASPOON SHAOXING WINE
- 3 TABLESPOONS VEGETABLE BROTH (STOCK, PAGE 92)
- 1 TEASPOON CORNSTARCH (CORNFLOUR)
- ¼ TEASPOON SESAME OIL
- STEAMED RICE (PAGE 540), TO SERVE

* Bring a large saucepan of water to a boil, add the cauliflower florets, and blanch for 3 minutes. Drain and rinse under cold running water until cooled.
* Combine the flour, ½ teaspoon salt, baking powder, 1 teaspoon vegetable oil, and 4 tablespoons water in a bowl and mix into a paste. Add the cauliflower and toss to coat.
* Heat 2 cups (16 fl oz/475 ml) vegetable oil in a wok or deep saucepan to 300°F/150°C, or until a cube of bread browns in 1½ minutes. Add the cauliflower, using chopsticks to disperse the pieces rapidly to prevent sticking, and deep-fry for about 3 minutes until light brown. Use a slotted spoon to carefully remove the florets from the oil and drain on paper towels.
* Pour out most of the oil, leaving about 1 tablespoon in the wok. Add the bell pepper, sugar, the remaining ½ teaspoon salt, and the wine. Stir-fry for 1 minute over high heat, until the pepper has softened.
* Mix the vegetable broth (stock), cornstarch (cornflour), and 1 tablespoon water in a small bowl and stir this mixture into the wok. Bring to a boil, stirring, for 30 seconds to thicken the sauce. Stir in the cauliflower, add the sesame oil, and season with salt to taste. Transfer to a serving plate and serve with rice.

瑶柱焖节瓜
FUZZY MELON WITH
DRIED SCALLOPS

REGION: GUANGDONG
PREPARATION TIME: 10 MINUTES,
  PLUS 15 MINUTES SOAKING TIME
COOKING TIME: 30 MINUTES
SERVES: 4

* In a small heatproof bowl, soak the dried scallops in ½ cup (4 fl oz/120 ml) cold water for 15 minutes. Drain, then remove the small hard muscle. Tear into shreds and return to the water. Add the ginger juice and sugar.
* Place the bowl in a collapsible pot or bamboo steamer over a pot of boiling water. Steam, covered, for 10 minutes.
* Heat the vegetable oil in a wok or large skillet (frying pan) over medium heat, add the garlic, and stir-fry for 2 minutes until fragrant. Add the fuzzy melon and the scallop mixture, then toss thoroughly. Add the chicken broth (stock) and bring to a boil. Reduce to low heat and simmer, covered, for about 20 minutes, or until the fuzzy melon is tender. Using a slotted spoon, transfer the fuzzy melon to a serving plate.
* Combine the cornstarch (cornflour) with 1 tablespoon water in a small bowl and add the mixture to the wok. Bring to a boil, stirring, for 30 seconds to thicken. Drizzle in the sesame oil, then pour the sauce over the fuzzy melon. Serve with rice.

- ¼ CUP (1 OZ/25 G) DRIED SCALLOPS
- 1 TABLESPOON GINGER JUICE
- ½ TEASPOON GRANULATED SUGAR
- 2 TABLESPOONS VEGETABLE OIL
- 1 CLOVE GARLIC, FINELY CHOPPED
- 1 LB 5 OZ/600 G FUZZY MELON, PEELED AND CUT INTO ¾-INCH/ 1.5-CM-THICK SLICES
- 1 CUP (8 FL OZ/250 ML) CHICKEN BROTH (STOCK, PAGE 90)
- 1 TEASPOON CORNSTARCH (CORNFLOUR)
- ½ TEASPOON SESAME OIL
- STEAMED RICE (PAGE 540), TO SERVE

素卷肘
WILD YAM ROLLS

REGION: SHANDONG
PREPARATION TIME: 20 MINUTES
COOKING TIME: 10 MINUTES
SERVES: 8

* Place the whole yams in a collapsible pot or bamboo steamer over a pot of boiling water. Steam, covered, for 10 minutes. Remove and leave to cool. Peel the yams and place in a large bowl.
* Use a fork to mash the yams to a paste. Add the soy sauces, salt, sugar, five-spice powder, wine, chicken broth (stock), and 1½ tablespoons sesame oil.
* Trim the tofu skins into four 4 x 8-inch/1 x 20-cm pieces. Place one piece of tofu skin on a sheet of aluminum foil. Spread some of the yam paste evenly onto the tofu skin and roll it into a ¾-inch/2-cm-wide tube. Wrap the foil around to enclose the roll. Repeat with the remaining tofu skins and paste until you have four rolls.
* Place the rolls in a collapsible pot or bamboo steamer over a pot of boiling water. Steam, covered, for 10 minutes. Leave to cool briefly and then take out the rolls and carefully remove the foil. Brush the rolls with the remaining sesame oil, cut into bite-size pieces, transfer to a plate and serve with rice.

- 1 LB/450 G WILD YAMS, UNPEELED AND RINSED
- 1 TABLESPOON LIGHT SOY SAUCE
- ½ TABLESPOON DARK SOY SAUCE
- ½ TEASPOON SALT
- ½ TEASPOON GRANULATED SUGAR
- 1 TEASPOON FIVE-SPICE POWDER
- ½ TEASPOON RICE WINE
- 4 TABLESPOONS CHICKEN BROTH (STOCK, PAGE 90)
- 2 TABLESPOONS SESAME OIL
- 2 (ABOUT 20 INCHES/50 CM) SHEETS TOFU SKIN
- 1 TABLESPOON CORNSTARCH (CORNFLOUR)
- STEAMED RICE (PAGE 540), TO SERVE

地三鲜
POTATOES, EGGPLANTS, AND PEPPERS

- 1 LARGE POTATO, CUT INTO 1-INCH/2.5-CM CHUNKS
- 1 SMALL EGGPLANT (AUBERGINE), CUT INTO 1-INCH/2.5-CM CHUNKS
- 1½ TEASPOONS SALT
- 2 CUPS (16 FL OZ/475 ML) VEGETABLE OIL
- 2 GREEN BELL PEPPERS, SEEDED AND CUT INTO 1-INCH/2.5-CM CHUNKS
- ½ TABLESPOON LIGHT SOY SAUCE
- 1 TEASPOON GRANULATED SUGAR
- 1 TEASPOON CORNSTARCH (CORNFLOUR)
- ½ TEASPOON SHREDDED GINGER
- 4 CLOVES GARLIC, SLICED
- 1 TABLESPOON RICE WINE
- STEAMED RICE (PAGE 540), TO SERVE

* Soak the potatoes in a bowl of cold water until ready to use.
* Fill a bowl with 2 cups (16 fl oz/500 ml) water and add the eggplant (aubergine) and 1 teaspoon salt. Soak for 15 minutes.
* Heat the oil in a wok or deep saucepan to 300°F/150°C, or until a cube of bread browns in 1½ minutes. Add the green bell peppers and deep-fry for about 15 seconds. Use a slotted spoon to carefully remove the peppers from the oil and drain on paper towels.
* Drain and pat the potatoes dry with paper towels. Add to the oil and deep-fry for about 4 minutes until golden brown. Use a slotted spoon to carefully transfer the potatoes to a plate lined with paper towels.
* Drain and pat the eggplants dry with paper towels. Heat the oil to about 350°F/180°C, or until a cube of bread browns in 30 seconds, add the eggplants, and deep-fry for 2 minutes. Use a slotted spoon to carefully transfer the eggplants to a plate lined with paper towels.
* Combine the soy sauce, sugar, remaining ½ teaspoon salt, and cornstarch (cornflour) in a bowl and mix into a sauce. Set aside.
* Pour out most of the oil, leaving about 1 tablespoon in the wok over medium-high heat. Add the ginger and garlic and stir-fry for 1–2 minutes until fragrant. Add the potatoes, eggplants, and green peppers, increase to high heat, and stir-fry for 1 minute.
* Add the wine and sauce to the wok. Bring to a boil, stirring, for 30 seconds to thicken the sauce. Transfer to a serving plate and serve with rice.

REGION: BUDDHIST VEGETARIAN
PREPARATION TIME: 10 MINUTES,
  PLUS 10 MINUTES SOAKING TIME
COOKING TIME: 10 MINUTES
SERVES: 4

鱼香脆皮茄子
EGGPLANTS IN FRAGRANT SAUCE

- 1 EGGPLANT (AUBERGINE), PEELED AND CUT INTO ¾ × ¾ × 2-INCH/ 1.5 × 1.5 × 5-CM STRIPS
- 1 TEASPOON SALT
- 3 TABLESPOONS PLUS 1 TEASPOON CORNSTARCH (CORNFLOUR)
- ½ TABLESPOON GRANULATED SUGAR
- 1 TABLESPOON LIGHT SOY SAUCE
- 2 TABLESPOONS BLACK OR BALSAMIC VINEGAR
- 2 CUPS (16 FL OZ/475 ML) VEGETABLE OIL
- 1 GREEN CAYENNE PEPPER, SEEDED AND CUT INTO ¾ × 2-INCH/1.5 × 5-CM STRIPS
- 1 RED CAYENNE PEPPER, SEEDED AND CUT INTO ¾ × 2-INCH/1.5 × 5-CM STRIPS
- ¼ OZ/10 G GINGER (ABOUT ¾-INCH/ 2-CM-LENGTH PIECE), SHREDDED
- 1 TABLESPOON CHILI SAUCE
- STEAMED RICE (PAGE 540), TO SERVE

* Combine the eggplant (aubergine), salt, and 2 cups (16 fl oz/475 ml) water and soak for 10 minutes. Drain the eggplant, transfer it to a bowl, and mix with 3 tablespoons cornstarch (cornflour).
* Combine the sugar, soy sauce, and vinegar and mix into a sauce.
* Heat the oil in a wok or large skillet (frying pan) over medium-high heat to about 340°F/170°C. Add the eggplant strips and deep-fry for about 3 minutes until golden brown. Use a slotted spoon to carefully remove the eggplant from the oil and drain on paper towels.
* Add the peppers to the oil in the wok and deep-fry for about 10 seconds. Drain the peppers, then transfer to a plate.
* Pour out most of the oil, leaving about 1 tablespoon in the wok. Add the ginger and chili sauce and stir-fry over medium-high heat for 1 minute until fragrant. Add the reserved sauce and bring to a boil.
* Mix 1 teaspoon cornstarch with 1 tablespoon water and stir the mixture into the sauce. Bring to a boil, stirring, for 30 seconds to thicken. Add the eggplants and peppers and toss rapidly to mix thoroughly. Transfer to a serving plate and serve with rice.

甜酸茄子
EGGPLANTS IN SWEET AND SOUR SAUCE

REGION: BUDDHIST VEGETARIAN
PREPARATION TIME: 10 MINUTES
COOKING TIME: 10 MINUTES
SERVES: 2

* Rinse and pat the eggplants (aubergines) dry with paper towels. Make cuts in the eggplant at a space of ¼ inch/5 mm and ¾ inch/2 cm deep. As you make the cuts, roll each eggplant by about 15 degrees so that it resembles a snake.
* To make the batter, combine all the ingredients and 2 tablespoons water and mix well.
* Heat the oil in a wok or deep saucepan to 300°F/150°C, or until a cube of bread browns in 1½ minutes. Dip the eggplants in the batter and carefully place in the hot oil. Deep-fry for 2–3 minutes until golden brown. Use a slotted spoon to carefully remove the eggplants from the oil and drain on paper towels.
* Combine the sugar and vinegar in a small saucepan and stir over medium heat for 2–3 minutes until the sugar is dissolved. Pour over the eggplants and serve with rice.

• 2 JAPANESE EGGPLANTS (AUBERGINES)
• 1 CUP (8 FL OZ/250 ML) VEGETABLE OIL
• 3 TABLESPOONS BROWN SUGAR
• 3 TABLESPOONS RED VINEGAR
• STEAMED RICE (PAGE 540), TO SERVE

FOR THE BATTER:
• 1½ TABLESPOONS ALL-PURPOSE (PLAIN) FLOUR
• ½ TABLESPOON CORNSTARCH (CORNFLOUR)
• ⅛ TEASPOON BAKING SODA (BICARBONATE OF SODA)
• ¼ TEASPOON SALT
• ¼ TABLESPOON VEGETABLE OIL

梅菜蒸三寸心
CHOY SUM WITH PRESERVED MUSTARD

REGION: SHUNDE
PREPARATION TIME: 10 MINUTES
COOKING TIME: 10 MINUTES
SERVES: 4

* Rinse the mustard heart in water and soak in a bowl of cold water for 5 minutes. Trim, then chop into small pieces. Put the choy sum on a heatproof plate.
* Combine the mustard heart, ginger, and oil in a small bowl and mix well. Arrange the mustard heart and ginger evenly on top of the choy sum.
* Place the plate in a collapsible pot or bamboo steamer over a pot of boiling water. Steam, covered, for 10 minutes. Serve with rice.

• 2 OZ/50 G SWEET PRESERVED MUSTARD HEARTS
• 1 LB 5 OZ/600 G CHOY SUM, STEMS ONLY
• 1 OZ/25 G GINGER (ABOUT 2-INCH/5-CM-LENGTH PIECE), SHREDDED
• 2 TABLESPOONS VEGETABLE OIL
• STEAMED RICE (PAGE 540), TO SERVE

焖酿苦瓜
STUFFED BITTER MELON

- 1 LB/450 G UNCOOKED SHRIMP (PRAWNS), SHELLED AND DEVEINED
- 2 TEASPOONS SALT
- 1 TABLESPOON FERMENTED BLACK BEANS, RINSED AND CHOPPED
- 1 TABLESPOON GARLIC, CHOPPED
- 1 TABLESPOON GRANULATED SUGAR
- 1 TEASPOON LIGHT SOY SAUCE
- 2 TABLESPOONS PLUS 1 TEASPOON VEGETABLE OIL
- 1 LB 5 OZ/600 G BITTER MELON
- 1 EGG WHITE, BEATEN
- 1 TABLESPOON PORK FATBACK, DICED
- ¼ TEASPOON GROUND WHITE PEPPER
- 2 TEASPOONS CORNSTARCH (CORNFLOUR)
- 1 TABLESPOON SHAOXING WINE
- ½ TEASPOON SESAME OIL
- STEAMED RICE (PAGE 540), TO SERVE

* Rub the shrimp (prawns) with 1 teaspoon salt and rinse. Drain on paper towels to absorb excess water and wrap in a dish towel. Refrigerate for 1 hour.
* Combine the fermented black beans, garlic, sugar, soy sauce, and 1 teaspoon vegetable oil into a black bean paste in a bowl.
* Trim off the ends of the bitter melon and cut into 1-inch/2.5-cm-thick rings. Remove the seeds. Mix the bitter melon with ½ teaspoon salt and marinate for 5 minutes.
* Bring a large saucepan of water to a boil, add the bitter melon, and blanch for 1 minute. Drain and rinse under cold running water.
* Put the shrimp on a cutting board. Using the back of a knife, press down repeatedly to mash the shrimp roughly. Chop the shrimp a few times with the blunt edge of the knife, transfer to a bowl, and add ½ teaspoon salt. Add 1 teaspoon egg white and stir with chopsticks in a single direction for 1 minute until gummy in consistency. Add the pork fatback, white pepper, and 1 teaspoon cornstarch (cornflour) and mix well into a shrimp patty. Pick up the patty with one hand and smash it repeatedly against the bowl, five to six times until sticky and elastic.
* Dredge the inside of the bitter melon rings with the remaining cornstarch and stuff each piece with the shrimp patty until full. Use a spoon to smooth the patty surface.
* Heat 2 tablespoons vegetable oil in a wok or large skillet (frying pan) over medium heat, stir in the black bean paste, and fry for 1 minute until fragrant. Sprinkle in the wine, add ½ cup (4 fl oz/120 ml) water, and bring to a boil. Add the stuffed bitter melon, reduce to low heat, and simmer, covered, for 10 minutes. Do not turn the bitter melon over.
* Transfer the stuffed bitter melons to a serving plate. Increase to high heat and cook for another 2–3 minutes until the sauce is reduced by a third. Stir in the sesame oil. Drizzle the sauce over the bitter melon. Serve with rice.

酿南瓜花
STUFFED PUMPKIN FLOWERS

REGION: GUANGXI
PREPARATION TIME: 20 MINUTES,
  PLUS 20 MINUTES SOAKING TIME
COOKING TIME: 15 MINUTES
SERVES: 4–6

* Put the mushrooms in a bowl, cover with cold water, and soak for at least 20 minutes, or until softened. Remove the mushrooms, squeeze dry, and discard the stems. Chop the softened mushrooms.
* Remove the stamens and floral axis from each flower. Gently tear off the sepals (the green part attached to the stem, which hold the petals together) on the outsides of the petals.
* Combine the pork, fish, mushrooms, tofu, scallion (spring onion), ¼ teaspoon salt, and sesame oil in a bowl and mix. Divide the filling equally into 24 portions and stuff each flower with one portion of the filling. Leave the flower opened.
* Fan out the flowers on a large heatproof plate. Place the plate of flowers in a collapsible pot or bamboo steamer over a pot of boiling water. Steam, covered, for 7 minutes, then drain the water from the plate.
* Put the chicken broth (stock) into a skillet (frying pan). Bring to a boil over high heat, then stir in the remaining ¼ teaspoon salt. Mix the cornstarch (cornflour) with 1 tablespoon water, then stir the mixture into the sauce. Bring to a boil, stirring, for 30 seconds to thicken. Drizzle the sauce over the flowers. Serve with rice.

- 2 DRIED BLACK MUSHROOMS
- 24 MALE PUMPKIN OR ZUCCHINI FLOWERS, RINSED
- 5 OZ/150 G GROUND (MINCED) PORK
- 2 OZ/50 G WHITE FISH FILLET, CHOPPED
- 5 OZ/150 G FIRM TOFU, DRAINED
- 1 SCALLION (SPRING ONION), CHOPPED
- ½ TEASPOON SALT
- 1 TEASPOON SESAME OIL
- ¼ CUP (2 FL OZ/60 ML) CHICKEN BROTH (STOCK, PAGE 90)
- 1 TEASPOON CORNSTARCH (CORNFLOUR)
- STEAMED RICE (PAGE 540), TO SERVE

椰汁香芋南瓜煲
PUMPKIN AND TARO CASSEROLE

REGION: HONG KONG
PREPARATION TIME: 15 MINUTES
COOKING TIME: 25 MINUTES
SERVES: 4

* Place the taro and pumpkin in a collapsible pot or bamboo steamer over a pot of boiling water. Steam, covered, for 10 minutes.
* Heat the oil in a Dutch oven (casserole) over medium heat, add the ginger, and fry for 1 minute until fragrant. Add the taro, pumpkin, and ½ cup (4 fl oz/120 ml) water, bring to a boil, and then reduce to medium-low heat. Add the scallions (spring onions), cover, and simmer for 10 minutes.
* Add the salt and coconut milk, stir, and cook for another 2 minutes until the sauce thickens.
* Serve in the Dutch oven with rice.

- 7 OZ/200 G TARO, CUT INTO 1½ × ¾-INCH/4 × 2-CM CHUNKS
- 7 OZ/200 G PUMPKIN, CUT INTO 1½ × ¾-INCH/4 × 2-CM CHUNKS
- 1 TABLESPOON VEGETABLE OIL
- ¼ OZ/5 G GINGER (ABOUT ½-INCH/ 1-CM-LENGTH PIECE), SLICED
- 2 SCALLIONS (SPRING ONIONS), STEMS ONLY, CHOPPED
- ½ TEASPOON SALT
- SCANT 1 CUP (7 FL OZ/200 ML) COCONUT MILK
- STEAMED RICE (PAGE 540), TO SERVE

番茄滑蛋
TOMATOES WITH
SCRAMBLED EGGS

- 2 TOMATOES
- 3 LARGE EGGS, SEPARATED
- 4 TABLESPOONS VEGETABLE OIL
- ½ TEASPOON SALT
- ¼ OZ/5 G GINGER (ABOUT ½-INCH/
  1-CM-LENGTH PIECE), SHREDDED
- 1 TABLESPOON KETCHUP
- 1 TEASPOON GRANULATED SUGAR
- ½ TEASPOON CORNSTARCH
  (CORNFLOUR)

* Score the base of the tomatoes. Bring a small saucepan of water to a boil, add the tomatoes, and heat for 1–2 minutes. Immediately transfer to a bowl of ice water. When the tomatoes are cool enough to handle, peel away the skin, then roughly chop and drain the extra juice.
* Beat the egg whites in a small bowl until foamy, add 1 tablespoon oil, and beat again until fully combined. Beat in the egg yolks and ¼ teaspoon salt.
* Heat 2 tablespoons oil in a wok or large skillet (frying pan) over high heat to about 340°F/170°C, or until a cube of bread browns in 45 seconds. (The oil needs to be relatively hot in order to cook the eggs with the heat turned off.) Once hot, turn off the heat and pour in the eggs.
* Using a spatula (fish slice), push the eggs to one side of the wok to form layers of cooked eggs. Transfer the eggs to a plate when they are just under cooked. (If the oil has cooled down before the eggs are cooked, put the wok back on low heat to finish cooking the eggs.)
* Use the remaining 1 tablespoon oil in the wok to stir-fry the ginger over medium heat for a few seconds, and then add the tomatoes, ketchup, ¼ teaspoon salt, and sugar and stir-fry for 1 minute. Combine the cornstarch (cornflour) and 1 teaspoon water. Bring to a boil, stirring, for 30 seconds to thicken the sauce. Place the cooked tomatoes on top of the eggs. Using chopsticks, gently mix the tomatoes and eggs slightly before serving.

丝瓜蛤蜊

RIDGED LUFFA
WITH CLAMS

REGION: TAIWAN
PREPARATION TIME: 5 MINUTES
COOKING TIME: 10 MINUTES
SERVES: 4

* Roll-cut the luffa.
* Bring a saucepan of water to a boil, add the clams, and cook for 1 minute until they open up. Drain and discard those that do not open.
* Heat the vegetable oil in a wok or large skillet (frying pan) over medium heat, add the ginger, and stir-fry for 1 minute until fragrant. Add the luffa, clams, salt, sugar, and 3 tablespoons water and bring to a boil. Reduce to low heat and sauté, covered for 2 minutes. Stir in the scallions (spring onions).
* Mix the cornstarch (cornflour) with 1 tablespoon water in a small bowl and stir this mixture into the wok. Bring to a boil, stirring, for 30 seconds to thicken the sauce. Stir in sesame oil and transfer to a plate. Serve with rice.

- 1 LB 2 OZ/500 G RIDGED LUFFA, RIDGES PEELED BUT SKIN LEFT ON
- 11 OZ/300 G CLAMS, SCRUBBED CLEAN
- 2 TABLESPOONS VEGETABLE OIL
- 1 OZ/25 G GINGER (ABOUT 2-INCH/ 5-CM-LENGTH PIECE), SHREDDED
- 1 TEASPOON SALT
- ½ TEASPOON GRANULATED SUGAR
- 2 SCALLIONS (SPRING ONIONS), SHREDDED
- 1 TEASPOON CORNSTARCH (CORNFLOUR)
- ⅛ TEASPOON SESAME OIL
- STEAMED RICE (PAGE 540), TO SERVE

干贝烩丝瓜

LUFFA WITH
DRIED SCALLOPS

REGION: HUNAN
PREPARATION TIME: 10 MINUTES
COOKING TIME: 5 MINUTES
SERVES: 4

* Soak the dried scallops in a small heatproof bowl with water for 5 minutes to soften. Drain and remove the hard adductor muscle on the side of the scallops by gently pushing downward. Place the bowl in a collapsible pot or bamboo steamer over a pot of boiling water. Steam, covered, for 10 minutes. Set aside to cool.
* Tear the scallops into shreds. Reserve the steamed juices and set both aside.
* Remove the seeds from the luffa and cut the flesh into 2 × ¼-inch/5 × 0.5-cm pieces.
* Heat the vegetable oil in a wok or large skillet (frying pan) over high heat. Add the luffa and stir-fry for about 30 seconds. Put in the salt, scallops, steamed juices, and 3 tablespoons water and bring to a boil. Reduce to low heat, and cook for 2–3 minutes until the luffa is translucent.
* Mix the cornstarch (cornflour) with ½ tablespoon water in a small bowl and stir the mixture into the wok. Bring to a boil, stirring, for 30 seconds to thicken the sauce. Mix in the sesame oil and white pepper. Transfer to a plate and serve with rice.

- ¼ CUP (1 OZ/25 G) DRIED SCALLOPS
- 2¼ LB/1 KG RIDGED LUFFA, RIDGES PEELED OFF BUT SKIN LEFT ON
- 2 TABLESPOONS VEGETABLE OIL
- ½ TEASPOON SALT
- ½ TEASPOON CORNSTARCH (CORNFLOUR)
- ½ TEASPOON SESAME OIL
- ⅛ TEASPOONS GROUND WHITE PEPPER
- STEAMED RICE (PAGE 540), TO SERVE

REGION: SICHUAN
PREPARATION TIME: 10 MINUTES
   PLUS 15 MINUTES MARINATING
COOKING TIME: 10 MINUTES
SERVES: 4
📷 PAGE 453

鱼香茄子
EGGPLANT IN
GARLIC SAUCE

- 2 EGGPLANTS (AUBERGINES), HALVED LENGTHWISE AND THEN CUT INTO ¾-INCH/1.5-CM-WIDE STRIPS
- 1 TABLESPOON SALT
- 3½ OZ/100 G GROUND (MINCED) PORK
- 1 TEASPOON LIGHT SOY SAUCE
- 2 CUPS (16 FL OZ/475 ML) VEGETABLE OIL
- 1 TABLESPOON CHOPPED GINGER
- 1 TABLESPOON GRATED GARLIC
- 2 TABLESPOONS CHOPPED SCALLIONS (SPRING ONIONS)
- ½ TEASPOON SICHUAN PEPPERCORNS, CRUSHED
- 1 TABLESPOON PIXIAN CHILI PASTE, CHOPPED
- 1 TABLESPOON RICE WINE
- 2 TEASPOONS GRANULATED SUGAR
- 2 TABLESPOONS BLACK OR BALSAMIC VINEGAR
- 1 TEASPOON CORNSTARCH (CORNFLOUR)
- ½ TEASPOON SESAME OIL
- CILANTRO (CORIANDER) LEAVES, TO GARNISH (OPTIONAL)
- STEAMED RICE (PAGE 540) OR NOODLES, TO SERVE

* Soak the eggplants (aubergines) in 4¼ cups (34 fl oz/1 liter) water and the salt for 15 minutes. Drain, rinse under cold running water, and pat the eggplants dry with paper towels.
* Meanwhile, combine the pork with the light soy sauce and 1 tablespoon water in a bowl. Marinate for 15 minutes.
* Heat the vegetable oil in a wok or deep saucepan to 340°F/170°C, or until a cube of bread browns in 45 seconds. Add the eggplants and deep-fry, in batches, for 3–5 minutes. Use a slotted spoon to carefully remove the eggplants from the oil and drain on paper towels.
* Pour out most of the oil, leaving about 2 tablespoons in the wok. Add the ginger, garlic, and scallions (spring onions), and stir-fry for 30 seconds until fragrant. Toss in the Sichuan peppercorns and chili paste and cook for 1 minute over medium heat.
* Add the pork and stir-fry rapidly for 1 minute. Sprinkle in the wine, add the sugar, vinegar, and 2 tablespoons water. Bring to a boil. Reduce to medium heat, put in the eggplants, and simmer, covered, for 1–2 minutes.
* Mix the cornstarch (cornflour) with ½ tablespoon water and stir this mixture into the wok. Bring to a boil, stirring, for 30 seconds to thicken the sauce. Finally mix in the sesame oil and transfer to a serving plate. Garnish with cilantro (coriander), if using. Serve with rice or noodles.

EGGPLANT IN GARLIC SAUCE

REGION: HONG KONG
PREPARATION TIME: 10 MINUTES,
  PLUS 15 MINUTES SOAKING TIME
COOKING TIME: 5 MINUTES
SERVES: 4

丝瓜云耳炒肉片
RIDGED LUFFA
WITH PORK

- ½ CUP (¼ OZ/10 G) DRIED BLACK FUNGUS
- 1 LB 5 OZ/600 G RIDGED LUFFA, RIDGES PEELED BUT SKIN ON
- 5 OZ/150 G PORK TENDERLOIN, SLICED
- 1 TEASPOON LIGHT SOY SAUCE
- 1 TEASPOON GRANULATED SUGAR
- ¼ TEASPOON GROUND WHITE PEPPER
- 2 TEASPOONS CORNSTARCH (CORNFLOUR)
- 2 TABLESPOONS VEGETABLE OIL
- ¼ OZ/10 G GINGER (ABOUT ¾-INCH/ 2-CM-LENGTH PIECE), SLICED
- 2 CLOVES GARLIC, SLICED
- 3 SHALLOTS, QUARTERED
- ¼ TEASPOON SALT
- ½ TEASPOON SESAME OIL
- STEAMED RICE (PAGE 540), TO SERVE

* Cover the black fungus with cold water and soak for about 15 minutes until soft. Tear it into small pieces and set aside.
* Bring a saucepan of water to a boil, add the fungus, and blanch for 3 minutes. Drain the black fungus, then set aside.
* Rinse the luffa and roll-cut it into small chunks.
* Combine the pork, soy sauce, sugar, white pepper, and 2 tablespoons water and marinate for 5 minutes. Mix in 1 teaspoon cornstarch (cornflour).
* Heat the vegetable oil in a wok or large skillet (frying pan) over medium-high heat. Add the ginger, garlic, and shallots and stir-fry for 1 minute until fragrant. Add the pork and stir-fry for about 4 minutes until cooked through.
* Put in the luffa and stir-fry for 1 minute, then add the salt and black fungus, and toss to mix all the ingredients.
* Mix the remaining 1 teaspoon cornstarch with 1 tablespoon water and stir the mixture into the sauce to thicken it. Drizzle over the sesame oil, stir, and transfer to a plate. Serve with rice.

REGION: GUANGDONG
PREPARATION TIME: 5 MINUTES
COOKING TIME: 5 MINUTES
SERVES: 2

豆豉酱焗苦瓜
BITTER MELON WITH
BLACK BEAN PASTE

- 3 CLOVES GARLIC, 2 CLOVES CHOPPED AND 1 CLOVE SLICED
- 1 TABLESPOON FERMENTED BLACK BEANS, RINSED AND CHOPPED
- ½ TEASPOON GRANULATED SUGAR
- 2 TABLESPOONS VEGETABLE OIL
- 11 OZ/300 G BITTER MELON, SKIN PARED, CORE DISCARDED, AND CUT INTO CHUNKS
- ¼ TEASPOON SALT
- 1 TABLESPOON RICE WINE
- STEAMED RICE (PAGE 540), TO SERVE

* Combine the chopped garlic, black beans, sugar, and 1 tablespoon oil to make a black bean paste.
* Heat the remaining 1 tablespoon oil in a wok or large skillet (frying pan). Add the sliced garlic and stir-fry over medium heat for 1 minute until fragrant. Put in the bitter melon and salt, then toss lightly. Add the black bean paste—do not stir. Add 2 tablespoons water, cover, reduce to low heat, and simmer for 2 minutes.
* Add the wine, then increase to medium heat, and stir-fry the bitter melon for 1–2 minutes until most of the liquid has evaporated. Transfer to a serving plate and serve with rice.

甜水瓜烙

SWEET LUFFA

PANCAKE

REGION: CHAOZHOU
PREPARATION TIME: 20 MINUTES,
  PLUS 5 MINUTES SOAKING TIME
COOKING TIME: 10 MINUTES
SERVES: 4

* Rinse the luffa and cut it into 2-inch/5-cm-long strips.
* Cover the preserved turnips in cold water and soak for 5 minutes. Rinse, drain and then chop it into small pieces.
* Put the peanuts into a dry skillet (frying pan), toast them over medium heat, and shake occasionally for 3–4 minutes until brown. Transfer to a bowl, remove any bran, then crush the peanuts. Mix in 1 tablespoon sugar.
* Toast the sesame seeds in a small pan over medium heat and shake occasionally for 3–5 minutes. Transfer to a bowl.
* Mix the luffa strips, preserved turnips, and the remaining 3 tablespoons sugar in a large bowl and set aside for 15 minutes. Stir in the sweet potato starch and ½ cup (4 fl oz/120 ml) water and mix thoroughly to make a luffa batter.
* Heat 2 tablespoons oil over medium heat in a flat non-stick skillet (frying pan). Stir the luffa batter, then pour it into the skillet. Smooth out the surface with a rubber spatula (fish slice). Cook for 2–3 minutes until the underside of the pancake is cooked. Then flip it over, drizzle the remaining tablespoon oil along the side of the skillet, and cook for another 2–3 minutes until the second side is cooked. Transfer the luffa pancake to a serving plate. Sprinkle the crushed peanuts and sesame seeds over the surface of the pancake to serve.

- 14 OZ/400 G EGYPTIAN LUFFA, RIDGES PEELED
- 3 TABLESPOONS PRESERVED TURNIPS
- ⅓ CUP (2 OZ/50 G) SHELLED PEANUTS
- 4 TABLESPOONS GRANULATED SUGAR
- 1 TABLESPOON WHITE SESAME SEEDS
- 2 OZ/50 G SWEET POTATO STARCH OR 3 TABLESPOONS CORNSTARCH (CORNFLOUR)
- 3 TABLESPOONS VEGETABLE OIL

素蟹黃豆腐

VEGETARIAN "CRAB MEAT" WITH TOFU

- 2 POTATOES, CUT INTO ¾-INCH/2-CM-THICK SLICES
- 1 LARGE CARROT, CUT INTO ¾-INCH/2-CM-THICK SLICES
- 2 EGGS, SEPARATED
- 1½ TEASPOONS SESAME OIL
- 1 SALTED DUCK EGG
- 7 OZ/200 G SILKEN TOFU, CUT INTO ¾-INCH/2-CM CUBES
- 1 TEASPOON LIGHT SOY SAUCE
- 1 TEASPOON SALT
- 2 TABLESPOONS VEGETABLE OIL
- 1 TABLESPOON GINGER, GRATED
- 1 TEASPOON GRANULATED SUGAR
- 2 TEASPOONS ZHENJIANG VINEGAR OR BALSAMIC VINEGAR
- STEAMED RICE (PAGE 540), TO SERVE

* Bring a pot of water to a boil, add the potatoes and carrots, and cook for 15 minutes, or until cooked through. Drain, then crush with a fork. Set aside.
* Put the egg yolks in a bowl with ½ teaspoon sesame oil and beat thoroughly. Set aside.
* Add the egg white from the salted duck egg to the egg whites and beat until fluffy. Set aside. Mash the salted duck egg yolk into irregular pieces.
* Put the tofu in a bowl with 2 cups (16 fl oz/475 ml) water and ½ teaspoon salt. Let soak for 30 minutes, then drain and place the tofu on a heatproof plate. Mix the tofu with the soy sauce and ½ teaspoon sesame oil.
* Place the plate in a collapsible pot or bamboo steamer over a pot of boiling water. Steam, covered, for 3 minutes. Drain the water from the plate and set the tofu aside.
* Heat the vegetable oil in a wok or large skillet (frying pan). Add the egg whites, breaking them up with a spatula (fish slice), and stir-fry over medium heat for 1–2 minutes until cooked. Remove from the wok and set aside on a plate.
* Put in the ginger and salted duck egg yolk and stir-fry for another minute. Add the potatoes, carrots, remaining ½ teaspoon salt, sugar, and vinegar, and stir-fry for another 1–2 minutes.
* Add the remaining ½ teaspoon sesame oil and cooked egg whites. Toss all the ingredients together and remove the wok from heat. Mix in the raw egg yolks, add the tofu, and serve with rice.

焦盐菠菜心

DEEP-FRIED
SPINACH

REGION: HUNAN
PREPARATION TIME: 10 MINUTES
COOKING TIME: 5 MINUTES
SERVES: 4-6

* To clean the spinach, fill a sink or large bowl with cold water, and then let sit for 1 minute. Drain and repeat twice.
* Beat the egg whites until foamy. Stir in the egg yolks, ham, dried shrimp (prawns), flour, cornstarch (cornflour), and salt and mix into a batter.
* Heat the vegetable oil in a wok or deep saucepan over medium-high heat to 340°F/170°C, or until a cube of bread browns in 45 seconds. Dip the spinach into the batter, then deep-fry for about 2–3 minutes until crispy. Use a slotted spoon to carefully remove the spinach from the oil and drain on paper towels.
* Sprinkle the ground Sichuan pepper on the spinach and drizzle over the sesame oil. Serve with a side of ketchup.

- 3 BUNCHES YOUNG SPINACH (ABOUT 1 LB 5 OZ/600 G), ROOTS TRIMMED
- 3 EGGS, SEPARATED
- ½ OZ/15 G CURED HAM, CHOPPED
- ½ TABLESPOON DRIED SHRIMP, CHOPPED
- ½ CUP (2 OZ/50 G) ALL-PURPOSE (PLAIN) FLOUR
- 2½ TABLESPOONS CORNSTARCH (CORNFLOUR)
- ½ TEASPOON SALT
- 3 CUPS (25 FL OZ/750 ML) VEGETABLE OIL
- ¼ TEASPOON GROUND SICHUAN PEPPER
- ½ TEASPOON SESAME OIL
- 2 TABLESPOONS KETCHUP, TO SERVE

锅塌菠菜

SPINACH POUCHES

REGION: SHANDONG
PREPARATION TIME: 15 MINUTES
COOKING TIME: 10 MINUTES
SERVES: 4

* Remove the root and trim the stems of the spinach, leaving about ¾ inch/2 cm of stem. Rinse and drain.
* Using a sharp and heavy knife, cut the chicken across the grain into thin slices, then press down with the body of the knife firmly to mash the slices, and chop the chicken into a paste. Alternatively, do this in a food processor.
* Combine the chicken, pork fatback, ginger, and ¼ teaspoon salt in a large bowl. Set aside.
* Beat the egg whites in a small bowl until foamy, and then stir in the cornstarch (cornflour) to create a batter. Dip a spinach leaf into the egg-white batter, spread some chicken paste on the surface, and fold the spinach leaf in half lengthwise into a stuffed spinach pouch. Repeat with the remaining spinach leaves.
* Heat the oil in a wok or large skillet (frying pan) to 275°F/140°C, or until a cube of bread turns golden in 2 minutes. Add the spinach pouches in batches, brown both sides, and drain on paper towels.
* Return the pouches to the wok, add the wine, chicken broth (stock), and remaining ½ teaspoon salt. Bring to a boil over high heat, reduce to low heat, then simmer for 1–2 minutes.
* Serve immediately with rice.

- 3½ OZ/100 G SPINACH
- 3½ OZ/100 G BONELESS, SKINLESS CHICKEN BREAST
- 1 OZ/30 G PORK FATBACK, FINELY CHOPPED
- ½ TEASPOON CHOPPED GINGER
- ¾ TEASPOON SALT
- 2 EGG WHITES
- 2 TEASPOONS CORNSTARCH (CORNFLOUR)
- 2 TABLESPOONS VEGETABLE OIL
- 1 TABLESPOON SHAOXING WINE
- ½ CUP (4 FL OZ/120 ML) CHICKEN BROTH (STOCK, PAGE 90)
- STEAMED RICE (PAGE 540), TO SERVE

干煸虾子茭白
WATER BAMBOO
WITH SHRIMP ROE

- 1 LB 5 OZ/600 G WATER BAMBOO STEMS
- 2 TABLESPOONS DRIED SHRIMP
- 2 OZ/50 G GROUND (MINCED) PORK
- 3 TABLESPOONS LIGHT SOY SAUCE
- 1 TEASPOON GRANULATED SUGAR
- 2 TABLESPOONS VEGETABLE OIL
- 1 TABLESPOON SICHUAN PEPPERCORNS
- 1 TEASPOON GRATED GINGER
- 3 TABLESPOONS SICHUAN PRESERVED MUSTARD GREENS, RINSED, TRIMMED, AND CHOPPED
- 1 TEASPOON ZHENJIANG VINEGAR OR BALSAMIC VINEGAR
- ¼ TEASPOON SESAME OIL
- 4 TABLESPOONS DRIED SHRIMP ROE
- 2 TABLESPOONS CHOPPED SCALLION (SPRING ONION)
- STEAMED RICE (PAGE 540), TO SERVE

* To prepare the water bamboo stems, remove the outer shells and use a vegetable peeler to shave away the green skin until you reach the white part. Rinse and cut the water bamboo stems into small chunks. Bring a saucepan of water to a boil over high heat, add the bamboo stems, and blanch for 1 minute and drain.

* Soak the dried shrimp in a small bowl of water for about 5 minutes. Drain and chop the shrimp finely. Put ½ teaspoon finely chopped shrimp in a bowl with the ground (minced) pork, ½ teaspoon soy sauce, and ½ teaspoon sugar. Combine well and set aside.

* Heat the vegetable oil in a wok or large skillet (frying pan) over low heat. Add the water bamboo and stir-fry for 3–4 minutes until golden brown. Transfer to a plate and set aside.

* Put the Sichuan peppercorns in the oil remaining in the wok, and cook over low heat for 1–2 minutes until fragrant. Use a slotted spoon to remove the pepper and discard. Add the ginger, remaining dried shrimp, and ground pork and stir-fry for another 1–2 minutes until pork is thoroughly cooked. Stir in the preserved mustard greens, remaining ½ teaspoon sugar and soy sauce, water bamboo, vinegar, and sesame oil and mix thoroughly. Add the shrimp roe, toss quickly, transfer to a serving plate, and top with the scallion (spring onion). Serve with rice.

虾酱炒通菜
WATER SPINACH
WITH SHRIMP PASTE

REGION: CHAOZHOU
PREPARATION TIME: 5 MINUTES
COOKING TIME: 5 MINUTES
SERVES: 4

* Bring a large saucepan of water to a boil and add
  1 teaspoon oil. Add the water spinach and blanch for
  30 seconds. Remove the greens and immediately flush
  with cold running water until cooled. Drain and set aside.
* Combine the shrimp paste and 1 tablespoon water and
  mix well.
* Heat the remaining 2 tablespoons oil in a wok or large
  skillet (frying pan) over high heat. Add the shallots, chile,
  and garlic and stir-fry for 1 minute until fragrant. Add
  the shrimp paste mixture, salt, sugar, and wine. Put in
  the water spinach and toss rapidly for about 30 seconds.
  Transfer to a serving plate and serve with rice.

• 2 TABLESPOONS PLUS 1 TEASPOON
  VEGETABLE OIL
• 11 OZ/300 G WATER SPINACH
• 2 TEASPOONS SHRIMP PASTE
• 3 SHALLOTS, QUARTERED
• 1 RED CHILE, SEEDED AND SHREDDED
• 2 CLOVES GARLIC, SLICED
• ½ TEASPOON SALT
• ½ TEASPOON GRANULATED SUGAR
• ½ TABLESPOON SHAOXING WINE
• STEAMED RICE (PAGE 540), TO SERVE

虾米虎皮椒
PEPPERS WITH
DRIED SHRIMP

REGION: HAKKA
PREPARATION TIME: 10 MINUTES
COOKING TIME: 10 MINUTES
SERVES: 4

* Soak the dried shrimp in a small bowl of water for about
  5 minutes. Drain and set aside.
* Remove the stem from the peppers but do not cut them
  open. Use a toothpick or skewer to pierce the surface of
  the peppers all over and pat dry with paper towels.
* Heat the tablespoons oil in a wok or large skillet (frying
  pan) over medium heat, add the peppers, and fry for
  6–7 minutes until the peppers are soft and wrinkled.
  Remove the peppers and pour out the excess oil from
  the wok, leaving 1 teaspoon.
* Heat the oil over medium-high heat, add the ginger and
  dried shrimp and stir-fry for 1–2 minutes until fragrant.
  Put in the peppers, soy sauce, salt, and sugar and toss
  well. Mix in the vinegar, transfer to a serving plate, and
  serve with rice.

• 2 TABLESPOONS DRIED SHRIMP
• 8 LARGE HOT (CAYENNE) PEPPERS,
  RINSED
• 3 TABLESPOONS VEGETABLE OIL
• 1 TABLESPOON SHREDDED GINGER
• 1 TEASPOON LIGHT SOY SAUCE
• ½ TEASPOON SALT
• 1 TEASPOON GRANULATED SUGAR
• 1 TABLESPOON BLACK OR BALSAMIC
  VINEGAR
• STEAMED RICE (PAGE 540), TO SERVE

REGION: YUNNAN
PREPARATION TIME: 15 MINUTES
COOKING TIME: 5 MINUTES
SERVES: 4
PAGE 461

云腿炒苦瓜
BITTER MELON
WITH HAM

- 1 LB 2 OZ/500 G BITTER MELON, SEEDED, HALVED LENGTHWISE, AND THINLY SLICED
- 1½ TEASPOONS SALT
- 2 TABLESPOONS VEGETABLE OIL
- 1 TEASPOON CHOPPED GARLIC
- 5 OZ/150 G YUNNAN HAM OR OTHER CURED HAM, THINLY SLICED
- 2 OZ/50 G CAYENNE PEPPERS, SEEDED AND DICED
- 1½ TEASPOONS GRANULATED SUGAR
- ½ TEASPOON GROUND WHITE PEPPER
- STEAMED RICE (PAGE 540), TO SERVE

* Combine the bitter melon with 1 teaspoon salt and marinate for 10 minutes, then rinse and drain.
* Heat the oil in a wok or large skillet (frying pan) over medium heat. Add the garlic and stir-fry for 1 minute until fragrant.
* Put in the ham, peppers, and bitter melon and stir-fry for another 1 minute. Season with the remaining ½ teaspoon salt, sugar, and white pepper. Stir, then transfer to a serving plate. Serve with rice.

REGION: HAKKA
PREPARATION TIME: 15 MINUTES
COOKING TIME: 10 MINUTES
SERVES: 4

咸蛋炒苦瓜
BITTER MELON
WITH SALTED EGG

- 11 OZ/300 G BITTER MELON
- 1 SALTED DUCK EGG
- 1 TABLESPOON VEGETABLE OIL
- 2 CLOVES GARLIC, SLICED
- ½ TEASPOON SALT
- 1 TEASPOON CRUSHED ROCK SUGAR
- 1 PRESERVED DUCK EGG, SHELLED AND CUT INTO 16 PIECES
- 1 SCALLION (SPRING ONION), CHOPPED
- PINCH OF GROUND WHITE PEPPER
- STEAMED RICE (PAGE 540), TO SERVE

* Rinse the bitter melon, cut it in half lengthwise, and clean out and discard the pulp and seeds. Cut the flesh into ½-inch/1-cm-thick slices.
* Bring a saucepan of water to a boil, add the salted duck egg and boil for 7–8 minutes until hard boiled. Remove the egg from the water and, when cool enough to handle, shell the egg. Cut it open and carefully separate the egg white from the yolk. Cut the egg white into small pieces and crush the yolk.
* Heat the oil in a wok or large skillet (frying pan) over medium heat. Add the garlic and stir-fry for 1–2 minutes until golden.
* Add the salted egg white and bitter melon and toss well. Stir in the salt, rock sugar, and ½ cup (4 fl oz/120 ml) water. Bring to a boil, cover, and simmer for about 1 minute.
* Stir in the preserved egg and salted egg yolk and stir-fry for about 2 minutes until the sauce thickens. Add the scallion (spring onion) and white pepper and transfer to a plate. Serve with rice.

BITTER MELON WITH HAM

REGION: SHUNDE
PREPARATION TIME: 15 MINUTES,
   PLUS 20 MINUTES SOAKING TIME
COOKING TIME: 20 MINUTES
SERVES: 4

十锦肉

SHUNDE MIXED
SALAD

- 4 DRIED BLACK MUSHROOMS
- 3½ OZ/100 G LEAN PORK, CUT INTO FINE STRIPS
- 1 TEASPOON LIGHT SOY SAUCE
- ½ CUP (¼ OZ/10 G) DRIED BLACK FUNGUS
- 1 CUP (8 FL OZ/250 ML) VEGETABLE OIL
- 1 EGG, BEATEN
- ¼ CUP (1¼ OZ/30 G) SHELLED PEANUTS
- ⅛ OZ/5 G MUNG BEAN VERMICELLI
- 2 OZ/50 G TARO, PEELED AND CUT INTO FINE STRIPS
- 2 OZ/50 G CHIVES, CUT INTO 2-INCH/5-CM LENGTHS
- ½ CARROT, CUT INTO FINE STRIPS
- ½ TEASPOON SALT
- 2 OZ/50 G JÍCAMA, PEELED AND CUT INTO FINE STRIPS
- STEAMED RICE (PAGE 540), TO SERVE

* Put the mushrooms in a bowl, cover with cold water, and soak for at least 20 minutes, or until softened. Remove the mushrooms, squeeze dry, and discard the stems. Cut the mushrooms into fine strips.
* Combine the pork with the soy sauce and marinate for 10 minutes.
* Cover the black fungus in cold water and soak for 15 minutes. Drain, then cut the black fungus into strips.
* Heat 1 tablespoon oil in a small skillet (frying pan) over medium heat. Pour the egg into pan, tilting the pan around to create a thin crepe. Cook for 2 minutes, then turn over and cook for another 2 minutes. When cooled, cut into strips.
* Heat the remaining oil in a wok or deep saucepan over low heat. Add the peanuts and deep-fry for 4–5 minutes until crispy. Use a slotted spoon to carefully remove the peanuts from the oil and drain on paper towels.
* Heat the oil to 300°F/150°C, or until a cube of bread browns in 1½ minutes. Add the vermicelli and deep-fry for 20 seconds, or until the vermicelli puffs up. Use a slotted spoon to carefully remove the vermicelli from the oil and drain on paper towels.
* Put the taro strips into the hot oil and deep-fry over medium heat for 3–4 minutes until crispy. Use a slotted spoon to carefully remove the taro from the oil and drain on paper towels.
* Put the pork strips into the hot oil and deep-fry for about 3 minutes, or until cooked through. Use a slotted spoon to carefully remove the pork from the oil and drain on paper towels.
* Pour out most of the oil, leaving about 1 tablespoon in the wok. Add the mushrooms and stir-fry over high heat for about 30 seconds. Add the black fungus, chives, carrot, salt, and pork, toss for about 30 seconds, then transfer the mixture to a large bowl.
* Put the egg strips, jícama, and taro into the bowl and mix well with the other ingredients. Transfer the ingredients to a serving plate and add the vermicelli and peanuts on top. Serve with rice.

冬菇烩竹笙

MUSHROOMS AND
BAMBOO FUNGUS

REGION: GUANGDONG
PREPARATION TIME: 10 MINUTES,
    PLUS 20 MINUTES SOAKING AND
    15 MINUTES MARINATING TIME
COOKING TIME: 15 MINUTES
SERVES: 4

* Put the mushrooms in a bowl, cover with cold water, and soak for at least 20 minutes, or until softened. Remove the mushrooms, squeeze dry, and discard the stems. Reserve the mushroom soaking water.
* Combine the mushrooms, 1 tablespoon ginger juice, and soy sauce in a heatproof bowl and marinate for 10 minutes. Mix in 2 tablespoons vegetable oil, seal tightly with aluminum foil, place the bowl of mushrooms in a collapsible pot or bamboo steamer over a pot of boiling water. Steam, covered, for 10 minutes.
* Bring a small saucepan of water to a boil, add the bamboo fungus and 1 tablespoon ginger juice, and blanch for 2 minutes. Drain and rinse under cold running water and gently squeeze by hand to remove excess water.
* Heat the remaining vegetable oil in a wok or large skillet (frying pan), add the garlic, and stir-fry over medium heat for 2–3 minutes until fragrant. Add the bamboo fungus and button mushrooms, sprinkle in the wine, pour in the chicken broth (stock), and bring to a boil over high heat. Stir in the black mushrooms along with the reserved mushroom soaking water, then add the oyster sauce, sugar, and salt and stir-fry for 2 minutes. Reduce to medium heat and simmer, uncovered, for 2–3 minutes until reduce by half.
* Mix the cornstarch (cornflour) with 3 tablespoons cold water in a small bowl and stir the mixture into the wok. Bring to a boil, stirring, for about 30 seconds to thicken the sauce.
* Drizzle over the sesame oil, transfer to a serving plate, and serve with rice.

- 8 DRIED BLACK MUSHROOMS
- 2 TABLESPOONS GINGER JUICE
- 1 TABLESPOON LIGHT SOY SAUCE
- 4 TABLESPOONS VEGETABLE OIL
- 8 BAMBOO FUNGUS, CHILLED OR DEFROSTED IF FROZEN
- 3 CLOVES GARLIC, SLICED
- 8 LARGE WHITE BUTTON MUSHROOMS, BRUSHED AND CLEANED
- 1 TABLESPOON SHAOXING WINE
- ½ CUP (4 FL OZ/120 ML) CHICKEN BROTH (STOCK, PAGE 90)
- 1 TABLESPOON OYSTER SAUCE
- ½ TEASPOON GRANULATED SUGAR
- ½ TEASPOON SALT
- 1 TABLESPOON CORNSTARCH (CORNFLOUR)
- ½ TEASPOON SESAME OIL
- STEAMED RICE (PAGE 540), TO SERVE

二冬白雪
MUSHROOMS AND
BAMBOO SHOOTS

- 6 DRIED BLACK MUSHROOMS
- 1 CUP (5 OZ/130 G) SLICED BAMBOO SHOOTS
- ¼ CARROT, SLICED
- 1 TABLESPOON VEGETABLE OIL
- 1 TABLESPOON SHAOXING WINE
- ½ TEASPOON SALT
- 4 TABLESPOONS VEGETABLE BROTH (STOCK, PAGE 92)
- ⅓ CUP (1 OZ/25 G) SUGAR SNAPS, STRINGY PARTS REMOVED
- ½ TEASPOON CORNSTARCH (CORNFLOUR)
- 1 TEASPOON SESAME OIL
- STEAMED RICE (PAGE 540), TO SERVE

* Put the mushrooms in a bowl, cover with cold water, and soak for at least 20 minutes, or until softened. Squeeze gently, remove, and discard the stems.
* Bring a saucepan of water to a boil, add the bamboo and carrot, and blanch for 2 minutes. Drain and set aside.
* Heat the vegetable oil in a wok or large skillet (frying pan), add the mushrooms, bamboo shoots, carrot, wine, salt, and vegetable broth (stock), and bring to a boil. Stir in the sugar snaps.
* Mix the cornstarch (cornflour) with ½ tablespoon water in a small bowl and stir this mixture into the wok. Bring to a boil, stirring, for about 30 seconds to thicken the sauce. Mix in sesame oil and transfer to a serving plate. Serve with rice.

椒盐蘑菇
OYSTER MUSHROOMS
WITH SPICED SALT

- 1 TEASPOON SALT
- ½ TEASPOON GROUND SICHUAN PEPPER
- 1 CUP (8 FL OZ/250 ML) VEGETABLE OIL
- 14 OZ/400 G OYSTER MUSHROOMS, RINSED AND TORN INTO LONG STRIPS
- 6 TABLESPOONS ALL-PURPOSE (PLAIN) FLOUR

* Heat the salt in a dry skillet (frying pan) over medium heat for 2 minutes. Take the skillet off the heat and let the salt cool for about 1 minute, then stir in the ground Sichuan pepper.
* Heat the oil in a wok or deep saucepan to 300°F/150°C, or until a cube of bread browns in 1½ minutes. Toss the mushrooms in the flour to coat, then deep-fry for 2–3 minutes until light brown. Use a slotted spoon to carefully remove the mushrooms from the oil and drain on paper towels.
* Transfer the mushrooms to a serving plate and serve with the spiced salt.

香菜拌木耳
BLACK FUNGUS AND
CILANTRO SALAD

REGION: NORTHEAST
PREPARATION TIME: 10 MINUTES,
  PLUS 15 MINUTES SOAKING AND
  30 MINUTES CHILLING TIME
COOKING TIME: 10 MINUTES
SERVES: 4–6

* Soak the fungus in a small bowl of cold water for
  15 minutes until softened. Remove and discard the
  hard stems at the base. Rinse well.
* Bring a small saucepan of water to a boil, add the
  fungus, and blanch for 3 minutes. Drain in a colander
  and shake well to remove excess water.
* Combine the black fungus, chile, oyster sauce, and sugar
  in a large bowl and mix well. Refrigerate for 30 minutes
  until cooled.
* Toast the sesame seeds in a small pan over medium
  heat and shake occasionally for 3–5 minutes, or until
  golden brown. Set aside.
* Remove the black fungus from the refrigerator and mix
  in the sesame oil. Sprinkle with toasted sesame seeds and
  the cilantro (coriander) and serve.

- ¾ CUP (½ OZ/15 G) DRIED BLACK
  FUNGUS
- 1 RED CHILE, SEEDED AND CHOPPED
- 1 TABLESPOON OYSTER SAUCE
- ½ TEASPOON GRANULATED SUGAR
- ½ TABLESPOON WHITE SESAME SEEDS
- 1 TEASPOON SESAME OIL
- 12 OZ/350 G CILANTRO (CORIANDER),
  CHOPPED

厚菇大芥菜
HEAD MUSTARD
WITH MUSHROOMS

REGION: CHAOZHOU
PREPARATION TIME: 15 MINUTES, PLUS
  20 MINUTES MARINATING TIME
COOKING TIME: 20 MINUTES
SERVES: 4

* Put the mushrooms in a bowl, cover with cold water, and
  soak for at least 20 minutes, or until softened. Remove the
  mushrooms, squeeze dry, and discard the stems. Put them
  back into the bowl with the soy sauce and marinate for
  10 minutes. Mix in 1 tablespoon oil.
* Bring a saucepan of water to a boil, add the head mustard
  slices, and simmer for 5 minutes. Drain and set aside.
* Heat the remaining 1 tablespoon oil in a Dutch oven
  (casserole) over high heat, add the pork, and fry for
  3–4 minutes until the fat is released. Add the whole garlic
  cloves and stir-fry for 1 minute until fragrant, then add the
  mushrooms, chicken broth (stock), and head mustard.
  Bring to a boil, then reduce to low heat and simmer,
  covered, for 5 minutes, or until the head mustard is tender.
  Season with the salt and discard the pork.
* Serve the head mustard and mushrooms in the Dutch oven
  with rice.

- 8 LARGE DRIED BLACK MUSHROOMS
- 1 TEASPOON LIGHT SOY SAUCE
- 2 TABLESPOONS VEGETABLE OIL
- 1 HEAD MUSTARD, ABOUT 1 LB/450 G,
  STEM ONLY, CUT INTO THICK SLICES
- 5 OZ/150 G SKIN-ON PORK BELLY, CUT
  INTO SLICES
- 6 CLOVES GARLIC
- 2 CUPS (16 FL OZ/475 ML) CHICKEN
  BROTH (STOCK, PAGE 90)
- ½ TEASPOON SALT
- STEAMED RICE (PAGE 540), TO SERVE

REGION: YUNNAN
PREPARATION TIME: 15 MINUTES
COOKING TIME: 5 MINUTES
SERVES: 4

夜来香炒鸡油菌
CHANTERELLE
WITH TUBEROSE

- 12 OZ/350 G CHANTERELLE MUSHROOMS
- 5 OZ/150 G TUBEROSE, RINSED AND DRAINED
- 2 OZ/50 G PORK TENDERLOIN, CUT INTO STRIPS
- ½ TEASPOON SALT
- 1 TEASPOON CORNSTARCH (CORNFLOUR)
- 1 EGG WHITE
- 9 OZ/250 G LARD
- ½ TEASPOON GROUND WHITE PEPPER
- STEAMED RICE (PAGE 540), TO SERVE

* Clean and rinse the mushrooms and squeeze them to remove excess water. Cut the mushrooms along their lengths into strips.
* Use paper towels to dry the tuberose as much as possible.
* Mix the pork tenderloin, ¼ teaspoon salt, ½ teaspoon cornstarch (cornflour), and the egg white.
* Heat the lard in a wok or large skillet (frying pan) to about 275°F/140°C. Add the pork and stir-fry for 30 seconds, then transfer to a plate lined with paper towels.
* Pour out most of the lard, leaving about 2 tablespoons in the wok. Heat the lard over high heat. Add the mushrooms and stir-fry rapidly for 1 minute, then stir in the pork and tuberose. Add the remaining ¼ teaspoon salt and the white pepper.
* Mix the remaining ½ teaspoon cornstarch with 1 tablespoon water and stir the mixture into the mushrooms and pork. Bring to a boil, stirring, for about 30 seconds to thicken the sauce. Transfer to a serving plate. Serve with rice.

REGION: SHANGHAI
PREPARATION TIME: 10 MINUTES
COOKING TIME: 5 MINUTES
SERVES: 4

青椒凤尾菇
MUSHROOMS WITH
BELL PEPPERS

- 11 OZ/300 G OYSTER MUSHROOMS, TORN APART
- 1 TEASPOON SALT
- 2 TEASPOONS SHAOXING WINE
- 1 TABLESPOON CORNSTARCH (CORNFLOUR)
- 3 TABLESPOONS VEGETABLE OIL
- 1 GREEN BELL PEPPERS, SEEDED AND CUT INTO ¾-INCH/2-CM DICE
- 3 TABLESPOONS VEGETABLE BROTH (STOCK, PAGE 92)
- 1 TEASPOON SESAME OIL
- STEAMED RICE (PAGE 540), TO SERVE

* Bring a saucepan of water to a boil, add the mushrooms, and blanch for 1 minute. Drain, rinse, and press the mushrooms to remove most of the water. Transfer the mushrooms to a bowl, mix with ½ teaspoon salt, 1 teaspoon wine, and 2 teaspoons cornstarch (cornflour).
* Heat the vegetable oil in a wok or large skillet (frying pan) over medium heat. Add the mushrooms and bell peppers and stir-fry for 15 seconds. Remove from wok.
* Put the vegetable broth (stock), remaining ½ teaspoon salt, and 1 teaspoon wine in the wok. Mix the remaining 1 teaspoon cornstarch with 1 tablespoon water in a small bowl and stir this mixture into the wok. Bring to a boil, stirring, for about 30 seconds to thicken the sauce. Return the mushrooms and peppers to the wok and add the sesame oil. Transfer to a serving plate and serve with rice.

VEGETABLES, TOFU & EGGS

蠔油鮮草菇

STRAW MUSHROOMS
IN OYSTER SAUCE

REGION: HONG KONG
PREPARATION TIME: 10 MINUTES
COOKING TIME: 15 MINUTES
SERVES: 4–6

* Bring a large saucepan of water to a boil. Add the bok choy and blanch for 1 minute, then rinse under cold running water. Drain and set aside.
* Heat 2½ tablespoons chicken broth (stock) in a wok or large skillet (frying pan) over medium-low heat, add the mushrooms, and simmer for 2 minutes. Use a slotted spoon to transfer the mushrooms to a plate. Discard the chicken broth.
* Heat the vegetable oil in the wok over medium-high heat, add the garlic, and fry for 1 minute until golden brown. Remove and discard the garlic. Put in the mushrooms, ginger juice, oyster sauce, sugar, salt, and the remaining 2½ tablespoons chicken broth and bring to a boil.
* Mix the cornstarch (cornflour) with ½ tablespoon water in a small bowl and stir this mixture into the wok. Bring to a boil, stirring, for about 30 seconds to thicken the sauce. Sprinkle in the white pepper and sesame oil. Place the mushrooms in the center of a large serving plate and surround them with the bok choy. Serve with rice.

- 11 OZ/300 G GREEN BOK CHOY
- 5 TABLESPOONS CHICKEN BROTH (STOCK, PAGE 90)
- 1 (15 OZ-/425-G) CAN STRAW MUSHROOMS, DRAINED
- 2 TABLESPOONS VEGETABLE OIL
- 4 CLOVES GARLIC, CRUSHED
- 1 TABLESPOON GINGER JUICE
- 1½ TABLESPOON OYSTER SAUCE
- 1 TEASPOON GRANULATED SUGAR
- ¼ TEASPOON SALT
- ½ TEASPOON CORNSTARCH (CORNFLOUR)
- ¼ TEASPOON GROUND WHITE PEPPER
- ½ TEASPOON SESAME OIL
- STEAMED RICE (PAGE 540), TO SERVE

467

REGION: BUDDHIST VEGETARIAN
PREPARATION TIME: 5 MINUTES,
   PLUS 20 MINUTES SOAKING TIME
COOKING TIME: 10 MINUTES
SERVES: 4

素蚂蚁上树
VEGETABLES OVER VERMICELLI

- 2 DRIED BLACK MUSHROOMS
- 2 OZ/50 G KAOFU, TORN INTO SMALLER PIECES
- 2¾ OZ/75 G MUNG BEAN VERMICELLI, CUT INTO 4-INCH/10-CM LENGTHS
- 3 CUPS (25 FL OZ/750 ML) VEGETABLE OIL
- ¼ CUP (1 OZ/25 G) FINELY CHOPPED BAMBOO SHOOTS
- ½ TEASPOON SALT
- 1 TABLESPOON LIGHT SOY SAUCE
- 1 TEASPOON SHAOXING WINE
- SCANT 1 CUP (7 FL OZ/200 ML) HOT VEGETABLE BROTH (STOCK, PAGE 92)
- 1 TEASPOON CORNSTARCH (CORNFLOUR)
- 1 TABLESPOON SESAME OIL
- STEAMED RICE (PAGE 540), TO SERVE

* Put the mushrooms in a bowl, cover with cold water, and soak for at least 20 minutes, or until softened. Remove the mushrooms, squeeze dry, and discard the stems. Finely chop the mushrooms. Strain the mushroom soaking water into a small bowl and set aside.
* Preheat the oven to 300°F/150°C/Gas Mark 2.
* Put the kaofu on a baking sheet and bake for 15 minutes until it is dry enough to break up by hand. When it is cool enough to handle, break up the kaofu into a powder.
* Tie a kitchen string loosely around the center of the vermicelli lengths to form a bundle.
* Heat the vegetable oil in a wok or deep saucepan to 300°F/150°C, or until a cube of bread browns in 1½ minutes. Put in the bundle of vermicelli in the oil and deep-fry for about 20 seconds until thoroughly puffed into fine white noodles. Transfer the bundle to a serving plate and remove the string.
* Pour out most of the oil, leaving about 1 tablespoon in the wok. Add the mushrooms, kaofu powder, bamboo shoots, salt, soy sauce, wine, mushroom soaking water, and vegetable broth (stock). Bring the broth to a boil, then reduce to low heat, and simmer for about 2 minutes.
* Mix the cornstarch (cornflour) with 1 tablespoon water and add to the wok. Bring to a boil, stirring, for about 30 seconds to thicken the sauce. Stir in sesame oil, then pour the mixture over the vermicelli. Serve with rice.

口蘑锅巴
MUSHROOM SAUCE OVER SIZZLING CRISPY RICE

REGION: SICHUAN
PREPARATION TIME: 5 MINUTES
COOKING TIME: 10 MINUTES
SERVES: 2

Crispy rice is the crust formed at the bottom of the cooker when rice is cooked in a casserole. Packaged crispy rice is now available in some supermarkets that sell Asian foods.

* Heat the vegetable broth (stock) in a saucepan. Add the mushrooms, bamboo shoots, salt, soy sauce, and wine and bring to a boil. Put in the spinach, reduce to low heat, and simmer for about 2 minutes until wilted. Mix the cornstarch with 1 tablespoon water, then stir the mixture into the pan. Bring to a boil, stirring, for about 30 seconds to thicken the sauce.
* Heat the oil in a wok or deep saucepan to 300°F/150°C, or until a cube of bread browns in 1½ minutes. Add the crispy rice, and deep-fry for 3–4 minutes until golden.
* Transfer the crispy rice to a large serving plate and pour over the sauce. Serve with rice.

- 1 CUP (8 FL OZ/250 ML) VEGETABLE BROTH (STOCK, PAGE 92)
- 2 PORTOBELLO MUSHROOMS, CUT INTO ¹⁄₁₂-INCH/2-MM-THICK SLICES
- ½ CUP (2 OZ/50 G) SLICED BAMBOO SHOOTS, DRAINED
- ½ TEASPOON SALT
- 2 TEASPOONS SOY SAUCE
- 2 TEASPOONS SHAOXING WINE
- 3 CUPS (3½ OZ/100 G) PACKED BABY SPINACH
- 1 TEASPOON CORNSTARCH (CORNFLOUR)
- 1 CUP (8 FL OZ/250 ML) VEGETABLE OIL
- 3½ OZ/100 G CRISPY RICE, BROKEN INTO 1½-INCH/4-CM SQUARES
- STEAMED RICE (PAGE 540), TO SERVE

香菇盒
MUSHROOM SANDWICHES

REGION: ANHUI
PREPARATION TIME: 15 MINUTES
COOKING TIME: 15 MINUTES
SERVES: 6

* Put the mushrooms in a bowl, cover with cold water, and soak for at least 20 minutes, or until softened. Remove the mushrooms, squeeze dry, and discard the stems.
* Meanwhile, make the filling. Combine all the ingredients but only ½ teaspoon cornstarch (cornflour) and mix well. Divide the filling into 6 equal portions.
* Place the mushrooms on a cutting board, face down, and brush the underside with 1 teaspoon cornstarch. Put the filling on six mushrooms, cover with the other 6 to form mushroom sandwiches, and put on a heatproof plate.
* Place the plate in a collapsible pot or bamboo steamer over a pot of boiling water. Steam, covered, for 10 minutes. Drain the water from the plate. Set aside and keep warm.
* Put the chicken broth (stock) and soy sauce in a saucepan and bring to a boil. In a small bowl, mix the remaining ½ teaspoon cornstarch with ½ tablespoon water and stir this mixture into the wok. Bring to a boil, stirring, for about 30 seconds to thicken the sauce. Add the sesame oil and drizzle the sauce on the top of the sandwiches. Serve with rice.

- 12 DRIED BLACK MUSHROOMS (OF SIMILAR SIZE)
- ¼ CUP (2 FL OZ/60 ML) CHICKEN BROTH (STOCK, PAGE 90)
- 1 TEASPOON LIGHT SOY SAUCE
- 1 TEASPOON SESAME OIL
- STEAMED RICE (PAGE 540), TO SERVE

  FOR THE FILLING:
- 2 OZ/60 G GROUND (MINCED) LEAN PORK
- 1 TABLESPOON CHOPPED HAM
- 2 TEASPOONS CHOPPED SCALLIONS (SPRING ONIONS)
- ¼ TEASPOON SALT
- ¼ TEASPOON GRANULATED SUGAR
- 2 TEASPOONS CORNSTARCH (CORNFLOUR)
- ½ BEATEN EGG
- 1 TEASPOON VEGETABLE OIL

REGION: BUDDHIST VEGETARIAN
PREPARATION TIME: 15 MINUTES,
   PLUS 20 MINUTES SOAKING TIME
COOKING TIME: 1 HOUR 15 MINUTES
SERVES: 4

素炒鳝丝

SAUTÉED BLACK MUSHROOMS

- 3½ OZ/100 G DRIED BLACK MUSHROOMS
- 1 TABLESPOON LIGHT SOY SAUCE
- 1 TABLESPOON GINGER JUICE
- 1 CUP (8 FL OZ/250 ML) PLUS 2 TABLESPOONS VEGETABLE OIL
- 1¼ CUPS (5 OZ/150 G) CORNSTARCH (CORNFLOUR)
- ¾ CUP (3 OZ/90 G) SLICED BAMBOO SHOOTS, DRAINED
- 1 TABLESPOON SESAME OIL
- ½ TEASPOON WHITE VINEGAR
- STEAMED RICE (PAGE 540), TO SERVE

  FOR THE SAUCE:
- 4 SPRIGS CILANTRO (CORIANDER), CUT INTO 1½-INCH/4-CM LENGTHS
- 2 SCALLIONS (SPRING ONIONS), SHREDDED INTO 1½-INCH/4-CM LENGTHS
- ⅛ OZ/5 G GINGER (ABOUT ½-INCH/ 1-CM-LENGTH PIECE), SHREDDED INTO 1½-INCH/4-CM LENGTHS
- 1 TABLESPOON SESAME OIL
- 2 TEASPOONS SHAOXING WINE
- ½ TEASPOON SALT
- ¼ TEASPOON GROUND WHITE PEPPER

* Put the mushrooms in a bowl, cover with cold water, and soak for at least 20 minutes, or until softened. Remove the mushrooms, squeeze dry, and discard the stems.
* Put the mushrooms in a heatproof bowl and mix in the soy sauce, ginger juice, and 2 tablespoons vegetable oil. Place the bowl in a collapsible pot or bamboo steamer over a pot of boiling water. Steam, covered, for 1 hour. (Add more water to the pot if needed.)
* Transfer the mushrooms to a colander to drain and let cool, then cut them into ⅛-inch/3-mm-thick strips.
* To make the sauce, combine all the ingredients in a bowl, mix well, and set aside.
* Heat the remaining 1 cup (8 fl oz/250 ml) vegetable oil in a wok or large skillet (frying pan) over medium-high heat to about 340°F/170°C, or until a cube of bread browns in 45 seconds. Add the cornstarch (cornflour) into the colander of mushrooms and toss a few times to coat the strips. Shake off the excess cornstarch.
* Put the coated mushroom strips into the oil and deep-fry for 3–4 minutes until the mushrooms are firm and crunchy. Add the bamboo shoots and deep-fry for about 30 seconds. Use a slotted spoon to carefully remove the mushrooms and bamboo shoots from the oil and drain on paper towels. Pour the oil out of the wok.
* Return the mushrooms and bamboo shoots to the wok, add the sauce, and sauté over high heat for 3 minutes, or until most of the sauce has evaporated. Stir in the sesame oil and vinegar and transfer to a serving plate. Serve immediately with rice.

红烧牛肝菌
SAUTÉED PORCINI
MUSHROOMS

REGION: YUNNAN
PREPARATION TIME: 15 MINUTES
COOKING TIME: 5 MINUTES
SERVES: 4

* Scrape the stem of the mushrooms to clean off the dirt and wipe with a damp dish towel or paper towel. Cut the mushrooms into large pieces.
* Combine the pork, ¼ teaspoon salt, ¼ teaspoon white pepper, and ½ teaspoon cornstarch (cornflour) in a bowl. Add the egg white and mix thoroughly.
* Heat the vegetable oil in a wok or deep saucepan to 265°F/130°C. Add the porcini mushrooms and deep-fry for about 1 minute. Use a slotted spoon to transfer the mushrooms to a colander to drain.
* Put the pork into the hot oil and cook for about 30 seconds. Use a slotted spoon to carefully remove the pork from the oil and drain on paper towels.
* Pour out most of the oil, leaving about 1 teaspoon in the wok. Add the garlic, ginger, and scallion (spring onion) and stir-fry over high heat for 1 minute until fragrant. Add the peppers and stir-fry for 30 seconds, put in the mushrooms, pork, pickled vegetables, remaining ¼ teaspoon salt, soy sauce, sugar, ¼ teaspoon white pepper, and chicken broth (stock), and cook for 2 minutes. In a small bowl, mix the remaining 1 teaspoon cornstarch with 1 tablespoon water and stir this mixture into the wok. Bring to a boil, stirring, for about 30 seconds to thicken the sauce.
* Stir in the sesame oil and transfer to a serving plate. Serve with rice.

- 12 OZ/350 G FRESH PORCINI MUSHROOMS
- 2 OZ/60 G PORK TENDERLOIN, SLICED
- ½ TEASPOON SALT
- ½ TEASPOON GROUND WHITE PEPPER
- ½ TABLESPOON CORNSTARCH (CORNFLOUR)
- ½ EGG WHITE
- 2 CUPS (16 FL OZ/475 ML) VEGETABLE OIL
- 2 CLOVES GARLIC
- 2 GINGER SLICES
- 1 SCALLION (SPRING ONION), CUT INTO 2-INCH/5-CM LENGTHS
- ½ RED BELL PEPPER, SEEDED AND DICED
- 1 CAYENNE PEPPER, SEEDED AND DICED
- 3 TABLESPOONS PICKLED VEGETABLES, CUT INTO SMALL PIECES
- 1 TEASPOON LIGHT SOY SAUCE
- 1 TEASPOON GRANULATED SUGAR
- 2 TABLESPOONS CHICKEN BROTH (STOCK, PAGE 90)
- ½ TABLESPOON SESAME OIL
- STEAMED RICE (PAGE 540), TO SERVE

REGION: BUDDHIST VEGETARIAN
PREPARATION TIME: 10 MINUTES,
   PLUS 20 MINUTES SOAKING TIME
COOKING TIME: 10 MINUTES
SERVES: 4

素脆鱔

CRISPY
MUSHROOMS

- 3½ OZ/100 G LARGE DRIED BLACK MUSHROOMS
- 4 TABLESPOONS CORNSTARCH (CORNFLOUR)
- 3 TABLESPOONS VEGETABLE BROTH (STOCK, PAGE 92)
- 2 TABLESPOONS BLACK OR BALSAMIC VINEGAR
- 4 TEASPOONS GRANULATED SUGAR
- 2 TEASPOONS LIGHT SOY SAUCE
- ½ TEASPOON SALT
- 1 CUP (8 FL OZ/250 ML) VEGETABLE OIL
- ¼ OZ/10 G GINGER (ABOUT ¾-INCH/ 2-CM-LENGTH PIECE), FINELY CHOPPED
- 1 TABLESPOON SESAME SEEDS, TOASTED
- STEAMED RICE (PAGE 540), TO SERVE

* Put the mushrooms in a bowl, cover with cold water, and soak for at least 20 minutes, or until softened. Remove the mushrooms, squeeze dry, and discard the stems. Cut the mushrooms into ½-inch/2-mm-thick strips. Put them in the bowl and mix in the cornstarch (cornflour).

* Combine the vegetable broth (stock), vinegar, sugar, soy sauce, and salt in a small bowl and mix well.

* Heat the oil in a wok or skillet (frying pan) over medium heat to about 340°F/170°C, or until a cube of bread browns in 45 seconds. Add the mushrooms in small batches and shallow-fry for 3 minutes, or until golden brown or crispy. Use a slotted spoon to carefully remove the mushrooms from the oil and drain on paper towels.

* Pour out most of the oil, leaving about 1 tablespoon in the wok over medium heat. Add the ginger and stir-fry for 1 minute until fragrant. Add the sauce and bring to a boil. Increase to high heat and boil for about 4 minutes, or until the sauce is reduced by half.

* Add the mushrooms and toss rapidly to coat them in the sauce. Transfer to a serving plate and top with the toasted sesame seeds. Serve with rice.

山桃仁冬菇
MUSHROOMS WITH
PEACH KERNELS

REGION: NORTHEAST
PREPARATION TIME: 5 MINUTES,
  PLUS 20 MINUTES SOAKING TIME
COOKING TIME: 1 HOUR 15 MINUTES
SERVES: 4

* Put the mushrooms in a bowl, cover with cold water, and soak for at least 20 minutes, or until softened. Remove the mushrooms, squeeze dry, and discard the stems.
* Bring a saucepan of water to a boil, add the peach kernels, and blanch for 4–5 minutes until the skins begin to wrinkle. Drain and rinse under cold running water. Peel and dry the peach kernels thoroughly using paper towels.
* Put the peach kernels into a wok or deep saucepan, add enough vegetable oil to cover the kernels, and deep-fry over medium-low heat for 5–10 minutes until the kernels are crunchy. Use a slotted spoon to carefully remove the kernels from the oil and drain on paper towels. Discard the vegetable oil.
* Heat the sesame oil over medium heat. Add the ginger slices and stir-fry for 1 minute until fragrant. Put in the mushrooms and vegetable broth (stock), bring to a boil, reduce to low heat and simmer for 1 hour. Stir frequently to prevent burning. Transfer the mushrooms to a bowl.
* Heat the remaining 2 tablespoons oil in the wok over high heat. Add the chopped ginger and stir-fry for 1 minute until fragrant. Put in the mushrooms and peach kernels. Add the soy sauce, sugar, and salt. Mix the cornstarch (cornflour) with 1 tablespoon water and stir this mixture into the wok. Bring to a boil, stirring for 30 seconds to thicken the sauce. Transfer to a serving plate and serve with rice.

- 2 OZ/50 G DRIED BLACK MUSHROOMS
- 1 CUP (5 OZ/150 G) PEACH KERNELS
- 2 TABLESPOONS VEGETABLE OIL, PLUS EXTRA FOR DEEP-FRYING
- 2 TEASPOONS SESAME OIL
- ¾ OZ/20 G GINGER (ABOUT 1-INCH/ 2.5-CM-LENGTH PIECE), HALF SLICED AND HALF CHOPPED
- 1 CUP (8 FL OZ/250 ML) VEGETABLE BROTH (STOCK, PAGE 92)
- 1 TEASPOON LIGHT SOY SAUCE
- ½ TEASPOON GRANULATED SUGAR
- ¼ TEASPOON SALT
- 1 TEASPOON CORNSTARCH (CORNFLOUR)
- STEAMED RICE (PAGE 540), TO SERVE

REGION: HAKKA
PREPARATION TIME: 10 MINUTES,
  PLUS 30 MINUTES SOAKING TIME
COOKING TIME: 3-4 MINUTES
SERVES: 4

客家小炒
HAKKA-STYLE
STIR FRY

- 1½ OZ/40 G DRIED SQUID
- ½ TABLESPOON COARSE SALT
- 7 OZ/200 G PORK TENDERLOIN, CUT INTO THICK STRIPS
- 1 TEASPOON GRANULATED SUGAR
- 2 TEASPOONS LIGHT SOY SAUCE
- ½ TEASPOON CORNSTARCH (CORNFLOUR)
- 1 TEASPOON PLUS 2 TABLESPOONS VEGETABLE OIL
- 1 RED CHILE, SEEDED AND SLICED
- 1 TEASPOON SHA CHA SAUCE
- 1 TABLESPOON RICE WINE
- 7 OZ/200 G CHIVES, CUT INTO 2-INCH/5-CM LENGTHS
- 1 STALK CHINESE CELERY, LEAVES DISCARDED, CUT INTO 2-INCH/5-CM LENGTHS
- ⅛ TEASPOON GROUND WHITE PEPPER
- STEAMED RICE (PAGE 540), TO SERVE

* Combine the dry squid, salt, and 2 cups (16 fl oz/475 ml) cold water and soak for 30 minutes. Rinse under cold running water. Remove the thin membrane from the squid and slice the squid horizontally into ½-inch/ 2-mm-thick strips.
* Combine the pork strips, sugar, and 1 teaspoon soy sauce, and marinate for 10 minutes. Mix in the cornstarch and 1 teaspoon oil.
* Heat 1 tablespoon oil in a wok or large skillet (frying pan). Add the pork strips and stir-fry over high heat for 1 minute, or until cooked through. Transfer to a plate.
* Add the remaining 1 tablespoon oil to the wok, add the squid and red chile, and stir-fry rapidly over high heat for about 30 seconds. Add the sha cha sauce and sprinkle wine along the side of the wok. Put in the chives, Chinese celery, and pork and toss for about 1 minute. Add the remaining 1 teaspoon soy sauce and the white pepper, stir well, and transfer to a serving plate. Serve with rice.

REGION: HONG KONG
PREPARATION TIME: 5 MINUTES
COOKING TIME: 5 MINUTES
SERVES: 4

清炒番薯叶
STIR-FRIED
YAM LEAVES

- 9 OZ/250 G YAM LEAVES OR SPINACH LEAVES
- 1 TABLESPOON VEGETABLE OIL
- 2 CLOVES GARLIC, CHOPPED
- 1 RED CHILE, SEEDED AND CUT INTO CHUNKS
- ¼ TEASPOON SALT

* Rinse and trim the yam leaves so that only about ¾ inch/2 cm of the stems remain below the leaves.
* Heat the oil in a wok or large skillet (frying pan). Add the garlic and chile and stir-fry over low heat for 1 minute until fragrant. Put in the yam leaves and stir-fry rapidly over medium heat for another 2 minutes, just until the leaves are cooked. Add the salt and stir-fry for another minute. Transfer to a serving plate and serve.

素蟹粉

MOCK CRAB
MEAT

REGION: BUDDHIST VEGETARIAN
PREPARATION TIME: 5 MINUTES
COOKING TIME: 20 MINUTES
SERVES: 4

* Bring a pot of water to a boil, add the potatoes and carrots, and cook for 15 minutes, or until cooked through. Drain, then crush with a fork.
* Heat 3 tablespoons oil in a wok or large skillet (frying pan) over medium heat. Add the ginger and stir-fry for 1 minute until fragrant. Add the potatoes and carrots, ¼ teaspoon salt, and the white pepper and stir-fry for about 1 minute. Reduce to low heat and stir-fry for another 2 minutes. Add the sugar and vinegar and stir rapidly to blend all the ingredients. Transfer to a serving plate.
* Heat the remaining 1 tablespoon oil in a clean wok over medium heat. Add the mushrooms, the remaining ¼ teaspoon salt, and vegetable broth (stock) and bring to a boil. Simmer for about 30 seconds. Mix the cornstarch (cornflour) with 1 tablespoon water, then stir the mixture into wok. Bring to a boil, stirring, for about 30 seconds to thicken the sauce . Add the scallion (spring onion) and stir to mix. Adjust salt to taste. Pour the mushrooms and sauce over the potatoes and carrots. Serve with rice.

- 3 POTATOES, CUT INTO ¾-INCH/2-CM-THICK SLICES
- 2 CARROTS, CUT INTO ¾-INCH/2-CM-THICK SLICES
- 4 TABLESPOONS VEGETABLE OIL
- ¼ OZ/10 G GINGER (ABOUT ¾-INCH/2-CM-LENGTH PIECE), CHOPPED
- ½ TEASPOON SALT, PLUS EXTRA TO TASTE
- ⅛ TEASPOON GROUND WHITE PEPPER
- 1 TABLESPOON GRANULATED SUGAR
- 1 TABLESPOON BLACK OR BALSAMIC VINEGAR
- 1 CUP (6½ OZ/180 G) CANNED STRAW MUSHROOMS, DRAINED AND SLICED
- SCANT ½ CUP (3½ FL OZ/100 ML) VEGETABLE BROTH (STOCK, PAGE 92)
- 1 TEASPOON CORNSTARCH (CORNFLOUR)
- 1 TABLESPOON CHOPPED SCALLION (SPRING ONION)
- STEAMED RICE (PAGE 540), TO SERVE

南乳清斋
VEGETABLES WITH RED BEAN CURD

- 6 DRIED BLACK MUSHROOMS
- ½ CUP (¼ OZ/10 G) BLACK FUNGUS
- 1 SNOW FUNGUS
- ¾ OZ/20 G MUNG BEAN VERMICELLI
- ½ NAPA CABBAGE, CUT INTO 2-INCH/5-CM CHUNKS
- 2 TABLESPOONS VEGETABLE OIL
- 1½ OZ/40 G GINGER (ABOUT 2½-INCH/6-CM-LENGTH PIECE), SLICED
- 1 CUBE RED BEAN CURD
- 1⅔ CUPS (14 FL OZ/400 ML) VEGETABLE BROTH (STOCK, PAGE 92)
- ½ CUP (1¼ OZ/30 G) SHELLED GINKGO NUTS
- 5 OZ/150 G FRIED BEAN CURD STICKS (SEE NOTE), CUT INTO 1¼-INCH/3-CM SECTIONS
- ½ CARROT, SLICED
- 2 TABLESPOONS VEGETARIAN OYSTER SAUCE OR LIGHT SOY SAUCE
- 1 TEASPOON SALT
- 1 TEASPOON GRANULATED SUGAR
- 5 OZ/150 G SUGAR SNAPS, TRIMMED AND STRINGS REMOVED
- STEAMED RICE (PAGE 540), TO SERVE

* Put the mushrooms in a bowl, cover with cold water, and soak for at least 20 minutes, or until softened. Remove the mushrooms, squeeze dry, and discard the stems. Strain the soaking water through a strainer (sieve) and reserve.
* Cover the black and snow fungus in cold water and soak for 15 minutes. Drain the fungus and discard the stems. Tear the snow fungus into 1¼-inch/3-cm-square pieces.
* Soak the vermicelli in a bowl of hot water for about 5 minutes to soften. Drain and set aside.
* Separate the cabbage leaves from the stems.
* Heat the oil in a wok or large skillet (frying pan) over medium-high heat. Add the ginger and stir-fry for 1 minute until fragrant. Add the red bean curd, crush it, then stir in the cabbage stems, mushroom soaking water, and vegetable broth (stock) and bring to a boil.
* Put the ginkgo nuts, mushrooms, snow and black fungus, bean curd sticks, carrot, and cabbage leaves into the wok. Stir in the oyster sauce, salt, and sugar. Bring to a boil, cover, and simmer over low heat for 15 minutes.
* Add the vermicelli, stir, then add the sugar snaps. Cover and simmer for 5 minutes. Transfer to a serving plate and serve with rice.

NOTE:
Fried bean curd sticks are available in Asian markets. If not available, heat 2 cups (16 fl oz/475 ml) vegetable oil in a wok to 300°F/150°C, or until a cube of bread browns in 1½ minutes. Add the bean curd sticks, and deep-fry for 3 minutes, or until puffed up.

大豆芽炒肉松

SOYBEAN SPROUTS WITH GROUND PORK

REGION: GUANGDONG
PREPARATION TIME: 45 MINUTES
COOKING TIME: 10 MINUTES
SERVES: 4

* Combine the pork fatback, ground pork, soy sauce, cornstarch (cornflour), and ½ tablespoon oil in a bowl.
* Cut the sprouts into ½-inch/1-cm lengths. Place the seeds into a dry wok or large skillet (frying pan) and stir-fry over low heat for 3 minutes, or until most of the liquid has evaporated. Remove the seeds from wok and set aside.
* Heat 1 tablespoon oil in a clean wok over high heat, stir in the seeds and carrot, then put in the sprouts, ginger juice, and rice wine and stir-fry for 1 minute, or until the sprouts turn translucent. Drain, then transfer to a serving plate.
* Heat the remaining 1 tablespoon oil in the wok over medium heat and stir-fry the garlic for 1 minute until fragrant. Add the pork mixture and stir-fry over high heat for 2 minutes, or until done.
* Stir in the soybean seeds, sprouts, and salt and stir-fry over high heat for 1 minute until the liquid has evaporated. Transfer to a serving plate and serve with rice.

- 2 OZ/50 G PORK FATBACK, FINELY CHOPPED
- 5 OZ/150 G LEAN GROUND (MINCED) PORK, FINELY CHOP
- ½ TEASPOON LIGHT SOY SAUCE
- ½ TEASPOON CORNSTARCH (CORNFLOUR)
- 2½ TABLESPOONS VEGETABLE OIL
- 3¾ CUPS (11 OZ/300 G) SOYBEAN SPROUTS, ROOT ENDS REMOVED AND SEEDS SEPARATED FROM STEMS
- ⅓ CARROT, CHOPPED
- 1 TEASPOON GINGER JUICE
- 1 TEASPOON RICE WINE
- 2 CLOVES GARLIC, GRATED
- ½ TEASPOON SALT
- STEAMED RICE (PAGE 540), TO SERVE

REGION: HONG KONG
PREPARATION TIME: 15 MINUTES,
  PLUS 20 MINUTES SOAKING TIME
COOKING TIME: 45 MINUTES
SERVES: 4

釀冬菇
STUFFED BLACK MUSHROOMS

- 10 DRIED BLACK MUSHROOMS
- 1 TABLESPOON LIGHT SOY SAUCE
- 1½ TEASPOONS GRANULATED SUGAR
- 1 TABLESPOON CORNSTARCH (CORNFLOUR)
- 3 CUPS PLUS 2 TABLESPOONS (25 FL OZ/750 ML) VEGETABLE OIL
- 1 LARGE POTATO, CUT INTO ¾-INCH/ 2-CM SLICES
- 3 WATER CHESTNUTS, CHOPPED
- 1–2 TABLESPOONS FINELY CHOPPED CARROT
- ¼ TEASPOON SALT
- GROUND WHITE PEPPER, TO TASTE
- STEAMED RICE (PAGE 540), TO SERVE

FOR THE BATTER:
- 3 TABLESPOONS ALL-PURPOSE (PLAIN) FLOUR
- 1 TABLESPOON CORNSTARCH (CORNFLOUR)
- ¼ TEASPOON BAKING SODA (BICARBONATE OF SODA)
- ½ TEASPOON SALT
- ½ TABLESPOON VEGETABLE OIL

* Cover the mushrooms in boiling water and soak for at least 20 minutes. Remove the mushrooms, squeeze dry, and discard the stems.
* In a heatproof bowl, combine 8 mushrooms, the soy sauce, 1 teaspoon sugar, and cornstarch (cornflour) and mix well. Stir in 1 tablespoon oil.
* Place the bowl into a collapsible pot or bamboo steamer over a pot of boiling water. Steam, covered, for 15 minutes over high heat. Set aside to cool.
* Place the potato slices in a collapsible pot or bamboo steamer over a saucepan of boiling water and steam, covered, for 20 minutes. Transfer the potatoes to a bowl and mash them.
* Meanwhile, dice the 2 remaining mushrooms.
* Heat 1 tablespoon oil in a wok or large skillet (frying pan). Add the diced mushrooms, water chestnuts, and carrot and stir-fry for 2 minutes. Stir in the salt, the remaining ½ teaspoon sugar, and the white pepper. Add the mashed potato and blend it with the other ingredients to make a filling.
* To make the batter, combine all the ingredients and 4 tablespoons water in a large bowl and mix well.
* Stuff the steamed mushrooms with the filling.
* Heat the remaining 3 cups (25 fl oz/750 ml) oil in a wok or deep saucepan over medium heat to about 300°F/150°C, or until a cube of bread browns in 1½ minutes. Dip the stuffed mushrooms into the batter, transfer them to the hot oil in the wok, and deep-fry the stuffed mushrooms for 4 minutes, or until golden brown. Use a slotted spoon to carefully remove the mushrooms from the oil and drain on paper towels. Serve with rice.

三丝干巴菌
STIR-FRIED GANBA
FUNGUS

REGION: YUNNAN
PREPARATION TIME: 30 MINUTES
COOKING TIME: 5 MINUTES
SERVES: 4

* Put the fungus into a bowl and rub thoroughly with ¼ teaspoon salt. Rinse the fungus strips with water, then return to a clean bowl and add the flour. Rub it into the fungus strips thoroughly, then flush with water to remove all dirt and impurities. Squeeze the fungus strips to remove excess water.
* Place the fungus into a collapsible pot or bamboo steamer over a pot of boiling water. Steam, covered, for 5 minutes. Set aside to cool.
* Put the cornstarch (cornflour) into a bowl. Add 1 tablespoon water, stir, then let the starch settle. Pour out the water to leave a wet starch. Stir in the egg white to create a batter. Add the chicken strips and mix well.
* Heat 2 tablespoons oil in a wok or large skillet (frying pan) over medium heat. Remove the chicken strips from the batter, put them into the wok, and stir-fry for 30 seconds. Transfer to a plate.
* Put the fungus into the wok over medium heat and stir-fry for about 15 seconds. Transfer to a plate.
* Heat the remaining 1 tablespoon oil in a wok over medium-high heat stir-fry the garlic for 1 minute until fragrant. Add the ham, cayenne pepper, and chicken and stir-fry for 3–4 minutes, or until cooked through. Add the ganba fungus, toss, and transfer to a serving plate. Serve with rice.

- 7 OZ/200 G FRESH GANBA FUNGUS, CLEANED AND TORN INTO THIN STRIPS
- 1 TEASPOON SALT
- 1 TEASPOON ALL-PURPOSE (PLAIN) FLOUR
- 1 TEASPOON CORNSTARCH (CORNFLOUR)
- ½ EGG WHITE, BEATEN
- 2 CHICKEN BREASTS, CUT INTO THIN STRIPS
- 3 TABLESPOONS VEGETABLE OIL
- 5–6 CLOVES GARLIC, CHOPPED
- 3 OZ/80 G COOKED YUNNAN HAM, CUT INTO THIN STRIPS
- ½ CAYENNE PEPPER, CUT INTO THIN STRIPS
- STEAMED RICE (PAGE 540), TO SERVE

REGION: HUNAN
PREPARATION TIME: 10 MINUTES
COOKING TIME: 5 MINUTES
SERVES: 4

肉末酸豆角
PICKLED BEANS
WITH PORK

- 5 OZ/150 G GROUND (MINCED) PORK
- 1 TEASPOON LIGHT SOY SAUCE
- ½ TEASPOON GRANULATED SUGAR
- ½ TEASPOON CORNSTARCH (CORNFLOUR)
- 1 TABLESPOON VEGETABLE OIL
- 2 CLOVES GARLIC, CRUSHED
- 2 RED CHILES, SEEDED AND CUT INTO STRIPS
- 9 OZ/250 G PICKLED STRING BEANS, RINSED AND CHOPPED
- STEAMED RICE (PAGE 540), TO SERVE

* Combine the ground (minced) pork, soy sauce, sugar, and 2 tablespoons water in a bowl. Marinate for 5 minutes, then mix in the cornstarch (cornflour).
* Heat the oil in a wok or large skillet (frying pan) over low heat. Add the garlic and chiles and stir-fry for 1 minute until fragrant. Put in the pork and stir-fry rapidly for another 2–3 minutes over high heat until cooked through. Add the pickled string beans and stir-fry for another minute. Transfer to a serving plate and serve with rice.

REGION: BUDDHIST VEGETARIAN
PREPARATION TIME: 5 MINUTES
COOKING TIME: 10 MINUTES
SERVES: 2

雪菜毛豆
SOYBEANS WITH TOFU AND
PRESERVED MUSTARD GREENS

- 11 OZ/300 G FRESH SOYBEANS, PODDED
- 7 OZ/200 G PRESERVED MUSTARD GREENS, RINSED
- 2 TABLESPOONS VEGETABLE OIL
- 1 TABLESPOON CHOPPED GINGER
- 1 PIECE SEMI-DRIED TOFU, CUT INTO ½-INCH/1-CM DICE
- 1 RED BELL PEPPER, SEEDED AND CUT INTO ½-INCH/1-CM DICE
- ½ TEASPOON SALT
- ½ TEASPOON GRANULATED SUGAR
- 1 TEASPOON LIGHT SOY SAUCE
- 1 TEASPOON SESAME OIL
- STEAMED RICE (PAGE 540), TO SERVE

* Bring a large saucepan of water to a boil, add the soybeans, and blanch for 2 minutes. Drain and rinse under cold running water.
* Squeeze the mustard greens to remove excess water, then trim and chop them up.
* Heat the vegetable oil in a wok or large skillet (frying pan) over medium-high heat. Add the ginger and stir-fry for about 30 seconds until fragrant. Add the soybeans, mustard greens, and tofu and sauté for about 3 minutes. Add the bell pepper, salt, sugar, and soy sauce, and sauté for about 1 minute. Stir in the sesame oil, transfer to a serving plate, and serve with rice.

VEGETABLES, TOFU & EGGS

栗子烧面筋
WHEAT GLUTEN
WITH CHESTNUTS

REGION: BUDDHIST VEGETARIAN
PREPARATION TIME: 5 MINUTES,
  PLUS 10 MINUTES SOAKING TIME
COOKING TIME: 20 MINUTES
SERVES: 4

* Heat the vegetable oil in a wok or large skillet (frying pan)
  over high heat. Add the ginger and stir-fry for 1 minute
  until fragrant. Add the wheat gluten, chestnuts, soy sauce,
  sugar, and 4 tablespoons water and bring to a boil.
* Reduce to medium heat and sauté for about 5 minutes, or
  until the sauce is completely absorbed. Stir in the sesame
  oil and transfer to a serving plate. Serve with rice.

- 2 TABLESPOONS VEGETABLE OIL
- 1 TABLESPOON CHOPPED GINGER
- 5 OZ/150 G WHEAT GLUTEN, CUT INTO
  1 × 1½-INCH/2.5 × 4-CM PIECES,
  ¼ INCH/5 MM THICK
- 1¼ CUP (5 OZ/150 G) SHELLED
  CHESTNUTS
- 1½ TABLESPOONS LIGHT SOY SAUCE
- 2 TEASPOONS GRANULATED SUGAR
- ½ TEASPOONS SESAME OIL
- STEAMED RICE (PAGE 540), TO SERVE

栗子烧大葱
BEIJING SCALLIONS
WITH CHESTNUTS

REGION: SHANXI
PREPARATION TIME: 15 MINUTES
COOKING TIME: 20 MINUTES
SERVES: 4

* Soak the dried shrimp in a small bowl of water for about
  5 minutes. Drain and set aside.
* Heat the oil in a wok or large skillet (frying pan).
  Add the Beijing scallions and stir-fry over low heat
  for 1–2 minutes until fragrant. Use a slotted spoon
  to transfer the scallions to a plate.
* With the remaining oil in the wok, stir-fry the garlic and
  scallion (spring onion) for 1–2 minutes until fragrant.
  Add the pork, salt, and soy sauce and stir-fry for another
  2–3 minutes, or until the pork is cooked through.
* Put the pork in the center of a heatproof bowl, scatter
  the shelled chestnuts around the pork, and top with the
  Beijing scallions and shrimp. Sprinkle with the sugar.
* Place in a collapsible pot or bamboo steamer over a pot
  of boiling water. Steam, covered, for 15 minutes. Remove
  and drain the sauce to another bowl.
* Cover the bowl of pork with a plate and using dish towels,
  invert the contents onto a serving plate. (Alternatively, use
  tongs to transfer the contents.) Pour the reserved sauce on
  top of the pork. Serve with rice.

- ½ TABLESPOON DRIED SHRIMP
- 2 TABLESPOONS VEGETABLE OIL
- 1 LB 5 OZ/600 G BEIJING SCALLIONS
  OR SCALLIONS (SPRING ONIONS), CUT
  INTO 2-INCH/5-CM LENGTHS
- 2 CLOVES GARLIC, SLICED
- 1 SCALLION (SPRING ONION),
  SHREDDED
- 5 OZ/150 G PORK TENDERLOIN, THINLY
  SLICED
- ½ TEASPOON SALT
- 1 TEASPOON LIGHT SOY SAUCE
- ¾ CUP (3½ OZ/100 G) SHELLED
  CHESTNUTS
- 1 TABLESPOON GRANULATED SUGAR
- STEAMED RICE (PAGE 540), TO SERVE

REGION: HAKKA
PREPARATION TIME: 45 MINUTES
COOKING TIME: 5 MINUTES
SERVES: 4
📷 PAGE 483

炒算盘子
STIR-FRIED ABACUS BEADS

- 2 TABLESPOONS DRIED SHRIMP
- 11 OZ/300 G TARO, CUT INTO SMALL PIECES
- 1¼ CUPS (5 OZ/150 G) TAPIOCA STARCH
- ½ TEASPOON SALT
- 2 TABLESPOONS VEGETABLE OIL, PLUS EXTRA TO GREASE
- 3 SHALLOTS, FINELY CHOPPED
- 1 RED CHILE, SEEDED AND FINELY CHOPPED
- 1 TEASPOON SHRIMP PASTE
- 1 TEASPOON GRANULATED SUGAR
- 2 SCALLIONS (SPRING ONIONS), SHREDDED PLUS EXTRA TO GARNISH
- STEAMED RICE (PAGE 540), TO SERVE

Traditionally, Hakka people live frugally and women are often in charge of managing the household finances. Making the mashed taro into abacus shapes was meant to impart the importance of financial management. The skills to make this dish are still being taught to Hakka children as part of their education in some parts of the world.

* Soak the dried shrimp in a bowl of warm water for 5 minutes, then finely chop.
* Place the taro in a heatproof bowl in a collapsible pot or bamboo steamer over a pot of boiling water. Steam, covered, for 30 minutes. Carefully remove and use a fork to mash.
* Add the tapioca starch, then gradually add ¾ cup (6 fl oz/ 175 ml) water and knead by hand to form a piece of dough. Set aside for 30 minutes.
* Grease a large plate with oil.
* Put 1 tablespoon oil in a large bowl and set aside.
* Roll a small piece of dough (about ⅛ oz/5 g) into a small ball. Flatten the ball slightly and use your thumb and forefinger in the center of the ball to make a dent in the center to resemble an abacus bead. Put the bead on the greased plate. Repeat with the remaining dough.
* Bring a large saucepan of water to a boil. Add the beads and cook for 1 minute. Once the beads float to the surface, use a slotted spoon to transfer the beads to the prepared bowl. Roll the beads in the oil to prevent them from sticking together.
* Heat a flat nonstick skillet (frying pan) and add the beads. Fry for 1–2 minutes over medium heat until the beads are lightly brown. Transfer to a serving plate.
* Heat the remaining 1 tablespoon oil in a skillet (frying pan) over medium heat, add the dried shrimp, shallots, chile, shrimp paste, and sugar. Add the beads and stir to mix.
* Transfer to a serving plate and top with the scallions (spring onions). Serve with rice or for breakfast.

STIR-FRIED ABACUS BEADS

顺德小炒
SHUNDE
STIR-FRY

- 5 OZ/150 G BONELESS, SKIN-ON
  PORK BELLY
- 1 TEASPOON SALT
- 2 TABLESPOONS VEGETABLE OIL
- 2¾ OZ/75 G TARO, CUT INTO 1½-INCH/
  4-CM STRIPS
- 3 GINGER SLICES
- 2¾ OZ/75 G FLOWERING CHIVES,
  FLOWERS DISCARDED, CUT INTO
  1½-INCH/4-CM LENGTHS
- 1 RED CHILE, SEEDED AND CUT INTO
  STRIPS
- 1 TEASPOON LIGHT SOY SAUCE
- 2¾ OZ/75 G YELLOW CHIVES, CUT INTO
  1½-INCH/4-CM LENGTHS
- STEAMED RICE (PAGE 540), TO SERVE

* Combine the pork with the salt and marinate for
  30 minutes. Rinse under cold running water and drain.
* Put the pork into a large saucepan and add enough water
  to cover it completely. Bring to a boil over high heat, reduce
  to low heat, and simmer, covered, for 10 minutes. Drain and
  rinse under cold running water, then slice.
* Heat the oil in wok or skillet (frying pan) over medium
  heat, add the taro, and pan-fry for 4 minutes, or until
  crispy. Remove the taro and set aside.
* Add the ginger to the wok and stir-fry over high heat for
  30 seconds. Put in the pork and stir-fry until browned, then
  add the flowering chives, chiles, and soy sauce. Continue to
  stir-fry for another 30 seconds. Stir in the yellow chives and
  taro and toss thoroughly. Serve with rice.

VEGETABLES, TOFU & EGGS

香酥荔芋卷

CRISPY
TARO ROLL

REGION: BUDDHIST VEGETARIAN
PREPARATION TIME: 15 MINUTES
COOKING TIME: 40 MINUTES
SERVES: 4

* Place the taro into a collapsible pot or bamboo steamer over a pot of boiling water. Steam, covered, over high heat for 30 minutes. Transfer the taro to a bowl and mash with a fork while it is hot.
* Add the salt, sugar, white pepper, and 1 tablespoon cornstarch (cornflour) to make a thick but spreadable paste. Add a little water if necessary to achieve the right consistency. Divide the paste into 4 equal portions.
* Bring a saucepan of water to a boil, add the carrot, and cook for about 2 minutes until just tender. Drain.
* Mix the remaining ½ teaspoon cornstarch with ½ teaspoon water to use as a sealing agent.
* Put a piece of tofu sheet on a bamboo mat (like those used to make sushi rolls). Spread a portion of taro paste across the sheet, leaving about ½ inch/1 cm at one end free of the paste. Place a sheet of plastic wrap (clingfilm) on the taro paste and use your hands to smooth out the paste to ensure an even thickness. Use a rolling pin to roll the taro paste into a thin sheet across the tofu sheet.
* Put a stick of carrot (use more than one if they are not long enough to span the length of the tofu sheet) on the taro paste at one end of the sheet and, with the aid of the bamboo mat, roll up the tofu sheet into a tight roll with the paste and carrot inside. Brush the tofu skin on one end of the roll with the sealing agent and gently press to seal the roll. Trim the two ends of the roll. Repeat with the remaining tofu sheets and taro paste. Cut the taro rolls into ¾-inch/1.5-cm slices.
* Heat the oil in a wok or a deep saucepan. Add the taro roll slices and deep-fry for 1–2 minutes until crispy on the outsides. Use a spider strainer to remove the sliced taro roll and drain on paper towels. Transfer the taro rolls to a serving plate. Serve with ketchup as a dip, if desired.

- 11 OZ/300 G TARO, PEELED AND CUT INTO ½-INCH/1-CM CUBES
- ½ TEASPOON SALT
- ½ TEASPOON GRANULATED SUGAR
- ¼ TEASPOON GROUND WHITE PEPPER
- 1 TABLESPOON PLUS ½ TEASPOON CORNSTARCH (CORNFLOUR)
- 1 CARROT, CUT INTO FOUR LONG ½ × ½-INCH/1 × 1-CM STICKS
- 4 TOFU SHEETS, CUT INTO FOUR 8-INCH/20-CM SQUARES
- 2 CUPS (16 FL OZ/475 ML) VEGETABLE OIL
- KETCHUP, TO SERVE (OPTIONAL)

REGION: SHUNDE
PREPARATION TIME: 10 MINUTES
COOKING TIME: 10 MINUTES
SERVES: 4

大良煎藕餅
PAN-FRIED LOTUS ROOT PATTIES

- 7 OZ/200 G LOTUS ROOT, PEELED AND ENDS TRIMMED
- 3½ OZ/100 G GROUND (MINCED) PORK
- ½ TEASPOON LIGHT SOY SAUCE
- ¼ TEASPOON GRANULATED SUGAR
- PINCH OF WHITE PEPPER
- 1 DUCK LIVER SAUSAGE, CHOPPED
- ½ EGG, BEATEN
- 1 BUNCH CILANTRO (CORIANDER), CHOPPED
- 1½ TABLESPOON CORNSTARCH (CORNFLOUR)
- 3 TABLESPOONS VEGETABLE OIL, PLUS EXTRA FOR OILING
- STEAMED RICE (PAGE 540), TO SERVE

* To prepare the lotus root, use a chopstick to clean the channels and rinse thoroughly under cold running water. Chop.
* Combine the pork, soy sauce, sugar, and white pepper in a large bowl. Using chopsticks, stir the mixture in a single direction for about 1 minute until a gummy patty is formed. Stir in the sausage, lotus root, egg, cilantro (coriander), and cornstarch (cornflour) and mix well. With wet hands, form the mixture into 8–9 balls.
* Heat the oil in a skillet (frying pan) over low heat and add the lotus root balls one at a time.
* Oil the back of a spatula (fish slice) and use it to gently flatten each ball into a patty, about 2 inches/5 cm in diameter. Pan-fry the patties for 4 minutes on each side, or until golden brown. Serve with rice.

REGION: SHUNDE
PREPARATION TIME: 15 MINUTES
COOKING TIME: 30 MINUTES
SERVES: 4

牛肉薯仔餅
POTATO PANCAKE WITH BEEF

- 1 LARGE POTATO, CUT INTO ½-INCH/ 1.5-CM SLICES
- 2 CLOVES GARLIC, CHOPPED
- 3½ OZ/100 G GROUND (MINCED) BEEF
- 1 SHALLOT, CHOPPED
- ¼ TEASPOON SALT
- PINCH OF GROUND WHITE PEPPER
- 1 TABLESPOON VEGETABLE OIL
- 1 EGG, BEATEN

This delicious dish can be part of a family-style meal or eaten as a snack. Steaming the potatoes allows for better control over how much water is absorbed, which affects the texture.

* Put the potatoes on a heatproof plate. Scatter over the chopped garlic and place in a collapsible pot or bamboo steamer over a pot of boiling water. Steam, covered, for 20 minutes.
* Transfer the potatoes to a bowl and mash with a fork. Mix in the beef, shallot, salt, and white pepper.
* Roll 8 potato balls and flatten them into pancakes about ½ inch/1 cm thick and 2 inches/5 cm in diameter.
* Heat the oil in a large skillet (frying pan). Brush each pancake with the beaten egg and pan-fry over medium-low heat for 3–4 minutes until golden brown. Flip over and pan-fry for another 3–4 minutes. Serve.

金玉满堂

POTATO AND
CARROT MASH

REGION: BUDDHIST VEGETARIAN
PREPARATION TIME: 10 MINUTES,
   PLUS 20 MINUTES SOAKING TIME
COOKING TIME: 20 MINUTES
SERVES: 4

* Cover the mushrooms in boiling water and soak for at least 20 minutes. Remove the mushrooms, squeeze dry, and discard the stems. Cut the mushrooms into very fine strips.
* Put the potatoes and carrots into a large saucepan, cover with water, and bring to a boil. Boil for about 15 minutes until tender. Mash the potatoes and carrots.
* Bring a saucepan of water to a boil over high heat, add the peas, and blanch for 2 minutes. Drain.
* Put the potatoes, carrots, mushrooms, and bamboo shoots into a large bowl. Add the salt, wine, and sugar and blend into a paste.
* Heat 2 tablespoons oil in a wok. Add the paste and stir-fry over medium heat until all the ingredients are fully blended with the oil. Add the remaining 1 tablespoon oil and continue stirring, then mix in the peas. Stir in the vinegar, then transfer to a serving plate. Serve with rice.

- 3 DRIED BLACK MUSHROOMS
- 2 POTATOES, PEELED
- 3 CARROTS, CHOPPED
- ¼ CUP (1¼ OZ/30 G) SLICED BAMBOO SHOOTS
- ⅓ CUP (2 OZ/50 G) FRESH OR FROZEN PEAS
- ½ TEASPOON SALT
- 2 TABLESPOONS SHAOXING WINE
- 1 TABLESPOON GRANULATED SUGAR
- 3 TABLESPOONS VEGETABLE OIL
- 2 TEASPOONS WHITE VINEGAR
- STEAMED RICE (PAGE 540), TO SERVE

REGION: SHUNDE
PREPARATION TIME: 10 MINUTES,
   PLUS 10 MINUTES SOAKING TIME
COOKING TIME: 15 MINUTES
SERVES: 4

家乡蒸藕粉
STEAMED
LOTUS ROOTS

- 1 TABLESPOON DRIED SHRIMP
- 1 LB/450 G LOTUS ROOTS, PEELED AND
  ENDS TRIMMED
- ½ TEASPOON SALT
- 1½ TEASPOONS SWEET POTATO STARCH
- 3 TABLESPOONS VEGETABLE OIL
- STEAMED RICE (PAGE 540), TO SERVE

* Rinse the dried shrimp, then cover them in cold water and
  soak for 10 minutes. Drain the shrimp and chop finely.
* To prepare the lotus root, use a chopstick to clean the
  channels and rinse thoroughly under cold running water.
  Coarsely chop.
* Put the lotus roots into a blender or food processor, add
  4 tablespoons water, and process until coarse in texture.
* Transfer the grated lotus roots to a bowl and drain off any
  excess water. Add the salt, sweet potato starch, and oil
  and mix well, then transfer to a deep heatproof plate and
  arrange the dried shrimp on top.
* Cover the plate with aluminum foil. Place the plate in a
  collapsible pot or bamboo steamer over a pot of boiling
  water. Steam, covered, for 15 minutes. Serve with rice.

REGION: GUANGDONG
PREPARATION TIME: 20 MINUTES
COOKING TIME: 10 MINUTES
SERVES: 6-8

火腿冬瓜夹
STEAMED HAM AND WINTER
MELON SANDWICHES

- 1 LB 5 OZ/600 G WINTER MELON
- 3½ OZ/100 G CURED HAM, SLICED
  INTO 16 EQUAL PIECES
- 1 TABLESPOON HONEY
- 4 GINGER SLICES
- 1 CUP (8 FL OZ/250 ML) CHICKEN
  BROTH (STOCK, PAGE 90)
- STEAMED RICE (PAGE 540), TO SERVE

* Peel the winter melon but leave a trace of green on
  the surface. Cut into 4 equal-size chunks and remove the
  rind and seeds.
* For each chunk of melon, cut into 4 equal pieces, and make
  a deep cut on each piece to allow space to insert a piece
  of ham.
* In a small heatproof bowl, combine the ham slices with
  honey and place in a collapsible pot or bamboo steamer
  over a pot of boiling water. Steam, covered, for 3 minutes.
* Insert a slice of ham into each piece of melon to form
  a sandwich and arrange the sandwiches in a shallow
  heatproof bowl. Place the ginger on top of the sandwiches,
  pour over the chicken broth (stock), and steam for
  10 minutes. Remove and discard the ginger before
  serving with rice.

虾米肉碎蒸莲藕丝

LOTUS ROOT
WITH PORK

REGION: HONG KONG
PREPARATION TIME: 10 MINUTES
COOKING TIME: 8 MINUTES
SERVES: 4

* Soak the dried shrimp in a small bowl of water for
  15 minutes. Drain, chop, and set aside.
* Combine the ground (minced) pork, white pepper,
  and ½ teaspoon soy sauce in a large bowl. Mix well
  and set aside.
* To prepare the lotus root, use a chopstick to clean the
  channels and rinse thoroughly under cold running water.
  Use a spiral vegetable slicer to create long strands
  (alternatively, cut the lotus root into long thin strips)
  and put in a bowl. Add the cornstarch (cornflour),
  sugar, and 1 teaspoon soy sauce, then stir well.
* Mix the lotus root, pork, and shrimp and transfer to a
  heatproof plate. Stir in the oil and place in a collapsible
  pot or bamboo steamer over a pot of boiling water.
  Steam, covered, for about 8 minutes. Carefully remove
  from the steamer, top with chopped scallion (spring onion),
  and serve with rice.

- 1½ TABLESPOONS DRIED SHRIMP
- 3½ OZ/100 G GROUND (MINCED)
  PORK, FINELY CHOPPED
- ½ TEASPOON GROUND WHITE PEPPER
- 1½ TEASPOONS LIGHT SOY SAUCE
- 16 OZ/450 G LOTUS ROOT, PEELED
  AND ENDS TRIMMED
- ½ TABLESPOON CORNSTARCH
  (CORNFLOUR)
- ½ TEASPOON GRANULATED SUGAR
- 1 TABLESPOONS VEGETABLE OIL
- 2 TABLESPOONS CHOPPED SCALLION
  (SPRING ONION)
- STEAMED RICE (PAGE 540), TO SERVE

清蒸萝卜丸

STEAMED RADISH BALLS

REGION: HAKKA
PREPARATION TIME: 15 MINUTE
COOKING TIME: 10 MINUTES
SERVES: 4 (MAKES ABOUT 30)

* Combine the radish, cornstarch (cornflour), and ¼ teaspoon
  salt in a large bowl and set aside for 5 minutes.
* In a separate bowl, combine the ground (minced) pork,
  remaining ¼ teaspoon salt, and white pepper.
* Take a tablespoon of shredded turnip in one hand, squeeze
  it gently to rid of excess moisture and wrap the turnip
  around ½ teaspoon of the pork to form a small turnip ball.
  Continue with the remaining ingredients.
* Place the stuffed radish balls in a collapsible pot or bamboo
  steamer over a pot of boiling water. Steam, covered, for
  10 minutes. Remove and sprinkle over the chopped scallions
  (spring onions). Serve with rice.

- 11 OZ/300 G DAIKON RADISH,
  SHREDDED
- 6½ TABLESPOONS CORNSTARCH
  (CORNFLOUR)
- ½ TEASPOON SALT
- 2 OZ/60 G GROUND (MINCED) PORK
- PINCH OF GROUND WHITE PEPPER
- 2 SCALLIONS (SPRING ONIONS),
  CHOPPED
- STEAMED RICE (PAGE 540), TO SERVE

粟米番薯斋粥
VEGETARIAN CONGEE WITH CORN AND SWEET POTATO

- ¾ CUP (5½ OZ/160 G) LONG-GRAIN RICE, RINSED
- ½ TEASPOON SALT, PLUS EXTRA TO TASTE
- ½ TABLESPOON VEGETABLE OIL
- 1 LB 2 OZ/500 G SWEET POTATOES, PEELED AND CUT INTO ¾-INCH/2-CM DICE
- 1 (14-OZ/400-G) CAN CREAM OF CORN

* Combine the rice, salt, and oil in a large bowl and soak for 20 minutes.
* Bring 12½ cups (5¼ pints/3 liters) water to a boil in a large pot. Add the rice mixture and cook, uncovered, over high heat for 15 minutes.
* Add the sweet potato and cook over high heat for 45 minutes to 1 hour until the rice and sweet potato are completely cooked. Stir frequently to prevent sticking.
* Add the corn, bring to a boil, and cover, then turn off the heat and let stand for 10 minutes. Stir the rice, adjust the seasoning to taste, and then ladle into individual bowls.

腊味香芋煲
TARO WITH CURED MEATS

- 1 LB 5 OZ/600 G TARO, CUT INTO ½-INCH/1-CM-THICK PIECES
- 3½ OZ/100 G CHINESE CURED BACON
- 1 CHINESE SAUSAGE
- 1 CURED DUCK LEG
- 2 TABLESPOONS VEGETABLE OIL
- ¾ OZ/20 G GINGER (ABOUT 1-INCH/ 2.5-CM-LENGTH PIECE), SLICED
- 3 CLOVES GARLIC, SLICED
- ½ CUP (4 FL OZ/120 ML) COCONUT MILK
- 3 SCALLIONS (SPRING ONIONS), STEMS ONLY, CHOPPED
- 1 TEASPOON SALT
- STEAMED RICE (PAGE 540), TO SERVE

* Place the taro in a collapsible pot or bamboo steamer over a pot of boiling water. Steam, covered, for 10 minutes. Carefully remove and set aside.
* Put the bacon, sausage, and duck leg into a large heatproof bowl and steam for 10 minutes. Carefully remove and cool. When cooled, slice the bacon and sausage and cut the duck leg into chunks.
* Heat the oil in a Dutch oven (casserole) over medium heat, add the ginger and garlic, and stir-fry for 1 minute until fragrant. Stir in the cured meats, pour in 5 tablespoons water, and bring to a boil over high heat.
* Add the taro, stir lightly, reduce to low heat, and simmer, covered, for 2 minutes. Stir in the coconut milk, scallions (spring onions), and salt, then cover and cook for 1 minute. Turn off the heat and allow to simmer in the residual heat for 5 minutes. Serve in the Dutch oven with rice.

TARO WITH CURED MEATS

REGION: ANHUI
PREPARATION TIME: 20 MINUTES,
  PLUS 20 MINUTES SOAKING TIME
COOKING TIME: 15 MINUTES
SERVES: 4

李鸿章杂烩

CHOP
SUEY

- 1¼ OZ/30 G DRIED BEAN CURD STICKS
- 2 DRIED BLACK MUSHROOMS
- 5 OZ/150 G WHITE FISH FILLETS, CUT INTO BITE-SIZE PIECES
- ½ TEASPOON SALT
- ¼ TEASPOON GROUND WHITE PEPPER
- 2 SKINLESS, BONELESS CHICKEN THIGHS, CUT INTO 2 × ½-INCH/5 × 1-CM SLICES
- 2 OZ/50 G COOKED HAM, CUT INTO 2 × ½-INCH/5 × 1 CM-SLICES
- ¾ CUP (3 OZ/90 G) SLICED BAMBOO SHOOTS, DRAINED
- 1 SCALLION (SPRING ONION), CUT INTO 2-INCH/5-CM LENGTHS
- ½ OZ/15 G GINGER (ABOUT ¾-INCH/ 2-CM-LENGTH PIECE), SLICED
- 1 TABLESPOON LIGHT SOY SAUCE
- 1 TABLESPOON SHAOXING WINE
- ⅔ CUP (¼ PINT/150 ML) CHICKEN BROTH (STOCK, PAGE 90)
- 2 TABLESPOONS VEGETABLE OIL
- 2 OZ/50 G SNOW PEAS, TRIMMED, STRINGS REMOVED
- 1 TEASPOON CORNSTARCH (CORNFLOUR)
- STEAMED RICE (PAGE 540), TO SERVE

The full name for chop suey is Li Hung Zhang Chop Suey. Li was a top official in the Qing Dynasty and in charge of military, economic, and foreign affairs. In 1896, Li attended the crowning ceremony of Nicholas II of Russia, followed by a visit to the United States. The Chinese dinner he hosted for American officials was so successful that people later tried to find out what had been served. Li's response was *chop suey*, meaning "many things put together."

* Cover the bean curd sticks in cold water and soak for 20 minutes until softened. Drain the sticks and cut them into 2-inch/5-cm lengths.
* Put the mushrooms in a bowl, cover with cold water, and soak for at least 20 minutes, or until softened. Remove the mushrooms, squeeze dry, and discard the stems. Thinly slice.
* Meanwhile, in a blender, combine the fish, ¼ teaspoon salt, and the white pepper and process into a paste. With wet hands, form the fish paste into ¾-inch/2-cm fish balls.
* Place the fish balls in a collapsible pot or bamboo steamer over a pot of boiling water. Steam, covered, for 5 minutes.
* Put the fish balls, bean curd sticks, and mushrooms into a dry wok or large skillet (frying pan). Add the chicken, ham, bamboo shoots, scallion (spring onion), ginger, soy sauce, wine, the remaining ¼ teaspoon salt, the chicken broth (stock), and oil and bring to a boil. Cover, reduce to low heat, and simmer for 10 minutes. Add the snow peas and simmer for another 2 minutes.
* Mix the cornstarch with 1 tablespoon water, then stir the mixture into the wok. Bring to a boil, stirring, for about 30 seconds to thicken the sauce. Transfer to a serving plate and serve with rice.

芋头糕
TARO
PUDDING

REGION: GUANGDONG
PREPARATION TIME: 45 MINUTES
COOKING TIME: 1 HOUR 30 MINUTES
SERVES: 4

This is one of the many favorite festive dishes prepared during Chinese New Year in Guangdong and Hong Kong. It is also served as dim sum when guests come calling during the holidays.

- 1 LB 5 OZ/600 G TARO ROOT, CUT INTO ½-INCH/1-CM CUBES
- 5 TABLESPOONS DRIED SHRIMP
- 1 CHINESE SAUSAGE
- 6 TABLESPOONS TAPIOCA STARCH
- 1 TEASPOON SALT
- ¼ TEASPOON GROUND WHITE PEPPER
- ½ CUP (2¾ OZ/75 G) RICE FLOUR

* Divide the taro into 2 portions. Place 1 portion in a collapsible pot or bamboo steamer over a pot of boiling water. Steam, covered, for 30 minutes. Carefully transfer the taro to a bowl and mash to a paste. Steam the remaining portion for 15 minutes and set aside.
* Meanwhile, soak the dried shrimp in a bowl with 1 cup (8 fl oz/250 ml) cold water for 5 minutes until softened. Strain the soaking water in a bowl and chop the shrimp.
* Place the sausage in a collapsible pot or bamboo steamer over a pot of boiling water. Steam, covered, for 3 minutes. Remove and cut into thin slices. Set aside.
* Combine the taro paste and tapioca starch and mix, then add the salt, white pepper, and ⅓ cup (2½ fl oz/75 ml) shrimp soaking water. Mix well. Add the rice flour and the remaining shrimp water and mix again. Mix in the steamed taro cubes, dried shrimp, and sliced Chinese sausage. Put the mixture into a loaf pan. Place in a collapsible pot or bamboo steamer over a pot of boiling water. Steam, covered, for 1 hour. (Add more water to the pot if needed). Remove and set aside to cool completely.
* Cut the taro pudding into ½-inch/1-cm-thick slices. Heat a large skillet (frying pan) and fry over medium-high heat for 2–3 minutes until slightly browned. Turn over and fry for 2 minutes. Serve as breakfast or as part of dim sum.

REGION: BUDDHIST VEGETARIAN
PREPARATION TIME: 10 MINUTES
COOKING TIME: 20 MINUTES
SERVES: 4

银杏香笋
GINKGO NUTS WITH
BAMBOO SHOOTS

- 1½ CUPS (5 OZ/150 G) SHELLED GINKGO NUTS
- 2¼ OZ/60 G FRESH BAMBOO SHOOTS, CUT INTO CHUNKS (OR ½ CUP CANNED BAMBOO SHOOTS, SLICED)
- 1 TABLESPOON VEGETABLE OIL
- ¼ TEASPOON SALT
- PINCH OF GROUND WHITE PEPPER
- ½ RED BELL PEPPER, SEEDED AND CUT INTO ¾-INCH/2-CM SQUARES
- ½ GREEN BELL PEPPER, SEEDED AND CUT INTO ¾-INCH/2-CM SQUARES
- STEAMED RICE (PAGE 540), TO SERVE

* Bring a saucepan of water to a boil, add the ginkgo nuts, and boil for 15 minutes. Drain and rinse the kernels, then rub them to remove the skins.
* If using fresh bamboo shoots, bring a saucepan of water to a boil, add the bamboo shoots, and blanch for 2 minutes. Drain and rinse under cold running water.
* Heat the oil in a wok or large skillet (frying pan) over medium heat. Add the ginkgo nuts and bamboo shoots and stir-fry for 1 minute. Season with the salt and white pepper, then add the peppers and toss for 30 seconds. Transfer to a serving plate and serve with rice.

NOTE:
Ginkgo nuts should be consumed in moderation. See Glossary for more information.

REGION: BUDDHIST VEGETARIAN
PREPARATION TIME: 20 MINUTES,
   PLUS 15 MINUTES SOAKING TIME
COOKING TIME: 10 MINUTES
SERVES: 4

白璧青云
ASPARAGUS
AND TOFU

- 1 CUP (1 OZ/25 G) DRIED BLACK FUNGUS
- ½ OZ/15 G BLACK MOSS
- 7 OZ/200 G FIRM TOFU, DRAINED AND MASHED INTO A PASTE
- 2 TEASPOONS SALT
- 1 TABLESPOON SHAOXING WINE
- 1 TABLESPOON VEGETABLE OIL
- 1 BUNCH (ABOUT 7 OZ/200 G) ASPARAGUS, TRIMMED AND CUT DIAGONALLY INTO 1-INCH/2.5-CM LENGTHS
- 1½ CUPS (12 FL OZ/350 ML) VEGETABLE BROTH (STOCK, PAGE 92)
- 1 TEASPOON SESAME OIL
- STEAMED RICE (PAGE 540), TO SERVE

* Cover the black fungus in cold water and soak for 15 minutes. Remove the softened black fungus and cut it into fine shreds.
* Cover the black moss in cold water and soak for about 15 minutes. Remove the softened black moss, drain, and squeeze dry. Chop the black moss and put it into a heatproof bowl.
* Add the mashed tofu, 1 teaspoon salt, and 2 teaspoons wine. Place the bowl in a collapsible pot or bamboo steamer on a pot of boiling water and steam, covered, for about 5 minutes. Set aside to cool, then cut into ¾ × ¾ × 1-inch/1.5 × 1.5 × 2.5-cm pieces.
* Heat the vegetable oil in a wok or large skillet (frying pan) over medium heat. Stir in the asparagus, black fungus, remaining 1 teaspoon salt, 1 teaspoon wine, and the vegetable broth (stock) and bring to a boil. Put in the tofu and black moss pieces, reduce to low heat, and simmer for 2–3 minutes. Stir in the sesame oil, transfer to a serving bowl, and serve with rice.

VEGETABLES, TOFU & EGGS

雪里蕻干烧冬笋
PRESERVED MUSTARD GREENS
WITH BAMBOO SHOOTS

REGION: BUDDHIST VEGETARIAN
PREPARATION TIME: 10 MINUTES,
   PLUS 5 MINUTES SOAKING TIME
COOKING TIME: 5 MINUTES
SERVES: 4

* Cover the mustard greens in water and soak for 5 minutes. Drain, rinse well, and then squeeze to remove excess water. Trim, then chop the greens.
* If using fresh bamboo shoots, bring a saucepan of water to a boil, add the bamboo shoot, and blanch for 1 minute. Drain and rinse under cold running water.
* Heat the vegetable oil in a wok or large skillet (frying pan) over high heat. Add the ginger and stir-fry for 1 minute until fragrant. Add the mustard greens and bamboo shoots and stir-fry for about 2 minutes.
* Add the salt, sugar, and 4 tablespoons water to the wok and sauté for 1 minute. Mix the cornstarch (cornflour) with 1 tablespoon water, then mix into the wok. Bring to a boil, stirring, for about 30 seconds to thicken the sauce.
* Drizzle over the sesame oil and transfer to a serving plate. Serve with rice.

- 5 OZ/150 G PRESERVED MUSTARD GREENS
- 1 LB 2 OZ/500 G (ABOUT 3 CUPS CANNED BAMBOO SHOOTS) FRESH BAMBOO SHOOTS, CUT INTO 1½-INCH/4-CM-LONG MATCHSTICKS
- 2 TABLESPOONS VEGETABLE OIL
- ¼ OZ/10 G GINGER (ABOUT ¾-INCH/ 2-CM-LENGTH PIECE), CHOPPED
- ½ TEASPOON SALT
- 2 TEASPOONS GRANULATED SUGAR
- 1 TEASPOON CORNSTARCH (CORNFLOUR)
- 1 TEASPOON SESAME OIL
- STEAMED RICE (PAGE 540), TO SERVE

油焖春笋
BRAISED BAMBOO
SHOOTS

REGION: ZHEJIANG
PREPARATION TIME: 10 MINUTES
COOKING TIME: 15 MINUTES
SERVES: 2

* Cut off and discard ½ inch/1 cm from the base of the shoots.
* Heat the vegetable oil in a wok or large skillet (frying pan) over low heat, add the Sichuan peppercorns, and stir-fry for 2–3 minutes until fragrant. Remove the Sichuan peppercorns and discard.
* Add the bamboo shoots to the wok and stir-fry over medium heat for about 1 minute. Stir in the soy sauce, sugar, and 4 tablespoons water and bring to a boil. Reduce to low heat and simmer, covered, for 5 minutes until the bamboo shoots are tender. Increase to high heat and stir-fry for 1 minute until the sauce thickens slightly and clings to the bamboo shoots. Drizzle in the sesame oil and serve with rice.

- 14 OZ/400 G FRESH SPRING BAMBOO SHOOTS (OR 3 CUPS CANNED BAMBOO SHOOTS, SLICED AND DRAINED)
- 1 TABLESPOON VEGETABLE OIL
- 1 TEASPOON SICHUAN PEPPERCORNS
- 2 TEASPOONS DARK SOY SAUCE
- 2 TEASPOONS GRANULATED SUGAR
- 1 TEASPOON SESAME OIL
- STEAMED RICE (PAGE 540), TO SERVE

火腿蚕豆
FAVA BEANS
WITH HAM

- 2 TABLESPOONS LARD
- 1¾ CUPS (11 OZ/300 G) FAVA (BROAD) BEANS
- 3½ OZ/100 G HAM, ½-INCH/1-CM SQUARES
- ¼ TEASPOON SALT
- 4 TABLESPOONS CHICKEN BROTH (STOCK, PAGE 90)
- 1 TEASPOON CORNSTARCH (CORNFLOUR)
- 1 TABLESPOON SESAME OIL
- STEAMED RICE (PAGE 540), TO SERVE

* Heat the lard in a wok or large skillet (frying pan) over medium heat. Add the fava (broad) beans and toss rapidly for about 30 seconds. Stir in the ham and salt, then add the chicken broth (stock). Bring to a boil, then sauté for about 1 minute.
* Mix the cornstarch (cornflour) with 1 tablespoon water, then stir the mixture into the wok. Bring to a boil, stirring, for about 30 seconds to thicken the sauce.
* Drizzle over the sesame oil. Transfer to a serving bowl and serve with rice.

翡翠虾仁
SHRIMP WITH
SUGAR SNAPS

- 9 OZ/250 G UNCOOKED SHRIMP (PRAWNS), SHELLED AND DEVEINED
- 1½ TEASPOON SALT
- 1 EGG WHITE, BEATEN
- 2 TEASPOONS RICE WINE
- ¼ TEASPOON GROUND WHITE PEPPER
- 1 TEASPOON CORNSTARCH (CORNFLOUR)
- 3 TABLESPOONS CHICKEN BROTH (STOCK, PAGE 90)
- 2 CUPS (16 FL OZ/475 ML) VEGETABLE OIL
- 3½ OZ/100 G SUGAR SNAPS, PODDED
- STEAMED RICE (PAGE 540), TO SERVE

* Rub the shrimp (prawns) with 1 teaspoon salt for about 30 seconds, rinse, and drain. Pat with paper towels to absorb excess moisture and put them in a clean dish towel. Refrigerate for 1 hour.
* Transfer the shrimp into a bowl, add the egg white and ¼ teaspoon salt, and mix well.
* In another bowl, combine the wine, white pepper, ¼ teaspoon salt, cornstarch (cornflour), and chicken broth (stock) into a sauce.
* Heat the oil in a wok or deep saucepan to 265°F/130°C. Add the shrimp, stir, and deep-fry for about 30 seconds until they begin to turn pink. Use a slotted spoon to remove the shrimp from the oil and drain on paper towels.
* Pour out the oil, return the shrimp to the wok, and add the peas and sauce. Sauté over high heat for 4 minutes, or until all the sauce has evaporated. Transfer to a serving plate. Serve with rice.

FAVA BEANS WITH HAM

BAMBOO SHOOTS
IN CHILI OIL

REGION: BUDDHIST VEGETARIAN
PREPARATION TIME: 10 MINUTES
COOKING TIME: 5 MINUTES
SERVES: 4

- 1 LB 5 OZ/600 G FRESH BAMBOO SHOOTS OR (5 CUPS CANNED BAMBOO SHOOTS, SLICED)
- 3 TABLESPOONS SESAME OIL
- 1 TEASPOON SICHUAN PEPPERCORNS
- 2 TEASPOONS LIGHT SOY SAUCE
- ¼ TEASPOON SALT
- SCANT ½ CUP (3½ FL OZ/100 ML) VEGETABLE BROTH (STOCK, PAGE 92)
- 2 TABLESPOONS CHILI OIL

* Cut off and discard the bamboo shoot bases about 1½ inch/4 cm from the tops, leaving only the tender tips. (Omit this step if using canned bamboo shoots.) Cut each bamboo shoot tip lengthwise into 12 or 16 strips.
* If using fresh bamboo shoots, bring a large saucepan of water to a boil, add the bamboo shoots, and blanch for 1 minute. Drain and rinse under cold running water. Slice.
* Heat the sesame oil in a wok or large skillet (frying pan) over medium heat. Add the bamboo shoots and Sichuan peppercorns and stir-fry for about 30 seconds. Add the soy sauce, salt, and vegetable broth (stock), cover, and simmer for 2 minutes.
* Uncover and simmer for about 4 minutes, or until the sauce is reduced to a quarter. Transfer to a serving plate.
* Heat the chili oil in a small skillet, drizzle it over the shoots, and set aside to cool. Serve at room temperature.

虾子油焖冬笋

BAMBOO SHOOTS
WITH SHRIMP ROE

REGION: ZHEJIANG
PREPARATION TIME: 20 MINUTES
COOKING TIME: 30 MINUTES
SERVES: 6

- 2¼ LB/1 KG FRESH BAMBOO SHOOTS
- 2 CUPS (16 FL OZ/475 ML) VEGETABLE OIL
- 1½ TABLESPOONS SHRIMP ROE
- 1 TABLESPOON LIGHT SOY SAUCE
- 1 TEASPOON SALT
- 1 TEASPOON GRANULATED SUGAR
- ½ CUP (4 FL OZ/120 ML) CHICKEN BROTH (STOCK, PAGE 90)
- 1 TEASPOON SESAME OIL
- STEAMED RICE (PAGE 540), TO SERVE

* Cut open the outer skin of the bamboo shoot, lengthwise, and peel to reveal the tender shoot. Cut off and discard the base leaving only the tender part and smooth out the surface with a knife.
* Slice each bamboo shoot lengthwise into 4 wide slices. On each slice, make 4–5 cuts on each piece, but keeping it linked at the tip so that it looks like a fan.
* Heat the vegetable oil in a wok or deep saucepan to 300°F/150°C, or until a cube of bread browns in 1½ minutes. Add the bamboo and deep-fry for 5 minutes, or until light brown. Use a slotted spoon to carefully remove the bamboo shoots from the oil and drain on paper towels.
* Pour out most of the oil, leaving about 2 tablespoons in the wok. Add the bamboo shoots, shrimp roe, soy sauce, salt, sugar, and chicken broth (stock), then bring to a boil. Reduce to low heat and simmer, covered, for 15–20 minutes. Increase to high heat and cook, uncovered, for 5 minutes, or until the sauce has reduced and thickened. Stir in the sesame oil then transfer the bamboo shoots to a serving plate. Serve with rice.

香辣四季豆
BEANS IN
FRAGRANT SAUCE

REGION: BUDDHIST VEGETARIAN
PREPARATION TIME: 5 MINUTES
COOKING TIME: 10 MINUTES
SERVES: 4

* Heat the vegetable oil in a wok or deep saucepan to 300°F/150°C, or until a cube of bread browns in 1½ minutes. Add the mung bean vermicelli in batches and deep-fry for 20 seconds until puffed up. Use a slotted spoon to carefully remove the vermicelli from the oil and drain on paper towels.
* Reheat the oil to about 340°F/170°C, or until a cube of bread browns in 45 seconds. Add the French beans and deep-fry for about 3 minutes. Use a slotted spoon to carefully remove the beans from the oil and drain on paper towels.
* Pour out most of the oil, leaving about 2 tablespoons in the wok. Add the scallion (spring onion), ginger, and pickled chiles and stir-fry over medium heat for about 30 seconds until fragrant. Add the chili bean baste and continue to stir-fry for 30 seconds. Put in the beans, soy sauce, salt, sugar, and vegetable broth (stock) and bring to a boil. Add the vermicelli, sauté for 1 minute, then stir in the vinegar.
* Mix the cornstarch (cornflour) with 1 tablespoon water, then stir the mixture into the wok. Bring to a boil, stirring, for about 30 seconds to thicken the sauce.
* Drizzle over the sesame oil, stir, and transfer to a serving plate. Serve with rice.

- 2 CUPS (16 FL OZ/475 ML) VEGETABLE OIL
- 3½ OZ/100 G MUNG BEAN VERMICELLI
- 5 OZ/150 G FRENCH BEANS, STALK ENDS TRIMMED AND STRINGS REMOVED
- 1 SCALLION (SPRING ONION), CUT INTO 2-INCH/5-CM LENGTHS AND SHREDDED
- ⅛ OZ/5 G GINGER (ABOUT ½-INCH/ 1-CM-LENGTH PIECE), SHREDDED
- ⅛ OZ/5 G PICKLED CHILES, SHREDDED
- 1 TABLESPOON PIXIAN CHILI BEAN PASTE, CHOPPED
- 1 TEASPOON LIGHT SOY SAUCE
- ½ TEASPOON SALT
- 1 TEASPOON GRANULATED SUGAR
- SCANT ½ CUP (3½ FL OZ/100 ML) VEGETABLE BROTH (STOCK, PAGE 92)
- 1 TABLESPOON BLACK OR BALSAMIC VINEGAR
- 1 TEASPOON CORNSTARCH (CORNFLOUR)
- 1 TEASPOON SESAME OIL
- STEAMED RICE (PAGE 540), TO SERVE

干煸四季豆
STIR-FRIED GREEN BEANS

- 2 CUPS (16 FL OZ/475 ML) VEGETABLE OIL
- 11 OZ/300 G GREEN BEANS, STRINGY PARTS REMOVED AND CUT INTO 2-INCH/5-CM LENGTHS
- 4 DRIED CHILES, HALVED LENGTHWISE
- 2 CLOVES GARLIC, CHOPPED
- ¼ TEASPOON CRUSHED SICHUAN PEPPERCORNS
- 1 OZ/30 G GROUND (MINCED) PORK, FINELY CHOPPED
- 1 OZ/30 G SICHUAN PRESERVED MUSTARD GREENS, CHOPPED
- 1 TEASPOON LIGHT SOY SAUCE
- 1 TABLESPOON RICE WINE
- 1 TEASPOON GRANULATED SUGAR
- STEAMED RICE (PAGE 540), TO SERVE

* Heat the oil in a wok or deep saucepan to 300°F/150°C, or until a cube of bread browns in 1½ minutes. Add the green beans and deep-fry for 2 minutes until they begin to wrinkle. Use a slotted spoon to carefully remove the beans from the oil and drain on paper towels.
* Pour out most of the oil, leaving only about 2 tablespoons in the wok. Add the chiles, garlic, and Sichuan peppercorns and stir-fry over medium heat 1 minute until fragrant.
* Add the pork and stir-fry for 4–5minutes over medium heat, until cooked through. Stir in the mustard greens, soy sauce, wine, and sugar and stir-fry for 30 seconds.
* Increase to high heat, add the beans, and toss well. Transfer to a serving plate and serve with rice.

炒豆角松
GREEN BEANS WITH BARBECUE PORK

- 2 EGGS
- 1 TEASPOON SALT
- ⅔ CUP (3½ OZ/100 G) SHELLED RAW PEANUTS
- 2 TABLESPOONS VEGETABLE OIL
- 7 OZ/200 G GREEN BEANS, TRIMMED AND CUT INTO ½-INCH/1-CM CUBES
- 1 TABLESPOON GINGER JUICE
- 1 TEASPOON RICE WINE
- 3½ OZ/100 G BARBECUE PORK (PAGE 394), CHOPPED INTO ½-INCH/1-CM DICE
- ½ TEASPOON SESAME OIL
- 1 HEAD ICEBERG LETTUCE, LEAVES SEPARATED AND TRIMMED INTO CUP SHAPES (OPTIONAL)

* Beat the eggs with ½ teaspoon salt in a small bowl.
* Put the peanuts in a small skillet (frying pan) and dry-roast over medium-low heat for 2–3 minutes until fragrant. Transfer the peanuts to a plate and, when cool enough to handle, remove the skins.
* Heat the vegetable oil in a wok or large skillet (frying pan) over high heat, add the beans, and stir-fry for about 1 minute. Stir in the remaining ½ teaspoon salt, the ginger juice, wine, and pork. Making a space in the center of the wok, then pour in the eggs and stir rapidly to scramble.
* Add the peanuts and sesame oil, toss, and transfer to a serving plate. Serve with the lettuce leaves, if using, as wraps.

VEGETABLES, TOFU & EGGS

GREEN BEANS WITH BARBECUE PORK

REGION: GUANGDONG
PREPARATION TIME: 5 MINUTES
COOKING TIME: 3 MINUTES
SERVES: 2

炒豆苗
STIR-FRIED
PEA SHOOTS

- 4 CUPS (11 OZ/300 G) PEA SHOOTS, RINSED
- 3 TABLESPOONS VEGETABLE OIL
- 2 CLOVES GARLIC, CRUSHED
- ¼ TEASPOON SALT
- STEAMED RICE (PAGE 540), TO SERVE

* Put the pea shoots in a colander to drain. Shake the colander to remove as much water from the pea shoots as possible.
* Heat the oil in a wok or large skillet (frying pan) over high heat. Add the garlic and stir-fry for 1 minute until golden. Put in the pea shoots and stir-fry rapidly until they begin to soften. Add the salt and stir-fry for another minute. Transfer to a serving plate and serve with rice.

REGION: HONG KONG
PREPARATION TIME: 10 MINUTES,
   PLUS 20 MINUTES SOAKING TIME
COOKING TIME: 5 MINUTES
SERVES: 4

青豆粟米炒肉碎
PORK WITH PEAS
AND CORN

- 2 DRIED BLACK MUSHROOMS
- 5 OZ/150 G GROUND (MINCED) PORK
- 1 TEASPOON LIGHT SOY SAUCE
- 1 CUP (5 OZ/150 G) PEAS
- 2 TABLESPOONS VEGETABLE OIL
- SCANT 1 CUP (5 OZ/150 G) CORN
- ½ TEASPOON SALT
- STEAMED RICE (PAGE 540), TO SERVE

* Put the mushrooms in a bowl, cover with cold water, and soak for at least 20 minutes, or until softened. Remove the mushrooms, squeeze dry, and discard the stems. Dice the mushrooms.
* Combine the pork and soy sauce in a bowl and mix well.
* Bring a small saucepan of water to a boil, add the peas, and blanch for 1 minute. Drain.
* Heat the oil in a wok or a large skillet (frying pan) over medium-high heat. Add the mushrooms and stir-fry for 1 minute. Add the ground pork and stir-fry for 2 minutes until cooked through.
* Put the peas, corn, and salt into the wok, toss for another 2 minutes, then transfer the mixture to a serving plate. Serve with rice.

软烧豆腐
BRAISED
TOFU

REGION: SHANDONG
PREPARATION TIME: 5 MINUTES
COOKING TIME: 30 MINUTES
SERVES: 4

* Bring 4¼ cups (34 fl oz/1 liter) water to a boil in a large saucepan. Add the tofu and ½ teaspoon salt, reduce to medium heat, and simmer for 1 minute. Drain and set aside.
* Heat the sesame oil in a skillet (frying pan), add the Sichuan peppercorns, and stir-fry for 2–3 minutes until fragrant. Remove and discard the peppercorns.
* Add the sugar and cook over low heat for 2 minutes until caramelized. Put in the tofu and stir gently to color. Add the scallion (spring onion), ginger, soy sauce, wine, remaining ½ teaspoon salt, and vegetable broth (stock) and bring to a boil. Reduce to low heat and simmer, uncovered, for 10 minutes, or until the sauce thickens. Using a fork, pierce small holes in the tofu to allow some of the sauce into the tofu.
* Stir in the Sichuan pepper oil and transfer to a serving plate. Serve with rice.

- 1 LB 2 OZ/500 G FIRM TOFU, DRAINED AND CUT INTO ¾-INCH/2-CM CUBES
- 1 TEASPOON SALT
- 3 TABLESPOONS SESAME OIL
- 1 TEASPOON SICHUAN PEPPERCORNS
- 2 TABLESPOONS GRANULATED SUGAR
- 1 SCALLION (SPRING ONION), CHOPPED
- 1 TEASPOON CHOPPED GINGER
- 1 TABLESPOON LIGHT SOY SAUCE
- 1 TEASPOON SHAOXING WINE
- ½ CUP (4 FL OZ/125 ML) VEGETABLE BROTH (STOCK, PAGE 92)
- 1 TEASPOON SICHUAN PEPPER OIL
- STEAMED RICE (PAGE 540), TO SERVE

辣子豆腐
TOFU IN FRAGRANT
SAUCE

REGION: SHAANXI
PREPARATION TIME: 10 MINUTES
COOKING TIME: 10 MINUTES
SERVES: 4

* Heat 1 cup (8 fl oz/250 ml) water in a wok or large skillet (frying pan), add the tofu, spinach, salt, and soy sauce and bring to a boil. Reduce to medium heat and simmer for about 5 minutes. Mix the cornstarch (cornflour) with 1 tablespoon water and add it to the wok. Bring to a boil, stirring, for about 30 seconds to thicken the sauce. Transfer to a deep serving plate.
* Heat the oil in a clean wok. Add the Beijing scallions and stir-fry over medium heat for 2 minutes until slightly brown. Add the chili powder and stir rapidly for about 1 minute until fragrant. Stir in the ground Sichuan pepper, then arrange the mixture on top of the tofu on the plate. Serve with rice.

- 11 OZ/300 G FIRM TOFU, DRAINED AND CUT INTO 1¼ × ¾ × ½-INCH/3 × 1.5 × 1-CM PIECES
- ⅛ CUP (1 OZ/25 G) SPINACH, CUT INTO 1¼-INCH/3-CM STRIPS
- ½ TEASPOON SALT
- 1 TABLESPOON LIGHT SOY SAUCE
- 1 TEASPOON CORNSTARCH (CORNFLOUR)
- 2 TABLESPOONS VEGETABLE OIL
- 2 BEIJING SCALLIONS OR 6 SCALLIONS (SPRING ONIONS), CUT INTO 1¼-INCH/3-CM LENGTHS, THEN HALVED LENGTHWISE
- 1 TABLESPOON CHILI POWDER
- ¼ TEASPOON GROUND SICHUAN PEPPER
- STEAMED RICE (PAGE 540), TO SERVE

REGION: BUDDHIST VEGETARIAN
PREPARATION TIME: 10 MINUTES,
    PLUS 20 MINUTES SOAKING TIME
COOKING TIME: 30 MINUTES
SERVES: 4

黄焖豆腐
TOFU IN
BROWN SAUCE

- 6 DRIED BLACK MUSHROOMS
- 1½ TEASPOONS LIGHT SOY SAUCE
- 2 TEASPOONS GRANULATED SUGAR
- 1½ TABLESPOONS CORNSTARCH
  (CORNFLOUR)
- 2 CUPS (16 FL OZ/475 ML) PLUS
  1 TEASPOON VEGETABLE OIL
- ⅓ CUP (2 OZ/50 G) SLICED BAMBOO
  SHOOTS, DRAINED
- 1 LB 2 OZ/500 G FIRM TOFU, DRAINED
  AND CUT INTO 2 × 1 × ½-INCH/
  5 × 2.5 × 1-CM PIECES
- ⅛ OZ/5 G GINGER (ABOUT ½-INCH/
  1-CM-LENGTH PIECE), CHOPPED
- 1 TEASPOON SHAOXING WINE
- ½ TEASPOON SALT
- 1 CUP (8 FL OZ/250 ML) VEGETABLE
  BROTH (STOCK, PAGE 92)
- 1 TABLESPOON SESAME OIL
- STEAMED RICE (PAGE 540), TO SERVE

* Put the mushrooms in a bowl, cover with cold water, and soak for at least 20 minutes, or until softened.
* In a heatproof bowl, combine the mushrooms with ½ teaspoon soy sauce, ½ teaspoon sugar, and ½ tablespoon cornstarch (cornflour). Stir in 1 teaspoon vegetable oil. Place the bowl in a collapsible pot or bamboo steamer over a pot of boiling water. Steam, covered, for 15 minutes.
* Bring a saucepan of water to a boil, add the bamboo shoots, and blanch for 1 minute. Drain and rinse under cold running water.
* Heat the remaining 2 cups (16 fl oz/475 ml) vegetable oil in a wok or deep saucepan to 340°F/170°C, or until a cube of bread browns in 45 seconds. Toss the tofu pieces in 2 teaspoons cornstarch, then deep-fry until golden brown. Use a slotted spoon to carefully remove the tofu from the oil and drain on paper towels.
* Pour out most of the oil, leaving about 1 tablespoon in the wok. Add the ginger and stir-fry over medium-high heat for 1 minute until fragrant. Stir in the mushrooms, bamboo shoots, and wine. Add the tofu, salt, remaining 1 teaspoon soy sauce, and 1½ teaspoons sugar, and the vegetable broth (stock). Bring to a boil, then reduce to low heat and simmer for about 1 minute until the tofu softens.
* Increase to high heat and cook for 3 minute, or until the sauce has been reduced to ½ cup (4 fl oz/120 ml). Mix the remaining 1 teaspoon cornstarch with 1 tablespoon water and stir the mixture into the wok. Bring to a boil, stirring, for about 30 seconds to thicken the sauce
* Stir in the sesame oil and transfer to a plate. Serve with rice.

溜腐皮
BRAISED
TOFU SHEETS

REGION: BUDDHIST VEGETARIAN
PREPARATION TIME: 10 MINUTES,
   PLUS 5 MINUTES SOAKING TIME
COOKING TIME: 10 MINUTES
SERVES: 2

* Cover the tofu sheets in cold water and soak for 5 minutes until soft. Drain, then cut into 1¼ × ¾-inch/3 × 2-cm pieces.
* Heat the oil in a wok or large skillet (frying pan) over medium heat. Put in the tofu sheets and shallow-fry for about 3 minutes until the sheets are crispy but not browned. Use a slotted spoon to carefully remove the tofu sheets from the oil and drain on paper towels.
* Pour out most of the oil, leaving about 1 teaspoon in the wok. Add the ginger and stir-fry over medium heat for about 30 seconds until fragrant. Add the vegetable broth (stock), soy sauce, and salt and bring to a boil.
* Put in the mushrooms, bamboo shoots, and tofu sheets and return to a boil. Mix the cornstarch (cornflour) with 2 tablespoons water and stir the mixture into the wok. Bring to a boil, stirring, for about 30 seconds to thicken the sauce. Serve.

- 10 TOFU SHEETS
- 3 TABLESPOONS VEGETABLE OIL
- 1 TEASPOON CHOPPED GINGER
- 2 CUPS (16 FL OZ/475 ML) VEGETABLE BROTH (STOCK, PAGE 92)
- 1 TEASPOON LIGHT SOY SAUCE
- ¼ TEASPOON SALT
- 3½ OZ/100 G SHIITAKE MUSHROOMS, CUT INTO ½-INCH/1-CM-THICK SLICES
- ⅓ CUP (2 OZ/50 G) SLICED BAMBOO SHOOTS, DRAINED
- 1 TABLESPOON CORNSTARCH (CORNFLOUR)

梅菜焖豆腐
TOFU WITH PRESERVED
MUSTARD GREENS

REGION: TAIWAN
PREPARATION TIME: 5 MINUTES
COOKING TIME: 15 MINUTES
SERVES: 4

* Dust the tofu with the cornstarch (cornflour).
* Heat the vegetable oil in a wok or deep saucepan over to 340°F/170°C, or until a cube of bread browns in 45 seconds. Add the tofu pieces and deep-fry for 4 minutes, or until golden. Use a slotted spoon to carefully remove the tofu from the oil and drain on paper towels.
* Pour out most of the oil, leaving about 1 tablespoon in the wok. Add the garlic and stir-fry over medium heat for 1 minute until fragrant. Add the ground (minced) pork, increase to high heat, and stir-fry for about 1 minute, separating any lumps of pork.
* Add the mustard greens and stir-fry for about 1 minute. Add the chicken broth (stock), sugar, salt, and white pepper and bring to a boil. Stir in the tofu, bring the broth to a boil, then reduce the heat, cover and simmer for about 3–4 minutes. Stir in the sesame oil, transfer to a serving plate, and serve with rice.

- 1 LB 2 OZ/500 G FIRM TOFU, DRAINED AND CUT INTO 2¼ × 1¼ × ¾-INCH/ 6 × 3 × 1.5-CM PIECES
- 1 TABLESPOON CORNSTARCH (CORNFLOUR)
- 2 CUPS (16 FL OZ/475 ML) VEGETABLE OIL
- 7 CLOVES GARLIC, FINELY CHOPPED
- 3½ OZ/100 G GROUND (MINCED) PORK
- 5 OZ/150 G PRESERVED MUSTARD GREENS, TRIMMED, RINSED AND CHOPPED
- ½ CUP (4 FL OZ/120 ML) CHICKEN BROTH (STOCK, PAGE 90)
- 2 TABLESPOONS GRANULATED SUGAR
- ⅓ TEASPOON SALT
- ½ TEASPOON GROUND WHITE PEPPER
- 1 TEASPOON SESAME OIL
- STEAMED RICE (PAGE 540), TO SERVE

炸豆腐丸子
DEEP-FRIED
TOFU BALLS

- 1 TABLESPOON DRIED SHRIMP
- 9 OZ/250 G FIRM TOFU, DRAINED
- 1 BUNCH CILANTRO (CORIANDER), FINELY CHOPPED
- 1 SCALLION (SPRING ONION), GREEN PART ONLY, FINELY CHOPPED
- ½ TEASPOON SICHUAN PICKLED MUSTARD, FINELY CHOPPED
- 1 TEASPOON GINGER, FINELY CHOPPED
- 1 TEASPOON SALT
- ½ TEASPOON GROUND SICHUAN PEPPER
- 1 TEASPOON TIANMIANJIANG
- 1 EGG
- 2 TABLESPOON CORNSTARCH (CORNFLOUR)
- 4½ CUPS (34 FL OZ/1 LITER) VEGETABLE OIL
- STEAMED RICE (PAGE 540), TO SERVE
- KETCHUP, TO SERVE (OPTIONAL)

FOR THE SPICED PEPPER SALT:
- ½ TEASPOON SALT
- ¼ TEASPOON GROUND SICHUAN PEPPER

* Soak the dried shrimp in a bowl of cold water for 5 minutes. Drain, then finely chop and set aside.
* Put the tofu into a large bowl and mash it with a fork. Stir in the dried shrimp, cilantro (coriander), scallion (spring onion), pickled mustard, ginger, salt, ground Sichuan pepper, tianmianjiang, and egg. Mix thoroughly and then stir in the cornstarch (cornflour). Form the tofu mixture into 1¼-inch/3-cm-diameter balls.
* Heat the oil in a wok or deep saucepan to 340°F/170°C, or until a cube of bread browns in 45 seconds. Add the tofu balls and deep-fry for 3 minutes, or until slightly brown in color. Use a slotted spoon to carefully remove the balls from the oil and drain on paper towels.
* Reheat the oil to 340°F/170°C and return the tofu balls to the wok. Deep-fry for another minute until the balls are golden brown. Use a slotted spoon to carefully remove the balls from the oil and drain on paper towels.
* To make the spiced pepper salt, mix the ingredients. Serve the tofu balls with rice, ketchup, if using, and spiced pepper salt.

DEEP-FRIED TOFU BALLS

冬菇烩豆腐
TOFU AND MUSHROOMS

- 2 TABLESPOONS PEAS
- 2 TABLESPOONS VEGETABLE OIL
- 9 OZ/250 G TOFU, CUT INTO
  1½-INCH/4-CM SQUARES, ABOUT
  ¼ INCH/5 MM THICK
- 1 TABLESPOON LIGHT SOY SAUCE
- 1 TEASPOON GRANULATED SUGAR
- 1 TEASPOON SALT
- 2 TEASPOONS RICE WINE
- 6 TABLESPOONS VEGETABLE BROTH
  (STOCK, PAGE 92)
- 1 TABLESPOON CORNSTARCH
  (CORNFLOUR)
- 4 DRIED BLACK MUSHROOMS, SOAKED
  IN COLD WATER TO SOFTEN, STEMS
  REMOVED
- 1 TEASPOON SESAME OIL
- STEAMED RICE (PAGE 540), TO SERVE

* Bring a small saucepan of water to a boil over high heat, add the peas, and blanch for 1 minute. Drain and rinse.
* Heat 1 tablespoon vegetable oil in a wok or large skillet (frying pan) over medium heat. Add the tofu and fry for 3 minutes, or until lightly browned on both sides. Stir in the soy sauce, sugar, ½ teaspoon salt, 1 teaspoon wine, and 4 tablespoons vegetable broth (stock). Reduce to low heat and simmer for 5 minutes until the sauce has reduced by half.
* Mix ½ tablespoon cornstarch (cornflour) with 1 tablespoon water in a small bowl and stir this mixture into the sauce. Bring to a boil, stirring, for about 30 seconds to thicken the sauce. Transfer to a serving plate.
* Add the remaining 1 tablespoon vegetable oil to the wok and stir-fry the mushrooms and peas over high heat for 1 minute. Add the remaining 1 teaspoon wine, ½ teaspoon salt and 2 tablespoons vegetable broth and bring to a boil. Mix together the remaining ½ tablespoon cornstarch and 1 tablespoon water and stir this mixture in the wok. Add the sesame oil. Bring to a boil, stirring, for about 30 seconds to thicken sauce. Pour over the tofu on the plate and serve with rice.

湘潭包子豆腐
XIANGTAN-STYLE
TOFU

- 1 OZ/25 G SHAOXING PRESERVED
  MUSTARD GREENS
- 2 TABLESPOONS VEGETABLE OIL
- 1 LB 5 OZ/600 G FIRM TOFU, DRAINED
  AND CUT INTO 32 CUBES
- 1 LEEK, CUT INTO 1-INCH/2.5-CM
  LENGTHS
- 5 TABLESPOONS VEGETABLE BROTH
  (STOCK, PAGE 92)
- 2 TABLESPOONS CHILI OIL
- 2 TEASPOONS LIGHT SOY SAUCE
- ⅓ TEASPOON SALT
- 1 TEASPOON CORNSTARCH
  (CORNFLOUR)
- ½ TEASPOON SESAME OIL
- STEAMED RICE (PAGE 540), TO SERVE

* Soak the preserved mustard greens in a bowl of water for 15 minutes until soft. Rinse thoroughly, trim and cut into 1-inch/2.5-cm lengths.
* Heat the vegetable oil in a wok or large skillet (frying pan) over medium heat, add the tofu, and fry for 3 minutes, or until golden. Remove the tofu from the wok and set aside.
* Using the remaining oil in the wok, stir-fry the mustard greens over medium heat for 30 seconds. Return the tofu to the wok, add the leek, vegetable broth (stock), chili oil, soy sauce, and salt and stir gently to mix. Bring to a boil, then reduce to medium heat and simmer, covered, for 2 minutes.
* Mix the cornstarch (cornflour) with 1 tablespoon water in a small bowl and stir this mixture into the wok. Bring to a boil, stirring, for about 30 seconds to thicken the sauce. Drizzle in the sesame oil and transfer to a plate. Serve immediately with rice.

白起豆腐
BAIQI TOFU

REGION: SHANXI
PREPARATION TIME: 10 MINUTES
COOKING TIME: 20 MINUTES
SERVES: 4

Baiqi was a renowned general of the Qin Kingdom (which evolved into the Qin Empire) during the Warring States over 2,300 years ago. In a battle with the Zhao Kingdom, Baiqi slaughtered over 400,000 of their troops and led the Qin army to victory. He was much-hated by the Zhao people, who created this dish years later to express their hatred. The tofu is traditionally roasted over a charcoal flame and then steamed to symbolize the death of Baiqi through burning and drowning.

- 1 LB 2 OZ/500 G FIRM TOFU, DRAINED AND CUT INTO 1-INCH/2.5-CM CUBES
- 2 TABLESPOONS VEGETABLE OIL
- 2 TEASPOONS FINELY CHOPPED GINGER
- 4 CLOVES GARLIC, CHOPPED
- 2 QUANTITIES SOYBEAN CRISPS (PAGE 52)
- ⅔ CUP (3½ OZ/100 G) CORNMEAL
- 2 TEASPOONS SALT
- STEAMED RICE (PAGE 540), TO SERVE

* Preheat the broiler (grill). Plate the tofu on a wire rack and broil (grill) for 3–4 minutes. Turn over each piece of tofu and broil for another 3–4 minutes until brown.
* Heat the oil in a wok or large skillet (frying pan) over medium-high. Add the ginger and garlic and stir-fry for 1 minute until fragrant. Stir in the soybean crisps, cornmeal, and salt and stir-fry for another minute until combined.
* Arrange the tofu on a heatproof plate and place in a collapsible pot or bamboo steamer over a pot of boiling water. Steam, covered, for 5 minutes.
* Remove the tofu from the steamer and transfer to a serving plate. Top with the crispy soybean mixture and serve with rice.

REGION: HUNAN
PREPARATION TIME: 15 MINUTES,
    PLUS 10 MINUTES SOAKING TIME
COOKING TIME: 10 MINUTES
SERVES: 4

焦溜豆腐丸
DEEP-FRIED TOFU
BALLS IN SAUCE

- 1 LB 2 OZ/500 G FIRM TOFU, RINSED AND DRAINED
- 2 OZ/50 G MUNG BEAN VERMICELLI
- ¾ CUP (3½ OZ/100 G) ALL-PURPOSE (PLAIN) FLOUR
- 1 EGG
- ½ TEASPOON SALT
- 2 TEASPOONS CHOPPED SCALLION (SPRING ONION)
- PINCH OF GROUND WHITE PEPPER
- 2 CUPS (16 FL OZ/475 ML) VEGETABLE OIL
- 5 TABLESPOONS VEGETABLE BROTH (STOCK, PAGE 92)
- 1 TEASPOON LIGHT SOY SAUCE
- 1 TEASPOON CORNSTARCH (CORNFLOUR)
- STEAMED RICE (PAGE 540), TO SERVE

* Place the tofu in a bowl and coarsely mash with a fork.
* Soak the mung bean vermicelli in a bowl of cold water for about 10 minutes until softened. Drain, chop, and add to the tofu.
* Stir in the flour, egg, salt, 1 teaspoon chopped scallion (spring onion), and white pepper. Using your hands, mix well and set aside.
* Heat the oil in a wok or deep saucepan to 340°F/170°C, or until a cube of bread browns in 45 seconds. Scoop out a generous tablespoon of the mixture and shape it into a 1-inch/2.5-cm-diameter ball, adding more mixture if necessary. Use a spoon to carefully lower the balls, in batches, into the hot oil and deep-fry for 3–4 minutes until golden brown. Use a slotted spoon to carefully remove the tofu balls from the oil and drain on paper towels.
* Pour out most of the oil, leaving about 1 tablespoon in the wok. Add the vegetable broth (stock) and bring to a boil. Stir in the soy sauce and the remaining chopped scallion.
* Mix the cornstarch (cornflour) and 1 tablespoon water in a small bowl and stir this mixture into the wok. Bring to a boil, stirring, for about 30 seconds to thicken the sauce.
* Drizzle the sauce over the tofu balls and serve with rice.

宫保豆腐
GONGBAO
TOFU

REGION: SICHUAN
PREPARATION TIME: 20 MINUTES
COOKING TIME: 15 MINUTES
SERVES: 4

* Put the tofu in a bowl, add 2 cups (16 fl oz/475 ml) water and ½ teaspoon salt, and soak for 15 minutes. Drain and dry with paper towels.
* Dice the tofu into ½-inch/1.5-cm cubes, transfer to a bowl, and then add the egg, cornstarch (cornflour), and remaining ½ teaspoon salt. Set aside.
* In a separate bowl, combine the chili bean paste, pickled chiles, and sesame oil.
* Heat 3 tablespoons vegetable oil in a wok or skillet (frying pan) over low heat, add the peanuts, and fry for 5 minutes, or until toasted and crunchy. Remove to a plate to cool.
* Heat the remaining 1 tablespoon oil in the wok over medium heat. Add the tofu and pan-fry for 3–4 minutes, or until slightly firm. Use a slotted spoon to carefully remove the tofu from the oil and drain on paper towels.
* With the remaining oil in the wok, stir-fry the ginger, scallion (spring onion), chili bean paste and pickled chiles until fragrant. Add the soy sauce, sugar, and ½ cup (4 fl oz/125 ml) water and sauté until the sauce thickens. Gently stir in the tofu and peanuts, then drizzle in the wine. Transfer to a serving plate and serve with rice.

- 1 LB 2 OZ/500 G FIRM TOFU, DRAINED
- 1 TEASPOON SALT
- 1 EGG, BEATEN
- 2 TABLESPOONS CORNSTARCH (CORNFLOUR)
- 2 TABLESPOONS PIXIAN CHILI BEAN PASTE, ROUGHLY CHOPPED
- ¾ OZ/20 G PICKLED CHILES, CHOPPED
- 1 TABLESPOON SESAME OIL
- 4 TABLESPOONS VEGETABLE OIL
- ⅓ CUP (2 OZ/50 G) PEANUTS, SHELLED AND HUSKED
- 1 TEASPOON CHOPPED GINGER
- 1 SCALLION (SPRING ONION), CHOPPED
- 1 TEASPOON LIGHT SOY SAUCE
- 1 TABLESPOON GRANULATED SUGAR
- 2 TABLESPOONS SHAOXING WINE
- STEAMED RICE (PAGE 540), TO SERVE

REGION: SICHUAN
PREPARATION TIME: 20 MINUTES,
  PLUS 5 MINUTES SOAKING TIME
COOKING TIME: 5 MINUTES
SERVES: 4
📷 PAGE 513

麻婆豆腐
MAPO TOFU

- 1 LB/450 G FIRM TOFU, DRAINED AND CUT INTO ¾-INCH/2-CM CUBES
- 1 TEASPOON SALT
- 3 TABLESPOONS VEGETABLE OIL
- 3½ OZ/100 G GROUND (MINCED) PORK
- 1 TEASPOON FERMENTED BLACK BEANS, RINSED AND CHOPPED
- 1 TABLESPOON PIXIAN CHILI PASTE, CHOPPED
- 2 TEASPOONS CHOPPED GINGER
- 2 TEASPOONS CHOPPED GARLIC
- 1 TEASPOON CHILI POWDER
- 2 TEASPOONS LIGHT SOY SAUCE
- ½ TEASPOON GRANULATED SUGAR
- ½ TABLESPOON CORNSTARCH (CORNFLOUR)
- 1 TEASPOON SESAME OIL
- 2 SCALLIONS (SPRING ONIONS), CHOPPED
- ½ TEASPOON GROUND SICHUAN PEPPER
- STEAMED RICE (PAGE 540), TO SERVE

* Soak the tofu in a bowl of hot water, add ½ teaspoon salt, and set aside for 5 minutes. Drain.
* Heat the vegetable oil in a wok or large skillet (frying pan) over medium heat, add the pork, and stir-fry for 2–3 minutes until most of the liquid has evaporated.
* Put in the fermented black beans, chili paste, ginger, and garlic. Stir in the chili powder, add 4 tablespoons water, and bring to a boil.
* Add the tofu, gently stir, and reduce to low heat. Simmer, covered, for about 1 minute. Stir in the soy sauce, sugar, and the remaining ½ teaspoon salt.
* Mix the cornstarch (cornflour) with 1 tablespoon water in a small bowl and stir this mixture into the wok. Bring to a boil, stirring, for about 30 seconds to thicken the sauce. Add the sesame oil and scallions (spring onions), toss, and transfer to a serving bowl. Sprinkle over the ground Sichuan pepper and serve with rice.

REGION: BUDDHIST VEGETARIAN
PREPARATION TIME: 10 MINUTES
COOKING TIME: 10 MINUTES
SERVES: 4

炒豆腐脑
MASHED TOFU STEW

- 3 TABLESPOONS VEGETABLE OIL
- ⅛ OZ/5 G GINGER (ABOUT ½-INCH/ 1-CM-LENGTH PIECE), SLICED
- ⅓ CARROT, GRATED
- 1 SCALLION (SPRING ONION), CHOPPED
- 1 LB 2 OZ/500 G TOFU, MASHED
- 2¾ CUPS (23 FL OZ/700 ML) HOT VEGETABLE BROTH (STOCK, PAGE 92)
- ½ TEASPOON SALT
- 1 TABLESPOON CORNSTARCH
- 1 SPRIG CILANTRO (CORIANDER), LEAVES ONLY

* Heat 1 tablespoon oil in a wok or large skillet (frying pan) over low heat. Add the ginger and fry for 2 minutes until crispy. Discard ginger and reserve the oil.
* Heat 2 tablespoons oil in the wok. Add the grated carrot and deep-fry over low heat for 2–3 minutes. Strain the carrot oil through a fine strainer (sieve). Discard the carrots and return the oil to the wok.
* Heat the carrot oil over medium-high heat. Add the scallion (spring onion) and stir-fry for 1 minute until fragrant. Add the tofu and stir until the oil and tofu are thoroughly blended.
* Add the vegetable broth (stock) and salt and bring to a boil. Mix the cornstarch (cornflour) with 3 tablespoons water and add this mixture to the wok. Bring to a boil, stirring, for about 30 seconds to thicken the sauce. Drizzle the reserved ginger oil over the soup and top with cilantro (coriander) leaves to serve.

MAPO TOFU

REGION: FUJIAN
PREPARATION TIME: 15 MINUTES, PLUS
  30 MINUTES MARINATING TIME
COOKING TIME: 10 MINUTES
SERVES: 2

- 5 OZ/150 G GROUND (MINCED) PORK
- ½ TEASPOON SALT
- ½ TEASPOON GRANULATED SUGAR
- 3 DRIED BLACK MUSHROOMS
- 1 LB 2 OZ/500 G FIRM TOFU, DRAINED
- 2 OZ/50 G SICHUAN PRESERVED
  MUSTARD GREENS, RINSED, TRIMMED
  AND CHOPPED
- PINCH OF GROUND WHITE PEPPER
- 1 TABLESPOON CORNSTARCH
  (CORNFLOUR)
- ½ CUP (2 OZ/60 G) OATMEAL
- 1 CUP (8 FL OZ/250 ML)
  VEGETABLE OIL
- WORCESTERSHIRE SAUCE OR SWEET
  AND SOUR SAUCE (PAGE 169), TO SERVE

* Combine the ground (minced) pork, salt, sugar, and
  1 tablespoon water in a bowl and marinate for 30 minutes.
  Stir with chopsticks in one direction, until the pork begins
  to turn gummy.
* Put the mushrooms in a bowl, cover with cold water, and
  soak for at least 20 minutes, or until softened. Remove and
  discard the stems and chop.
* Pat dry the tofu with paper towels, then break it up into
  chunks. Add to the bowl of pork, then stir in the preserved
  mustard, mushrooms, white pepper, and cornstarch
  (cornflour) in one direction until well blended. Form 12 balls.
* Roughly grind the oatmeal in a food processor and transfer
  to a plate. Roll the tofu balls in the oatmeal to coat and
  place on a plate.
* Heat the oil in a wok or deep saucepan to 300°F/150°C,
  or until a cube of bread browns in 1½ minutes. Carefully
  lower the tofu balls, a few at a time, into the oil and deep-
  fry for 3–4 minutes until golden brown. Serve with either
  Worcestershire sauce or sweet and sour sauce.

八公山豆腐
BAGONGSHAN
TOFU

REGION: ANHUI
PREPARATION TIME: 10 MINUTES,
  PLUS 10 MINUTES SOAKING TIME
COOKING TIME: 10 MINUTES
SERVES: 4

- ½ CUP (¼ OZ/10 G) DRIED BLACK
  FUNGUS
- ½ CUP (2 OZ/50 G) PLUS 1 TEASPOON
  CORNSTARCH (CORNFLOUR)
- 9 OZ/250 G FIRM TOFU, DRAINED AND
  CUT INTO ¾-INCH/2-CM CUBES
- 2 CUPS (16 FL OZ/475 ML) VEGETABLE
  OIL
- 1 TABLESPOON DRIED SHRIMP ROE
- ¼ CUP (1 OZ/25 G) SLICED BAMBOO
  SHOOTS, DRAINED
- 1 SCALLION (SPRING ONION), CUT
  INTO ¾-INCH/2-CM LENGTHS
- 3 TABLESPOONS LIGHT SOY SAUCE
- ⅓ TEASPOON SALT
- STEAMED RICE (PAGE 540), TO SERVE

* Cover the black fungus in cold water and soak for about
  10 minutes, or until soft. Drain, then tear into 1¼-inch/
  3-cm squares.
* Mix ½ cup (2 fl oz/60 ml) cornstarch (cornflour) with
  3 tablespoons water. Add the tofu and stir until well coated.
* Heat the oil in a wok or deep saucepan to about 300°F/150°C,
  or until a cube of bread browns in 45 seconds. Add the tofu
  and deep-fry for 2–3 minutes until golden. Use a slotted
  spoon to remove the tofu and drain on paper towels.
* Pour out most of the oil, leaving about 1 tablespoon in the
  wok. Add the shrimp roe, bamboo shoots, black fungus,
  and scallion and stir-fry over medium heat for 30 seconds.
  Add the tofu, soy sauce, salt, and 3 tablespoons water and
  bring to a boil.
* Mix the remaining 1 teaspoon cornstarch with 1 tablespoon
  water and stir the mixture into the wok. Bring to a boil,
  stirring, for about 30 seconds to thicken the sauce. Transfer
  the mixture to a serving plate and serve with rice.

金相玉

STIR-FRIED TOFU
AND PORK

REGION: JIANGXI
PREPARATION TIME: 20 MINUTES
COOKING TIME: 15 MINUTES
SERVES: 4

* Place the tofu on a heatproof plate and into a collapsible pot or bamboo steamer over a pot of boiling water. Steam, covered, for 5 minutes. Drain the water from the plate, and set aside.
* Combine the pork, light soy sauce, and ½ teaspoon cornstarch (cornflour) in a bowl and mix well. Set aside.
* Divide the tofu into two portions and cut one portion into ⅛-inch/3-mm-wide strips. Cut the remaining portion into very thin slices and pat dry with paper towels.
* Heat 2 tablespoons vegetable oil in a wok or skillet (frying pan) over medium heat, add the tofu slices, and pan-fry for 3–4 minutes until golden brown. Remove from wok and cut the slices into ⅛-inch/3 mm-thin strips.
* Using the oil already in the wok over high heat, stir-fry the ginger and scallions (spring onions) for 1–2 minutes until fragrant. Add the pork and stir-fry for 3–4 minutes until cooked through.
* Add the fried and unfried tofu strips, black fungus, cayenne peppers, and bamboo shoots. Sprinkle the wine, then add the chicken broth (stock), dark soy sauce, and salt and stir well.
* Mix the cornstarch with 1 tablespoon water in a small bowl and stir this mixture into the wok. Bring to a boil, stirring, for about 30 seconds to thicken the sauce. Stir in the sesame oil and white pepper. Transfer to a serving plate and serve with rice.

• 1 LB 2 OZ/500 G FIRM TOFU, DRAINED
• 2¾ OZ/75 G PORK TENDERLOIN, CUT INTO FINE STRIPS
• ½ TEASPOON LIGHT SOY SAUCE
• 1½ TEASPOON CORNSTARCH (CORNFLOUR)
• 3 TABLESPOONS VEGETABLE OIL
• ¾ OZ/20 G GINGER (ABOUT 1-INCH/ 2.5-CM-LENGTH PIECE), CHOPPED
• 2 SCALLIONS (SPRING ONIONS), CHOPPED
• ½ CUP (¼ OZ/10 G) DRIED BLACK FUNGUS, SOAKED IN WATER TO SOFTEN, STEMS DISCARDED, AND CAPS CUT INTO FINE STRIPS
• 2 CAYENNE PEPPERS, SEEDED AND CUT INTO FINE STRIPS
• ⅔ CUP (9 OZ/250 G) SLICED BAMBOO SHOOTS, DRAINED
• 1 TABLESPOON RICE WINE
• 2 TABLESPOONS CHICKEN BROTH (STOCK, PAGE 90)
• 1 TEASPOON DARK SOY SAUCE
• ½ TEASPOON SALT
• ¼ TEASPOON SESAME OIL
• ⅛ TEASPOON GROUND WHITE PEPPER
• STEAMED RICE (PAGE 540), TO SERVE

REGION: BUDDHIST VEGETARIAN
PREPARATION TIME: 10 MINUTES
COOKING TIME: 10 MINUTES
SERVES: 2

梅菜素扣肉
PRESERVED MUSTARD HEARTS WITH TOFU

- 2¾ OZ/75 G PRESERVED SWEET MUSTARD HEARTS
- 1 TABLESPOON GRANULATED SUGAR
- ½ TABLESPOON SHAOXING WINE
- ½ TABLESPOON GINGER JUICE
- 2 TABLESPOONS VEGETABLE OIL
- 2 PIECES SEMI-DRIED TOFU (ABOUT (2 OZ/50 G TOTAL), EACH CUT INTO 12 SLICES
- STEAMED RICE (PAGE 540), TO SERVE

* Cover the mustard hearts with cold water and soak for 5 minutes. Rinse under cold running water. Squeeze out excess water. Trim the mustard hearts, then chop and put them into a bowl. Mix in the sugar, wine, and ginger juice and stir in the oil.
* Line the inside of a 2-cup (17-fl oz/500-ml) heatproof bowl with the tofu slices. Add the chopped mustard hearts and smooth out their surface. Seal the bowl with aluminum foil.
* Place the bowl in a collapsible pot or bamboo steamer over a pot of boiling water. Steam, covered, for 10 minutes.
* Remove and drain the sauce to another bowl. Cover the bowl of tofu and mustard hearts with a plate and using dish towels, invert the tofu and vegetables onto a serving plate (Alternatively, use tongs to transfer the contents). Pour the sauce on top of the tofu and serve with rice.

REGION: BEIJING
PREPARATION TIME: 10 MINUTES
COOKING TIME: 15 MINUTES
SERVES: 4

锅塌豆腐
DEEP-FRIED TOFU

- 1 LB 2 OZ/500 G FIRM TOFU, DRAINED
- 1 SCALLION (SPRING ONION), FINELY CHOPPED
- 1 TEASPOON FINELY CHOPPED GINGER
- 2 TEASPOONS SHAOXING WINE
- 3 CUPS (25 FL OZ/750 ML) VEGETABLE OIL
- 3 TABLESPOONS ALL-PURPOSE (PLAIN) FLOUR
- 2 EGGS, BEATEN
- SCANT ½ CUP (3½ FL OZ/100 ML) CHICKEN BROTH (STOCK, PAGE 90)
- 1 TEASPOON SALT
- 1 TEASPOON SESAME OIL
- STEAMED RICE (PAGE 540), TO SERVE

* Cut the tofu lengthwise into two, then crosswise into ¼-inch/5-mm-thick pieces. Place the tofu on a plate and sprinkle ½ teaspoon chopped scallions (spring onions), ½ teaspoon chopped ginger, and 1 teaspoon wine.
* Heat the vegetable oil in a wok or deep saucepan to 300°F/150°C, or until a cube of bread browns in 1½ minutes. Dredge the tofu with flour, then dip it into the beaten egg. Carefully lower the tofu into the oil and deep-fry for 2–3 minutes until golden brown. Use a slotted spoon to carefully remove the tofu from the oil and drain on paper towels. Trim off any loose egg strands.
* Pour out most of the oil, leaving about 2 tablespoons in the wok. Add the remaining scallions and ginger and stir-fry over medium-high heat for 1 minute until fragrant. Add the chicken broth (stock), salt, remaining wine, and deep-fried tofu and bring to a boil. Stir-fry over medium-low heat until the liquid has completely evaporated.
* Gently stir in the sesame oil and transfer to a serving plate. Serve with rice.

VEGETABLES, TOFU & EGGS

鸡火干丝

SEMI-DRIED TOFU WITH CHICKEN AND HAM

REGION: JIANGSU
PREPARATION TIME: 30 MINUTES
COOKING TIME: 2½–3 HOURS
SERVES: 4

This is a classical dish of Yangzhou in the Jiangsu Province and was one of many dishes served to the Emperor Qianlong in the Qing Dynasty during one of his south China tours.

* Bring 8½ cups (68 fl oz/2 liters) water to a boil in a large saucepan, add the chicken and ginger slices, cover, and return to a boil over high heat. Turn off the heat and let the chicken steep in the hot water, covered, for 30 minutes. Use tongs to remove the chicken and let it cool.
* Transfer the chicken to a cutting board, back facing down, and use a sharp knife to cut out the chicken breasts. Tear the breasts into fine strands and set aside.
* Return the remainder of the chicken to the saucepan. Bring the pan of chicken and broth (stock) to a boil and cook, uncovered, for another 2 hours over low heat, or until about 3 cups (25 fl oz/750 ml) chicken broth remains. Add ½ teaspoon salt.
* Use a ladle to skim away the oil from the surface of the broth, remove from the heat, then pour the broth into a cheesecloth (muslin)-lined sieve (strainer) set over a bowl. Reserve for later use.
* Meanwhile, soak the ham in cold water for 30 minutes, then rinse and drain. Soak the tofu in a bowl with 2 cups (16 fl oz/475 ml) water and 1 teaspoon salt for 30 minutes. Drain.
* Place the ham in a collapsible pot or bamboo steamer over a pot of boiling water. Steam, covered, for 5 minutes. Remove the ham and slice into very thin strips.
* Place the tofu in a saucepan, add fresh water to cover, and bring to a boil for 2 minutes. Drain.
* Bring 3 cups (25 fl oz/750 ml) reserved chicken broth (stock) to a boil in a clean saucepan, add the shredded chicken and ham, and cook over medium heat for 5 minutes. Stir in the tofu and simmer for 5 minutes, then add the sesame oil. Transfer to a serving bowl and serve.

- 1 (2½-LB/1.2-KG) WHOLE CHICKEN
- ¼ OZ/5 G GINGER (ABOUT ½-INCH/ 1-CM-LENGTH PIECE), SLICED
- 1½ TEASPOONS SALT
- ¾ OZ/20 G JINHUA OR SMITHFIELD HAM
- 2 SEMI-DRIED TOFU, TRIMMED OF THE HARD SKIN AND SLICED INTO THIN STRIPS
- ½ TEASPOON SESAME OIL

蟹粉豆腐
TOFU WITH CRAB MEAT
AND CRAB ROE

- 3 SALTED DUCK EGGS
- 2 TABLESPOONS VEGETABLE OIL
- 2 OZ/50 G GINGER (ABOUT 3-INCH/ 7.5-CM-LENGTH PIECE), CHOPPED
- ⅔ CARROT, GRATED
- 1 TEASPOON SALT
- 1 TEASPOON GRANULATED SUGAR
- 1 TEASPOON ZHENJIANG OR BALSAMIC VINEGAR
- 2 TOFU, DRAINED AND CUT INTO ½-INCH/1.5-CM PIECES
- 2 TEASPOONS CORNSTARCH (CORNFLOUR)
- 3 TABLESPOONS CRAB MEAT AND TOMALLEY
- 1½ TABLESPOONS CRAB ROE
- CHOPPED CILANTRO (CORIANDER) AND SCALLIONS (SPRING ONIONS), TO GARNISH (OPTIONAL)

* Place the salted duck eggs in a collapsible pot or bamboo steamer over a pot of boiling water. Steam, covered, for 5 minutes. Carefully remove and cool.
* Discard the egg whites. Put the egg yolks in a bowl and crush with the back of a fork. Set aside.
* Heat the oil in a wok or large skillet (frying pan). Add the ginger and carrot and stir-fry over medium heat for 1 minute until fragrant. Put in three-quarters of the salted egg yolks and 4 tablespoons water, bring to a boil, and season with salt, sugar, and vinegar. Add the tofu, stir gently, and cook for 30 seconds.
* Mix the cornstarch (cornflour) with 2 tablespoons water in a small bowl and stir this mixture into the wok. Bring to a boil, stirring, for about 30 seconds to thicken the sauce. Transfer to a serving bowl.
* Add 2 tablespoons water to the wok, bring to a boil, and stir in the crab meat and tomalley and the remaining salted egg yolks. Dish out and put on top of the tofu. Finish with a sprinkling of crab roe, cilantro (coriander), and scallions (spring onions), if using.

香椿拌豆腐
TOFU WITH SALTED
TOONA SHOOTS

- ¼ CUP (2 OZ/50 G) SALTED CHINESE TOONA SHOOTS, RINSED
- 1 TABLESPOON SESAME PASTE
- 9 OZ/250 G FIRM TOFU, DRAINED AND CUT INTO ½-INCH/1-CM CUBES
- 1 TEASPOON SESAME OIL
- ½ TEASPOON SALT
- STEAMED RICE (PAGE 540), TO SERVE

* Soak the Chinese toona shoots in a bowl of cold water, covered, for 15 minutes.
* Bring a large saucepan of water to a boil, add the toona, and blanch 30 seconds. Drain and rinse under cold running water. Finely chop and set aside.
* Put the sesame paste into a bowl and stir in 1 teaspoon water.
* In a serving bowl, combine the tofu, toona, sesame paste, sesame oil, and salt. Mix and serve at room temperature with rice.

VEGETABLES, TOFU & EGGS

TOFU WITH CRAB MEAT AND CRAB ROE

REGION: SHANDONG
PREPARATION TIME: 10 MINUTES
COOKING TIME: 15 MINUTES
SERVES: 4

炒豆腐泥
TOFU MASH

- 4 TABLESPOONS VEGETABLE OIL
- 11 OZ/300 G SOFT TOFU, DRAINED AND MASHED
- 2½ TABLESPOONS DRIED SHRIMP, SOAKED IN WATER UNTIL SOFT, DRAINED, AND CHOPPED
- 1 OZ/25 G PRESERVED MUSTARD GREENS, TRIMMED, RINSED, AND CHOPPED
- 2 TABLESPOONS SHAOXING WINE
- ½ SCALLION (SPRING ONION), CHOPPED
- ½ TEASPOON CHOPPED GINGER
- ⅛ TEASPOON SALT
- 2 TABLESPOONS CHICKEN BROTH (STOCK, PAGE 90)
- 2 CHINESE LEEKS, CUT INTO 1½-INCH/4-CM LENGTHS
- ½ TEASPOON CORNSTARCH (CORNFLOUR)
- 1 TEASPOON SESAME OIL
- STEAMED RICE (PAGE 540), TO SERVE

* Heat 2 tablespoons vegetable oil in a wok or large skillet (frying pan) over medium low heat, add the mashed tofu, and stir-fry for 3 minutes to remove most of the moisture. Remove from the wok and set aside. Wipe the wok with paper towels.
* Add 1 tablespoon vegetable oil and stir-fry the dried shrimp over medium-high heat for 1 minute until aromatic. Add the mustard greens and 1 tablespoon wine, then stir-fry for another 2–3 minutes until most of the moisture has evaporated. Remove from the wok and divide the shrimp-and-mustard greens mixture into 2 portions.
* Heat the remaining 1 tablespoon vegetable oil in the wok, add the scallion (spring onion) and ginger, and stir-fry over high heat for 1 minute until fragrant. Add the tofu paste, 1 portion of the mustard greens mixture, put in the remaining 1 tablespoon wine, salt, and chicken broth (stock), and then stir in the leeks.
* Mix the cornstarch (cornflour) with ½ tablespoon water in a small bowl and stir this mixture into the wok. Bring to a boil, stirring, for about 30 seconds to thicken the sauce.
* Drizzle over the sesame oil and transfer to a serving a plate. Top with the shrimp and mustard greens. Serve with rice.

REGION: GUANGDONG
PREPARATION TIME: 5 MINUTES,
   PLUS 10 MINUTES SOAKING TIME
COOKING TIME: 10 MINUTES
SERVES: 6–8

椒盐豆腐
TOFU WITH
SPICED SALT

- 1 LB 2 OZ/500 G FIRM TOFU, DRAINED AND CUT INTO ¾-INCH/2-CM CUBES
- 1 TEASPOON SALT
- 2 CUPS (16 FL OZ/475 ML) VEGETABLE OIL
- 4 TABLESPOONS ALL-PURPOSE (PLAIN) FLOUR
- 2 SCALLIONS (SPRING ONIONS), CHOPPED
- 2 CLOVES GARLIC, CHOPPED

  FOR THE SPICED SALT:
- 1 TEASPOON SALT
- ½ TEASPOON FIVE-SPICE POWDER
- 1 TEASPOON SHAJIANG POWDER
- ½ TEASPOON CHILI POWDER

* Soak the tofu in 2 cups (16 fl oz/475 ml) water, add the salt, and set aside for 10 minutes. Drain the tofu.
* To make the spiced salt, heat the salt in a dry saucepan over medium heat for 2 minutes, then remove the pan from the heat, mix in the remaining spiced salt ingredients, and set aside.
* Heat the oil in a wok or large skillet (frying pan) to about 265°F/130°C. Dust the tofu cubes with the flour, then deep-fry for about 2–3 minutes until brown.
* Pour out most of the oil, leaving 1 tablespoon in the wok. Add the scallions (spring onions) and garlic and stir-fry over medium heat for 1 minute until fragrant. Add the fried tofu, toss to mix it with the other ingredients, then mix in 1 teaspoon of the spiced salt. Transfer to a serving plate.

鸡汁百页包

TOFU ROLL IN
CHICKEN BROTH

REGION: SHANGHAI
PREPARATION TIME: 30 MINUTES
COOKING TIME: 15 MINUTES
SERVES: 4

* In a large bowl, combine 4¼ cups (34 fl oz/1 liter) water and the baking soda (bicarbonate of soda). Add the tofu sheets and soak for 15 minutes until the sheets become an off-white color. Rinse thoroughly in water.
* Bring a large saucepan of water to a boil over high heat, add the cabbage, and blanch for 3 minutes. Using a slotted spoon, transfer the cabbage to a colander and rinse under cold running water. Squeeze the water from the cabbage and chop.
* Reboil the water in the pan over high heat. Cut the leaves from the Chinese leeks, add to the water, and leave for 15 seconds, until softened. Using a slotted spoon, remove the leaves immediately.
* When cool enough to handle, cut each leaf in half lengthwise down the center and set aside (these will be used to secure the tofu rolls).
* To prepare the filling, combine the pork, shrimp (prawns), cabbage, salt, sugar, soy sauce, white pepper, and cornstarch (cornflour) and mix well. Divide the filling into 16 equal portions.
* Cut each tofu sheet into quarters. Put one portion of filling along one edge of a tofu sheet, roll halfway, tuck in the ends, then continue to roll. Repeat with the remaining tofu wraps and filling. Tie each tofu roll with a piece of the reserved leek leaf.
* Bring the chicken broth (stock) to a boil in a saucepan, add the tofu roll, reduce to low heat, cover, and simmer for 10 minutes. Transfer the tofu rolls and chicken broth to a shallow bowl and serve with rice.

- 1 TEASPOON BAKING SODA (BICARBONATE OF SODA)
- 4 TOFU SHEETS
- 7 OZ/200 G NAPA CABBAGE, LEAVES SEPARATED
- 1 BUNCH CHINESE LEEKS
- 9 OZ/250 G GROUND (MINCED) PORK
- 2 OZ/50 G UNCOOKED SHRIMP (PRAWNS), SHELLED, DEVEINED, AND COARSELY CHOPPED
- ½ TEASPOON SALT
- ½ TEASPOON GRANULATED SUGAR
- 1 TEASPOON LIGHT SOY SAUCE
- PINCH OF GROUND WHITE PEPPER
- 1 TABLESPOON CORNSTARCH (CORNFLOUR)
- 2 CUPS (16 FL OZ/475 ML) CHICKEN BROTH (STOCK, PAGE 90)
- STEAMED RICE (PAGE 540), TO SERVE

521

翡翠素方
VEGETABLE ROLL

- 1 TABLESPOON WHITE SESAME SEEDS
- 1 DRIED TOFU SKIN (ABOUT
  20 INCHES/50 CM), SOFTENED
  ACCORDING TO PACKAGE
  INSTRUCTIONS
- 2 CUPS (1 LB/450 G) PACKED SPINACH
  LEAVES OR ANY OTHER LEAFY
  VEGETABLE
- 4 DRIED BLACK MUSHROOMS,
  SOAKED IN WATER UNTIL SOFT, STEMS
  DISCARDED, AND CAPS FINELY SLICED
- 4 TABLESPOONS SHREDDED CARROT
  (OPTIONAL)
- 1 TABLESPOON PORCINI MUSHROOM
  POWDER
- ¾ TEASPOON SALT
- ½ TEASPOON SESAME OIL
- 1 EGG, BEATEN
- 1 TABLESPOON VEGETABLE OIL
- CILANTRO (CORIANDER), TO GARNISH
  (OPTIONAL)

* Toast the sesame seeds in a small pan over medium heat and shake occasionally for 3–5 minutes or until golden brown. Set aside.
* Fold the tofu skin into a quadrant and trim the sides to create 4 square pieces.
* Bring a large saucepan of water to a boil over high heat, add the spinach, and blanch for 30 seconds. Drain and rinse under cold running water. Use your hands to squeeze out excess moisture. Coarsely chop the leaves.
* For the filling, combine the spinach, mushrooms, carrots (if using), porcini powder, sesame seeds, salt, and sesame oil in a bowl. Divide the filling into 4 equal portions.
* Brush some egg onto a piece of tofu skin, place the filling along one edge of the rectangle. Roll the skin, tucking in the edges, then finish rolling it up.
* Heat the vegetable oil in a large skillet (frying pan), add the vegetable rolls, and brown on both sides over medium-low heat for 4–6 minutes, then remove from the pan and drain on paper towels. Cut each roll into 5 pieces before serving. Garnish with cilantro (coriander), if using.

烫干丝
YANGZHOU TOFU
SALAD

- 2 YANGZHOU SEMI-DRIED TOFU PIECES
  1 TEASPOON SALT
- 2 TABLESPOONS LIGHT SOY SAUCE
- 1 TABLESPOON ZHENJIANG OR
  BALSAMIC VINEGAR
- 1 TEASPOON GRANULATED SUGAR
- 2 TABLESPOONS SESAME OIL
- ¼ OZ/10 G GINGER (ABOUT ¾-INCH/
  2-CM-LENGTH PIECE), SHREDDED
- 1 SPRIG CILANTRO (CORIANDER),
  CHOPPED

* Rinse the tofu and trim all the sides to remove the hardened skin. Slice the tofu into 1/12-inch/2-mm-thick slices, then again to make 1/12-inch/2-mm thick strips.
* Soak the tofu strips in 2 cups (16 fl oz/475 ml) water, add the salt, and set aside for 30 minutes. Transfer to a colander to drain.
* Combine the soy sauce, vinegar, sugar, and sesame oil in a bowl to make a sauce.
* Bring 2 cups (16 fl oz/475 ml) water to a boil. Pour the boiling water over the tofu in the colander. Let drain.
* Put the tofu into a bowl, then top with the sauce, ginger, and cilantro (coriander).

VEGETABLE ROLL

REGION: HAKKA
PREPARATION TIME: 15 MINUTE
 PLUS 3 HOURS SOAKING TIME
COOKING TIME: 20 MINUTES
SERVES: 4

东江豆腐煲
HAKKA-STYLE
TOFU CASSEROLE

- ½ CUP (3½ OZ/100 G) DRIED SOYBEANS
- 1 CUP (8 FL OZ/250 ML)
  VEGETABLE OIL
- 1 OZ/30 G SALTED FISH
- 7 OZ/200 G GROUND (MINCED) PORK
- 3 SCALLIONS (SPRING ONIONS) STEMS
  ONLY, CHOPPED
- 1 LB 2 OZ/500 G FIRM TOFU, DRAINED
- 2 CUPS (16 FL OZ/475 ML) CHICKEN
  BROTH (STOCK, PAGE 90)
- 2 STALKS CHINESE LEEKS, CUT INTO
  2½-INCH/6-CM LENGTHS AND STEMS
  FLATTENED
- 1 TEASPOON SALT
- PINCH OF GROUND WHITE PEPPER
- STEAMED RICE (PAGE 540), TO SERVE

* Soak the soybeans in a bowl of cold water for 3 hours.
  Drain.
* Heat the oil in a wok or large skillet (frying pan) to 300°F/
  150°C, or until a cube of bread browns in 1½ minutes.
  Add the soybeans and deep-fry for 3–4 minutes until crispy.
  Use a slotted spoon to carefully remove the soybeans
  from the oil and drain on paper towels. Pour out most
  of the oil from the wok, leaving about 2 tablespoons.
  Set aside.
* Place the salted fish in a collapsible pot or bamboo steamer
  over a pot of boiling water. Steam, covered, for 3 minutes.
  Carefully remove and cool briefly. When cool enough to
  handle, take off the skin and remove all the bones. Put the
  salted fish flesh into a large bowl and combine with the
  pork and scallions (spring onions). Stir with chopsticks in
  one direction until the filling mixture becomes gummy.
* Cut the tofu into 8 rectangular pieces. Use a spoon to
  hollow out part of each piece and fill with the pork filling.
* Heat the oil in the wok over medium heat, add the tofu,
  meat-side down, and pan-fry for 2 minutes until golden
  brown. Set aside.
* Heat a Dutch oven (casserole), put in the chicken broth
  (stock), Chinese leek, salt, and white pepper and bring
  to a boil.
* Add the fried tofu and soybeans, reduce to low heat and
  simmer, covered, for 15 minutes. Serve with rice.

总督豆腐
VICEROY
TOFU

REGION: HEBEI
PREPARATION TIME: 10 MINUTES,
 PLUS 15 MINUTES SOAKING TIME
COOKING TIME: 10 MINUTES
SERVES: 4

Li Hung Zhang, a high official in the Qing Dynasty. was the viceroy of Hebei. As a food connoisseur, Li was very demanding and this tofu dish was one of his favorites.

* Soak the dried scallop in ¼ cup (2 fl oz/50 ml) water for 15 minutes. Drain the scallop and tear it into strands. Strain the water through a fine strainer (sieve) and reserve.
* Mix 2 tablespoons cornstarch (cornflour) with the flour, then toss the tofu cubes in the mixture to lightly coat.
* Heat the oil in a wok or large skillet (frying pan) over medium-high heat. Add the tofu cubes and deep-fry for 4 minutes, or until golden brown. Drain the tofu and transfer to a serving plate.
* Pour out most of the oil, leaving about 2 tablespoons in the wok. Add the ginger, garlic, and pickled chiles and stir-fry over medium-high heat for 1 minute until fragrant. Add the ground (minced) pork and stir-fry for 2 minutes, or until the pork is fully cooked. Stir in the chili sauce, wine, salt, sugar, soy sauce, and the scallop soaking water and bring to a boil.
* Stir in the shrimp roe and scallop strands. Mix 1 teaspoon cornstarch (cornflour) with 1 tablespoon water, then stir this mixture into the wok. Bring to the boil, stirring, for about 30 seconds to thicken the sauce. Add the scallion (spring onion), toss well, then pour the sauce over the tofu on the plate. Serve with rice.

- 1 DRIED SCALLOP
- 2 TABLESPOONS PLUS 1 TEASPOON CORNSTARCH (CORNFLOUR)
- 2 TABLESPOONS ALL-PURPOSE (PLAIN) FLOUR
- 9 OZ/250 G FIRM TOFU, CUT INTO ¾-INCH/2-CM CUBES
- 1 CUP (8 FL OZ/250 ML) VEGETABLE OIL
- ⅛ OZ/5 G GINGER (ABOUT ½-INCH/ 1-CM-LENGTH PIECE), CHOPPED
- 2 CLOVES GARLIC, CHOPPED
- ¼ OZ/10 G PICKLED CHILES, CHOPPED
- 2 OZ/50 G GROUND (MINCED) PORK
- 1 TABLESPOON CHILI SAUCE
- 1 TABLESPOON RICE WINE
- ¼ TEASPOON SALT
- 1 TEASPOON GRANULATED SUGAR
- 1 TABLESPOON LIGHT SOY SAUCE
- 1 TEASPOON SHRIMP ROE
- 1 SCALLION (SPRING ONION), CHOPPED
- STEAMED RICE (PAGE 540), TO SERVE

REGION: ANHUI
PREPARATION TIME: 30 MINUTES, PLUS
  1 HOUR REFRIGERATION TIME
COOKING TIME: 10 MINUTES
SERVING: 6
📷 PAGE 527

朱洪武豆腐
ZHU HONGWU
TOFU

- 3½ OZ/100 G UNCOOKED SHRIMP
  (PRAWNS), SHELLED AND DEVEINED
- 3½ OZ/100 G GROUND (MINCED) PORK
- 1 TEASPOON SALT
- 2 TABLESPOONS CORNSTARCH
  (CORNFLOUR)
- ¼ TEASPOON GROUND WHITE PEPPER
- 9 OZ/250 G FIRM TOFU, DRAINED
- 4 EGG WHITES
- 3 CUPS (25 FL OZ/750 ML)
  VEGETABLE OIL
- SCANT ½ CUP (3½ FL OZ/100 ML)
  CHICKEN BROTH (STOCK, PAGE 90)
- 1 TEASPOON SHAOXING WINE
- 1 TABLESPOON ZHENJIANG OR
  BALSAMIC VINEGAR
- 1 TABLESPOON GRANULATED SUGAR
- 1 TABLESPOON CHOPPED SCALLIONS
  (SPRING ONIONS)
- 1 TABLESPOON CHOPPED GINGER
- STEAMED RICE (PAGE 540), TO SERVE

This dish was named after Zhu Yuanzhang (1328–1398), a monk turned founder and emperor of the Ming Dynasty. Legend has it that Zhu was a beggar when he was young and a kind-hearted restaurant owner used to offer him tofu to satisfy his hunger. When Zhu became emperor, he frequently asked his palace cooks to make this dish.

* Roll the shrimp in a clean dish towel and refrigerate for 1 hour.
* Combine the pork, ¼ teaspoon salt, and 2 tablespoons water in a bowl and marinate for 15 minutes. Mix in ½ teaspoon cornstarch (cornflour) and set aside.
* Remove the shrimp from the dish towel and place them on a cutting board. Use a heavy cleaver to flatten and chop the shrimp into a paste. Put the shrimp paste into a large bowl, add the white pepper and ¼ teaspoon salt, and mix with the pork.
* Using chopsticks, stir the mixture in a single direction until it becomes gluey in texture. Divide into 12 portions.
* Cut the tofu into 24 rectangular slices, measuring 1½ × ¾ × ¹/₁₂ inches/4 × 2 × 0.2 cm. Place 12 pieces on a large plate and spread one portion of the paste evenly on each piece. Top each tofu piece with another tofu piece to form a tofu sandwich. Set aside.
* Beat the egg whites in a small bowl until fluffy, add ½ tablespoon cornstarch, and mix to form an egg batter.
* Heat the oil in a wok or deep saucepan to 300°F/150°C, or until a cube of bread browns in 1½ minutes. Dip each tofu sandwich into the egg batter, one at a time, and carefully place in the hot oil. Deep-fry for 2–3 minutes until firm. Use a slotted spoon to carefully remove the tofu sandwich from the oil, and drain on paper towels.
* Reheat the oil to about 340°F/170°C, or until a cube of bread browns in 45 seconds. Carefully lower the tofu sandwiches and deep-fry for 1–2 minutes until golden brown. Use a slotted spoon to carefully remove the sandwiches from the oil and drain on paper towels. Pour out the oil from the wok and save it for other uses.
* Pour the chicken broth (stock) into the wok and bring to a boil over high heat. Add the wine, vinegar, sugar, and the remaining ½ teaspoon salt. Reduce to low heat, put in the tofu sandwiches, and bring to a boil. Mix the remaining 1 teaspoon cornstarch with 1 tablespoon water in a small bowl and stir in this mixture. Bring to a boil, stirring, for about 30 seconds, to thicken the sauce. Transfer the tofu sandwiches and sauce to a plate. Serve with rice.

ZHU HONGWU TOFU

大良炒鲜奶
DALIANG BATTERED
SHRIMP

- 1 OZ/300 G UNCOOKED SHRIMP
  (PRAWNS), SHELLED AND DEVEINED
- 1 TABLESPOON CORNSTARCH
  (CORNFLOUR)
- 1 TABLESPOON SALT
- ¼ OZ/10 G CURED HAM
- SCANT 1 CUP (7 FL OZ/200 ML)
  MILK
- 6 EGG WHITES
- 2 TABLESPOONS VEGETABLE OIL
- 1 TABLESPOON PINE NUTS
- STEAMED RICE (PAGE 540), TO SERVE

* Rub the shrimp (prawns) with ½ tablespoon cornstarch (cornflour), rinse, and pat dry with paper towels. Put the shrimp in a bowl and sprinkle with salt. Allow to marinate in the refrigerator for 30 minutes.
* Bring 4¼ cups (34 fl oz/1 liter) water to a boil in a large saucepan. Add the shrimp and blanch for 2 minutes until done. Remove the shrimp to a colander and drain.
* Place the ham on a heatproof plate in a collapsible pot or bamboo steamer over a pot of boiling water. Steam, covered, for 3 minutes. Allow the ham to cool, chop, and set aside.
* Combine the remaining ½ tablespoon cornstarch and 1 tablespoon milk in a large bowl. Mix well to form a wet starch. Stir in the remaining the milk.
* Beat the egg whites in a small bowl until smooth. Strain the egg whites through a fine mesh strainer (sieve) to remove the foam. Add the strained egg whites and shrimp to the milk mixture to make a batter.
* Heat the oil in a skillet (frying pan) over medium-high heat to about 340°F/170°C, or until a cube of bread browns in 45 seconds. Turn off the heat. Wait about 1 minute for the oil to cool, add the shrimp and batter, pouring it slowly into the center of the oil.
* When the milk begins to coagulate, use the back of a spatula (fish fry) to push the shrimp batter, allowing the mixture to coagulate layer by layer. If the mixture coagulates too slowly or has stopped coagulating altogether, turn the heat on to low, and continue to push with the spatula until all the mixture is coagulated. Transfer the shrimp to a plate and top with the pine nuts and the chopped ham. Serve with rice.

煎芙蓉蛋

EGG
FOO YUNG

REGION: HONG KONG
PREPARATION TIME: 5 MINUTES
COOKING TIME: 10 MINUTES
SERVES: 4

* Bring a saucepan of water to a boil, add the shrimp (prawns), and blanch for 1 minute. Use a slotted spoon and transfer them to a strainer (sieve) to drain. Rinse under cold running water.
* Add the bean sprouts to the water and blanch for 15 seconds, drain and rinse immediately.
* Beat the eggs in a bowl and mix in the shrimp, bean sprouts, and pork. Stir in the salt and 1 teaspoon oil.
* Heat the remaining 4 teaspoons oil in a skillet (frying pan) and tilt the pan from side to side. Pour in the egg mixture, allowing it to spread across the surface of the skillet, and fry over medium-high heat for 3–4 minutes until just done. Use a spatula (fish slice) to flip over and pan-fry for another 3 minutes, or until completely cooked. Serve with rice.

- 5 OZ/150 G UNCOOKED SHRIMP (PRAWNS), SHELLED AND DEVEINED
- 2¼ CUPS (2¾ OZ/75 G) BEAN SPROUTS, STEM ONLY
- 4 EGGS
- ¼ QUANTITY (OR 3 OZ/100 G) BARBECUE PORK (PAGE 394), CUT INTO THICK STRIPS
- ½ TEASPOON SALT
- 5 TEASPOONS VEGETABLE OIL
- STEAMED RICE (PAGE 540), TO SERVE

菜脯韭菜煎蛋

OMELET WITH PRESERVED
TURNIPS AND CHIVES

REGION: HAKKA
PREPARATION TIME: 10 MINUTES
COOKING TIME: 5 MINUTES
SERVES: 4

* Mix the tapioca starch with 2 tablespoons water in a small bowl, let it settle, and then slowly drain away the water, leaving behind a wet starch.
* Beat the eggs in another small bowl, then mix in the wet starch, salt, and sesame oil.
* Heat 1 tablespoon vegetable oil in a wok or large skillet (frying pan over medium heat). Add the preserved turnips and chives and stir-fry over medium heat for 1 minute until fragrant. Add the turnip and chives to the egg batter and mix well.
* Heat the remaining 2 tablespoons vegetable oil in the skillet (frying pan). Pour in the egg batter and cook over medium heat for 3–4 minutes until both sides are brown. Transfer the omelet to a serving plate and serve with rice.

- 1 TABLESPOON TAPIOCA STARCH OR CORNSTARCH (CORNFLOUR)
- 3 EGGS
- ½ TEASPOON SALT
- ¼ TEASPOON SESAME OIL
- 3 TABLESPOONS VEGETABLE OIL
- 3 TABLESPOONS SWEET PRESERVED TURNIPS, RINSED AND CHOPPED
- 5 OZ/150 G CHINESE CHIVES, CUT INTO 2¾-INCH/7-CM LENGTHS
- STEAMED RICE (PAGE 540), TO SERVE

煎蛋角

PORK OMELET

- 3½ OZ/100 G GROUND (MINCED) PORK
- ½ TEASPOON SALT
- ½ TEASPOON GRANULATED SUGAR
- 1½ TEASPOON CORNSTARCH
  (CORNFLOUR)
- 2 TABLESPOONS VEGETABLE OIL
- 3 TABLESPOONS SWEET PRESERVED
  TURNIPS, CHOPPED
- 4 EGGS
- PINCH OF GROUND WHITE PEPPER
- STEAMED RICE (PAGE 540), TO SERVE

* Combine the pork, salt, sugar, and 1 tablespoon water in a bowl and marinate for 10 minutes.
* Meanwhile, mix 2 tablespoons water with the cornstarch (cornflour) in a small bowl and stir well. After the starch has settled, slowly pour out the excess water leaving a wet starch.
* Heat 1 tablespoon oil in a wok or large skillet (frying pan) and add the pork and sweet preserved turnips. Stir-fry the pork and turnip over high heat for 2 minutes, then drain off the excess water and oil. Remove to a bowl and set aside.
* Beat eggs in a small bowl and add them to the wet starch to make an egg batter.
* Wipe the wok with paper towels and heat the remaining 1 tablespoon oil over medium-low heat. Add 1 tablespoon of the egg batter and immediately tilt the wok so that the batter forms a small round in the center. Put a spoonful of the minced pork and preserved turnips on one side of the egg batter round. Gently shake the wok from side to side to prevent the egg batter from sticking to the bottom, and cook for 2 minutes.
* Just before the omelet is cooked, use a spatula (fish slice) to gently fold one half over the top of the pork filling to form a half-moon shape and press the edges down lightly to seal. Flip the omelet over and lightly brown the other side for another 2 minutes. Transfer the omelet to a serving plate. Repeat with the remaining egg batter and filling until done. Serve with rice.

虾仁炒滑蛋
SCRAMBLED EGGS
WITH SHRIMP

REGION: GUANGDONG
PREPARATION TIME: 10 MINUTES
COOKING TIME: 5 MINUTES
SERVES: 4

* Season the shrimp (prawns) with ½ teaspoon salt and rub well, then rinse.
* Bring a saucepan of water to a boil, add the shrimp, and blanch for 1 minute. Drain and rinse under cold water.
* Beat the egg whites until fluffy. Add the lard and stir to mix. Add the egg yolks and remaining salt, and beat well, then mix in the shrimp.
* Heat the oil in a wok or large skillet (frying pan) to 340°F/170°C, or until a cube of bread browns in 45 seconds. Once hot, turn off the heat and pour in the eggs. Using a spatula (fish slice), push the eggs and shrimp to one side of the wok to form layers of cooked eggs. Transfer to a plate when the eggs are just under cooked. (If the oil has cooled down before the eggs are cooked, put the wok back on low heat to finish cooking the eggs.) Transfer to a plate and serve immediately. Serve with rice.

- 5 OZ/150 G UNCOOKED SHRIMP (PRAWNS), SHELLED AND DEVEINED
- 1 TEASPOON SALT
- 5 EGGS, SEPARATED
- 1 TABLESPOON MELTED LARD
- 2 TABLESPOONS VEGETABLE OIL
- STEAMED RICE (PAGE 540), TO SERVE

雪夜桃花
SCRAMBLED EGG WHITES
WITH SHRIMP

REGION: HENAN
PREPARATION TIME: 20 MINUTES, PLUS
   15 MINUTES STANDING TIME
COOKING TIME: 10 MINUTES
SERVES: 4

* Put the shrimp (prawns) into a bowl with the salt and set aside for 15 minutes. Bring a small saucepan of water to a boil over high heat, add the shrimp, and blanch for 1 minute. Drain and set aside to cool.
* Beat the egg whites in a medium bowl until foamy.
* Mix the cornstarch (cornflour) with 2 tablespoons water in a small bowl. After the starch has settled, slowly pour out the excess water leaving a wet starch.
* Filter the egg whites through a fine strainer (sieve) and stir in the wet starch to make a batter. Add the shrimp and mix well.
* Heat the 2 tablespoons oil in a wok or large skillet (frying pan) to 325°F/170°C, or until a cube of bread browns in 45 seconds. Turn off heat. Wait 1 minute to allow the oil to cool slightly, then pour the batter into the center of the wok. When batter begins to coagulate, use the back of a spatula (fish slices) to push the batter slowly and repeatedly, creating folds, until all the batter has coagulated. If needed, turn on to low heat and finish cooking the eggs to achieve soft scrambled egg. Transfer to a plate and top with the chopped ham. Serve with rice.

- 5 OZ/150 G UNCOOKED SHRIMP (PRAWNS), SHELLED AND DEVEINED
- 1 TEASPOON SALT
- 12 EGG WHITES
- 4 TABLESPOONS CORNSTARCH (CORNFLOUR)
- 2 TABLESPOONS VEGETABLE OIL
- ¼ OZ/10 G COOKED CURED HAM, CHOPPED
- STEAMED RICE (PAGE 540), TO SERVE

PREPARATION TIME: 5 MINUTES
COOKING TIME: 3-4 HOURS
SERVES: 8
📷 PAGE 533

茶叶蛋
TEA EGGS

- 8 EGGS
- 2 TABLESPOONS BLACK TEA LEAVES
- 1 TABLESPOON FIVE-SPICE POWDER
- 3 TABLESPOONS LIGHT SOY SAUCE
- 1 TEASPOON SALT
- 1 TABLESPOON GRANULATED SUGAR
- STEAMED RICE (PAGE 540), TO SERVE

* Put the eggs in 8½ cups (68 fl oz/2 liters) water in a saucepan and bring to a boil, then reduce to low heat and simmer for 5 minutes. Remove the eggs and flush under cold water until cool.
* Gently crack the eggs so that cracks show all over the eggs. Do not peel eggs.
* Boil 4¼ cups (1¾ pints/1 liter) water in a saucepan with the tea leaves, five-spice powder, soy sauce, salt, and sugar for 5 minutes. Add the eggs and return to a boil. Reduce to low heat, cover the saucepan, and simmer for 5 minutes.
* Turn off the heat and leave the eggs to steep in the sauce for 3–4 hours. Peel the eggs and serve.

REGION: HONG KONG
PREPARATION TIME: 10 MINUTES
COOKING TIME: 5 MINUTES
SERVES: 4

黑松露酱玉子豆腐
EGG TOFU WITH BLACK TRUFFLE SAUCE

- 11 OZ/300 G EGG TOFU
- 1 EGG, BEATEN
- 1 TABLESPOON VEGETABLE OIL
- 2 TABLESPOONS CORNSTARCH (CORNFLOUR)
- 3 TABLESPOONS BLACK TRUFFLE SAUCE
- 2 TABLESPOONS CHOPPED SCALLIONS (SPRING ONIONS)

* Carefully remove the egg tofu packet and cut the egg tofu into ½-inch/1.5-cm-thick slices.
* Heat the oil in a large skillet (frying pan).
* Lightly dredge each egg tofu slice with the cornstarch (cornflour), dip into the beaten egg, and add to the skillet. Pan-fry over low heat for 2–3 minutes until golden brown on both sides. Use a slotted spoon to carefully remove the egg tofu from the oil and drain on paper towels.
* Drizzle over a little black truffle sauce on each egg tofu piece and scatter with the chopped scallions (spring onions).

REGION: GUANGDONG
PREPARATION TIME: 10 MINUTES,
  PLUS 10 MINUTES SOAKING TIME
COOKING TIME: 20 MINUTES
SERVES: 4

粉丝虾米蒸水蛋
STEAMED EGGS
WITH DRIED SHRIMP
AND VERMICELLI

- ¾ OZ/20 G MUNG BEAN VERMICELLI
- 2 TABLESPOONS DRIED SHRIMP, RINSED
- 4 EGGS
- ¼ TEASPOON SALT
- STEAMED RICE (PAGE 540), TO SERVE

* Soak the mung bean vermicelli in a bowl of cold water for 10 minutes to soften. Drain, cut into 2½-inch/6-cm lengths, and place into a shallow heatproof bowl.
* Put the shrimp into a saucepan with 1 cup (8 fl oz/250 ml) water, bring to a boil over low heat for 1 minute, turn off heat and let the shrimp steep in the hot water for 10 minutes. Remove the shrimp and strain the liquid from the pan into a bowl and set aside to cool for later use. Place the shrimp evenly on top of the vermicelli.
* In a bowl, combine the shrimp liquid and enough water to make 2½ cups (18 fl oz/550 ml). Beat the eggs in a large bowl. Add the shrimp liquid and the salt, pour the mixture over the shrimp and vermicelli, and seal with microwave-safe plastic wrap (clingfilm). Place in a collapsible pot or bamboo steamer over a pot of water. Bring to a boil, then reduce to a simmer, and steam, covered, for about 15 minutes, or until the eggs are firm. If not, steam for another 2–3 minutes.
* Remove the plastic wrap and serve with rice.

榨菜肉松蒸滑蛋
STEAMED EGGS WITH PRESERVED MUSTARD AND PORK FLOSS

REGION: HONG KONG
PREPARATION TIME: 10 MINUTES
COOKING TIME: 10 MINUTES
SERVES: 4

* Combine the tofu with ¼ teaspoon salt in a bowl. Set aside for 10 minutes, then drain.
* Soak the preserved mustard greens in a bowl of water for 5 minutes. Drain, trim and chop.
* Beat the eggs and strain through a fine strainer (sieve) to remove the foam. Stir in the chicken broth (stock) and remaining ¼ teaspoon salt, then add the tofu and transfer to a shallow heatproof bowl. Top with the preserved mustard greens. Seal with aluminum foil and place in a collapsible pot or bamboo steamer over a pot of boiling water. Steam, covered, for 10 minutes.
* Lift off the wrap and top the eggs with the pork floss and scallions (spring onions). Serve with rice.

• 9 OZ/250 G SOFT TOFU, DRAINED AND CUT INTO ½-INCH/1.5-CM DICE
• ½ TEASPOON SALT
• ¼ OZ/10 G SICHUAN PRESERVED MUSTARD GREENS
• 2 EGGS
• 1 CUP (8 FL OZ/240 ML) CHICKEN BROTH (STOCK, PAGE 90)
• 3 TABLESPOONS PORK FLOSS
• 2 SCALLIONS (SPRING ONIONS), CHOPPED
• STEAMED RICE (PAGE 540), TO SERVE

炒桂花翅
VERMICELLI WITH EGGS

REGION: GUANGDONG
PREPARATION TIME: 10 MINUTES
COOKING TIME: 5 MINUTES
SERVES: 4

* Soak the mung bean vermicelli in a bowl of cold water for 5 minutes. Drain and cut into 3–inch/7.5-cm lengths.
* Bring a saucepan of water to a boil over high heat, add the bean sprouts and cook for 15 seconds. Drain immediately.
* Beat the eggs with the salt in a small bowl.
* Heat the oil in nonstick skillet (frying pan). Add the ham, and stir-fry over medium-low heat for 1 minute. Put in the vermicelli and stir-fry for another 3–4 minutes, adding the chicken broth (stock) gradually, until the vermicelli is soft. Add enough broth so that the vermicelli is soft enough to be cut with chopsticks. Slowly add the eggs into the skillet and stir constantly so that the eggs do not form lumps.
* Add the bean sprouts and toss lightly to mix with the vermicelli. Serve with rice.

• 2 OZ/50 G MUNG BEAN VERMICELLI
• ½ CUP (2 OZ/50 G) BEAN SPROUTS
• 2 DUCK EGGS OR CHICKEN EGGS
• ½ TEASPOON SALT
• 2 TABLESPOONS VEGETABLE OIL
• 1 OZ/30 G CURED HAM, CUT INTO STRIPS
• ½ CUP (4 FL OZ/120 ML) CHICKEN BROTH (STOCK, PAGE 90)
• STEAMED RICE (PAGE 540), TO SERVE

RICE CONGEE

&

NOODLES

RICE, CONGEE & NOODLES

REGIONS: ALL
PREPARATION TIME: 5 MINUTES, PLUS
   10 MINUTES STANDING TIME
COOKING TIME: 20 MINUTES
SERVES: 3–4

白米饭
STEAMED RICE

- 2 CUPS (14 OZ/400 G) LONG-GRAIN RICE

A rice cooker is essential kitchen equipment in every Chinese household but if you do not have one, steamed rice can be easily prepared on a stove.

* Rinse the rice under cold running water to wash away the starch.
* Bring 1½ cups (12 fl oz/375 ml) water to boil in a small saucepan. Stir in the rice and return to a boil over medium-high heat.
* Reduce to low heat and steam, covered, for 16–18 minutes until the rice is tender and all the water has been absorbed.
* Let stand, covered, for 10 minutes. Serve.

REGION: HONG KONG
PREPARATION TIME: 15 MINUTES,
   PLUS 30 MINUTES SOAKING TIME
COOKING TIME: 20 MINUTES
SERVES: 4

海味三宝腊味饭
STEAMED RICE WITH CURED MEAT AND SEAFOOD

- 1 DRIED OCTOPUS
- 2 TABLESPOONS LARGE DRIED SHRIMP, RINSED AND DRAINED
- ¼ CUP (¼ OZ/10 G) DRIED WHITEBAIT, RINSED AND DRAINED
- 1 TABLESPOON GINGER JUICE
- 2 TABLESPOONS PLUS 1 TEASPOON VEGETABLE OIL
- 6 CLOVES GARLIC, CHOPPED
- 1½ CUPS (11 OZ/300 G) LONG-GRAIN RICE, RINSED AND DRAINED
- 2 CHINESE SAUSAGES, SLICED DIAGONALLY INTO ¼-INCH/5-MM PIECES
- 2 OZ/50 G CHINESE CURED BACON
- 1 TEASPOON SALT

* Soak the dried octopus in a bowl of cold water for 30 minutes until softened, then cut into bite-size pieces.
* Combine the dried shrimp, whitebait, octopus, ginger juice, and 1 teaspoon oil in a small bowl. Set aside.
* Heat the remaining 2 tablespoons oil in a wok or large skillet (frying pan) over medium-high heat, add the garlic, and stir-fry for 1 minute until fragrant. Add the rice and stir-fry for 1 minute. Add 2¼ cups (18 fl oz/550 ml) water and bring to a boil, then reduce to low heat and cook, covered, for 10 minutes until most of the water has been absorbed. (Alternatively, use a rice cooker.)
* Stir in the dried shrimp, whitebait, and octopus together with the Chinese sausages and bacon. Re-cover and cook for 5 minutes until the rice is done. Transfer to a serving platter and serve immediately.

荷叶饭
RICE IN A
LOTUS LEAF

REGION: GUANGDONG
PREPARATION TIME: 10 MINUTES,
  PLUS 45 MINUTES SOAKING TIME
COOKING TIME: 30 MINUTES
SERVES: 4

* Soak the dried lotus leaf in a bowl of cold water for about 45 minutes until softened. Rinse under cold running water and pat dry with a clean dish towel. Lay out the lotus leaf on a steaming rack and brush with oil. Set aside.
* Meanwhile, soak the mushrooms in a bowl of cold water for 20 minutes until softened. Soak the dried scallops in a separate bowl with ½ cup (4 fl oz/120 ml) cold water for 15 minutes. Drain the scallops, then remove the small hard muscle. Remove the mushrooms, squeeze dry, and discard the stems and the soaking water.
* In another bowl, combine the chicken, 1 teaspoon soy sauce, the sugar, cornstarch (cornflour), and ½ tablespoon oil. Mix well and marinate for 10 minutes.
* Heat 1 tablespoon oil in a small skillet (frying pan), add the eggs, moving the skillet so that the eggs create a thin layer on the surface, and fry over medium heat for 1–2 minutes until cooked. Cut into strands and set aside.
* Heat 1 tablespoon oil in a wok or large skillet over medium-high heat, add the mushrooms, chicken, and shrimp (prawns), and stir-fry for 2 minutes until chicken is nearly cooked through and the shrimp turn pink. Add the scallops and duck, then toss and stir-fry for another minute until the scallops are cooked through. Remove from the wok and set aside on a plate.
* In the same wok, heat the remaining 2 tablespoons oil over medium-high heat and stir-fry the shallots for 1–2 minutes. Add the rice, egg strands, fish sauce, and remaining 1 teaspoon soy sauce and stir-fry for 1 minute. Mix in the cooked ingredients and toss well.
* Put the fried rice on the lotus leaf, wrap into a square bundle and place in a collapsible pot or bamboo steamer over a pot of boiling water. Steam, covered, for 20 minutes. Carefully cut open the lotus leaf, sprinkle the scallion (spring onion) over the top of the rice, and serve. (The lotus leaf is not to be consumed.)

- 1 DRIED LOTUS LEAF
- 4½ TABLESPOONS VEGETABLE OIL, PLUS EXTRA FOR BRUSHING
- 2 DRIED BLACK MUSHROOMS
- 2 DRIED SCALLOPS
- 4 BONELESS, SKINLESS CHICKEN THIGHS, CUT INTO SMALL BITE-SIZE PIECES
- 2 TEASPOONS LIGHT SOY SAUCE
- ½ TEASPOON GRANULATED SUGAR
- 1 TEASPOON CORNSTARCH (CORNFLOUR)
- 2 EGGS, BEATEN
- 3½ OZ/100 G UNCOOKED SHRIMP (PRAWNS), SHELLED AND DEVEINED
- 3½ OZ/100 G ROAST DUCK, DICED
- 2 SHALLOTS, CHOPPED
- 4 CUPS (23 OZ/650 G) COOKED RICE
- 1 TEASPOON FISH SAUCE
- 1 SCALLION (SPRING ONION), CHOPPED, TO SERVE

REGION: HAINAN
PREPARATION TIME: 15 MINUTES
COOKING TIME: 45 MINUTES
SERVES: 4
PAGE 543

海南鸡饭
HAINAN CHICKEN RICE

- 1 (1 LB 5-OZ/600-G) CORN-FED CHICKEN
- 1 CUP (8 FL OZ/250 ML) CHICKEN BROTH (STOCK, PAGE 90)
- 1 TABLESPOON VEGETABLE OIL
- 6 CLOVES GARLIC, CHOPPED
- 1½ CUPS (11 OZ/300 G) LONG-GRAIN RICE, RINSED AND DRAINED
- 1 LEMONGRASS STALK, CUT INTO 2-INCH/5-CM LENGTHS
- 2 TABLESPOONS COCONUT MILK
- CILANTRO (CORIANDER), TO GARNISH (OPTIONAL)
- SLICED RED CHILE, TO GARNISH (OPTIONAL)

FOR THE MARINADE:
- ½ TABLESPOON SALT
- ½ TABLESPOON GINGER JUICE
- ½ TABLESPOON SHAOXING WINE

FOR THE SPICY DIPPING SAUCE:
- 1 CLOVE GARLIC, FINELY CHOPPED
- ½ RED CHILE, CHOPPED
- 2 TABLESPOONS WHITE VINEGAR

FOR THE GINGER-SCALLION DIPPING SAUCE:
- SCANT ½ CUP (3½ FL OZ/100 ML) CANOLA (RAPESEED) OIL
- 1 TABLESPOON GRATED GINGER
- 1 TEASPOON SALT, TO TASTE
- ¼ CUP FINELY CHOPPED SCALLIONS (SPRING ONIONS)

* Combine the marinade ingredients in a small bowl, then rub the marinade over the chicken. Place the chicken in a heatproof bowl and put into a collapsible pot or bamboo steamer over a pot of boiling water. Steam, covered, for 15–20 minutes, or until cooked through. Remove the chicken and set aside. Strain the strained chicken juices into a measuring cup. Add enough chicken broth (stock) to the measuring cup so that it measures 2¼ cups (17 fl oz/ 500 ml). Set aside.
* Heat the oil in a wok or large skillet (frying pan) over medium-high heat, add the garlic, and stir-fry for 1 minute until fragrant. Add the rice and stir until well coated in oil.
* Transfer the rice to a large saucepan. Add the chicken broth and lemongrass on top, bring to a boil, and simmer over low heat for 15–20 minutes. (Alternatively, use a rice cooker.) When most of the broth has been absorbed, stir in the coconut milk. Cook for another 5 minutes, or until the rice is tender, then remove the lemongrass.
* To make the spicy dipping sauce, combine the ingredients and set aside.
* To make the ginger-scallion sauce, heat the oil in a small saucepan over medium heat, add the ginger and salt, and stir in the scallion (spring onion) for 20–30 seconds. Transfer to a small bowl and set aside.
* Slice the chicken, place on a serving plate, garnish with the cilantro (coriander) and sliced red chiles, if using, and serve with the rice and dipping sauces.

RICE, CONGEE & NOODLES

HAINAN CHICKEN RICE

REGION: SHANGHAI
PREPARATION TIME: 10 MINUTES,
 PLUS 1 HOUR SOAKING TIME
COOKING TIME: 20–30 MINUTES
SERVES: 4
PAGE 545

上海菜饭
SHANGHAI PORK AND
VEGETABLE RICE

- 3½ OZ/100 G SALTED PORK
- 3½ OZ/100 G GREEN BOK CHOY
- 1 TABLESPOON VEGETABLE OIL
- 2 OZ/50 G PORK FATBACK, DICED
- 3 CLOVES GARLIC, CHOPPED
- 2 CUPS (14 OZ/400 G) LONG-GRAIN
  RICE, RINSED AND DRAINED

* Soak the salted pork in a bowl of cold water for 1 hour.
  Drain, then cut into ⅛-inch/3-mm-thick slices.
* Bring a large saucepan of water to a boil, add the bok choy,
  and blanch for 1–2 minutes. Drain and rinse under cold
  running water, then chop.
* Heat the oil in a wok or large skillet (frying pan) over low
  heat, add the pork fatback, and stir-fry for 4–5 minutes
  until crispy. Transfer the pork to a plate and set aside.
* Add the garlic and stir-fry for 30 seconds until fragrant,
  then add the rice and continue to stir-fry 30 seconds.
  Add 3 cups (25 fl oz/750 ml) water and stir once. Bring
  to a boil, add the salted pork, then reduce to low heat and
  cook, covered, for 15–20 minutes until the rice is cooked.
  (Alternatively, use a rice cooker.) Stir in the bok choy, cover,
  and let stand for 3 minutes. Transfer to a serving plate,
  garnish with the pork, then serve.

REGION: HONG KONG
PREPARATION TIME: 10 MINUTES,
 PLUS 45 MINUTES SOAKING TIME
COOKING TIME: 55 MINUTES
SERVES: 4

蒜蓉中虾笼仔蒸饭
STEAMED RICE
WITH SHRIMP

- 1 DRIED LOTUS LEAF, RINSED
- 2 TABLESPOONS VEGETABLE OIL, PLUS
  EXTRA FOR BRUSHING
- 1 HEAD GARLIC, CLOVES SEPARATED
  AND CHOPPED
- 1½ CUPS (11 OZ/300 G) LONG-GRAIN
  RICE, RINSED AND SOAKED IN COLD
  WATER FOR 1 HOUR
- 1 TEASPOON SALT
- 11 OZ/300 G UNCOOKED SHRIMP
  (PRAWNS), WITH HEAD AND SHELL ON
  AND CLAWS AND LEGS TRIMMED

* Soak the dried lotus leaf in a bowl of cold water for about
  45 minutes until softened. Rinse under cold running water
  and pat dry with a clean dish towel. Lay out the lotus leaf
  on a steaming rack and brush with oil. Set aside.
* Heat 1 tablespoon oil in a wok or large skillet (frying pan)
  over medium heat, add 1 tablespoon of the garlic, and
  stir-fry for 1–2 minutes until fragrant. Drain, then add the
  rice and ½ teaspoon salt and mix well.
* Spread the rice across the leaf. Put the rack in a collapsible
  pot or bamboo steamer over a pot of boiling water. Steam,
  covered, for 45 minutes, or until the rice is cooked.
* Meanwhile, cut along the length of the shrimp (prawns) to
  open the shell. Hold the two sides of each shrimp and bend
  them toward the back to break the shell and keep open.
* Combine the remaining chopped garlic, ½ teaspoon salt,
  and 1 tablespoon oil into a bowl, then spread some of the
  mixture over each shrimp. Put the shrimp on top of the rice
  in the bamboo steamer and steam for another 5 minutes
  until the shrimp are pink and cooked through. Serve. (The
  lotus leaf is not to be consumed.)

RICE, CONGEE & NOODLES

SHANGHAI PORK AND VEGETABLE RICE

REGION: CHAOZHOU
PREPARATION TIME: 10 MINUTES
COOKING TIME: 20 MINUTES
SERVES: 2-4

香葱珠蚝焗饭
RICE WITH OYSTERS
AND PORK

- 1 LB 5 OZ/600 G SMALL OYSTER
- 1 TABLESPOON CORNSTARCH
  (CORNFLOUR)
- 1 TABLESPOON GINGER JUICE
- 1½ TEASPOONS SALT
- ½ TEASPOON GROUND WHITE PEPPER
- 2 OZ/50 G GROUND (MINCED) PORK
- 1 TABLESPOON VEGETABLE OIL
- 2 CLOVES GARLIC, CHOPPED
- ¾ CUP (5 OZ/150 G) LONG-GRAIN
  RICE, RINSED AND DRAINED
- ½ SCALLION (SPRING ONION),
  CHOPPED

  FOR THE SAUCE:
- 3 TABLESPOONS LIGHT SOY SAUCE
- 1 TABLESPOON DARK SOY SAUCE
- 1 TABLESPOON CHICKEN BROTH
  (STOCK, PAGE 90)
- ½ TEASPOON GRANULATED SUGAR
- ½ TEASPOON SESAME OIL

* Shuck the oysters, then pick out any fragments of shell and rub with the cornstarch (cornflour). Rinse well.
* Bring a large saucepan of water to a boil, add the oysters, and blanch for 30 seconds, then drain.
* Combine the oysters, ginger juice, ½ teaspoon salt, and white pepper in a bowl and mix well. Set aside.
* In a separate bowl, combine the pork and ½ teaspoon salt and mix well.
* Heat the oil in a wok or large skillet (frying pan), add the garlic, and stir-fry for 30 seconds until fragrant. Stir in the rice and the remaining ½ teaspoon salt.
* Combine the rice and 1¼ cups (10 fl oz/300 ml) water in a saucepan and stir once. Bring to a boil, then reduce to low heat, and cook, covered, for 10 minutes. (Alternatively, use a rice cooker.) Mix in the pork and oysters and cook for another 5 minutes, or until the rice is tender and the pork is cooked through.
* Put the sauce ingredients into a small saucepan and bring to a boil over medium-high heat. Stir the sauce into the rice. Transfer to a serving plate, top with the scallion (spring onion), and serve.

REGION: HONG KONG
PREPARATION TIME: 10 MINUTES,
  PLUS 30 MINUTES SOAKING TIME
COOKING TIME: 10 MINUTES
SERVES: 4

章鱼鸡粒炒饭
CHICKEN FRIED RICE
WITH DRIED OCTOPUS

- 3½ OZ/100 G DRIED OCTOPUS
- 3 BONELESS CHICKEN THIGHS, CUT
  INTO ¾-INCH/2-CM DICE
- 2 TEASPOONS LIGHT SOY SAUCE
- ½ TEASPOON GRANULATED SUGAR
- 1 TEASPOON CORNSTARCH
  (CORNFLOUR)
- 2 TABLESPOONS PLUS 1 TEASPOON
  VEGETABLE OIL
- 1 SLICE GINGER, CHOPPED
- ⅓ CUP (2 OZ/50 G) PEAS
- 4 CUPS (23 OZ/650 G) COOKED
  LONG-GRAIN RICE, RINSED, LUMPS
  BROKEN UP, AND DRAINED
- 1 SCALLION (SPRING ONION),
  CHOPPED

* Soak the dried octopus in a bowl of cold water for 30 minutes until softened.
* Meanwhile, in a separate bowl, combine the chicken, 1 teaspoon soy sauce, the sugar, and cornstarch (cornflour) and marinate for 15 minutes.
* Drain the octopus and cut it into ½-inch/1-cm dice. Transfer to a bowl and add 1 teaspoon oil.
* Heat 2 tablespoons oil in a wok or large skillet (frying pan) over medium-high heat. Add the ginger and stir-fry 1 minute until fragrant. Add the chicken, octopus, and peas and stir-fry for 2 minutes, or until the chicken is cooked through.
* Stir in the cooked rice and the remaining 1 teaspoon soy sauce and toss rapidly for 2 minutes until the rice is heated through. Add the scallion (spring onion), stir, and transfer to a plate to serve.

RICE, CONGEE & NOODLES

福建炒饭
FUJIAN-STYLE
FRIED RICE

REGION: FUJIAN
PREPARATION TIME: 15 MINUTES,
   PLUS 20 MINUTES SOAKING TIME
COOKING TIME: 10 MINUTES
SERVES: 4

* Put the mushrooms in a bowl, cover with cold water, and soak for at least 20 minutes, or until softened. Remove the mushrooms, squeeze dry, and discard the stems. Chop the flesh and set aside.
* Meanwhile, in a small bowl, soak the dried scallops in ½ cup (4 fl oz/120 ml) cold water for 15 minutes. Drain, then remove the small hard muscle. Tear into shreds and reserve the soaking water.
* Combine the chicken and ¼ teaspoon salt in a bowl, mix well, and set aside to marinate for 10 minutes.
* Beat the egg in a large bowl, add the remaining ¼ teaspoon salt, and mix in the cooked rice.
* Heat 1½ tablespoons vegetable oil in a wok or large skillet (frying pan) over high heat, add the rice, and stir-fry for 2–3 minutes. Remove to a serving plate and set aside.
* Heat the remaining 1½ tablespoons oil over medium-high heat, add the garlic, and stir-fry for 30 seconds until fragrant. Add the chicken, mushrooms, scallops, shrimp (prawns), and Chinese broccoli and stir-fry for 2–3 minutes until all the ingredients are fully cooked. Add the soy sauce, sugar, and scallop water and bring to a boil.
* Mix the cornstarch (cornflour) with 2 tablespoons water in a small bowl and stir this mixture into the wok. Bring to a boil, stirring, for 30 seconds to thicken the sauce.
* Drizzle in the sesame oil, toss well, and pour over the fried rice. Transfer to a serving plate and serve.

• 4 DRIED BLACK MUSHROOMS
• 2 DRIED SCALLOPS
• 2 BONELESS, SKINLESS CHICKEN THIGHS, CHOPPED
• ½ TEASPOON SALT
• 1 EGG
• 4 CUPS (23 OZ/650 G) COOKED LONG-GRAIN RICE, RINSED, LUMPS BROKEN UP, AND DRAINED
• 3 TABLESPOONS VEGETABLE OIL
• 1 CLOVE GARLIC, SLICED
• 5 OZ/150 G UNCOOKED SHRIMP (PRAWNS), SHELLED, DEVEINED, AND CHOPPED
• 2 CHINESE BROCCOLI STEMS, SLICED
• 1 TABLESPOON LIGHT SOY SAUCE
• ½ TEASPOON GRANULATED SUGAR
• 1 TABLESPOON CORNSTARCH (CORNFLOUR)
• 1 TEASPOON SESAME OIL

REGION: HONG KONG
PREPARATION TIME: 5 MINUTES, PLUS
  15 MINUTES MARINATING TIME
COOKING TIME: 20 MINUTES
SERVES: 2–3
📷 PAGE 549

三文鱼芦笋野菌饭
RICE WITH SALMON
AND ASPARAGUS

- 5½ OZ/160 G SALMON FILLET, SKIN-ON
- 2 TEASPOONS MIRIN
- 2 TEASPOONS LIGHT SOY SAUCE, PLUS
  EXTRA TO SERVE
- 8 MOREL MUSHROOMS OR SHIITAKE
  MUSHROOMS
- 1¼ CUPS (9 OZ/250 G) LONG-GRAIN
  RICE, RINSED AND DRAINED
- ½ TEASPOON SALT
- 1 TABLESPOON OLIVE OIL
- 2½ CUPS (20 FL OZ/600 ML) CHICKEN
  BROTH (STOCK, PAGE 90)
- 4 ASPARAGUS SPEARS, TRIMMED

* Put the salmon in a larger freezer bag, add the mirin and soy sauce, and seal. Shake and mix well so that the salmon is coated and marinate in the refrigerator for 15 minutes.
* Meanwhile, soak the mushrooms in 4 tablespoons cold water for 10 minutes. With the mushrooms still in the water, snip them open with a pair of scissors and clean the insides. Remove the mushrooms and strain the soaking liquid into a small bowl. Set aside.
* Put the rice, salt, and olive oil into a saucepan, add the mushroom soaking water and the chicken broth (stock), then stir to mix. Bring to a boil, add the mushrooms, and cook until most of the water has been absorbed, about 5 minutes. Add the salmon and asparagus, reduce to low heat, and cook for another 5–10 minutes over low heat, covered, until the rice is fully cooked. Turn off the heat and let stand for another 5 minutes until the salmon is cooked through. Serve immediately with soy sauce, if desired.

客家水粄
HAKKA RICE PUDDING

- 1 TABLESPOON VEGETABLE OIL,
  PLUS EXTRA FOR GREASING
- ⅔ CUP (3½ OZ/100 G) RICE FLOUR
- ½ TEASPOON SALT
- 2 TABLESPOONS DRIED SHRIMP
- 2 SHALLOTS, CHOPPED
- 1 CHINESE SAUSAGE, CHOPPED
- 2 TABLESPOONS SWEET PRESERVED
  TURNIPS, CHOPPED
- ½ TEASPOON LIGHT SOY SAUCE
- 1 TEASPOON GRANULATED SUGAR
- 2 OZ/50 G CHIVES, CUT INTO
  ½-INCH/1-CM LENGTHS
- GROUND WHITE PEPPER, TO TASTE

* Grease 4 heatproof bowls with oil and keep them warm in a steamer.
* Mix the rice flour and salt in a large bowl. In a separate heatproof bowl, combine ½ cup (4 fl oz/120 ml) cold water with 1½ cups (12 fl oz/350 ml) boiling water, then immediately pour it into the flour mixture. Stir with chopsticks to blend.
* Pour the mixture into the prepared rice bowls, stir lightly, then cover each bowl with aluminum foil to seal it. Steam, covered, for 15 minutes.
* Meanwhile, soak the dried shrimp in a bowl of cold water for 5 minutes until softened. Drain, then chop.
* Heat the oil in a wok or large skillet (frying pan), add the shallots, and stir-fry over medium heat for 1–2 minutes until browned. Stir in the sausage, preserved turnip, and shrimp, then add the soy sauce and sugar, and toss well. Add the chives and season with white pepper.
* Carefully remove the bowls of rice pudding from the steamer. Divide the topping equally amongst each bowl. Serve hot.

RICE, CONGEE & NOODLES

RICE WITH SALMON AND ASPARAGUS

西炒饭
HONG KONG
FRIED RICE

- 1 CARROT, DICED
- 3½ OZ/100 G COOKED HAM, DICED
- ⅓ CUP (2 OZ/50 G) FROZEN PEAS
- 2 EGGS, BEATEN
- 3 CUPS (1 LB 2 OZ/500 G) COOKED LONG-GRAIN RICE, RINSED, LUMPS BROKEN UP, AND DRAINED
- 1 TABLESPOON VEGETABLE OIL
- ½ ONION, DICED
- 5 OZ/150 G SHELLED UNCOOKED SHRIMP (PRAWNS), DEVEINED AND DICED
- 1 TEASPOON SALT
- 3 TABLESPOONS KETCHUP

* Bring a small saucepan of water to a boil, add the carrot, and blanch for 2 minutes. Drain and rinse under cold running water. Transfer to a bowl, then add the ham and peas.
* Mix the eggs with the cooked rice in a large bowl.
* Heat the oil in a wok or large skillet (frying pan) over medium-high heat, add the onion, and stir-fry for 5–7 minutes until softened. Add the shrimp (prawns) and stir-fry for about 2 minutes until just cooked. Put in the rice-and-egg mixture, salt, and ketchup and stir-fry for 3–4 minutes until the eggs and shrimp are cooked. Add the ham and vegetables and toss thoroughly for another 2 minutes. Transfer to individual bowls or a serving plate, then serve.

干巴菌炒饭
FRIED RICE WITH GANBA

- 3½ OZ/100 G FRESH GANBA MUSHROOMS OR ¼ OZ/10 G DRIED, RINSED THOROUGHLY
- ½ TEASPOON SALT
- 1 TEASPOON ALL-PURPOSE (PLAIN) FLOUR
- 1 EGG
- 2¼ CUPS (12 OZ/350 G) COOKED LONG-GRAIN RICE, RINSED, LUMPS BROKEN UP, AND DRAINED
- 2 TABLESPOONS VEGETABLE OIL

The Ganba mushroom, also known as the dried beef mushroom, grows in the forests of Yunnan. Available only in July and August, they are prized by locals. If using dried Ganba, skip steps 1 and 2.

* Use a small knife to scrape the mushrooms clean of dirt. Tear the mushrooms into thin strips, put into a bowl, and rub thoroughly with ¼ teaspoon salt, then rinse.
* Add the flour to the mushrooms, rub thoroughly, and rinse to remove any remaining impurities. Squeeze dry to remove any excess water.
* Place the mushrooms in a collapsible pot or bamboo steamer over a pot of boiling water. Steam, covered, for 5 minutes until cooked through. Set aside.
* Beat the egg with the remaining ¼ teaspoon salt in a large bowl, then add the rice and mix thoroughly.
* Heat the oil in a wok or large skillet (frying pan) over medium-high heat. Add the rice and stir-fry 3–4 minutes until the rice grains separate and the egg is cooked. Add the mushrooms and stir-fry rapidly for 30 seconds, or until fragrant (do not overcook). Transfer to a serving plate.

RICE, CONGEE & NOODLES

HONG KONG FRIED RICE

REGION: HONG KONG
PREPARATION TIME: 15 MINUTES,
  PLUS 1 HOUR SOAKING TIME
COOKING TIME: 30 MINUTES
SERVES: 2
📷 PAGE 553

焗猪扒饭
BAKED PORK CHOPS OVER RICE

- 1 TABLESPOON PLUS ½ TEASPOON SALT
- 2 BONE-IN PORK LOIN CHOPS, ABOUT ¾-INCH/2-CM THICK
- 2 TABLESPOONS FROZEN PEAS
- 2 EGGS, LIGHTLY BEATEN
- 1¼ CUPS (4½ OZ/125 G) BREADCRUMBS
- 2¼ CUPS (12 OZ/350 G) COOKED LONG-GRAIN RICE, RINSED, LUMPS BROKEN UP, AND DRAINED
- 1 CUP (8 FL OZ/250 ML) VEGETABLE OIL
- ½ ONION, THINLY SLICED
- 2 TOMATOES, CHOPPED

  FOR THE SAUCE:
- 3 TABLESPOONS KETCHUP
- 1 TABLESPOON GRANULATED SUGAR
- 2½ TEASPOONS CORNSTARCH (CORNFLOUR)
- ¾ TEASPOON SALT

* Combine 1 cup (8 fl oz/250 ml) water with 1 tablespoon salt in a large bowl. Add the pork chops and soak for 1 hour.
* Bring a saucepan of water to a boil, add the peas, and blanch for 1 minute. Drain and set aside.
* Preheat the oven to 350°F/180°C/Gas Mark 4.
* To make the sauce, combine all the ingredients and ½ cup (4 fl oz/120 ml) water in a bowl, mix well, and set aside.
* Drain and rinse the pork chops under cold running water, then pat dry with paper towels. Brush the pork chops with the beaten eggs and dip them into the breadcrumbs.
* Combine the rice, ½ teaspoon salt, and remaining beaten eggs in a large bowl.
* Heat the oil in a wok or skillet (frying pan) over medium-high heat, add the pork chops, and shallow-fry for 4 minutes on each side until golden brown and just cooked through. Remove the pork chops and set aside.
* Pour out most of the oil, leaving 1 tablespoon in the wok. Heat the oil over medium-high heat, add the rice, and stir-fry for 2–3 minutes until well coated in oil. Put the fried rice into a Dutch oven (casserole) and place the pork chops on top.
* Give the wok a wipe with a paper towel, add 1 tablespoon oil, and stir-fry the onion over medium heat for 5 minutes until softened. Add the peas, tomatoes, and the sauce, then bring to a boil over high heat. Pour the sauce over the pork chops and rice. Transfer to the oven and cook for 20 minutes, or until slightly brown and cooked through.

BAKED PORK CHOPS OVER RICE

REGION: HONG KONG
PREPARATION TIME: 10 MINUTES, PLUS
  5 MINUTES MARINATING TIME
COOKING TIME: 10 MINUTES
SERVES: 4
📷 PAGE 555

香葱肉碎虾酱炒饭
FRIED RICE WITH BEEF
AND SHRIMP PASTE

- 3 CUPS (1 LB 2 OZ/500 G) COOKED LONG-GRAIN RICE
- 7 OZ/200 G GROUND (MINCED) BEEF
- ½ TABLESPOON SHRIMP PASTE
- 1 TEASPOON GRANULATED SUGAR
- 2 TABLESPOONS VEGETABLE OIL
- 1 TABLESPOON CHOPPED GINGER
- ½ TEASPOON SALT
- ½ SCALLION (SPRING ONION), CHOPPED

  FOR THE MARINADE:
- 1 TEASPOON LIGHT SOY SAUCE
- 1 TEASPOON CORNSTARCH (CORNFLOUR)
- ½ TEASPOON GRANULATED SUGAR
- PINCH OF GROUND WHITE PEPPER

* Rinse the rice under cold running water to wash away the starch and to break up any lumps, then drain.
* Combine the marinade ingredients in a large bowl, add the ground (minced) beef, and marinate for 5 minutes.
* Combine the shrimp paste and sugar in a small bowl, stir in 1 tablespoon water to thin out, and set aside.
* Heat the oil in a wok or large skillet (frying pan) over medium-high heat, add the ginger, and stir-fry for 1 minute until fragrant. Add the ground beef and shrimp-sugar paste and stir-fry rapidly for another minute. Finally, add the rice and salt, then toss thoroughly for another 5 minutes until the beef is cooked and the rice is heated through. Stir in the scallion (spring onion) and transfer to serving bowls to serve.

糯米蒸排骨
SPARERIBS WITH
GLUTINOUS RICE

- ¾ CUP (5 OZ/150 G) GLUTINOUS RICE, RINSED
- 1 CUBE RED BEAN CURD, MASHED WITH A FORK
- 2 CLOVES GARLIC, CHOPPED
- 1 SCALLION (SPRING ONION), CHOPPED, PLUS EXTRA TO GARNISH
- 1 TABLESPOON LIGHT SOY SAUCE
- 1 TEASPOON RICE WINE
- ½ TEASPOON GRANULATED SUGAR
- 1 TEASPOON SALT
- ½ TEASPOON CORNSTARCH (CORNFLOUR)
- 11 OZ/300 G PORK SPARERIBS, CUT INTO SMALL CHUNKS, RINSED, AND DRAINED
- 1 TABLESPOON VEGETABLE OIL

* In a heatproof bowl, combine the rice with 2 cups (16 fl oz/475 ml) boiling water and set aside for 1 hour. Rinse under cold running water and drain.
* Meanwhile, in a large bowl, combine the bean curd, garlic, scallion (spring onion), soy sauce, wine, sugar, salt, cornstarch (cornflour), and 2 tablespoons water and mix well. Add the spareribs and marinate for 15 minutes.
* Heat the oil in a wok or large skillet (frying pan) over medium heat, add the spareribs and marinade, and cook for about 1 minute. Stir in the rice.
* Line a collapsible pot or bamboo steamer with a sheet of aluminum foil. Pour the spareribs-and-rice mixture onto the foil, then set over a pot of boiling water. Steam, covered, for 1½ hours until the rice and spareribs are cooked. (Add more water to the pot if needed.)
* Garnish with chopped scallion and transfer to a serving plate.

FRIED RICE WITH BEEF AND SHRIMP PASTE

REGION: GUANGDONG
PREPARATION TIME: 10 MINUTES,
    PLUS 20 MINUTES SOAKING TIME
COOKING TIME: 30 MINUTES
SERVES: 3-4
[📷] PAGE 557

生炒糯米饭
STIR-FRIED
GLUTINOUS RICE

- 1 CUP (7 OZ/200 G) GLUTINOUS RICE,
  RINSED
- 2 TABLESPOONS VEGETABLE OIL
- 3 DRIED BLACK MUSHROOMS
- 2 TABLESPOONS DRIED SHRIMP
- 1 CHINESE SAUSAGE
- 1 CHINESE DUCK LIVER SAUSAGE
- 3½ OZ/100 G CHINESE CURED BACON
- 1 TABLESPOON LIGHT SOY SAUCE
- ½ TEASPOON SALT
- 1 TEASPOON GRANULATED SUGAR
- 1 SCALLION (SPRING ONION),
  CHOPPED, PLUS EXTRA TO GARNISH

* Soak the glutinous rice in 3 cups (25 fl oz/750 ml) boiling water for 20 minutes. Rinse under cold running water and rub gently to remove the starch from the surface of the rice. Rinse again, drain, and mix well with 1 tablespoon oil.
* Meanwhile, put the mushrooms in a bowl, cover with cold water, and soak for at least 20 minutes, or until softened. Remove the mushrooms, squeeze dry, and discard the stems. Cut into thin slices. In another small bowl, soak the dried shrimp in cold water for 5 minutes. Drain and cut into small pieces. Strain the mushroom and shrimp soaking water for later use.
* Put the sausages and cured bacon into a large saucepan and add enough water to cover them completely. Bring to a boil over high heat and blanch for 1 minute. Drain. When cool enough to handle, slice and set aside.
* Combine the soy sauce, salt, and sugar in a small bowl and mix well.
* Heat the remaining 1 tablespoon oil in a wok or large skillet (frying pan) over medium heat, add the sausages, cured bacon, mushrooms, and shrimp, and stir-fry for 1 minute until fragrant. Remove from the wok and set aside on a plate until needed.
* Reheat the oil in the wok and stir-fry the glutinous rice over medium-low heat, turning the rice constantly with a spatula (fish slice). Gradually pour in the mushroom and shrimp soaking water, 2 tablespoons at a time, until the rice has absorbed the liquid and is thoroughly cooked through, about 20 minutes. Add the ingredients from the plate and the sauce, and stir-fry for another 2–3 minutes until well mixed with the rice.
* Stir in the scallion (spring onion) and transfer to a serving bowl, then garnish with the extra scallion and serve.

STIR-FRIED GLUTINOUS RICE

REGION: JIANGSU
PREPARATION TIME: 10 MINUTES,
    PLUS 1 HOUR SOAKING TIME
COOKING TIME: 1 HOUR
SERVES: 2-3
📷 PAGE 559

扬州炒饭
YANGZHOU
FRIED RICE

- 1¼ CUPS (9 OZ/250 G) LONG-GRAIN RICE, RINSED AND DRAINED (SEE NOTE)
- 2½ TABLESPOONS VEGETABLE OIL
- 3½ OZ/100 G UNCOOKED SHRIMP (PRAWNS), SHELLED AND DEVEINED
- 4 EGGS, SEPARATED
- 1 TEASPOON SALT
- ½ QUANTITY BARBECUE PORK
- (PAGE 394), DICED
- 1 SCALLION (SPRING ONION), CHOPPED

This dish dates back to the late sixth century when it was created by Yang Shu, a top government official during Emperor Yang's reign in the Sui Dynasty. The dish was originally called "Golden Nugget Rice" because each rice grain was enveloped in golden egg yolk.

* Combine the rice, ½ tablespoon oil, and 2 cups (16 fl oz/ 475 ml) water in a saucepan and stir once. Bring to a boil, then reduce to low heat, and cook, covered, for about 15–20 minutes, or until the rice is tender. (Alternatively, use a rice cooker.)
* Bring a saucepan of water to a boil over high heat, add the shrimp (prawns), and blanch for 2 minutes. Drain and set aside.
* Combine 2 egg whites, 4 egg yolks, and ½ teaspoon salt in a small bowl and beat together.
* Slowly pour the eggs into the rice and, using chopsticks, stir until each grain of rice is coated in egg.
* Heat the remaining 2 tablespoons oil in a wok or large skillet (frying pan) over medium-high heat, add the rice, and stir-fry until each grain of rice is covered with oil. Turn off the heat and stir-fry for another 2 minutes until the eggs are cooked. Add the shrimp, barbecue pork, and ½ teaspoon salt, and toss for another 2–3 minutes. Stir in the chopped scallion (spring onion) and transfer to a serving bowl or plate and serve.

NOTE:
Alternatively, 3 cups (1 lb 2 oz/500 g) of day-old rice can be used. Rinse the rice with water to wash away the starch and to break up any lumps, then drain. Skip step 1 of the recipe.

YANGZHOU FRIED RICE

REGION: HONG KONG
PREPARATION TIME: 10 MINUTES
COOKING TIME: 15 MINUTES
SERVES: 4

鸳鸯炒饭
HONEYMOON
FRIED RICE

- 1 BONELESS, SKINLESS CHICKEN BREAST, CUT INTO THIN STRIPS
- 1½ TEASPOONS CORNSTARCH (CORNFLOUR)
- 5 OZ/150 G SHELLED UNCOOKED SHRIMP (PRAWNS), DEVEINED
- 2 TABLESPOONS PEAS
- 3 TABLESPOONS VEGETABLE OIL
- ½ ONION, THINLY SLICED
- 2 EGGS, BEATEN
- 4 CUPS (1 LB 8½ OZ/700 G) COOKED LONG-GRAIN RICE, RINSED, LUMPS BROKEN UP, AND DRAINED
- 2 TABLESPOONS KETCHUP
- 1 TEASPOON GRANULATED SUGAR
- ½ TEASPOON SALT
- SCANT ½ CUP (3½ FL OZ/100 ML) MILK
- PINCH OF GROUND WHITE PEPPER

Also known as "yin-yang rice," the honeymoon rice is topped with a tangy red sauce over one half of the dish and a creamy white sauce on the other, forming the shape of the yin-yang symbol. It is often served at the end of a wedding banquet in Hong Kong.

* Combine the chicken strips, ½ teaspoon cornstarch (cornflour), and 1 tablespoon water in a bowl and mix.
* Bring a saucepan of water to a boil, add the shrimp (prawns), and blanch for 2 minutes. Drain.
* Bring a saucepan of water to a boil, add the peas, and blanch for 1 minute. Drain.
* Heat 1 tablespoon oil in a wok or large skillet (frying pan) over medium-high heat, add the chicken strips, and stir-fry for about 1 minute, then add the onion, and stir-fry for 1 minute, or until soft. Transfer the mixture to a plate.
* Clean the wok and heat 1 tablespoon oil over medium-high heat. Add the shrimp and stir-fry for about 1 minute. Add the peas, toss together, then transfer to a plate.
* Heat the remaining 1 tablespoon oil in a wok over medium-high heat. Add the eggs and stir-fry for 1 minute until half cooked. Add the rice and stir-fry for another minute, or until mixed together and fully cooked. Transfer the mixture to a shallow serving bowl.
* Put the ketchup and scant 1 cup (7 fl oz/200 ml) water into a clean wok and bring to a boil. Add the sugar, ¼ teaspoon salt, and the cooked chicken and onion and return to a boil. Mix ½ teaspoon cornstarch with 1 tablespoon water, add this mixture to the chicken, and stir-fry for about 30 seconds to thicken the sauce. Transfer to the bowl and cover one half of the fried rice.
* Pour the milk and scant ½ cup (3½ fl oz/100 ml) water into a clean wok and bring to a boil. Add the remaining ¼ teaspoon salt, white pepper, and the shrimp and peas, then return to a boil. Mix the remaining ½ teaspoon cornstarch with 1 tablespoon water and stir this mixture into the wok. Bring to a boil, stirring, for about 30 seconds to thicken sauce. Pour the mixture over the other half of the fried rice. Serve.

菠萝鸡粒炒饭
CHICKEN AND PINEAPPLE
FRIED RICE

REGION: HONG KONG
PREPARATION TIME: 10 MINUTES, PLUS
  15 MINUTES MARINATING TIME
COOKING TIME: 10 MINUTES
SERVES: 2–3

* Transfer the rice to a bowl, stir in the beaten egg, and set aside until needed.
* In another bowl, combine the chicken, sugar, cornstarch (cornflour), and 1 teaspoon soy sauce. Season with a little salt and marinate 15 minutes.
* Heat the oil in a wok or large skillet (frying pan), add the ginger, and stir-fry over medium-high heat for 1 minute until fragrant. Add the chicken and Chinese broccoli, then stir-fry for 2–3 minutes until the chicken is cooked. Add the bell pepper, pineapple chunks, rice, and remaining 1 teaspoon soy sauce. Stir well and fry for 3–4 minutes until the egg is cooked through. Add the scallions (spring onions) and toss. Transfer the rice to a serving platter and serve.

NOTE:
For a more traditional approach, use a fresh pineapple. Using a sharp knife, hollow out the pineapple half and leave the shell intact for the serving bowl. Remove the "eyes" of the pineapple, then cut out and discard the core. Cut the pineapple into chunks, place in a bowl with 1 cup (8 fl oz/250 ml) water and ½ teaspoon salt, and soak for 2 minutes. Drain, then add the pineapple, as instructed above. When ready to serve, transfer the rice into the pineapple shell.

- 3 CUPS (1 LB 2 OZ/500 G) COOKED LONG-GRAIN RICE, RINSED, LUMPS BROKEN UP, AND DRAINED
- 1 EGG, BEATEN
- 3 BONELESS, SKINLESS CHICKEN THIGHS, DICED
- ½ TEASPOON GRANULATED SUGAR
- 1 TEASPOON CORNSTARCH (CORNFLOUR)
- 2 TEASPOONS LIGHT SOY SAUCE
- 2 TABLESPOONS VEGETABLE OIL
- 1 TEASPOON CHOPPED GINGER
- 2 OZ/50 G CHINESE BROCCOLI STEMS OR ASPARAGUS STALKS, THINLY SLICED
- ½ RED BELL PEPPER, SEEDED AND DICED
- 1 (8-OZ/225-G) CAN PINEAPPLE CHUNKS, DRAINED
- 2 SCALLIONS (SPRING ONIONS), CHOPPED
- SALT, TO TASTE

REGION: HONG KONG
PREPARATION TIME: 10 MINUTES, PLUS
  20 MINUTES MARINATING TIME
COOKING TIME: 30 MINUTES
SERVES: 2
📷 PAGE 563

腊肠鸡煲仔饭
RICE WITH CHICKEN AND SAUSAGE IN A CASSEROLE

- 1 LB 5 OZ/600 G CHICKEN PIECES, CUT INTO 1½ × ¾-INCH/4 × 2-CM PIECES (BONE-IN)
- 1 TEASPOON LIGHT SOY SAUCE
- 1 TABLESPOON GINGER JUICE
- 1 TABLESPOON CORNSTARCH (CORNFLOUR)
- 2 TABLESPOONS VEGETABLE OIL
- 6 CLOVES GARLIC, CHOPPED
- ¾ CUP (5 OZ/150 G) LONG-GRAIN RICE, RINSED AND DRAINED
- 2 CHINESE SAUSAGES, CUT DIAGONALLY INTO ½-INCH/1-CM-THICK SLICES
- 2 SCALLIONS (SPRING ONIONS), CHOPPED
- 1 TABLESPOON SHREDDED GINGER
- 2-3 CILANTRO (CORIANDER) STEMS, TO GARNISH (OPTIONAL)

  FOR THE SAUCE:
- 1 TABLESPOON DARK SOY SAUCE
- 3 TABLESPOONS LIGHT SOY SAUCE
- 1 TABLESPOON CHICKEN BROTH (STOCK, PAGE 90)
- ½ TEASPOON GRANULATED SUGAR
- ½ TEASPOON SESAME OIL

* Combine the chicken pieces, soy sauce, and ginger juice in a bowl and marinate in the refrigerator for 20 minutes. Mix in the cornstarch (cornflour).
* Heat 1 tablespoon oil in a wok or large skillet (frying pan) over medium-high heat, add the chicken, and stir-fry for about 2-3 minutes until browned. Transfer to a plate.
* Heat the remaining 1 tablespoon oil in a clean wok over medium heat, add the garlic, and stir-fry for 1 minute until fragrant. Add the rice and stir-fry for another 30 seconds.
* Transfer the rice mixture to a Dutch oven (casserole). Add a scant 1 cup (7½ fl oz/225 ml) water and cook, uncovered, over high heat for 3-4 minutes until most of the water has been absorbed.
* Put in the sausages and chicken, then top with the scallions (spring onions) and ginger. Cover the Dutch oven and cook over low heat for 20 minutes until the chicken and rice are cooked through.
* Combine the sauce ingredients in a small saucepan and bring to a boil over medium-high heat. Serve the sauce alongside the rice casserole. Garnish with cilantro (coriander) stems, if using.

RICE WITH CHICKEN AND SAUSAGE IN A CASSEROLE

REGION: HONG KONG
PREPARATION TIME: 5 MINUTES, PLUS
  10 MINUTES MARINATING TIME
COOKING TIME: 20 MINUTES
SERVES: 2–3

咸鱼肉饼煲仔饭
RICE WITH PORK AND SALTED FISH IN A CASSEROLE

- 5 OZ/150 G PORK TENDERLOIN, SLICED
- 1 TABLESPOON LIGHT SOY SAUCE
- 1 TEASPOON GRANULATED SUGAR
- 1 TABLESPOON CORNSTARCH (CORNFLOUR)
- 2 TABLESPOONS VEGETABLE OIL
- ¾ CUP (5 OZ/150 G) LONG-GRAIN RICE, RINSED AND DRAINED
- 1¼ OZ/30 G CHINESE SALTED FISH, RINSED AND DRAINED
- ¼ OZ/10 G (ABOUT ¾-INCH/2-CM-LENGTH PIECE) SHREDDED GINGER

* In a bowl, combine the pork, soy sauce, ½ teaspoon granulated sugar, the cornstarch (cornflour), and 2 tablespoons water and marinate for 10 minutes. Stir in 1 tablespoon oil.
* Put the rice into a Dutch oven (casserole). Add 1 cup (8 fl oz/250 ml) water, bring to a boil over high heat, and cook, uncovered, for 3–4 minutes until most of the water has been absorbed.
* Arrange the pork slices on the rice, then arrange the salted fish on top of the pork. Top with the ginger, remaining ½ teaspoon sugar, and remaining 1 tablespoon oil. Cover, reduce to low heat, and cook for about 10–15 minutes until the rice and pork are cooked through.
* Remove the salted fish and pork to a plate to serve separately, with the rice alongside.

REGION: HONG KONG
PREPARATION TIME: 10 MINUTES, PLUS
  10 MINUTES MARINATING TIME
COOKING TIME: 25 MINUTES
SERVES: 4

窝蛋牛肉煲仔饭
EGG AND BEEF RICE CASSEROLE

- 7 OZ/200 G GROUND (MINCED) BEEF
- 1 TABLESPOON LIGHT SOY SAUCE
- ½ TABLESPOON OYSTER SAUCE
- ½ TEASPOON GRANULATED SUGAR
- 1 TABLESPOON SWEET POTATO STARCH OR CORNSTARCH (CORNFLOUR)
- 2 TABLESPOONS VEGETABLE OIL
- 2 CUPS (14 OZ/400 G) LONG-GRAIN RICE, RINSED AND DRAINED
- 1 EGG

FOR THE SWEET SOY SAUCE:
- 1 TABLESPOON DARK SOY SAUCE
- 1 TABLESPOON CHICKEN BROTH (STOCK, PAGE 90)
- ½ TEASPOON GRANULATED SUGAR
- ½ TEASPOON SESAME OIL

* Combine the beef, soy and oyster sauces, sugar, and 4 tablespoons water in a large bowl and marinate for 10 minutes.
* Add the sweet potato starch and mix well, then add the oil and mix again. Using your hands, form the beef mixture into a large round patty.
* Place the rice in a Dutch oven (casserole), add 3 cups (25 fl oz/750 ml) water, and bring to a boil over high heat. Cook, uncovered, for 3–4 minutes until most of the water has been absorbed.
* Place the meat patty on top of the rice, cover, reduce to low heat, and cook for 15 minutes until the meat is properly cooked through.
* Uncover and crack the egg onto the meat patty. Cover, turn off the heat, and stand for another 3–5 minutes.
* Meanwhile, to make the sauce, combine ingredients in a small saucepan over medium heat and stir until the sugar is dissolved. Sprinkle the sauce on top of the patty and rice before serving.

RICE, CONGEE & NOODLES

豉汁白鳝煲仔饭
RICE WITH EEL AND BLACK BEAN SAUCE IN A CASSEROLE

REGION: HONG KONG
PREPARATION TIME: 20 MINUTES
COOKING TIME: 30 MINUTES
SERVES: 3–4

* In a bowl, combine the black beans, chile, half the garlic, the sugar, soy sauce, and 1 tablespoon oil. Set aside.
* Using a sharp knife, cut off and discard the head of the eel. Sprinkle with 1 teaspoon salt and the cornstarch (cornflour) and rub off the mucus from the skin. Rinse under cold running water and drain. Cut the eel in half lengthwise along the body, then cut each piece into 2 lengths. Cut the eel into ½-inch/1-cm-thick slices and mix with the black bean sauce.
* Heat the remaining 1 tablespoon oil in a Dutch oven (casserole) over medium heat, add the remaining half of the chopped garlic, rice, and the remaining ½ teaspoon salt, and stir-fry for 1–2 minutes until fragrant.
* Add 2 cups (16 fl oz/475 ml) water, bring to a boil, and simmer, uncovered, for 15–20 minutes, or until most of the water has been absorbed. Place the eel on top of the rice, cover, and cook over low heat for 12 minutes.
* Combine the sauce ingredients in a small saucepan and bring to a boil over medium-high heat. Pour the sauce over the rice and serve in the Dutch oven.

* 2 TABLESPOONS FERMENTED BLACK BEANS, RINSED AND CHOPPED
* 1 RED CHILE, SEEDED AND CHOPPED
* 6 CLOVES GARLIC, CHOPPED
* 1 TEASPOON GRANULATED SUGAR
* 2 TABLESPOONS LIGHT SOY SAUCE
* 2 TABLESPOONS VEGETABLE OIL
* 1 (1 LB 5-OZ/600-G) FRESHWATER EEL
* 1½ TEASPOONS SALT
* 1 TABLESPOON CORNSTARCH (CORNFLOUR)
* 1½ CUPS (11 OZ/300 G) LONG-GRAIN RICE, RINSED AND DRAINED

FOR THE SAUCE:
* 3 TABLESPOONS LIGHT SOY SAUCE
* 1 TABLESPOON DARK SOY SAUCE
* 1 TABLESPOON CHICKEN BROTH (STOCK, PAGE 90)
* ½ TEASPOON GRANULATED SUGAR
* ½ TEASPOON SESAME OIL

羊肉手抓饭
RICE AND LAMB CASSEROLE

REGION: XINJIANG
PREPARATION TIME: 10 MINUTES,
  PLUS 20 MINUTES SOAKING TIME
COOKING TIME: 40 MINUTES
SERVES: 4

* Soak the rice in a bowl of cold water for 20 minutes. Drain and set aside.
* Heat the oil in a Dutch oven (casserole) over medium-high heat, add the ginger and garlic, and stir-fry for 1 minute until fragrant. Stir in the lamb and fry for 2–3 minutes until browned. Add the onions and carrot, then stir in the wine, white pepper, salt, and soy sauce. Mix well and remove from the Dutch oven.
* Add the rice and 2 cups (16 fl oz/475 ml) water, then bring to a boil over high heat. Return the lamb and vegetables to the Dutch oven, reduce to low heat, and cook, covered, for about 30 minutes, or until the lamb and rice are cooked through. Mix in the scallions (spring onions) and cumin. Serve in the Dutch oven.

* 1½ CUPS (11 OZ/300 G) LONG-GRAIN RICE
* 1 TABLESPOON VEGETABLE OIL
* ¼ OZ/10 G GINGER (ABOUT ¾-INCH/ 2-CM-LENGTH PIECE), SLICED
* 2 CLOVES GARLIC, CHOPPED
* 11 OZ/300 G BONELESS LAMB, DICED INTO ½-INCH/1-CM CUBES
* 2 ONIONS, CHOPPED
* 1 CARROT, DICED
* ½ TABLESPOON RICE WINE
* ½ TEASPOON GROUND WHITE PEPPER
* 1½ TEASPOONS SALT
* 2 TEASPOONS LIGHT SOY SAUCE
* 2 SCALLIONS (SPRING ONIONS), CHOPPED
* 1 TABLESPOON GROUND CUMIN

豉汁排骨煲仔飯
RICE AND SPARERIBS
IN A CASSEROLE

- 2 TABLESPOONS FERMENTED BLACK BEANS, RINSED AND CHOPPED
- 6 CLOVES GARLIC, CHOPPED
- 2 TABLESPOONS LIGHT SOY SAUCE
- 1 TEASPOON GRANULATED SUGAR
- 2 TABLESPOONS VEGETABLE OIL
- 1 LB 5 OZ/600 G PORK SPARERIBS, CUT INTO BITE-SIZE PIECES
- 1 TABLESPOON CORNSTARCH (CORNFLOUR)
- ¾ CUP (5 OZ/150 G) LONG-GRAIN RICE, RINSED AND DRAINED
- ½ TEASPOON SALT
- SCALLIONS (SPRING ONIONS) AND SLICED RED CHILE, TO GARNISH (OPTIONAL)

FOR THE SAUCE:
- 3 TABLESPOONS LIGHT SOY SAUCE
- 1 TABLESPOON DARK SOY SAUCE
- 1 TABLESPOON CHICKEN BROTH (STOCK, PAGE 90)
- ½ TEASPOON GRANULATED SUGAR
- ½ TEASPOON SESAME OIL

* Combine the black beans, 1 tablespoon chopped garlic, soy sauce, sugar, and 1 tablespoon oil in a large bowl and mix well.
* In a separate bowl, mix the spareribs with 4 tablespoons water, stir in the cornstarch (cornflour), and tip into the bowl of black beans.
* Heat the remaining 1 tablespoon oil in a Dutch oven (casserole), add the remaining garlic, and stir-fry over medium heat for 1 minute until fragrant. Stir in the drained rice and the salt. Pour in 1 cup (8 fl oz/250 ml) water, bring to a boil, and reduce to low heat. Simmer, uncovered, for 3–4 minutes until most of the water has been absorbed. Add the spareribs and black beans, reduce to low heat, and cook, covered, for 20 minutes, or until the spareribs and rice are cooked through.
* Combine the sauce ingredients in a small saucepan and bring to a boil over high heat. Pour the sauce over the spareribs and serve straight from the Dutch oven. Garnish with scallions (spring onions) and sliced chiles, if using.

RICE AND SPARERIBS IN A CASSEROLE

白粥
PLAIN
CONGEE

- ¾ CUP (5½ OZ/150 G) LONG-GRAIN
  RICE, RINSED AND DRAINED
- ½ TEASPOON SALT, PLUS EXTRA
  TO TASTE
- ½ TABLESPOON VEGETABLE OIL

* Combine all the ingredients in a bowl and let stand for
  20 minutes.
* Put 14 cups (112 fl oz/3½ liters) water into a large saucepan
  and bring to a boil over high heat. Add the rice and bring
  to another boil. Reduce to a simmer, uncovered, for
  1¼ hours until the rice is broken down and porridge-like.
  (Stir occasionally to prevent it from sticking to the bottom.)
* Cover and let stand for another 15 minutes.
* Congee can be served as is, seasoned with salt, or as an
  accompaniment to meat, fish, or vegetable dishes.

生菜鲮鱼球粥
CONGEE WITH
FISH BALLS

- 11 OZ/300 G UNSALTED DACE FISH,
  FINELY CHOPPED
- 1 TEASPOON SALT, PLUS EXTRA
  TO TASTE
- ¼ TEASPOON GRANULATED SUGAR
- ¼ TEASPOON GROUND WHITE PEPPER
- 1 TABLESPOON CORNSTARCH
  (CORNFLOUR)
- 2 QUANTITIES PLAIN CONGEE (ABOVE)
- ½ HEAD LETTUCE, SHREDDED

* In a bowl, combine the fish, salt, sugar, and white pepper
  and marinate for 30 minutes. Add the cornstarch
  (cornflour) and mix thoroughly into a fish paste.
* Bring the congee to a boil in a saucepan over high heat.
  Use your hands to scoop a handful of the fish paste and
  squeeze it through the hole formed by the thumb and index
  finger, making a small fish ball. Drop the fish ball into the
  congee. Repeat with the remaining fish paste. Turn off the
  heat, cover, and let stand for 5 minutes.
* Boil the congee for another 5 minutes until the fish balls
  are cooked through, then season with extra salt. Stir in the
  lettuce, ladle into bowls, and serve immediately.

生滚鸡粥

CHICKEN CONGEE

REGION: HONG KONG
PREPARATION TIME: 5 MINUTES, PLUS
   30 MINUTES MARINATING TIME
COOKING TIME: 20 MINUTES
SERVES: 4

* Combine the chicken, ginger juice, soy sauce, salt, and
  sugar in a large bowl and marinate for 30 minutes.
  Stir in the cornstarch (cornflour) and vegetable oil.
* Bring the congee to a boil in a large saucepan over high
  heat. Stir in the chicken, then turn off the heat, cover,
  and let stand for 10 minutes.
* Return the congee to a boil, then reduce to low heat, and
  cook for 5 minutes, or until the chicken is cooked through.
  Take the pan off the heat, drizzle over the sesame oil, and
  mix in the lettuce. Season with extra salt to taste, then
  transfer to individual serving bowls and serve.

- 1 LB 5 OZ/600 G BONELESS, SKINLESS
  CHICKEN, CUT INTO ¾ × 1½-INCH/
  2 × 4-CM PIECES
- 2 TABLESPOONS GINGER JUICE
- 2 TABLESPOONS LIGHT SOY SAUCE
- 1 TEASPOON SALT, PLUS EXTRA
  TO TASTE
- 1 TEASPOON GRANULATED SUGAR
- 1 TABLESPOON CORNSTARCH
  (CORNFLOUR)
- 1 TABLESPOON VEGETABLE OIL
- 2 QUANTITIES PLAIN CONGEE
  (PAGE 568)
- 1 TEASPOON SESAME OIL
- ½ HEAD ICEBERG LETTUCE, SHREDDED

菜干猪骨粥

CONGEE WITH DRIED BOK CHOY AND SPARERIBS

REGION: GUANGDONG
PREPARATION TIME: 10 MINUTES,
   PLUS 4 HOURS MARINATING TIME
COOKING TIME: 1 HOUR 50 MINUTES
SERVES: 4

* Rub 3 teaspoons salt all over the spareribs and marinate
  in the refrigerator for 4 hours. Rinse off the salt, then drain.
* Meanwhile, cut off and discard the root section of the dried
  bok choy and soak in cold water for 1 hour. Rinse, drain, and
  cut into ¾-inch/2-cm lengths.
* Combine the rice, the remaining ½ teaspoon salt, and the
  oil in a bowl and set aside for 20 minutes.
* Put the spareribs into a stockpot, add 12½ cups (100 fl oz/
  3 liters) water. Bring to a boil over high heat, reduce to
  medium heat, and simmer for 20 minutes. Skim the froth
  and scum off the surface, if needed. Add the rice and boil
  over high heat for 15 minutes.
* Stir in the bok choy and simmer for 1 hour.
* Cover the pot, turn off the heat, and let stand for 10 minutes
  before serving.

- 3½ TEASPOONS SALT
- 11 OZ/300 G PORK SPARERIBS,
  CUT INTO SMALL PIECES
- 2 OZ/50 G DRIED BOK CHOY
- ¾ CUP (5½ OZ/160 G) LONG-GRAIN
  RICE, RINSED AND DRAINED
- 1 TABLESPOON VEGETABLE OIL

REGION: GUANGDONG
PREPARATION TIME: 10 MINUTES,
   PLUS 1 HOUR SOAKING TIME
COOKING TIME: 10 MINUTES
SERVES: 4
📷 PAGE 571

荔灣艇仔粥

LAIWAN-STYLE
CONGEE

- 3½ OZ/100 G DRIED SQUID, SOAKED IN WATER AND DRAINED
- ½ TEASPOON SALT
- ⅓ CUP (2 OZ/50 G) PEANUTS
- 1 TABLESPOON VEGETABLE OIL, PLUS EXTRA FOR DEEP-FRYING
- ⅛ OZ/5 G MUNG BEAN VERMICELLI
- 11 OZ/300 G WHITE FISH FILLETS, THINLY SLICED
- 2 QUANTITIES PLAIN CONGEE (PAGE 568)
- ¾ OZ/20 G GINGER (ABOUT 1-INCH/2.5-CM-LENGTH PIECE), SHREDDED
- 1 SCALLION (SPRING ONIONS), SHREDDED, TO SERVE

FOR THE PORK RIND:
- ¾ CUP (3½ OZ/100 G) PORK RINDS
- 2 SLICES GINGER
- 1 SCALLION (SPRING ONION), CUT INTO 1½-INCH/4-CM LENGTHS
- ½ TEASPOON SALT

FOR THE BEEF:
- 5 OZ/150 G GROUND (MINCED) BEEF
- 1 TEASPOON SALT
- 1 TEASPOON GRANULATED SUGAR
- ½ TEASPOON GROUND WHITE PEPPER

* Bring a large saucepan of water to a boil, then add the squid and salt. Simmer for 2 minutes, then drain and rinse. Cut into strips and set aside.
* Fill the same pan with water and bring to a boil. Add the pork rind ingredients and cook over medium-high heat for 4–5 minutes. Remove the pork rind and soak in a bowl of cold water for at least 1 hour, drain, and then cut into strips.
* Put the peanuts into a wok or deep saucepan and add enough oil to cover. Deep-fry the peanuts over medium-low heat for 3–4 minutes until crunchy. Use a slotted spoon to carefully remove the peanuts and drain on paper towels. Set aside to cool.
* Re-heat the oil remaining in the wok and gently add the vermicelli, a little at a time, and deep-fry over low heat (about 300°F/150°C) for 30 seconds until golden and puffed up. Drain on paper towels and set aside.
* Combine all beef ingredients and 4 tablespoons water in a bowl. Add the fried vermicelli and mix well by hand.
* Mix the fish with 1 tablespoon oil.
* Bring the congee to a boil in a large saucepan, add the beef mixture, squid, pork rind, and ginger, and season with salt. Stir for about 1 minute until cooked through. Ladle the mixture into each bowl. Top with the fried peanuts and shredded scallion (spring onion). Serve.

TAIWAN-STYLE CONGEE

生滚田鸡粥
CONGEE
WITH FROG LEGS

- 1 LB 5 OZ/600 G FROG LEGS, SKINNED, RINSED, AND CUT INTO BITE-SIZE PIECES
- 1 TABLESPOON GINGER JUICE
- 2 TABLESPOONS LIGHT SOY SAUCE
- 1 TEASPOON GRANULATED SUGAR
- ½ TEASPOON GROUND WHITE PEPPER
- 1 TABLESPOON CORNSTARCH (CORNFLOUR)
- 1 TABLESPOON VEGETABLE OIL
- 2 QUANTITIES PLAIN CONGEE (PAGE 568)
- ½ HEAD ROMAINE (COS) LETTUCE, SHREDDED
- 1 TEASPOON SESAME OIL
- SALT, TO TASTE

* Combine the frog legs, ginger juice, soy sauce, sugar, and white pepper in a bowl. Use your hands to combine well and marinate in the refrigerator for 30 minutes.
* Add the cornstarch (cornflour), then stir in the vegetable oil.
* Bring the congee to a boil in a large saucepan, stir in the frog mixture, and then turn off the heat. Cover and let stand for 5 minutes until the frog legs are cooked through.
* Bring the congee to another boil over high heat and stir in the lettuce.
* Add the sesame oil, season with salt to taste, and serve in a soup tureen or individual bowls.

柴鱼花生粥
CONGEE WITH TUNA
AND PEANUTS

- 1½ OZ/40 G DRIED SKIPJACK TUNA OR BONITA FLAKES
- ⅓ CUP (2¼ OZ/60 G) PEANUTS
- 2 QUANTITIES PLAIN CONGEE (PAGE 568)
- 5 OZ/150 G GROUND (MINCED) PORK
- ½ TEASPOON LIGHT SOY SAUCE
- ½ TEASPOON CORNSTARCH (CORNFLOUR)
- 2 SCALLIONS (SPRING ONIONS), CHOPPED
- SALT, TO TASTE

Dried skipjack tuna is often used in China and Japan as a flavoring agent for soups. In fact, it is a key ingredient in the classic seasoning, miso.

* Rinse the dried skipjack tuna, then soak it in bowl of warm water for 15 minutes. Drain the tuna and cut it into 1-inch/2.5-cm-square pieces.
* Bring a saucepan of water to a boil, add the tuna and peanuts, and boil for 10 minutes. Drain the tuna and peanuts.
* Bring the congee to a boil in a saucepan, add the tuna and peanuts, and continue to boil for another 30 minutes.
* Meanwhile, in a bowl, combine the pork, soy sauce, and cornstarch (cornflour) and marinate for 15 minutes.
* Stir the pork into the congee, then turn off the heat, cover, and let stand for 10 minutes until the pork is cooked through. Season with salt to taste, then ladle the congee into soup tureens or individual bowls. Garnish with chopped scallions (spring onions).

蠔仔肉碎粥
CONGEE WITH OYSTERS
AND PORK

REGION: CHAOZHOU
PREPARATION TIME: 10 MINUTES, PLUS
  20 MINUTES SOAKING TIME
COOKING TIME: 5 MINUTES
SERVES: 4

* Put the mushrooms in a bowl, cover with cold water, and soak for at least 20 minutes, or until softened. Remove the mushrooms, squeeze dry, and discard the stems. Cut into thin slices.
* Meanwhile, soak the rice in a bowl of hot water for about 5 minutes, then drain and set aside.
* Rub the oysters with 1 teaspoon cornstarch (cornflour) and pick out any fragments of shell. Rinse well under cold running water. Bring a saucepan of water to a boil, add the oysters, and blanch for 30 seconds. Drain and set aside.
* In a bowl, combine the pork, the remaining ½ teaspoon cornstarch, and ½ teaspoon salt. Marinate for 15 minutes.
* Heat the oil in a nonstick skillet (frying pan), add the dried flounder, and pan-fry over medium heat for 1–2 minutes until crispy. Set aside.
* Bring the chicken broth (stock) to a boil in a large saucepan. Add the pork and mushrooms, reduce to medium-low heat, stir, and simmer for 2 minutes until the pork is cooked through. Add the rice and bring to a boil.
* Put in the oysters, Chinese celery, preserved turnip, and remaining 1 teaspoon salt. Boil for 1 minute and then add the flounder. Stir in the white pepper just before serving.

- 3 DRIED BLACK MUSHROOMS
- 2¼ CUPS (12 OZ/350 G) COOKED RICE
- 9 OZ/250 G PEARL OR SMALL OYSTERS, SHUCKED AND DRAINED
- 1½ TEASPOONS CORNSTARCH (CORNFLOUR)
- 3 OZ/80 G GROUND (MINCED) PORK
- 1½ TEASPOONS SALT
- 2 TABLESPOONS VEGETABLE OIL
- ¼ OZ/10 G DRIED FLOUNDER FLESH, CUT INTO ½-INCH/1.5-CM CUBES
- 4¼ CUPS (1¾ PINTS/ LITER) CHICKEN BROTH (STOCK, PAGE 90)
- 1 TABLESPOON CHOPPED CHINESE CELERY OR CILANTRO (CORIANDER)
- 2 TEASPOONS CHOPPED PRESERVED TURNIP
- PINCH OF GROUND WHITE PEPPER

生滾牛肉粥
CONGEE
WITH BEEF

REGION: GUANGDONG
PREPARATION TIME: 5 MINUTES, PLUS
  15 MINUTES SOAKING TIME
COOKING TIME: 10 MINUTES
SERVES: 4

* Combine the beef with 3 tablespoons cold water in a bowl and soak for 15 minutes.
* Pour out the excess water, then mix in the garlic and cornstarch (cornflour).
* Bring the congee to a boil in a large saucepan over high heat, add the beef, and cook for 1–2 minutes until cooked through. Season with salt to taste and ladle into the serving bowls. Sprinkle with the white pepper and drizzle over the sesame oil.

- 11 OZ/300 G BEEF TENDERLOIN, VERY THINLY SLICED, OR GROUND (MINCED) BEEF
- 3 CLOVES GARLIC, CHOPPED
- 1 TABLESPOON CORNSTARCH (CORNFLOUR)
- 2 QUANTITIES PLAIN CONGEE (PAGE 568)
- ¼ TEASPOON GROUND WHITE PEPPER
- 1 TEASPOON SESAME OIL
- SALT, TO TASTE

皮蛋瘦肉粥
CONGEE WITH PORK AND PRESERVED DUCK EGGS

- 5 OZ/150 G LEAN PORK, SLICED
- 1 TABLESPOON SALT
- ½ TABLESPOON CORNSTARCH (CORNFLOUR)
- ½ TABLESPOON VEGETABLE OIL
- 2 QUANTITIES PLAIN CONGEE (PAGE 568)
- 2 PRESERVED DUCK EGGS, CHOPPED
- 2 SCALLIONS (SPRING ONIONS), CHOPPED, TO GARNISH

* Combine the pork and salt in a bowl and marinate in the refrigerator for at least 2 hours.
* Rinse the pork, drain, and return it to the bowl. Mix in the cornstarch (cornflour) and oil.
* Bring the congee to a boil in a saucepan, then turn off the heat. Separate the pork slices and gradually drop them into the pan. Cover and let stand for 10 minutes until the pork is cooked through. Do not stir.
* Stir in the preserved duck eggs and ladle into a soup tureen or individual bowls. Garnish with scallions (spring onions).

糯米麦粥
CONGEE WITH GLUTINOUS RICE AND WHEAT

- ¾ CUP (5 OZ/150 G) WHEAT BERRIES
- 1 CUP (7 OZ/200 G) GLUTINOUS RICE
- 1 SLICE GINGER
- 2 TABLESPOONS ROCK SUGAR, CRUSHED

This sweet congee can be served at breakfast or as a snack. In addition to its nourishing properties, it also soothes an upset stomach.

* Soak the wheat berries in a bowl of cold water for 8 hours.
* Soak the rice in a separate bowl of water for 4 hours. Drain both.
* In a large saucepan, combine the ginger, rice, wheat berries, and 10½ cups (4¼ pints/2.5 liters) water and bring to a boil. Cook, uncovered, over medium heat for 10 minutes. Reduce to low heat, cover, and cook for another 1 hour 20 minutes until porridge-like and tender.
* Add the rock sugar and stir until dissolved. Serve in individual bowls.

生滚猪肝鱼片粥
CONGEE WITH PORK
LIVER AND FISH

REGION: GUANGDONG
PREPARATION TIME: 15 MINUTES,
  PLUS 1 HOUR SOAKING TIME
COOKING TIME: 10 MINUTES
SERVES: 4

* Soak the pork liver in a bowl of cold water for about 1 hour, changing the water 2–3 times and occasionally pressing the liver gently to force out the blood. Drain, then cut the pork liver into ¼-inch/5-mm-thick slices. Combine the liver and half the ginger in a bowl and mix.
* Sprinkle the fish with the salt and set aside for 10 minutes.
* Rinse the fish and pat dry with paper towels and then thinly slice. Combine the fish, the remaining ginger, white pepper, and oil in a bowl and mix well.
* Bring the congee to a boil in a large saucepan over high heat. Stir in the pork liver and fish, cover then turn off the heat, and let stand for 4 minutes until the liver and fish are cooked through.
* Ladle into individual bowls and garnish with chopped cilantro (coriander).

• 11 OZ/300 G PORK LIVER
• 2 OZ/50 G GINGER (ABOUT 3-INCH/7.5-CM-LENGTH PIECE), SHREDDED
• 11 OZ/300 G WHITE FISH FILLETS
• ½ TEASPOON SALT, PLUS EXTRA TO TASTE
• PINCH OF GROUND WHITE PEPPER
• 1 TABLESPOON VEGETABLE OIL
• 2 QUANTITIES PLAIN CONGEE (PAGE 568)
• 1 BUNCH CILANTRO (CORIANDER), CHOPPED, TO GARNISH

小米粥
MILLET CONGEE

REGION: INNER MONGOLIA
PREPARATION TIME: 20 MINUTES
COOKING TIME: 45 MINUTES
SERVES: 4

This ancient cereal grain has been used in northeast China and Inner Mongolia since the Shang Dynasty in 1,600 BC. In fact, Chairman Mao and the Red Army were dependent on millet as sustenance while fighting the Kuomintang and the invading Japanese. It is gluten free and high in protein.

* Rinse the millet and soak in a bowl of cold water for 15 minutes. Drain.
* Bring 8½ cups (68 fl oz/2 liters) water to a boil in a large saucepan. Add the millet, and cook, uncovered, over medium-high heat for about 30 minutes. Turn off the heat, cover, and stand for 10 minutes until porridge-like.
* Flavor with salt or sugar.

• ½ CUP (3½ OZ/100 G) FOXTAIL MILLET
• SALT OR SUGAR, TO TASTE

REGION: GUANGDONG
PREPARATION TIME: 5 MINUTES
COOKING TIME: 15 MINUTES
SERVES: 4

姜丝鱼腩粥
CONGEE WITH FISH BELLY

- 1 LB 5 OZ/600 G FISH BELLY
- 1½ OZ/40 G GINGER (ABOUT 2½-INCH/6-CM-LENGTH PIECE), SHREDDED
- 1 TABLESPOON VEGETABLE OIL
- 2 QUANTITIES PLAIN CONGEE (PAGE 568)
- 1 TEASPOON SALT
- 1 SCALLION (SPRING ONION), CHOPPED

* Rinse the fish belly in cold water and remove the black membrane on the flesh. Rinse and cut into ½-inch/1-cm-thick chunks. Place in a bowl, then add the ginger and oil.
* Bring the congee to a boil in a large saucepan, then season with the salt and add the fish belly. Stir, then turn off the heat, cover, and let stand for 10 minutes. Return the congee to a boil and remove from the heat once the fish is cooked through. Ladle into a soup tureen or into individual bowls and garnish with the chopped scallion (spring onion).

REGION: TAIWAN
PREPARATION TIME: 25 MINUTES
COOKING TIME: 40 MINUTES
SERVES: 4
📷 PAGE 577

台湾红烧牛肉面
TAIWAN-STYLE BEEF NOODLES

- 1 TOMATO
- 1 STAR ANISE
- ½–1 TEASPOON SICHUAN PEPPERCORNS
- 1 TABLESPOON VEGETABLE OIL
- 1 TEASPOON SLICED GINGER
- 1 TABLESPOON RED DISTILLED GRAIN SAUCE
- 1 TABLESPOON BEAN PASTE
- 1 LB 2 OZ/500 G BEEF SHANK
- 1 TABLESPOON SHAOXING WINE
- 1 TABLESPOON DARK SOY SAUCE
- ½ TABLESPOON LIGHT SOY SAUCE
- ½ TEASPOON SALT
- 1 TEASPOON GRANULATED SUGAR
- 7 OZ/200 G DRIED WHEAT NOODLES
- 3 CUPS (25 FL OZ/750 ML) HOT BEEF BROTH (STOCK, PAGE 90)
- 2 SCALLIONS (SPRING ONIONS), CHOPPED, TO GARNISH
- CILANTRO (CORIANDER), TO GARNISH (OPTIONAL)

* Score the base of the tomato. Bring a small saucepan of water to a boil, add the tomato, and heat for 1–2 minutes. Immediately transfer to a bowl of ice water. When the tomato is cool enough to handle, peel away the skin. Chop, then set aside.
* Place the star anise and Sichuan peppercorns into a spice bag.
* Heat the oil in a wok or large skillet (frying pan) over medium-high heat, add the ginger, and stir-fry for 1 minute until fragrant. Add the red distilled grain sauce, bean paste, and beef shank and stir-fry for another 2–3 minutes, just until the beef is browned. Pour in the wine and enough water to cover the beef. Increase to high heat and bring to a boil, then reduce to low heat. Add the spice bag and chopped tomato. Stir, cover, and simmer for 30 minutes until the beef is tender. Add the soy sauces, salt, and sugar.
* Discard the ginger and spice bag and use a pair of tongs to remove the beef shank from the sauce. Cut the beef into thick pieces, then return it to the sauce.
* Meanwhile, bring a large saucepan of water to a boil, then add the noodles. Cook according to the package directions, or until tender. Drain, then divide the noodles among serving bowls. Ladle the beef and broth over the noodles and garnish with scallions (spring onions) and cilantro (coriander), if using.

TAIWAN-STYLE BEEF NOODLES

REGION: SHANGHAI
PREPARATION TIME: 10 MINUTES,
    PLUS 1 HOUR MARINATING TIME
COOKING TIME: 10 MINUTES
SERVES: 2
📷 PAGE 579

上海排骨面
SHANGHAI PORK CHOP NOODLE SOUP

- 2 PORK LOIN CHOPS
- 1 CUP (8 FL OZ/250 ML) VEGETABLE OIL
- 4 GREEN BOK CHOY
- 11 OZ/300 G FRESH SHANGHAI NOODLES
- ¼ TEASPOON SALT
- ½ TEASPOON SESAME OIL
- 2½ CUPS (18 FL OZ/550 ML) HOT PORK BROTH (STOCK, PAGE 91)
- 1 TABLESPOON CHOPPED SCALLION (SPRING ONION), TO GARNISH

FOR THE MARINADE:
- 1 TABLESPOON SHAOXING WINE
- 1 TABLESPOON CHOPPED GARLIC
- 2 TEASPOONS LIGHT SOY SAUCE
- 1 TEASPOON GRANULATED SUGAR
- ½ TEASPOON GROUND WHITE PEPPER

* Use a meat mallet or the back of a heavy knife to repeatedly pound the pork chops to tenderize. Combine the pork and marinade ingredients in a bowl and marinate in the refrigerator for 1 hour.
* Heat the vegetable oil in a wok or large skillet (frying pan) to 340°F/170°C, or until a cube of bread browns in 45 seconds. Gently lower the pork chops into the oil and deep-fry for 3–4 minutes until golden brown and cooked through. Use a slotted spoon to carefully remove the chops from the oil and drain on paper towels. Set aside.
* Bring a large saucepan of water to a boil over high heat and blanch the bok choy for 3 minutes. Drain.
* Bring another large saucepan of water to a boil, then add the noodles. Cook according to the package directions until just tender. Drain, then divide among serving bowls.
* Put the bok choy on top of the noodles, season both with the salt and sesame oil, then ladle over the pork broth (stock). Sprinkle over the scallion (spring onion). Serve the pork chop separately on a plate or slice and place on top of the noodles.

蟹肉片儿面
CRAB MEAT SOUP WITH CRISPY WONTON WRAPPERS

- 2 CUPS (16 FL OZ/475 ML) VEGETABLE OIL
- 16 CANTONESE-STYLE WONTON WRAPPERS, CUT INTO ¾-INCH/ 2-CM SQUARES
- 2½ CUPS (20 FL OZ/600 ML) CHICKEN BROTH (STOCK, PAGE 90)
- ¾ CUP (5 OZ/150 G) STRAW MUSHROOMS, TRIMMED AND HALVED
- 1 TEASPOON SALT
- ⅓ CUP (5 OZ/150 G) CRAB MEAT
- ¼ TEASPOON SESAME OIL
- ½ TEASPOON GROUND WHITE PEPPER
- 1½ OZ/40 G YELLOW CHIVES, CUT INTO ¾-INCH/2-CM LENGTHS

* Heat the vegetable oil in a wok or deep saucepan to 300°F/150°C, or until a cube of bread browns in 1½ minutes. Gently lower in the wonton wrappers, in batches, and deep-fry for 1–2 minutes until crispy. Use a slotted spoon to remove the wonton squares from the oil and drain on paper towels.
* Bring the chicken broth (stock) to a boil in a medium saucepan, add the mushrooms and salt, and bring to a boil.
* Put in the crab meat, return to a boil, and stir in the sesame oil and white pepper.
* Put the chives into a tureen. Pour the chicken broth with the crab meat over the chives.
* Serve the soup with the wonton squares on the side—guests can add them to the broth just before eating.

SHANGHAI PORK CHOP NOODLE SOUP

番茄蛋汤面

NOODLE SOUP WITH
TOMATO AND EGGS

- 1 LARGE TOMATO
- 2 EGGS, SEPARATED
- 2 TABLESPOONS PLUS 1 TEASPOON
  VEGETABLE OIL
- ½ TEASPOON SALT
- 5 OZ/150 G DRIED EGG NOODLES
- 2 CUPS (16 FL OZ/475 ML) CHICKEN
  BROTH (STOCK, PAGE 90)
- ⅛ OZ/5 G GINGER (ABOUT ½-INCH/
  1-CM-LENGTH PIECE), SHREDDED
- ½ TEASPOON GRANULATED SUGAR

* Score the base of the tomato. Bring a small saucepan of
  water to a boil, add the tomato, and heat for 1–2 minutes.
  Immediately transfer to a bowl of ice water. When the
  tomato is cool enough to handle, peel away the skin. Chop,
  then set aside.
* Beat the egg whites in a bowl until foamy. Add 1 teaspoon
  oil, ¼ teaspoon salt, and the egg yolks and beat again until
  fully blended.
* Bring a large saucepan of water to a boil over high heat.
  Add the noodles and cook according to the package
  direction until tender. Drain and put into a bowl.
* Bring the chicken broth (stock) to a boil in a saucepan,
  then ladle it over the noodles.
* Heat 1 tablespoon oil in a wok or large skillet (frying pan)
  over medium-high heat, add the ginger, and stir-fry for
  2 minutes until fragrant. Put in the tomato, sugar, and
  remaining ¼ teaspoon salt and stir-fry for about
  1–2 minutes. Remove from the wok and set aside on a plate.
* Wipe the wok with paper towel and heat the remaining
  1 tablespoon oil over medium-high heat. Pour in the beaten
  eggs and turn the heat off immediately. Scramble until the
  eggs are just cooked but slightly runny. Finally, stir in the
  tomato mixture and spoon on top of the noodles. Serve
  immediately.

羊肉烩面

NOODLE SOUP
WITH MUTTON

- 5 OZ/150 G DRIED WHEAT NOODLES
- 1 TEASPOON VEGETABLE OIL
- 3 SCALLIONS (SPRING ONIONS), CUT
  INTO 2-INCH/5-CM LENGTHS
- 1 TEASPOON LIGHT SOY SAUCE
- ½ TEASPOON SALT
- ¼ TEASPOON SESAME OIL
- PINCH OF GROUND WHITE PEPPER
- 11 OZ/300 G BONELESS MUTTON OR
  LAMB, THINLY SLICED

* Bring a large saucepan of water to a boil, then add the
  noodles. Cook according to the package directions until
  tender. Drain and set aside.
* Heat the vegetable oil in the same saucepan over medium
  heat and stir-fry the scallions (spring onions) until soft.
  Pour in 2 cups (16 fl oz/475 ml) water, bring to a boil, and
  add the soy sauce, salt, sesame oil, and white pepper.
  Stir the mutton into the soup, separate the slices with
  a chopstick, and then add the noodles. Simmer for about
  2 minutes until the mutton is cooked through. Transfer to
  individual bowls and serve immediately.

冬菇素汤面
VEGETARIAN
NOODLE SOUP

REGION: HONG KONG
PREPARATION TIME: 5 MINUTES,
  PLUS 20 MINUTES SOAKING TIME
COOKING TIME: 15 MINUTES
SERVES: 2

* Put the mushrooms in a bowl, cover with cold water, and soak for at least 20 minutes, or until softened. Remove the mushrooms, squeeze dry, and discard the stems. Return the mushrooms to the bowl, add the sugar and soy sauce, and marinate for at least 5 minutes until needed.
* Bring a large saucepan of water to a boil, then add the noodles. Cook according to the package directions until just tender. Drain, then divide among serving bowls.
* Bring another saucepan of water to a boil over high heat, add the vegetables and cook until tender. (Carrots will require a longer blanching time than leafy greens.) Drain the vegetables and put in the noodle bowls.
* Heat the vegetable broth (stock) in a saucepan. Add the mushrooms and bring to a boil over high heat. Reduce to medium heat, and cook for 5 minutes. Add the salt, adjust the seasoning to taste, then ladle the broth into the bowls and top with the mushrooms. Serve.

- 6 DRIED BLACK MUSHROOMS
- ½ TEASPOON GRANULATED SUGAR
- 1 TEASPOON LIGHT SOY SAUCE
- 3½ OZ/100 G DRIED WHEAT NOODLES
- 3½ OZ/100 G ASSORTED VEGETABLES (CARROTS, LEAFY GREENS, OR BROCCOLI), CHOPPED INTO EQUAL-SIZE PIECES
- 3 CUPS (25 FL OZ/750 ML) VEGETABLE BROTH (STOCK, PAGE 92)
- ¼ TEASPOON SALT, PLUS EXTRA TO TASTE

嫩鸡煨面
SHANGHAI CHICKEN
NOODLE SOUP

REGION: SHANGHAI
PREPARATION TIME: 10 MINUTES
COOKING TIME: 15 MINUTES
SERVES: 2

* Combine the chicken, salt, and white pepper in a bowl and mix well.
* Bring a large saucepan of water to a boil, then add the noodles. Cook according to the package directions until just tender. Drain and set aside.
* Bring the chicken broth (stock) and 1 cup (8 fl oz/250 ml) water to a boil in a saucepan over high heat. Add the chicken and cook for 3 minutes until the chicken is cooked through. Add the noodles to the soup, reduce to low heat, and cook for another minute.
* Season with extra salt and pepper, then ladle the soup and noodles into a large serving bowl.

- 2 BONELESS, SKINLESS CHICKEN THIGHS, CUT INTO BITE-SIZE PIECES
- ½ TEASPOON SALT, PLUS EXTRA TO TASTE
- PINCH OF GROUND WHITE PEPPER, PLUS EXTRA TO TASTE
- 3½ OZ/100 G DRIED SHANGHAI NOODLES
- 2 CUPS (16 FL OZ/475 ML) CHICKEN BROTH (STOCK, PAGE 90)

REGION: HONG KONG
PREPARATION TIME: 5 MINUTES
COOKING TIME: 15 MINUTES
SERVES: 4
📷 PAGE 583

雪菜火鸭丝汤米粉
VERMICELLI WITH ROAST DUCK IN SOUP

- 7 OZ/200 G DRIED RICE VERMICELLI
- 3 CUPS (25 FL OZ/750 ML) CHICKEN BROTH (STOCK, PAGE 90)
- ½ TEASPOON SALT
- 1 TABLESPOON VEGETABLE OIL
- 1 CLOVE GARLIC, SLICED
- 5 OZ/150 G PRESERVED MUSTARD GREENS, RINSED, TRIMMED, AND CHOPPED
- 1 RED CHILE, SEEDED AND FINELY SLICED (OPTIONAL)
- ½ SMALL ROAST DUCK, MEAT SHREDDED
- 1 TEASPOON CORNSTARCH (CORNFLOUR)

  FOR THE SAUCE:
- 2 TEASPOONS LIGHT SOY SAUCE
- 1 TEASPOON GRANULATED SUGAR
- 1 TEASPOON SESAME OIL

* Bring a large saucepan of water to a boil and add the vermicelli. Cover, turn off the heat, and let stand for 10 minutes until softened. Using chopsticks, stir the vermicelli to prevent it from sticking, then drain.
* Put the chicken broth (stock), salt, and 2 cups (16 fl oz/ 475 ml) water in a large saucepan and bring to a boil. Add the vermicelli, return to a boil, and then transfer everything to a soup tureen.
* Heat the vegetable oil in a wok or large skillet (frying pan) over high heat, add the garlic, and stir-fry 1 minute until golden. Add the mustard greens and chile, if using, and stir-fry for 1 minute. Stir in the roast duck and sauce ingredients, add 4 tablespoons water, and bring to a boil.
* Mix the cornstarch (cornflour) with 1 tablespoon water in a small bowl and stir this mixture into the wok. Bring to a boil, stirring, for 30 seconds to thicken the sauce, then pour over the vermicelli.

REGION: HONG KONG
PREPARATION TIME: 10 MINUTES
COOKING TIME: 15 MINUTES
SERVES: 2

虾球汤面
NOODLE SOUP WITH SHRIMP

- 6-8 UNCOOKED SHRIMP (PRAWNS), SHELLED AND DEVEINED
- ¾ TEASPOON SALT, PLUS EXTRA TO TASTE
- 3½ OZ/100 G DRIED EGG NOODLES
- 2 CUPS (16 FL OZ/475 ML) CHICKEN BROTH (STOCK, PAGE 90)
- 2¾ OZ/75 G YELLOW CHIVES, CUT INTO 2-INCH/5-CM LENGTHS

* Cut the shrimp (prawns) lengthwise along the back. Rub with ½ teaspoon salt, then rinse thoroughly and drain.
* Bring a large saucepan of water to a boil, then add the noodles. Cook according to the package directions until just tender. Drain.
* Meanwhile, put the chicken broth (stock) in a saucepan and bring to a boil. Add the noodles and return to a boil. Transfer the noodles to serving bowls.
* Bring the broth to a boil, add the shrimp, chives, and remaining ¼ teaspoon salt, and boil for 1–2 minutes until the shrimp are fully cooked. Season with extra salt to taste. Pour the shrimp and broth over the noodles in the bowls to serve.

VERMICELLI WITH ROAST DUCK IN SOUP

松茸火腿烩伊面
YI-NOODLES WITH MUSHROOMS AND CHINESE BACON

- 3–4 FRESH MATSUTAKE MUSHROOMS
- ¾ OZ/20 G CHINESE CURED BACON
- 7 OZ/200 G YI-NOODLES
- 1 TABLESPOON VEGETABLE OIL
- ½ CUP (4 FL OZ/120 ML) CHICKEN BROTH (STOCK, PAGE 90)
- 1 TABLESPOON MATSUTAKE MUSHROOM POWDER
- 1 TABLESPOON OYSTER SAUCE
- ½ TABLESPOON DARK SOY SAUCE

* Use a damp cloth to clean the mushrooms and then tear them into strips.
* Place the bacon in a collapsible pot or bamboo steamer over a pot of boiling water. Steam, covered, for 5 minutes. Drain, then slice the bacon into thin strips.
* Bring a large saucepan of water to a boil, then add the noodles. Using chopsticks, stir and separate the noodles, then drain immediately and rinse under cold running water.
* Heat the oil in a wok or skillet (frying pan) over medium-high heat, add the bacon, and stir-fry for 1 minute. Add the mushrooms and the chicken broth (stock), then bring to a boil and reduce to low heat.
* Add the mushroom powder and oyster and soy sauces.
* Put in the noodles, then stir gently for 1–2 minutes until the sauce thickens and most of it has been completely absorbed by the noodles. Serve.

干烧伊面
BRAISED YI-NOODLES

- 1¼ CUPS (9 OZ/250 G STRAW MUSHROOMS), RINSED AND HALVED
- 9 OZ/250 G YI-NOODLES
- 1½ TABLESPOONS OYSTER SAUCE
- 1 TABLESPOON VEGETABLE OIL
- 2 CLOVES GARLIC, GRATED
- 1 TEASPOON SHAOXING WINE
- 5 OZ/150 G CHIVES, CUT INTO 2½-INCH/6-CM LENGTHS
- ½ TEASPOON SESAME OIL

  FOR THE SAUCE:
- 1 TABLESPOON LIGHT SOY SAUCE
- 1 TEASPOON DARK SOY SAUCE
- ½ TEASPOON GRANULATED SUGAR
- 1 CUP (8 FL OZ/250 ML) CHICKEN BROTH (STOCK, PAGE 90)

* If using fresh straw mushrooms, bring a large saucepan of water to a boil over high heat, add the mushrooms, and blanch for 1 minute. Drain and rinse under cold running water. Set aside.
* Fill the same pan with plenty of water and bring to a boil. Add the noodles, using chopsticks to stir and separate them, and cook for 1 minute. Drain and put the noodles on a serving plate.
* Mix all the sauce ingredients in a small bowl.
* Heat the vegetable oil in a wok or large skillet (frying pan) over medium heat, add the garlic, and stir-fry for 1 minute until fragrant. Add the straw mushrooms and wine, then stir-fry for another minute. Add the sauce, bring to a boil, and then stir in the noodles and chives. Reduce to low heat and stir continuously for 3–4 minutes, or until the noodles have absorbed most of the liquid. Drizzle in the sesame oil, transfer to the serving plate, and serve.

YI-NOODLES WITH MUSHROOMS AND CHINESE BACON

REGION: BEIJING
PREPARATION TIME: 10 MINUTES, PLUS
  20 MINUTES SOAKING TIME
COOKING TIME: 15 MINUTES
SERVES: 2

打卤面
NOODLES WITH
PORK AND GRAVY

- 4 DRIED BLACK MUSHROOMS
- ½ CUP (¼ OZ/10 G) DRIED BLACK FUNGUS
- 2 OZ/50 G PORK TENDERLOIN
- 5 OZ/150 G DRIED WHEAT NOODLES
- 2 TABLESPOONS VEGETABLE OIL
- ½ CUCUMBER, SLICED
- 1 NAPA CABBAGE LEAF, SHREDDED
- ½ CARROT, SLICED
- 2 CUPS (16 FL OZ/475 ML) PORK BROTH (STOCK, PAGE 91)
- ½ TEASPOON SALT
- 1 TABLESPOON LIGHT SOY SAUCE
- 1 TABLESPOON CORNSTARCH (CORNFLOUR)
- ½ TEASPOON SESAME OIL
- 1 EGG, LIGHTLY BEATEN

FOR THE PORK MARINADE:
- ½ TEASPOON LIGHT SOY SAUCE
- ½ TEASPOON CORNSTARCH (CORNFLOUR)
- ¼ TEASPOON GRANULATED SUGAR

* Put the mushrooms in a bowl, cover with cold water, and soak for at least 20 minutes, or until softened. Remove the mushrooms, squeeze dry, and discard the stems. Cut the mushrooms into slices and tear the black fungus into bite-size pieces. Set both aside.
* Meanwhile, combine all the marinade ingredients and 1 tablespoon water in a small bowl. Add the pork and marinate for 15 minutes.
* Bring a large saucepan of water to a boil, then add the noodles. Cook according to the package directions until just tender. Drain, then divide among serving bowls.
* Heat the vegetable oil in a wok or large skillet (frying pan) over medium heat. Add the pork, mushrooms, cucumber, black fungus, Napa cabbage, and carrot and stir-fry for 2–3 minutes. Pour in the pork broth (stock), 1 cup (8 fl oz/250 ml) water, the salt, and soy sauce and cook for 3 minutes, or until the pork is cooked through.
* Mix the cornstarch (cornflour) with 3 tablespoons water in a small bowl and stir this mixture into the wok. Bring to a boil, stirring, for 30 seconds to thicken the sauce. Drizzle in the sesame oil.
* Drizzle in the beaten egg and use chopsticks to stir, making strands of egg. Pour the meat and gravy over the noodles, then serve.

REGION: HONG KONG
PREPARATION TIME: 5 MINUTES
COOKING TIME: 15 MINUTES
SERVES: 4

虾子烩面
BRAISED NOODLES
WITH SHRIMP ROE

- 11 OZ/300 G DRIED THIN EGG NOODLES
- 2 TABLESPOONS VEGETABLE OIL
- ½ OZ/20 G GINGER (ABOUT 1-INCH/2.5-CM-LENGTH PIECE), SHREDDED
- 2 TABLESPOONS SHRIMP ROE
- 1 CUP (8 FL OZ/250 ML) CHICKEN BROTH (STOCK, PAGE 90)
- 2 TABLESPOONS OYSTER SAUCE
- 2 SCALLIONS (SPRING ONIONS), SHREDDED
- 1 TEASPOON SESAME OIL

* Bring a saucepan of water to a boil, then add the noodles. Cook according to the package directions until just tender. Drain, rinse under cold running water, and set aside.
* Heat the vegetable oil in a wok or large skillet (frying pan) over medium-high heat, add the ginger, and stir-fry for 1–2 minutes until fragrant. Put in the shrimp roe and stir-fry for 30 seconds. Add the chicken broth (stock) and bring to a boil. Stir in the oyster sauce and noodles and mix well.
* Reduce to low heat and stir-fry for 2–3 minutes until the broth has been completely absorbed by the noodles.
* Sprinkle in the scallions (spring onions) and drizzle over the sesame oil. Stir well, transfer to a serving plate, and serve.

黄鱼煨面

NOODLE SOUP
WITH CORVINA

REGION: SHANGHAI
PREPARATION TIME: 15 MINUTES,
   PLUS 30 MINUTES CHILLING TIME
COOKING TIME: 35 MINUTES
SERVES: 2

* Remove any pinbones from the fillet. On a plate lined with paper towels, combine the fillets and ½ teaspoon salt and wrap around more paper towels to cover. Refrigerate for 30 minutes to firm up the fish.
* Meanwhile, in a small skillet (frying pan), heat the mustard greens over low heat to remove most of the moisture. Take off the heat, put in a bowl, and mix in the sugar. Set aside.
* Heat the oil in a large saucepan over high heat, add the ginger, reserved fish head and bones, wine, and 2 cups (16 fl oz/475 ml) boiling water, and bring to a boil. Reduce to medium-low heat and simmer for 10–15 minutes until the broth turns white.
* Strain the broth and discard the ginger, fish head, and bones. Pour the broth back into the pan, add the mustard greens and bamboo shoots, and bring to a boil. Reduce to medium heat and simmer for 10 minutes until the flavors have mingled and the shoots are tender.
* Meanwhile, bring a large saucepan of water to a boil, then add the noodles. Cook over medium heat until just tender. Drain. Set aside.
* Cut the fillets into bite-size chunks and put into a bowl. Add the ginger juice and white pepper and mix well.
* Put the noodles in the soup, then add the fish fillets and remaining ½ teaspoon salt. Bring to a boil, reduce to low heat, and simmer for about 3 minutes, or until the fish is cooked through. Divide the noodles between bowls, ladle over the soup, and serve.

- 1 (1-LB/450-G) CORVINA (YELLOW CROAKER) FISH, CLEANED, FILLETED, AND HEAD AND BONES RESERVED
- 1 TEASPOON SALT
- 3½ OZ/100 G PRESERVED MUSTARD GREENS, TRIMMED, RINSED, AND CHOPPED
- 1 TEASPOON GRANULATED SUGAR
- 1 TEASPOON VEGETABLE OIL
- ⅛ OZ/5 G GINGER (ABOUT ½-INCH/ 1-CM-LENGTH PIECE), SLICED
- 1 TEASPOON SHAOXING WINE
- 2 OZ/50 G BAMBOO SHOOTS, CUT INTO THIN STRIPS
- 11 OZ/300 G FRESH SHANGHAI NOODLES
- 1 TABLESPOON GINGER JUICE
- PINCH OF GROUND WHITE PEPPER

REGION: CHAOZHOU
PREPARATION TIME: 10 MINUTES, PLUS
 10 MINUTES MARINATING TIME
COOKING TIME: 10 MINUTES
SERVES: 4
📷 PAGE 589

炒粿条

CHAR KWAY
TEOW

- 5 OZ/150 G PORK TENDERLOIN, SLICED
- 1 TEASPOON SALT
- PINCH OF GROUND WHITE PEPPER
- 1 TEASPOON CORNSTARCH
  (CORNFLOUR)
- 1 LB/450 G FRESH RICE NOODLES
- 2 TABLESPOONS LIGHT SOY SAUCE
- 3 TABLESPOONS PLUS 1 TEASPOON
  VEGETABLE OIL
- 1 CLOVE GARLIC, CHOPPED
- 1 CHINESE SAUSAGE, CUT DIAGONALLY
  INTO ¼-INCH/5-MM-THICK SLICES
- 15 OZ/150 G UNCOOKED SHRIMP
  (PRAWNS), SHELLED AND DEVEINED
- 2 SHALLOTS, SLICED
- 1 RED CHILE, SEEDED AND SHREDDED
- ½ TABLESPOON CURRY POWDER
- 1 TEASPOON GRANULATED SUGAR
- 1 EGG
- 1½ CUPS (5 OZ/150 G) BEAN SPROUTS
- 1 TABLESPOON CRISPY GARLIC (PAGE
  195), TO SERVE

* Combine the pork, ½ teaspoon salt, the white pepper, cornstarch (cornflour), and 1 tablespoon water in a bowl and marinate for 10 minutes.
* Meanwhile, put the rice noodles into a bowl. Separate the strands of the rice noodles and stir in the soy sauce. Set aside.
* Add 1 teaspoon oil to the marinated pork and mix well.
* Heat 1 tablespoon oil in a wok or large skillet (frying pan) over medium-high heat, add the garlic, and stir-fry for 1 minute until fragrant. Add the pork, increase to high heat, and stir-fry for 1 minute. Add the sausage and shrimp (prawns) and stir-fry for about 2 minutes until all the ingredients are fully cooked. Transfer to a plate.
* Heat 1 tablespoon oil in a clean wok over medium heat, add the shallots, chile, and curry powder, and stir-fry over low heat for 1 minute until fragrant.
* Stir in ¼ cup (2 fl oz/50 ml) water and increase to high heat. Add the rice noodles, sugar, and remaining ½ teaspoon salt and toss to mix well.
* Push the noodles to the sides of the wok, leaving an opening in the center. Add the remaining 1 tablespoon oil, then crack the egg into it. Stir for 2–3 minutes until the egg is cooked and mixed with the rice noodles.
* Add the bean sprouts, pork, sausage, and shrimp. Mix well, then transfer to a serving plate, top with the crispy garlic, and serve.

CHAR KWAY TEOW

REGION: SICHUAN
PREPARATION TIME: 10 MINUTES
COOKING TIME: 10 MINUTES
SERVES: 2
📷 PAGE 591

担担面
DAN DAN
NOODLES

- 2 TABLESPOONS VEGETABLE OIL
- 4 TABLESPOONS SICHUAN PRESERVED MUSTARD GREENS, TRIMMED, RINSED, AND CHOPPED
- 5 OZ/150 G GROUND (MINCED) BEEF OR PORK
- 3 TEASPOONS LIGHT SOY SAUCE
- 7 OZ/200 G DRIED RICE NOODLES
- 2 TABLESPOONS SESAME PASTE, MIXED WITH 2 TABLESPOONS WATER
- 2 TABLESPOONS SICHUAN PEPPER OIL
- 4 TABLESPOONS CHILI OIL
- ½ CUP (4 FL OZ/120 ML) HOT CHICKEN BROTH (STOCK, PAGE 90)
- ⅓ CUP (2 OZ/50 G) PEANUTS, TOASTED AND CRUSHED
- 1 SCALLION (SPRING ONION), CHOPPED

Dan Dan noodles is a classic Sichuan dish, which is prepared with pork or beef and a spicy sauce made with chili oil and preserved vegetables. As with most Sichuan recipes, adjust the spiciness with the amount of oil and peppercorns used.

* Heat 1 tablespoon vegetable oil in a wok or large skillet (frying pan) over medium-high heat, add the mustard greens, and stir-fry for 3–4 minutes until fragrant. Set aside.
* Combine the beef or pork and 1 teaspoon soy sauce in a bowl. Heat the remaining 1 tablespoon vegetable oil in a clean wok over medium-high heat, add the ground meat, and stir-fry for 3–4 minutes until cooked through.
* Meanwhile, bring a large saucepan of water to a boil, then add the noodles. Cook according to the package directions until just tender. Drain, then divide among serving bowls.
* Divide the sesame paste, preserved mustard greens, meat, remaining 2 teaspoons soy sauce, and the Sichuan and chili oils between the noodle bowls. Ladle over the hot chicken broth (stock), then top with the crushed peanuts and chopped scallion (spring onion).

REGION: HONG KONG
PREPARATION TIME: 10 MINUTES
COOKING TIME: 20 MINUTES
SERVES: 2–3

雞絲冷麵
CHILLED NOODLES
WITH CHICKEN

- 5 OZ/150 G DRIED EGG NOODLES
- 2 BONELESS, SKINLESS CHICKEN BREASTS
- 1 TEASPOON WHITE SESAME SEEDS
- 2 TEASPOONS SESAME OIL
- 1 SMALL CUCUMBER, SHREDDED
- 1 SMALL CARROT, SHREDDED

  FOR THE SAUCE:
- 3 TABLESPOONS HOISIN SAUCE
- 3 TABLESPOONS SESAME PASTE
- 1½ TABLESPOONS LIGHT SOY SAUCE
- 1½ TABLESPOONS OYSTER SAUCE
- 1½ TABLESPOONS BLACK OR BALSAMIC VINEGAR
- 1½ TABLESPOONS GRANULATED SUGAR

* Bring a large saucepan of water to a boil, then add the noodles. Cook the noodles according to the package directions until just tender, separating the noodles with chopsticks. Drain, rinse, and refrigerate until cooled.
* In the same saucepan, add 4¼ cups (34 fl oz/1 liter) water and bring to a boil. Add the chicken and return to a boil. Cover, turn the heat off, and let stand for 10 minutes until cooked. Cut the chicken into strips and refrigerate.
* Toast the sesame seeds in a small pan over medium heat and shake occasionally for 3–5 minutes, or until golden brown. Set aside.
* To make the sauce, combine all the ingredients and 3 tablespoons cold water and mix well.
* Combine the noodles with the sesame oil, add the cucumber and carrot, and top with the shredded chicken.
* Pour the sauce over the noodles, sprinkle over the sesame seeds, and serve.

RICE, CONGEE & NOODLES

DAN DAN NOODLES

拉条子

HAND-PULLED
NOODLES

- 1 (5-OZ/150-G) LEG OF LAMB, SLICED
- ½ TEASPOON LIGHT SOY SAUCE
- 1 TABLESPOON VEGETABLE OIL, PLUS
  EXTRA FOR GREASING
- 1 SLICE GINGER
- 1 ONION, SLICED
- 1 TOMATO, CUT INTO CHUNKS
- ½ TEASPOON SALT
- ½ TEASPOON GRANULATED SUGAR
- 1 EGG, BEATEN
- ½ TEASPOON CORNSTARCH
  (CORNFLOUR)

FOR THE HAND-PULLED NOODLES:
- 1½ CUPS (5 OZ/150 G) CAKE FLOUR
  OR ALL-PURPOSE (PLAIN) FLOUR,
  PLUS EXTRA IF NEEDED
- ½ TEASPOON SALT

* To make the hand-pulled noodles, combine the flour and salt in a large bowl. Gradually pour in 5 tablespoons warm water, little by little, and mix until fully combined—do not add all the water at once. The dough should be a little dry to the touch. If the dough is too wet, add more flour.
* Bring the dough together and knead on a lightly floured surface for about 1 minute until the surface is smooth and the texture springy. Shape the dough into a smooth ball and return to the bowl. Cover with a dish towel and proof in a warm place for 20 minutes.
* Take out the dough and knead for about 1 minute (being careful not to over-knead, which will make it more difficult to "pull" the noodles into strands) and shape it into a ball. Return to the bowl, cover with a clean dish towel, and proof for another 20 minutes.
* Transfer the dough to an oiled surface. Cut the dough into 4 pieces and roll each piece into a 24-inch/60-cm log shape. Oil each piece, then return them to the bowl, cover, and let stand for another 20 minutes. The dough can be refrigerated until ready for use.
* When ready to make the noodles, take a piece of dough, roll it into a long, thin strand (about the diameter of a chopstick), and gently stretch to arm's length. Set aside and repeat with the remaining pieces of dough. You want to work quickly to ensure an even thickness of noodles.
* Bring a large saucepan of water to a boil over high heat. Lower each noodle into the pan, stretching it as it goes in. Use chopsticks to disperse the noodles in the water. Cook for 4–5 minutes until just tender, then rinse under cold running water. Drain well and divide the noodles between the serving bowls.
* Combine the lamb and soy sauce in a bowl and marinate for 5 minutes.
* Heat the oil in a wok or large skillet (frying pan) over medium-high heat, add the ginger, and stir-fry for 1 minute until fragrant. Add the onion and stir-fry for another 5–6 minutes until softened. Add the lamb and stir-fry for 2 minutes until cooked.
* Stir in the tomato, salt, sugar, and ½ cup (4 fl oz/120 ml) water and bring to a boil. Slowly pour the egg into the wok and stir.
* Mix the cornstarch (cornflour) with ½ tablespoon water in a small bowl and stir this mixture into the wok. Bring to a boil, stirring, for 30 seconds to thicken the sauce, then pour over the noodles and serve.

鳝糊面

NOODLES
WITH EEL

REGION: SHANGHAI
PREPARATION TIME: 20 MINUTES
COOKING TIME: 10 MINUTES
SERVES: 2

* Using a sharp knife, cut off and discard the head of the eel. Cut the eel open down the entire length of its body and remove the spine. Sprinkle with the coarse salt and cornstarch (cornflour) and rub off the mucus from the skin. Rinse under cold running water and drain. Dry with paper towels, then cut the eel into 2 × ½-inch/5 × 1.5-cm pieces.
* Bring a large saucepan of water to a boil. Turn off the heat, then add the eel and stir rapidly for about 10 seconds. Immediately remove the eel from the water, using a slotted spoon, then rinse under cold running water and drain.
* Combine the salt, soy sauce, and sugar in a small bowl and mix well into a sauce. Set aside.
* Heat 1 teaspoon vegetable oil in a wok or large skillet (frying pan) over medium-low heat, add the pork fatback, and stir-fry for 1–2 minutes until crispy. Use a slotted spoon to discard the crispy pork.
* Add ½ tablespoon vegetable oil to the wok and heat over high heat. Add the ginger and eel and stir-fry rapidly for 1 minute. Sprinkle in the wine, add the sauce, and toss for another 1 minute until the eel pieces are cooked through.
* Add the bean sprouts and stir-fry for another minute until softened and slightly crunchy. Stir in the white pepper and transfer to a serving plate.
* Arrange the eel on the plate and add the chopped garlic in the center.
* Wipe the wok clean with paper towels and add the remaining ½ tablespoon vegetable oil and 1 tablespoon sesame oil. Heat over medium-high heat until hot, then pour the hot oil over the chopped garlic.
* Meanwhile, bring a large pot of water to a boil and cook the noodles according to the package directions until tender. Divide the noodles between the serving bowls and serve alongside the stir-fried eel.

- 1 (1 LB 2-OZ/500-G) FRESHWATER EEL
- ½ TEASPOON COARSE SALT
- 1 TABLESPOON CORNSTARCH (CORNFLOUR)
- ½ TEASPOON SALT
- 2 TABLESPOONS LIGHT SOY SAUCE
- 1 TEASPOON GRANULATED SUGAR
- 1 TABLESPOON PLUS 1 TEASPOON VEGETABLE OIL
- 1 TABLESPOON CHOPPED PORK FATBACK
- ⅛ OZ/5 G GINGER (ABOUT ½-INCH/ 1-CM-LENGTH PIECE), SHREDDED
- 1 TEASPOON SHAOXING WINE
- 1 CUP (3½ OZ/100 G) BEAN SPROUTS
- ¼ TEASPOON GROUND WHITE PEPPER
- 2 CLOVES GARLIC, CHOPPED
- 1 TABLESPOON SESAME OIL
- 11 OZ/300 G FRESH OR DRIED SHANGHAI NOODLES

REGION: FUJIAN
PREPARATION TIME: 15 MINUTES,
   PLUS 20 MINUTES SOAKING TIME
COOKING TIME: 20 MINUTES
SERVES: 4
📷 PAGE 595

福建炒米粉
FUJIAN-STYLE
VERMICELLI

- 4 DRIED BLACK MUSHROOMS
- 2 TABLESPOONS DRIED SHRIMP
- 7 OZ/200 G XIN ZHU OR ANY TYPE OF DRIED RICE VERMICELLI
- 1½ CUPS (5 OZ/150 G) BEAN SPROUTS
- 4 TABLESPOONS VEGETABLE OIL
- 2 EGGS, BEATEN
- 1 TABLESPOON LIGHT SOY SAUCE
- ½ TEASPOON SALT
- 1 TEASPOON GRANULATED SUGAR
- 1 TABLESPOON BLACK OR BALSAMIC VINEGAR
- 3 SHALLOTS, SLICED
- 1 (5-OZ/150-G) PORK BELLY, SLICED
- 1 TABLESPOON CORNSTARCH (CORNFLOUR)
- 2½ OZ/65 G CHIVES, CUT INTO 1½-INCH/4-CM LENGTHS
- 2 TABLESPOONS CRISPY GARLIC (PAGE 195)

* Put the mushrooms in a bowl, cover with cold water, and soak for at least 20 minutes, or until softened. Remove the mushrooms, squeeze dry, and discard the stems. Cut into thin strips.
* Meanwhile, soak the dried shrimp in ½ cup (4 fl oz/120 ml) cold water for about 10 minutes. Strain the soaking water into a bowl and reserve.
* Put the vermicelli into a large saucepan and add enough water to cover it completely. Bring to a boil over high heat and immediately turn off the heat. Stand for 10 minutes. Use chopsticks to disperse the vermicelli, then drain and rinse under cold running water. Drain and set aside.
* Bring a saucepan of water to a boil over high heat, add the bean sprouts, and blanch for 30 seconds. Remove and drain. Set aside.
* Heat 1 tablespoon oil in a wok or large skillet (frying pan) over medium heat, add the eggs, and spread out into a thin layer. Cook for 1–2 minutes until cooked through. Remove, cool, and cut into thin strips.
* Combine the soy sauce, salt, sugar, vinegar, and reserved shrimp soaking water in a small bowl to make a sauce.
* Heat 2 tablespoons oil in a wok, add the vermicelli, and stir-fry over medium heat for 3–4 minutes until lightly browned. Transfer to a plate. Heat the remaining 1 tablespoon oil and stir-fry the shallots for 1–2 minutes until fragrant. Add the pork belly, dried shrimp, and mushrooms and cook for 2 minutes, or until cooked through.
* Mix the cornstarch (cornflour) with 2 tablespoons water in a small bowl and stir this mixture into the wok. Bring to a boil, stirring, for about 30 seconds to thicken the sauce. Add the shrimp sauce, stir in the chives, bean sprouts, and eggs, and top with the vermicelli. Transfer to a serving plate and scatter over the crispy garlic.

FUJIAN-STYLE VERMICELLI

REGION: BEIJING
PREPARATION TIME: 10 MINUTES, PLUS
  10 MINUTES MARINATING TIME
COOKING TIME: 10 MINUTES
SERVES: 4
📷 PAGE 597

炸酱面
NOODLES WITH SPICY BROWN SAUCE

- 7 OZ/200 G LEAN PORK, CUT INTO THIN STRIPS
- 2 TEASPOONS LIGHT SOY SAUCE
- ½ TEASPOON GRANULATED SUGAR
- 1 TABLESPOON PLUS 1 TEASPOON CORNSTARCH (CORNFLOUR)
- 3 TABLESPOONS VEGETABLE OIL
- 3 CLOVES GARLIC, CHOPPED
- 1 TABLESPOON CHOPPED SICHUAN PRESERVED MUSTARD GREENS, TRIMMED, RINSED, AND CHOPPED
- 2 TABLESPOONS HOISIN SAUCE
- 1 TABLESPOON CHILI SAUCE
- 1 TABLESPOON KETCHUP
- ½ TEASPOON SALT
- ½ TEASPOON DARK SOY SAUCE
- 1 LB 5 OZ/600 G DRIED WHEAT NOODLES
- ⅓ CUCUMBER, SHREDDED

* Combine the pork, 1 teaspoon light soy sauce, the sugar, 1 teaspoon cornstarch (cornflour), and 1 tablespoon water in a bowl, mix well, and marinate for 10 minutes. Mix in 1 tablespoon oil.
* Heat the remaining 2 tablespoons oil in a wok or large skillet (frying pan) over medium-high heat, add the garlic, and stir-fry for 1 minute until fragrant. Add the pork, preserved mustard greens, hoisin and chili sauces, ketchup, and remaining 1 teaspoon light soy sauce. Stir-fry for another 2–3 minutes until the pork is cooked through. Add the salt and ½ cup (4 fl oz/120 ml) water, bring to a boil, and then stir in the dark soy sauce.
* In a small bowl, mix the remaining 1 tablespoon cornstarch with 2 tablespoons water and stir this mixture into the wok. Bring to a boil, stirring, for 30 seconds to thicken the sauce.
* Meanwhile, bring a large saucepan of water to a boil, then add the noodles. Cook according to the package directions until just tender. Drain, then transfer to a large bowl or 4 individual serving bowls. Pour over the brown sauce, top with the shredded cucumber, and serve.

葱油拌面
NOODLES WITH SHALLOT OIL

- 1⅓ TABLESPOON VEGETABLE OIL
- 1¼ OZ/30 G PORK FATBACK, CUT INTO PEA-SIZE PIECES
- 4 SHALLOTS, QUARTERED AND LIGHTLY CRUSHED
- 4 CLOVES GARLIC, CHOPPED
- 11 OZ/300 G FRESH EGG NOODLES
- 1 TABLESPOON LIGHT SOY SAUCE
- 1 TABLESPOON FISH SAUCE

* Heat 1 teaspoon oil in a saucepan over medium-high heat, add the pork fatback, and pan-fry for 4–5 minutes until crisp. Remove the crispy pork and drain on paper towels.
* Add the shallots and garlic to the pan and pan-fry over medium heat for 2 minutes until slightly brown. Transfer the shallot and garlic oil to a bowl. Discard the garlic and shallots.
* Bring a large saucepan of water to a boil, add the fresh noodles, and cook for 30 seconds. Drain and mix with the remaining 1 tablespoon oil. Drain, then divide among serving bowls.
* Sprinkle over the soy sauce, fish sauce, and garlic-shallot oil. Mix well and top with the crispy pork. Serve immediately.

NOODLES WITH SPICY BROWN SAUCE

煎炒麵底
PAN-FRIED EGG
NOODLES

- 14 OZ/400 G FRESH EGG NOODLES OR
  7 OZ/200 G DRIED EGG NOODLES
- 3 TABLESPOONS VEGETABLE OIL

* Bring a large saucepan of water to a boil, add the fresh noodles, and cook for 30 seconds. (If using dried noodles, cook according to the package directions until just tender.) Drain and mix with 1 tablespoon oil.
* Heat the remaining 2 tablespoons oil in a large nonstick skillet (frying pan), add the noodles, distributing them evenly, and pan-fry for 3-4 minutes over medium heat until golden brown. Do not stir—keep the skillet moving all the time to ensure even cooking. Flip the noodles over and cook for another 3-4 minutes until brown.

煎米粉底
PAN-FRIED RICE
VERMICELLI

- 7 OZ/200 G DRIED RICE VERMICELLI
- 3 TABLESPOONS VEGETABLE OIL

This recipe is a basis for many of the stir-fried dishes such as Scrambled Eggs and Shrimp over Vermicelli (page 603). It is never served on its own.

* Bring a large saucepan of water to a boil and add the vermicelli. Cover, turn off the heat, and let stand for 10 minutes. Uncover, then use chopsticks to stir and separate the vermicelli to prevent sticking. Drain, then stir in 1 tablespoon oil.
* Heat the remaining 2 tablespoons oil in a large nonstick skillet (frying pan) over medium heat, add the vermicelli, and pan-fry for 3-4 minutes until light brown and crispy. Do not stir—keep the skillet moving all the time to ensure even cooking. Flip the noodles over and cook for another 3-4 minutes until brown.

虾面

SHRIMP

NOODLES

REGION: FUJIAN
PREPARATION TIME: 5 MINUTES
COOKING TIME: 10 MINUTES
SERVES: 4

* Bring a saucepan of water to a boil, add the shrimp
  (prawns), and blanch for 2 minutes until they are pink
  and cooked through. Drain and set aside.
* Meanwhile, bring a large saucepan of water to a boil, then
  add the noodles. Cook according to the package directions,
  until just tender. Drain, then divide among serving bowls.
* Using the same large saucepan, bring water to a boil over
  high heat. Add the bean sprouts and blanch for 30 seconds.
  Drain and divide among the serving bowls.
* Put the shrimp and eggs into the bowls.
* Heat the broth (stock) in a saucepan, add the fish sauce,
  and bring to a boil. Ladle the broth into the bowls and serve
  immediately.

- 12 UNCOOKED SHRIMP (PRAWNS),
  SHELLED AND DEVEINED
- 14 OZ/400 G THIN DRIED EGG
  NOODLES
- 1 CUP (3/12 OZ/100 G) BEAN SPROUTS
- 2 HARD-BOILED EGGS, HALVED
- 4¼ CUPS (34 FL OZ/1 LITER) SHRIMP
  BROTH (STOCK, PAGE 92)
- 4 TABLESPOONS FISH SAUCE

鮪魚米粉

VERMICELLI

WITH TUNA

REGION: TAIWAN
PREPARATION TIME: 10 MINUTES
COOKING TIME: 10 MINUTES
SERVES: 4

* Combine the chicken broth (stock), salt, and 1 cup
  (8 fl oz/250 ml) water in a bowl. Stir well and set aside.
* Place the tuna in a bowl and use a fork to break it up.
* Heat 1 tablespoon oil in a wok or skillet (frying pan) over
  medium-low heat and add the beaten egg. Tilt the skillet so
  that the egg evenly covers the surface, making an omelet.
  Cook for 1–2 minutes on each side until golden. Remove and
  slice the egg into thin strands.
* Heat the remaining 2 tablespoons oil in the same wok over
  medium heat and stir in the shredded carrot and the tuna.
  Stir-fry for 1 minute.
* Pour in the chicken broth mixture and bring to a boil, then
  add the vermicelli and stir. Reduce to low heat and cook,
  stirring continuously, for about 3–4 minutes, or until all of
  the sauce is absorbed by the vermicelli.

NOTE:
Taiwan Xin Zhu rice vermicelli does not require presoaking.
If using other varieties of rice vermicelli, bring a large
saucepan of water to a boil and add the vermicelli. Cover,
turn off the heat, and let stand for 10 minutes. Uncover,
then use chopsticks to stir and separate the vermicelli to
prevent sticking. Drain, then stir in 1 tablespoon oil.

- 1 CUP (8 FL OZ/250 ML) CHICKEN
  BROTH (STOCK, PAGE 90)
- 1 TEASPOON SALT
- 1 (6-OZ/170-G) CAN TUNA, DRAINED
- 3 TABLESPOONS VEGETABLE OIL
- 1 EGG, BEATEN
- 1 CARROT, SHREDDED
- 5 OZ/150 G XIN ZHU OR ANY DRIED
  RICE VERMICELLI (SEE NOTE)

REGION: GUANGDONG
PREPARATION TIME: 10 MINUTES,
    PLUS 20 MINUTES SOAKING TIME
COOKING TIME: 30 MINUTES
SERVES: 4
📷 PAGE 601

银芽肉丝炒面
STIR-FRIED NOODLES WITH PORK AND BEAN SPROUTS

- 3 DRIED BLACK MUSHROOMS
- 11 OZ/300 G LEAN PORK, SLICED
- 1 TEASPOON LIGHT SOY SAUCE
- ½ TEASPOON GROUND WHITE PEPPER
- 3 TABLESPOONS VEGETABLE OIL
- 1½ CUPS (5 OZ/150 G) BEAN SPROUTS
- 5 OZ/150 G YELLOW CHIVES, CUT INTO
  1½-INCH/4-CM LENGTHS
- 1 TABLESPOON OYSTER SAUCE
- ½ TEASPOON GRANULATED SUGAR
- 1 TABLESPOON CORNSTARCH
  (CORNFLOUR)
- ½ TEASPOON SESAME OIL
- 1 QUANTITY PAN-FRIED EGG NOODLES
  (PAGE 598)

* Put the mushrooms in a bowl, cover with cold water, and soak for at least 20 minutes, or until softened. Remove the mushrooms, squeeze dry, and discard the stems. Strain the mushroom water into a cup and set aside.
* Meanwhile, in a bowl, combine the pork, soy sauce, white pepper, and 1 tablespoon vegetable oil and marinate for 10 minutes.
* Bring a pot of water to a boil over high heat, add the bean sprouts, and blanch for 10–15 seconds. Drain and rinse under cold running water. Set aside.
* Heat the remaining 2 tablespoons oil in a wok or large skillet (frying pan), add the pork and stir-fry for 2 minutes over high heat until cooked through. Add the mushrooms and yellow chives, and toss thoroughly.
* Put in the oyster sauce, sugar, and 4 tablespoons reserved mushroom water. Bring to a boil. Mix the cornstarch (cornflour) with 2 tablespoons water in a small bowl and stir this mixture into the wok. Bring to a boil, stirring, for 30 seconds to thicken the sauce.
* Add the bean sprouts and sesame oil, stir, and put on top of the pan-fried egg noodles to serve.

REGION: HONG KONG
PREPARATION TIME: 5 MINUTES
COOKING TIME: 10 MINUTES
SERVES: 4

豉油王炒面
NOODLES WITH SPECIAL SOY SAUCE

- 12 OZ/350 G FRESH EGG NOODLES
- 4 TABLESPOONS VEGETABLE OIL
- 1 TABLESPOON LIGHT SOY SAUCE
- 1½ TABLESPOONS DARK SOY SAUCE
- 1 TABLESPOON OYSTER SAUCE
- ½ TEASPOON GRANULATED SUGAR
- ½ ONION, SHREDDED
- 1½ CUPS (5 OZ/150 G) BEAN SPROUTS
- 2¾ OZ/75 G CHIVES, CUT INTO
  2½- INCH/6-CM LENGTHS
- ½ TEASPOON SALT
- 2 TABLESPOONS CHICKEN BROTH
  (STOCK, PAGE 90)

* Bring a large saucepan of water to a boil, add the fresh noodles, and cook for 30 seconds. Drain and mix with 1 tablespoon oil.
* Combine the soy sauces, oyster sauce, and sugar in a small bowl and mix well to make a sauce. Set aside.
* Heat 2 tablespoons oil in a wok or large skillet (frying pan), add the onion, and stir-fry over high heat until softened. Put in the bean sprouts and chives, then season with the salt. Remove from the wok and set aside.
* Add the remaining 1 tablespoon oil to the wok, add the noodles and special soy sauce, and stir-fry for another 2 minutes. Add the chicken broth (stock) and bean sprouts, and stir-fry for another minute until well mixed. Serve.

RICE, CONGEE & NOODLES

STIR-FRIED NOODLES WITH PORK AND BEAN SPROUTS

南乳猪手捞面
NOODLES WITH
PORK KNUCKLE

- 1 (1 LB 5-OZ/600-G) PORK KNUCKLE
- ¼ OZ/10 G GINGER (ABOUT ¾-INCH/ 2-CM-LENGTH PIECE), SLICED
- 1 TEASPOON SICHUAN PEPPERCORNS
- 2 CUBES RED BEAN CURD
- 1 TABLESPOON RED BEAN CURD JUICE
- 2 TABLESPOONS VEGETABLE OIL
- 2 TABLESPOONS SHAOXING WINE
- 1 TEASPOON DARK SOY SAUCE
- ½ TEASPOON SALT
- 1 TEASPOON GRANULATED SUGAR
- 7 OZ/200 G DRIED EGG NOODLES

* Use a knife to scrape the pork knuckle clean and rinse under cold running water. Put the pork knuckle into a large saucepan and add enough water to cover completely. Bring to a boil over high heat and blanch for 5 minutes. Drain and rinse under cold running water. Chop into chunks and set aside.

* Fill the same large saucepan with water and bring to a boil. Add the pork knuckle, 4 ginger slices, and the Sichuan peppercorns and bring the water to another boil over high heat. Reduce to low heat and simmer for 2 hours, or until tender. Drain and rinse the pieces thoroughly under cold running water.

* Put the red bean curd, bean curd juice, and 4 tablespoons water into a food processor or blender. Blend to make a sauce, transfer to a bowl, and set aside.

* Heat the oil in a wok or large skillet (frying pan) over medium-high heat, add the remaining ginger slices, and stir-fry for 1 minute until fragrant. Put in the pork knuckle pieces, wine, red bean curd sauce, and soy sauce and stir-fry for 1 minute. Pour in enough water to cover the pork knuckle and bring to a boil. Season with the salt and sugar, reduce to medium-low heat, and simmer, uncovered, for 15 minutes until the sauce thickens.

* Meanwhile, bring a large saucepan of water to a boil, then add the noodles. Cook according to the package directions until just tender. Drain, then divide among serving bowls. Add the pork knuckles pieces to each bowl, drizzle over the sauce, and serve.

菜薳牛肉炒河

FRIED NOODLES
WITH BEEF

REGION: GUANGDONG
PREPARATION TIME: 10 MINUTES,
   PLUS 10 MINUTES SOAKING TIME
COOKING TIME: 10 MINUTES
SERVES: 3–4

* Combine the beef with 4 tablespoons water in a bowl
  and soak for 10 minutes. Pour out the excess water, then
  mix in 1 teaspoon cornstarch (cornflour).
* Meanwhile, put the rice noodles into a bowl. Separate
  the strands of noodles and stir in the soy sauce.
* Heat 1 tablespoon vegetable oil in a wok or large skillet
  (frying pan) over high heat, add the ginger, and fry for
  1 minute until fragrant. Add the choy sum and stir-fry
  1–2 minutes until just tender. Season with the salt, toss,
  and then transfer to a plate.
* Wipe the wok with paper towels, then heat the remaining
  2 tablespoons vegetable oil over high heat. Add the beef
  and stir-fry for 2–3 minutes, just until half done. Add the
  oyster sauce and 4 tablespoons water, then bring to a boil.
* In a small bowl, mix the remaining 2 teaspoons cornstarch
  with 2 tablespoons water and stir this mixture into the wok.
  Bring to a boil, stirring, for 30 seconds to thicken the sauce.
* Return the choy sum to the wok, add the noodles, and stir-
  fry over high heat for 1 minute. Add the sesame oil, stir, and
  transfer to a serving plate.

- 5 OZ/150 G BEEF FLANK STEAK, SLICED
- 1 TABLESPOON CORNSTARCH
  (CORNFLOUR)
- 1 LB/450 G FRESH RICE NOODLES
- 1 TEASPOON LIGHT SOY SAUCE
- 3 TABLESPOONS VEGETABLE OIL
- ¾ OZ/20 G GINGER (ABOUT
  1-INCH/2.5-CM-LENGTH PIECE),
  SLICED
- 11 OZ/300 G CHOY SUM, KEEPING
  ONLY THE TENDER PART, ABOUT
  4-INCHES/10-CM FROM THE TOP
- ½ TEASPOON SALT
- 2 TABLESPOONS OYSTER SAUCE
- 1 TEASPOON SESAME OIL

滑蛋虾仁煎米粉

SCRAMBLED EGGS AND
SHRIMP OVER VERMICELLI

REGION: HONG KONG
PREPARATION TIME: 15 MINUTES
COOKING TIME: 5 MINUTES
SERVES: 4

* Bring a large saucepan of water to a boil, add the shrimp
  (prawns), and blanch for 2 minutes. Drain and set aside.
* Beat the egg whites in a small bowl until foamy, add
  1 teaspoon oil, the salt, and the egg yolks, and then beat
  again. Mix in the shrimp.
* Heat 2 tablespoons oil in a wok or large skillet (frying pan)
  over high heat. (The oil needs to be hot enough to cook the
  eggs with the heat turned off.) Turn off the heat and pour
  in the egg mixture.
* Using a spatula (fish slice), fold the eggs over onto
  themselves in the wok for about 2 minutes, layer by layer,
  as a layer is formed on the surface. Always follow the same
  direction while folding. (If the oil has cooled down before
  the eggs are cooked, put the wok back over low heat to
  finish cooking the eggs.)
* Put the vermicelli on a serving plate, then add the prawn
  and egg mixture on top. Serve immediately.

- 11 OZ/300 G SHELLED UNCOOKED
  SHRIMP (PRAWNS), DEVEINED
- 6 EGGS, SEPARATED
- 2 TABLESPOONS PLUS 1 TEASPOON
  VEGETABLE OIL
- ½ TEASPOON SALT
- 1 QUANTITY PAN-FRIED RICE
  VERMICELLI (PAGE 598)

REGION: SHANGHAI
PREPARATION TIME: 10 MINUTES, PLUS
   15 MINUTES MARINATING TIME
COOKING TIME: 10 MINUTES
SERVES: 4
[📷] PAGE 605

京葱肉片炒年糕
GLUTINOUS RICE CAKES WITH PORK AND BEIJING SCALLIONS

- 5 OZ/150 G PORK, SLICED
- ½ TEASPOON LIGHT SOY SAUCE
- ½ TEASPOON GRANULATED SUGAR
- ½ TEASPOON CORNSTARCH (CORNFLOUR)
- 2½ TABLESPOONS VEGETABLE OIL
- 1 BEIJING SCALLION OR 3 SCALLIONS (SPRING ONIONS), CUT DIAGONALLY
- 1½ TABLESPOONS BEAN PASTE
- 11 OZ/300 G GLUTINOUS RICE CAKES, RINSED AND CUT INTO ¼-INCH/5-MM SLICES
- ½ TEASPOON SALT
- ½ TEASPOON SESAME OIL

* Combine the pork, soy sauce, sugar, and 2 tablespoons water in a bowl and marinate for 15 minutes. Stir in the cornstarch (cornflour) and add ½ tablespoon vegetable oil.

* Heat the remaining 2 tablespoons oil in a wok or large skillet (frying pan) over medium heat, add the scallion, and stir-fry for 1–2 minutes until soft. Transfer to a plate.

* Add the bean paste to the wok and stir over medium-high heat, then put in the pork and continue to stir-fry for 2 minutes until just cooked through. Add 2 tablespoons water and the glutinous rice cakes and stir-fry for another 1–2 minutes until the water has been absorbed. Stir in another 2 tablespoons water and the salt and stir-fry until the rice cakes are softened. Stir in the scallions (spring onions) and sesame oil, then transfer to a plate and serve.

味菜牛肉丝炒米粉
VERMICELLI WITH BEEF AND PRESERVED MUSTARD GREENS

- 9 OZ/250 G DRIED RICE VERMICELLI
- 1 TEASPOON SALT
- 4 TABLESPOONS VEGETABLE OIL
- 1 RED CHILE, CHOPPED
- 2 CLOVES GARLIC, CHOPPED
- 1 TABLESPOON FERMENTED BLACK BEANS, RINSED AND COARSELY CHOPPED
- ½ TEASPOON GRANULATED SUGAR
- 5 OZ/150 G BEEF FLANK STEAK, CUT INTO THIN STRIPS
- 3½ OZ/100 G PRESERVED MUSTARD GREENS, TRIMMED, RINSED, AND CHOPPED
- 2 TABLESPOONS LIGHT SOY SAUCE
- 1 TABLESPOON CORNSTARCH (CORNFLOUR)
- 1 TEASPOON SESAME OIL

* Bring a large saucepan of water to a boil and add the vermicelli and salt. Cover, turn off the heat, and let stand for 10 minutes to soften the vermicelli. Using chopsticks, stir the vermicelli to prevent it from sticking. Drain, then stir in 1 tablespoon vegetable oil.

* Combine the chile, garlic, black beans, and sugar in a small bowl and mix well. Heat 2 tablespoons vegetable oil in a wok or large skillet (frying pan) over medium heat, add the vermicelli, and pan-fry for 3–4 minutes until slightly crispy. Flip over and cook for another 4–5 minutes until brown. Remove the vermicelli to a plate and set aside.

* Add 1 tablespoon vegetable oil to the wok and stir-fry the black bean mixture for 1 minute until fragrant.

* Increase to high heat, stir in the beef, add the mustard greens, soy sauce, and ½ cup (4 fl oz/120 ml) water, then bring to a boil and cook for 1–2 minutes, or until the beef is just cooked through.

* Mix the cornstarch (cornflour) with 2 tablespoons water in a small bowl and stir this mixture into the wok. Bring to a boil, stirring, for 30 seconds to thicken the sauce. Add the vermicelli, toss, and drizzle in the sesame oil. Serve.

RICE, CONGEE & NOODLES

GLUTINOUS RICE CAKES WITH PORK AND BEIJING SCALLIONS

REGION: GUANGDONG
PREPARATION TIME: 10 MINUTES,
   PLUS 10 MINUTES SOAKING TIME
COOKING TIME: 10 MINUTES
SERVES: 3
📷 PAGE 607

豉椒牛河
RICE NOODLES WITH BEEF
AND BLACK BEAN SAUCE

- 7 OZ/200 G BEEF FLANK STEAK, SLICED
- 2 TEASPOONS CORNSTARCH
  (CORNFLOUR)
- 3 TABLESPOONS VEGETABLE OIL
- 1 LB/450 G FRESH RICE NOODLES
- 2 TABLESPOONS LIGHT SOY SAUCE
- 2 TABLESPOONS FERMENTED BLACK
  BEANS, RINSED AND CHOPPED
- 2 CLOVES GARLIC, CHOPPED
- 1 RED CHILE
- 1 TEASPOON GRANULATED SUGAR
- 1 GREEN BELL PEPPER, SEEDED AND
  CUT INTO CHUNKS
- 1 TEASPOON SESAME OIL

* Combine the beef with 4 tablespoons water in a bowl and soak for 10 minutes. Pour out the excess water, then mix in 1 teaspoon cornstarch (cornflour) and ½ tablespoon vegetable oil.
* Meanwhile, put the rice noodles into a bowl. Using chopsticks, separate the strands of the noodles and stir in ½ tablespoon soy sauce.
* Combine the black beans, garlic, and chile in a bowl. Mix in the sugar and ½ tablespoon vegetable oil.
* Heat the remaining 2 tablespoons vegetable oil in a wok or large skillet (frying pan) over medium heat, add the black bean mixture, and stir-fry for 1 minute until fragrant. Put in the beef and stir-fry for another 2–3 minutes, just until half done. Add the bell pepper, the remaining 1½ tablespoons soy sauce, and 5 tablespoons water and bring to a boil.
* Mix the remaining 1 teaspoon cornstarch with 2 tablespoons water in a small bowl and stir this mixture into the wok. Bring to a boil, stirring, for 30 seconds to thicken the sauce.
* Put in the rice noodles and stir-fry over high heat for 2 minutes until the noodles are heated through and well mixed.
* Stir in the sesame oil, transfer to a serving plate, and serve.

RICE NOODLES WITH BEEF AND BLACK BEAN SAUCE

REGION: HONG KONG
PREPARATION TIME: 5 MINUTES
COOKING TIME: 5 MINUTES
SERVES: 4
📷 PAGE 609

XO辣椒酱炒肠粉
RICE ROLLS WITH CHILI SAUCE

- 2 TABLESPOONS VEGETABLE OIL
- 2 CLOVES GARLIC, CHOPPED
- 2 TABLESPOONS CHILI SAUCE (SUCH AS XO SAUCE)
- 1 LB/450 G FRESH RICE ROLLS, CUT INTO 1½-INCH/4-CM LENGTHS
- 1 TEASPOON SESAME OIL
- CILANTRO (CORIANDER), TO GARNISH (OPTIONAL)

* Heat the vegetable oil in a wok or large skillet (frying pan) over medium-high heat, add the garlic, and stir-fry 1 minute until fragrant. Put in the chili sauce and stir-fry for another minute. Add the rice rolls and sesame oil, increase to high heat, and stir-fry for another 1–2 minutes until well mixed. Transfer to a serving plate, garnish with cilantro (coriander), if using, and serve as breakfast or as part of dim sum.

REGION: CHAOZHOU
PREPARATION TIME: 15 MINUTES
COOKING TIME: 15 MINUTES
SERVES: 3-4

潮州煎面
CHAOZHOU-STYLE NOODLES

- 1 LB 2 OZ/500 G FRESH EGG NOODLES
- 1 TABLESPOON SALT
- 4 TABLESPOONS VEGETABLE OIL
- 2 EGG YOLKS, BEATEN
- 2 OZ/50 G YELLOW CHIVES, CUT INTO ¾-INCH/2-CM LENGTHS
- 2 TABLESPOONS RED VINEGAR, TO SERVE
- 2 TABLESPOONS GRANULATED SUGAR, TO SERVE

* Bring a large saucepan of water to a boil, add the fresh noodles and salt, and cook for 30 seconds. Drain and mix with 1 tablespoon oil. Rinse under cold running water, drain, and transfer the noodles to a bowl. Add egg yolks and stir.
* Heat 1 tablespoon oil in a wok or large skillet (frying pan) over medium-high heat, add the chives, and stir-fry for 1 minute until softened. Remove from the wok, then set aside.
* Heat the remaining 2 tablespoons oil in a skillet over medium heat, add the noodles, stirring to coat them in the oil, and spread out evenly in the skillet.
* Place a similar-size, flat-base saucepan of water on top of the noodles to press down the noodles as they fry.
* Reduce to low heat and fry the noodles for 4–5 minutes until one side is golden brown. Remove the pan of water, then flip the noodles over and add the pan of water on top. Cook for another 4–5 minutes until golden brown.
* Transfer the noodles to a serving plate and scatter with the yellow chives. Serve with the vinegar and sugar, separately, on the side.

RICE ROLLS WITH CHILI SAUCE

REGION: SHANGHAI
PREPARATION TIME: 5 MINUTES, PLUS
  5 MINUTES MARINATING TIME
COOKING TIME: 15 MINUTES
SERVES: 2
📷 PAGE 611

上海粗炒
STIR-FRIED SHANGHAI
NOODLES

- 3½ OZ/100 G LEAN PORK, SLICED
- 2 TABLESPOONS LIGHT SOY SAUCE
- 1 TEASPOON GRANULATED SUGAR
- 1 TEASPOON CORNSTARCH
  (CORNFLOUR)
- 2½ TABLESPOONS VEGETABLE OIL
- 11 OZ/300 G SHANGHAI NOODLES
- 3 NAPA CABBAGE LEAVES, SHREDDED
- ½ TABLESPOON DARK SOY SAUCE
- 1 TEASPOON SESAME OIL

* Combine the pork, ½ tablespoon light soy sauce, ½ teaspoon sugar, the cornstarch (cornflour), and ½ tablespoon vegetable oil in a bowl. Mix well and marinate for 5 minutes.
* Meanwhile, bring a large saucepan of water to a boil, then add the noodles. Cook according to the package directions, until tender. Drain and rinse under cold running water.
* Bring a saucepan of water to a boil over high heat. Add the Napa cabbage and blanch for 2 minutes until tender. Drain.
* Heat the remaining 2 tablespoons oil in a wok or large skillet (frying pan) over medium heat, add the pork, and stir-fry for 2 minutes until cooked through. Put in the drained noodles and stir-fry for 2 minutes. Add the Napa cabbage, remaining ½ teaspoon sugar, remaining 1½ tablespoons light soy sauce, and the dark soy sauce. Stir-fry for 2 minutes until well combined. Stir in the sesame oil, transfer to a serving plate, and serve.

STIR-FRIED SHANGHAI NOODLES

DESSERTS

DESSERTS

REGION: TIANJIN
PREPARATION TIME: 5 MINUTES, PLUS
 15 MINUTES SOAKING AND
 4 HOURS STANDING TIME
COOKING TIME: 10 MINUTES
SERVES: 8
📷 PAGE 617

琥珀桃仁
CARAMELIZED
WALNUTS

- 2 CUPS (9 OZ/250 G) WALNUTS, SHELLED
- GENEROUS 1 CUP (9 OZ/250 G) GRANULATED SUGAR
- 3 CUPS (25 FL OZ/750 ML) VEGETABLE OIL
- SESAME SEEDS, TO GARNISH (OPTIONAL)

* Soak the walnuts in a bowl of warm water for 15 minutes. Drain, then combine the walnuts and sugar in a clean bowl. Stand for 4 hours, stirring and mixing 2–3 times.
* Pick out the walnuts and shake off the excess sugar. Discard the sugar.
* Heat the oil in a wok or deep saucepan to 350°F/180°C, or until a cube of bread browns in 30 seconds. Carefully add the walnuts and deep-fry until they are caramel in color. Use a slotted spoon to transfer the walnuts to a colander to drain, then spread out onto a large tray to cool.
* Sprinkle with sesame seeds, if using, and serve.

REGION: BEIJING
PREPARATION TIME: 10 MINUTES,
 PLUS AT LEAST 6 HOURS SOAKING TIME
COOKING TIME: 1 HOUR 10 MINUTES
SERVES: 4

酸梅汤
SMOKED PLUM
SOUP

- 4 SMOKED PLUMS
- 4 SMOKED DATES (OPTIONAL)
- 15 DRIED HAWTHORN APPLE
- 1 SMALL LICORICE ROOT
- 1 TABLESPOON DRIED OSMANTHUS FLOWERS (OPTIONAL)
- 1 CUP (7 OZ/200 G) BROWN SUGAR, PLUS EXTRA TO TASTE

* Put the plums and dates, if using, in a medium bowl, add 2 cups (16 fl oz/475 ml) cold water, and soak for at least 6 hours, preferably overnight.
* Use scissors to snip the plums and dates open. Put them in a stainless steel stockpot or clay pot (see Note), along with the soaking liquid and 8½ cups (68 fl oz/2 liters) water. Add the dried hawthorn apple and licorice to the pot.
* Bring the water to a boil over high heat, reduce to medium heat, and simmer, covered, for 1 hour. Sprinkle in the Osmanthus flowers, if using, stir a few times, and turn the heat off. Cover and let sit for 5 minutes.
* Drain the liquid through a fine-mesh sieve (strainer) into a pitcher (jug), stir in the sugar, and adjust the sweetness to taste. (You need just enough sugar to offset the sourness of the plums but not so much that it masks it.) Chill well before serving.

NOTE:
Aluminum can react violently with acid. To avoid any risk, we recommend a clay pot or stainless steel saucepan.

CARAMELIZED WALNUTS

REGION: JIANGSU
PREPARATION TIME: 20 MINUTES,
  PLUS 1 HOUR SOAKING TIME
COOKING TIME: 3 HOURS
SERVES: 4

桂花糖藕

HONEYED LOTUS ROOTS
IN SWEET OSMANTHUS

- ½ CUP (3½ OZ/100 G) GLUTINOUS RICE, RINSED
- 1¾ LB/800 G LOTUS ROOTS, RINSED
- 2 TABLESPOONS CRUSHED ROCK SUGAR
- 2 TABLESPOONS OSMANTHUS SUGAR

* Soak the glutinous rice in a bowl of cold water for 1 hour. Drain.
* Cut off the 2 ends of each lotus root, so that each cut piece is about 1½ inches/4 cm long and reserve.
* Using chopsticks, clean the channels inside the lotus roots and rinse them thoroughly in water. Replace one end of each lotus root as a cover and fix them it in place with toothpicks (cocktail sticks). Put spoonfuls of the rice into the lotus root so that they are about 80 percent full. Cover the other end of the lotus roots with the other cut-off pieces and fix in place with toothpicks.
* Transfer the stuffed lotus roots to a nonmetallic pot, add enough water to cover the roots, and bring to a boil. Reduce to medium-low heat and simmer, covered, for 2 hours.
* Add the rock sugar to the pot and simmer for another 30 minutes. Add the Osmanthus sugar and cook over low heat for 15–20 minutes until you have a syrup. Remove the lotus roots and set aside to cool. Remove the toothpicks, then cut the lotus roots into ¼-inch/5-mm slices. Transfer to a serving plate. Pour the Osmanthus sugar syrup over the lotus roots and serve.

REGION: ANHUI
PREPARATION TIME: 10 MINUTES
COOKING TIME: 1 HOUR 10 MINUTES
SERVES: 4

蜜汁红芋

TARO IN HONEYED
SAUCE

- 4 OZ/120 G ROCK SUGAR
- 4 SMALL TARO ROOTS (ABOUT 3 OZ/80 G EACH), PEELED AND CUT LENGTHWISE IN HALF
- 1 TABLESPOON HONEY

* Heat scant 1 cup (7 fl oz/200 ml) water in a nonstick saucepan over medium heat. Add the rock sugar and stir until dissolved. Add the taro and honey, bring to a boil over high heat, and skim any froth off the surface.
* Reduce to low heat, cover, and simmer for about 1 hour until the sauce has thickened to a syrup. Stir occasionally to prevent it from burning.
* Transfer the taro to individual bowls, pour over the syrup, and serve.

蜜汁弥猴桃

KIWI FRUIT IN
HONEYED SAUCE

REGION: ANHUI
PREPARATION TIME: 10 MINUTES
COOKING TIME: 5 MINUTES
SERVES: 6

* Make a ½-inch/1-cm hole at one end of each kiwi.
* Put the dates into a food processor and process into a paste, then stuff it into the holes in the kiwis.
* Heat the oil in a wok or deep saucepan to 265°F/130°C. Gently lower the kiwis and deep-fry for 1 minute. Use a slotted spoon to carefully remove the kiwis from the oil and drain on paper towels.
* Bring ½ cup (4 fl oz/120 ml) water to a boil in a saucepan over high heat, then stir in the granulated sugar and honey. Combine the cornstarch (cornflour) with 2 tablespoons water in a small bowl and stir this mixture into the saucepan. Bring to a boil, stirring, for 30 seconds until the syrup thickens.
* Coat the deep-fried kiwis in the honeyed sauce, then sprinkle over the Osmanthus sugar. Put the kiwi in 6 individual bowls and serve.

- 6 KIWI FRUITS, PEELED
- 3 SUGARED DATES, PITTED
- 1 CUP (8 FL OZ/250 ML) VEGETABLE OIL
- 4 TABLESPOONS GRANULATED SUGAR
- 1 TABLESPOON HONEY
- 1 TABLESPOON CORNSTARCH (CORNFLOUR)
- 1 TABLESPOON OSMANTHUS SUGAR

糯米红枣

JUJUBE DATES STUFFED WITH
GLUTINOUS RICE FLOUR

REGION: SHANGHAI
PREPARATION TIME: 20 MINUTES
COOKING TIME: 20 MINUTES
SERVES: 4-6

* Combine ½ cup (4 fl oz/120 ml) water with the flour in a bowl and knead into a dough.
* Cut the dough into small pieces. Stuff the dates with the pieces of dough.
* Place the stuffed dates in a collapsible pot or bamboo steamer over a pot of boiling water. Steam, covered, for 20 minutes.
* Meanwhile, combine the sugar, ginger juice, and ½ cup (4 fl oz/120 ml) water in a small saucepan and cook over low heat for 10–15 minutes until a thick syrup forms. Roll the dates in the syrup and transfer to serving plate. Serve.

- ½ CUP (3½ OZ/100 G) GLUTINOUS RICE FLOUR
- 2 CUPS (11 OZ/300 G) JUJUBE DATES, RINSED AND PITTED
- 3 TABLESPOONS CRUSHED ROCK SUGAR
- 1 TEASPOON GINGER JUICE

REGION: BEIJING
PREPARATION TIME: 15 MINUTES,
   PLUS 8 HOURS SOAKING AND
   4 HOURS CHILLING TIME
COOKING TIME: 1 HOUR 30 MINUTES
SERVES: 6–8
📷 PAGE 621

豌豆黄
SPLIT PEA PUDDING

- 1⅓ CUPS (11 OZ/300 G) DRIED YELLOW SPLIT PEAS
- 2 SHEETS LEAF GELATIN (ABOUT ¼ OZ/6 G)
- VEGETABLE OIL, FOR GREASING
- ⅓ CUP (4 OZ/120 G) GRANULATED SUGAR
- PINCH OF SALT
- RASPBERRIES, TO SERVE (OPTIONAL)

* Soak the dried split peas in a large bowl of cold water for 8 hours. Drain.
* Place the peas in a large saucepan, add 4¼ cups (34 fl oz/ 1 liter) water, and bring to a boil over high heat. Reduce to medium heat and simmer for 45–60 minutes until the peas are very soft. Drain, transfer the peas to a blender, and blend to a puree.
* Soak the leaf gelatin in a small bowl of tepid water for 10 minutes, to soften.
* Grease an 8-inch/20-cm square pan with oil.
* Pass the peas through a fine strainer (sieve) into a clean saucepan, then add the sugar and salt. Gently cook over medium heat, stirring constantly, for 10–15 minutes to remove any moisture. The mixture is ready when it is starchy in consistency and clings onto the rubber spatula (fish slice) if lifted. Turn the heat off.
* Drain the leaf gelatin, squeeze lightly, then add it to the pan. Stir to melt and distribute evenly.
* Pour the peas into the prepared pan. Place a sheet of plastic wrap (clingfilm) on top and smooth over the surface. Set aside to cool to room temperature, then chill in the refrigerator for at least 4 hours. To serve, loosen the edges with a knife, invert the pudding onto a clean work surface, and cut into pieces. Transfer to a serving plate and decorate with raspberries, if using.

SPLIT PEA PUDDING

REGION: HONG KONG
PREPARATION TIME: 10 MINUTES
    PLUS 10 MINUTES SOAKING AND
    ABOUT 7 HOURS CHILLING TIME
COOKING TIME: 5 MINUTES
SERVES: 8
📷 PAGE 623

椰汁糕
COCONUT
PUDDING

- 6 SHEETS LEAF GELATIN (ABOUT ½ OZ/15 G)
- ½ CUP (4 FL OZ/120 ML) MILK
- ½ CUP (4 FL OZ/120 ML) COCONUT MILK
- 2 EGG WHITES
- FEW DROPS OF LEMON JUICE
- ¼ CUP (2 OZ/50 G) SUPERFINE (CASTER) SUGAR

This jelly-like pudding is similar to bavarois, but without the egg yolks, and whipped egg whites are used in place of whipped cream. A relatively high quantity of gelatin is used to give the dessert a sliceable texture.

* Line a 2-cup (16-fl oz/475-ml) mold with plastic wrap (clingfilm). Set aside.
* Soak the leaf gelatin in a small bowl of tepid water for about 10 minutes to soften.
* Pour the milk into a small saucepan and bring to almost-boiling point over medium-low heat. When it begins to bubble, remove the pan from the heat. Squeeze the softened gelatin sheets gently to remove excess water, then add them to the pan. Stir gently to melt the gelatin. Add the coconut milk to the pan and stir again.
* Transfer the mixture to a large bowl and place it over a bowl of ice to chill it, stirring from time to time until the mixture has a jelly-like consistency and starts to set at the edges (but is not yet a solid mass). It should be thick, yet still runny enough for the meringue to be folded into it. If at any point the mixture becomes too solid, warm it through in the microwave for a few seconds. Set aside.
* Combine the egg whites and a few drops of lemon juice in a large bowl and beat with an electric beater until the egg whites start to form soft peaks. Gradually add the sugar and beat until the meringue is glossy and holds soft peaks again.
* Give the coconut mixture a final stir to loosen it, then carefully fold in the meringue in a few additions. Pour the mixture into the prepared mold and refrigerate for at least 6 hours to set.
* Cover the mold with a plate and invert to release the pudding onto the plate. Cut it into cubes and serve.

COCONUT PUDDING

炒三不粘
RICH EGG CUSTARD

- 4 EGGS, SEPARATED
- 1 TEASPOON CORNSTARCH
  (CORNFLOUR)
- ⅓ CUP (2 OZ/60 G) GRANULATED
  SUGAR
- ½ TABLESPOON OSMANTHUS SUGAR
- 5 TABLESPOONS LARD

* Beat the egg yolks and 2 egg whites in a small bowl until
  blended. Save the remaining egg whites for another recipe.
* Combine the cornstarch (cornflour) with 1 tablespoon
  water in a small bowl. Set aside for 5 minutes, or until the
  starch settles, then pour out the water to leave wet starch.
* Pour the granulated sugar into a small saucepan, add a
  scant ½ cup (3½ fl oz/100 ml) water, and bring to a boil.
  Reduce to a simmer and cook for 15 minutes, or until the
  sugar is completely dissolved. Set aside to cool completely.
* Add the syrup, Osmanthus sugar, and wet starch to the
  bowl of eggs and mix well.
* Heat 4 tablespoons lard in a wok or large skillet (frying
  pan) over low heat (about 240°F/120°C on a candy [sugar]
  thermometer). Add the mixture and use a wooden spoon to
  stir it over very low heat for 2–3 minutes. Gradually add the
  remaining 1 tablespoon lard, stirring continuously, and cook
  for 5–6 minutes until the custard thickens and coats the
  back of the spoon. Serve hot in individual bowls.

REGION: CHAOZHOU
PREPARATION TIME: 20 MINUTES,
    PLUS 20 MINUTES SOAKING AND
    30 MINUTES STANDING TIME
COOKING TIME: 45 MINUTES
SERVES: 4

糕烧杂锦
SUGARED
TIDBITS

- 1 CUP (4 OZ/120 G) FRESH
  CHESTNUTS, SHELLED
- 2 CUPS (16 FL OZ/475 ML)
  VEGETABLE OIL
- 7 OZ/200 G PUMPKIN, PEELED AND
  CUT INTO 1¼-INCH/3-CM DICE
- 7 OZ/200 G TARO, PEELED AND CUT
  INTO 1¼-INCH/3-CM DICE
- 2 SWEET POTATOES (ABOUT 7 OZ/
  200 G), PEELED AND CUT INTO
  1¼-INCH/3-CM DICE
- 1⅓ CUPS (11 OZ/300 G) GRANULATED
  SUGAR
- 1½ CUPS (7 OZ/200 G) SHELLED
  GINKGO NUTS, CORES REMOVED
- ¾ CUP (5 OZ/150 G) WATER
  CHESTNUTS

* Soak the chestnuts in a bowl of hot water for 20 minutes
  to remove the inner skin.
* Heat the oil in a wok or deep saucepan to 300°F/150°C,
  or until a cube of bread browns in 1½ minutes. Add the
  pumpkin and deep-fry for 4–5 minutes until golden brown.
  Use a slotted spoon to carefully remove the pumpkin
  from the oil and drain on paper towels. Deep-fry the taro,
  sweet potatoes, and fresh chestnuts for 4–5 minutes, then
  combine in a bowl with ¼ cup (2 oz/50 g) sugar and let
  stand for 30 minutes.
* Put 2 cups (16 fl oz/475 ml) water in a large saucepan,
  then add the ginkgo nuts and remaining sugar. Bring
  to a boil over high heat, reduce to low heat, and simmer
  for 30 minutes until the water is reduced by half.
* Add all the deep-fried ingredients to the saucepan and
  simmer for 10 minutes until the liquid has thickened into
  a syrup. Drain the water chestnuts, stir into the pot, and
  simmer for about 1 minute. Serve.

芝麻糕
STEAMED SESAME CAKE

REGION: GUANGDONG
PREPARATION TIME: 15 MINUTES
COOKING TIME: 50 MINUTES
SERVES: 4

* Combine the water chestnut flour with 1 cup (8 fl oz/ 250 ml) water in a large bowl, mix well, and set aside.
* In another large bowl, add the sesame paste, sugar, and salt and beat to loosen the sesame paste. Gradually and very slowly, add 2 cups (16 fl oz/475 ml) water to the sesame paste, a little at a time, beating well to remove any lumps. You need to form an emulsion and once the mixture becomes a soup-like consistency, gradually add the rest of the water.
* Stir the mixture and strain through a fine-mesh strainer (sieve) to remove any lumps, using a spoon to press down on the mixture. Combine the chestnut mixture and sesame batter and beat to form a smooth batter.
* Grease an 8-inch/20-cm square baking pan with oil and place on a steaming rack in a wok. Bring the water to a boil over medium-high heat, then use a ladle to add ½ cup (4 fl oz/120 ml) sesame batter to the pan. Cover and steam over high heat for 5 minutes. Add another layer of sesame batter and steam for another 6 minutes. Repeat again until you have 7–8 layers. It should feel firm to the touch.
* Carefully remove the pan from the steamer and set aside to cool completely. Use your fingers to gently loosen the edges of the cake from the pan and invert onto a serving plate. Cut into squares to serve. Decorate with toasted sesame seeds, if desired.

NOTE:
This recipe uses black sesame paste, which can be found at Asian grocery stores, but you can also make your own by processing toasted black sesame seeds in a food processor until it forms a paste.

- 1½ CUPS (6 OZ/175 G) WATER CHESTNUT FLOUR
- 6 TABLESPOONS UNSWEETENED BLACK SESAME PASTE (SEE NOTE)
- ½ CUP (3½ OZ/100 G) GRANULATED SUGAR
- PINCH OF SALT
- VEGETABLE OIL, FOR GREASING
- TOASTED SESAME SEEDS, TO DECORATE (OPTIONAL)

REGION: HAKKA
PREPARATION TIME: 10 MINUTES
COOKING TIME: 1 HOUR
SERVES: 4
📷 PAGE 627

花生麻糬
PEANUT
MOCHI

- ½ CUP (2 OZ/50 G) RAW PEANUTS, SHELLED
- 4 TABLESPOONS WHITE SESAME SEEDS
- 4 TABLESPOONS BROWN SUGAR
- ½ CUP (3½ OZ/100 G) GLUTINOUS RICE FLOUR

* Toast the peanuts in a small pan over low heat for 6–7 minutes until fragrant. Transfer to a plate to cool. In the same pan, toast the sesame seeds over medium heat and shake occasionally for 3–5 minutes, or until golden brown. Put the nuts into a food processor and process until finely ground. Transfer to a bowl. Repeat with the sesame seeds. Combine the two ground mixtures, add the sugar, and mix well. Set aside.

* Put the rice flour in a large bowl, gradually add ½ cup (4 fl oz/120 ml) water, and knead until a dough is formed. Take out a piece of dough (about one-ninth) and place it in a collapsible pot or bamboo steamer over a pot of boiling water. Steam, covered, for 30 minutes until sticky and cooked through.

* Combine the steamed dough with the remaining dough in the bowl and knead well.

* Using your hands, roll out balls of about ¾ inch/2 cm in diameter and put them on a heatproof plate. Transfer to the collapsible pot or bamboo steamer and steam over a pot of boiling water, covered, for 30 minutes.

* Remove and cool until the mochi is cool enough to handle. Roll the steamed mochi in the ground peanut-and-sesame mixture until fully coated. Serve.

REGION: GUANGXI
PREPARATION TIME: 10 MINUTES
COOKING TIME: 5 MINUTES
SERVES: 4

桂花马蹄露
WATER CHESTNUT SOUP
WITH OSMANTHUS SUGAR

- 2 OZ/50 G ROCK SUGAR
- 1½ CUPS (11 OZ/300 G) WATER CHESTNUTS, PEELED, RINSED, AND COARSELY CHOPPED
- 2 TABLESPOONS OSMANTHUS SUGAR
- 1 TABLESPOON WATER CHESTNUT FLOUR

* Bring 3 cups (25 fl oz/750 ml) water to a boil in a large saucepan, add the rock sugar, and stir to dissolve.

* Put the water chestnuts into the pan, return to a boil, and stir in the Osmanthus sugar.

* Mix the water chestnut flour with 3 tablespoons water in a small bowl and stir this mixture into the soup. Bring the mixture to a boil, then take the pan off the heat and transfer into individual serving bowls. Serve warm.

PEANUT MOCHI

椰丝红豆麻薯

COCONUT AND
RED BEAN MOCHI

FOR THE MOCHI BATTER:
- SCANT 1 CUP (6¼ OZ/180 G) GLUTINOUS RICE FLOUR
- 2 TABLESPOONS RICE FLOUR
- 1¼ OZ/30 G WHEAT STARCH
- ¼ CUP (2 OZ/50 G) GRANULATED SUGAR
- ¼ CUP (2 FL OZ/60 ML) COCONUT MILK

FOR THE FILLING:
- 1 CUP (11 OZ/300 G) RED (ADZUKI) BEAN PASTE, DIVIDED AND ROLLED INTO FIFTEEN ¾-OZ/20-G BALLS, CHILLED

TO FINISH:
- ½ CUP (3½ OZ/100 G) GLUTINOUS RICE FLOUR
- 1 CUP (4 OZ/120 G) DRIED SHREDDED (DESICCATED) COCONUT, FOR COATING

* Add the glutinous rice flour to a dry wok or large skillet (frying pan) and stir-fry over low heat for a few minutes until it smells slightly toasted. Remove the pan from the heat and set aside to cool completely.
* Meanwhile, mix together all the ingredients for the mochi batter in a heatproof bowl. Gradually add ¾ cup (6 fl oz/ 175 ml) water until the mixture has a pourable consistency, like heavy (double) cream. Add up to 4 teaspoons more water, if necessary, to thin out.
* Place the bowl, uncovered, on a steaming rack in a wok of boiling water, cover, and steam over high heat for 20 minutes.
* Remove the bowl from the wok and beat the mochi vigorously for 1 minute with a wooden spoon or rubber spatula (fish slice) to increase the elasticity and chewiness. Cool the mochi until still warm but touchable.
* To assemble the mochis, place the cooked glutinous rice flour, shredded (desiccated) coconut, and scant ½ cup (3½ fl oz/100 ml) water in separate bowls. Remove the chilled red (adzuki) bean filling from the refrigerator.
* Dust your hands with the cooked flour and take a lump of the warm cooked dough (about 1¼ oz/35g). Place a damp clean dish towel over the remaining cooked dough to prevent it from drying out. Flatten the piece of mochi dough in the center with your thumb and gradually stretch the dough outward to create a hole for the filling. Place a red bean ball into the hole. Dust your hands (especially your thumbs) with a little more cooked flour and push the dough upward around the filling to cover it. Pinch the dough together firmly at the top to seal in the filling. Roll the mochi between your palms to form a ball.
* Dip the mochi in the bowl of water quickly, ensuring the entire surface is moistened. Lift it out with a fork and immediately roll the ball in the coconut—the water helps the coconut flakes stick onto the mochi. Transfer the mochi to a plate.
* Repeat the process to make 15 mochis in total and serve. The texture is at its best on the day of making, after which the mochis will begin to harden.

芝麻汤圆
GLUTINOUS RICE BALLS WITH BLACK SESAME FILLING

REGION: ZHEJIANG
PREPARATION TIME: 30 MINUTES,
    PLUS 1 HOUR CHILLING AND
    10 MINUTES RESTING TIME
COOKING TIME: 15 MINUTES
SERVES: 4

* To make the filling, toast the sesame seeds in a small pan over medium heat and shake occasionally for 3–5 minutes or until fragrant. Set aside to cool.
* Mix the sesame seeds with the granulated sugar into a blender or food processor and grind into a powder. Transfer the mixture to a bowl and mix in the lard. Refrigerate for about 1 hour until the filling is firm.
* Divide into 20 portions and roll each into a ball. Place on a baking sheet and refrigerate until ready to use.
* Put the glutinous rice flour into a large bowl, gradually add ½ cup (4 fl oz/120 ml) boiling water, and stir with chopsticks until flaky. Knead the mixture into a dough (at this point, the dough will appear to be quite dry). Rest for 10 minutes, then knead until it is soft and smooth. Add a little flour if necessary to achieve the correct texture. The dough should be soft and dry, and not stick to the hands. Divide the dough into 20 portions.
* Take a portion of dough, roll it into a ball in your palms, then make a dent in the center of the ball with your thumb. Put a sesame ball into the dent and fold the dough over the sesame ball to enclose it completely. Press the dough together at the top to seal in the filling. Roll it into a smooth ball. Repeat with the remaining dough and filling. Set aside.
* Heat 2 cups (16 fl oz/475 ml) water in a saucepan, add the brown sugar and ginger juice, and bring to a boil to make a ginger tea. Stir to dissolve the sugar. Pour the tea into 4 bowls.
* Bring 6¼ cups (2½ pints/1.5 liters) water to a boil in a large saucepan. Using a slotted spoon, carefully lower the glutinous rice balls, in batches, into the water and return to a boil. Stir to ensure the rice balls do not stick to the bottom. Cook for about 4–5 minutes, or until the rice balls float to the surface. Remove them with a slotted spoon, divide evenly among the bowls, and serve.

- ½ CUP (3½ OZ/100 G) GLUTINOUS RICE FLOUR
- ¼ CUP (2 OZ/50 G) BROWN SUGAR
- 2 TABLESPOONS GINGER JUICE

FOR THE FILLING:
- 2¼ TABLESPOONS BLACK SESAME SEEDS
- 3½ TABLESPOONS GRANULATED SUGAR
- 2 TABLESPOONS LARD

REGION: GUANGDONG
PREPARATION TIME: 20 MINUTES,
  PLUS 4 HOURS SETTING TIME
COOKING TIME: 30 MINUTES
MAKES: 8
📷 PAGE 631

炸鲜奶
FRIED MILK
CUSTARDS

- VEGETABLE OIL, FOR GREASING AND DEEP-FRYING
- 2 CUPS (16 FL OZ/475 ML) MILK
- ½ CUP (2 OZ/50 G) CORNSTARCH (CORNFLOUR)
- 2 EGG WHITES
- ALL-PURPOSE (PLAIN) FLOUR, FOR DUSTING
- ½ CUP (3½ OZ/100 G) GRANULATED SUGAR, PLUS EXTRA TO SPRINKLE

FOR THE BATTER:
- 1¼ CUPS (5 OZ/150 G) ALL-PURPOSE (PLAIN) FLOUR
- ½ CUP (2 OZ/50 G) CORNSTARCH (CORNFLOUR)
- ½ TEASPOON SALT
- 2 TEASPOONS BAKING POWDER
- 1 CUP (8 FL OZ/250 ML) COLD OR SPARKLING WATER, AS NEEDED

A crispy coating is key to this tasty, melt-in-your-mouth dessert. It's best to serve each batch immediately, then fry the remaining custards as required. If left to sit, they will go soggy.

* Grease a 4 × 6-inch/10 × 15-cm baking pan.
* To make the custard, beat together ½ cup (4 fl oz/120 ml) milk with the cornstarch (cornflour) in a mixing bowl until the cornstarch is dissolved. Add the egg whites and beat again until smooth.
* Pour the remaining 1½ cups (12 fl oz/350 ml) milk into a medium saucepan, add the sugar, and bring to a boil over medium-low heat. When the milk begins to bubble, pour a third of it over the egg mixture and beat continuously. Gradually pour in the remaining milk and continue to beat.
* Return the custard mixture to the pan and bring to a boil over medium-low heat. Simmer for 2–3 minutes, beating continuously, until the mixture thickens and clings to a wooden spoon. Immediately scrape the mixture into the prepared baking pan, press a sheet of plastic wrap (clingfilm) on the surface, and smooth down. Let cool and refrigerate, covered, for at least 4 hours.
* Next, make the batter. Combine the flour, cornstarch, salt, and baking powder in a large bowl. Make a well in the center, then pour in the water, a little at a time, and beat to a pourable consistency (you may not need all the water).
* Use a butter knife to gently loosen it away from the baking pan and invert the pan onto a clean work surface. Cut the custard in eight 2 x 1-inch/5 x 2.5-cm pieces. Place about 4 tablespoons flour for dusting in a shallow bowl.
* Pour enough oil into a wok or deep saucepan to fill no more than a third. Heat to 350°F/180°C, or until a cube of bread browns in 30 seconds. Take 4 custards and dust them in the flour and then in the batter. Coat evenly, lift out, and let the excess drip off. (If the batter does not drip off, add a little more water to make it a little thinner.) Gently lower into the hot oil and deep-fry for 2–3 minutes until light golden. Using a slotted spoon, turn the custards frequently to ensure even cooking and prevent them from sticking to the bottom of the wok. Carefully remove the custards from the oil and drain on paper towels. Repeat with the remaining custards. Sprinkle with sugar while hot, gently toss, and serve.

FRIED MILK CUSTARDS

福果芋泥
TARO PASTE WITH
GINKGO NUTS

- ¾ CUP (6 OZ/160 G) GRANULATED SUGAR
- 1 CUP (5 OZ/150 G) GINKGO NUTS, SHELLED, HALVED AND CORES REMOVED
- 1 LB 5 OZ/600 G TARO, PEELED AND ENDS TRIMMED
- ⅔ CUP (5 FL OZ/150 ML) VEGETABLE OIL

* Pour 1 cup (8 fl oz/250 ml) water into a small saucepan and add 3 tablespoons sugar. Bring to a boil and add the ginkgo nuts. Return to a boil, then reduce to low heat, and simmer for 10 minutes until the sugar dissolves to make a syrup. Turn off the heat and set aside.
* Use a chopstick to clean the channels of the lotus root, then thoroughly rinse under cold running water. Slice into ½-inch/1-cm-thick pieces. Put the taro on a large heatproof plate, spread out to a single layer, and transfer to a collapsible pot or bamboo steamer over a pot of boiling water. Steam, covered, for 1 hour. (Add more water to the pot if needed.) Carefully transfer the taro to a large bowl and mash it into a paste while still hot.
* Heat 5 tablespoons oil in a nonstick pan over medium heat, add the taro paste and remaining sugar, and mix well. Gradually add 1½ cups (12 fl oz/350 ml) water and 4 tablespoons oil, stir, and mash the taro paste until smooth. Add the remaining 1 tablespoon oil and stir well.
* Mix half of the ginkgo nuts into the taro paste and dish out into small bowls. Scatter the remaining ginkgo nuts over each bowl and serve.

琥珀莲子
LOTUS SEED
WITH LONGAN

- 24 DRIED LOTUS SEEDS
- 24 FRESH LONGAN, PEELED AND SEEDED
- 1 TEASPOON VEGETABLE OIL
- 2 TABLESPOONS GRANULATED SUGAR
- ¾ OZ/20 G ROCK SUGAR
- 1 TABLESPOON OSMANTHUS SUGAR

* Soak the dried lotus seeds in a bowl of cold water for about 4 hours, or until soft.
* Bring 4¼ cups (34 fl oz/1 liter) water to a boil in a large saucepan. Add the lotus seeds, reduce to low heat, and simmer, covered, for 30 minutes. Strain the lotus water into a bowl and reserve for later use.
* Insert a lotus seed into each longan.
* Heat the oil in a saucepan, add the granulated sugar, and stir over low heat for 2 minutes until melted and caramel in color. Add the reserved lotus water and bring to a boil.
* Stir in the stuffed longan and rock sugar and simmer for about 1 hour, covered, until the liquid is syrupy. Stir in the Osmanthus sugar, then transfer to individual bowls and serve with the syrup on the side.

绿豆沙
MUNG BEAN
SOUP

REGION: GUANGDONG
PREPARATION TIME: 5 MINUTES, PLUS
  4 HOURS SOAKING TIME
COOKING TIME: 1 HOUR
SERVES: 4

This sweet dessert soup is served both at home and after meals at Chinese restaurants. Cantonese people like to add an herb called common rue to the dish, but with its strong aroma and a bitter note, it's a divisive ingredient that people either love or hate. If you'd like to use it, add ¼ oz/10 g at the last 30 minutes of cooking.

- ½ CUP (4 OZ/120 G) MUNG BEANS
- SPLASH OF LEMON JUICE OR WHITE VINEGAR
- ½ CUP (4 OZ/120 G) BROWN SUGAR, OR TO TASTE

* Put the mung beans in a large bowl, fill with cold water, and soak for at least 4 hours.
* Drain the beans, then put in a large saucepan with 6¼ cups (50 fl oz/1.5 liters) cold water and a splash of lemon juice (this helps to retain the bright green color of the mung beans). Bring to a boil, then reduce the heat and simmer, uncovered, over medium heat for 1 hour until the beans are softened. Add the sugar to taste and serve hot or cold.

豆沙锅饼
PANCAKES STUFFED
WITH RED BEAN PASTE

REGION: BEIJING
PREPARATION TIME: 10 MINUTES
COOKING TIME: 15 MINUTES
SERVES: 4-8 (MAKES 2 PANCAKES)

* Combine the eggs and flour in a medium bowl and mix well. Gradually pour in ½ cup (4 fl oz/120 ml) cold water and stir to make a batter.
* Heat an 8-inch/20-cm nonstick skillet (frying pan) over low heat and brush with a little oil. Ladle in half the batter, tilting the pan to spread the batter evenly on the bottom, and cook over low heat for 2–3 minutes on each side until cooked through. Transfer to a plate and make a second pancake using all but 1 tablespoon of the remaining batter.
* Spread half the red (adzuki) bean paste onto a pancake, fold the edges toward the center to form a square, then fold in half so you have a rectangular shape. Seal the edges with some of the remaining batter and gently press to complete the seal. Repeat with the remaining pancake.
* Heat the oil in a wok or deep saucepan to 340°F/170°C, or until a cube of bread browns in 45 seconds. Gently lower in the pancakes, one at a time, and deep-fry for 2 minutes until golden brown. Use tongs to carefully remove the pancake from the oil and drain on paper towels. Slice the pancakes into 1¼-inch/3-cm-wide strips and serve.

- 2 EGGS, BEATEN
- ¾ CUP (3 OZ/80 G) ALL-PURPOSE (PLAIN) FLOUR
- 3 CUPS (25 FL OZ/750 ML) VEGETABLE OIL
- ½ CUP (5 OZ/150 G) RED (ADZUKI) BEAN PASTE
- PINCH OF SALT

笑口枣

LAUGHING DONUT HOLES

- 2 TABLESPOONS LARD OR UNSALTED BUTTER
- 2¼ CUPS (11 OZ/300 G) ALL-PURPOSE (PLAIN) FLOUR
- ½ TEASPOON BAKING POWDER
- ½ TEASPOON BAKING SODA (BICARBONATE OF SODA)
- ⅔ CUP (5 OZ/140 G) GRANULATED SUGAR
- 1 EGG, BEATEN
- 6 TABLESPOONS WHITE SESAME SEEDS
- 8½ CUPS (68 FL OZ/2 LITERS) VEGETABLE OIL

* Melt the lard in a skillet (frying pan) and set aside to cool.
* Sift the flour, baking powder, and baking soda (bicarbonate of soda) onto a pastry board or clean work surface. Make a well in the center and add the sugar, egg, lard, and 4 tablespoons cold water. Using your hands, gently bring the flour toward the center of the board and push down to form a dough. Using a scraper, gently fold the dough for 4–5 minutes, press down with your hands—do not knead the dough otherwise gluten will form and the right texture won't be achieved.
* Cut the dough into strips and then into small pieces, each weighing about ¼ oz/7 g. Roll each piece into a small dough ball, dampen the balls with a little water, and roll them in the sesame seeds. Roll each dough ball again, using your fingers to press the sesame seeds firmly into the dough.
* Heat the oil in a wok or deep saucepan to 300°F/150°C, or until a cube of bread browns in 1½ minutes. Put the dough balls, in batches, onto a spider strainer or a large slotted spoon and carefully lower the balls into the hot oil. Reduce the heat to 265°F/130°C and deep-fry for 2 minutes, stirring occasionally with chopsticks, or until the donuts have opened up. Increase the heat to 300°F/150°C, and cook for 1 minute, or until golden brown. Use a slotted spoon to carefully remove them and drain on paper towels. Repeat with the remaining dough balls.
* They can be served immediately or stored in an airtight jar where they will keep for 2–3 days.

酒醉核桃仁

WALNUTS IN WINE SAUCE

- 5 OZ/150 G ROCK SUGAR, CRUSHED
- 2 TABLESPOONS HONEY
- 1 EGG WHITE
- 2 CUPS (9 OZ/250 G) WALNUTS
- 3 TABLESPOONS KAOLIANG WINE

* Combine the rock sugar, honey, and ⅔ cup (5 fl oz/150 ml) warm water in a bowl and stir until the sugar is dissolved.
* Beat the egg white and pour it through a strainer (sieve) to filter the foam. Stir the egg white into the sugar syrup.
* Bring a scant 1 cup (7 fl oz/200 ml) water to a boil in a saucepan. Stir in the syrup and return to a boil. Add the walnuts and return to a boil. Stir in the kaoliang wine, then transfer the mixture into 4 small bowls and serve.

LAUGHING DONUT HOLES

REGION: JIANGSU
PREPARATION TIME: 30 MINUTES
COOKING TIME: 20 MINUTES
SERVES: 4

文思豆腐南瓜羹
WENSI TOFU
PUMPKIN SOUP

- 9 OZ/250 G SILKEN TOFU
- 1 LB 2 OZ/500 G PUMPKIN, PEELED, SEEDED, AND CUT INTO BITE-SIZE PIECES
- 1½ OZ/40 G ROCK SUGAR, CRUSHED

* Place the tofu on a cutting board, then halve it. Cut each piece lengthwise into 3 equal pieces for a total of 6 pieces.
* Put some water on 1 piece of tofu and thinly slice. Gently press with the body of the knife on one end of the row so the slices lie on their sides. Sprinkle water on the tofu slices and cut them into thin, hair-like strands. Put the tofu strands into a large bowl of cold water and use chopsticks to gently disperse them. Repeat with the remaining tofu pieces. Use chopsticks to lift the tofu strands and gently drop them into 4 individual serving bowls. Set aside.
* Place the pumpkin in a collapsible pot or bamboo steamer over a pot of boiling water. Steam, covered, for 15 minutes. Remove the pumpkin and allow to cool briefly.
* Put the pumpkin into a blender or food processor, add 3 cups (25 fl oz/750 ml) water, and blend into a thick puree.
* Transfer the puree to a large saucepan and bring to a boil over high heat. Use a large spoon to skim off the foam from the surface of the soup. Add the rock sugar and stir for 5 minutes until the sugar has dissolved. Transfer the soup into the separate serving bowls.
* Disperse the strands gently with chopsticks and serve hot or cold.

桂花鲜栗羹

CHESTNUT SOUP WITH OSMANTHUS FLOWER

REGION: ZHEJIANG
PREPARATION TIME: 30 MINUTES,
  PLUS 20 MINUTES SOAKING TIME
COOKING TIME: 30 MINUTES
SERVES: 4

* If using fresh chestnuts, remove the outer husk of the chestnuts. Put the chestnuts in a bowl, add boiling water to cover, and soak for 20 minutes. Peel off the skin. Dice the chestnuts into ½-inch/1-cm cubes.
* Bring a saucepan of water to the boil and add the chestnuts. Reduce the heat to low and cook for 25 minutes. Remove and drain.
* Heat 2 cups (17 fl oz/475 ml) water in a saucepan and bring to a boil. Add the chestnuts and sugars, then simmer for about 3 minutes.
* Combine the lotus root flour and 2 tablespoons water in a bowl. Gradually add the mixture to the soup and stir to blend. Divide the soup between 4 bowls and garnish with dried flowers.

* 1½ CUPS (5 OZ/150 G) FRESH CHESTNUTS OR 1 CUP (4 OZ/120 G) CANNED CHESTNUTS, DRAINED
* 2 TEASPOONS OSMANTHUS SUGAR
* 5 TABLESPOONS GRANULATED SUGAR
* 1 TABLESPOON LOTUS ROOT OR WATER CHESTNUT FLOUR
* ½ TEASPOON DRIED OSMANTHUS FLOWERS, TO GARNISH

枣莲炖雪哈

HASMA WITH LOTUS SEEDS AND JUJUBE DATES

REGION: ZHEJIANG
PREPARATION TIME: 30 MINUTES, PLUS
  8 HOURS SOAKING TIME
COOKING TIME: 1 HOUR 5 MINUTES
SERVES: 4

* Cover the hasma in 2 cups (16 fl oz/475 ml) water and soak for about 8 hours, or until the hasma look like balls of cotton. With a pair of tweezers, carefully pick out and discard any grit.
* Meanwhile, cover the dried lotus seeds in warm water and soak for about 1 hour. Drain, then pick out and discard the heart of the seeds. Rinse the seeds.
* Put the hasma into a saucepan and add 2 cups (16 fl oz/ 475 ml) water and the ginger juice. Bring to a boil over high heat and blanch for 5 minutes. Drain.
* Combine the hasma, lotus seeds, dates, and rock sugar in a sealable heatproof bowl and add 2 cups (16 fl oz/ 475 ml) water. Seal, then place the bowl in a collapsible pot or bamboo steamer over a pot of boiling water. Steam, covered, for 1 hour. (Add more water to the pot if needed.)
* Transfer to 4 bowls and serve.

* ¼ OZ/10 G DRIED HASMA
* ½ CUP (½ OZ/15 G) DRIED LOTUS SEEDS
* 1 TABLESPOON GINGER JUICE
* 8–10 JUJUBE DATES (ABOUT ½ OZ/ 15 G), PITTED
* 2¼ OZ/60 G ROCK SUGAR

REGION: GUANGDONG
PREPARATION TIME: 5 MINUTES,
    PLUS 1 HOUR SOAKING TIME
COOKING TIME: 15 MINUTES
SERVES: 4
📷 PAGE 639

芝麻糊
BLACK SESAME
SOUP

- GENEROUS ½ CUP (4 OZ/120 G) GLUTINOUS RICE, RINSED
- 1½ CUPS (9 OZ/250 G) BLACK SESAME SEEDS
- GRANULATED SUGAR, TO TASTE

* Put the glutinous rice in a large bowl, add 4¼ cups (34 fl oz/1 liter) cold water, and soak for 1 hour.
* Put the black sesame seeds into a skillet (frying pan) and toast over low heat for 4–5 minutes until fragrant. Be careful not to burn the seeds as they will become bitter.
* Transfer the toasted sesame seeds, glutinous rice, and its soaking water to a blender or food processor and blend until smooth. Use a fine-mesh strainer (sieve) to strain the contents into a bowl, using a large spoon to press down and extract most of the juice from the seeds. Discard the seeds.
* Pour the sesame juice into a cheesecloth (muslin)-lined bowl, then transfer the soup to a saucepan and bring to a slow boil over medium heat. Stir continuously, add the sugar to taste, then serve.

REGION: BEIJING
PREPARATION: 10 MINUTES, PLUS
    15 MINUTES SOAKING TIME
COOKING: 25 MINUTES
SERVES: 4
📷 PAGE 639

核桃酪
WALNUT
SOUP

- 1¾ CUPS (7 OZ/200 G) SHELLED WALNUTS
- ¼ CUP (2 OZ/50 G) LONG-GRAIN RICE
- ⅓ CUP (2 OZ/50 G) JUJUBE DATES, RINSED AND PITTED
- 1 CUP (7 OZ/200 G) GRANULATED SUGAR, OR TO TASTE

* Soak the walnuts in a bowl of warm water for 15 minutes. Drain.
* In a separate bowl, soak the rice in water for 15 minutes. Drain and set aside.
* Bring a small saucepan of water to a boil over high heat, add the dates, and simmer for 15 minutes. Remove the pits and skin and discard them, then mash the flesh.
* Combine the walnuts, rice, and jujube dates in a blender, add a scant 1 cup (7 fl oz/200 ml) water, and blend into a walnut paste. Transfer to a saucepan, add the sugar and 2 cups (16 fl oz/475 ml) water, and bring to a boil over high heat. Reduce to low heat and simmer, stirring constantly, for 5 minutes until the flavors are blended. Serve warm.

BLACK SESAME SOUP (TOP) AND WALNUT SOUP (BOTTOM)

GREEN TEA AND WATER CHESTNUT DESSERT

REGION: ANHUI
PREPARATION TIME: 5 MINUTES, PLUS
  5 MINUTES STANDING TIME
COOKING TIME: 5 MINUTES
SERVES: 2

- 5 TABLESPOONS GREEN TEA LEAVES
- 2 TABLESPOONS CORNSTARCH
  (CORNFLOUR)
- 2 CUPS (16 FL OZ/475 ML)
  VEGETABLE OIL
- 10 WATER CHESTNUTS, PEELED AND
  CUT INTO THIN STRIPS
- 3 TABLESPOONS CONFECTIONERS'
  (ICING) SUGAR

* Put the tea leaves into a bowl and add 1 cup (8 fl oz/250 ml) hot water. Cover and steep for about 5 minutes.
* Pour out the tea and reserve the tea leaves. Pat the leaves with paper towels to absorb excess moisture. Mix in 2 teaspoons cornstarch (cornflour).
* Heat the oil in a wok or deep saucepan to 300°F/150°C, or until a cube of bread browns in 1½ minutes. Add the tea leaves and deep-fry for about 30 seconds. Use a slotted spoon to carefully remove the tea leaves from the oil immediately (otherwise they will burn) and drain on paper towels.
* In a small bowl, combine the water chestnuts with the remaining 4 teaspoons cornstarch. Reheat the oil and deep-fry the water chestnuts for 2–3 minutes until they are light brown in color, then remove and drain.
* Arrange the tea leaves in the center of a serving plate and dust with confectioners' (icing) sugar. Scatter the water chestnuts around the leaves. Mix the tea leaves and water chestnuts just before serving.

NOTE:
This dish uses the sprouts of Jingting green tea from the mountains of Anhui. Longjing tea from Zhejiang or other green teas can be used as well.

HONEY LOCUST SEED DESSERT

REGION: YUNNAN
PREPARATION TIME: 10 MINUTES,
  PLUS 8 HOURS SOAKING TIME
COOKING TIME: 20 MINUTES
SERVES: 2-3

- ¾ OZ/20 G HONEY LOCUST SEEDS
- 2 SNOW FUNGUS (ABOUT 2 OZ/50 G)
- 4 JUJUBE DATES, RINSED, PITTED, AND
  CUT INTO PIECES
- 2 OZ/50 G ROCK SUGAR

* Rinse the honey locust seeds in cold water, then soak in ½ cup (4 fl oz/120 ml) water for 8 hours.
* Cover the snow fungus in hot water and soak for about 30 minutes. Rinse the snow fungus and trim off the firm part at the base. Tear the fungus into small pieces.
* Bring 3 cups (25 fl oz/750 ml) water to a boil in a large pot. Add the jujube dates, snow fungus, and rock sugar, reduce to low heat, and cook for 15 minutes.
* Add the honey locust seeds together with the soaking water, bring to a boil over high heat, then reduce to low heat, and simmer for 5 minutes. Serve.

DESSERTS

蛋白杏仁茶
ALMOND TEA WITH
EGG WHITES

REGION: GUANGDONG
PREPARATION TIME: 20 MINUTES,
    PLUS 4 HOURS SOAKING TIME
COOKING TIME: 5 MINUTES
SERVES: 4

Almond tea is a misnomer for this dish since apricot kernels are used, not almonds. Its name is derived from the fact that the flavor of apricot kernels is similar to that of almonds and the name is easier to remember. It is also called a tea rather than a soup because it is so thin. There is a version of the recipe, which includes rice, making it altogether thicker so it can properly be called a soup.

- 1¼ CUPS (9 OZ/250 G) SWEET APRICOT KERNELS
- 3 EGG WHITES
- 2 OZ/50 G ROCK SUGAR, CRUSHED

* Rinse the apricot kernels under cold running water. Drain, then soak in a bowl of cold water for 4 hours.
* Beat the egg whites in a large bowl until fluffy.
* Drain the apricot kernels and put them into a blender or food processor. Add 1 cup (8 fl oz/250 ml) water and process to a smooth paste.
* Add another 3 cups (25 fl oz/750 ml) water to the blender and blend for 2 minutes until smooth. Line a strainer (sieve) with cheesecloth (muslin) and place it over a large bowl. Pour the kernel milk into the strainer and use a spoon to press down on the kernel pulp, extracting as much milk as possible. Set aside.
* Return the kernel pulp to the blender, pour in a scant ½ cup (3½ fl oz/100 ml) water and blend for 2 minutes. Strain through the cheesecloth again and combine with the reserved kernel milk. Set aside. Discard the kernel pulp.
* Heat the apricot kernel milk in a pot over medium heat and bring to a boil. Add the rock sugar, then very slowly stir in the beaten egg whites. Serve hot or cold.

REGION: HONG KONG
PREPARATION TIME: 15 MINUTES, PLUS
  15 MINUTES STANDING TIME
COOKING TIME: 15 MINUTES
SERVES: 6
📷 PAGE 643

杨枝甘露
MANGO, POMELO,
AND SAGO DESSERT

- ¼ CUP (1 OZ/30 G) SAGO
- 4 RIPE MANGOES, PEELED, STONE REMOVED, AND CUT INTO CHUNKS
- SCANT ½ CUP (3½ FL OZ/100 ML) COCONUT MILK
- 4 TABLESPOONS EVAPORATED MILK, PLUS EXTRA TO SERVE
- ¼ CUP (2 OZ/50 G) GRANULATED SUGAR
- 5 POMELO OR PINK GRAPEFRUIT SEGMENTS

* Add the sago and 1¼ cups (10 fl oz/300 ml) water to a small saucepan and bring to a boil. Reduce to low heat and cook for 10 minutes. Cover, turn off the heat, and stand for 15 minutes.
* Rinse the sago under cold running water to get rid of any starch. Put the sago into a large bowl, add enough cold water to cover it, and refrigerate.
* In a food processor, combine two-thirds of the mango, the coconut milk, and evaporated milk and process until the mixture is smooth. Transfer to a bowl and refrigerate.
* Mix the sugar with 4 tablespoons hot water in a small saucepan and stir over low heat for 2–3 minutes, or until syrupy. Set aside to cool.
* Peel off the membrane from the pomelo or pink grapefruit segments and shred (or separate the flesh into chunks).
* Remove the sago from the refrigerator and drain. Add the sago, pomelo, and sugar syrup to the mango puree and gently mix. Divide into separate bowls, drizzle with evaporated milk, top with the reserved mango, and serve.

鲜奶炖蛋白
MILK CUSTARD
WITH EGG WHITES

- 6 EGG WHITES
- 1⅔ CUPS (14 FL OZ/400 ML) MILK
- 5 TEASPOONS GRANULATED SUGAR

* Beat the egg whites in a bowl until smooth and pour through a fine-mesh strainer (sieve) into a bowl.
* Add the milk and sugar to the bowl, and stir until the sugar has dissolved completely.
* Divide the mixture between 4 heatproof bowls and seal with aluminum foil or microwave-safe plastic wrap (clingfilm). Place the bowls in a collapsible pot or bamboo steamer over a pot of boiling water. Reduce to a gentle simmer, and steam, covered, for 10 minutes, or until the custard is set. Serve.

MANGO, POMELO, AND SAGO DESSERT

REGION: GUANGDONG
PREPARATION TIME: 5 MINUTES,
    PLUS 10 MINUTES SETTING TIME
COOKING TIME: 5 MINUTES
SERVES: 4
📷 PAGE 645

豆腐花
TOFU
PUDDING

- ½ TEASPOON GYPSUM POWDER
  (FIBROSUM CALCIUM SULFATE,
  SEE NOTE)
- 2 TEASPOONS CORNSTARCH
  (CORNFLOUR)
- 4¼ CUPS (34 FL OZ/1 LITER)
  UNSWEETENED SOY MILK (SEE NOTE)
- BROWN SUGAR OR SYRUP, TO SERVE

* To make the setting solution, Combine the gypsum powder, cornstarch (cornflour), and 4 tablespoons tepid water in a large bowl and mix well until dissolved. Set aside.
* Heat the soy milk in a large saucepan over low heat until it reaches 185°F/85°C. (The temperature is important to ensure the pudding will set.) Remove the pan from the heat immediately.
* Stir the setting solution. Lift the saucepan 12 inches/30 cm above the setting solution, then pour the hot soy milk into the bowl. The process should only take 3–4 seconds. Quickly use a large spoon or rubber spatula (fish slice) to make an "o" motion in the bowl to help distribute the setting solution evenly. Cover the bowl with a large plate or plastic wrap (clingfilm) and let stand for at least 10 minutes.
* The soy milk should set to a light, wobbly consistency. Carefully scoop the pudding into bowls and serve warm or cold with the sugar or syrup on top.

NOTE:
Gypsum powder is available at Chinese herbal shops or at some Asian grocery stores.
It is essential that you use unsweetened soy milk that is free from additives and emulsifiers.

REGION: GUANGDONG
PREPARATION TIME: 5 MINUTES,
    PLUS 4 HOURS SOAKING TIME
COOKING TIME: ABOUT 2 HOURS
SERVES: 4

红豆沙
RED BEAN
SOUP

- GENEROUS 1 CUP (7 OZ/200 G) RED
  (ADZUKI) BEANS
- 2 DRIED TANGERINE PEELS
- 3½ OZ/100 G ROCK SUGAR, OR TO
  TASTE
- EVAPORATED MILK OR VANILLA ICE
  CREAM, TO SERVE

* Put the red (adzuki) beans into a bowl, cover with plenty of cold water, and soak for 4 hours.
* Soak the dried tangerine peels in cold water for 10 minutes to soften, then drain. Using a knife, scrape to remove the pith. Cut into smaller pieces.
* Drain the beans, put them into a large saucepan with 8½ cups (68 fl oz/2 liters) water, and bring to a boil. Add the tangerine peel. Reduce to medium heat and simmer for about 2 hours, uncovered. Stir frequently to prevent the beans from sticking to the bottom of the pan.
* Add the sugar to taste. Ladle into bowls and serve with evaporated milk or vanilla ice cream.

TOFU PUDDING

 645

REGION: HONG KONG
PREPARATION TIME: 10 MINUTES, PLUS
   15 MINUTES STANDING TIME
COOKING TIME: 1 HOUR
SERVES: 8

焗西米布丁
BAKED TAPIOCA
PUDDING

- ⅔ CUP (7 OZ/200 G) LOTUS SEED PASTE OR RED (ADZUKI) BEAN PASTE
- ½ CUP (3 OZ/80 G) DRY TAPIOCA
- BUTTER, FOR GREASING

FOR THE CUSTARD CREAM:
- ½ CUP (4 FL OZ/120 ML) MILK
- 3 TABLESPOONS CUSTARD POWDER
- 2 TABLESPOONS CORNSTARCH (CORNFLOUR)
- ¼ CUP (2 OZ/50 G) GRANULATED SUGAR
- 1 CUP (8 FL OZ/250 ML) COCONUT MILK
- 1½ TABLESPOONS (¾ OZ/20 G) UNSALTED BUTTER
- 3 EGGS

A Chinese twist on a traditional British dessert—this Cantonese version is elevated with a lotus seed or red (adzuki) bean filling to make a warming dessert.

* Line an 8-inch/20-cm square baking pan with plastic wrap (clingfilm). Spread the lotus seed paste evenly across the bottom, leaving a ¾-inch/2-cm border. Place another sheet of plastic wrap on top and press down gently to make an even layer. Transfer the wrapped paste to a large plate and chill in the refrigerator.
* Meanwhile, bring a large saucepan of water to a boil over high heat. Add the tapioca and boil over high heat for 10–15 minutes until the pearls are translucent with traces of an uncooked white center. Turn off the heat, cover, and let stand for 10 minutes. The tapioca should be transparent, but it is okay if some white bits still remain since they will be cooked further in the oven.
* Drain the tapioca using a strainer (sieve) and rinse well under cold running water to wash off the starch. Rinse until the tapioca is cool. Set aside.
* Place an oven rack in the center of the oven and preheat the oven to 400°F/200°C/Gas Mark 6. Grease the baking pan and set aside.
* To make the custard cream, combine the milk, custard powder, cornstarch (cornflour), and sugar in a medium saucepan and mix with a rubber spatula (fish slice) until smooth. Add the coconut milk and butter. Set the pan over medium heat and slowly heat the mixture. Keep stirring for about 5–7 minutes until thickened. Add the drained tapioca and stir continuously for another 2 minutes until the mixture comes away from the surface of the pan.
* Remove the pan from the heat and beat in an egg, ensuring it is fully incorporated and the mixture is smooth. Repeat with the remaining eggs. The mixture should be glossy and smooth.
* Spread half of the tapioca mixture into the prepared pan. Take the lotus seed filling out of the refrigerator, unwrap it, and place it over the tapioca mixture. Cover with the remaining tapioca mixture and smooth out the top with a piece of plastic wrap. Bake for 30–35 minutes until golden brown and a toothpick (cocktail stick) inserted into the center comes out clean. If the top is not golden enough, change the oven setting to broil and brown it for 5 minutes until golden. Remove the pudding from the oven and let cool for 15 minutes before serving.

焗椰汁年糕

BAKED GLUTINOUS RICE PUDDING WITH COCONUT MILK

REGION: HONG KONG
PREPARATION TIME: 10 MINUTES
COOKING TIME: 1 HOUR
SERVES: 8

* Preheat the oven to 340°F/170°C/Gas Mark 3½.
* Beat the eggs with the sugar in a large bowl, then mix in the evaporated milk. Add the glutinous rice flour, in batches, stirring gently in one direction with a large wooden spoon until completely blended. Gradually stir in the coconut milk.
* Grease an 8 × 4-inch (20 × 10-cm) loaf pan. Line it with a piece of parchment (baking) paper. Pour in the batter and bake for 20 minutes. Reduce the temperature to 300°F/150°C/Gas Mark 2 and bake for another 40–45 minutes, or until golden and cooked through.
* Remove the pudding from the oven and let cool. Peel away the parchment paper, slice, and serve.

- 5 EXTRA LARGE (LARGE) EGGS
- 1 CUP (7 OZ/200 G) GRANULATED SUGAR
- ½ CUP (4 FL OZ/120 ML) EVAPORATED MILK
- SCANT 1½ CUPS (10 OZ/280 G) GLUTINOUS RICE FLOUR, SIFTED
- 1¼ CUPS (10 FL OZ/300 ML) COCONUT MILK
- BUTTER, FOR GREASING

中式挞皮

SWEET TART PASTRY

REGION: HONG KONG
PREPARATION TIME: 10 MINUTES
  PLUS 30 MINUTES FREEZING TIME
MAKES: 23 OZ/650 G DOUGH

This basic pastry dough is similar to a sweet pie crust (*pâte sucrée*), but Chinese bakers often incorporate skimmed milk powder to their dough for a milkier taste. It is difficult to make a smaller quantity of the dough, but it freezes well and any remaining dough can be reserved for later use.

* Using an electric beater, cream the butter, sugar, and salt together for 3–4 minutes until smooth and creamy. Add the egg and skimmed milk powder, if using, to the butter mixture and beat until emulsified.
* Use a rubber spatula (fish slice) to blend in the flour in 3 separate additions. Be sure to scrape up the flour at the bottom of the bowl.
* Knead the dough a few times so that it comes together smoothly. Divide the dough into 4 equal portions. Press down on each piece of dough so that it forms a disk and tightly wrap each of them in plastic wrap (clingfilm). Chill in the freezer for 30 minutes, then roll out the dough for immediate use. Alternatively, double-wrap each in plastic wrap to freeze. To use, thaw the frozen dough and then lightly knead.

- 1 CUP (8 OZ/225 G) UNSALTED BUTTER, AT ROOM TEMPERATURE
- ½ CUP (2¼ OZ/60 G) CONFECTIONERS' (ICING) SUGAR
- ¼ TEASPOON SALT
- 1 EGG
- ⅓ CUP (2 OZ/50 G) SKIMMED MILK POWDER (OPTIONAL)
- 2⅓ CUPS (11½ OZ/320 G) ALL-PURPOSE (PLAIN) FLOUR

REGION: HONG KONG
PREPARATION TIME: 20 MINUTES,
  PLUS 30 MINUTES CHILLING AND
  15 MINUTES COOLING TIME
COOKING TIME: 20 MINUTES
SERVES: 6
🖻 PAGE 649

蛋撻
HONG KONG-STYLE
EGG TARTS

- 2½ TABLESPOONS GRANULATED SUGAR
- ½ TEASPOON CUSTARD POWDER
  OR ¼ TEASPOON CORNSTARCH
  (CORNFLOUR)
- 2 GOOD-QUALITY EGGS, PLUS 1 EGG
  YOLK
- ⅓ CUP (2½ FL OZ/75 ML) MILK
- ¼ QUANTITY SWEET TART PASTRY
  (PAGE 647)

These iconic tarts are descendants of the British custard tart, except that the Hong Kong version is smaller and much less creamy. The custard powder prevents the filling from overbaking. If you do not have custard powder, use cornstarch (cornflour) instead.

* Combine the sugar and ⅔ cup (5 fl oz/150 ml) water in a small saucepan, bring to a boil, and stir until the sugar is fully dissolved. (It is crucial that the sugar is melted so that the custard has a smooth sheen after baking.) Remove the pan from the heat and let the syrup cool to room temperature.
* Mix the custard powder with 1 tablespoon cooled syrup in a large bowl until a paste is formed. (Any leftover syrup can be reserved for future use.) Add the eggs and the extra yolk. and beat gently until smooth. Stir in the milk.
* Pass the custard through a fine-mesh strainer (sieve) into a bowl to remove any undissolved particles. Skim any froth off the surface.
* This quantity of filling can be used to make six large 3-inch/ 7.5-cm tarts or twelve small 1½-inch/4-cm tarts. To make the larger tarts, divide the dough into six 1¼-oz/35-g portions. For the smaller tart, divide the dough into twelve ½-oz/15-g portions.
* Lightly knead a portion of dough a few times so that it becomes pliable. Roll out the dough between 2 sheets of plastic wrap (clingfilm) to a circle that is about ½ inch/ 1 cm larger than the cups in your pan, with a ¹⁄₁₂ inch/2 mm thickness. (The thinner the dough, the crispier the tart.) Remove the top sheet of plastic wrap and invert the dough onto a tart pan. Press the dough into the sides, remove the plastic wrap, then trim the top with a knife. Press on the sides gently so the dough extends slightly above the rim of the pan. Repeat for the remaining tarts, then chill in the refrigerator for at least 30 minutes.
* Preheat the oven to 425°F/220°C/Gas Mark 7. Position an oven rack in the lower third of the oven. Place a heavy baking sheet on the rack to preheat.
* Remove the lined tart pans from the refrigerator. Stir the custard, then pour it into each tart pan until it almost reaches the top. Bake for 10 minutes, or until golden and the pastry starts to set.
* Reduce the temperature to 350°F/180°C/Gas Mark 4. Bake for another 5–7 minutes until the filling is slightly wobbly in the center. Let the tarts cool for at least 15 minutes before serving.

DESSERTS

HONG KONG-STYLE EGG TARTS

REGION: HONG KONG
PREPARATION TIME: 15 MINUTES,
  PLUS 30 MINUTES RESTING TIME
COOKING TIME: 15–20 MINUTES
SERVES: 12
[📷] PAGE 651

椰撻
COCONUT
TARTS

- ¼ QUANTITY SWEET TART PASTRY
  (PAGE 647)
- CANDIED (GLACÉ) CHERRIES, HALVED,
  TO DECORATE (OPTIONAL)

FOR THE FILLING:
- 1 CUP (4 OZ/100 G) DRIED SHREDDED
  (DESICCATED) COCONUT
- 2½ TABLESPOONS (1¼ OZ/30 G)
  UNSALTED BUTTER, MELTED
- 2 EGGS
- 4 TABLESPOONS MILK
- 1¼ TEASPOONS BAKING POWDER
- 1½ TEASPOONS CUSTARD POWDER
  (OPTIONAL)
- ¼ CUP PLUS 2 TEASPOONS (2¼ OZ/
  60 G) GRANULATED SUGAR

A staple in Hong Kong bakeries, these delicious tarts have a coconut filling akin to a frangipane. Traditionally, custard powder is used to make the filling, but this is purely optional.

* Put all the filling ingredients into a large bowl and mix well until thick and creamy. Set aside for 30 minutes.
* Place an oven rack in the center of the oven. Preheat the oven to 375°F/190°C/Gas Mark 5.
* This quantity of filling can be used to make six large 3-inch/ 7.5-cm tarts or twelve small 1½-inch/4-cm tarts. To make the larger tarts, divide the dough into six 1¼-oz/35-g portions. For the smaller tart, divide the dough into twelve ½-oz/15-g portions.
* Lightly knead a portion of dough a few times so that it becomes pliable. Roll out the dough between 2 sheets of plastic wrap (clingfilm) to a circle that is about ½ inch/ 1 cm larger than the cups in your pan, with a $1/12$ inch/2 mm thickness. (The thinner the dough, the crispier the tart.) Remove the top sheet of plastic wrap and invert the dough onto a tart pan. Press the dough into the sides, remove the plastic wrap, then trim the top with a knife. Press on the sides gently so the dough extends slightly above the rim of the pan. Repeat for the remaining tarts, then chill in the refrigerator for at least 30 minutes.
* Spoon the coconut filling into the lined pans until they are three-quarters full. Place a small piece of plastic wrap (clingfilm) over the filling in each tart and press down gently to spread the filling evenly in the pastry case. Remove the plastic wrap, make crosshatch marks across the top, and top with a candied (glacé) cherry half, if using.
* Bake for 15–20 minutes (depending on the size of your tart pans) until the pastry is a golden brown and the coconut filling is set. Serve warm or at room temperature.

COCONUT TARTS

REGION: AMERICAN CHINESE
PREPARATION TIME: 20 MINUTES,
  PLUS 30 MINUTES CHILLING TIME
COOKING TIME: 25-30 MINUTES
MAKES: 24 COOKIES
📷 PAGE 653

杏仁饼
ALMOND
COOKIES

- GENEROUS 3 CUPS (12 OZ/350 G) ALL-PURPOSE (PLAIN) FLOUR
- 2 TEASPOONS BAKING POWDER
- ½ TEASPOON BAKING SODA (BICARBONATE OF SODA)
- 1 CUP (7 OZ/200 G) LARD
- ¾ CUP (5 OZ/150 G) GRANULATED SUGAR
- ¼ TEASPOON SALT
- 2 TEASPOONS ALMOND EXTRACT
- 2 EGGS, 1 SEPARATED
- ABOUT 24 ALMONDS, LIGHTLY TOASTED (OPTIONAL)

A high ratio of leavening agent gives the cookies an airy, open crumb. Traditionally, lard is used, but if you cannot get hold of it or must avoid it for dietary reasons, substitute it with a half quantity of butter and a half quantity of vegetable shortening. The extra egg white serves to hold the dough together, otherwise the texture of the cookies will be too crumbly.

* To make the dough, mix together the flour, baking powder, and baking soda (bicarbonate of soda) in a large bowl.
* Put the lard, sugar, salt, and almond extract in a separate large bowl and use an electric mixer to mix for 4–5 minutes until pale and fluffy.
* Add the whole egg plus 1 egg white and beat again until the mixture has emulsified. Fold in the flour mixture in three or four additions.
* Knead the dough gently a few times to bring it together. Wrap it in plastic wrap (clingfilm), transfer to the refrigerator, and chill for at least 30 minutes.
* Preheat the oven to 400°F/200°C/Gas Mark 6. Line 3 large baking sheets with parchment (baking) paper.
* Take 1 tablespoon of dough and roll it between your palms to form a round ball, then place this on a prepared baking sheet. Repeat with the remaining dough, arranging the balls evenly on the prepared baking sheets, spacing them at least 1½ inches/4 cm apart. Flatten each ball into a circle that is approximately 2½ inches/6 cm wide and ½ inch/ 1 cm thick.
* Combine the remaining egg yolk with 1 teaspoon water and mix well. Using a pastry brush, glaze each dough circle with the egg wash. Place an almond on each circle, if using, and press down gently.
* Bake for 10 minutes, then reduce the heat to 350°F/180°C/ Gas Mark 4 and bake for another 15–20 minutes until the cookies are golden brown and baked through (or the cookies will not be crisp).
* Remove from the oven and set aside to cool. Serve immediately or store in an airtight container for up to 3 days.

ALMOND COOKIES

REGION: HONG KONG
PREPARATION TIME: 20 MINUTES
 PLUS 30 MINUTES RESTING TIME
COOKING TIME: 30 MINUTES
MAKES: 32
📷 PAGE 655

核桃酥
WALNUT COOKIES

- ½ CUP (4 OZ/120 G) BUTTER, ROOM TEMPERATURE
- ¼ CUP (2 OZ/50 G) GRANULATED SUGAR
- ¼ CUP (2 OZ/50 G) BROWN SUGAR
- 1 EGG, BEATEN
- SCANT 2 CUPS (8 OZ/225 G) ALL-PURPOSE (PLAIN) FLOUR
- ½ TEASPOON BAKING SODA (BICARBONATE OF SODA)
- 1 TEASPOON BAKING POWDER
- PINCH OF SALT
- ½ CUP (2½ OZ/65 G) SHELLED WALNUTS, BROKEN, PLUS EXTRA TO DECORATE (OPTIONAL)

* Preheat the oven to 350°F/180°C/Gas Mark 4.
* Beat the butter and sugars together until smooth. Add 2 tablespoons egg and mix until fully blended.
* Sift the flour, baking soda (bicarbonate of soda), baking powder, and salt into a large bowl. Sift again. Add to the wet mixture, in batches, and mix into a dough. Stir in the broken walnuts. Transfer the dough to a baking sheet, shape into a disk, and let rest for 30 minutes.
* Divide the dough into 32 portions. Roll each portion into a ball in your palms and flatten slightly into a small round cookie. Top each circle, if desired, with a piece of broken walnut and transfer to a baking sheet.
* Mix the remaining beaten egg with 1 tablespoon water to make an egg wash. Brush the tops of the cookies.
* Bake for 18 minutes. Reduce the oven temperature to 325°F/160°C/Gas Mark 3 and bake for another 13 minutes until baked through.
* Remove from the oven and set aside to cool. Serve immediately or store in an airtight container for up to 3 days.

花生酥
PEANUT CRISP COOKIES

- 1 CUP (4 OZ/120 G) CAKE FLOUR
- ¼ TEASPOON BAKING POWDER
- ⅓ CUP (1½ OZ/40 G) CONFECTIONERS' (ICING) SUGAR
- ⅓ CUP (2½ OZ/65 G) PEANUT BUTTER
- 4 TABLESPOONS CORN OIL
- ¼ TEASPOON SALT
- 16 PEANUTS, SHELLED AND HALVED, TO DECORATE
- 1 EGG, BEATEN

* Preheat the oven to 300°F/150°C/Gas Mark 2.
* Sift the flour, baking powder, and sugar into a large bowl.
* In a separate bowl, mix the peanut butter with the oil, add the salt and the sifted flour mixture, and blend until the dough is smooth and will not stick to your fingers. Divide the dough into 32 portions.
* Roll a portion of dough into a ball in your hands, then flatten it into a small, round cookie. Place half a peanut on top. Repeat with the remaining dough portions.
* Add 1–2 teaspoons water to the beaten egg and mix to make an egg wash. Brush the top of each cookie with the egg wash and transfer to a baking sheet. Bake for 20–22 minutes, or until golden.
* Remove from the oven and set aside to cool. Serve immediately or store in an airtight container for up to 3 days.

GUEST CHEFS

GUEST CHEFS

CHAN YAN TAK

·

LUNG KING HEEN

FOUR SEASONS HOTEL HONG KONG, 8 FINANCE STREET, CENTRAL, HONG KONG, CHINA

*

Combining textures and flavors with inventive presentations, Executive Chef Chan Yan Tak is the first Chinese chef to receive three Michelin stars for his intricately designed menu at Four Season's Lung King Heen. One of the most celebrated chefs in China, Chef Tak is best known for introducing Western ingredients into Chinese dishes.

PREPARATION TIME: 10 MINUTES, PLUS
   10 MINUTES MARINATING TIME
COOKING TIME: 10 MINUTES
SERVES: 2

黑蒜大千鸡
"DAXIAN" BLACK GARLIC CHICKEN

- 10½ OZ/300 G BONELESS, SKINLESS CHICKEN, CUT INTO BITE-SIZE CHUNKS
- 1½ TABLESPOONS LIGHT SOY SAUCE
- 1 TEASPOON CORNSTARCH (CORNFLOUR)
- 1 TABLESPOON VEGETABLE OIL
- 2 CLOVES GARLIC, SLICED
- 2 SHALLOTS, SLICED
- ½ ONION, SLICED
- 2 DRIED CHILES, CUT INTO ½-INCH/ 1-CM SEGMENTS
- 1 RED CLUSTER PEPPER, FINELY CHOPPED
- 1 OZ/25 G BLACK GARLIC, CHOPPED
- 1 TABLESPOON FERMENTED BLACK BEANS, RINSED AND CHOPPED
- 1 TEASPOON DARK SOY SAUCE
- ½ TEASPOON GRANULATED SUGAR
- 2 STALKS CILANTRO (CORIANDER),

* Combine the chicken, 1 tablespoon light soy sauce, cornstarch (cornflour), and 4 tablespoons water in a bowl and marinate for 10 minutes.
* Heat the oil in a wok or large skillet (frying pan) over medium-high heat, add the chicken, and cook for 3–4 minutes, or until cooked through. Transfer to a plate.
* In the same wok, add the garlic, shallots, onion, dried chiles, and red pepper and sauté over medium-high heat for 1 minute or until fragrant. Put in the black garlic, black beans, and chicken, then add the remaining ½ tablespoon light soy sauce, dark soy sauce, and sugar and stir-fry until thoroughly combined. Add the remaining cornstarch, then stir in the cilantro (coriander). Transfer to a serving plate and serve.

番茄奶冻
TOMATO
BLANCMANGE

PREPARATION TIME: 20 MINUTES,
PLUS 30 MINUTES SOAKING AND
6 HOURS CHILLING TIME
MAKES: 10 CUPS

The preparation of this blancmange has two parts: the base is a tomato pudding and the top is a fresh mousse.

* For the tomato pudding, combine the basil seeds and enough water to cover them and soak for 30 minutes, then strain.
* Score the base of the tomatoes. Bring a small saucepan of water to a boil, add the tomatoes, and heat for 1–2 minutes. Immediately transfer to a bowl of ice water. When cool enough to handle, peel away the skin.
* Put the tomatoes in a blender, add a scant 2 cups (15 fl oz/450 ml) water, and puree. Combine the granulated sugar and gelatin powder, add the mixture to the blender, and mix well.
* Transfer the mixture to a saucepan and bring to a boil. Immediately turn off the heat and set aside to cool. (It will cool more rapidly if placed in water).
* Add the sweet whipped topping to make a paste. Transfer 3¾ oz/110 g of the mixture to a pan, stir in a heaping tablespoon of the basil seeds, and mix thoroughly. Refrigerate the mixture at a temperature ranging between 32–40°F/0–4°C for 1 hour, or until set.
* For the blancmange, combine the sugar and the gelatin powder in a small saucepan. Gradually pour in the milk and bring to a boil over medium-high heat, stirring continuously. Remove from the heat, allow to cool, and then add the sweet whipped topping to make a paste.
* Once the tomato base has set, add 1¼ oz/36 g of blancmange on top and then return the mixture to the refrigerator and chill for 3 hours.
* Decorate with mint leaves and serve.

FOR THE TOMATO PUDDING:
* 1½ TEASPOONS SWEET BASIL SEEDS
* 4–5 TOMATOES
* ¾ CUP (5 OZ/150 G) GRANULATED SUGAR
* 1½ TABLESPOONS GELATIN POWDER
* ⅓ CUP (2½ OZ/75 G) SWEET WHIPPED TOPPING
* MINT LEAVES, TO GARNISH

FOR THE BLANCMANGE:
* 2 TABLESPOONS GRANULATED SUGAR
* ½ TABLESPOON GELATIN POWDER
* 1 CUP (8 FL OZ//250 ML) MILK
* 3 TABLESPOONS SWEET WHIPPED TOPPING

蒜虾春卷

GARLIC AND PRAWN SPRING ROLLS

- ⅔ CUP (2¾ OZ/80 G) SELF-RAISING FLOUR
- 30 (8-INCH/20 CM) SPRING ROLL WRAPPERS
- 3 CUPS (25 FL OZ/750 ML) VEGETABLE OIL, FOR DEEP FRYING

FOR THE SHRIMP (PRAWN) FILLING:
- 1 LB 5 OZ/600 G UNCOOKED SHRIMP (PRAWNS), PEELED AND DEVEINED
- 4 TEASPOONS CORNSTARCH (CORNFLOUR), PLUS EXTRA FOR BRUSHING
- ⅓ CUP (2½ OZ/75 ML) VEGETABLE OIL
- 25 CLOVES GARLIC (ABOUT 2¾ OZ/ 80 G), CHOPPED
- 1¼ TEASPOONS SALT
- ¾ TEASPOON GROUND WHITE PEPPER
- 4 TEASPOONS GRANULATED SUGAR
- 1 TEASPOON CHICKEN STOCK POWDER
- ½ TEASPOON SESAME OIL
- 2¾ OZ/80 G PORK FATBACK, FINELY CHOPPED

FOR THE VEGETABLE FILLING:
- 10½ OZ/300 G CHINESE BROCCOLI OR CHOY SUM, FINELY CHOPPED
- ⅔ TEASPOON SALT
- 2½ TEASPOONS SUGAR
- ½ TEASPOON CHICKEN STOCK POWDER
- 1½ TABLESPOONS VEGETABLE OIL
- 12–14 CLOVES GARLIC, CHOPPED

* To make the shrimp (prawn) filling, put the shrimp into a bowl and mix with the cornstarch (cornflour). Rinse under cold running water, then drain and set aside.
* Heat 4 tablespoons vegetable oil in a wok or large skillet (frying pan) over medium-high heat, add the garlic, and cook for 30 seconds, or until fragrant. Turn off the heat and set aside to cool.
* Use paper towels to pat dry the shrimp, then transfer them to a bowl. Add the salt, white pepper, and 1 tablespoon vegetable oil and mix well by hand. Add the sugar, chicken stock powder, sesame oil, pork fatback, and the garlic and mix well. Set aside.
* To make the vegetable filling, combine all the ingredients together in a bowl and mix well.
* In a small bowl, combine the self-raising flour and a scant ½ cup (3½ fl oz/100 ml) water and mix into a paste. Set aside.
* To make the spring rolls, place a wrapper on a clean work surface and add 2 tablespoons of shrimp filling along one side. Add 2 teaspoons of vegetable filling along the same edge, then roll up the wrapper and fold in the edges. Brush the open edge with the flour paste to seal. Repeat with the remaining wrappers and filling.
* Heat the vegetable oil in a wok or deep saucepan to 340°F/170°C, or until a cube of bread browns in 45 seconds. Gently lower the spring rolls, in batches, into the hot oil and deep-fry for 3 minutes, using chopsticks to turn them around. Increase the heat to 350°F/180°C, or until a cube of bread browns in 30 seconds. Deep-fry for a 1 minute, until golden. Use a slotted spoon to remove the spring rolls from the hot oil and drain on paper towels. Serve immediately.

THOMAS CHEN

·

TUOME

536 EAST 5TH STREET, NEW YORK, NY 10009, UNITED STATES

Chinese-American chef Thomas Chen was born and raised in New York. After attending culinary school, he spent a number of years at Eleven Madison Park before opening his first restaurant. His work at Tuome focuses on offering an ingredient-driven contemporary American menu that showcases his classic culinary training and Asian upbringing. Since opening, Thomas and the restaurant have continued to receive praise from consumers and media alike.

*

红鲷鱼酸辣汤
RED SNAPPER WITH
HOT & SOUR SOUP

PREPARATION TIME: 30 MINUTES
COOKING TIME: 45 MINUTES
SERVES 2

* Heat the oil in a large saucepan over medium heat, add the ginger and garlic, and stir for 2 minutes until fragrant. Add the onions, carrots, celery, scallions (spring onions), and chile and stir-fry for 6–7 minutes, or until softened. Add the tomato paste and stir for 30 seconds, then pour in the wine and cook for 2 minutes until reduced.
* Pour the chicken broth (stock) into the pan and bring to a boil over high heat, then reduce to low heat and simmer for 15 minutes. Add the soy sauce and vinegar.
* In a small bowl, combine the cornstarch (cornflour) with 1½ tablespoons water and stir this mixture into the pan. Bring to a boil, stirring, for about 30 seconds to thicken the soup. Strain, discard the vegetables, and return the broth to the pan.
* Add the bamboo shoots and mushrooms. Slowly drizzle in the beaten egg and use chopsticks to stir, making strands of egg.
* Salt the fish fillets and put them in a collapsible pot or bamboo steamer over a pot of boiling water. Bring to a boil, then reduce to a simmer and gently steam, covered, for 6–8 minutes until cooked through. Season with salt.
* Ladle the soup into 2 shallow bowls, top each with a fish fillet, and garnish with cilantro (coriander). Serve.

- 1 TABLESPOON CANOLA (RAPESEED) OIL
- 2 TABLESPOONS GINGER, SLICED
- 2–3 CLOVES GARLIC, CRUSHED
- ½ CUP DICED ONIONS
- ½ CUP SLICED CARROTS
- ½ CUP SLICED CELERY
- ¼ CUP CHOPPED SCALLIONS (SPRING ONIONS)
- 1 BIRD'S EYE CHILE, SPLIT
- 1 TEASPOON TOMATO PASTE
- ½ CUP (4 FL OZ/120 ML) SHAOXING WINE
- 4 CUPS (32 FL OZ/950 ML) CHICKEN BROTH (STOCK)
- 2 TABLESPOONS LIGHT SOY SAUCE
- 1 TABLESPOON RED WINE VINEGAR
- 1 TABLESPOON CORNSTARCH (CORNFLOUR)
- ¼ CUP BAMBOO SHOOTS, DICED
- 1 CUP (2 OZ/60 G) ENOKI MUSHROOMS, TRIMMED
- 1 EGG, BEATEN
- 2 (6-OZ/170-G) RED SNAPPER FILLETS
- ¼ CUP CILANTRO (CORIANDER) LEAVES, TO GARNISH
- SALT, TO TASTE

FRIED CHICKEN WITH GENERAL TSO'S HONEY

PREPARATION TIME: 20 MINUTES,
PLUS 12 HOURS MARINATING TIME
COOKING TIME: 15 MINUTES
SERVES: 4

FOR THE BUTTERMILK CHICKEN:
- 4 CUPS (32 FL OZ/950 ML) BUTTERMILK
- ½ TEASPOON SRIRACHA®
- ¼ TEASPOON ONION POWDER
- ¼ TEASPOON GARLIC POWDER
- ¼ TEASPOON GINGER POWDER
- ¼ TEASPOON SALT, PLUS EXTRA TO TASTE
- 8 BONELESS, SKINLESS CHICKEN THIGHS, CUT INTO 1-INCH/2.5-CM CUBES
- CANOLA (RAPESEED) OIL, FOR FRYING

FOR THE HONEY SAUCE:
- ½ CUP (4 FL OZ/120 ML) HONEY
- 2 TEASPOONS LIGHT SOY SAUCE
- 1 TEASPOON SAMBAL OELEK
- ¼ TEASPOON FINELY CHOPPED GARLIC

FOR THE FLOUR MIXTURE:
- 4 CUPS (17½ OZ/500 G) ALL-PURPOSE (PLAIN) FLOUR
- 2 CUPS (8 OZ/225 G) CORNSTARCH (CORNFLOUR)
- ¼ TEASPOON GARLIC POWDER
- ¼ TEASPOON WHITE PEPPER
- ¼ TEASPOON FINE SALT

* In a large mixing bowl, combine the buttermilk, Sriracha®, onion powder, garlic powder, ginger powder, and salt and mix well. Add the chicken thighs and refrigerate for 12 hours.
* To make the honey sauce, combine all the ingredients, mix well, and set aside.
* To make the flour mixture, combine all the ingredients in a large bowl and stir to mix.
* Heat the oil in a wok or deep saucepan to 340°F/170°C, or until a cube of bread browns in 45 seconds. Dip the chicken in the flour mixture and toss to coat. Gently lower the chicken, in batches, into the hot oil, and deep-fry for 2 minutes. Use a slotted spoon or mesh strainer (sieve) to remove the chicken and drain on a wire rack. Set aside for 2 minutes.
* Reheat the oil to 340°F/170°C, then gently lower the chicken and re-fry for another 2 minutes, until the chicken is cooked through. Season with salt to taste.
* Transfer the chicken to a serving plate and serve with the honey sauce on the side.

虾仁腊肠炒饭
CHINESE SAUSAGE AND SHRIMP FRIED RICE

PREPARATION TIME: 20 MINUTES,
PLUS 12 HOURS CHILLING TIME
COOKING TIME: 20 MINUTES
SERVES: 2

* Bring a saucepan of water to boil, add the rice, and boil for 6 minutes over high heat, stirring occasionally. Strain the rice and cool in the refrigerator for 12 hours.
* Heat 1 tablespoon oil in a wok or large skillet (frying pan) over low heat. Add the ginger and cook for about 2 minutes until fragrant. Add the shishito peppers, beech mushrooms, garlic chives, scallions (spring onions), and dried shrimp. Sauté over high heat for 2 minutes until the vegetables are tender.
* Add the shrimp (prawns) and cook for 2–3 minutes until pink. Transfer the mixture to a bowl and set aside.
* Heat 1 tablespoon oil in a small skillet (frying pan) over high heat, add the eggs, and scramble for 2–3 minutes, or until just done. Using a spatula (fish slice), break up the scrambled eggs into small pieces and transfer them to the bowl of vegetables and shrimp.
* In a clean wok, cook the Chinese sausage over medium heat (no need for oil as the sausage will render as it cooks) for 1–2 minutes until crispy. Transfer the sausage to the bowl of ingredients, leaving the rendered fat in the pan.
* Add the remaining 2 tablespoons oil to the wok. Heat over high heat, add the rice, and stir-fry continuously until all the rice is coated with oil and warmed through, breaking up any large lumps with the spatula.
* Put in the reserved bowl of ingredients, soy sauce, fish sauce, and sambal oelek, mix well, then season with salt to taste and mix well. Transfer to a serving plate and serve.

- 2 CUPS (14 OZ/400 G) LONG-GRAIN RICE, RINSED
- 4 TABLESPOONS CANOLA (RAPESEED) OIL
- 1 TABLESPOON FINELY CHOPPED GINGER
- 7 SHISHITO PEPPERS, SLICED
- ½ CUP (1 OZ/30 G) BEECH MUSHROOMS, SEPARATED
- ½ CUP SLICED GARLIC CHIVES, CUT INTO ¼-INCH/3-MM SEGMENTS
- 3 SCALLIONS (SPRING ONIONS), SLICED
- 2 TEASPOONS DRIED SHRIMP
- 5 UNCOOKED SHRIMP (PRAWNS), SHELLED, DEVEINED, AND BUTTERFLIED
- 2 EGGS, BEATEN
- 2 CHINESE SAUSAGES, SLICED
- 2 TEASPOONS LIGHT SOY SAUCE
- 2 TEASPOONS FISH SAUCE
- 2 TEASPOONS SAMBAL OELEK
- SALT, TO TASTE

KATHY FANG

·

HOUSE OF NANKING

919 KEARNY STREET, SAN FRANCISCO, CA 94133, UNITED STATES

*

The Fang family has been at the forefront of Chinese cuisine in San Francisco since opening House of Nanking in 1988. This popular restaurant, treasured for its classic, home-style dishes, has an ardent following of locals, tourists, city notables, and celebrities. Kathy grew up in the kitchen of House of Nanking and has emerged from her renowned culinary family as chef and co-owner of Fang, a Chinese restaurant in San Francisco, which she opened with her father Peter Fang in 2011.

PREPARATION TIME: 5 MINUTES
COOKING TIME: 50 MINUTES
SERVES: 2

宫保三文鱼
KUNG PAO SALMON
WITH BROCCOLI

- 1 LARGE SWEET POTATO, PEELED AND CUT INTO 1-INCH/2.5-CM CUBES
- 2 TABLESPOONS EXTRA-VIRGIN OLIVE OIL
- 2 TEASPOONS GROUND CINNAMON
- 3 CUPS (1 LB 2 OZ/500 G) BROCCOLI FLORETS
- 1 (8-OZ/225-G) SKINLESS SALMON FILLET, CUT INTO 1-INCH CUBES
- 2 TABLESPOONS ROASTED UNSALTED PEANUTS
- THINLY SLICED SCALLIONS (SPRING ONIONS), TO GARNISH
- SALT AND GROUND BLACK PEPPER

  FOR THE SAUCE:
- ½ CUP (4 FL OZ/120 ML) LIGHT SOY SAUCE
- ¼ CUP (4 FL OZ/120 ML) WHITE VINEGAR
- 1 TABLESPOON AGAVE SYRUP
- 1 TEASPOON GINGER
- ½ TEASPOON MINCED GARLIC
- ½ TEASPOON CHILI FLAKES
- ½ TEASPOON SRIRACHA®

* Preheat the oven to 375°F/190°C/Gas Mark 5.
* Put the sweet potato on a baking sheet, add ½ tablespoon oil add ground cinnamon, and toss to combine. Season with salt and pepper and spread out the sweet potato in a single layer. Bake for 15–20 minutes, or until softened.
* Meanwhile, combine the broccoli and ½ tablespoon oil in a large bowl, season with salt and pepper, and toss.
* Push the sweet potato to one side of the baking sheet, add the broccoli to the other side, and arrange in a single layer. Bake for another 10–15 minutes, or until tender.
* To make the sauce, combine all the ingredients in a small bowl and mix well.
* Heat 1 tablespoon oil in a wok or large skillet (frying pan) over high heat, then add the salmon and pan-fry for 3–5 minutes until browned on all sides. Transfer the salmon to a plate and set aside.
* Add the sauce to the pan and simmer for 2–4 minutes, or until thickened. Reduce to medium heat, add the salmon , broccoli, and sweet potato and cook for 3 minutes, turning gently to coat.
* Transfer the mixture to a serving plate and top with peanuts and scallions (spring onions).

港式咖喱虾仁炒饭
HONG KONG-STYLE CURRY FRIED RICE WITH SHRIMP

PREPARATION TIME: 5 MINUTES
COOKING TIME: 8 MINUTES
SERVES: 2

* Heat 1 teaspoon oil in a nonstick skillet (frying pan) over high heat. Add the eggs and scramble until well done. Transfer to a bowl and set aside.
* Heat 1 teaspoon oil in the same skillet over medium-high heat, add the curry powder, ginger, and garlic, and stir for 30–45 seconds until fragrant. Add the shrimp (prawns) and stir-fry for 1 minute. Stir in the peas, rice, lettuce, scallions (spring onions), fish sauce, salt, and sugar. Mix well.
* Drizzle in the remaining 1 teaspoon oil, reduce to medium-high heat, and stir until well mixed. Add the egg and Sriracha® or chili paste, if using, and stir.
* Transfer to a serving plate and serve.

- 1 TABLESPOON CANOLA (RAPESEED) OR SOYBEAN OIL
- 3 EGGS, BEATEN
- 1 TABLESPOON YELLOW CURRY POWDER
- 1 TABLESPOON GRATED GINGER
- 1 TEASPOON CHOPPED GARLIC
- ½ CUP (2 OZ/60 G) CHOPPED BOILED SHRIMP (PRAWNS)
- ¼ CUP (2 OZ/60 G) PEAS OR SOY BEANS
- 2 CUPS (11½ OZ/320 G) COOKED WHITE RICE
- 1 CUP (3 OZ/80 G) SHREDDED ROMAINE OR ICEBERG LETTUCE
- 2 SCALLIONS (SPRING ONIONS), CHOPPED
- 1 TEASPOON FISH SAUCE
- PINCH OF SALT
- PINCH OF GRANULATED SUGAR
- 1 TEASPOON SRIRACHA® OR CHILI PASTE (OPTIONAL)

酸辣土豆丝
HOT AND SOUR POTATO THREADS

PREPARATION TIME: 8 MINUTES
COOKING TIME: 7 MINUTES
SERVES: 2

* Combine the potatoes and the salt in a large bowl and toss. Add enough water to cover and set aside for 5 minutes, then drain.
* Heat the oil in a wok or large skillet (frying pan) over high heat, add the potatoes, and stir-fry until the potatoes are coated in oil. Put in the remaining ingredients and 1 tablespoon water, then cook for 5 minutes, stirring continuously to prevent the potatoes from sticking to the pan and overcooking.
* Transfer the mixture to a serving plate, season with extra chili oil to taste, and garnish with black sesame seeds, if using.

- 2 FLOURY POTATOES (SUCH AS RUSSETS), PEELED AND CUT INTO THIN STRIPS
- 1 TEASPOON SALT
- 1 TABLESPOON CANOLA (RAPESEED) OR SOYBEAN OIL
- 4 TABLESPOONS WHITE VINEGAR
- 2 TEASPOONS GRANULATED SUGAR
- 1 TEASPOON CHILI PASTE OR SAMBAL
- 1 TEASPOON CHILI FLAKES
- 1 TEASPOON CHILI OIL, PLUS EXTRA TO TASTE
- BLACK SESAME SEEDS, TO GARNISH (OPTIONAL)

KONG KHAI MENG

•

LA CHINE

WALDORF ASTORIA HOTEL, 540 LEXINGTON AVENUE, NEW YORK, NY 10022, UNITED STATES

*

At La Chine, traditional French techniques are paired with the best ingredients under the direction of culinary director David Garcelon and seasoned executive chef Kong Khai Meng. Meng, a Singapore native, has more than 20 years experience at some of Asia's most acclaimed Chinese restaurants.

PREPARATION TIME: 35 MINUTES
COOKING TIME: 40 MINUTES
SERVES: 1

蜜汁鲈鱼
CHILEAN SEA BASS WITH HONEY AND SOY GLAZE

- 1 (5-OZ/150-G) SEA BASS FILLET, SKIN ON
- 3 TABLESPOONS LIGHT SOY SAUCE
- 1 TABLESPOON POTATO STARCH
- 1 EGG WHITE
- 3½ TABLESPOONS VEGETABLE OIL
- 9 OZ/250 G BEECH MUSHROOMS, TRIMMED AND SEPARATED
- 1 SPEAR ASPARAGUS, CUT DIAGONALLY INTO 1¼-INCH/3-CM LENGTHS
- ½ TABLESPOON PEAS
- SALT AND PEPPER

FOR THE HONEY AND SOY GLAZE:
- SCANT 3 CUPS (23 FL OZ/680 ML) PREMIUM LIGHT SOY SAUCE
- GENEROUS 2 CUPS (17 FL OZ/500 ML) DARK SOY SAUCE
- GENEROUS 2 CUPS (17 FL OZ/500 ML) MAGGI® SEASONING
- 2⅔ TABLESPOONS SESAME OIL
- ⅓ CUP (2¾ OZ/80 G) OYSTER SAUCE
- 2 CUPS (14 OZ/400 G) GRANULATED SUGAR
- 2 TEASPOONS CHICKEN STOCK POWDER
- 1¾ CUPS (14½/430 ML) GOOD-QUALITY ORGANIC HONEY

* Preheat an oven to 350°F/180°C/Gas Mark 4.
* To make the glaze, put all the ingredients, except the honey, and 2¾ cups (22 fl oz/700 ml) water in a large saucepan. Place over a double boiler and simmer for 25–30 minutes, or until thick enough to coat a spoon. Add the honey and remove from the heat. Set aside.
* Combine the sea bass and soy sauce and marinate for 8 minutes. Transfer the fish to an ovenproof dish, skin side down, and bake for 7 minutes. Brush a thin layer of the glaze and bake for another 5 minutes, until cooked through.
* In the meantime, heat the honey and soy glaze over low heat. Mix the potato starch and 1 tablespoon water, then add this mixture to the sauce to thicken.
* Bring a small saucepan of water to a boil over medium-high heat. Add the egg white and 3 tablespoons vegetable oil and poach. Strain, then return the egg to the pan, season with salt and pepper, and sauté for 1 minute, until soft and tender. Transfer to a serving plate.
* Heat ½ tablespoon vegetable oil in a small skillet (frying pan) over medium-high heat, add the asparagus, peas, and mushrooms, and cook for 2 minutes. Season with salt and pepper.
* Place the sea bass on top of the egg white and surround the fish with the vegetables. Drizzle over the honey and soy glaze and served immediately. (The remaining glaze can be stored in the refrigerator for up to 30 days.)

酸菜
PICKLED NAPA CABBAGE

PREPARATION TIME: 10 MINUTES,
PLUS 26 HOURS MARINATING TIME
MAKES: 2¾ LB/1.8 KG

* Combine the cabbage and 1¾ cups (17½ oz/500 g) salt in a large bowl and let stand for 2 hours, or until soft tender. Rinse the salted cabbage under cold running water to remove the salt and crisp the cabbage. Drain in a colander and set aside.
* In a blender, combine the carrot, chile, garlic, remaining 4 teaspoons salt, sugar, rice vinegar, and fermented bean curd and process until a paste is formed.
* Combine the cabbage and the paste, mix well, and marinate in the refrigerator for at least 24 hours.

- 1 (2¾-LB/1.8-KG) NAPA CABBAGE, TRIMMED TO 3-INCH/7.5-CM-LONG PIECES
- SCANT 2 CUPS (18½ OZ/520 G) KOSHER SALT
- 1 LARGE CARROT, SLICED
- 3–4 LONG RED CHILE, SLICED
- 10 CLOVES GARLIC
- ²/₃ CUP (4½ OZ/130 G) GRANULATED SUGAR
- SCANT 1 CUP (7 FL OZ/200 ML) RICE VINEGAR
- 5 OZ/140 G FERMENTED BEAN CURD

干炸马鲛鱼
CRISPY SPANISH MACKEREL, PICKLED NAPA CABBAGE, AND SMOKED SOY DRESSING

PREPARATION TIME: 20 MINUTES
COOKING TIME: 3 HOURS 15 MINUTES
SERVES: 6

* To make the dressing, heat the oil in a saucepan over medium-high heat, add the shallots and ginger, and fry for 1–2 minutes, or until lightly seared. Add the remaining ingredients and 4¼ cups (34 fl oz/1 liter) water and bring to a boil. Reduce to medium-low heat and simmer for 3 hours, or until thickened. Strain and store in the refrigerator.
* Combine the mackerel, light soy sauce, and wine and marinate for 30 minutes. Drain, then pat dry.
* Heat the oil in a wok or deep saucepan to 215°F/100°C, gently lower the mackerel, and deep-fry for 3–5 minutes, or until cooked through and still moist. Use a slotted spoon to remove the mackerel and transfer to paper towel to drain.
* Toss with 3 tablespoons smoked soy dressing, plate with pickled Napa cabbage, and serve.

- 5 OZ/140 G SPANISH MACKEREL FILLETS, SKIN-ON AND CUT INTO 6 PIECES
- 1½ TEASPOONS LIGHT SOY SAUCE
- 1¼ TEASPOONS SHAOXING WINE
- 3 CUPS (25 FL OZ/750 ML) VEGETABLE OIL
- 6 PIECES PICKLED NAPA CABBAGE (SEE ABOVE)

FOR THE SMOKED SOY DRESSING:
- 3½ TABLESPOONS VEGETABLE OIL
- ½ SMALL SHALLOT, SLICED
- 2 OZ/60 G GINGER (ABOUT 3-INCH/ 7.5-CM-LENGTH PIECE), SLICED
- 1 SMALL SCALLION (SPRING ONION)
- GENEROUS 2 CUPS (17 FL OZ/500 ML) PREMIUM SOY SAUCE
- 16 OZ/ 450 G ROCK SUGAR
- 1½ CUPS (10½ OZ/300 G) GRANULATED SUGAR
- ²/₃ CUP (5 FL OZ/150 G) MALTOSE
- ²/₃ CUP (5 OZ/150 ML) HUADIAO (SHAOXING YELLOW) RICE WINE
- 2–3 BAY LEAVES
- 3 STAR ANISE
- 1 CINNAMON STICK

PREPARATION TIME: 15 MINUTES
COOKING TIME: 10 MINUTES
SERVES: 2

黑椒牛排
BEEF TENDERLOIN, HICKORY WALNUTS, BLACK PEPPER GLAZE

- 1 (7¾-OZ/220-G) BEEF TENDERLOIN, CUT INTO 1¼-INCH/3-CM CUBES
- 1 TABLESPOON BROWN BEAN PASTE
- 2 TEASPOONS GRANULATED SUGAR
- 1 TEASPOON POTATO STARCH
- 3⅓ TABLESPOONS VEGETABLE OIL
- ¼ RED BELL PEPPER, SEEDED AND CUT INTO 1¼-INCH/3-CM SQUARES
- ¼ YELLOW BELL PEPPER, SEEDED AND CUT INTO 1¼-INCH/3-CM SQUARES
- 1¾ TABLESPOONS (1 OZ/25 G) BUTTER
- 2-3 CLOVES GARLIC, SLICED
- ½ SMALL RED ONION, CUT INTO 1¼-INCH/3-CM SQUARES
- 3 CIPOLLINI ONIONS, PEELED, CUT IN HALF, AND LAYERS SEPARATED
- ⅓ LEEK, CUT INTO THIN STRIPS
- ½ TEASPOON COARSE BLACK PEPPER
- ⅛ OZ/3 G LIN'AN HICKORY WALNUTS

FOR THE BLACK PEPPER GLAZE:
- 3⅓ CUPS (27 FL OZ/800 ML) MAGGI® SEASONING
- 1 CUP (8 FL OZ/250 ML) WORCESTERSHIRE SAUCE
- 3½ TABLESPOONS CHICKEN STOCK POWDER
- 4 CUPS (2¼ LB/1 KG) KETCHUP
- 2⅔ CUPS (18½ OZ/520 G) GRANULATED SUGAR

* Combine the beef, brown bean paste, sugar, and potato starch in a small bowl and marinate in the refrigerator until ready to use.
* To make the black pepper glaze, combine all the ingredients in a bowl, mix, and set aside.
* Heat the vegetable oil in a wok or large skillet (frying pan) over medium-high heat, add the bell peppers, and cook for 1–2 minutes until softened. Transfer to a plate and set aside.
* In the same wok, heat the butter over medium-high heat, add the beef, and sear for 2 minutes on each side until browned and medium rare. Transfer to a plate.
* In a clean wok, add the garlic and both onions and sauté over medium-high heat for 1 minute until fragrant. Add the leeks and black pepper and sauté for another 1 minute.
* Add the beef tenderloin and ½ tablespoon glaze and increase to high heat, then add the peppers and sauté for 1–2 minutes. Transfer to a serving plate and sprinkle over the hickory walnuts.

NOTE:
The extra glaze can be stored in the refrigerator for up to 3 days.

TONY LU

·

MANDARIN ORIENTAL PUDONG

111 PUDONG S ROAD, PUDONG, SHANGHAI, CHINA

Celebrated Shanghai chef Tony Lu was born and raised in Shanghai, and gained experience in several high-end Cantonese restaurants before rising to international fame with Fu1039, Fu1088, and Fu1015. Fu1015 was included on the 2013 and 2014 "Asia's 50 Best Restaurants" list sponsored by San Pellegrino, while Fu1088 was acclaimed as one of Food & Wine China's "Best 50 Restaurants in China" in 2010 and 2011. As the Chef Consultant at Mandarin Oriental Pudong, Shanghai's Yong Yi Ting, Chef Lu serves authentic Jiang Nan cuisine, which celebrates the culinary styles of Shanghai and its neighboring provinces, Jiangsu and Zhejiang.

*

烟熏鲳鱼

SMOKED POMFRET WITH SWEET SOY SAUCE

PREPARATION TIME: 15 MINUTES, PLUS
25 MINUTES MARINATING TIME
COOKING TIME: 25 MINUTES
SERVES: 2–3

* In a large bowl, combine 1½ tablespoons light soy sauce, and rice wine, then add the fish and marinate for 25 minutes.
* Heat 1 tablespoon vegetable oil in a wok or large skillet (frying pan) over medium-high heat. Add the ginger, scallions (spring onions), and dried chiles and sauté for 30 seconds until fragrant. Add 2 cups (16 fl oz/475 ml) water and bring to a boil, then add the hoisin sauce, sugar, 1½ tablespoons light soy sauce, dark soy sauce, rice wine, and sesame oil and simmer for 20 minutes. Strain and set aside.
* Heat the vegetable oil in a wok or deep saucepan to 350°F/180°C, or until a cube of bread browns in 30 seconds. gently lower the sliced fish into the oil, and fry for 3 minutes on each side until golden brown and cooked through. Use a slotted spoon to carefully transfer the fish from the oil to the sauce. Coat the fish in the sauce, then transfer to a serving dish.

- 3 TABLESPOONS LIGHT SOY SAUCE
- 1⅔ TABLESPOONS HUADIAO (SHAOXING YELLOW) RICE WINE
- 1 (17½-OZ/500-G) WHOLE POMFRET, CLEANED, FILLETED AND CUT INTO THICK SLICES
- 3 CUPS (25 FL OZ/740 ML) PLUS 1 TABLESPOON VEGETABLE OIL
- ¼ OZ/10 G GINGER (ABOUT ¾-INCH/ 2-CM-LENGTH PIECE), SLICED
- 3 SCALLIONS (SPRING ONIONS)
- 2 DRIED CHILES
- ⅓ CUP (2¾ OZ/80 G) HOISIN SAUCE
- ⅓ CUP (2¾ OZ/80 G) GRANULATED SUGAR
- 1 TABLESPOON DARK SOY SAUCE
- 2 TEASPOONS SESAME OIL
- 2 BAY LEAVES
- 3 STAR ANISE

黑松露鲍鱼红烧肉焖饭
RICE WITH SOY-BRAISED PORK BELLY, ABALONE, AND MOREL MUSHROOMS IN A BLACK TRUFFLE SAUCE

- 1 (10½-OZ/300-G) SKIN-ON PORK BELLY
- 1 TABLESPOON VEGETABLE OIL
- 1 MOREL MUSHROOM
- 1 TABLESPOON VEGETABLE OIL
- ⅛ OZ/5 G GINGER (ABOUT ½-INCH/ 1-CM-LENGTH PIECE), PEELED AND CHOPPED
- 1 TABLESPOON HUADIAO (SHAOXING YELLOW) RICE WINE
- 2 TABLESPOONS YELLOW BEAN SOY SAUCE
- 2 TEASPOONS DARK SOY SAUCE
- 1 CUP (8 FL OZ/250 ML) MEAT STOCK (PAGE 90-91)
- ¾ CUP (5 OZ/150 G) GRANULATED SUGAR
- ¼ CUP (2 OZ/60 G) LONG-GRAIN RICE
- 1 FRESH ABALONE, SHELLED AND RINSED
- 1 TEASPOON BLACK TRUFFLE SAUCE
- 1 TEASPOON POTATO STARCH
- 1 FRESH BLACK TRUFFLE, SLICED

* Bring a saucepan of water to a boil, add the pork belly, and boil for 3 minutes. Drain, then cool and cut into ten 1-oz/30-g squares.
* In a small bowl, combine the morel mushrooms and enough hot water to cover and soak for 1 hour until the mushrooms swell.
* Meanwhile, heat the oil in a wok or large skillet (frying pan) over low heat, add the pork and ginger, and stir-fry for 2-3 minutes until the meat is tight. Add the rice wine, yellow bean soy sauce, dark soy sauce, broth (stock), sugar, and a generous 2 cups (17 fl oz/500 ml) water and simmer over low heat for 1 hour.
* Combine the rice and 2⅓ tablespoons water in a heatproof bowl, cover with aluminum foil, and place in a collapsible pot or bamboo steamer over a pot of boiling water. Steam, covered, for 15 minutes until cooked through.
* Add the morel mushroom, the abalone, and the black truffle sauce to the pork belly mixture and stew for another 5 minutes. Combine the potato starch and 1 teaspoon water and stir this mixture into the wok. Bring to a boil, stirring, for about 30 seconds to thicken the sauce. Place on the steamed rice, scattering a few slivers of black truffle on top, and serve.

ANTHONY LUI

·

THE FLOWER DRUM

17 MARKET LANE, MELBOURNE, VIC 3000, AUSTRALIA

In China, "flower drum" is known as a traditional dance famous for its beauty and elegance. In 1975, Gilbert Lau opened The Flower Drum as a humble desire to serve good Cantonese food to the people in Australia. Gilbert's high standards for both himself and his staff allowed Cantonese cuisine to penetrate the tough Australian food market, ultimately establishing a Chinese restaurant that would rival the dominant European cuisines. Under the helm of executive chef Anthony Lui, the restaurant continues to be a respected culinary destination.

*

蟹肉蒸豆腐
STEAMED SILKEN TOFU
WITH CRAB MEAT

PREPARATION TIME: 10 MINUTES
COOKING TIME: 10 MINUTES
SERVES: 6

* In a bowl, combine the crab meat, shrimp (prawns), potato flour, salt, and white pepper and mix thoroughly until smooth and firm. Add the tofu, scallion (spring onion), and sesame oil and mix well.
* Lightly coat each Chinese soup spoon with vegetable oil. Use the spoons to scoop the tofu mixture and put the spoons in a collapsible bowl or bamboo steamer over a pot of boiling water. Steam, covered, for about 4–5 minutes, until the shrimp are cooked through. Remove the parcels from each spoon, using a toothpick to loosen if necessary.
* Heat ½ tablespoon vegetable oil in a skillet (frying pan) over medium-high heat, add the steamed tofu parcels, and fry for about 2 minutes, or until golden brown. Transfer to a serving plate.
* In a small saucepan, combine the chicken broth (stock), soy sauce, and oil until just boiling. Pour the sauce over the tofu and serve immediately.

- 3½ OZ/100 G UNCOOKED SHRIMP (PRAWNS), SHELLED, DEVEINED, AND FINELY CHOPPED
- 1 TEASPOON POTATO FLOUR
- ¼ TEASPOON SALT
- PINCH OF GROUND WHITE PEPPER
- 2 (4½-OZ/130-G) EGG TOFU, MASHED
- 1 SCALLION (SPRING ONION), CHOPPED
- ½ TEASPOON SESAME OIL
- ¼ CUP (4 OZ/120 G) COOKED KING CRAB MEAT
- 12 HEATPROOF CHINESE SOUP SPOONS
- ½ TABLESPOON VEGETABLE OIL, PLUS EXTRA FOR COATING

FOR THE SAUCE:
- ¼ CUP (2 OZ/60 ML) CHICKEN BROTH (STOCK, PAGE 90)
- 1½ TABLESPOONS LIGHT SOY SAUCE
- ½ TEASPOON VEGETABLE OIL

耗油香菇烤鸡

PAN-FRIED CHICKEN STUFFED MUSHROOMS WITH OYSTER SAUCE

- 7 OZ/200 G SKINLESS, BONELESS CHICKEN BREAST OR THIGH, MINCED
- ⅔ TEASPOON SALT
- 1⅔ TABLESPOONS POTATO FLOUR, PLUS EXTRA FOR BRUSHING
- ½ EGG WHITE
- ½ TEASPOON GINGER JUICE
- 2 TABLESPOONS FINELY CHOPPED WATER CHESTNUTS
- 12 SWISS BROWN MUSHROOMS (ABOUT 2-INCH/5-CM DIAMETER), STEMS REMOVED
- ½ TABLESPOON VEGETABLE OIL
- 8 BOK CHOY, OUTER LEAVES REMOVED, TO GARNISH

FOR THE SAUCE:
- ½ CUP (4 FL OZ/120 ML) CHICKEN BROTH (STOCK, PAGE 90)
- 1 TABLESPOON HIGH-QUALITY OYSTER SAUCE
- ¼ TEASPOON DARK SOY SAUCE
- ⅔ TEASPOON POTATO FLOUR
- ½ TEASPOON SESAME OIL
- ⅔ TABLESPOON SHAOXING WINE

* Bring a saucepan of water to a boil, add the bok choy, and blanch for 2–3 minutes. Drain, then set aside.
* In a food processor, combine the chicken, salt, potato flour, egg white, and ginger juice and mix well for 1 minute. Add 2½ teaspoons water and mix for 1 minute. Repeat the process 3 times.
* Use a long spoon or spatula (fish slice) to bring the mixture to the center of the mixing bowl and mix for another 5 minutes. Add the water chestnuts and stir until combined. Divide the mixture into 12 portions.
* Use a spoon to create a cavity in each mushroom. Brush the inside of the mushrooms with potato flour, then stuff each mushroom with the chicken mixture until a smooth mound is formed.
* Heat the oil in a large skillet (frying pan) over medium heat. Add the mushrooms, in batches if necessary, stuffing side down. Cover and cook for 4 minutes, until browned and just cooked through. Turn over, cover, and cook for another 3 minutes, until the chicken is cooked through and the mushrooms are slightly softened.
* Combine all the sauce ingredients in a small bowl and add this mixture to the wok. Gently toss the mushrooms and cook until the sauce is bubbling and thickened.
* Transfer the mushrooms to a serving plate and decorate with the bok choy. Pour over the sauce and serve immediately.

烤乳鸽

ROAST SQUAB WITH PORT WINE SAUCE

PREPARATION TIME: 15 MINUTES,
    PLUS 30 MINUTES REFRIGERATING
    AND 3 HOURS MARINATING TIME
COOKING TIME: 30 MINUTES
SERVES: 4

* Trim off the head and feet from each squab.
* Combine the salt and sugar in a small bowl. Gently rub the mixture over the squabs, insides and outside, and refrigerate for 30 minutes.
* Combine the squabs and the port in a large bowl and marinate for 3 hours, turning the squabs over 1–2 times.
* Reserve ½ cup (4 fl oz/120 ml) of port. Transfer the squab and the remaining port into a large pot and cook over medium heat for 15 minutes, turning the squabs every 2–3 minutes to prevent the skin from sticking to the bottom of the pan. Remove the squabs, then cook the sauce until thick and syrupy. Set aside.
* Combine the soy sauce and 2 teaspoons water and rub the mixture over the squabs.
* In the meantime, preheat an oven to 475°F/240°C/Gas Mark 9. Place the squabs, breast side up, on a baking sheet and roast for 7–8 minutes. Turn over, add half the sauce and the remaining ¼ cup (2 fl oz/50 ml) port, then flip over the squabs, breast-side down, and roast for another 5 minutes, or until golden brown and cooked through. Remove the squabs from the oven and set aside to cool.
* When cool enough to handle, cut each squab in half, cut each half into 3–4 pieces, and place on a serving platter. Spoon over the remaining sauce and serve.

• 4 (17½ OZ/500-G) SQUABS, CLEANED
• 2½ CUPS (20 FL OZ/600 ML) PORT
• 2 TABLESPOONS SALT
• 4 TABLESPOONS GRANULATED SUGAR
• 1 TEASPOON LIGHT SOY SAUCE

MOK KIT KEUNG

·

SHANG PALACE

KOWLOON SHANGRI-LA HOTEL, 64 MODY ROAD, TSIM SHA TSUI EAST, KOWLOON, HONG KONG, CHINA

*

Chef Mok Kit Keung—the executive chef of the hotel's Michelin-starred Shang Palace—trained in traditional Cantonese cuisine at a young age, and has prepared meals for the King Mohammed VI of Morocco, the president of Russia, the former and current prime ministers of Singapore, and many other prominent dignitaries. He has also received a number of culinary accolades, including the Gold Medal Award in Chinese Cuisine from the Restaurant Association of Singapore in 2001 and 2004, the Gold Medal Award in the Food Hotel Asia 2008 Imperial Challenge, and numerous other recognitions over the years.

PREPARATION TIME: 10 MINUTES
COOKING TIME: 5 MINUTES
SERVES 4

黑松露鮮蟹肉炒鮮奶蛋白
FRESH MILK AND EGG WHITE WITH CRAB MEAT AND BLACK TRUFFLE

- 5 EGG WHITES
- ⅔ CUP (5 FL OZ/150 ML) LIGHT (SINGLE) CREAM
- 4 TABLESPOONS ALASKAN KING CRAB MEAT
- 2 CUPS (16 FL OZ/475 ML) VEGETABLE OIL
- ¼ OZ/7 G RICE VERMICELLI
- 1 EDIBLE FLOWER, TO GARNISH
- FRISÉE, TO GARNISH
- SLICED BLACK TRUFFLE, TO SERVE

  FOR THE SEASONING:
- ⅓ TEASPOON SALT
- ¼ TEASPOON CHICKEN STOCK POWDER
- ¼ TEASPOON CHICKEN BROTH (STOCK)
- ¾ TABLESPOON CORNSTARCH (CORNFLOUR)
- 3 TABLESPOONS WATER

* Combine the egg whites, cream, and seasoning ingredients in a bowl, mix well, and set aside.
* Put the crab meat in a small bowl, add enough hot water to cover it, and stir. Drain, then add the crab meat to the egg white mixture.
* Heat the vegetable oil in a wok or deep saucepan to 350°F/ 180°C, or until a cube of bread browns in 30 seconds. Add the vermicelli and deep-fry for 10 seconds, until crispy. Transfer to a serving plate.
* Put a third of the egg white mixture into the wok and stir-fry for 1–2 minutes, until cooked. Place the egg white mixture on top of the vermicelli. Add half of the remaining egg white mixture into the wok, stir-fry for 1–2 minutes until cooked, and place on top of the vermicelli. Repeat with the remaining egg white mixture.
* Garnish with edible flower and frisée, then serve with sliced black truffle.

酥炸牡蛎

DEEP-FRIED OYSTER AND CRISPY RICE WITH PORT WINE

PREPARATION TIME: 15 MINUTES
COOKING TIME: 5 MINUTES
SERVES: 1

* In a small bowl, combine the oyster and cornstarch (cornflour).
* Bring a small saucepan of water to a boil, add the oyster, and poach for 1 minute. Use a slotted spoon to remove the oyster and drain on paper towels.
* To make the dry batter, combine all the ingredients in a small bowl and mix well.
* In another small bowl, combine 2 tablespoons dry batter, 1 teaspoon vegetable oil, and 1½ tablespoons water. Stir to make a wet batter.
* Coat the oyster in the dry batter, then dip in the wet batter, and then back again in the dry batter. Heat 2 cups (16 fl oz/475 ml) oil in a wok or deep saucepan to 340°F/170°C, or until a cube of bread browns in 45 seconds. Add the oyster and deep-fry for 2–3 minutes, or until it turns golden brown. Use a slotted spoon to remove the oyster and drain on paper towels.
* In the same wok, add the crispy rice and deep-fry for about 1 minute, or until golden brown and crispy. Place the lettuce leaf on a plate, then place the crispy rice on top. Set aside.
* Add the remaining ½ teaspoon vegetable oil to the wok over medium-high heat and sauté the garlic and shallot for 30 seconds until fragrant. Add the seasoning ingredients, then the oyster and stir well until coated.
* Place the oyster on the lettuce cup and garnish with the scallions (spring onion) and edible flower.

- 1 AMERICAN OYSTER, SHUCKED
- 1 TABLESPOON CORNSTARCH (CORNFLOUR)
- 1 LETTUCE LEAF
- 2 CUPS (16 FL OZ/465 ML) PLUS 1½ TEASPOONS VEGETABLE OIL
- ⅛ OZ/6 G CRISPY RICE
- ½ TEASPOON MINCED GARLIC
- ½ TEASPOON SHALLOT
- SHREDDED SCALLIONS (SPRING ONIONS), TO GARNISH
- EDIBLE FLOWERS, TO GARNISH

FOR THE DRY BATTER:
- 3¾ TABLESPOONS ALL-PURPOSE (PLAIN) FLOUR
- 1 TEASPOON BAKING POWDER
- ½ TEASPOON BAKING SODA ¾ TABLESPOON CORNSTARCH (CORNFLOUR)

FOR THE SEASONING:
- 4 TEASPOONS SWEET AND SOUR SAUCE
- 1 TEASPOON PORT
- ¼ TEASPOON CHICKEN STOCK POWDER

梅酒排骨

STEWED IBERICO SPARE RIBS WITH JAPANESE PLUM WINE

- 21 OZ/600 G IBERICO SPARE RIBS
- 1⅓ TABLESPOON LIGHT SOY SAUCE
- 1 TEASPOON CHICKEN STOCK POWDER
- 1½ TABLESPOONS CORNSTARCH (CORNFLOUR)
- 2 CUPS (16 FL OZ/475 ML) VEGETABLE OIL
- 2 TABLESPOONS JAPANESE PLUM WINE
- 1 EDIBLE MAPLE

FOR THE SAUCE:
- 3 PRESERVED RED PLUMS
- 3–4 SALTED DRIED PLUMS
- 3–4 SCALLIONS (SPRING ONIONS)
- 6 CLOVES GARLIC
- ¼ OZ/10 G GINGER (ABOUT ¾-INCH/ 2-CM-LENGTH PIECE)
- 2 SHALLOTS, SLICED
- 1 STAR ANISE
- 2 SOUR PLUMS
- 2 BAY LEAVES
- ¼ TEASPOON PLUM POWDER
- 1 TEASPOON CHICKEN STOCK POWDER
- 2½ TEASPOONS OYSTER SAUCE
- 2 OZ/55 G ROCK SUGAR
- 2⅔ TABLESPOONS RICE WINE

* Bring a large saucepan of water to a boil and add the spare ribs. Reduce to medium-low heat and simmer for 1 hour. Drain and let cool.
* When cool enough to handle, cut the ribs into 4–6 pieces. Season the spare ribs with the soy sauce, chicken stock powder, and cornstarch (cornflour).
* Heat the oil in a wok or large skillet (frying pan) over medium-high heat, add the spare ribs, and deep-fry for 3–4 minutes until golden brown. Use a slotted spoon to remove and drain on paper towels. Remove all the oil from the wok.
* Heat the wok over medium-high heat, add the ribs, the sauce ingredients, and enough water to cover the ribs. Bring to a boil, reduce to medium-low heat, and simmer, covered, for 1½ hours until the ribs are tender. Add the Japanese plum wine.
* Transfer the ribs on a serving plate. Strain the sauce, drizzle over the ribs, and garnish with edible maple. Serve.

TONG CHEE HWEE

·

HAKKASAN

8 HANWAY PLACE, LONDON W1T 1HD, UNITED KINGDOM

Chef Tong Chee Hwee started his career when he was discovered, at the age of 18, in Singapore while overseeing the kitchens at the Ritz-Carlton. In 2001, Tong moved to London to become head chef at Hakkasan and is currently the executive head chef for Hakkasan, Yauatcha, and HKK restaurants in London, which are renowned for serving high-end tasting menus that celebrate the diversity of Chinese cuisine by reviving and modernizing traditional recipes.

*

醉鸡卷

DRUNKEN CHICKEN ROLL

PREPARATION TIME: 30 MINUTES,
  PLUS 14 HOURS MARINATING TIME
COOKING TIME: 20 MINUTES
SERVES: 4

* Heat the chicken broth (stock) in a large saucepan over medium-high heat until warmed through. Remove from the heat, add both wines, and set aside to cool.
* Pat the chicken dry with paper towels, then put them in a bowl. Add the salt and ginger juice and marinate for 2 hours.
* Place a leg on a piece of plastic wrap (clingfilm), skin side down, and roll it tightly. Repeat with the remaining chicken legs.
* Place the legs with the plastic wrap in a collapsible bowl or bamboo steamer over a pot of boiling water. Steam, covered, for 15 minutes and let cool.
* When cool enough to handle, remove the plastic wrap and transfer to a bowl. Pour over the chicken broth and marinate for 12 hours.
* Slice the chicken, then transfer to a serving plate and garnish with cilantro (coriander).

* 2½ CUPS (20 FL OZ/600 ML) CHICKEN BROTH (STOCK, PAGE 90)
* ½ CUP (4 FL OZ/120 ML) SHAOXING WINE
* 2½ TABLESPOONS KWAI WINE
* 6 BONELESS, FREE-RANGE CHICKEN LEGS
* 2½ TEASPOONS CASTER SUGAR
* 4 TEASPOONS SALT
* 1 TABLESPOON GINGER JUICE
* CILANTRO (CORIANDER), TO GARNISH

茶香烟熏神户牛肉

TEA-SMOKED
WAGYU BEEF

PREPARATION TIME: 30 MINUTES
COOKING TIME: 1 HOUR 30 MINUTES
SERVES: 4

- 3¼ LB/1.5 KG WAGYU SHORT RIBS, DEBONED AND CUT IN HALVES
- 2 TABLESPOONS POTATO STARCH
- VEGETABLE OIL SPRAY, FOR FRYING
- 3 CLOVES GARLIC
- ¼ OZ/10 G GINGER (ABOUT ¾-INCH/ 2-CM-LENGTH PIECE)
- 2 SMALL SCALLIONS (SPRING ONIONS), CHOPPED
- 3½ OZ/100 G JAPANESE YAM OR PUMPKIN, CUT INTO CHUNKS AND PAN-FRIED (OPTIONAL)
- 1½ TABLESPOONS JASMINE TEA LEAVES
- ¼ CUP (2½ OZ/50 G) BROWN SUGAR
- ¾ CUP (3½ OZ/100 G) COOKED RICE

FOR THE SAUCE:
- 3 TABLESPOONS SOY SAUCE
- 2 TABLESPOONS KETCHUP
- 4 TEASPOONS RICE VINEGAR
- 1 OZ/25 G ROCK SUGAR
- 3 TABLESPOONS PLUS 1 TEASPOON SHAOXING WINE
- 1 BLACK CARDAMOM POD
- 2 TABLESPOONS RED YEAST RICE

* In a bowl, combine the short ribs and potato starch and gently coat the beef.
* Spray the vegetable oil to coat the wok or large skillet (frying pan) and heat over medium heat. Add the beef and pan-grill for 2 minutes, until golden. Transfer the beef to a plate.
* Clean the wok and spray more vegetable oil. Sauté the garlic, ginger, and scallions (spring onions) over medium-high heat for 1 minute until fragrant.
* To make the sauce, combine all the ingredients and 8½ cups (64 fl oz/2 liters) water in a large saucepan and bring to a boil.
* Add the short ribs to the saucepan and boil for 1 hour–1¼ hours, covered, until soft and tender. Use a slotted spoon to transfer the beef to a plate and let cool. Cut into smaller pieces, if desired.
* Boil the remaining sauce in the saucepan for 30 minutes, until reduced to 1¼ cups (10 fl oz/250 ml). Strain, then return to the saucepan. Add the beef and bring to a boil, stirring continuously. Add the Japanese yam, if using.
* Line a wok with a large piece of aluminum foil, then add the sugar, steamed rice, and tea leaves, and place a rack over the mixture, making sure that it doesn't touch. Heat over low-medium heat until it begins to smoke, then place the ribs on the rack. Cover, reduce to low heat to prevent too much smoke, and smoke for 10 minutes. Serve.

松露香醋海鲈鱼

WILD SEA BASS WITH TRUFFLE VINEGAR

PREPARATION TIME: 20 MINUTES, PLUS
30 MINUTES MARINATING TIME
COOKING TIME: 5 MINUTES
SERVES: 4

* To make the sauce, combine all the ingredients and ¼ cup (4 fl oz/120 ml) water in a blender, then transfer to a saucepan and bring to a boil. Set aside.
* Put the fish, zucchini (courgette), pumpkin, ginger, potato starch, egg white, and the salt in a large bowl, mix well, and marinate for 30 minutes. Add 2 tablespoons oil.
* Heat 1 teaspoon oil in a skillet (frying pan) over medium-high heat, then add the fish, skin-side down, and pan-fry for 2 minutes on each side until nearly cooked through. Set aside. Transfer the fish to a plate lined with paper towels to drain.
* In the same pan, heat 1 teaspoon oil over medium heat, add the garlic, and sauté for 30 seconds or until fragrant. Add the fish and pan-fry for 1 minute, then add the vegetable-and-ginger mixture. Adjust the seasoning to taste.
* Transfer to a serving plate and serve with the fish sauce.

- 6 (3½-OZ/100-G) WILD SEA BASS FILLETS, SKIN ON
- 3½ OZ/100 G ZUCCHINI (COURGETTE), INTO 2-INCH/5-CM STRIPS
- 3½ OZ/100 G PUMPKIN, CUT INTO 2-INCH/5-CM STRIPS
- ¼ OZ/10 G GINGER (ABOUT ¾-INCH/ 2-CM-LENGTH PIECE), CUT INTO 2-INCH/5-CM STRIPS
- 2 TEASPOONS POTATO STARCH
- ½ EGG WHITE, BEATEN
- ½ TEASPOON SALT, PLUS EXTRA TO TASTE
- 2 TABLESPOONS PLUS 2 TEASPOONS VEGETABLE OIL

FOR THE FISH SAUCE:
- 2⅓ TABLESPOONS BALSAMIC TRUFFLE VINEGAR
- 2 TABLESPOONS LIGHT SOY SAUCE
- 2½ TEASPOONS GRANULATED SUGAR
- 1 TEASPOON SHAOXING WINE
- ¾ TEASPOON MAGGI® SEASONING SAUCE
- ½ TEASPOON SQUID SAUCE
- ½ TEASPOON DARK SOY SAUCE
- CHOPPED CILANTRO (CORIANDER)

JOEL WATANABE

·

BAO BEI CHINESE BRASSERIE

163 KEEFER STREET, VANCOUVER, BC V6A 1X3, CANADA

*

In January 2010, Bao Bei opened its doors and immediately gained the public's attention with its innovative take on modern Chinese cuisine. Chef Joel Watanabe's creative approach to Asian ingredients, incorporating classic French with Japanese techniques, brings a rich and subtle touch to all his dishes. His style has garnered him a faithful local and international following.

PREPARATION TIME: 20 MINUTES, PLUS 20 MINUTES STANDING TIME
COOKING TIME: 2¼–3¼ HOURS
MAKES: 10

狮子头
LION'S HEAD MEATBALLS

- ⅛ OZ/5 G (ABOUT ½-INCH/1-CM-LENGTH PIECE) GINGER, PEELED
- 4 TABLESPOONS SHAOXING WINE
- 2 CUPS (9 OZ/250 G) PLUS 1½ TABLESPOONS CORNSTARCH (CORNFLOUR)
- 2½ LB/1 KG GROUND PORK BUTT (SHOULDER), ABOUT 30% FAT
- 1 BUNCH SCALLIONS (SPRING ONIONS), FINELY CHOPPED
- 2 EGG WHITES, BEATEN
- 2 TABLESPOONS PREMIUM LIGHT SOY SAUCE
- 2½ TEASPOONS TOASTED SESAME OIL, PLUS EXTRA TO TASTE
- 4¼ CUPS (34 FL OZ/1 LITER) CANOLA (RAPESEED) OIL
- 1 HEAD NAPA CABBAGE, CUT CROSSWISE INTO 1-INCH/4-CM PIECES
- 8½ CUPS (64 FL OZ/2 LITERS) CHICKEN BROTH (STOCK, PAGE 90)
- GROUND WHITE PEPPER, TO TASTE

* Preheat the oven to 380°F/195°C/Gas Mark 5.
* In a blender, process the ginger and ½ tablespoon water to make a paste. Transfer to a small bowl and set aside.
* Put the Shaoxing wine and 1¾ tablespoons cornstarch (cornflour) into a large bowl. Add the pork, scallions (spring onions), egg whites, soy sauce, and sesame oil, then season with white pepper and mix well until the mixture is gummy. (Alternatively, use a stand mixer with the paddle attachment and mix on medium speed for 2 minutes.) With damp hands, shape the mixture into ten 3-inch/7.5-cm-diameter balls.
* Pour enough canola (rapeseed) oil into a wok or deep saucepan until it is 1-inch/2.5-cm deep and heat to 325°F/170°C, or until a cube of bread browns in 45 seconds.
* Put 2 cups (9 oz/250 g) cornstarch in a shallow bowl, then add a meatball and coat generously. Repeat with the remaining meatballs. Gently lower the meatballs, in batches, into the hot oil and shallow-fry for 4–5 minutes, until golden all over. Use a slotted spoon to carefully remove the meatballs from the oil and drain on paper towels.
* Put 3 layers of cabbage on the bottom of a large Dutch oven (casserole), then place the meatballs on top of the cabbage, packed together snugly. Cover with another 3 layers of cabbage, then add enough chicken broth (stock) to cover the meatballs and cabbage. Cover and place in the oven for 2–3 hours, or until the internal temperature of the meatballs reaches 170°F/75°C. Remove from oven and let stand, covered, for 20 minutes. Serve the meatballs in bowls with a little broth and cabbage.

芥菜肉丝炒年糕
STICKY RICE CAKES WITH PRESERVED MUSTARD GREENS AND PORK

PREPARATION TIME: 20 MINUTES,
PLUS 2 DAYS MACERATING TIME
COOKING TIME: 20 MINUTES
MAKES: 2

* To make the preserved mustard greens, combine the salt and sugar in a bowl. Place a layer of the salt mixture in a large sterilized jar, put a layer of greens on top, and then add another layer of salt. Continue the layering process until all the vegetables are used.
* Place a weight on the mustard greens, cover, and set aside in a cool, dry place to macerate for 2 days.
* In a bowl, combine the pork loin, 1 teaspoon soy sauce, ½ teaspoon sugar, and 1 teaspoon sesame oil.
* Bring a small saucepan of water to a boil, add the wood ear fungus, and then reduce to medium heat and simmer for 5 minutes. Transfer to a bowl of ice water and strain.
* Bring a saucepan of water to a boil, add the bamboo shoots, and blanch for 2 minutes. Drain and set aside.
* In a wok or large skillet (frying pan) over medium-high heat, add the pork loin and sauté for 2–3 minutes, until just cooked. Transfer the pork to a plate and set aside.
* Heat the canola (rapeseed) oil in a wok over medium-high heat, add the garlic, and fry for about 1 minute or until fragrant. Stir in the fungus, bamboo shoots, and 3 tablespoons mustard greens and cook for 5 seconds until warmed through.
* Add the rice cakes, the remaining 2 teaspoons sugar, ½ teaspoon soy sauce, 1½ teaspoons sesame oil, and chicken broth (stock). Cook on high heat for 10 minutes until the broth is reduced by half. Put in the pork and cook for 2–3 minutes, until the sauce is thick enough to coat the back of a spoon. Transfer to a serving bowl.
* To make the salted turnip omelet, combine the eggs, soy sauce, sugar, and salt in a small bowl and mix well.
* Melt the butter in a non-stick pan over medium-low heat. Once the butter begins to bubble, add the egg mixture and the salted turnip. Shake the pan vigorously in a circular motion to makes sure the eggs are evenly cooked. (The omelet should be a little bit runny in the middle.)
* Remove the pan from the heat and let sit for 1 minute, then gently roll the omelet into the bowl of rice cakes. Serve.

* 2 OZ/60 G PORK LOIN, CUT INTO THIN STRIPS
* 1½ TEASPOONS LIGHT SOY SAUCE
* 2½ TEASPOONS GRANULATED SUGAR
* 2½ TEASPOONS TOASTED SESAME OIL
* ⅛ OZ/5 G DRIED WOOD EAR FUNGUS
* 2 OZ/60 G FRESH BAMBOO, SLICED
* 1 TABLESPOON FINELY CHOPPED GARLIC
* 9 OZ/250 G GLUTINOUS RICE CAKES
* 1⅔ CUPS (14 FL OZ/400 ML) CHICKEN BROTH (STOCK, PAGE 90)
* 2 TABLESPOONS CANOLA (RAPESEED) OIL

FOR THE PRESERVED MUSTARD GREENS:
* 3 TABLESPOONS SALT
* 2 TABLESPOONS GRANULATED SUGAR
* 5 LB/2¼ KG MUSTARD GREENS, RINSED AND TRIMMED

FOR THE SALTED TURNIP OMELET:
* 3 EGGS
* 1½ TEASPOONS LIGHT SOY SAUCE
* PINCH OF GRANULATED SUGAR
* PINCH OF SALT
* 1½ TABLESPOONS UNSALTED BUTTER
* 1 TABLESPOON CHOPPED SALTED TURNIP

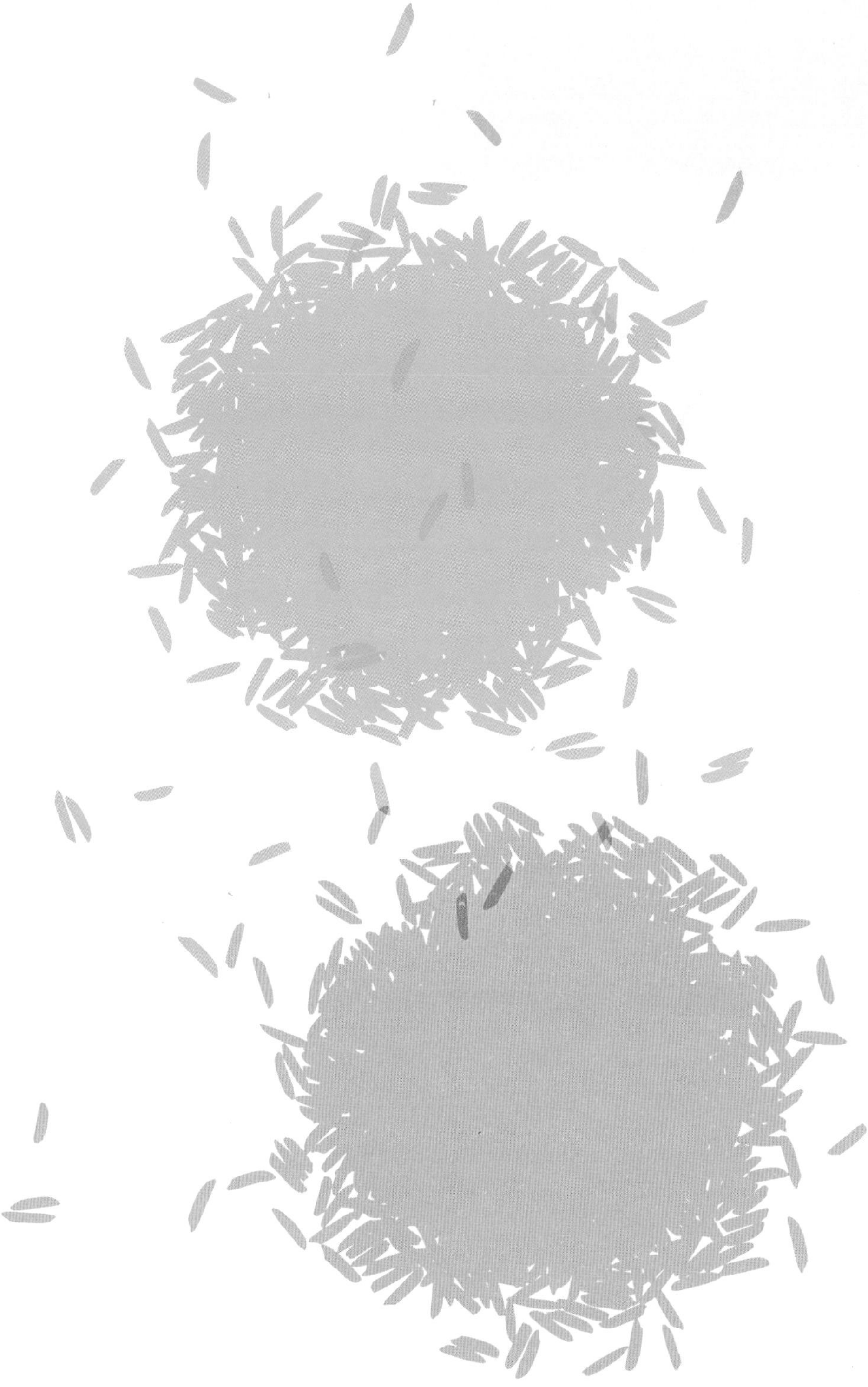

GLOSSARY - INDEX - BIBLIOGRAPHY - RECIPE NOTES

GLOSSARY

GLOSSARY

ABALONE (*BAO YU*, 鲍鱼)
This species of mollusk was traditionally the preserve of royalty. It has since become a popular, albeit expensive, festive treat, found in fresh, dried, or canned form at specialist stores and fishmongers. With a crunchy, squid-like texture, the flesh is delicate and buttery, releasing a similar sweetness to sea scallops. Among its other medicinal properties, abalone is thought to benefit the immune system.

ANGELICA ROOT (*DANG GUI*, 当归)
Pungent and slightly bitter in flavor, this herbal plant is widely consumed as a remedy for indigestion, and blood deficiency, among other ailments. It is largely grown in the Gansu Province of northwest China, and can be sourced in specialist and health stores.

APRICOT KERNELS (*XING REN*, 杏仁)
These seeds have long been consumed as a cure for coughs and colds. Apricot kernels come in two varieties, sweet and bitter, and are used in traditional Chinese cooking at a ratio of 4:1. The bitter kernels can be toxic when prepared incorrectly; therefore, only the sweet variety is used in the book.

ARROWROOT (*CHI GU*, 慈菇)
Frequently consumed at Chinese New Year, this seasonal root symbolizes prosperity and blessings for a male offspring according to Cantonese tradition. It resembles a garlic bulb and can be stir-fried, braised, or sliced into chips (crisps). If arrowroot is unavailable, it may be substituted with potatoes (similar starchy texture), water chestnuts, or jicama.

BAIJIU (*BAI JIU*, 白酒)
This kind of distilled spirit—which literally translates to "white alcohol"—has been brewed for centuries using ancient techniques of fermenting sorghum and other kinds of grain. It constitutes a large percentage of China's spirits market and if unavailable, vodka makes a decent substitute.

BAMBOO FUNGUS (*ZHU SHENG*, 竹笙)
This fungus is nutritious and prized for medicinal use in China. Also called "the botanical chicken," the fungus has a unique crunchy yet springy texture and a delicate flavor that requires little additional seasoning.

BAMBOO SHOOTS (*ZHU SUN*, 竹笋)
Delicate with earthy notes and a crunchy texture, these edible shoots are often added to stir-fries, braised dishes, salads, and soups. To prepare fresh shoots, remove the husks and be sure to blanch for 2–3 minutes to remove any toxins. Seasonal shoots such as winter bamboo shoots and spring shoots are highly prized for their tenderness but may be difficult to find. Canned and vacuum-packed varieties are available in select supermarkets and Asian food stores.

BEAN PASTE (*MIAN CHI*, 面豉)
Also known as *yuan shai chi* (原晒豉) or *mo yuan chi* (磨原豉), bean paste is a popular condiment in southern Chinese cooking. Bean paste is the by-product of soy sauce—once soy sauce has been extracted from fermented soybeans, the remains are the bean paste. Available at most Asian food stores, this dark brown paste lends favorable salty, sweet, and bitter notes to meat- and seafood-based stir-fries and stews.

BEAN SPROUTS (*YA CAI*, 芽菜)
Bean sprouts are made from sprouting beans, most commonly the greenish-capped mung beans.

BEIJING SCALLION
(*DA CONG*, 大葱 OR *JING CONG*, 京葱)
Sometimes labeled as Tokyo Negi or Welsh scallion, this popular and versatile vegetable from northern China is a cross between a leek and a scallion (spring onion), either of which can be used as an alternative. It can be eaten raw, stir-fried, or prepared with noodles.

BITTER MELON (*KU GUA*, 苦瓜)
Used as food or medicine, bitter melon (or bitter gourd) is a popular Asian pod vegetable with a uneven, knobbly, and ridged surface. Bitter melon may contain alkaloid substances such as quinine and morodicine, which causes intolerance in some people. Reduce its bitterness and toxicity by parboiling or soaking in saltwater for up to 10 minutes.

BLACK CARDAMOM (CAO GUO, 草果)

A distant relative of green cardamom, this warming spice is dried over an open fire and possesses a distinct smoky camphor aroma. Widely used across China, black cardamom can enhance the flavor of meat and fish, but it should be used sparingly to avoid overwhelming other dishes.

BLACK MOSS (FA CAI, 发菜)

Also known as "fat choy," this bacteria is harvested in the Gobi Desert and the Qinghai Plateau, dry black moss looks like black floss and is frequently used in Cantonese cooking. This rare and expensive product can be sourced online or in select Asian supermarkets. The moss should be soaked prior to cooking.

BLACK VINEGAR (see Vinegars)

BOK CHOY (BAI CAI, 白菜)

Bok choy, or pak choy, is a type of cabbage with smooth, dark-green leaves and a white stem. While it can be found fresh in most supermarkets, it is also available as a dried version called cai gan (菜乾), which follows a tradition of preserving to enhance flavor. The dried leaves should be soaked for an hour or so until soft, then rinsed and drained before use. Green bok choy (xiao tang cai, 小唐菜), known also as Shanghai bok choy or Shanghai greens, is distinguished by its green stem. If bok choy is unavailable, cabbage is an acceptable alternative.

BRAN DOUGH (KAOFU, 烤麸)

This Shanghai specialty is made from fermented and steamed gluten dough and sold in blocks. Spongy and tofu-like in texture, it will absorb sauces and flavors from other ingredients.

BROWN SUGAR (HONG TANG, 红糖)

This traditional sweetener, known as red sugar in China, is a key ingredient in sweet and sour sauces as well as desserts. It can be substituted white granulated sugar—cook in a dry skillet (frying pan) until it turns to caramel.

BROWN SUGAR BAR (PIAN TANG, 片糖)

Also known as brown sugar candy, these pressed bars are made from unrefined sugar can and lend a deep, complex flavor to many Chinese sweet and savory dishes. This is not to be confused with the similar-looking palm sugar, which are different.

CELTUCE (WOJU, 莴苣)

Variously known as "asparagus lettuce," "stem lettuce," or "celery lettuce," this plant is primarily cultivated for its stalk, which can be used fresh in salads or stir-fries.

Celtuce are harvested once their stems reach a certain length, making the leaves old, coarse, and less suited for cooking. They can be found in Asian food stores or substituted with celery.

CHAOZHOU PLUM PASTE (MEI GAO JIANG, 梅糕酱)

Made from plums, it is similar to plum sauce but with a more intense plum flavor. Plum sauce can be used as a substitute.

CHAOZHOU SALTED MUSTARD GREENS (CHAOZHOU XIAN CAI, 潮州咸菜)

Chaozhou is a city in the Guangdong Province of southeast China, a region famed for its preserved vegetables. Nutritionally rich and with a strong, peppery taste, these mustard greens are stored in brine and conventionally eaten as an appetizer or with congee for breakfast. Named xian cai in Chinese, meaning "salted vegetable," they are available canned or vacuum-packed.

CHILES (LA JIAO, 辣椒)

China is one of the world's largest chile producers, cultivating many varieties, which can be dried, chopped, crushed, and powdered. Bird's eye chiles, a favorite in Chinese cooking, are small, tapered, and available in red or green. They're fiery so only one or two are needed to give a dish some kick. If you prefer less heat in a recipe, a milder chile can be used.

CHILI BEAN PASTE (DOU BAN JIANG, 豆瓣酱)

Chili bean paste is a pantry essential, especially when it comes to Sichuan cuisine. Fava (broad) beans or soybeans are fermented with chiles to create a richly flavored basis for stir-fries, soups, and marinades, or as a condiment with rice.

CHILI OIL (LA YOU, 辣油)

This rich, red chili-infused vegetable oil can be drizzled over fried rice, noodles, and salads or used as a dipping sauce. Star anise, cinnamon, Sichuan peppercorns, and bay leaves may be added to deepen the flavor. Sichuan chili oil (hong you, 红油), known also as ash oil, is the Sichuan take on chili oil and boasts a rich sediment of Sichuan chiles, garlic, and star anise. Whether used as a dipping sauce for wontons or as a coating for stir-fried vegetables, the tingling notes of Sichuan chile add extra heat.

CHINESE BROCCOLI (JIE LAN, 芥兰)

Chinese broccoli, also known as gai lan, is a leafy vegetable with thick stalks and a small number of tiny flower heads not unlike broccoli. It can be substituted with rapini or broccoli.

CHINESE CELERY (*TANG QIN*, 唐芹)

The thin, hollow stems and feathery leaves of this plant carry a more intense, aromatic flavor than Western varieties. It is often used in soups and stir-fries, but Chinese celery can also be eaten raw as a piquant salad ingredient or a garnish. If unavailable, celery can be used as a substitute.

CHINESE CHIVES (*JIU CAI*, 韭菜)

Chinese chives, also known as garlic chives, are characterized by flat, tender, and dark leaves. They can be finely chopped as a seasoning, garnish, or dumpling filling, and their flavor mellows during cooking. Flowering chives (*jiu cai hua*, 韭菜花)—the stems and blossoms of the same plant—are used to add a crunchy texture and garlicky note to stir-fries.

CHINESE CURED BACON (*LA ROU*, 腊肉)

Curing is a traditional method of preserving meat and fish, especially in the southern part of China where the weather is warm and humid. To make Chinese cured bacon, pork belly (or at times with shoulder) is seasoned with soy sauce, brown sugar, and spices such as cinnamon, and then air-dried. It comes available both smoked and unsmoked.

CHINESE CURED SAUSAGE (*LA CHANG*, 腊肠)

A vast array of sausages is sold at Chinese markets, some available fresh, others cured to a hard, shriveled texture. Air-dried sausages are known in Cantonese as "lap cheong" or "wax sausages," a reference to their smooth outer texture. Some are made with liver (see Dried liver sausage, page 692), while others are seasoned with soy sauce, salt, sugar, and rose wine. Once cooked, the melted fat brings a rich sweetness to stir-fries and fried-rice dishes. They can also be steamed with rice.

CHINESE OLIVE VEGETABLE (*GAN LAN CAI*, 橄榄菜)

This local Guangdong delicacy is a preserve, which combines shredded mustard greens, olives, oil, and salt. Use it to flavor fried rice and dishes such as Shrimp with Chinese Olive Vegetables (page 181).

CHINESE SALTED FISH (*XIAN YU*, 咸鱼)

There is a long tradition in Chinese cuisine of salting and drying as a preservation method to manage surplus supplies of fresh fish. Dried fish was traditionally known as "poor man's food," because a small, flavorful scrap went a long way to enhance rice dishes. It pairs well with fried rice, noodles, or ground (minced) pork for steamed patties.

CHOY SUM (*CAI XIN*, 菜心)

A leafy vegetable, also known as flowering broccoli, choy sum can be lightly boiled, steamed, stir-fried, or used in soups. It can be replaced with Chinese broccoli, which has firmer stems.

COCONUT MILK (*YE NAI*, 椰奶)

The term "coconut" is thought to date back to the 16th-century Spanish term coco, meaning "to grin" (split coconuts resemble smiling faces). Popular and nutritious, it adds creaminess to curries and soups. Canned coconut milk is available in supermarkets and Asian food stores.

CONGEE (*ZHOU*, 粥)

Versatile and nourishing, congee is a rice porridge served as a classic Chinese breakfast and as comfort food throughout the day. While some people prefer it plain, it is more often prepared with a simple stock and enhanced with meat, fish, and vegetable accompaniments. Short-grain, long-grain, Arborio, and even brown rice can be used.

CURED DUCK (*LA YA*, 腊鸭)

A raw duck leg is salted and seasoned with spices and rice wine, then hung to slowly dry under the sun. It is dense in texture and brings an intensely concentrated duck flavor and delicate aroma to any dish. A common way of preparing the duck is to steam it with rice.

CURED FISH (*LA YU*, 腊鱼)

Cured fish is slightly salted fish that has been air-fried in the shade. This is not the same as salted fish, which is far saltier and fairly dry.

DACE (*LING YU ROU*, 鲮鱼肉)

The meat from this freshwater fish, also known as "mud carp," can be minced, seasoned, and rolled into patties, or ground into a batter for deep-fried vegetables. While the flesh is sweet and tender, it is dense with bones so it is often pulverized rather than served whole. A popular dace dish includes Dace with Daikon radish (page 158).

DAIKON RADISH (*LUO BO*, 萝卜)

Also known as Chinese turnip or lo bak, this mild-flavored radish has a long white root and fast-growing leaves. It features prominently in Chinese dishes such as Turnip Pudding (page 79), a favorite at dim sum.

DARK SOY SAUCE (see Soy sauce)

DISTILLED GRAIN SAUCE (*JIU ZAO*, 酒糟)

Distilled grain sauce is the cereal by-product from the distillation process. Red distilled grain sauce (*hong zao*, 红糟) is made of the dregs of red yeast rice after distillation, while white distilled grain sauce (*bai zao*, 白糟) is made from the remnants of glutinous rice. Both varieties are frequently used as marinades, especially in the coastal regions of Fujian, Zhejiang, and Jiangsu as well as in Taiwan.

DRIED ANCHOVIES (see Dried fish)

DRIED BLACK FUNGUS (*HEI MU ER*, 黑木耳)
Also known as "cloud ear" or "wood ear," this nutritious woodland fungus is lauded by Chinese herbalists for its circulation-boosting properties. Unlike the thick and coarse white-back wood ear fungus, dried black fungus is soft and tender, making it a popular ingredient in salads and braised and steamed dishes, where it tends to absorb the seasoning. It is usually sold dried and requires pre-soaking.

DRIED BLACK MUSHROOMS (*DONG GU*, 冬菇)
The Chinese name for dried black mushrooms is *dong gu*, which means "winter mushrooms." Dried shiitake mushrooms that grow in the north (北菇) break into flowery lines due to the intense cold and are considered to be the best. We recommend soaking dried mushrooms in cold water for least 20 minutes before use.

DRIED BOK CHOY (see Bok choy)

DRIED FISH (*YU GAN*, 鱼乾)
The Chinese believe that eating certain foods, including dried fish, on auspicious days such as the Chinese New Year brings them luck. Dried anchovies (*ding xiang yu gan*, 丁香鱼乾) impart a concentrated salty flavor to fish broths (stocks) or stir-fries, such as Stir-fried Pork with Anchovies (page 352). They are high in calcium and found in packets in Asian food stores. Dried flounder (*da di yu*, 大地鱼) is often salted and dried to hard strips known as "firewood." It flavors the broth (stock) for Hong Kong-style wonton soup and can be steamed, with ginger, soy, scallion (spring onion), and rice wine. If unavailable, other dried fish such as dried sole, cod, or haddock serve as decent substitutes. Fish maw (*yu du*, 鱼肚) or (*hua jiao*, 花胶), the dried bladder of a fish, is rich in collagen and protein and a delicacy in Chinese cuisine. Little in the way of taste, it provides texture while soaking up the surrounding flavors of a dish. Dry, rubbery, and translucent, it is available as a flat piece or hollow tubing and must be soaked until tender before use. Although they are both products of the same fish, *yu du* generally refers to cheap fish maw, whereas *hua jiao* is more expensive and a better-quality item.

DRIED FLOUNDER (see Dried fish)

DRIED HAW (*GAN SHAN ZHA*, 干山楂)
This small fruit grows on the Chinese hawthorn and is the size of a crabapple. Sour and sweet in flavor, it can be candied, dried, and used to make refreshing tonics such as Smoked Plum Soup (page 616).

DRIED LONGAN (see Longan)

DRIED LOTUS SEEDS (*GAN LIAN ZI*, 干莲子)
The shelled and dried seeds from this widely cultivated freshwater plant are a popular filling in sweet pastries—soups such as Lotus Seed with Longan (page 632)—and congee. Red (adzuki) bean and lotus seed soup is traditionally served to newlyweds; the latter ingredient symbolizing the birth of many children. Lotus seeds can be found canned, chilled, or dried in Asian food stores.

DRIED MUNG BEAN STARCH SHEETS
  (see Mung bean)

DRIED SEAFOOD (*HAI WEI*, 海味)
Dried shrimp, dried scallops (or conpoy), dried octopus, and dried oysters are used to deepen flavors in soups, stir-fries, and stews. There is particular demand for such ingredients in the festive run-up to Chinese New Year: briny dried oysters are a popular delicacy symbolizing good fortune. They should be soaked before use.

DRIED SCALLOPS (SEE DRIED SEAFOOD)

DRIED SHRIMP (*XIA MI*, 虾米)
Available in an array of shapes, colors, and sizes, dried shrimp are often used for their sweet and unusual umami-enhanced flavor. See also Dried seafood.

DRIED TANGERINE PEEL (*CHEN PI*, 陈皮)
This dried peel of a particular tangerine from Guangdong has been prized as a culinary ingredient and medicinal tonic for hundreds of years. The aromatic peel has to be aged for at least three years before use. The flavor becomes more intense with age and the older it is, the higher the cost.

DRIED WOLFBERRIES (*GOUQI*, 枸杞)
Also known as goji or lyceum berries, these "super fruits" are grown in northwestern China from the Ningxia region to Xinjiang. Packed with antioxidants and vitamins, they have long been recognized for their medicinal properties and are added to herbal soups and dishes. Packets of dried fruit can be found in most supermarkets, health stores, and Asian food stores.

DUCK LIVER SAUSAGE (*YA RUN CHANG*, 鸭润肠)
Duck liver sausage is made with duck liver and pork, marinated with salt, sugar, and wine, stuffed in a sausage casing, and then dried under the sun or roasted in an oven. With its high fat content, moist texture, and sweet, smoky taste, this sausage is a popular addition to clay-pot rice dishes and can also be steamed to accompany plain rice. Duck liver sausage is most commonly found dried and vacuum-packed.

EEL (*HUANG SHAN*, 黄鳝)
Rice field eel, also known as Asian swamp eel, is an elongated fish that is unwieldy when purchased whole, so tend to be sold skinned, gutted, and deboned. The meat is delicate and lean; its subtle taste lends itself perfectly to richer flavors. While the book features recipes with freshwater eel, Seafood Watch, a sustainable seafood advisory list, recommends that consumers avoid eating them due to significant pressures on the eel populations.

EGG TOFU (*YU ZI TOUFU*, 玉子豆腐)
Egg tofu is a flavorful tofu made with beaten eggs that are mixed with dashi, poured into molds, and then steamed.

FERMENTED BLACK BEANS (*DOU CHI*, 豆豉)
Fermented black beans are black soybeans, which have been soaked, steamed, fermented, salted, and dried. It is a popular ingredient for adding a salty, earthy depth to stews, steamed dishes, and stir-fries in southern China. They can also be ground to a paste or mashed with garlic.

FISH BELLY (*YU NAN*, 鱼腩)
Grass carp is a freshwater fish native to the areas along the Yangtze and Pearl Rivers in southern China. In Cantonese cuisine, the fish belly is steamed with ginger and onions and topped with soy sauce. If carp is not readily available, perch or bass can serve as a substitute.

FISH MAW (see Dried fish)

FISH MAW PUFFS (*SHA BAO YU DU*, 沙爆鱼肚)
Fish maw puffs are made from deep-fried fish maw.

FISH SAUCE (*YU LU*, 鱼露)
An amber-colored condiment made from fermented fish and brine, fish sauce should be used sparingly for its pungent smell and intense flavor. It is more often used in southeast Asian cuisine but will occasionally make an appearance in Chinese recipes.

FIVE-SPICE POWDER
   (*WU XIANG FEN*, 五香粉)
This popular, versatile, and widely available spice blend—a combination of peppercorns, star anise, cloves, cumin, and cinnamon—is an essential ingredient in a Chinese kitchen and creates the basis for marinades and dry rubs for roast meats. They can be purchased from large supermarkets and Asian food stores.

FLOWERING CHIVES (See Chinese chives)

FOXTAIL MILLET (*XIAO MI*, 小米)
Millet, a staple food with a long history of cultivation in China, comprises several varieties of grass-bearing small seeds. The husks of these seeds are removed during threshing to produce a gluten-free, easily-digestible alternative to other grains. High in minerals such as iron and magnesium, millet is boiled in water to create a simple, nutritious porridge such as Millet Congee (page 575). Packages of millet can be found in health stores and select supermarkets.

FROGS (*TIAN JI*, 田鸡)
Highly symbolic in Chinese culture as a mark of prosperity, good luck, or protection, frog meat is best deep-fried or in stir-fries and rice casseroles. The skin must be removed due to potential toxicities. Sea scallops or chicken can be used as substitutes.

FUZZY MELON (*JIE GUA*, 节瓜)
Part of the same family as winter melon, the fuzzy melon resembles a zucchini (courgette) with sparse hair on the skin, which should be peeled off before using. It is sweet and can be used in stir-fries, braised dishes, and soups.

GANBA FUNGUS (*GAN BA JUN*, 干巴菌)
This rare fungus is found in the sandy soils under pine trees in the Yunnan Province of southwest China. Also known as the dried beef mushroom, it brings a chewy texture and pungent, woody flavor to dishes such as Fried Rice with Ganba (page 550). Using a small knife, clean the ganba fungus to rid it of dirt and pick out any grass.

GARLIC SPROUTS (*SUAN TAI*, 蒜苔)
These flowering, green stems of the garlic plant are often sliced and sautéed, (with the tougher base discarded). They provide an aromatic addition to stir-fries, complementing pork, bell peppers and ginger. If unavailable, flowering chives serve as an alternative.

GINGER (JIANG, 姜)
Highly versatile and particularly common in Chinese cuisine, ginger can be peeled, sliced, grated, candied, and powdered—its fiery flavor pairs well with beef, pork, and seafood. Fresh ginger juice, which can be used as a meat tenderizer, is required for certain marinades and sauces. To prepare this at home, grate a peeled lump of ginger and strain the juice.

GINKGO NUTS (BAI GUO, 白果)
These pistachio-shaped seeds, extracted from the fruit of the ginkgo tree, are traditionally utilized in Chinese herbal medicine for their antioxidant and anti-aging properties. The nuts have a sweet, chestnut taste but should not be eaten raw. They are readily available, peeled and vacuum-packed, at Asian specialty food stores. Adults are advised not to consume more than eight nuts a day; exceeding this quantity risks poisoning.

GLUTINOUS RICE (NUO MI, 糯米)
Also known as sticky, sweet, or pearl rice, this grain is noted for its short kernels and high starch content. It can be steamed or stir-fried in savory dishes, but it is often used in desserts with red (adzuki) bean paste, coconut, and sesame. Glutinous rice flour (sometimes called sweet rice flour) can be used to make desserts such as glutinous rice cakes and Peanut Mochi (page 626).

GLUTINOUS RICE CAKES (NIAN GAO, 年糕)
Rice is ground up and kneaded into stiff white rolls that can be purchased in dried or frozen form. It can be made into savory dishes such as Glutinous Rice Cakes with Pork and Beijing Scallions (page 604), but it is more commonly used to prepare a festive dessert for Chinese New Year when it symbolizes prosperity.

GLUTINOUS RICE WINE (NUO MI JIU, 糯米酒)
Also known as fermented sticky rice wine, glutinous rice wine can be traced back to the Tang Dynasty. It is very thick and milky white in color.

HAIRY FIG (WU ZHI MAO TAO, 五指毛桃)
The hairy fig, *fiscus hirta*, is an evergreen shrub or small tree in southern China, Southeast Asia, and India, and the root of the shrub is used as an ingredient for Chinese herbal medicine. Flavored like coconut, it can be added to soups with chicken or pork.

HASMA (XUE GE GAO, 雪鸽膏)
This rare and expensive ingredient (also called hashima) from northeast China was once the preserve of emperors. The fat encasing the fallopian tubes of the Asiatic grass frog is dried and sold in pieces or flakes. Once reconstituted, they expand and become semi-transparent, with a glutinous texture and distinct smell. It can be stirred into sweet soups such as Hasma with Lotus Seeds and Jujube Dates (page 637).

HOISIN SAUCE (HAI XIAN JIANG, 海鲜酱)
Thick, black, and pungent, this popular condiment is made with fermented soybeans, garlic, chili, and sugar. Widely available in supermarkets and Asian food stores, use to marinate grilled meats or to serve as a simple dipping sauce—its sweet, smoky taste makes it a staple of southern Chinese cooking.

HONEY LOCUST SEED (XUE LIAN ZI, 雪莲子)
This legume tree, native to China, can be distinguished by the clusters of thorns that sprout from its trunk and branches. The pulp from the seed pods—bright green, strongly sweet, crisp, and succulent—are used in soups, congee, desserts, and as a drink.

JELLYFISH (HAI ZHE, 海蜇)
Certain edible species of jellyfish are enjoyed as a delicacy. The jellyfish is pickled or cured in salt and sold dried, after which it requires reconstitution prior to consumption. The upper dome area, rather than the tentacles, is conventionally used in cooking and commonly prepared as a cold salad at banquets. Consumers are advised to seek out the dried alternative from Asian food stores.

JICAMA (SHA GE, 沙葛)
Jicama spread to China from its native Mexico via trade routes. With a crisp, white flesh and sweet, starchy taste, it can be eaten raw or paired with meat or fish. Water chestnuts or Jerusalem artichokes can be used as substitutes.

JINHUA HAM (JIN HUA HUO TUI, 金华火腿)
This specialty has been produced for more than a thousand years and is named after its city of origin in Zhejiang. Salted and cured for more than three years, Jinhua ham is deep red and imparts an intensely rich flavor to broths (stocks), stews, and soups. At a pinch, it may be substituted with Smithfield ham.

JUJUBE DATES (HONG ZAO, 红枣)
Several hundred varieties of jujube dates exist. It is an essential component to traditional Chinese medicine— revered for its sweet and warm properties. They can be consumed fresh, cooked, candied. Packets of the dried fruit can be found in select Asian food stores.

KALIMERIS INDICA (*MA LAN TOU*, 马兰头)
This flowering plant of the Asteraceae family, which includes daisies and sunflowers, is found on hill slopes, riversides, roadsides, and unused farmland. Its leaves and stems are often combined with tofu in a simple and easy-to-make salad (page 50). It can be substituted with arugula (rocket).

KAOLIANG WINE (*GAO LIANG JIU*, 高粱酒)
This strong spirit, native to Zhigu in southeast China, is made from ancient distilling techniques using fermented sorghum. Also known as sorghum wine, or dubbed "Platinum Dragon," it is as clear as water with an alcohol content often exceeding 55 percent. Taiwan is also a major producer of this spirit.

LEMONGRASS (*XIANG MAO*, 香茅)
While the sweet, lemony scent is more associated with Thai curries, lemongrass is also used in China when paired with chicken, pork, or seafood. To prepare, the stems are generally cooked whole, sliced, or ground to a paste. The woody stalk is tougher than scallions (spring onions) and often discarded prior to serving. Fresh lemongrass is widely available year round, but lemongrass powder or lemon zest can be used as substitutes.

LICORICE ROOT (*GAN CAO*, 甘草)
This dried root, resembling fibrous twigs, is widely used in Chinese herbal medicine to tonify the spleen, aid indigestion, relieve heartburn, and cleanse the body of toxins. It is also used as a natural sweetener in tea, chewed in dried form, or blended with other herbs to harmonize their effects.

LIGHT SOY SAUCE (see Soy sauce)

LONGAN (*LONG YAN*, 龙眼)
Longan, which translates to "dragon's eye" in Chinese, is a fruit with a pale, yellowish shell and white, translucent flesh. This healthy snack serves as a skin revitalizer and comes available fresh, canned, preserved in syrup, jellied, or as a tea. It is also available in a dried form, which can be used to flavor sweet dessert soups or savory dishes such as Shrimp and Wolfberries in Wine Sauce (page 186).

LOTUS ROOT (*LIAN OU*, 莲藕)
Lotus grows in ponds and marshes with large heart-shape leaves held by long stems above the water. White, thick, and round with many channels inside, the roots are crunchy, tasty, and an important ingredient in vegetarian foods. If fresh lotus root is not available, dried or canned lotus root can be found in selected Asian food stores. Lotus root flour (*ou fen*, 藕粉) can be used as a starchy thickener for recipes such as Chestnut Soup with Osmanthus Flower (page 626).

LUFFA (*SI GUA*, 丝瓜)
Known also angled luffa, Chinese okra, and luffa squash, this long, ridged vegetable is similar to, and can be substituted with a zucchini (courgette). It soak up flavors very well.

MALTOSE (*MAI YA TANG*, 麦芽糖)
Maltose is a syrup made from germinated wheat, starch, and cane sugar. Thick, golden in color, and less sweet than regular syrup, it is often used in candy-making or as a glaze for barbecued meats.

MATSUTAKE MUSHROOM (*SONG RONG*, 松茸)
Native of China, matsutake mushrooms are large, firm mushrooms that sprout from the roots of pine trees. They impart a powerful, woody flavor and are best prepared in such a way as to preserve their distinct, spicy aroma. Portobello or shiitake mushrooms can be used as alternatives. Matsutake mushroom powder (*song rong fen*, 松茸粉) is the ground form of the dried mushroom, adding earthiness to rice dishes while enhancing mild-flavored fish and chicken.

MIRIN (see Rice wine)

MONK FRUIT (*LUO HAN GUO*, 罗汉果)
Traditionally grown in a forested and mountainous region of southern China, this sweet fruit is used in dry form as a sweetener.

MUNG BEAN (*LV DOU*, 绿豆)
These tiny, green beans feature widely in Chinese cuisine and have been cultivated for 3,000 years. They can be boiled in soups or ground to a paste for dumplings and cakes. Their crisp, white shoots add bite to spring rolls and stir-fries (see Bean sprouts). Dried mung bean sheets (*gan fen pi*, 干粉皮) come as thin, translucent dried sheets in a package. They do not require cooking but simply soak in boiling water until soft and jelly like. The sheets can also be made into transparent vermicelli known as glass or cellophane noodles (*fen si*, 粉丝), while the starch can also be jellied in desserts.

NOODLES (*MIAN*, 面 OR *FEN*, 粉)
Cheap, nutritious, and filling, noodles have stood the test of time: a 4,000-year-old sealed bowl was unearthed in northwest China in 2005, and global availability attests to the continued popularity of this

pantry staple. They can be spun from rice, wheat, mung bean, or sweet potato flour, with or without eggs, and range from golden yellow to translucent white. Whether fresh or dried, thick as ribbons or in thin vermicelli strands, there are hundreds of varieties of Chinese noodles as each region has its favorite way of making them.

ORANGE DAYLILY (HUANG HUA CAI, 黄花菜)
Daylilies are delicate, trumpet-shaped, edible flowers that are best consumed on the day they've been picked. When harvested and dried, they are known as golden needles. Some people are allergic to daylilies so it's best only to eat one lily, at first, as a precautionary measure.

OSMANTHUS FLOWER (GUI HUA, 桂花)
This popular flower, native from China to Southeast Asia, is known for its rich, long-lingering floral aroma and is often consumed dried—gan gui hua, 干桂花—as an herbal tea or in desserts. Osmanthus sugar (gui hua tang, 桂花糖) is made by combining the fragrant yellow flowers with sugar.

OYSTER SAUCE (HAO YOU, 蚝油)
This thick, brown condiment is popular in Cantonese cuisine and made from oysters that have been simmered until the reduced juices caramelize and are seasoned with other condiments. Sweet and salty with earthy undertones, this sauce is often drizzled over steamed leafy greens, doused over stir-fries, and rice dishes, or as a base for marinades.

PEACH KERNELS (TAO REN, 桃仁)
Peach kernels, or peach seeds, are believed to promote blood circulation. They taste and look like almonds, which can also be used as a substitute. Dried kernels can be found at Asian supermarkets.

PEANUTS (HUA SHENG, 花生)
Raw peanuts are unprocessed and can be boiled as a snack or deep-fried to garnish dish.

PICKLED CHILES (PAO JIAO, 泡椒)
Chiles are first washed and dried completely before putting into a sterile jar together with spices (star anise, Sichuan peppercorns, etc.) and sterilized water. One or two tablespoons of baijiu is added, then it is sealed and left to ferment for at least a week to allow. Pickled green chiles are often served as a condiment to accompany rice or noodle dishes. Some of the heat is subdued during the pickling process, replaced by a mild sweetness and mellow color. Fermentation adds a touch of sourness that enhances the flavor.

PICKLED GINGER (SUAN JIANG, 酸姜)
Ginger is thinly sliced and preserved in a pickling brine of salt, sugar, and white vinegar (see recipe on page 296) and fresh, young ginger works particularly well. In Chinese cuisine, it is used as a palate cleanser, in salad dressings, sauces, and marinades, or with preserved duck egg.

PICKLED POTHERB MUSTARD (XUE LI HONG, 雪里蕻)
Potherb mustards are generally seasoned with spices, preserved in brine, and served as a tangy pickle with stews and stir-fries. Traditionally, the greens were tightly packed in earthen pots and sealed to quicken fermentation, a process still practiced in many rural areas. Packets of the preserved greens can be sourced in select Asian food stores.

PICKLED VEGETABLES (PAO CAI, 泡菜)
Preservation techniques are entrenched in Chinese culinary history, with many simple recipes still conducted at home. In some regions, porcelain pickling urns have been fashioned for the sole purpose of preserving fresh produce to greatest effect. Sliced vegetables—such as carrots, celery, radishes, and cucumbers—are commonly pickled in combinations of brine, sugar, white vinegar, ginger, and spices such as star anise and Sichuan peppercorns. Also, each province has its regional traditions—Sichuan preserves tend to be spicier, while Cantonese pickles are vinegary and sweet.

PICKLED WINE SAUCE (ZAO LU, 糟卤)
Made by adding rice wine to red distilled grain sauce, pickled wine sauce (also known as pickle sauce) is a favorite condiment to add to precooked ingredients such as duck's tongue or pork knuckles. The result is a cold appetizer with a hint of wine flavor.

PIXIAN CHILI BEAN PASTE (PIXIAN DOU BAN JIANG, 郫县豆瓣酱)
This rich, reddish-brown chili bean paste is native to the Pixian region in Sichuan. Chiles, fava (broad) beans, salt, and flour are fermented for over a year, forging an intense taste incomparable to other bean pastes. It dissolves in broths (stocks), enriches sauces, and spices up marinades for meat and fish. It can also be served as a simple condiment.

PORK FATBACK (FEI ZHU ROU, 肥猪肉)
Pork fatback is cut into small pieces that do not melt when cooked and thus prevents the dish from being greasy. It can also be used to provide a smooth texture to the meat when cooking.

PORK FLOSS (ROU SONG, 肉松)

Pork floss—also known as rousong, meat wool, and meat floss—is a dried pork product with a light and fluffy texture similar to coarse cotton candy (candy floss). There are two common types of pork floss: pork *sung* and pork *fu*.

PRESERVED BLACK OLIVES (LAN JIAO, 榄角)

Whereas Mediterranean olives are commonly pressed for their oil, it is the nuts and fruit of the Chinese olive that are more generally consumed. Large and elongated in shape and tapered ends, the olives are first soaked in hot water until soft, then halved and pitted and marinated in salt.

PRESERVED DUCK EGG (PI DAN, 皮蛋)

Also referred to as "thousand-year-old eggs," "century eggs," or "millennium eggs," this delicacy dates back to the Ming Dynasty. Traditionally, the eggs were pickled in brine and buried in coals, chalk, and clay for many months, although time-saving techniques have since been honed. The yolks acquire a striking dark green color, rippled with concentric circles like the cross-section of a tree trunk, while the whites are amber and gelatinous. The pungent odor is a combination of sulfur and ammonia and the eggs are an acquired taste. They can be served as an appetizer with pickled ginger or with congee for breakfast.

PRESERVED KOHLRABI (DA TOU CAI, 大头菜)

Kohlrabi is a type of vegetable, distinguished by its squat green or purple bulb and shoots. Preserved kohlrabi (also known as salted kohrabi) is available sliced or shredded and preserved in brine.

PRESERVED LEMONS
(XIAN NING MENG, 咸柠檬)

Whole lemons are preserved in jars with salt, then stored for several months until they darken to a deep brown color. They may be added to congee, fish, and poultry dishes or served as a relish with chopped chile, garlic, and ginger.

PRESERVED MUSTARD GREENS

Preserved mustard greens can be served as an appetizer, used as an ingredient, or served in congee and every region has its own. Napa cabbage is often used in northern China and in the south, they use the mustard plant known as *jie cai*, which is slightly bitter and peppery in taste. Shaoxing preserved mustard greens (*Shaoxing mei gan cai*, 绍兴霉干菜) are pervasive in the cuisine of Shaoxing, a city in the eastern province of Zhejiang, and can be found dried in packets. They should be soaked for an extended period of time until soft, then thoroughly rinsed before use. Their powerful flavor enhances meat dishes and tofu. Sichuan preserved mustard greens (*ya cai*, 芽菜) are shredded tender stems of the mustard greens, which are preserved with salt and other spices. Chopped into small pieces, it is one of the main ingredients of the famous Dan Dan Noodles (page 590) and often used in stir-fried vegetables or in double-boiled pork dishes.

PRESERVED PINEAPPLE PASTE
(FENG LI JIANG, 凤梨酱)

Preserved pineapple paste is made by slowly cooking fresh pineapple, sugar, and lemon juice until thickened, then cooling the mixture in a jar. This sticky, golden jam is often prepared at home but can be purchased in shops selling Taiwanese foods.

PRESERVED TURNIPS (CAI PU, 菜脯)

Known also as salted turnip or preserved radish, Daikon radishes are cut, salted, and dried for preservation. Both crispy and salty, it is a favorite ingredient among the Hakka, Chaozhou, Fujian, Taiwanese, and northerners. It can be used in stir-fries and omelets or act as a savory garnish for congee.

PUNING BEAN PASTE
(PUNING DOU JIANG, 普宁豆酱)

This soybean product emerged from Puning in the Chaozhou region in Guangdong. The paste is often used with seafood or as a dip (see Fish Rice, page 129).

RED (ADZUKI) BEANS (HONG DOU, 红豆)

Sweet and nutty, this small red (adzuki) bean is indigenous to China and is often used in desserts such as Red Bean Soup (page 644). Red bean paste (*dou sha*, 红豆沙), sometimes referred to as anko, is a dark red, sweet bean paste available both mashed and smooth.

RED BEAN CURD (NAN RU, 南乳)

Cut into cubes and sold in jars, red bean curd is produced from the curdled milk of soybeans fermented in a solution of rice wine, salt, and red yeast rice. The fermentation process softens the curd, releasing an intense umami flavor popular in stir-fries and stews. Available in Asian food stores, this product is an essential addition to chicken and pork dishes, and is also eaten with congee at breakfast.

RED DISTILLED GRAIN SAUCE
(see Distilled grain sauce)

RED VINEGAR (see Vinegars)

RED YEAST RICE (*HONG QU MI*, 红曲米)
Used in China for over a thousand years in medicine, red yeast rice (also known as red rice) is rice that has been fermented with a type of yeast and adds a vibrant red color to a dish. Some commercial supplements have been found to contain high levels of the toxin citrinin and we recommend cherry juice or cranberry juice as acceptable substitutes.

RICE WINE (*MI JIU*, 米酒)
Arguably, the second-most popular condiment after soy sauce, rice wine is used to tenderize meats, marinate seafood, and impart flavor to food. Shaoxing wine (*Shaoxing jiu*, 绍兴酒)—one of the oldest types of wine in China—is a quality rice wine that is both consumed as a drink and added to marinades, soups, and stuffing. Produced in the Shaoxing region since the fifth century, it is enjoyed for its fragrant scent. Mirin (*wei lin*, 味醂) is a Japanese rice wine with a lower alcohol and higher sugar content than sake.

ROCK SUGAR (*BING TANG*, 冰糖)
These rocks of crystallized palm, beet, or cane sugar are golden or transparent in appearance and add sweetness to marinades, soups, teas, and congee. They are generally ground or dissolved prior to use and available in packets or boxes at Asian food stores. Granulated sugar can be used as an alternative.

SALTED DRIED PLUMS (*HUA MEI*, 话梅)
Plums are picked when ripe, then washed, dried, marinated in a sugar solution. This process is repeated several times until the plum is dried but soft and sweet. Salted dried plums are a delicious snack but they can also be prepared in dishes such as Trotters with Salted Dried Plums (page 372).

SALTED DUCK EGG (*XIAN DAN*, 咸蛋)
The historic practice of preserving duck eggs in brine continues to this day, with many variations on the traditional method. The high fat content and vibrant color of duck egg yolks means that they are particularly prized as an appetizer or with soups, stir-fries, and congee. These eggs can be found vacuum-packed or in boxes in Asian food stores.

SALTED PLUMS (*MEI ZI*, 梅子)
The popular Chinese salted plums (not to be confused with dried salted plums) are native to Guangdong province. The fruits have a complex flavor that is simultaneously sweet, sour, and salty with a tangy hint of fermentation and are used as an ingredient in plum sauces.

SALTED PORK (*XIAN ROU*, 咸肉)
Salted pork is pork that has been salted repeatedly over a period of time and then dried in a shady, cool place (unlike cured pork, which is sun- or oven-dried). Salted pork is soft and pink and has a salty, meaty flavor that can be used to flavor rice dishes such as Shanghai Pork and Vegetable Rice (page 544).

SALTED RUTABAGA (*DA TOU CAI*, 大头菜)
Also known as pickled rutabaga, this preserved vegetable is flavored with five-spice powder and comes available whole, cubed, diced, shredded, or minced. It is extremely salty and should be rinsed before use.

SALTED TOON SHOOTS (*YAN YAN XIANG CHUN*, 盐腌香椿)
The Chinese toon, or toona sinensis, is a leafy plant native to parts of northern and eastern China. Growing to 40 inches/100 cm in height, the plant is extensively cultivated for its aromatic, peppery shoots. Toon shoots can be purchased frozen or salted, although the latter variety should be rinsed and soaked to remove excess salt before use. Toon shoots pair well with tofu and sesame oil or in stir-fries, egg dishes, and pickles.

SEA CUCUMBERS (*HAI SHEN*, 海参)
This species of echinoderm, a family including starfish and sea urchins, has a thick, elongated body and spiky tentacles. Its popular Chinese name, meaning "ginseng of the sea," denotes its use as a tonic to nourish the blood, cleanse the kidney, and promote general well-being. Due to its mild taste, sea cucumber absorbs the richer flavors of broths and stews, blending particularly well with Beijing scallions, cabbage, shiitake mushrooms, and pork. Dried or fresh varieties can be purchased online and in select Asian food stores, although expect a high price tag.

SESAME OIL (*ZHI MAN YOU*, 芝麻油)
Over 5,000 years ago, the Chinese burned this oil as a light source. Today, this highly versatile oil is a pantry staple, widely available in supermarkets and specialist food stores. A product of toasted sesame seeds, it brings a rich, nutty flavor to fish and meat marinades, sauces, dressings, and dips and can be drizzled over a host of rice and noodle dishes.

SESAME PASTE (*ZHIMA JIANG*, 芝麻酱)
While tahini is popular in much North African and Middle Eastern cuisine, many Chinese recipes also call for a form of sesame paste. Toasted sesame seeds are ground and blended with oil and seasoning, to create a rich paste used for coating noodles, steamed vegetables or grilled meats.

SESAME SEEDS (ZHI MA, 芝麻)

The tiny, flat seeds of this oil seed crop add a gentle crunch when scattered over dishes or combined with soy sauce, garlic and ginger. Yellow, red, and black varieties are also available. They make a popular ingredient for desserts such as Laughing Donuts (page 634).

SHA CHA SAUCE (SHA CHA JIANG, 沙茶酱)

This rich condiment, popular in Cantonese cuisine, is widely used as a marinade for grilled meats and may be labeled barbecue sauce in some food stores. A blend of soybean oil, garlic, shallots, chiles, and dried shrimp, it is high in protein and slightly spicy. Sha cha sauce works well in meaty stir-fries such as Beef in Sha Cha Sauce (page 405).

SHAJIANG (SHA JIANG, 沙姜)

Also known as Kaempferia galangal, kencur, or aromatic ginger, the gnarled roots are cultivated primarily in southern China. Ginger-like in taste and texture, they add tang to stir-fries and pastes. Shajiang can be used as a marinade for meats, in dips, and in brines. Shajiang powder (sha jiang fen, 沙姜粉) is sometimes known as "sand ginger." Similar to powdered ginger but more pungent, it is commonly used as an optional ingredient in five-spice powder.

SHAOXING PRESERVED MUSTARD GREENS
(see Preserved mustard greens)

SHAOXING WINE (see Rice wine)

SHRIMP PASTE (XIA JIANG, 虾酱)

In southeast China and other Southeast Asian countries (called balacan in Malaysia and Indonesia), finely ground shrimp (prawns) was traditionally salted and fermented under the sun. This salty, pungent paste enhances stir-fries, soups, and rice dishes.

SHRIMP ROE (XIA ZI, 虾子)

This classic seasoning consists of shrimp (prawn) eggs dried to a powder-like consistency. The vibrant red roe impart an intense umami flavor to egg noodles, blanched leafy greens, and tofu. A simple Hong Kong dish pairs Braised Noodles with Shrimp Roe (page 586).

SICHUAN CHILI OIL (See Chili oil)

SICHUAN PEPPERCORNS (HUA JIAO, 花椒)

Not actually a peppercorn but rather a dried, red-brown berry from a prickly species of ash tree, this highly distinctive and versatile seasoning is common in the spicy cuisine of western China. Enjoyed for their mouth-numbing, tongue-tingling bite, Sichuan peppercorns can be found in whole or ground form. (Grinding them in a pestle and mortar releases a stronger burst of flavor than the pre-powdered version.) Ground Sichuan pepper, a key ingredient in five-spice powder, imparts warmth to meat, fish, and tofu dishes.

SICHUAN PRESERVED MUSTARD GREENS
(see Preserved mustard greens)

SOYBEAN CRISPS (DOU SU, 豆酥)

Soybean crisps are made from the dregs of soybeans used to make soy milk, which have been roasted to remove most of the moisture and then stir-fried in oil until crispy. Its crispiness and distinct soy flavor add a level of complexity onto the flavor of meat and seafood dishes. See recipe on page 52.

SNAILS (LUO, 螺)

Marine snails can be found in Asian markets with fresh seafood. Meaty and flavorful, they are best stir-fried with spices and wine. Most of them are exported from Vietnam and can be sourced from selected Vietnamese food stores.

SOYBEAN SPROUTS (HUANG DOU YA, 黄豆芽)

While mung bean sprouts are generally used more widely, soybean sprouts are a reliable alternative and rich in protein and vitamins. Longer than mung bean sprouts, they have distinctive yellow grains and a crunchy, nutty texture—perfect for stir-fries and salads.

SOY SAUCE (CHI YOU, 豉油)

This condiment of fermented soybeans, salt, water, and barley or wheat flour adds instant depth of flavor to savory dishes. Light soy sauce (sheng chou, 生抽) is commonly used in Chinese cooking as a general flavor enhancer. Soybeans are mixed with flour, salt and water, fermented, and baked under hot sun in a closed container for about one year. Salty with a thin, watery consistency, it is a staple of dips, dressings, and marinades. Dark soy sauce (lao chou, 老抽) is made from light soy sauce with the addition of caramel, making it sweet and dark—ideal for a rich, deeper flavor and color in stews.

STAR ANISE (BA JIAO, 八角)

Widely cultivated in southern China, this rust-brown dried fruit is a dominant ingredient in five-spice powder. It imparts a warm, aniseed flavor to slow-cooked dishes and is generally removed before serving. Star anise works well in meat and poultry dishes and can be added to marinades, glazes, and slow-cooked soups and stews.

STRAW MUSHROOMS (CAO GU, 草菇)
These small grayish-brown mushrooms are also known as "paddy straw mushrooms" because they are cultivated on the rice straw used in paddy fields. Tender and with a mild flavor, they are often combined with tofu or stir-fried with strips of beef. If located in Asian food stores, they are most likely to be found dried or canned.

SUGARED DATES (MI ZAO, 蜜枣)
Fresh jujube dates are soaked in a sugar solution to absorb the sweetness and then dried. It is most often used as an ingredient in soups.

SWEET POTATO LEAVES (FAN SHU YE, 番薯叶)
Generally available during the summer months, these mild and tender greens are often flash-fried or steamed to preserve their nutrients. We recommend to stir-fry the leaves with garlic and soy sauce or oyster sauce, but they can also be served over rice or mixed into soups.

SWEET POTATO STARCH (FAN SHU FEN, 番薯粉)
This fine powder from the starch of dehydrated sweet potatoes is used as a thickening agent in soups. The dried potatoes are also ground to produce gluten-free flour used in making steamed buns or noodles (see Sweet potato vermicelli below). Yam flour, a similar product, is available in some stores, and cornstarch (cornflour), tapioca, or arrowroot are possible substitutes.

SWEET POTATO VERMICELLI (HONG SHU FEN TIAO, 红薯粉条)
With a similar texture to mung bean vermicelli, these noodles are gray when dried but turn translucent after cooking. Also popular in Korean cuisine, these gluten-free noodles pair well with stir-fried meat and vegetables and can also be used in a salad mixed with garlic and chili oil. If unavailable, mung bean vermicelli can be used as a substitute.

SWEET PRESERVED TURNIPS (TIAN LU OBO, 甜萝卜)
Similar to preserved turnips (page 696), this sweeter version is less salty.

TAPIOCA STARCH (MU SHU FEN, 木薯粉)
Tapioca starch comes from the dried root of the cassava plant, a resilient crop native to Brazil and grown throughout Asia. This slightly sweet, gluten-free flour can thicken soups, sauces, and dips. The starch is also available in small pearls, which can be used in desserts such as Baked Tapioca Pudding (page 646).

TARO (YU TOU, 芋头)
This tropical plant, cultivated for its edible starchy roots, is a staple in Asia. Creamy white with a nutty flavor, it should always be cooked to avoid potentially harmful effects when consumed raw. Taro root appears frequently in stews and desserts or in cakes enjoyed at New Year.

TARO PASTE (YU NI, 芋泥)
Taro paste is a popular derivative of the root. Steamed, pureed, and flavored with sugar and vegetable or coconut oil, it can be prepared at home or found in select Asian food stores.

TIANJIN PRESERVED CABBAGE (DONG CAI, 冬菜)
The northern province of Tianjin is renowned for its highly developed methods of vegetable preservation. To make this preserve, a local variety of cabbage, known for its thin and slender leaves, is shredded, mixed with garlic and salt, and compressed in brown earthenware jars. It is used in stuffings and garnishes for beef and fish dishes as well as in congees and broths (stocks).

TIANMIANJIANG (TIAN MIAN JIANG, 甜面酱)
Made from fermented flour, tianmianjiang is popular in several regions of China. The balance between sweetness and saltiness varies from region to region, but it is generally a thick and smooth paste similar to hoisin sauce. Use tianmianjiang as a base for stir-fries or as a dip to accompany Peking duck. It can be found in tubs or packets in Asian food stores.

TOFU (DOU FU, 豆腐)
This widely-used, high-protein ingredient is a staple in Chinese cuisine and essential to vegetarian diets. To prepare tofu, soy milk from soaked soybeans is strained and curdled in blocks. Variations on this simple procedure account for the spectrum of tofu products: silken, soft, regular, extra-firm, and spiced, all of which differ in density and flavor. Firm tofu is a safe bet for stir-fries, as they hold their shape, whereas delicate silken tofu will easily break in dishes such as a classic Mapo Tofu (page 512). Tofu will often absorb the surrounding flavors of savory broths and stir-fries and carries ginger, soy sauce, and chile particularly well. Sliced into blocks or cubes, it can be stuffed and deep-fried for extra crispiness.

TOFU PUFFS (DOU FU BU, 豆腐卜)
Found in the refrigerated section of Asian food stores, these puffs come in many shapes and sizes. They function similarly to conventional tofu, sponging up flavors and sticky meat juices in stews. They can be purchased fresh or dried and reconstituted.

TOFU SHEETS (*FU PI*, 腐皮)

When soy milk is boiled, a delicate skin materializes on the surface, which can be extracted and dried to form yellow sheets. These tofu sheets are often used in making dim sum. Tofu sheets can also be dried to a crisp to become crispy tofu sticks or sheets (*fu zhu*, 腐竹), also known as bean curd sheets or yuba. They can be found in Asian food stores.

TOFU WRAPS (*BAI YE*, 百页)

Many layers of tofu skins are pressed together to form a thick tofu skin which is often used as a wrapper to make meat rolls or tied into knots to use in a soup like yan du xian (page 113). Packets of these dried skins appear in Asian food stores, and the wraps should be soaked to soften before they are used.

TUBEROSE (*YE XIANG HUA*, 夜香花)

In China, tuberose is called "night fragrant jade" because it blooms at night and its floral scent is extracted for perfumery. It has tall spiked stems with numerous tubular blooms and cream-colored flowers.

VINEGARS (*CU*, 醋)

White vinegar (*bai mi cu*, 白米醋) is a colorless vinegar with high acidity, giving it a flavor that is more similar to regular vinegar. It can be used to round out rich, meaty stews or as a vinaigrette. Black vinegar (*hei cu*, 黑醋) is made from fermented rice or other grains. The woody, smoky character of this condiment makes it a popular dipping sauce and a welcome addition to rice, noodles, marinades, and stir-fries. Rich with mellow tones, black vinegar is also drunk as a health tonic. Zhenjiang vinegar (*Zhenjiang cu*, 镇江醋) is a popular type of black vinegar native to the city of Zhenjiang. It is often combined with sugar in braised meat and fish to provide a sweet and sour flavor. In stir-fries, it is thought to preserve nutrients and add crispiness. Balsamic vinegar may be used as a substitute for any type of black vinegar. Red vinegar (*da hong zhe cu*, 大红浙醋), also known as Zhejiang vinegar, uses fermented rice with the addition of food color to give it a red color.

WATER BAMBOO (*JIAO BAI*, 茭白)

Water bamboo, also called "wild rice stem," is a typical Chinese vegetable shaped like narrow bamboo shoots. To prepare the water bamboo stems, remove the outer shells and use a vegetable peeler to shave away the green skin until you reach the white flesh.

WATER CHESTNUTS (*MA TI*, 马蹄)

Native to Asia, this aquatic vegetable grows in marshes and is not actually a chestnut, despite the resemblance in size and color. Slightly sweet and crispy, water chestnuts are commonly found canned in supermarkets and Asian food stores. A source of potassium and fiber, they are a nutritious addition to stir-fries, salads, and steamed dishes. Dried water chestnuts can be finely ground to produce water chestnut flour (*ma ti fen*, 马蹄粉), a white and gluten-free powder used to thicken soups and stews or as a batter for deep-frying.

WATER SHIELD (*CHUN CAI*, 莼菜)

This aquatic herb, also known as the water lily, floats on the surface and is widely distributed in Asia and North America. Traditionally, its edible leaves are had in soups and stews. While lacking a distinctive taste, its rich green hues visually enhance dishes.

WATER SPINACH (*WEN CAI*, 蕹菜)

Known also as "morning glory" or oong choi, these mild, sweet-flavored greens have hollow stems, which remain relatively crunchy even after cooking. See Water Spinach with Shrimp Paste (page 459).

WHEAT GLUTEN (*MIAN JIN*, 面筋)

Also known as gluten balls, wheat gluten is made by mixing flour with water and salt, then stirring continuously until a thick and gummy ball is formed. It can be deep-fried as puffs (油面筋) or fermented and steamed as bran dough, a popular ingredient in Shanghainese cooking (see Bran dough, page 689). Wheat gluten is available in cans and may be found in select Asian markets.

WHEAT STARCH (*XIAO MAI DIAN FEN*, 小麦淀粉)

Wheat starch is commonly used with rice and glutinous rice flours to make a variety of dumpling wrapper.

WHITE-BACK WOOD EAR FUNGUS (*BAI BEI MU ER*, 白背木耳)

This nutritious woodland fungus is lauded for its circulation-boosting properties and iron component. While this fungus brings little in the way of flavor, its crispy texture makes it a popular addition to soups and stews. Usually sold dried, it requires pre-soaking and can be found in Asian food stores.

WHITE DISTILLED GRAIN SAUCE (see Distilled grain sauce)

WILD YAMS (*HUAI SHAN*, 淮山)

The Chinese variety of these starchy, edible tubers has a tough brown skin and white flesh and can be used in traditional herbal medicine to treat conditions related to the stomach, spleen, and kidneys. They can be boiled, fried, or mashed and added to soups, stir-fries, and congee. They are available fresh or in powdered form.

WINTER MELON (*DONG GUA*, 冬瓜)
Also known as wax gourd, this large, mild-tasting fruit grows on the vine and has a firm, white flesh that softens when cooked—especially in soups and stews.

WONTON WRAPPERS (*HUN TUN PI*, 馄饨皮)
Wonton wrappers, or skins, are made with flour and water and used to wrap wontons and dumplings. There are two different types of skins available in Asian markets: Cantonese wrappers are thin and more suited for dishes such as Sichuan-Style Wontons in Red Oil (page 64) while Shanghainese wrappers are thick and best used in recipes including Pork and Vegetable Wontons (page 59).

XIN ZHU RICE VERMICELLI
    (*XINZHU MI FEN*, 新竹米粉)
These thin, translucent, wind-dried noodles are a staple in the northern Taiwanese city of Hsinchu. Made from ground rice rather than mung bean starch, they are soaked, drained, and tossed in stir-fries with thinly sliced pork, shiitake mushrooms, carrot, and shrimp. See Vermicelli with Tuna (page 599).

XO CHILI SAUCE (*XO LA JIAO JIANG*, XO辣椒酱)
Named after XO, the highest grading in Cognac, this high-quality condiment originates from Hong Kong and does not actually contain any cognac or alcohol. Instead, it is made from a mixture of dried seafood, herbs, and spices. A regular chili sauce may be substituted but it will not have the same umami flavor.

YAK BUTTER (*SU YOU*, 酥油)
This dairy product is a specialty of Tibet. The milk from the yak is churned to produce a rich butter with a high fat content, closer to cheese in density. Yak butter tea is a popular part of the Himalayan diet.

YELLOW CHIVES (*JIU HUANG*, 韭黄)
Known also as hot bed chives, yellow chives are available during the summer and are cultivated under covers to achieve their distinctive leaves, which retain their yellow pigment without turning green. Their fragrance is mild and sweet compared to garlicky Chinese chives.

YI-NOODLES (*YI MIAN*, 伊面)
A type of flat Cantonese egg noodle made from wheat flour, yi-noodles have been deep-fried to create a golden yellow color and chewy, spongy texture. The noodles can be boiled, stir-fried, or used in soups or salads.

YUNNAN HAM (*YUNNAN HUO TUI*, 云南火腿)
The western province of Yunnan is highly regarded for its traditional method of dry-curing pork with salt. Robust flavors make this ham a simple yet delicious appetizer when eaten on its own, but its saltiness also pairs well with winter melon in soups such as Crab Meat and Winter Melon Soup (page 110). The ham is soaked before use to remove excess salt, and prosciutto or lardons can be used as an alternative.

ZHEJIANG VINEGAR (see Vinegars)

ZHENJIANG VINEGAR (see Vinegars)

ZHUHOU SAUCE (*ZHU HOU JIANG*, 柱候酱)
Also known as chu hou sauce, this combination of soybeans, garlic, ginger, sesame paste, and spices is ideal for braising meats and vegetables. Bean sauce is a reasonable substitute.

INDEX

BIBLIOGRAPHY

Ang, Audra. *To the People, Food Is Heaven: Stories Of Food And Life In A Changing China*. Lyons Press, New York, 2012.

Anhuisheng, Zhiliangjianduju. "Zhongguo huicai baiozhun" 中国徽菜标准 [China's Anhui Cuisine Standard]. Anhui Kexue Jishu Chubanshe, 2009.

Barclay, Eliza. *Chow Under Mao: Surviving China's Cultural Revolution on Local Food*. http://www.npr.org/sections/thesalt/2012/01/19/145456950/surviving-chinas-cultural-revolution-on-seasonal-local-food, 2012.

Chen, Mengyin. "Yuecai suyuan lu" 粤菜溯源录 [History of Cantonese Dishes]. Yinshi Tiandi Chubanshe, 1989.

Chen, Mengyin. "Shijing Vol. 1–5" 食经 一至五册 [Shijing Volumes 1–5]. The Commercial Press, 2008.

CIA The World Factbook. https://www.cia.gov/library/publications/resources/the-world-factbook.

Claiborne, Craig & Lee, Virginia. *The Chinese Cookbook*. André Deutsch, London, 1973.

Dikötter, Frank. *Mao's Great Leap to Famine*. http://www.nytimes.com/2010/12/16/opinion/16iht-eddikotter16.html, 2010.

Dunlop, Fuchsia. *Every Grain of Rice: Simple Chinese Home Cooking*. Bloomsbury, London, 2012.

Dunlop, Fuchsia. *Sichuan Cookery*. Michel Joseph, London, 2001.

Dunlop, Fuchsia. *The Revolutionary Chinese Cookbook*. Ebury Press, London, 2006.

Farrer, James (editor). *The Globalization of Asian Cuisines: Transnational Networks and Culinary Contact Zones*. Palgrave Macmillan, 2015.

Gong, Sasha & Seligman, Scott D. *The Cultural Revolution Cookbook*. Earnshaw Books, 2011.

Hahn, Emily. *The Cooking of China*. Time-Life Books, 1968.

Höllmann, Thomas O. *The Land of the Five Flavors: A Cultural History of Chinese*. Columbia University Press, 2014.

Hom, Ken & Huang, Ching-He. *Exploring China: A Culinary Adventure*. BBC Books, London, 2012.

Hong, Lihe. "Gan cai xin pu" 贛菜新谱 [New Recipes of Jiangxi Cuisine]. Jiangxi Kexue Jishu Chubanshe, 1997.

Jing, Hong & Wu, Hua. "Jingdian yinshi zhanggu" 经典饮食掌故 [Classic Cuisine Anecdotes]. Baihua Wenyi Chubanshe, 1991.

Jisheng, Yang. *China's Great Shame*. http://www.nytimes.com/2012/11/14/opinion/chinas-great-shame.html, 2012.

Li, Kai & Feng, Yong. "Chuancai chushi shouce" 川菜厨师手册 [Handbook of Sichuan Chefs]. Sichuan Kexue Jishu Chubanshe, 2010.

Li, Xiin. "Chuancai pengren shidian" 川菜烹饪事典 [Dictionary of Sichuan Cooking]. Sichuan Kexue Jishu Chubanshe, 2009.

Li, Zhaoxia, "Zhongguo miandian cidian" 中国面点辞典 [Chinese Noodles Dictionary]. Shanxi Science and Technology Press, 1991.

Li, Zhaoxia. "Zhongguo pengren jifa cidian" 中国烹饪技法辞典 [Dictionary of Chinese Cooking Techniques]. Shanxi Science and Technology Press, 2014.

Li, Zhaoxia. "Zhongguo Shicai cidian" 中国食材辞典 [Dictionary of Chinese Ingredients]. Shanxi Science and Technology Press, 2000.

Liu, Feng Tong, " Zhongguo caipu daquan" 中国菜谱大全 [Chinese Recipes Collection]. Tianjin Science and Technology Press, 2014.

Liu, Junru. *Chinese food*. Cambridge University Press, 2011.

Liu, Zihua. "Liu zihua chuancai dajiangtang" 刘自华川菜大讲堂 [Liu Zihuan Sichuan Lectures]. Yanbiandaxue Chubanshe, 1991.

Pan, Yingjun, "Yuechu baodian shicai pian" 粤厨宝典食材篇 [Cantonese Kitchen Collection: Ingredients]. Lingnan Meishu Chubanshe, 2009.

Pan, Yingjun. "Yuechu baodian weibu pian" 粤厨宝典味部篇 [Guangdong Kitchen Collection: Recipes]. Lingnan Meishu Chubanshe, 2009.

Perry, Neil. *Balance & Harmony: Asian Food*. Murdoch Books, Sydney, 2000.

Reilly, Fiona. *Essential Shanghai Street Food: 14 Must-eat Dishes*. http://www.seriouseats.com/2015/05/essential-shanghai-china-street-food-dishes.html, 2015.

Shun Wah, Annette & Aitkin, Greg. *Banquet: Ten Courses to Harmony*. Doubleday, 1999.

Simoons, Frederick J. *Food in China : a cultural and historical inquiry*. CRC Press, Boca Raton, 1991.

Sun, Jiaxiang and Zhao, Jianmin. "Zhongguo lucai wenhua" 中国鲁菜文化 [China Shandong Culinary Culture]. Shanxi Kexue Jishu Chubanshe, 1991.

Xiao, Fan. "Zhongguo pengren cidian" 中国烹饪辞典 [Dictionary of Chinese Cooking]. Zhongguo Shangye Chubanshe, 1992.

Xue, Jiachen. "Sushi lueshuo" 素食略说 [Brief Discussion of Vegetarian Dishes]. Zhongguo Shenge Chubanshe,1984.

Yao, Haiyang. "Zhengzong kongfucai" 正宗孔府菜 [Authentic Confucian Dishes]. Shandong Kexue Jishu Chubanshe, 1991.

Yao, Haiyang. "Jiachang lucai" 家常鲁菜 [Shandong Home Cooking]. Shandong Kexue Jishu Chubanshe, 2010.

Young, Grace & Richardson, Alan. *The Breath of a Wok*. Simon & Schuster, New York, 2004.

Zhang, Faming. "Jingchu shicui" 荆楚食萃 [Collection of Hubei Recipes]. Hubei Keji Chubanshe, 1988.

Zhang, Yunfu. "Zhongguo fo zhai" 中华佛斋 [Chinese Buddhist Vegetarian Dishes]. Qingdao Chubanshe Youxiangongsi, 2014.

Zhongguo Pengren Baikequanshu. "Zhongguo da baikequanshu chubanshe" 中国烹饪百科全书 [Encyclopedia of Chinese Cooking]. China Encyclopedia Publishing House, 2000.

Zhongguo Pengren Xiehui. "Zhongguo pengtiao jifa jicheng" 中国烹调技法集成 (Collection of Chinese Cooking Techniques). Yinshi Tiandi Chubanshe, 2006.

RECIPE NOTES

- Butter should always be unsalted.
- Eggs, vegetables, and fruits are assumed to be large (UK: medium) size, unless otherwise specified.
- Milk is always whole (full-fat), unless otherwise specified.
- Garlic cloves are assumed to be large; use two if yours are small.
- A fresh crab is always saltwater crab, unless otherwise specified.
- We strongly recommend using a cooking thermometer for accurate temperatures. To test whether your deep-frying oil is hot enough, add a cube of stale bread. If it browns in 30 seconds, the temperature is 350–375°F (180–190°C), about right for most frying. Exercise a high level of caution when following recipes involving any potentially hazardous activity, including the use of high temperature and open flames. In particular, when deep-frying, add the food carefully to avoid splashing, wear long sleeves, and never leave the pan unattended.
- Cooking and preparation times are for guidance only, as individual ovens vary. If using a fan (convection) oven, follow the manufacturer's directions concerning oven temperatures.
- Some recipes include raw or very lightly cooked eggs. These should be avoided particularly by the elderly, infants, pregnant women, convalescents, and anyone with an impaired immune system.
- Some recipes contain potentially harmful ingredients when not prepared properly or consumed in excess—such as red yeast rice, ginkgo nuts, and apricot kernels. These should be avoided particularly by the elderly, infants, pregnant women, convalescents, and anyone with an impaired immune system.
- Ginkgo nuts can be poisonous when served in large quantities—adults should consume no more than eight per day.
- Both imperial and metric measures are used in this book. Follow one set of measurements throughout, not a mixture, as they are not interchangeable.
- All spoon measurements are level. 1 teaspoon = 5 ml; 1 tablespoon = 15 ml. Australian standard tablespoons are 20 ml, so Australian readers are advised to use 3 teaspoons in place of 1 tablespoon when measuring small quantities.
- When no quantity is specified, for example of oils, salts, and herbs used for finishing dishes, quantities are discretionary and flexible.

PHAIDON PRESS LIMITED
REGENT'S WHARF
ALL SAINTS STREET
LONDON N1 9PA

PHAIDON PRESS INC.
65 BLEECKER STREET
NEW YORK, NY 10012

PHAIDON.COM

FIRST PUBLISHED 2016
© 2016 PHAIDON PRESS LIMITED

ISBN: 978 0 7148 7224 7

A CIP CATALOGUE RECORD FOR THIS BOOK
IS AVAILABLE FROM THE BRITISH LIBRARY AND
THE LIBRARY OF CONGRESS.

COMMISSIONING EDITOR: EMILIA TERRAGNI
PROJECT EDITOR: MICHELLE MEADE
PRODUCTION CONTROLLER: ADELA CORY
DESIGN AND ILLUSTRATIONS: JULIA HASTING
TYPESETTER: GEMMA WILSON
RECIPE PHOTOGRAPHER: DL ACKEN

PHOTO CREDITS: ABLE IMAGES/ALAMY STOCK PHOTO
240-241; MELINDA CHAN/GETTY IMAGES 38-39; CHINA
PHOTO PRESS/GETTY STOCK IMAGES 614-615; DE
AGOSTINI EDITORIAL/GETTY IMAGES 20-21; JAMES
HARDY/GETTY IMAGES 16-17; ROBERT HARDING/ALAMY
STOCK PHOTO 8-9; ANTON HAZEWINKEL/GETTY IMAGES
44-45; NOVARC IMAGES/ALAMY STOCK PHOTOS 538-
539; ZHANG PENG/GETTY STOCK IMAGES 88-89, 436-38,
658-59; ALEX SEGRE/ALAMY STOCK PHOTO 26-27;
IMAGE SOURCE/GETTY IMAGES 32-33; KEREN SU/GETTY
STOCK IMAGES 314-315; RAWPIXEL LTD/GETTY IMAGES
718-719; TC YUEN/GETTY STOCK IMAGES 684-685; CM
CHRISTOPHER WONG/GETTY STOCK IMAGES 126-127

THE "CRAB" SYMBOL IN THE FISH & SEAFOOD CHAPTER
(PAGES 124-237) IS BY CHARLOTTE VOGEL AND THE
"PIG" SYMBOL IN THE MEAT CHAPTER (PAGES 312-433)
IS BY ADAM ZUBIN BOTH FROM THENOUNPROJECT.COM

PRINTED IN CHINA

We would like to take this opportunity to thank Madam
Li Yuanjun 李元君女士 for recommending us to Phaidon
Press, giving us the opportunity to work on this book. We
would also like to thank Mr. W. O. Lai 黎华安先生 and
Ms. Cesilia Lai 黎诗思女士 for their assistance in research
as well as Mrs. Elaine Ma 马廖千睿女士 and Mr. Henry
Chow 周达勋先生 for their contributions to the Desserts
chapter. Without their help, we could not have met our
deadlines. We would like to show our appreciation to
the entire Phaidon team, for providing us with guidance
and advice, and whose professionalism and hard work
helped make this book possible.

The publisher would like to thank Clement Chan, Salima
Hirani, Sophie Hodgkin, Steve Kwan, Isobel McLean,
Cecilia Molinari, Jo Murray, Ellie Smith, Tracey Smith, and
Kate Wanwimolruk for their contributions to the book.